GUATEMALA

AL ARGUETA

GUATEMALA

Píchucalco
Ixtacomitán
Rayón
Tuxtla Gutiérrez
San Cristóbal de las Casas
Ocosingo
Palenque
Chancalá
Comitán

MEX 195
MEX 199
MEX 307

Presa de la Angostura

Pijijiapán

MEX 200

Ciudad Cuauhtémoc
La Mesilla
Gracias a Dios

MEX 190

TOLL ROAD
Río Grijalva

M E X I C O

El Naranjo
EL PERÚ
Río San Pedro
PIEDRAS NEGRAS
Río Usumacinta
Sierra del Lacandón
YAXCHILÁN
Cooperativa Bethel
Benemérito de las Américas
DOS PILAS

MEX 307

Playa Grande (Cantabal)
Sierra de los Cuchumatanes
Río Negro (Río Chixoy)
Sierra de Chamea

Todos Santos Cuchumatán
TOJCUNENCHÉN
ZACULEU
Huehuetenango
Nebaj
Sacapulas
Cobán
Purulhá
CAJYUP
Salamá

INTERAMERICANA

Volcán Tacaná 4,093m
Volcán Tajumulco 4,220m

CA 1

UTATLÁN (K'UMARCAAJ)
Santa Cruz del Quiché
Chichicastenango
Joyabaj
Sierra de Chuacús
MIXCO VIEJO

San Marcos
Quetzaltenango
Volcán Santa María
TOTONICAPÁN
SOLOLÁ
IXIMCHÉ
Panajachel
Lago de Atitlán
KAMINALJUYÚ
GUATEMALA CITY

Tapachula
El Catmen
Ciudad Tecún Umán
Ciudad Hidalgo
TAKALIK ABAJ
CHUITINAMIT
Santiago Atitlán
Volcán Atitlán
Volcán Santa María
La Antigua Guatemala
Volcán de Agua
Volcán Acatenango
Amatitlán

Tilapa
Retalhuleu
CA 2
Volcán de Fuego
EL BAÚL/BILBAO
Santa Lucía Cotzumalguapa
Escuintla
Cuilapa

Champerico
Río Samalá
Río Madre Vieja
LA DEMOCRACIA (MONTE ALTO)
Chiquimulilla
CARRETERA AL PACÍFICO

Sipacate
Puerto San José
Iztapa
Monterrico
Las Lisas

P A C I F I C   O C E A N

Río Suchiate

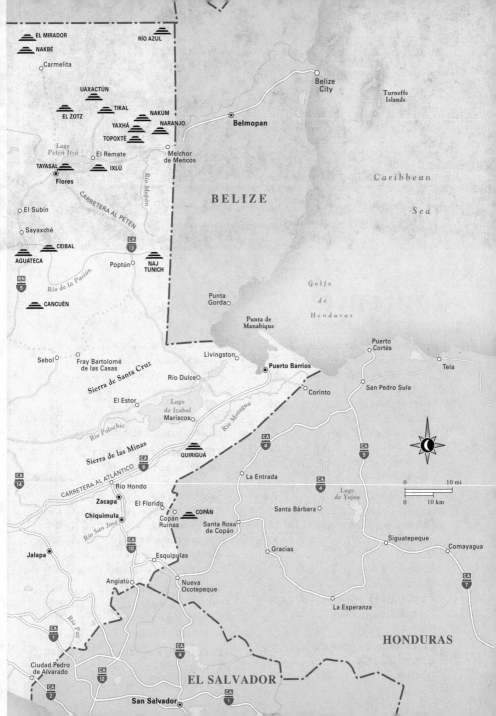

Contents

Guatemala has always been the stuff of legend. Wherever you go, you will sense its magic. When you leave its cosmopolitan capital, Guatemala City, the green landscape unfolds before you—its misty mountains, pine forests, and agricultural fields look like something out of a fairytale. You might visit a highland market where Mayan crafts are sold, or climb an active volcano to witness a lava light show. In a fancy Antigua restaurant, you can dine beneath Spanish colonial arches set beside a gurgling fountain, as live music from modern dance clubs floats through the warm air.

Despite the beauty of its landscape, the richness of its culture, and its diversity of flora and fauna, Guatemala is a country that remains the playground of a few fortunate souls. It's not an easy place to navigate, no doubt. Like much of Latin America, the country still struggles with endemic poverty and inequality. Shantytowns sprawl in the shadows of luxury high-rise condos, while a citizen movement clamors for political reform.

Whatever the outcome, I can tell you I've never loved my country more. I love its majestic mountains, conical volcanoes, sweltering jungles full of half-excavated Mayan pyramids, black-sand beaches, and the sense of magic that permeates everyday life here. Come see it for yourself: Discover the mysteries of this magical land.

Clockwise from top left: fountain in Antigua's El Convento; colorful detail at Casa Palopó in Santa Catarina Palopó; authentic Guatemalan cuisine; cabin at Las Lagunas Boutique Hotel in Petén; Mayan people from the Huehuetenango highlands; active Fuego Volcano.

Planning Your Trip

Where to Go

Guatemala City

The largest city in Central America, Guatemala City has long history of being overlooked by travelers. Among its numerous attractions are recommended **museums**, vibrant **nightlife**, and a range of **excellent restaurants** and **accommodations**. The **Zona Viva** is the place to go for nightlife, pleasant streetside cafés, and some of Latin America's finest restaurants.

La Antigua Guatemala

La Antigua is a **UNESCO World Heritage Site** thanks to its sublime collection of convents, churches, and monasteries. It features Guatemala's loveliest town plaza, graced by the elegant facade of the **Catedral de Santiago,** and its pleasant cobblestone streets are lined with restaurants, accommodations, and shops housed in beautiful old colonial homes. The surroundings are perfectly suited to **outdoor recreational activities.**

The Western Highlands

The Western Highlands boast not only Central America's highest **mountains and volcanoes,** but also its most authentic and vibrant **indigenous culture.** You'll find colorful **Mayan markets,** quaint mountain villages, and gorgeous alpine scenery. On the shores of spectacular **Lake Atitlán** are three volcanoes and several Mayan villages. Guatemala's second-largest city, **Quetzaltenango,** is a popular language-school destination, while **Chichicastenango** is home to Guatemala's most famous market. An emerging eco- and cultural tourism scene can be found in the **Ixil Triangle.**

The Pacific Coast

On the western end of the Pacific Coast, **Retalhuleu** is a hot spot thanks to the twin theme parks of **Xocomil** and **Xetulul.** **Birdwatchers** and **nature lovers** will find several private reserves, including a fantastic lodge built on the ninth terrace of the Mayan site of **Takalik Abaj.** East along the coast, you'll find the small village of **Sipacate,** home to Guatemala's emerging surf scene, and **Iztapa,** Guatemala's sailfishing capital. **Monterrico** is the region's most popular resort town.

El Oriente and Izabal

The dry plains of El Oriente are populated by ladino cowboys and cattle ranchers. Heading east toward Izabal is the Caribbean town of **Puerto Barrios,** the gateway for adventures to the seaside Garífuna town of **Lívingston,** the **Belize cayes,** and tranquil **Río Dulce.**

If You Have . . .

- **A WEEKEND:** Spend your time in Antigua Guatemala.

- **ONE WEEK:** Add Pacaya Volcano and Lake Atitlán or Tikal.

- **TWO WEEKS:** Add Atitlán and Tikal; visit Quetzaltenango and Cobán, saving some time for the museums in Guatemala City. If Quetzaltenango is too chilly, head to the Pacific Coast.

- **THREE WEEKS:** Enjoy all of the above at a more leisurely pace, adding Río Dulce and Lívingston.

Top: El Mirador's La Danta temple at twilight; **bottom left:** the ruins of Yaxhá in Petén; **bottom right:** detail of the tropics in Río Dulce National Park.

© AVALON TRAVEL

Las Verapaces

Las Verapaces are Guatemala's green heartland. Here you'll find the country's best-preserved cloud forests in the **Sierra de las Minas Biosphere Reserve,** the **Cloud Forest Biological Corridor,** which includes the **Biotopo Mario Dary Rivera,** and the pleasant town of **Cobán.** Nearby attractions include the spectacular limestone pools of **Semuc Champey,** white-water rafting on the **Río Cahabón,** and splendid **Laguna Lachuá.**

Petén

Petén is to Guatemala what the Amazon rainforest is to Brazil. In this **lowland jungle frontier** are the remains of several Mayan cities. The best-known Mayan site is **Tikal,** a must-see. In addition to the impressive **temple pyramids,** Tikal and the neighboring **Maya Biosphere Reserve** harbor Mayan ruins and varied wildlife. **Flores,** occupying an island on **Lake Petén Itzá,** is a transportation and services hub rivaled by **El Remate,** along the road to Tikal.

flying over the Maya Biosphere Reserve

Know Before You Go

When to Go

Guatemala has two seasons—rainy and dry. The **rainy season** usually begins at the end of May; the summer months are characterized by short afternoon or early evening showers that clear up by nighttime. By September or October, however, the weather is often socked in for days. During these two months, many hotels offer discounts in hopes of filling their rooms. Some parts of the country, most prominently the Caribbean coast, are rainy throughout the year.

The **dry season** runs from November to early May. December through February are the coldest months, with cold fronts from the north bringing temperatures into the mid-60s for daytime highs in mountain areas such as Antigua, Quetzaltenango, and Guatemala City. Temps warm up dramatically in March and April. During this time, thick haze from heat, dust, and agricultural burning clouds the views of Guatemala's stunning mountain scenery.

The **high tourist season** runs from December to Holy Week (usually in April) with a **second high season** between mid-June and early September. **Language schools** in Quetzaltenango and Antigua are full with college students during the summer; rates go up accordingly. School lets out in late October, with **vacations** taking place until January. Families with children take over many of the popular destinations.

Passports

U.S. citizens will need a **passport** with at least six months' validity after arrival. Residents of other countries will also need **ticket documents** for onward or return travel.

Vaccinations

No vaccinations are required for entry into Guatemala, though it's a good idea to be up to date on rabies, typhoid, measles-mumps-rubella

Arco de Santa Catalina in La Antigua Guatemala

(MMR), yellow fever, tetanus, and hepatitis shots.

Transportation

Guatemala City's modern **La Aurora International Airport** has several daily flights from numerous U.S. gateways. **Mundo Maya International Airport** serves the northern department of Petén and the ruins of Tikal.

The majority of inter- and intracity buses are recycled U.S. school buses known as **"chicken buses"** (cargo often consists of live animals); however, robberies and armed hijacking are increasingly common. **Tourist shuttle buses** are more expensive, but are recommended for safety reasons.

Rental cars can be acquired in Guatemala City, Panajachel, Antigua, Quetzaltenango, Cobán, and Flores. Unless you plan to stick to urban areas such as Guatemala City and Antigua or along the Pan-American Highway,

it's probably best to rent a **four-wheel-drive** vehicle. **Taxicabs** are available in almost any town or city. When in smaller towns, the best way to find a taxi is in the central square, or *parque central*. Otherwise, it's always best to call a cab rather than hail one from the street.

What to Pack

Dress in layers: Pack an assortment of short-sleeved T-shirts, sweaters, fleece jackets and/or a light rain jacket, shorts, and pants. Quick-drying synthetic fabrics wick away moisture during strenuous hikes in the backcountry. In jungle areas where mosquitoes are rampant, stick to **light-colored and lightweight shirts** with long sleeves you can roll up and **lightweight travel pants**. Also pack **sunscreen, bug spray,** and a **wide-brimmed hat** or ball cap. **Footwear** is extremely important. For serious jungle hiking, high, military-style **boots** protect against mud and snakes.

The Best of Guatemala

If you have 10 days, you can enjoy the best that Guatemala has to offer. The following itinerary will help you see as much as you can in a short amount of time without running ragged. After all, it's a vacation.

Day 1

Fly in to **Guatemala City** around lunchtime. Take the afternoon to visit the **Archaeology Museum** or the **Museo Popol Vuh** and **Museo Ixchel** (next door to each other) for a crash course on the Mayan civilization. Enjoy dinner in one of Guatemala City's excellent restaurants.

Days 2-3

Take an early-morning flight out of Guatemala City to **Flores,** the gateway to the Mayan ruins of **Tikal,** in the northern Petén department. Tikal is the most famous of Guatemala's Mayan sites and boasts impressive temple pyramids. Spend all day exploring the ruins and enjoying the sublime jungle environment. You have the option of

staying at the park and seeing the sunrise over the rainforest from the top of Temple IV or heading back south to **Lake Petén Itzá,** where you can stay at the jungle chic **La Lancha**. The lake, with its turquoise waters and tropical forest ecosystem, makes a good alternative to staying at the ruins. Fly back to Guatemala City on the afternoon of the second day. Upon arrival, grab a shuttle bus or taxi from the airport to **Antigua,** Guatemala's old colonial capital, and check in at any of the city's fine accommodations.

Days 4-5

Grab breakfast or coffee from any of the coffee shops along the plaza. **Café Condesa** makes a fine choice for breakfast. Take some time to see Antigua's major sights. Return to your comfortable hotel room for some chill-out time before heading out to dinner. On the second day, head out to **Finca Filadelfia** for breakfast and take a tour of the coffee farm. Lunch is at your leisure, and you can also use the time to do some

La Lancha, an ecolodge on the shores of Lake Petén Itzá

Lake Atitlán

shopping. In the afternoon, head out with one of the groups making the **Pacaya Volcano climb** to see the lava light show. The trip returns late at night.

Days 6-7

Take a shuttle bus sometime around noon for **Panajachel,** on the shores of spectacular **Lake**

colorful dolls for sale in Chichicastenango

Atitlán. You also have the option of continuing to nearby **Santa Catarina Palopó** or **Santa Cruz La Laguna** if Panajachel doesn't suit your style. The afternoon is yours to explore or simply relax. If possible, plan for Day 7 to fall upon a Sunday or Thursday so you can grab a shuttle bus from Panajachel to Chichicastenango to see the colorful **Chichicastenango Market.** Return to Panajachel in the afternoon.

Days 8-10

It's up to you. Head to the other side of Lake Atitlán to **San Pedro, San Marcos,** or **Santiago** for some more highland Mayan culture amid splendid settings or any of the other Mayan villages around the lake. You can also stay right where you are and make day trips to the other villages. This will give you time to really enjoy the lake, as the pace of your visit to Atitlán thus far will have been a bit hurried. Take a shuttle bus back to **Guatemala City** on the afternoon of Day 9 and check in to your hotel. Savor the culinary delights offered at another one of the city's excellent restaurants before packing your purchases for the flight home the next day and turning in for the night. Be sure to leave room in your carry-on for the excellent duty-free shopping at La Aurora Airport.

Guatemala's Top Ten

- **La Antigua Guatemala** (page 86): This fascinating **colonial town** flanked by volcanoes is just an hour from the Guatemala City airport. Among the ruins of old convents destroyed by an 18th-century earthquake are brightly colored restored colonial structures housing some of the country's **best restaurants** and **fanciest hotels.** Explore the cobblestone streets on foot, on Segway, or by horse-drawn carriage.

- **Volcano Climbs** (page 98): Much of Guatemala's highland region is dotted with majestic volcanic guardians. Active **Pacaya Volcano** is a fairly easy climb that most anyone in reasonable shape can do. **Acatenango Volcano** is extremely difficult, but you'll get an unparalleled view of Guatemala's amazing scenery, complete with an unobstructed view of lava-spewing **Fuego Volcano** right next to it.

- **Lake Atitlán** (page 127): Compared by writer Aldous Huxley to Italy's Lake Como but with the added embellishment of three conical volcanoes, Lake Atitlán is spectacular. Its fringes are populated by **small towns** quickly gaining popularity with foreign travelers and residents, each with its own vibe.

- **Chichicastenango's Market** (page 154): This twice-weekly affair is Latin America's **largest outdoor market.** Much of it is local trade among Mayan people, but there is also considerable trade in **handicrafts.**

- **Iztapa and Monterrico** (pages 203 and 207): Guatemala's Pacific Coast offers warm weather year-round in addition to black-sand beaches. Iztapa is well known by anglers for its impressive yields of **sailfish** and billfish. In season (Dec.-Feb.) it also serves as the gateway for **whale-watching** tours. Monterrico (and the village of Hawaii to the east) is the site of **sea turtle conservation** efforts but also has become popular with travelers seeking sun, sand, and surf.

- **Río Dulce National Park** (page 249): This waterway connects Guatemala's Caribbean Coast to its largest lake. Its impressive **canyon** is lined with jungle scenery. There are numerous lodges from which to enjoy outdoor activities and the eponymous town at the mouth of the river's confluence is a popular **boat marina.** Also at the confluence with the Caribbean Sea is the charming Garífuna enclave of **Lívingston.**

Semuc Champey

- **Semuc Champey Natural Monument** (page 278): Slowly gaining more popularity (but still not mainstream due to its remote location and difficult access), the emerald green **limestone pools and waterfalls** of Semuc Champey are a huge hit with those who make it here.

- **Tikal National Park** (page 313): This impressive archaeological site is among the **finest in the Mayan world** and the exuberant tropical forest all around (full of wildlife) only adds to the allure.

- **Yaxhá** (page 329): This archaeological site has its own unique feel because it overlooks not only verdant forests but two large lagoons. The **sunsets** viewed from its tallest structures are amazing.

- **El Mirador** (page 332): Many people come to Guatemala just to see the Mayan ruins, so it's not surprising that three of the country's Top Ten must-sees are archaeological sites. Accessible only by helicopter or a two-day mule trek, the **pyramids** here are among the largest ancient structures in the world. The largest, La Danta Complex, is bigger (in volume) than Egypt's Great Pyramid.

Escape to La Antigua

Guatemala's close proximity to U.S. shores and easy access by air (just 2.5 hours from Houston or Miami; 5 hours from New York) makes it a great candidate for an international weekend getaway.

Day 1

Plan this day to be a Friday or Saturday. There are nonstop flights from New York/Newark on Saturdays (and now also Friday nights, in season). Most other gateway cities have multiple flights daily.

Arrive in Guatemala City around noon. Grab a shuttle van or taxi to **La Antigua** and check into your hotel. Take the afternoon to explore the cobblestone streets and a museum or two, do some shopping, and get a bite to eat in one of the excellent restaurants. Grab drinks or dinner from **Café Sky** or **Lava Terrace Bar** and watch the sun set behind the volcanoes.

Day 2

Grab an early breakfast and then hike up to the **Cerro de la Cruz** for a wonderful view of the city with Agua Volcano in the background. Alternatively (between December and February), head out early to go **whale-watching** on the Pacific Coast (one hour away). Have lunch and an afternoon round of golf at **La Reunión Antigua Golf Resort** and spend the night there. From your suite, enjoy views of Agua and Pacaya Volcanoes over your private plunge pool.

Day 3

Transfer to Guatemala City and its international airport. Depending on the time of departure, you may be able to visit one or several of the museums near the airport: the **Museo Nacional de Arqueología y Etnología** and the **Museo Popol Vuh** and **Museo Ixchel** (next door to each other). Allow some extra time at the airport for some duty-free shopping before you fly out.

a skillful weaver in La Antigua

Wonders of the Maya

travelers atop La Danta temple in El Mirador

In Guatemala, not only can you take in the ancient Mayan wonders from long before the arrival of the Spanish, you can also visit the Postclassic highland ceremonial sites that greeted the conquistadors upon their arrival in 1524.

Most of the Mayan ceremonial sites that were at their cultural zenith during these time periods can be found in the country's northern Petén region. Among the largest and most sophisticated cities from the Preclassic period is **El Mirador,** which flourished between 200 BC and AD 150. No self-respecting archaeology buff would come to Guatemala without visiting the ruins of **Tikal** at the center of a 575-square-kilometer (222-square-mile) national park protecting the historical site and surrounding rainforest ecosystem. Farther north is the interesting astronomical observatory at **Uaxactún.** West of Tikal are the sites of **Nakum** and **Yaxhá,** the latter of *Survivor* TV fame. Nakum is remote and little explored, though it harbors some fine Mayan temples. Yaxhá is now the second-most visited of Petén's Mayan sites. It's large and impressive, with the added beauty of a lagoon backdrop.

Real history buffs might want to check out the ceremonial sites found and subjugated by the Spanish at the time of the conquest, thus completing the picture of Guatemala's pre-Columbian archaeological heritage. When the Spanish arrived in Guatemala, they first secured an alliance with the Kaqchikel, who had their capital in **Iximché** in Guatemala's Western Highlands. The Spanish would eventually establish their first capital on the same site. You can visit the restored ruins of Iximché, very conveniently situated just a few kilometers from the Pan-American Highway about an hour from Guatemala City. Near the city of Huehuetenango, the inhabitants of the Mam ceremonial site of **Zaculeu** were done in by starvation after Pedro de Alvarado's brother laid siege to the city for two months.

Guatemala offers some of the best sailfishing in the world. Back on land, Guatemala City has at least four good golf courses—with another star player just one hour outside the city. Numerous sailfishing outfitters and accommodations can host your stay; virtually all of them have agreements with golf courses, allowing you to combine the two activities for a "surf and turf" vacation.

SAILFISHING AND WHALE-WATCHING

Your base for sailfishing will likely be Iztapa, about 90 minutes from Guatemala City. Sailfish Bay Lodge is among the best outfitters, with a lodge right on the beach. Another good option is Casa Vieja Lodge, near Puerto San José. You can fish from one to five days (or more) and then tack on an extra day or two for golf.

Guatemala is also a stopping point along the migration path of humpback whales, so you can take a morning for whale-watching in season (December-February). Other species you might spy include pilot whales, whale sharks, sea turtles, and bottlenose dolphins. Scheduled tours leave weekend mornings from Antigua Guatemala or Iztapa, beginning and ending in the Puerto Quetzal marina.

GOLF

Set on a former coffee plantation just 20 kilometers from Antigua, La Reunión Antigua Golf Resort is the only place in the world where you can enjoy a round of golf with a view of four volcanoes, two of which are active. Practice your swing at the driving range in the shadow of smoke-belching Fuego Volcano; its 18-hole, Pete Dye-designed

the greens at La Reunión's Fuego Maya golf course

Fuego Maya golf course takes its inspiration from the 19-month Mayan solar calendar. The adjacent 26-suite hotel offers fabulous accommodations and delectable culinary creations. You may never want to leave.

It's only an hour from La Reunión to Guatemala City, or 45 minutes to the Pacific Coast. You can easily combine a stay in Antigua or Guatemala City with some golf time; Guatemala's near-perfect climate makes golf possible almost any time of year. In the vicinity of Guatemala City, the best place to tee off is San Isidro Golf Club. The surrounding hillsides offer wonderful views of the city.

The Green Heartland

During the dry season (November-April), much of Guatemala starts to look parched and brown, especially beginning in January. If you yearn for greener pastures, this is where the country's brilliant microclimates come in. The area of Las Verapaces remains green and lush throughout most of the year, thanks to the almost year-round presence of a light mist known as *chipi-chipi*. The area is also largely covered in beautiful cloud forests, soaked in rains and shrouded in cloud more often than not. Below is a sampling of the region's myriad attractions.

Biotopo Mario Dary Rivera

Along the road leading from Guatemala City to Cobán (and only about an hour's drive from the

jungle river at Parque Ecológico Hun Nal Ye

latter) is the wonderful **Biotopo Mario Dary Rivera,** also known as the **Quetzal Biotope.** It grants easy access to this unique ecosystem for the casual visitor while providing a refuge for Guatemala's emblematic national bird. There are two trails for exploring and plenty of waterfalls along the path lined with ferns and tall trees festooned with bromeliads. There are several lodging and dining options nearby with private cloud forest sanctuaries of their own.

Sierra de las Minas

A destination for the serious hiker and outdoor enthusiast is **Sierra de las Minas Biosphere Reserve.** Some of the best hiking anywhere in Guatemala, and Central America for that matter, can be found here. Several trails wind through this remote wilderness, allowing the opportunity to spot quetzals, and explore the cloud forest habitat. Starting in the village of **Albores,** hook up with a local conservation organization **FUNDAECO** for hikes to nearby attractions like **Peña del Angel** and accommodations in its private biological station.

Parque Ecológico Hun Nal Ye

North of the regional services hub of **Cobán**

(the departmental capital of Alta Verapaz), a dirt-road turnoff from the main (paved) road leads across verdant pastures and rainforest-clad hillsides to the lovely **Parque Ecológico Hun Nal Ye.** A private reserve and working farm, the park offers many opportunities for outdoor exploration, including hikes to a pristine, **azure-colored river,** a raging **waterfall,** a **cenote** (limestone water-filled sinkhole), **four-wheeling** on designated areas of the property, and **horseback riding.** A small museum houses a replica of a magnificently carved stone Mayan box, which was stolen from the property but then returned. The original now resides in a museum in Guatemala City.

Laguna Lachuá

Continuing farther into the northern reaches of Alta Verapaz department, this circular **lagoon** surrounded by rainforests is somewhat remote but very much worth the effort. Its clear waters vary between an emerald and turquoise color, thanks to the limestone bedrock all around. Like the better-known sinkholes in Mexico's Yucatán Peninsula, to the north, it is thought to have been created by a meteor impact millions of years ago. It makes an idyllic place for **camping,**

the placid limestone pools of Semuc Champey

swimming in its cool waters, and simply admiring the scenery in **splendid isolation.**

Lanquín and Semuc Champey

In northeast Alta Verapaz, another dirt road veers off from the main road and leads to some of Guatemala's most beautiful, lesser-known sites. **Lanquín** is a small town about 12 kilometers from the junction with the main highway harboring several cool **ecolodges** and Lanquín's magnificent eponymous **caves.** It also serves as the starting point for **white-water rafting** trips on the Río Cahabón. The same dirt road continues another 11 kilometers to the absolutely gorgeous **pools** and **waterfalls** of **Semuc Champey,** passing the **K'an Ba caves** along the way.

Living It Up

Guatemala has some of the hippest digs anywhere on the planet. Equivalent accommodations elsewhere in the world would cost twice as much. You also can find some of Latin America's best restaurants in Guatemala. After all, Guatemala's wealthy elite needs somewhere to spend its money. If you're sick and tired of hotels that all pretty much look the same and enjoy the opportunity to check out unique **boutique hotels** and **jungle lodges** near worthwhile attractions, then this list is for you.

Guatemala City

The **Real InterContinental** is one of the city's hippest haunts. (George W. and Laura Bush stayed at the InterContinental during a visit in March 2007.) You can enjoy afternoon coffee at any one of the recommended Zona 10 cafés. For dinner, enjoy fusion cuisine at **Tamarindos** or **Jake's,** considered by *Travel + Leisure* magazine to be among the best restaurants in Latin America. You can also have dinner at **El Portal del Ángel** in the hills on the outskirts of town overlooking the city.

La Antigua Guatemala

Be sure to eat at least one meal at **Mesón Panza Verde,** known for its phenomenal cuisine and wonderful atmosphere among baroque arches. Among the fabulous properties to spend the night are **Posada del Ángel** and **El Convento.**

If you enjoy golfing (and even if you don't), head 20 kilometers outside of Antigua to **La Reunión Antigua Golf Resort** overlooking the Pacific Coast and in the shadow of four volcanoes.

Guatemala's wide diversity of ecosystems makes it a birding hot spot—more than 700 species of birds can be found here. Avid bird-watchers consider this paradise, though novices can easily center an entire Guatemala vacation around birding.

With its own private reserve on the southern slopes of Atitlán Volcano, **Los Tarrales** harbors forests ranging in altitude from 700 to 3,000 meters (2,300-9,800 feet) that include broadleaf and cloud forests. Bird species are correspondingly diverse and include horned guan, long-tailed manakin, Pacific parakeet, orange-fronted parakeet, and several species of hummingbirds. Near Retalhuleu, **Reserva Patrocinio** lies south of Santiaguito Volcano at an altitude between 750 and 850 meters (2,500-2,700 feet). It is a good place for observing birds found in lowland and middle elevations. A substantial network of trails leads through protected patches of forest interspersed with coffee and macadamia plantations. Hawks, vultures, and falcons abound, as do parrots and woodpeckers.

On the Pacific Coast, the best places for birding are the vast **Manchón Guamuchal** wetlands and the canals and mangrove swamps bordering **Monterrico.** Species found in both parks include great egrets, roseate spoonbill, blue heron, and belted kingfisher.

On the moist Caribbean Coast, the **Cerro San Gil Reserve** harbors more than 350 species of birds, including the black-and-white hawk-eagle and keel-billed motmot. More than 90 neotropical migrants, including the wood thrush and blue-winged warbler, winter in the area. Birding is excellent in the **Sierra de las Minas Biosphere Reserve,** particularly if you want to see Guatemala's national symbol, the elusive quetzal. If you'd like to spot birds in the cloud forest while keeping a comfortable base to come back to after a long day, visit **Chelemhá Cloud Forest Preserve,** with its wonderful Maya Cloud Forest Lodge. The preserve lies at altitudes rang-

berylline hummingbird

ing from 2,000 to 2,500 meters (6,500-8,200 feet). Found within its forests are at least 14 bird species endemic to Central America's Northern Highlands. A total of 145 bird species have been recorded here to date.

In Petén, it's hard to beat **Tikal National Park.** You'll see ocellated turkeys along the forest floor as well as keel-billed toucans and Montezuma's oropendola, among hundreds of other bird species, zipping about the forest canopy. The temple pyramids provide excellent vantage points for bird-watching. South of Tikal, on the shores of Lake Petén Itzá, **Cerro Cahuí** is also an excellent place for bird-watching with several waterbird species, including pied-billed grebe, herons, and northern jacana as well as the more typical rainforest birds such as toucans. Two trails wind through the forest with some excellent vantage points over the lake.

You won't want to leave, so plan on spending the night in one of the Suites Gran Clase, with a private infinity-edge plunge pool and views of Agua and Pacaya Volcanoes. When there's no reason to leave such a beautiful room, room service comes in handy.

Lake Atitlán

My favorite Lake Atitlán hotel is **Casa Palopó,** just outside the village of Santa Catarina Palopó and overlooking the lake. Leave your cares behind and enjoy the excellent service, allowing plenty of time to watch the light change on the volcanoes

Monkeys also enjoy Las Lagunas Boutique Hotel.

view of Lake Atitlán from Casa Palopó

or the wind dance across the lake throughout the day. If you've got the cash, rent out the entire **Villa Palopó**, higher up the hill. For a change of setting, stay at the lovely **Laguna Lodge, La Fortuna at Atitlán,** or **Villa Sumaya,** in Santa Cruz La Laguna.

The Pacific Coast
On the ninth terrace of Takalik Abaj, **Takalik Maya Lodge** gives you the option of staying in quaint jungle cottages painted with yellow and green frescoes or a converted coffee farmhouse overlooking a swimming pool and a coffee-drying patio. Explore the ruins by tractor-pulled trailer from the lodge. If you want to see Guatemala's version of Disney World, check out the well-executed **Xocomil** and **Xetulul** theme parks and stay across the street in the excellent **Hostal Palajunoj,** where you can choose among African, Indonesian, Mayan, and Southeast Asian-style accommodations. Eat at **Restaurante Kapa Hapa** overlooking the swimming pools. The Pacific Coast's most stylish digs are at **Dos Mundos Pacific Resort,** featuring cabanas with the feel of an

exclusive Mexican beach villa. Along the road from Monterrico to neighboring Iztapa are the exclusive **Villa Los Cabos** condominiums, where you can rent a villa overlooking the enormous horseshoe-shaped swimming pool and the sea.

Izabal
For the ultimate private getaway, head up the Río Tatín, a tributary of the Río Dulce, to **Rancho Corozal,** a sumptuous thatched-roof private villa beautifully furnished and decorated. Use the skiff to explore the surrounding jungle rivers or simply relax in the hammock lounge with a good book.

Petén
La Lancha, owned by movie director Francis Ford Coppola, is Petén's most exclusive hideaway. It enjoys a magnificent location on the shores of Lake Petén Itzá. Simply lounge by the pool overlooking the turquoise lake waters and beautiful jungle. Other, locally owned alternatives are **Las Lagunas Boutique Hotel,** on a 200-acre private reserve with several lagoons, and the stylish **Bolontiku Hotel Boutique.**

Guatemala City

Look for ★ to find recommended sights, activities, dining, and lodging.

Highlights

★ **Palacio Nacional de la Cultura:** At the heart of downtown Guatemala City, this former presidential palace now serves as a museum that offers a fascinating glimpse into the country's rich history (page 33).

★ **Zona Viva:** Guatemala City's most cosmopolitan sector, while offering some of the city's best hotels, is also a fun place for a meal and a night on the town (page 44).

★ **Museo Ixchel:** The city's finest museum is a wonderful tribute to Mayan culture and to Guatemala's famous textiles and traditional village attire (page 45).

★ **Museo Miraflores:** This excellent museum is dedicated to the ancient Mayan site of Kaminaljuyú, which occupied the valley in which Guatemala City now stands. Several of the site's temple mounds lie nearby (page 45).

★ **Museo Nacional de Arqueología y Etnología:** Before or after visiting Guatemala's fascinating Mayan sites, head to this museum to admire many of the original pieces once found there, including beautifully carved monuments and brilliant jade masks (page 46).

Due to its much-maligned international image, you'll probably be surprised when you first lay eyes on Guatemala City from the window of your airplane. Even if you've visited other Central American capitals, you'll be taken

by Guatemala City's beauty from the air. Bordered by a lake, forested mountains, and four volcanoes, the nation's capital is a bustling urban agglomeration of three million inhabitants occupying a broad valley and spilling into ravines and neighboring hillsides.

The beauty of its physical surroundings aside, Guatemala City, or "Guate," as it's more commonly called by locals, can seem polluted, noisy, and downright dodgy once you step onto its streets—however, the same can be said of New York or Mexico City. It's all a matter of getting acquainted with your surroundings and discovering the pleasant aspects of this mountain city. Among these are a temperate spring-like climate, a splendid scenic backdrop, excellent dining and entertainment options, and the opportunity to travel in relative comfort with all of the amenities of a cosmopolitan city.

If you give it a chance, you'll find that Guate grows on you after a while. As far as Latin American capitals go, you could certainly do worse. (Some travelers find other Central American capitals less agreeable.) As the region's largest and most cosmopolitan city, Guatemala City has a wide variety of accommodations and entertainment options suited to tastes, needs, and budget.

The remodeled La Aurora International Airport serves as a fitting gateway to Central America's largest city. Just minutes from the airport, you'll find most of the areas frequented by Guatemala's well-to-do and expat residents. Scattered among forest-clad ravines and sprawling east into neighboring mountainsides are Guatemala City's business, retail, and residential sectors. The northern part of the city is home to its downtown core, which has unfortunately seen better days as a colonial capital, but is also the ongoing focus of some much-needed urban renewal. Tumbling out into surrounding ravines and plateaus in the vicinity of the downtown core

Previous: Guatemala City's Zona 14; aerial view of Guatemala City's older districts. **Above:** Hard Rock Café Guatemala City.

Guatemala City

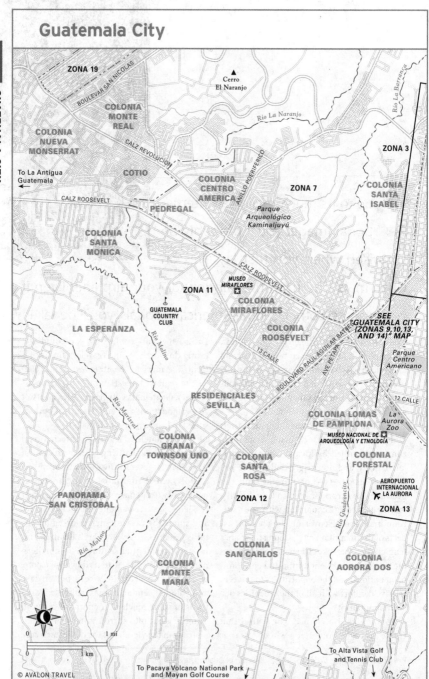

ZONA 19

BOULEVAR SAN NICOLAS

COLONIA
MONTE
REAL

COLONIA
NUEVA
MONSERRAT

CALZ REVOLUCION

COTIO

To La Antigua
Guatemala

CALZ ROOSEVELT

PEDREGAL

COLONIA
SANTA
MONICA

ZONA 11

GUATEMALA
COUNTRY
CLUB

LA ESPERANZA

Río Molino

RESIDENCIALES
SEVILLA

COLONIA
GRANAI
TOWNSON UNO

PANORAMA
SAN CRISTOBAL

Río Molino

COLONIA
MONTE
MARIA

▲ Cerro
El Naranjo

Río La Naranjo

ANILLO PERIFERICO

COLONIA
CENTRO
AMERICA

ZONA 7

Parque
Arqueológico
Kaminaljuyú

CALZ ROOSEVELT

MUSEO
MIRAFLORES

COLONIA
MIRAFLORES

COLONIA
ROOSEVELT

13 CALLE

BOULEVARD RAUL AGUILAR BATRES

AVE PETAPA

Río Marisral

COLONIA
SANTA
ROSA

ZONA 12

COLONIA
SAN CARLOS

Río La Barranca

ZONA 3

COLONIA
SANTA
ISABEL

SEE
"GUATEMALA CITY
(ZONAS 9,10,13,
AND 14)" MAP

Parque
Centro
Americano

12 CALLE

COLONIA LOMAS
DE PAMPLONA

MUSEO NACIONAL DE
ARQUEOLOGÍA Y ETNOLOGÍA

La
Aurora
Zoo

COLONIA
FORESTAL

AEROPUERTO
INTERNACIONAL
LA AURORA

ZONA 13

Río Guadronciito

COLONIA
AORORA DOS

0   1 mi

0   1 km

© AVALON TRAVEL

To Pacaya Volcano National Park
and Mayan Golf Course

To Alta Vista Golf
and Tennis Club

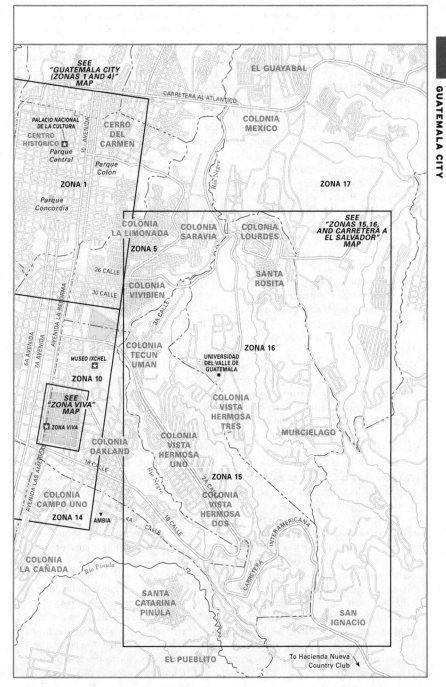

are the city's slums, while its industrial sectors lie mostly to the south and west. Chances are you won't be venturing into the these two sectors, just as you likely wouldn't hang out in a Brazilian *favela*.

It should be expected that a country of such great wealth (though poorly distributed) should have a modern capital with all the developed world comforts one would expect to find there. Great restaurants, museums, shops, and entertainment can all be found in this cosmopolitan capital. Like everything else in Guatemala, it all coexists side by side with some of the uglier realities. Things can look very different from one *zona* to the next. It's all there for you to see, and nowhere else in the country is this striking contrast of wealth and poverty so evident. Look at a visit to Guatemala City as a glimpse into the nation's culture, history, and politics, and a worthy introduction to a fascinating country of contrasts with unexpected surprises around every corner.

HISTORY

Guatemala City is in fact the fourth capital of Guatemala, the other three having been destroyed by natural disasters, including earthquakes and mudslides, or replaced by the establishment of Spanish-modeled urban centers, as in the case of the first highland capital Iximché. Like Iximché, the land now occupied by the modern-day urban center was once the site of a Mayan city that exercised considerable influence over trade routes for obsidian during Classic Mayan times thanks to an alliance with the central Mexican powerhouse of Teotihuacán. Kaminaljuyú, as the city was called, was first settled sometime around 400 BC. The early foundational cultures preceding the Mayan city established agriculture in the valley now occupied by Guatemala City and settled much of it, mostly in the western part of the valley. As with the other Classic Mayan sites, Kaminaljuyú was just a distant memory by the time the Spanish arrived on the scene in the 16th century.

The city's modern settlement dates to 1776, in the aftermath of the 1773 earthquakes of Santa Marta, which rocked the previous capital, now known as La Antigua Guatemala (The Old Guatemala, or "La Antigua" for short). Debate over whether or not to rebuild La Antigua raged for a few years, but in the end it was decided to start all over again in the neighboring Valle de la Ermita (Valley of the Hermitage), as the valley was known. An edict by Governor Martín Mayorga made the move official. It took a while for the new capital to catch on, as many Antigua residents refused to move despite Spanish decrees ordering the settlement of the new city. In 1800, the population of Guatemala City was only 25,000. The new city was laid out in a grid pattern, much like every other town established by the Spanish, with the construction of major public buildings including the Catedral Metropolitana (cathedral), Cabildo (Town Hall), and Palacio de los Capitanes Generales. Of these, only the cathedral remains standing.

Like its predecessor, Antigua Guatemala, the new Guatemalan capital would experience its own series of destructive earthquakes in December 1917, lasting into February of the following year. By this time, it seems, the population had come to terms with the fact that much of Guatemala lies upon one of the world's most active fault lines. The fault line would again wreak widespread havoc with another earthquake in 1976. Ironically, the most recent earthquake triggered wide-scale migration into the city, resulting in the establishment of many slums lining the city's numerous ravines, or *barrancos.*

The city grew tremendously throughout the 20th century, spreading from its original core (now known as the Centro Histórico) and spilling out into the surrounding *barrancos* and up into the mountains lining the western and eastern edges of the valley. Much of the country's industry is concentrated here, fueling economic migration from other parts of the country. The population of Guatemala City's metro area now reaches over four million.

CLIMATE

Guatemala City enjoys a delightful climate almost year-round. Its location in a valley at an altitude of 1,493 meters (4,897 feet) above sea level ensures that it never gets excessively warm, as do some other, low-lying Central American capitals. This pleasant climate has earned it the nickname "Land of Eternal Spring." It should be noted, however, that the nickname was coined during a long-gone era before the city's exponential growth, which has given rise to urban microclimates such as the urban heat island. The latter is caused when the direct tropical sun heats large expanses of pavement, which in turn heat the surrounding air masses, causing a phenomenon not unlike a large convection oven. The truth is that it can get somewhat hot here during April and May, what locals generally call *verano,* or summer, with daytime highs in the mid- to upper 80s. Longtime residents frequently remark about the increasingly warm summers, which they say have become much warmer than what was once typical. This is also the driest time of year, and the surrounding mountains can turn some rather parched shades of brown. Thermal inversions causing extreme haze are also quite typical this time of year, making Guatemala City look somewhat like a smaller version of Los Angeles. These occur frequently in valleys when a layer of warm air settles over a layer of cooler air lying close to the ground, holding this cooler air down and preventing pollutants from rising and scattering.

Between June and August, after the arrival of the rainy season, mornings are typically sunny and warm, giving way to increasing cloudiness and afternoon showers almost every day. September and October are increasingly rainy with entire stretches of cloudy or rainy days. In November the skies clear and become increasingly windy. Many people equate this time of year with kite-flying, and indeed the giant kite festival in the nearby towns of Sumpango and Sacatepéquez take place on the first of the month. December through February can be chilly here and elsewhere in mountainous parts of Guatemala with the arrival from the north of frequent cold fronts coinciding with the Northern Hemisphere's winter season. Bring some warm clothes if you're traveling to Guatemala City or elsewhere in the highlands during this time of year, as concrete houses with tile floors are the most popular form of architecture and aren't typically heated or carpeted, making it feel even colder.

PLANNING YOUR TIME

Upon international arrival into Guatemala, most travelers eager to make their way to the country's fascinating interior head straight to Antigua Guatemala, taking a shuttle bus from the airport and bypassing Guatemala City altogether. Whether at the beginning or end of your trip, a visit to the capital is crucial to understanding what makes this country tick. It is certainly worth spending some time here, and it can be an extremely rewarding destination after weeks spent in the countryside, offering fine restaurants, excellent museums, and all the comforts that a modern capital city has to offer. Guatemala City is also the country's transportation and business hub, so if you are trying to get around the country or are in Guatemala on business, you will find yourself on its streets sooner or later.

Most of the major attractions can be seen in a day or two. If you have more than two days to spend in Guatemala City, you might consider staying in Antigua to make better use of your time. Exceptions to this would be those in town for business looking for things to do after hours without taking a trip out of the city. Zona 10, conveniently near the airport, has some fine hotels and is home to a number of highly recommended museums. It is also one of the city's most attractive commercial and financial districts. A day strolling down pleasant Avenida La Reforma and sampling the Zona Viva's cafés, bars, nightclubs, and restaurants is a great way to cap off your visit to Guatemala.

ORIENTATION

Guatemala City's sprawl occupies about 400 square kilometers, filling a large valley scarred by deep ravines (known locally as *barrancos*) and surrounded by mountains and volcanoes. Its terrain gives the city a patchwork feel when viewed from the air, with parts of the city meandering fingerlike into the scarred landscape. The urban sprawl has also started migrating east and west into surrounding mountains. A large plateau atop the mountains abutting the city to the east is traversed by the Carretera a El Salvador (Road to El Salvador) and is one of the fastest-growing suburban sectors. The surrounding landscape is accentuated by the presence of active Pacaya Volcano, often visible at night, to the south. To the southwest, the cones of Agua, Fuego, and Acatenango Volcanoes can be seen rising above the mountain separating Guatemala City from neighboring Antigua Guatemala.

The city itself is divided into 25 zones, or *zonas*. Only a few of these hold any interest for the foreign visitor or resident. **Zonas 1 and 2** encompass the downtown sector, with **Zona 4** serving as a kind of transition zone between the original city core and newer business and residential sectors. **Zona 10** harbors the homes of wealthy elite, high-rise condominiums, hotels, restaurants, nightclubs, banks, and embassies. Moving south and abutting the airport, **Zona 14** is home to a large concentration of wealthy neighborhoods and high-rise condos. To the east and heading up the slopes of surrounding mountainsides lie residential **Zonas 15 and 16** and **Carretera a El Salvador.** Several of the city's *zonas* are separated from each other by natural boundaries, such as forested *barrancos*.

Unlike in Managua or San José, **street addresses** are very much in use here. Pay special attention when looking for street addresses, as the same street and house number can exist in more than one *zona*. Addresses usually begin with an avenue, or *avenida,* followed by a number with a dash. A typical street address would be something like: 7a Avenida 8-34 Zona 10. In this case, the "8" corresponds to the intersecting street number, or *calle.* The number after the dash is the house number. So the above address would be house number 34 between Eighth and Ninth Streets along 7th Avenue of Zona 10.

SAFETY

Guatemala City can be dodgy, though certain *zonas* are certainly safer than others. Most of the areas frequented by tourists are

the many contrasts of Guatemala City

The Feel and Vibe of Guatemala City

Guatemala City might feel quite intimidating and downright scary. While crime, pollution, and noise cannot be denied, you've made it this far, so you should probably check things out for yourself and see it through your own eyes.

Guatemala City is Central America's largest city, with an approximate metro area population approaching four million inhabitants. The good news concerning the city's size is that you really have no reason to venture into more than about a third of its area. Much of the sprawl constituting the sizable metro area is found outside the official city limits and is composed of Guatemalan working-class subdivisions, industrial parks, and slums. The nicer parts of town are also conveniently located adjacent to each other, in the eastern third of the city near the airport. The downtown core lies to the north of the city's newer sectors.

Perhaps most fascinating about Guatemala City are the constant juxtapositions evidencing this vibrant capital's status as a microcosm of Guatemala's larger wealth and class disparities. Tin-roofed shacks cling to forested hillsides just out of view from the wooden decks of $500,000 homes. Buses trundle slowly down tree-lined boulevards while late-model BMWs zip by in the passing lane. Maya from the highlands dressed in traditional garb wait for these buses under steel-and-glass bus stop shelters advertising French perfumes.

Guatemala City feels more like a real city and not an overgrown town (sorry, San José), with actual buildings occupying a somewhat impressive portion of the urban sprawl. These buildings house condos, banks, hotels, and offices, giving the city a very modern feel. You'll see Guatemala's well-to-do frequenting the cafés, bars, restaurants, and hotels found in these sectors, along with travelers and foreign residents. Guatemalans love to be seen dining out in fine restaurants and shopping at exclusive stores for the latest fashions.

A darker side of Guatemala City's flashy displays of wealth is the shotgun-toting guards you'll find stationed outside of banks, gas stations, and fast-food franchises. The congregating of suit-wearing bodyguards outside gyms, restaurants, and private schools would be downright comical were it not such a flagrant reminder of the specter of extortionary kidnapping. And then there's the barbed wire—lots of it—and iron bars adorning many of the city's houses, which lie bunkered away in cordoned-off neighborhoods guarded by access gates staffed by security personnel. It all takes some getting used to, but we're fairly adaptable as a species.

Good or bad, love it or hate it, Guatemala City is what it is. If it all gets to be too much, just head up into the hills east of the city and look at it from above. It seems a lot more peaceful that way, framed by low-lying clouds and its gorgeous volcanic backdrop. Spend a few minutes picking out your favorite locations and seeing how many different parts of the city you can identify. It's a sight for sore eyes.

relatively safe, though the downtown area is considerably less safe than Zonas 10 and 14 and purse snatching and pickpocketing are serious problems. Exercise common sense and caution when in public areas. Riding public buses is not usually a good idea, though the newer Transmetro mass transit system has proven safer and is certainly more efficient. Transmetro buses are bright green and not to be confused with the Transurbano bus system (similar to the municipal buses).

Pay careful attention when using ATMs. Some thieves have been so ingenious as to set up keypads at the entrance to ATM kiosks asking cardholders to enter their PIN numbers in order to gain access to the machine. You should never enter your PIN number anywhere other than on the ATM keypad itself.

Watch out for another common scam, particularly in the vicinity of the airport, whereby a "Good Samaritan" informs you of a flat tire on your car. If that is indeed the case, pull over in a well-lighted, public place if you can but do not stop in the middle of the road to change the tire. He may try to carjack you. If you are able to make it to a public place such as a gas station, have someone in your party stay inside the car while another checks all four tires. If a tire is indeed flat, stay inside of or close to your car while someone changes the tire for you (it's common for gas station attendants to change tires in Guatemala). The important thing is not to lose sight of the inside of your vehicle for a moment. Thieves can be extremely crafty at distracting you and getting into your car while you take care of the urgent business at hand. Locked doors may be a deterrent but are not going to stop the thieves if they've targeted you. For information on other precautions and common scams to watch out for while traveling in Guatemala, see the State Department's Consular Information Sheet online at http://travel.state.gov.

Sights

Sights are listed by city zone, the official format for divvying up the city's land area. Most of the city's historic sites are found within the Centro Histórico. Some of the nicer museums are found near the airport in Zona 13 and in the Miraflores area west of the city center in Zona 11.

CENTRO HISTÓRICO

The original core of Guatemala City, dating to its foundation, is composed of 1a to 17 Calle and 1a to 12 Avenida, known today as the Centro Histórico. Most of the architecture is neoclassical, a sharp departure from the baroque architecture found in the previous capital of Antigua Guatemala. Few of the original buildings remain, having largely been destroyed by earthquakes in 1917 and 1976 or modified with the passing of time. Yet some excellent examples of the original architecture can still be found, and there is an ongoing campaign to restore several historic buildings in the downtown core. This program, known as RenaCENTRO, is a collaboration between several entities, including the local municipality, INGUAT, the private sector, and Argentinean, Spanish, and French cooperation.

Guatemala City was once nicknamed "The Silver Teacup" for its urban Spanish Renaissance design and architecture, including elegant theaters, large colonial mansions, broad avenues, imposing churches, and charming side streets. Although they have aesthetically deteriorated, they are not beyond rescue. This is precisely RenaCENTRO's mission: a multifaceted, holistic approach to restoring the grandeur of Guatemala's colonial-era capital. The restoration inexorably hinges upon local economic reactivation. Given Guatemala's huge tourism potential, it seems only fitting that its capital would become a welcome stop along the visitor's path, although restoration remains an ongoing process.

Parque Central

In typical Spanish colonial fashion, the city was laid out around a central plaza with a Catholic church and government buildings surrounding it. It is also known as the Plaza de la Constitución. The **Parque Central** encompasses a large area between 6a and 7a Avenidas and 6a and 8a Calles. Alongside it are the Palacio Nacional de la Cultura, Catedral Metropolitana, and Portal del Comercio. The park is usually abuzz with shoe shiners and folks enjoying a stroll through its grounds, now largely composed of concrete blocks with little greenery after being remodeled in the mid-1980s to include an underground parking lot. A large Guatemalan flag dominates the plaza near a small, sadly neglected monument to the 1996 peace accords; it consists of a glass case that once enclosed a flame, which has long since burned out. South of the park, heading towards 9a Calle is **Portal del Comercio,** a commercial arcade recently restored as part of RenaCENTRO's ongoing gentrification projects. Novena Calle (between 6a and 7a Avenidas) has also been restored as a pedestrian thoroughfare known as Pasaje Aycinena.

★ Palacio Nacional de la Cultura

Boston's Fenway Park has its Green Monster and so does Guatemala City. The former presidential palace, built between 1939 and 1943 during the time of maniacal dictator Jorge Ubico, is a large, green stone structure with elements of colonial and neoclassical architecture. The 1996 peace accords between the government and URNG guerrillas were signed here and the building was subsequently converted into a museum. It is also sometimes used to host visiting dignitaries such as former president George W. Bush and actor Mel Gibson. With most of Guatemala's presidents preferring to live in other parts of the city, it has not housed a president during a term in office since the early 1990s.

The **Palacio Nacional de la Cultura** (tel. 2239-5000, 9am-noon and 2pm-5pm daily, $5) is one of Guatemala City's most interesting attractions, as it affords the visitor a glimpse into Guatemala's colonial and dictatorial legacy. After all, Guatemala City was once the capital of the entire Central American isthmus and nowhere else in the region were colonial institutions so embedded in the national fiber. Similarly, Guatemala's *caudillos* (military strongmen) needed a residence befitting their status as rulers of a quasifeudal kingdom, to which end the palace served them quite well.

You can take a guided tour of the palace so as to better appreciate the intriguing architecture, including some Moorish courtyards, frescoed arches made of carved stone, and artwork by several Guatemalan artists of the 1940s. As you climb the wood-and-brass main stairway, you can admire a mural by Alredo Gálvez Suárez depicting a romanticized take on Guatemalan history. Stained-glass windows by Julio Urruela Vásquez and Roberto González Goyri can be found adorning the palace in the second-floor banquet hall; they depict the virtues of good government. You might also be able to see the presidential balcony, which overlooks the plaza in classic dictatorial fashion.

A more modern-day attraction is the Patio de la Paz, where a stone sculpture of two hands commemorates the 1996 signing of the peace accords. A white rose held in the outstretched hands is changed at 11am by the palace guards once a week and on special occasions by visiting dignitaries. The rose used to be changed daily, but I guess it's one more thing we've lost to government cutbacks.

Catedral Metropolitana

The construction of Guatemala City's neoclassical **Catedral Metropolitana** (7a Avenida facing the plaza, 6am-noon and 2pm-7pm) began in 1782 and was completed in 1815, though the bell towers would not be completed until 1867. It has survived two earthquakes, a testament to its sturdy construction, even if it isn't exactly the prettiest of Guatemala's churches. The pillars on the church's facade are adorned with the names of many of Guatemala's disappeared, etched into the stone as a testament to the desire for justice, whether in this lifetime or the next. Inside, many of the altars and paintings adorning the church were brought here forcefully when the capital, along with its institutions, was officially moved to its current site from Antigua. The standout is the image of the Virgen del Perpetuo Socorro, Guatemala's oldest, brought into the country by Pedro de Alvarado in 1524.

Parque Centenario

Adjoining the larger central plaza, to the west, is the smaller **Parque Centenario,** with the Biblioteca Nacional (National Library) and Archivo General de Centroamérica (National Archive) bordering it. It occupies the former site of the Palacio Centenario, built to commemorate 100 years of independence from Spain. It briefly housed the National

Guatemala City (Zonas 1 and 4)

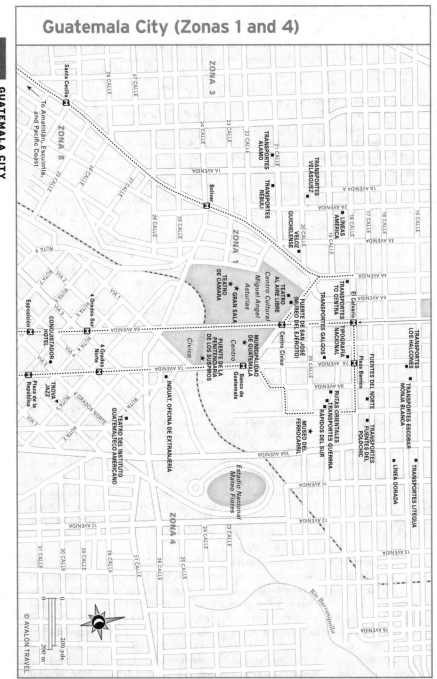

ZONA 3

28 CALLE
27 CALLE
24 CALLE
23 CALLE
22 CALLE

Santa Cecilia
ZONA 8
To Amatitlán, Escuintla, and Pacific Coast

21 CALLE

TRANSPORTES ÁLAMO
TRANSPORTES REBULI
TRANSPORTES VELÁSQUEZ

Bolívar

20 CALLE
LÍNEAS AMÉRICA
VELOZ QUICHELENSE
19 CALLE

18 CALLE
17 CALLE
16 CALLE
15 CALLE

1A AVENIDA
2A AVENIDA
3A AVENIDA

ZONA 1

Centro Cultural Miguel Ángel Asturias
★★ GRAN SALA
TEATRO DE CÁMARA
TEATRO AL AIRE LIBRE

4 Grados Sur
VÍA 1
RUTA 6
RUTA 3
VÍA 2
VÍA 3
VÍA 4

Exposición

CONQUISTADOR HOTEL

6A AVENIDA
RUTA 5
VÍA 5

4 Grados Norte

Plaza de la República

TROVA JAZZ

RUTA 4
A GRADOS NORTE
RUTA 2
VÍA 7

PUENTE DE SAN JOSÉ (MUSEO DEL EJÉRCITO)
TRANSPORTES TO CENTRA
TRANSPORTES GALGOS

El Calvario
4A AVENIDA
5A AVENIDA

TIPOGRAFÍA NACIONAL

Centro Cívico
Centro Cívico
PUENTE DE LA PENITENCIARÍA DE LOS SUSPIROS
MUNICIPALIDAD DE GUATEMALA
Banco de Guatemala

7A AVENIDA

Plaza Barrios
FUENTES DEL NORTE

TRANSPORTES LOS HALCONES
TRANSPORTES ESCOBAR
MONJA BLANCA

8A AVENIDA
9A AVENIDA
RUTAS ORIENTALES
TRANSPORTES GUERRA
RÁPIDOS DEL SUR

TRANSPORTES FUENTES DEL POLOCHIC

LÍNEA DORADA

TRANSPORTES LITEGUA

INGUAT, OFICINA DE EXTRANJERÍA
TEATRO DEL INSTITUTO GUATEMALTECO AMERICANO

MUSEO DEL FERROCARRIL

10A AVENIDA

Estadio Nacional Mateo Flores

11 AVENIDA

12 AVENIDA

13 AVENIDA

ZONA 4

31 CALLE
30 CALLE
29 CALLE
28 CALLE
27 CALLE
26 CALLE
25 CALLE

24 CALLE
23 CALLE

16 AVENIDA

Río Barranquilla

0   200 yds.
0   200 m

© AVALON TRAVEL

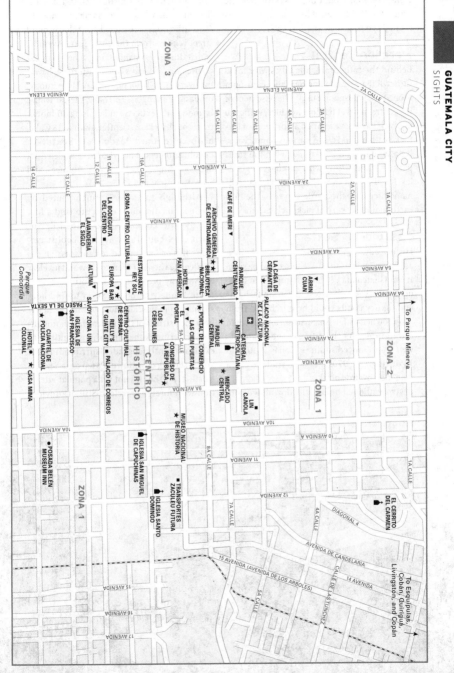

ZONA 3

To Parque Minerva

ZONA 2

To Esquipulas,
Cobán, Quiriguá,
Livingston, and Copán

EL CERRITO
DEL CARMEN

AVENIDA DE CANDELARIA

DIAGONAL 4

CALLE DE LAS LUNCHEZ

14 AVENIDA

5A CALLE

15 AVENIDA (AVENIDA DE LOS ARBOLES)

ZONA 1

POSADA BELEN
MUSEUM INN

HOTEL
COLONIAL

CASA MIMA

CUARTEL DE
POLICIA NACIONAL

IGLESIA DE
SAN FRANCISCO

SAVOY ZONA UNO

REILLY'S

GUATE CITY

PALACIO DE CORREOS

CENTRO CULTURAL
DE ESPAÑA

IGLESIA SAN MIGUEL
DE CAPUCHINAS

TRANSPORTES
ZACULEU FUTURA

IGLESIA SANTO
DOMINGO

MUSEO NACIONAL
DE HISTORIA

EUROPA BAR

ALTUNA

RESTAURANTE
REY SOL

SOMA CENTRO CULTURAL

LA BODEGUITA
DEL CENTRO

LAVANDERIA
EL SIGLO

Parque
Concordia

PASEO DE LA SEXTA

CENTRO
HISTÓRICO

ZONA 1

LOS
CEBOLLINES

PORTAL
DEL COMERCIO

LAS CIEN PUERTAS

CONGRESO DE
LA REPÚBLICA

PARQUE
CENTRAL

MERCADO
CENTRAL

LIN
CANOLA

PALACIO NACIONAL
DE LA CULTURA

CATEDRAL
METROPOLITANA

LA CASA DE
CERVANTES

ARRIN
CUAN

PARQUE
CENTENARIO

CAFE DE IMERI

ARCHIVO GENERAL
DE CENTROAMERICA

BIBLIOTECA
NACIONAL

HOTEL
PAN AMERICAN

Congress, whose building was burned to the ground in 1927. Its most interesting feature is a small acoustic shell amphitheater.

Mercado Central

Behind the cathedral is the city's **Mercado Central** (8a Avenida and 6a Calle, 6am-6pm Mon.-Sat., 9am-noon Sun.). The basement of the central market harbors produce, while the top two floors have a varied assortment of textiles, leather goods, and various handicrafts. It's a bit dark and bunkerlike, with the stalls packed to the ceiling with all kinds of goodies. It's also a bit overwhelming. The current market replaced the one destroyed by the 1976 earthquake. Be wary of pickpockets here.

Paseo de la Sexta

Historically, Sexta Avenida, otherwise known as "La Sexta," was the place to see and be seen. It was Guatemala City's most important thoroughfare, where the latest European fashions and luxury goods could be purchased from shops owned by Jewish, Spanish, and German immigrants. As the city expanded and its well-to-do moved south to Zonas 9, 10, and 13 during the 1970s, Sexta Avenida began a long, downward spiral.

As mentioned before, the downtown core of Guatemala City's historic Zona 1 has undergone urban renewal for some time now. In 2010 this process included the relocation of street vendors from the city's Sexta Avenida, at that time a disorganized mess choked by car traffic and sidewalks lined with those hawking everything from pirated DVDs to knock-off designer sunglasses. Today, the car traffic is gone and Sexta Avenida, along 10 blocks from the city's Plaza Central south to 18 Calle, has been renamed **Paseo de la Sexta.** An ongoing process, it has yielded remodeled art deco buildings, new lighting, sculptures, and a smattering of new cafés.

Although the area is much touted by the local media, don't expect to find a hip, trendy, and completely revamped downtown core. You also won't find cool streetside cafés or many good restaurants. This is Guatemala City, not Mexico City, and it's clear the wealthy prefer to stick to other parts of town. While you might expect to find new, slightly more upscale shops to line the newly upgraded streets of this pedestrian thoroughfare, the truth is the same shops continue to exist in slightly upgraded surroundings. If you're staying downtown, Paseo de la Sexta is worth a stop, but it's not yet a popular attraction with foreign travelers. Still, it provides

Paseo de la Sexta

a fascinating glimpse into the lives of working-class Guatemalan urbanites. Among the hubbub as you walk (or bike) down the thoroughfare, you'll find vendors curiously carrying full-sized and fully clothed mannequins on their backs or those selling ready-to-eat fruit and ceviche (only for the heartiest gringo stomachs). It's still not the safest part of town for a stroll, so be extra careful if you do venture out this way, as it's known for assorted riffraff, including pickpockets. There is a fair amount of police presence here, which is reassuring. The Transmetro now reaches this area, which makes it easier than ever to get to.

7a Avenida

Paralleling 6a Avenida is **7a Avenida,** with a variety of architectural highlights. Among these is the splendid **Palacio de Correos** (Central Post Office, 8:30am-5pm Mon.-Fri., 8:30am-1pm Sat.), at the corner of 7a Avenida and 12 Calle, featuring a large archway that reaches over to the building across the street. Also attractive is the nearby **Tipografía Nacional** (National Printing Press), at the corner of 7a Avenida and 18 Calle. It dates to 1894 and somewhat resembles a gingerbread house.

Both 6a and 7a Avenidas continue their straight course southward through Zonas 4 and 9 before ending at a series of archways marking the northern extreme of the airport runway.

Museums

One block east of the market and one block south on 10a Avenida is the **Museo Nacional de Historia** (9a Calle 9-70 Zona 1, tel. 2253-6149, museonh@hotmail.com, 9am-4:30pm Mon.-Fri., $1.50) with historical documents, clothing, and paintings, largely to do with Guatemala's tyrannical rulers. Among the more interesting exhibits are some photographs by Eadweard Muybridge, who visited and photographed the country in 1875. The museum is housed in a very attractive colonial building.

Casa Mima (8a Avenida 14-12 Zona 1, tel. 2253-6657, www.casamima.org, 10am-5pm Mon.-Sat., $3) offers a fascinating peek into the lives of Guatemala's upper middle class from generations past. The splendidly restored 19th-century town house is furnished in art deco, Victorian, and French neo-rococo styles. Guided tours are available and must be arranged one week in advance. **La Casa de Cervantes** (5a Calle 5-18 Zona 1, tel. 2251-8120, http://casadecervantes.com,

a detail from La Casa de Cervantes

free) showcases fair trade goods in Guatemala and has a gift shop, where you can purchase fair trade coffee, handicrafts, and even locally made kombucha. There's a small café with pleasant outdoor seating in an old courtyard and a bookstore packed with excellent titles documenting subjects of Guatemalan history and social justice. There are periodic exhibitions and special events. It's more of an information and cultural center than a museum but is certainly worth a look. It was being repainted with artwork from a local muralist during my last visit.

Train enthusiasts will enjoy **Museo del Ferrocarril** (in front of the intersection of 9a Avenida and 20 Calle, tel. 2232-9270, www.museofegua.com, 9am-4pm Tues.-Fri., 10am-4pm Sat.-Sun., $0.25), housed in a refurbished building that was once the city's train station. The state-run railways, known then as FEGUA, were privatized during the Arzú administration. Among the attractions are several steam engines, train cars, and exhibits of train paraphernalia, including some wonderful old photographs. Some cool classic cars are also on display here.

The **Centro Cultural de España** (6a Avenida 11-02 Zona 1, Edificio Lux, Nivel 2, tel. 2503-7500, www.cceguatemala.org, 10am-7pm Tues.-Fri., 10am-2pm Sat., free) shows movies most nights, hosts workshops and art exhibits, and has a small library. It makes a nice addition to the city's Paseo de la Sexta, having moved here from its old location at the now defunct 4 Grados Norte.

Churches

Several of the city's downtown churches have been restored in recent years and might be worth a stop to admire their noteworthy architecture. Construction on **Iglesia de San Francisco** (6a Avenida and 13 Calle Zona 1, 7am-noon and 2pm-7pm daily) began in 1800 and wasn't completed until 1851. Its charming light gray exterior has been worn down by the elements; inside are 18 altars of impressive quality. Another beautiful church is that of **Iglesia Santo Domingo** (12 Avenida

and 10a Calle), constructed between 1792 and 1808. In addition to its attractive architecture, it is known for its paintings, including one depicting the apparition of the Virgin Mary to Santo Domingo de Guzmán, after whom the capital of the Dominican Republic is named. (It is believed he received the rosary from her.) **El Cerrito del Carmen** (12 Avenida and 2a Calle Zona 1, 7am-noon and 2pm-6pm daily) denominates both the name of this hermitage and the hill on which it rests, with wonderful views of the downtown area. It dates to 1620 and is known for its image of a virgin of the same name embossed in silver, a gift from Carmelite nuns in the 17th century. Oil paintings by Tomás de Merlo adorn the inside of **Iglesia San Miguel de Capuchinas** (10 Avenida 10-51 Zona 1, 6am-noon and 2pm-7pm daily), with its transitional baroque-neoclassical architecture.

ZONA 2
Parque Minerva

As you head north along 6a Avenida and then Avenida Simeón Cañas, it's about 1.5 kilometers from the city center to Parque Minerva in the adjoining Zona 2 sector. The park here has some sporting facilities, including the **Estadio de Béisbol Enrique "Trapo" Torrebiarte,** where there are sometimes games on weekends. Its informal atmosphere is a bit like that of old-time minor league parks in the U.S. Midwest. Baseball is nowhere near as popular in Guatemala as in other parts of Central America, namely Nicaragua, but if you're a fan of the game, you might want to stop and check it out.

The park's main attraction, however, is also one of Guatemala's most unusual. The 2,000-square-meter **Mapa en Relieve** (Relief Map, Ave. Simeón Cañas Final, Hipódromo Del Norte, Zona 2, tel. 5632-5708, www.mapaenrelieve.org, 9am-5pm daily, $0.75) is built to 1:10,000 scale and was created in 1905, well before the invention of Google Earth. It gives you a good idea of the country's mountain topography and the contrasting flatness of Petén and neighboring Belize, which, of course, is included as part of Guatemala in accord with the long-standing border dispute. The scale of the mountains is somewhat exaggerated, with the volcanoes and peaks looking steep and pointy. There are observation towers from which you can get a better vantage point. The rivers and lakes are sometimes filled with water from built-in taps, making for an even more authentic experience. It makes a good stop if you're in Guatemala City before heading out to the interior and want to get a feel for the country's unique geography.

Museo de los Mártires

A fascinating glimpse into Guatemala's tragic (and largely unknown) history can be found in Zona 2's **Museo de los Mártires del Movimiento Sindical, Estudiantil y Popular de Guatemala** (1a. Calle 1-53 Zona 2, tel. 2232-4853, www.fafg.org, donations accepted). Forensic anthropology has come a long way in recent years in helping to identify the victims of Guatemala's 45,000 cases of forced disappearance during the civil war. The museum stands as a testament to the lives of almost 200 victims based on information found in a military archive detailing date of disappearance and death. There's a video presentation, clothing and personal items left behind by the victims, and a tribute to forensic anthropologists in their search for the truth. The victims' mug shots and file information are chillingly reproduced on a wall, giving a face and voice to the victims of Guatemala's dirty war.

ZONA 4

A revitalization program gave Zona 4 a distinct character in recent years with the establishment of a pedestrian thoroughfare known as 4 Grados Norte, lined with sidewalk cafés and restaurants during the day, doubling as bars at night. While it was a good idea in theory, it soon attracted a motley assortment of drug dealers and local riffraff. The restaurants and bars have mostly closed their doors, but the area is enjoying a renaissance as a center for technology-based businesses. The *New York Times* compared it to Silicon Valley in a 2011 story featuring the area's Campus Tec building. Dozens of new technology start-ups have sprung up here in recent years. Some of the postproduction for Hollywood movies now takes place here, including that for *The Chronicles of Narnia*.

Further adding luster to this area is the appearance of food trucks in a space fronting the pleasant **Plaza de La República** (7a

The disappeared from Guatemala's civil war are remembered at Zona 2's Museo de los Mártires.

Avenida y Ruta 5). The food trucks serving Chinese food, burgers, and tacos are a popular lunchtime option with workers in nearby office towers.

Zona 4's other main attraction is a dilapidated bus terminal for second-class buses, though this was expected to fall into disuse with the municipal government's plans to move all bus traffic out of the city.

Centro Cívico

As you head south from the downtown sectors of Zonas 1 and 2, you'll come to a transitional area between the old city core and some of the newer parts of town. Some guidebooks refer to the latter as the "new city," which to the best of my knowledge has never been used by locals to describe their city layout. As the city spread south from the central area, urban planners and architects decided to build around a concept of a civic center to house some of the more important government buildings. Thus was born the **Centro Cívico.** Today it houses Guatemala's **Corte Suprema de Justicia** (Supreme Court), **Banco de Guatemala** (Bank of Guatemala), **Municipalidad de Guatemala** (City Hall), and the administrative offices of the

Guatemala Tourist Commission (7a Avenida 1-17 Zona 4, 8am-4pm Mon.-Fri.). There's the occasional exhibit in the lobby and you can get some tourist information, including maps, but you're probably better off picking these up at the information kiosks at the international airport.

Centro Cultural Miguel Ángel Asturias

Inaugurated in 1968 and named after Guatemala's Nobel Prize-winning author, the capital's national theater is built on a hill once harboring the fort of San José de Buena Vista, destroyed by artillery fire during the October Revolution of 1944. The **Centro Cultural Miguel Ángel Asturias** (mcd.gob.gt/teatronacional) consists of a **Gran Sala** (Great Theater) with a seating capacity of 2,041, an outdoor amphitheater seating 2,500, the 320-seat **Teatro de Cámara** (Chamber Theater), and several smaller venues. It has some interesting architecture designed by Efrín Recinos, and its hilltop location overlooking the rest of the civic center gives it an air of grandeur. The center still hosts frequent events, including ballet and theater productions. Check local listings for more information.

Zona 4's Centro Cívico

ZONA 7
Parque Arqueológico Kaminaljuyú

This Mayan site occupied the valley where Guatemala City now stands. It was first settled sometime around 400 BC and grew to house an abundance of flat-topped pyramids (with the remains of nobility buried underneath) by AD 100. The first inhabitants of the site appear to have been some early cultures (Las Charcas, Miraflores, and Esperanza, dating from 1500 BC to AD 150), which established a foundation for the later development of the Classic Mayan culture here. These early cultures are characterized by the development of agriculture, weaving, pottery making, and ritual burial of the dead in temple mounds and shrines. Central to the city's rapid population growth was the construction of a series of irrigation canals drawing upon the ancient lake of Miraflores. Eventually the lake began to dry out, leading to widespread migration out of the city. Its Chol-speaking inhabitants are thought to have moved on to El Salvador and maybe even Copán, Honduras. The site's historical record fades out (momentarily) sometime between the 2nd and 3rd centuries AD.

With the rise of Central Mexico's Teotihuacán in the 5th century, the Guatemalan highlands received a large influx of invaders from the north. Here the invaders established their regional capital, constructing new temples and structures, and flourished with the control of trade networks around highly prized obsidian and jade. It is thought that, along with its powerful neighbor to the north, Kaminaljuyú exercised considerable influence over the Petén lowland sites, in particular Tikal. One of Tikal's rulers, Curl Nose, may actually have come from here in AD 387.

The site was first excavated in 1925 and yielded potsherds and clay figurines from the early cultures. Its larger extent and importance were discovered in 1935 when a local football team uncovered a buried structure after cutting away the edges of two inconspicuous mounds to lengthen their practice field. Today the site is really no more than a series of mounds. Though the site is in Zona 7 proper, the best place to see it is actually near the Museo Miraflores in adjacent Zona 11, where you can tour the excellent museum and see some temple mounds.

ZONA 9

Part of the city's newer sector, Zona 9 adjoins Zona 4 and is crossed by 6a and 7a Avenidas. Along 7a Avenida, on 2a Calle, is an Eiffel Tower-like monument commemorating the rule of Guatemala's liberal reformer Justo Rufino Barrios (1871-1885), known as **Torre del Reformador.** Wonderfully illuminated at night with a large spinning spotlight at its top, the steel tower serves as a nice backdrop for an annual December fireworks show. A bell at top is rung every year on June 30 in remembrance of the Liberal victory in the revolution of 1871. It was a project of the Ubico administration and was not a donation from France, as is commonly thought. The bell tower, however, was a gift from Belgium. Nearby, at the corner of 5a Calle and Avenida La Reforma is **Plaza Estado de Israel,** honoring the creation of the Jewish state with a giant Star of David sculpture.

Also along Avenida La Reforma, between 2a Calle and Calle Mariscal Cruz, is the **Jardín Botánico y Museo de Historia Natural** (Botanical Gardens and Natural History Museum, tel. 2334-6064, 8am-3pm Mon.-Fri., 9am-noon Sat., $1.50), managed by the Universidad de San Carlos. It's really only recommendable for the botanical gardens, which offer a nice respite from the chaotic traffic just beyond its walls. The plant species are all labeled in Spanish and Latin. Give the natural history museum a skip unless you're really into bad taxidermy.

At 7a Avenida and 12 Calle is the **Plazuela España,** a circular miniplaza circumvented by traffic and featuring a pretty fountain built in honor of Spain's King Carlos III in 1789. It originally was in the city's central park, where it had a large equestrian statue that disappeared shortly after independence from

Guatemala City (Zonas 9, 10, 13, and 14)

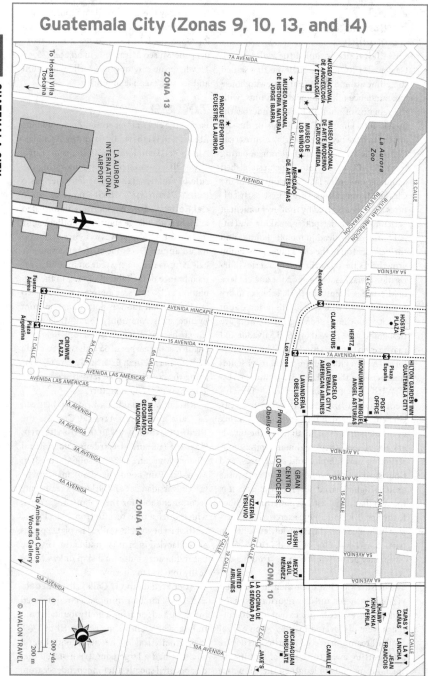

ZONA 13

To Hostal Villa Toscana

7A AVENIDA

MUSEO NACIONAL DE ARQUEOLOGÍA Y ETNOLOGÍA

MUSEO NACIONAL DE HISTORIA NATURAL JORGE IBARRA

MUSEO NACIONAL DE ARTE MODERNO CARLOS MERIDA

MUSEO DE LOS NIÑOS

PARQUE DEPORTIVO ECUESTRE LA AURORA

6A CALLE

MERCADO DE ARTESANÍAS

11 AVENIDA

La Aurora Zoo

13 CALLE

BOULEVAR LIBERACIÓN

LA AURORA INTERNATIONAL AIRPORT

5A AVENIDA

14 CALLE

Acueducto

CLARK TOURS

HERTZ

7A AVENIDA

16 CALLE

LAVANDERÍA

HOSTAL PLAZA

Plaza España

MONUMENTO A MIGUEL ÁNGEL ASTURIAS

HILTON GARDEN INN GUATEMALA CITY

POST OFFICE

BARCELO GUATEMALA CITY/ AMERICAN AIRLINES

Fuerza Aérea

Plaza Argentina

11 CALLE

CROWNE PLAZA

9A CALLE

AVENIDA HINCAPIÉ

15 AVENIDA

6A CALLE

Los Arcos

AVENIDA LAS AMÉRICAS

AVENIDA LAS AMÉRICAS

1A AVENIDA

2A AVENIDA

3A AVENIDA

4A AVENIDA

INSTITUTO GEOGRÁFICO NACIONAL

OBELISCO

Parque Obelisco

Obelisco

GRAN CENTRO LOS PRÓCERES

1A AVENIDA

2A AVENIDA

15 CALLE

14 CALLE

ZONA 14

To Ambia and Carlos Woods Gallery

10A AVENIDA

PIZZERÍA VESUVIO

2ª CALLE

19 CALLE

18 CALLE

SUSHI ITTO

MEXI/ SAÚL MÉNDEZ

ZONA 10

UNITED AIRLINES

LA COCINA DE LA SEÑORA PU

5A AVENIDA

6A AVENIDA

NICARAGUAN CONSULATE

17 CALLE

JAKE'S

CAMILLE

13 CALLE

TAPAS Y CAÑAS

KHAWP KHUN KHA/ LA PERLA

LA LANCHA

JEAN FRANCOIS

0 200 yds
0 200 m

© AVALON TRAVEL

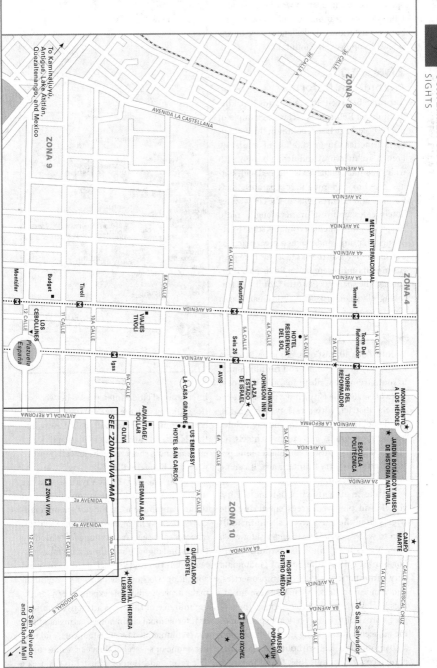

ZONA 8

ZONA 9

ZONA 4

ZONA 10

ZONA VIVA

To Kaminaljuyú,
Antigua, Lake Atitlán,
Quezaltenango, and Mexico

AVENIDA LA CASTELLANA

3a CALLE

3a CALLE A

1A AVENIDA

2A AVENIDA

3A AVENIDA

4A AVENIDA

5A AVENIDA

6A CALLE

MELVA INTERNACIONAL

Terminal

Montúfar

Budget

Tívoli

8A CALLE

Industria

6A AVENIDA

Torre Del
Reformador

1A CALLE

2A CALLE

LOS
CEBOLLINES

12 CALLE

Plazuela
España

11 CALLE

10a CALLE

VIAJES
TÍVOLI

7A AVENIDA

Seis 26

5A CALLE

4A CALLE

HOTEL
RESIDENCIA
DEL SOL

3A CALLE

2A CALLE

TORRE DEL
REFORMADOR

Igss

9A CALLE

AVIS

HOWARD
JOHNSON INN

PLAZA
ESTADO
DE ISRAEL

AVENIDA LA REFORMA

MONUMENTO
A LOS HÉROES

AVENIDA LA REFORMA

LA CASA GRANDE

ADVANTAGE/
DOLLAR

OLIVA

US EMBASSY

HOTEL SAN CARLOS

HEDMAN ALAS

6A
CALLE

7A CALLE

1A AVENIDA

3A CALLE A

2A AVENIDA

ESCUELA
POLITÉCNICA

JARDÍN BOTÁNICO Y MUSEO
DE HISTORIA NATURAL

SEE "ZONA VIVA" MAP

3a AVENIDA

4a AVENIDA

12 CALLE

11 CALLE

10a
CALLE

QUETZALROO
HOSTEL

6A AVENIDA

7A AVENIDA

HOSPITAL
CENTRO MÉDICO

CAMPO
MARTE

CALLE MARISCAL CRUZ

1A AVENIDA

6A AVENIDA

3A CALLE

To San Salvador

HOSPITAL HERRERA
LLERANDI

DIAGONAL 8

To San Salvador
and Oakland Mall

MUSEO IXCHEL

MUSEO
POPOL VUH

Spain. Its current location was a move by the Ubico administration. Some once-attractive but now deteriorated tile benches are on the sidewalks opposite the fountain.

ZONA 10
Avenida La Reforma

Running between 1a Calle and 20 Calle, Avenida La Reforma is a classic example of the 19th-century trend, common throughout Latin America's major capitals, of emulating French architectural and urban design with wide, tree-lined boulevards adorned with statues. This broad thoroughfare separates Zonas 9 and 10 and features some of the city's better hotels, cafés, and restaurants along its path. The wide, grassy median contains some interesting sculptures and makes a great place for a stroll or bike ride thanks to a new bike path running its entire length. La Reforma culminates at the spacious **Parque Obelisco,** featuring a large obelisk, a gigantic Guatemalan flag, palm trees, a fountain, and sitting areas.

★ Zona Viva

Within Zona 10, east of Avenida La Reforma all the way to 6a Avenida and running north to south from 10a Calle to 16 Calle, the **Zona Viva** is Guatemala City's most pleasant commercial district, with a variety of hip cafés, trendy boutiques, lively bars and nightclubs, excellent restaurants, and expensive hotels. It's Guatemala City at its best and after long periods in the country's hinterlands, it can be downright refreshing.

Unlike in downtown Guatemala City, you'll find plenty of trees sheltering the streets from the harsh tropical sun in addition to wide, pedestrian-friendly sidewalks. Zona Viva's many high-rise buildings harbor banks, offices, the bulk of Guatemala City's international hotel chain properties, and condominiums. None of these buildings is more than 20 stories high, as the airport's proximity limits vertical expansion of the adjacent areas, giving the neighborhood a cosmopolitan feel without the claustrophobic concrete-jungle look found in larger

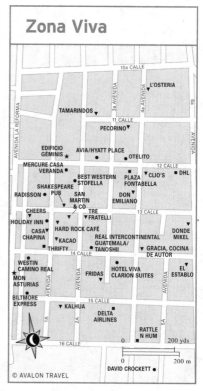

international cities. Interspersed between office buildings are the area's many dining and entertainment options and tucked away into the side streets are some of Guatemala's nicest residences sheltered behind walls, barbed wire, and bougainvillea.

During the day, Zona Viva's streets are mostly the haunt of businesspeople because of the area's prominence as the city's main financial district. By night, especially on weekends, it becomes the enclave of young folks heading to bars and nightclubs or dinner at a fancy restaurant. If you find yourself needing to spend a night or two in Guatemala City, you might make it a very enjoyable experience by checking into one of the area's attractive boutique or international chain hotels, eating at one of the recommended local restaurants, and taking in one or several of the nearby museums. The recent addition of a hostel to the area's accommodations means this is no longer just an option for wealthy travelers. It is also conveniently close to the airport.

★ Museo Ixchel

The city's most magnificent museum, **Museum Ixchel** (6a Calle Final Zona 10, tel. 2361-8081/2, www.museoixchel.org, 9am-5pm Mon.-Fri., 9am-1pm Sat., $4 adults, $2 students, $15-80 for guided tours in English) on the grounds of the Francisco Marroquín University, is dedicated to Mayan culture with an emphasis on weaving and traditional costumes. It's housed in a beautiful brick building built to resemble a Mayan *huipil*, or handwoven, embroidered blouse. On display are pre-Hispanic objects, photographs, handwoven fabrics, ceremonial costumes, weaving tools, and folk paintings by Guatemalan artist Andrés Curruchich. You'll find interactive multimedia displays, a café, bookstore, and *huipiles* for sale in the excellent gift shop. Displays are in English and Spanish. This museum is a must-see for anyone with even a casual interest in Mayan weaving, as it manages to condense the country's rich weaving heritage spanning a fairly vast geographical range into a single place with excellent displays and an attractive setting.

Museo Popol Vuh

Next door and also on the university campus is the similarly high-caliber **Museo Popol Vuh** (tel. 2361-2301, www.popolvuh.ufm.edu, 9am-5pm Mon.-Fri., 9am-1pm Sat., $4 adults, $2 students). Started in 1978 with a university donation by private collectors, it has been in its current location since 1997. The museum houses an impressive collection from Guatemala's archaeological record grouped in different rooms denoted by Preclassic, Classic, Postclassic, and Colonial themes. The highlight is in the Postclassic room with a replica of the *Dresden Codex,* one of only three Mayan books to survive their postconquest burning by the Spanish (the other two are the *Paris Codex* and the *Madrid Codex*).

ZONA 11
★ Museo Miraflores

The excellent **Museo Miraflores** (7a Calle 21-55 Zona 11, Paseo Miraflores, tel. 2470-3415, 9am-7pm Tues., Wed., Sun., 9am-8pm Thurs., Fri., Sat., $5 adults, $1 children and students) is dedicated to the history of the Mayan site of Kaminaljuyú. Just outside the museum's main entrance is a replica of an irrigation canal similar to those found throughout the Mayan city as early as 600 BC. Inside,

a statue of Nobel Prize laureate Miguel Ángel Asturias on Avenida La Reforma

the large window panels provide fantastic views of the stark contrast between old and new, with the green temple mound of structure B-V-3 flanked by modern glass buildings in the background. Also at the entrance is a scale model of what the city probably looked like in its heyday, built into the museum floor under a glass case. In the main exhibit area, you'll find a comprehensive history of Kaminaljuyú in English and Spanish as well as a burial display, pottery, jade jewelry, stone sculpture, and obsidian blades. There are also old photographs of the site's excavation and maps showing the large area once occupied by the ancient city. You are free to explore the temple mounds outside (steps are built into them). A few more temple mounds can be found in the vicinity of the museum, having been completely closed in by one of the city's larger shopping complexes. Among the latter are the ever-growing Galerías Miraflores, Paseo Miraflores, and Las Majadas.

ZONA 13

This area was once the site of a large farm known as La Aurora, which today gives its name to the zoo, airport, and adjacent horse track on the grounds of the former Hipódromo del Sur. The horse track has been reinvented as **Parque Deportivo Ecuestre La Aurora.**

Zona 13 also houses a number of fairly good museums, all adjacent to each other in a large complex, and the city's zoo.

La Aurora Zoo

Guatemala City's **La Aurora Zoo** (Boulevard Juan Pablo II Zona 13, tel. 2475-0894, http://aurorazoo.org.gt, 9am-5pm Tues.-Sun., $4 adults, $1.50 children) is modern and well run. Its grounds are a popular weekend destination for city dwellers from all walks of life. About 900 animals representing 110 species are housed in re-creations of their natural habitats, including African savannah, Asia, and tropical forest. There are leopards, lions, giraffes, Asian pachyderms, Bengal tigers, and jaguars and other species found in Guatemala's tropical forests. All cages have been removed from the park so as to provide visitors with the opportunity to see the animals free of visual obstructions. Check out the English teahouse dating to 1924. Penguins were the most recent addition to the zoo at last visit. Three Bengal tiger cubs were born and introduced to the public here in 2014, to the delight of spectators. They will likely find residency in a North American or European zoo by the time you read this, in an effort to maintain the gene pool of this highly endangered species.

Museo de los Niños

Right across the street is the **Museo de los Niños** (Children's Museum, 5a Calle 10-00 Zona 13, tel. 2475-5076, www.museodelosninos.com.gt, 8:30am-noon and 1pm-4:30pm Tues.-Fri., 9:30am-1:30pm and 2:30pm-6pm Sat.-Sun. and holidays, $5), housed in a pyramidal building, with educational exhibits and hands-on learning on themes such as civic values and teamwork. You'll also find a giant jigsaw puzzle of Guatemala, a music room, and trampolines. It's a popular school field trip.

★ Museo Nacional de Arqueología y Etnología

The city's **Museo Nacional de Arqueología y Etnología** (6a Calle y 7a Avenida Zona 13, tel. 2475-4399, www.munae.gob.gt, 9am-4pm Tues.-Fri., 9am-noon and 1:30pm-4pm Sat.-Sun., $7.50) houses an outstanding collection of original monuments from Guatemala's archaeological sites, including ceramics, carved rock sculptures and stelae from Kaminaljuyú, *barrigones* (Olmecoid stone figures with distended, bloated bellies) from the Pacific Coast sites, and stelae from the Petén sites. Among the latter are beautifully carved stelae and a spectacular hieroglyphic bench from Piedras Negras as well as stelae and hieroglyphic panels from Dos Pilas and Machaquilá. Another of the archaeology and ethnologgy museum's highlights is a splendid jade mask made famous on the cover of the September 1987 issue

a Maya stela on display in the Museo Nacional de Arqueología y Etnología

Rodolfo Abularach, reminiscent of Picasso's *Guernica*.

Museo Nacional de Historia Natural Jorge Ibarra

For all of Guatemala's rich ecology, it still lacks a comprehensive natural history museum to do it justice. The **Museo Nacional de Historia Natural Jorge Ibarra** (6a Calle 7-30 Zona 13, tel. 2472-0468, 9am-4pm Tues.-Fri., 9am-noon and 2pm-4pm Sat.-Sun., $1.50) makes an attempt but falls short. You'll find plenty of taxidermy as well as exhibits on several of the country's ecosystems. A standout is the photo exhibit on the Atitlán pied-billed grebe, extinct since 1987, and the attempt in the mid-20th century to save it.

ZONA 14

Guatemala City's boom district, Zona 14 has grown by leaps and bounds in recent years thanks to a plethora of new condos and office buildings built in this area. The sector's main feature is **Avenida Las Américas,** which is really just a continuation of Zona 9/10's Avenida La Reforma and boasts the same sylvan landscaping interspersed with monuments to Columbus and other historical figures centered around wide plazas. At the end of this avenue is a steep drop-off and Plaza Berlin, from which there are good views of the city's southern sprawl and Pacaya Volcano, along with some simple snack and drink stands. An addition to this plaza are three pieces of none other than the now-departed Berlin Wall, with a plaque commemorating liberty.

Avenida Las Américas parallels La Aurora Airport's runway. Branching off from the main artery are a number of side streets and residential areas. Two-story houses now share these streets with 20- and 30-story commercial and residential buildings. Between the airport runway and Avenida Las Américas is Avenida Hincapié, where the hangars of some of the domestic carriers and helicopter flights are housed just off its juncture with 18 Calle.

On Sundays, a stretch from Avenida Las

of *National Geographic*. The ethnology section has displays on traditional costumes and housing. The exhibits are not quite as modern or well executed as those in some other of the city's top museums, but the sheer significance of the original pieces found here makes a visit more than worthwhile.

Museo Nacional de Arte Moderno Carlos Mérida

Across the street is the city's **Museo Nacional de Arte Moderno Carlos Mérida** (tel. 2472-0467, 9am-4pm Tues.-Fri., 9am-noon and 1:30pm-4pm Sat.-Sun., $2.50), which focuses largely on the work of its namesake artist, including examples of his Cubist art and large murals. Mérida's Guatemala's most celebrated artist; his work also adorns the inside of several buildings in Guatemala City's Civic Center, including City Hall, with a giant mural known as *Canto a la Raza* (*Ode to the Race*), recently restored. Among the other interesting works found at the museum of modern art is one titled *La Peste* (*Pestilence*) by

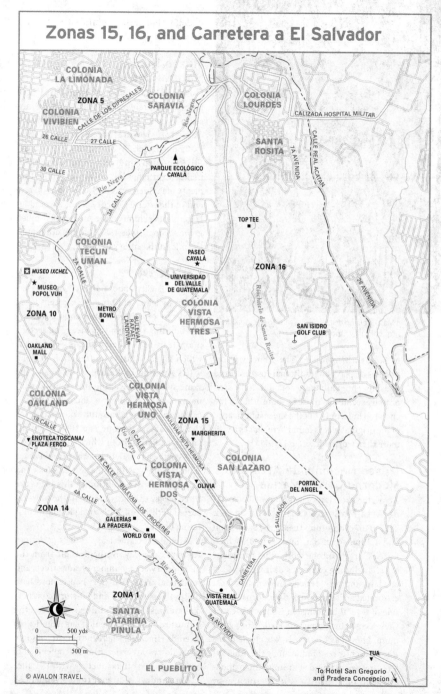

Zonas 15, 16, and Carretera a El Salvador

COLONIA LA LIMONADA

ZONA 5

COLONIA VIVIBIEN

COLONIA SARAVIA

COLONIA LOURDES

CALIZADA HOSPITAL MILITAR

26 CALLE

CALLE DE LOS CIPRESALES

27 CALLE

Rio Negro

SANTA ROSITA

CALLE REAL ACATAN

30 CALLE

3A CALLE

PARQUE ECOLÓGICO CAYALÁ

7A AVENIDA

TOP TEE

COLONIA TECUN UMAN

2A CALLE

PASEO CAYALÁ

ZONA 16

26 AVENIDA

★ MUSEO IXCHEL

★ MUSEO POPOL VUH

UNIVERSIDAD DEL VALLE DE GUATEMALA

Riachuelo de Santa Rosita

METRO BOWL

ZONA 10

COLONIA VISTA HERMOSA TRES

BULEVAR RAFAEL LANDIVAR

SAN ISIDRO GOLF CLUB

OAKLAND MALL

COLONIA OAKLAND

COLONIA VISTA HERMOSA UNO

18 CALLE

Rio Negro

0 CALLE

ZONA 15

BULEVAR VISTA HERMOSA

MARGHERITA

COLONIA SAN LAZARO

ENOTECA TOSCANA/ PLAZA FERCO

18 CALLE

BULEVAR LOS PROCERES

COLONIA VISTA HERMOSA DOS

OLIVIA

PORTAL DEL ANGEL

4A CALLE

ZONA 14

GALERIAS LA PRADERA

WORLD GYM

EL SALVADOR

CARRETERA A EL SALVADOR

Rio Pinula

ZONA 1

SANTA CATARINA PINULA

VISTA REAL GUATEMALA

8A AVENIDA

0   500 yds

0   500 m

TUA

EL PUEBLITO

To Hotel San Gregorio and Pradera Concepcion

© AVALON TRAVEL

Américas all the way to Avenida La Reforma's Plaza Israel is closed to pedestrian traffic, making for a very pleasant place to take a stroll.

ZONAS 15 AND 16

Also enjoying substantial growth due to new condos and office buildings are Zonas 15 and 16, on the eastern edge of Guatemala City bordering ravines and the hillside leading up to a neighboring plateau. In addition to the area's prominence as an affluent residential sector, it also houses joint retail/residential centers such as the ever-expanding **Paseo Cayalá** with condos, an outdoor shopping mall, gym, and even a driving range. It's pleasantly urbanized while feeling like you're well outside of the city core, seen off in the distance separated by deep gorges. Among the main thoroughfares is **Bulevar Vista Hermosa,** leading southeast out of the city.

Carretera a El Salvador

From Bulevar Vista Hermosa, the road winds out of the city and up a mountainside heading southeast, eventually making its way to neighboring El Salvador. The first 35 kilometers or so of this **Carretera a El Salvador** are Guatemala City's suburb extraordinaire.

After climbing up the mountains to the east of Guatemala City, the road eventually traverses a plateau, providing the perfect topographic conditions for the establishment of a virtual satellite city. The area around Carretera a El Salvador is also prime agricultural land. You'll find countless subdivisions springing up all over this fast-growing area, giving it all the feel of a U.S. suburb. The plateau lies at an altitude of about 2,135 meters (7,000 feet), so it's a bit cooler than Guatemala City and it also receives more rainfall during the rainy season. Those familiar with San José, Costa Rica, might find this area very similar to the Escazú suburbs near that city.

Although it's very much a residential area, you may find yourself visiting friends or staying at one of the hotels in this neck of the woods. Catering to the ever-increasing numbers of Guatemala City residents migrating to the surrounding suburbs, the area has at least one sizable shopping mall in **Pradera Concepción,** which adjoins the Condado Concepción shopping district. Between them, they boast a number of restaurants, PriceSmart warehouse shopping, WalMart, Sears, banks, car dealerships, a Starbucks, and even an IMAX movie theater. The selection of goods in local supermarkets

aerial view of Guatemala City's Zona 10 looking east to Zonas 15 and 16

is more upscale (with prices to match), so a lot of folks looking for favorite import items do their shopping up here. This area is also home to two of Guatemala's most upscale golf courses and one of the city's finest hotels. Also in this area, and once used as a little-known shortcut for getting out of the city, **Muxbal** has recently seen the rise of upscale shopping centers housing some of my favorite eateries.

Entertainment

NIGHTLIFE

Guatemala City has a fairly lively nightlife scene with bars, clubs, and music found mostly in the Zona Viva and downtown. There are plenty of places to dance to salsa and Latin beats in addition to rock and pop music. Electronica is also a big hit with Guatemalan partygoers. DJ Tiësto performs in Guatemala fairly frequently.

Bars

A good mix of bars in the downtown area caters to the city's bohemian population as well as to international travelers. In Zona 10, the Zona Viva sector centered around 16 Calle is the place to go if you want to hang out with the city's wealthy elite in the hippest establishments.

Downtown, **El Portal** (Portal del Comercio, 9a Calle, between 6a and 7a Avenidas, 10am-10pm Mon.-Sat.) is said to be the old stomping grounds of none other than Che Guevara, who lived in Guatemala City in the early 1950s. You'll find a long wooden bar and some wooden tables along with draft beers for about $2. The entrance is at the Portal del Comercio arcade ingress on the south side of the park along 6a Avenida. Nearby **Las Cien Puertas** (9a Calle between 6a and 7a Avenidas, Pasaje Aycinena, Zona 1, tel. 2232-8502, noon-2am Mon.-Sat.) is the city's quintessential bohemian hangout set in a restored colonial arcade. Enjoy tasty quesadillas and tacos when you get the munchies. **Europa Bar** (11 Calle 5-16, Edificio Testa, Local 201, tel. 2253-4929, 8am-midnight Mon.-Sat.) is a restaurant doubling as a bar that is popular with the expat crowd.

CNN and sports are on the cable TV, and the restaurant serves decent food, including the all-American staple breakfast of eggs, hash browns, bacon, and toast. **Reilly's GuateCity** (12 Calle 6-25 Zona 1, reillys.guatecity@gmail. com), a spin-off of the popular Irish pub in Antigua Guatemala, is also a good bet in downtown Guatemala City.

Zona Viva's motley assortment of upscale bars is constantly in flux. New places open and close all the time, and it's hard to keep up with all the changes, even if you live in Guatemala City. A classic expat hangout, **Shakespeare's Pub** (13 Calle and 1a Avenida, Torre Santa Clara II, Local 5, Zona 10, tel. 2331-2641, 11am-1am Mon.-Sat., 2pm-1am Sun.) appropriately advertises, "No tragedy, no comedy, just good times." **Cheers** (13 Calle 0-40 Zona 10, tel. 2368-2089, 9am-1am Mon.-Sat., 1pm-midnight Sun.) is a cool sports bar with scrumptious buffalo wings, frosty beer on tap, dartboards, pool tables, foosball, big-screen TVs, and classic rock on the stereo. **Rattle N Hum** (4a Avenida 16-11 Zona 10, noon-1am daily) is a fun, Australian-owned place often featuring live music. There's also tasty pub grub, and it's popular with locals and visitors alike.

Among the hotel bars, the InterContinental's **Maya Lounge** (14 Calle 2-51 Zona 10, tel. 2143-4444) bears mentioning for the cool vibe and chic modern-day Mayan decor. I also must note the bar at the **Hard Rock Café Guatemala City** (1a Avenida y 13 Calle Zona 10, Edificio Dubai Center, tel. 2332-3862, www.hardrock.com/cafes/guatemala-city, noon-12:30am Mon.-Sat., 11am-10pm Sun.) for its live music, the sheer variety and creativity of drink options, and the simple fact that it's one of the few places in Guatemala City with a cool outdoor patio bar. Antigua's popular **Monoloco** (16 Calle 1-01 Zona 10, CC Plaza Obelisco, tel. 2367-3283, www.restaurantemonoloco.com) now has a Guatemala City location with the same fun atmosphere and decent bar food.

Nightclubs

Like the bars, nightclubs are in constant flux, but here are some options that have been around for some time. In Zona 10, **Kalhua** (15 Calle and 1a Avenida, Zona 10, 8pm-3am Mon.-Sat., $5 cover) is one of Guatemala City's most popular clubs with a wealthy clientele and hip atmosphere spread out on four floors. I've had a great time dancing to electronica at **The Box Lounge Groove** (15 Calle y 4a Avenida, Zona 10, 5pm-1am Tues.-Sat.). It's on the small side, but its loyal clientele don't seem to mind squeezing in. **SOMA Centro Cultural** (11 Calle 4-27 Zona 1, tel. 2253-0406) is a good downtown option for music and a hip atmosphere. Also downtown, **Savoy Zona Uno** (12 Calle y Sexta Avenida 5-59 Zona 1, tel. 4040-4888) is wonderfully set in a derelict old building turned hipster haven.

There are street tacos and other munchies for sale on the ground floor.

Live Music

A popular place for live music in a wonderfully bohemian atmosphere is **La Bodeguita del Centro** (12 Calle 3-55 Zona 1, tel. 2230-1780, 8pm-2am Tues.-Sat., $4 cover on weekends). Besides live folk, rock, and jazz music, there are poetry readings, forums, and movies some nights. The atmosphere features posters the likes of Bob Marley and Che Guevara, as well as tons of Che-related memorabilia. Food is also served, with tasty chicken sandwiches. **TrovaJazz** (Vía 6 3-55 Zona 4, tel. 2267-9388, www.trovajazz.com) has live trova most evenings. It also serves food and coffee beverages. For live jazz, check out **La Esquina Jazz Café** (6a Avenida 0-15 Zona 2, tel. 2230-2859, noon-8pm Mon. and Thurs., noon-10pm Sat.-Sun).

PERFORMING ARTS

The **Centro Cultural Miguel Ángel Asturias** (24 Calle 3-81 Zona 4, tel. 2232-4042, 2232-4043, 2232-4044, or 2232-4045, mcd.gob.gt/teatro-nacional/) hosts ballet and a number of cultural events throughout the year. Check listings in the *Prensa Libre* newspaper

Hard Rock Café Guatemala City

or *Recrearte*, a free monthly publication widely available in tourist shops and hotels.

The **Teatro de la Cámara de la Industria** (Chamber of Industry Theater, Ruta 6, 9-21 Zona 4, tel. 2331-9191, showtimes 8:30pm Fri. and Sat., 5pm Sun., $8) usually has theater performances on weekends, mostly of satirical works.

For other cultural events, check the entertainment section of the useful Spanish-language website at www.deguate.com.

CINEMA

Guatemala City has a number of excellent movie theaters, with movies sometimes opening on the same day as their U.S. release. It's also (compared to the U.S.) a lot cheaper to go see a movie. The city's original IMAX movie theater is found at **Cines Pradera Concepción** (tel. 2329-2550, circuitoalba. com.gt), at the Pradera Concepción shopping mall along Km. 17.5 of Carretera a El Salvador, where you can have the IMAX theater experience for just $6. In one of the city's most popular shopping malls is **Cinépolis Miraflores** (Centro Comercial Miraflores, 21 Avenida 4-32 Zona 11, tel. 2378-2300, www.cinepolis. com.gt). Miraflores now also has an IMAX theater. Cinépolis (a Mexican chain) also has a location in Zona 10's **Oakland Mall** (Diagonal 6, 13-01 Zona 10, www.cinepo-lis.com.gt). Five of Oakland Mall's theaters are VIP lounges, in which you can order a meal and/or drink while you watch a movie. Other Cinépolis locations include **Cinépolis Cayalá** (Boulevard Rafael Landívar 10-05 Zona 16, Paseo Cayalá, tel. 2378-2300, www. cinepolis.com.gt) and **Cinépolis Portales** (Km. 4.5 Carretera al Atlántico Zona 17, Centro Comercial Portales, tel. 2378-2300, www.cinepolis.com.gt).

Not to be outdone, U.S. franchise Cinemark opened its first Guatemalan location at **Cinemark Eskala Roosevelt** (Calzada Roosevelt Km. 13.8 Zona 11, tel. 2250-7084, www.cinemarkca.com) featuring 3-D movies. There's a now a second location at **Cinemark Arkadia** (Boulevard Los Próceres, 18 Calle 26-21 Zona 10, www.cinemarkca.com) showing 3-D, D-BOX and XD movies.

Check the *Prensa Libre* newspaper or the theaters' websites for showtimes. Movies at all of these venues generally cost between $4 and $5, and all have stadium seating.

AMUSEMENT PARKS

The creators of Retalhuleu's (Pacific Coast) Xocomil and Xetulul theme parks have provided Guatemala City with a fun entertainment option in the form of **Mundo Petapa** (Avenida Petapa 42-36 Zona 12, tel. 2423-9000, www.irtra.org.gt, 9am-5pm Thurs.-Sat., 9am-6pm Sun., $13 adults, $7 children). There are plenty of rides (including a small roller coaster), swimming pools, a dinosaur-inspired playground, and a small zoo to keep kids and adults entertained. Food prices in the many kiosks and eateries are surprisingly reasonable for a theme park in an urban area. If adrenaline is your thing, check out **X Park** (Final Avenida Hincapié, Km. 11.5 Carretera a Boca del Monte, tel. 2380-2080, www.xpark. net, $2 admission, activities from $2.50), where there is bungee jumping, paintball, an obstacle course, and a climbing wall.

Have an outdoor adventure without going too far from Guatemala City at **Green Rush** (Km. 24 Carretera a El Salvador, tel. 5708-8801 or 5900-4291, www.greenrush.com.gt, 8am-8pm weekends, weekdays with prior reservation, $7 adults, $4 children; entrance includes access to trails, animal sanctuary, and relaxation areas). This ecoadventure park in the eastern hillsides flanking Guatemala City features 10 kilometers of trails and various outdoor activities that include archery ($2.50 and up), horseback riding ($2.50-13), and a zipline ($7). There's an animal sanctuary and a trail leading to a far-off waterfall. Services include a restaurant and picnic areas with gorgeous views over the Guatemala City valley. You can camp here with your own tent or go glamping in one of their souped-up safari tents ($121 d, including breakfast). The tents have private decks with lovely views and private bathrooms with hot-water showers.

Shopping

You can find almost anything you might possibly want or need in Guatemala City. In addition to many modern shopping malls stocked with the latest fashions and electronics, there are a number of department stores for household appliances and cosmetics. For grocery shopping, the local giant is Paiz, which was recently taken over by WalMart. La Torre is also a well-stocked local grocery chain. U.S.-style warehouse shopping is available at PriceSmart or at a number of local chains. Guatemalans love U.S.-made goods, which is easy to see given their wide availability. For organic grocery shopping and natural foods, head to **Orgánica** (Diagonal 6 16-23 Zona 10, tel. 2363-1819, 9am-7pm Mon.-Sat., and Km. 15.5 Carretera a El Salvador, Condado Concepción Fase 1 Local #21, tel. 6634-7077, 9am-6pm Mon.-Sat.). The website for all locations is www.organicastore.com.

CLOTHING STORES

In line with its fashionable cafés and expensive hotels, Guatemala City also features a number of attractive stores for window-shopping or picking up an outfit should you need something nice to wear for a fancy dinner or night out on the town. Two of the most fashionable retail outlets are the European chain **Mexx** (16 Calle 5-86 Zona 10, Plaza Magnolia, tel. 2368-0757, www.mexx.com, 10am-8pm daily) and the European-inspired menswear store **Saúl Méndez** (6a Avenida 15-64 Zona 10, tel. 2379-8722, www.saulemendez.com, 10am-8pm daily). Saúl Méndez, Mexx, and more recently, **Zara** (www.zara.com.gt), have locations in the following upscale shopping malls.

SHOPPING MALLS

Guatemala City has some excellent shopping malls carrying the most basic or most exclusive items one could need, in addition to fashionable boutiques and department stores. None of the latter (curiously) seem to result from Guatemalan investment. These include Simán (El Salvador), Carrion (Honduras), Figaly (Panama), and

Parque Comercial Las Majadas

Sears (United States). The city's largest shopping mall is **Pradera Concepción** (Km. 17.5 Carretera a El Salvador, 10am-7pm Mon.-Thurs. and 10am-9pm Fri.-Sat.), with a variety of familiar stores and restaurant chains including Sears and T.G.I. Friday's. It adjoins a smaller, open-air shopping center known as **Condado Concepción,** which features a Starbucks and an Applebee's in addition to several local chains. Opened in 2003 and expanded in 2006 and 2011, the sprawling **Galerías Miraflores** (21 Avenida 4-32 Zona 11, 10am-8pm Mon.-Thurs., 10am-9pm Fri.-Sat., 10am-7pm Sun.) also harbors some of Guatemala's most exclusive stores, including a Simán department store, the international Zara boutique, and a L'Occitane store. There's also an IHOP if you need your pancake fix. Across the way is the **Parque Comercial Las Majadas** shopping center with a Sears, Fetiche perfume store, and a T.G.I. Friday's. They've recently expanded with a new, very pleasant outdoor concept known as **Majadas ONCE** (tel. 2200-9696, www.majadas.com, 9am-9pm daily).

In Zona 10, east up the hill toward the Carretera a El Salvador, is **Galerías La Pradera** (20 Calle 25-85 Zona 10, tel. 2367-4136, 10am-8pm Mon.-Sat. and 10am-7pm Sun.), an upscale shopping mall remodeled in 2010-2011. Though not as upscale as its Zona Viva location might suggest, **Gran Centro Los Próceres** (16 Calle 2-00 Zona 10, tel. 2332-8742) nonetheless is conveniently situated near the major Zona 10 hotels. Also conveniently situated in Zona 10 (and brand-new) is **Arkadia Shopping** (Boulevard Los Próceres, 18 Calle 26-21 Zona 10, www.arkadiashopping.com, 10am-8pm Sun.-Thurs., 10am-9pm Fri.-Sat.).

Zona 10's most upscale shopping mall is also Guatemala City's nicest. **Oakland Mall** (Diagonal 6, 13-01 Zona 10, www.oakland-mall.com.gt, 10am-8pm Mon.-Thurs., 10am-9pm Fri.-Sat., 10am-7pm Sun.) features 170 stores spread across three floors, in addition to several movie theaters. Among its stores

the open-air style of Paseo Cayalá

and restaurants you'll find an aquarium, an impressive waterfall producing geometric shapes, and even a carousel imported from Italy. A Starbucks with plenty of outdoor seating fronts the street along its main entrance. Also in this sector is the very pleasant **Plaza Fontabella** (4a Ave. 12-59 Zona 10, tel. 6628-8600, www.plazafontabella.com), built as an outdoor mall in neocolonial style, where you can enjoy Guatemala's spring-like climate and a decent selection of stores and restaurants while strolling the cobblestone pedestrian walkways. Guatemala's first Carolina Herrera designer handbag store opened here in 2011. Convenient for shoppers coming in from neighboring Antigua due to its location on the southwestern edges of Guatemala City is **SanKris Mall** (Boulevard Principal de San Cristóbal, tel. 2300-0600, www.sankris.com.gt, 10am-8pm daily). It has a decent selection of stores and a World Gym.

In Zona 16, you'll find a fine example of the recent trend toward construction of outdoor pedestrian malls in warm-weather locales. **Paseo Cayalá** (Ciudad Cayalá, Zona 16, www.paseocayala.com.gt) is housed in a sprawling collection of whitewashed Spanish neocolonial buildings. There are numerous specialty stores in addition to cool restaurants and bars with outdoor patio seating fronting the cobblestone pedestrian thoroughfare. Three universities lie nearby, and the shopping district is part of a larger residential complex encompassing homes and student apartments. Recent additions include a movie theater, driving range, a World Gym, and a Starbucks. There are lovely views of the city's downtown core, off in the distance.

HANDICRAFTS

You can shop the jam-packed stalls in downtown Guatemala City's **Mercado Central** (8a Avenida and 6a Calle, 6am-6pm Mon.-Sat., 9am-noon Sun.) for textiles, *típica* clothing, and leather goods. A safer and more enjoyable option can be found near the airport and Zona 13 museums at the open-air **Mercado de Artesanías** (Boulevard Juan Pablo II, 8am-6pm Mon.-Sat., 8am-1pm Sun.), with a fairly wide assortment of handicrafts and tourist souvenirs.

Recommended retailers include **Lin Canola** (5a Calle 9-60 Zona 1, tel. 2232-0858, www.lin-canola.com, 9am-6pm Mon.-Fri.), where the assortment varies from home decorative items to jewelry and everything between. This store is especially recommended if you want to buy Guatemalan fabrics by the yard. Its Zona 10 location, **In Nola** (18 Calle 21-31 Zona 10, Boulevard Los Próceres, tel. 2367-2424, 8:30am-6:30pm Mon.-Fri. and 8:30am-1:30pm Sat.), is more modern and contains much the same in a better part of town.

Selling fashionable adaptations on traditional designs for the home, **Textura** (Diagonal 6, 13-63 Zona 10, tel. 2367-2098, 9:30am-7pm Mon.-Fri.., 9:30am-2:30pm Sat.) is especially recommended for its beautiful and colorful hammocks.

ART GALLERIES

If you want to take in the work of local artists, head to Guatemala's oldest art gallery, **Galería El Túnel** (16 Calle 1-01 Zona 10, Plaza Obelisco, tel. 2367-3284, www.galeriaeltunel.com.gt), featuring the work of more than 100 artists. Another good art gallery worth checking out is **el attico** (4a Avenida 15-45 Zona 14, tel. 2368-0853, www.elattico.com). **Fundación Rozas Botrán** (16 Calle 4-66 Zona 14, tel. 2366-7064, www.fundacionrozasbotran.org) has rotating painting, sculpture, and photography exhibits in its spacious gallery.

BOOKS

For a great atmosphere for unwinding with a cup of coffee or tea and a large selection of books (though mostly in Spanish), try **Sophos** (Plaza Fontabella, 4a Ave. 12-59 Zona 10, tel. 2419-7070, www.sophosenlinea.com, 9am-8pm Mon.-Sat., 10am-6pm Sun.). Also with plenty of books in Spanish is **Artemis Edinter** (www.artemisedinter.com) with several locations including Galerías Miraflores, Pradera Concepción, and Oakland Mall.

A number of bookstores cater to the expat community, stocking a variety of English-language books on their shelves. **Vista Hermosa Book Shop** (2a Calle 18-50, Vista Hermosa II, Zona 15, tel. 2369-1003, vhbookshop@intelnet.net.gt, 9am-1pm and 2pm-6pm Mon.-Sat.) has books in English and Spanish and is in a quiet residential sector east of Zona 10.

OUTDOOR GEAR

For anything you may have neglected to bring for your outdoor Guatemala adventures, head to **Big Mountain** (Centro Comercial Miraflores, 2do nivel, Kiosko K-96, tel. 2474-8547, www.bigmountainonline.com, 9am-8pm Mon.-Sun.), offering a good assortment of hiking, climbing, mountain biking, and camping gear, and name-brand outdoor clothing.

Another option for outdoor gear is The North Face (2nd floor of the Oakland Mall, Diagonal 6, 13-01 Zona 10, tel. 2336-6881, 10am-8pm Mon.-Thurs., 10am-9pm Fri.-Sat., 10am-7pm Sun.). There's also now a location at the Galerías Miraflores shopping mall.

Recreation

PARKS

The idea of a greenbelt is relatively new to Guatemalan city planners. Most of the city's parks tend to be plazas centered around churches. A refreshing alternative is that of Parque Ecológico Deportivo Cayalá (Calzada de la Paz, Zona 16, in front of the Cemaco warehouse, tel. 4561-8082 or 5744-4360, www.cayala.org, 8am-5:30pm Tues.-Sun., $5), where there are nature trails winding through the park's 24 acres of mostly forested land showcasing the flora and fauna of the city's *barrancos*. The urban oasis is privately run by ecological organization FUNDAECO and entry includes a visit to the Museo Metropolitano de Aves (Metropolitan Bird Museum). The museum showcases wooden versions of Guatemala's myriad bird species, including endemic and migratory birds.

On Sunday mornings, parts of Avenida Las Américas and Avenida La Reforma (from Plaza Eucarística to Plaza Israel) are closed to car traffic as part of the municipality's Pasos y Pedales initiative. Pedestrians, cyclists, inline skaters, and skateboarders take to the broad streets, while the green grass and plazas of the boulevards' wide central dividers serve as pleasant areas for rest and relaxation. A more recent development is the addition of a bike path running down the entire length of the wide, tree-and-grass strewn median of Avenida La Reforma all the way from Plaza El Obelisco to its northern extreme.

HEALTH CLUBS

There are a number of good gymnasiums, mostly U.S. franchises, where you can pay a day rate of about $7 to work out if you don't have a membership. World Gym (www.worldgym.com.gt) has four locations to choose from. Its Calzada Roosevelt location (Calzada Roosevelt 21-09 Zona 7, Centro Comercial Gran Vía Roosevelt, tel. 2475-2856) is conveniently across the street from Galerías Miraflores and the Grand Tikal Futura hotel. It also has a Zona 10 location (Boulevard Los Próceres 25-74 Zona 10, Gran Vía Pradera, tel. 2423-6000), a third location in the southwest suburbs of San Cristóbal (3ra. Calle Sector A-3, Boulevard San Cristóbal 6-72 Zona 8 de Mixco, SanKris Mall, tel. 2424-4848), and the newest location at Paseo Cayalá (Diagonal 35 Boulevard Austriaco 16-25 Zona 16, Cardales de Cayalá, tel. 2491-4333). All have a full gym and swimming pool. You can also work out at Gold's Gym (Pradera Concepción Mall, Km. 17.5 Carretera a El Salvador, tel. 6634-1240, www.goldsgym.com).

GOLF

Fans of golf will find some excellent golf courses in and around the city; those within private country clubs are usually still open to visitors. You can enjoy a round of golf surrounded by the country's spectacular mountain scenery as you play on narrow, sloping fairways lined with pine trees and a variety of other obstacles. Several of sportfishing outfitters have combined fishing and golf packages. If interested, contact The Great Sailfishing Company (tel. 7934-6220, or 877/763-0851 U.S., www.greatsailfishing.com) or Sailfish Bay Lodge (tel. 2426-3909 direct or 800/638-7405 U.S. reservations, www.sailfishbay.com). It's also possible to arrange a round of golf through the concierges at some of the city's finer hotels, including the Westin Camino

Real and InterContinental. Entry to all of these clubs is by prior authorization only. You'll need to call ahead or email.

In 2006 and 2007, Guatemala City's San Isidro Golf Club hosted the **NGA/Hooter's Pro Golf Tour,** which has become an annual event between the last week of February and the first week of March. Guatemala is also a major stop along the annual **Tour de las Américas** in February.

Guatemala City's exclusive Cayalá area is now home to a driving range, the first of its kind in Central America. **Top Tee** (Boulevard Austríaco 37-01, Arcadia de Cayalá, Zona 16, tel. 2300-0700, www.toptee.com.gt) has 38 driving stations, TV lounges for watching sports, and a well-stocked bar.

San Isidro Golf Club

Still officially within the city limits in Zona 16, **San Isidro Golf Club** (Finca San Isidro, Zona 16, tel. 2419-1200, www.clubcamp-estresanisidro.com) is the city's most modern and is in a quiet residential section in its eastern extremes. The 18-hole, par-72 course measures 6,640 yards and offers some truly spectacular views of Guatemala City flanked by Agua, Acatenango, and Fuego Volcanoes. Greens fees are $75, clubs rent for $15, a cart rental costs $20, and caddies are $15. The splendid facilities here include a restaurant overlooking the greens featuring a beautiful dining room with vaulted wooden ceiling, a gym, a squash court, and a swimming pool with lap lanes.

Hacienda Nueva Country Club

The 18-hole, 7,100-yard, par-72 golf course at **Hacienda Nueva Country Club** (Km. 25, Ruta Nacional 18, Carretera a Mataquescuintla, San José Pinula, tel. 6628-1000, www.haciendanueva.com, $75 Tues.-Fri., $90 weekends and holidays) is just outside the city near Carretera a El Salvador and set beautifully on the grounds of a 16th-century Jesuit monastery. There's a small chapel with original artwork where Mass is still held weekly. Facilities include nine tennis courts, two squash courts, tennis and golf pro shops, and a swimming pool that has won international design awards. The clubhouse has three dining areas, including a poolside snack bar, a casual dining room serving international dishes, and La Pérgola, an outdoor steakhouse overlooking the 18th hole. Fees include $15 for caddie service and $25 for cart rental. A limited number of golf clubs are available for rental at $15. There are also a driving range and putting green.

Alta Vista Golf and Tennis Club

The most challenging course can be found just down the road from Hacienda Nueva at **Alta Vista Golf and Tennis Club** (Km. 27, Ruta Nacional 18, Carretera a Mataquescuintla, San José Pinula, tel. 6661-1414, www.altavistagolf.com.gt, 7am-8pm Tues.-Sun., $75), where the 18-hole, par-71, slope-122 course is divided into two nine-hole sections. Additional challenges include 74 sand traps and two water traps with a route defined by 1,800 trees of varying species, adding a nice alpine touch to the incredible mountain views. The clubhouse is in a large and attractive three-story, English-style building with an elegant restaurant, a bar with pool table, an indoor swimming pool, three squash courts, and six tennis courts. Golf cart rentals cost $30, clubs are $15, and caddies $15.

Mayan Golf Course

South of the city in the neighboring district of Villa Nueva, **Mayan Golf Course** (Finca El Zarzal, Villa Nueva, tel. 6685-5800, www.mayangolfclub.com, $75) is Guatemala City's oldest, dating to 1918. The facilities here feel somewhat dated but have been well maintained. The 18-hole, par-72 golf course has exquisite views of Lake Amatitlán and Pacaya Volcano along its 7,092-yard length. Rental clubs and golf carts are available, and there is a café with a terrace overlooking the course. Additional sporting facilities include a bowling alley, tennis courts, a soccer field, volleyball court, and swimming pool.

Alta Vista Golf and Tennis Club offers one of Guatemala's most challenging courses.

BOWLING

Metro Bowl (2a Calle 15-93 Zona 15, on Vista Hermosa Boulevard, tel. 2243-2424, www.metrobowl.com.gt) is Central America's largest bowling alley, with 28 lanes. There are also eight pool tables and an area for video games. And, of course, there's a snack bar.

HORSEBACK RIDING/ EQUESTRIAN

Equestrian has become increasingly popular with Guatemala's well-to-do. In addition to the recently rehabilitated horse track known as **Parque Deportivo Ecuestre La Aurora**, next to the airport in Zona 13, there are a number of private facilities where equestrian and horseback riding are practiced. **Guate Equinos** (www.guateequinos.com, tel. 3163-8160 and 5305-7443) offers horseback riding lessons for all ages and instruction in all things equestrian on the grounds of the horse track at La Aurora and at its own facilities near a turnoff at km. 24.3 Carretera a El Salvador. Call or visit the website for a map of how to get here. **Club Ecuestre Vista Hermosa** (20 Avenida 21-00 Zona 16, Jacarandas de Cayalá, tel. 2261-0926, www.

clubecuestrevistahermosa.com) has three different tracks at its facility in Guatemala City's Cayalá area. For more on this sport of rising popularity in Guatemala, check out the Asociación Nacional de Ecuestres de Guatemala online at www.guatecuestres.com.

SPECTATOR SPORTS

Like other Latin Americans, Guatemalans are crazy about *fútbol.* The two most popular teams in the country's four-team national soccer league, denoted by the colors of their jerseys, are the Rojos (Municipales) and Cremas (Comunicaciones), who usually end up battling it out at the end of the season for the championship title. International games are also a big event, as Guatemala has never been to a World Cup. In recent years, it has gotten closer than it's ever been, and the postgame celebrations have spilled into the streets and lasted into the wee hours of the morning. Unfortunately, their high hopes have ended in bitter disappointment. Games can be seen at the **Estadio Mateo Flores** (10a Avenida, Zona 5), but be advised: The scene can get quite rowdy. In 1996, things got so out of hand that a stampede ensued when stands collapsed, killing 100 people. The soccer stadium has been remodeled in the aftermath. If you've always wanted to see a Latin American soccer match, you might want to check it out.

You can see baseball games at Parque Minerva's ballpark (Zona 2).

CITY TOURS

Traditional city tours can be arranged through any of the larger hotels or via **Clark Tours** (7a Avenida 14-76, Plaza Clark, Zona 9, tel. 2412-4700, www.clarktours.com). It has offices in the Westin Camino Real, Holiday Inn, and Barceló. For an urban adventure exploring Guatemala City on the ground level, consider a **bicycle tour** offered by local hostel **Quetzalroo** (6a Avenida 7-84 Zona 10, tel. 5746-0830, www.quetzalroo.com, $15

including bike rental). The tour varies depending on guests' interests and needs but you can expect to cover a lot of ground and see some interesting attractions through the eyes of well-informed local guide Marcos Romero-Close. The long version of the tour traverses Zonas 1, 2, 4, 10, 13, and 14 with stops at art galleries, coffee shops, a Zacapa Rum retail outlet, the Civic Center, Paseo de la Sexta, and various museums. Although Zona 10's Avenida La Reforma has a bike trail, most of the tour takes place on the gritty streets and sidewalks of Guatemala City. Helmets and reflective vests are provided. It's surprisingly safer on Guatemala City streets than you have been led to believe and Marcos has even hosted celebrities on the tour, including well-known Mexican singer Julieta Venegas.

Accommodations

Guatemala City has a wide variety of accommodations for all budgets. The major U.S. hotel chains have properties in Zonas 10, 11, and 13—close to the airport. Downtown is home to many of the city's budget accommodations.

CENTRO HISTÓRICO
$50-100

There are some real cheapies in downtown Guatemala City, traditionally the city's budget accommodation headquarters, though there are also some nice budget options outside the downtown area now, so there's really very little reason to stay in this somewhat dodgy part of town.

An exception located on a quiet side street is ★ **Posada Belén Museum Inn** (13 Calle "A" 10-30 Zona 1, tel. 2251-3478, www.posadabelen.com, $55-67 d), an 1873 home converted into a lovely museum inn. It has 10 rooms with tile floors tastefully decorated with Guatemalan bedspreads, paintings, and weavings. Its gracious hosts, René and Francesca, speak English and can help you

plan your journeys into Guatemala's rugged interior. Amenities include telephone and Internet access. All rooms have private bath and rates include breakfast. Other delicious homemade meals are available upon request. Oozing with history is the landmark **Hotel Pan American** (9a Calle 5-63 Zona 1, tel. 2232-6807, www.hotelpanamerican.com.gt, $55 d), which was once Guatemala City's go-to property, having been established by its namesake airline. Rooms have tile floors and are nicely decorated with Guatemalan artwork and furnishings. The dining room, serving international and Guatemalan dishes, is well known for its antique charm and elegance, with waiters wearing traditional village attire. It's also very well located, just steps away from bustling Paseo de la Sexta.

ZONA 4
$50-100

Conquistador Hotel (Vía 5, 4-68 Zona 4, tel. 2424-4444, hotelconquistador.com.gt, $90 d, including breakfast) was formerly a Ramada property. You'll find a lobby bar, the

Café Jardín serving a breakfast and lunch buffet, and La Pérgola serving fine international dishes for dinner.

ZONA 9
$50-100

The **Howard Johnson Inn** (Avenida La Reforma 4-22 Zona 9, tel. 2201-1111, www. hojo.com.gt, $95-103 d) comes with all the standard amenities you would expect from this international hotel chain, including air-conditioning, fan, nice wooden furniture, phone, and TV. There's a small restaurant in the lobby. Try to get a room facing the outside street.

$100-200

Among Guatemala City's numerous international hotel chain options is ★ **Barceló Guatemala City** (7a Avenida 15-45 Zona 9, tel. 800/227-2356, www.barceloguatemalacity.com, $125 d), with six different room types to choose from and all the standard comforts usually found in the Spanish hotel chain's properties. American and United Airlines have offices in the lobby of this former Marriott property.

The **Hilton Garden Inn Guatemala City** (13 Calle 7-65 Zona 9, tel. 2423-0909, http://hiltongardeninn3.hilton.com, from $119 d) is a winner for its sophisticated modern ambience. Amenities include a gym and restaurant. Its 110 rooms have air-conditioning.

ZONA 10
Under $50

The current Guatemala City favorite of the backpacking crowd is ★ **Quetzalroo Hostel** (6a Avenida 7-84 Zona 10, tel. 5746-0830, www.quetzalroo.com, $16-35). The owners take great pride in sharing their vast knowledge and enthusiasm for Guatemala and its capital city with visitors. For $16, you get a comfortable bed in a dorm room, shared bath, free wireless Internet, continental breakfast and free shuttle transport to the airport nearby. Private rooms with shared bath cost

$35 d per night. The hostel is conveniently situated in the heart of the Zona Viva. A fun add-on is a historical bike tour of Guatemala City. There's a cool rooftop patio with city views.

$50-100

Best Western Plus Hotel Stofella (2a Avenida 12-28 Zona 10, tel. 2410-8600, www. stofella.com, $100 d), a solid choice for business travelers, has rooms with fan or air-conditioning with breakfast included in the nightly rate. You'll find a lobby lounge, a fitness room with whirlpool tub, a bar, and in-room Internet connection. Offering many of the same services as its pricier sister hotels under the management of the Camino Real chain, **Biltmore Express** (15 Calle 0-31 Zona 10, tel. 2338-5000, hotelbiltmore.com.gt, $90 d) offers a continental breakfast and has comfortable rooms with broadband Internet. Guests can enjoy use of the nearby Westin Camino Real's swimming pool, whirlpool tub, and tennis and racquetball courts for an additional $10 a day. There's a free shuttle to and from the airport.

$100-200

Otelito (12 Calle 4-51 Zona 10, tel. 2339-1811, www.otelito.com, $140-200 d) is cool and hip but a bit noisy for some people's taste on account of a popular lobby lounge and nightclubs in its vicinity. There are 12 rooms, all named after local produce, housed in a modern home turned upscale hotel. The decor is minimalist with a different color scheme in evidence during each of the year's four seasons. It offers chill-out music playing on the speakers throughout the property, wireless Internet throughout, a business center, and a book exchange. Rooms feature nice artwork, 300-thread-count Egyptian cotton sheets, down pillows, air-conditioning, flat-screen cable TV, hardwood floors, and in-room chill-out music. Some have a minifridge. Walk-in showers feature tempered glass in lieu of shower curtains. There's a hip, frosted-glass lounge and restaurant (lunch and dinner daily, $7-12) downstairs. Popular Plaza Fontabella shopping mall is right across the street.

A top choice is the fabulous, 246-room ★ **Real InterContinental Guatemala** (14 Calle 2-51 Zona 10, tel. 2413-4444 or 800/835-4654 toll-free U.S., www.intercontinental.com, $125-485 d) with a wonderful lobby featuring Guatemalan paintings and sculpture, a sushi restaurant, a French café, and *boulangerie* and patisserie. The comfortable, stylish rooms feature in-room Internet access, down pillows, Egyptian cotton sheets, and flat-screen cable TV. Bathrooms have rain showerheads, and the safe deposit boxes are large enough to accommodate a laptop. There are free airport shuttles and a pleasant swimming pool on a deck overlooking the city. President George W. Bush and his wife, Laura, spent the night here during their 24-hour visit to Guatemala in March 2007.

Mercure Casa Veranda (12 Calle 1-24 Zona 10, tel. 2411-4100, www.mercure.com, $120 d) features all the amenities you'd come to expect from a reputable international hotel chain. Among the unique features of the property's 99 spacious suites are hardwood floors, Persian rugs, wireless Internet, and balconies with fantastic city views; some suites have full kitchens. The property also features a decent restaurant and bar.

A number of other international hotel chains are in this price category. Among them is the ever-reliable **Holiday Inn** (1a Avenida 13-22 Zona 10, tel. 2421-0000 or 800/009-9900 toll-free U.S., www.hinn.com.gt, $120 d), the landmark 271-room **Westin Camino Real** (14 Calle and Avenida La Reforma Zona 10, tel. 2333-3000, www.starwoodhotels.com, $149-329 d), and the business traveler-oriented, all-suite **Viva Clarion Suites** (tel. 2421-3333, www.clarionguatemala.com, $105-125 d).

The **Radisson** (1a Avenida 12-46 Zona 10, tel. 2421-5151 or 800/333-3333 toll-free U.S., www.radisson.com, $120 d) is another good business traveler option. All rooms have a minibar, in-room safe, large windows with city views, and in-room Internet access. There are also a gym, sauna, business center, and sushi restaurant/bar open 11am-midnight daily.

Conveniently near the U.S. embassy in a building oozing with European charm, **Hotel**

view of Zona 10 from the rooftop of Quetzalroo Hostel

San Carlos (Avenida La Reforma 7-89, Zona 10, tel. 2247-3000, www.hsancarlos.com, $90-175 d) offers 23 modern, comfortable rooms. The spacious suites are a good value and have hardwood floors and kitchenettes. There are also one- or two-bedroom apartments. At research time, U.S. hotel chains **Hyatt Place, Courtyard by Marriott,** and **La Quinta** announced plans for Guatemala City hotels to open in Zona 10 in 2016. The Hyatt Place project is particularly interesting, as it's part of a mixed use commercial, office, and residential complex known as AVIA encompassing three towers built round a plaza dotted with exuberant greenery. It will take up an entire city block, between 2nd and 3a Avenidas and 11 and 12 Calles.

ZONA 11
$100-200

Formerly the city's Hyatt Regency, the **Grand Tikal Futura** (Calzada Roosevelt 22-43 Zona 11, tel. 2410-0800, www.grand-tikalfutura.com.gt, $90-600 d) maintains high-quality standards and has comfortable, well-furnished rooms varying from standard rooms to stunning Diplomatic Suites. All have splendid views of the city and surrounding mountains. Restaurants include elegant La Molienda, serving international and Guatemalan dishes for breakfast, lunch, and dinner and the excellent Asia Grill and Wok serving lunch and dinner in a tropically inspired, casual atmosphere. There is a lobby bar, a fitness center with health-food bar, and a covered swimming pool with poolside service and city views.

ZONA 13 (AIRPORT)
Under $50

A number of inexpensive hotels all offering similar services are centered in a middle-class neighborhood near the airport. All offer free transport to and from the terminal as well as breakfast, though this varies from continental minimalist to a full-on Guatemalan feast. **Guatefriends B&B** (16 Calle 7-40 Zona 13, Aurora 1, tel. 5308-3275, $20) is run by a friendly couple. The rooms and property are decorated in bright colors that nod to Guatemala's colorful textiles and vivid Mayan culture. Among the nice extras are tasty home-cooked meals. **Dos Lunas Guest House** (21 Calle 10-92 Zona 13, Aurora II, tel. 2261-4248, www.hoteldoslunas.com, $18 pp) has nine basic rooms, all with shared bath, including a breakfast of eggs and toast. Reservations are necessary, as it's usually booked. **Hostal Los Lagos** (8a Avenida 15-85 Zona 13, tel. 2261-2809, www.loslagoshostal.com, starting $30 pp) has cheerful rooms with colorful paintings and several beds each. Rates include a complete breakfast of eggs and beans or cereal, and coffee or tea. You'll find Internet, cable TV, laundry, and baggage storage as well as two sitting rooms with bamboo furniture.

A notch above the rest of the lodgings in the airport neighborhood is ★ **Hostal Villa Toscana** (16 Calle 8-20, Aurora I, Zona 13, tel. 2261-2854, www.hostalvillatoscana.com, $52-68 d), a bed-and-breakfast where there are large, well-decorated rooms with private bathrooms and wireless Internet—there is even a suite with a balcony and volcano views. **Hotel Casa Blanca Inn** (15 Calle "C" 7-35, Aurora I, Zona 13, tel. 2261-3116, www.hotelcasablancainn.com, $40-55 d) is another good choice with pleasant, simply decorated rooms with big beds, reading lamps, and shared or private bathrooms. There is wireless Internet throughout and a pleasant patio bar.

$100-200

The 183-room **Crowne Plaza** (Avenida Las Américas 9-08 Zona 13, tel. 2422-5050 or 800/835-4654 toll-free U.S., www.ihg.com, $115 d) features rooms with the chain's Sleep Advantage, including deliciously comfortable beds, fine duvets, and your choice of seven different pillows. It has a business center with wireless Internet, a huge gym with excellent city views from the top floor, a sports bar with video poker and slot machines, and a heated

view from the Presidential Suite at Vista Real Guatemala

Carretera a El Salvador, tel. 2420-7720, www. vistareal.com, from $119 d) scores big points for its location on a bluff overlooking the city and its neocolonial architecture featuring Mexican artistic touches. Its 129 rooms are all comfortable and well furnished with some truly splendid features, including vaulted wooden ceilings and neocolonial archways in some rooms. The Suite Gran Clase rooms are a good value and substantially nicer than the Master Suites, which are only slightly less expensive. Check the website for special deals. Wireless Internet is offered throughout the property. There is a pleasant, though unheated, garden swimming pool. Its Restaurante Las Ventanas is one of the city's most exclusive, with a variety of international dishes served in an elegant dining room overlooking the hotel's gardens. Its well-stocked Bar Quinta Real is open 5pm-1am Monday-Saturday.

Well outside of Guatemala City but entirely worth the trip, ★ **San Gregorio Hotel & Spa** (Carretera a Santa Elena Barillas Km. 29.5, tel. 6634-3666, www.sangregoriospa. com, $120 d) is a modern, ecochic facility with 10 stylish rooms featuring hardwood floors, flat-screen TVs, Guatemalan textiles, wood accents, and views over Guatemala City valley to Lake Amatitlán and Agua Volcano. There's an indoor/outdoor swimming pool; the hotel's ecochic status is punctuated by the use of solar panels for water heating and rainwater collection for landscape irrigation. To get here, take the Carretera a El Salvador to a turnoff at Km. 25. You'll see a Texaco gas station; follow the road to Santa Elena Barillas another 4.5 kilometers. A sign for San Gregorio indicates the intersection where you'll make a right-hand turn to the lodge.

pool with whirlpool tub. The Los Volcanes restaurant, on the ground floor, serves international and local dishes à la carte or buffet style. There's a piano player at night. **Video Lotería Monte Carlo** (video gambling, 1pm-3am daily) is also based on the ground floor, featuring video poker and slot machines. Proceeds benefit the environmental foundation Monte Carlo Verde.

CARRETERA A EL SALVADOR (SUBURBS)
$100-200
Although a bit far from the action, the all-suite ★ **Vista Real Guatemala** (Km. 8.5

Food

Cosmopolitan Guatemala City features a variety of excellent eating establishments for every taste and budget, as well as some more familiar U.S. franchises. In recent years, Jake's received a spot on *Travel + Leisure* magazine's list of Top 10 Restaurants in Latin America.

CAFÉS

A profusion of new cafés has come and gone in the downtown area in recent years. Among those still in business is **Café de Imeri** (6a Calle 3-34 Zona 1, tel. 2232-3722, www.de-imeri.com, 8am-6:30pm Mon.-Sat.), which enjoys a loyal following owed to its delightful old-fashioned atmosphere and efficiently elegant service. The cakes and baked goods are top-notch, and there are good breakfasts, tacos, pasta, and salads. It makes a great place for lunch with a set menu for $4.

Saúl Café (several locations throughout the city in Miraflores, Oakland Mall, and Paseo Cayalá, www.saulemendez.com/site/es/gastronomia.html, $8-15) is a local chain serving delicious sweet and salty crepes, ice cream, sandwiches, salads, smoothies, and coffee in an eclectic atmosphere with relaxing music. Beer and wine are also served. **Caffé dei Fiori** (15 Avenida 15-66 Zona 10, tel. 2363-5888, www.caffedeifiori.com, $3-8) has been around since the 1970s in three prior Zona 10 locations. Its current incarnation features a pleasant covered patio where breakfasts, pizzas, pastas, salads, and sandwiches are served. Desserts include delicious tiramisu and *empanadas de piña*. Great espresso drinks round out the meal.

There are a number of local coffee shops with a widespread presence throughout Guatemala City. These include **& Café** and **Café Barista.** If you must, there are four Starbucks locations in upscale Guatemala City shopping malls.

LIGHT MEALS AND SWEETS

Popular with Guatemalans, **San Martin and Company** (13 Calle 1-62 Zona 10 and various locations in upscale shopping malls, www.sanmartinbakery.com/english, 6am-8pm Mon.-Sat.) is a bakery and café with pleasant outdoor seating on a terrace or ceiling fan-cooled dining room inside. There are scrumptious croissant sandwiches for breakfast as well as a variety of sandwiches, salads, and soups for lunch and dinner in the $3-5 range.

Chocolate lovers will find bliss at **Xocoli** (6a Avenida 9-19 Zona 10, tel. 2362-3251, www.xocoli.com, 8:30am-6:30pm Mon.-Fri., 9am-1pm Sat.). The Mayan world is, after all, the birthplace of chocolate, dating back to the use of cacao beans as currency in Mayan times. Quite possibly the best artisanal gelato outside of Italy, **Ríbola Gelato** (Plaza Vista Muxbal local 109, Km. 9.5 Antigua Carretera a El Salvador, tel. 6646-6948, www.ribola.com.gt) serves a variety of mouthwatering flavors made with ingredients imported from Italy.

SPANISH

At **Tapas y Cañas** (13 Calle 7-78 Zona 10, tel. 2388-2700, www.tapasycanas.com, lunch and dinner daily) you can savor delicious Spanish tapas. Try the *pinchos españoles* or the *albondigas de lomito*. A longtime local favorite, ★ **Altuna** (5a Avenida 12-31 Zona 1, tel. 2251-7185 and 10a Calle 0-45 Zona 10, tel. 2332-6576, www.restaurantealtuna.com, noon-10pm Tues.-Sat., noon-5pm Sun., $7-22) is also one of the city's fanciest offerings with impeccable service and an elegant atmosphere. Specialties include fish and seafood dishes, including paella and lobster, but the restaurant also serves land-based fare, including *jamón serrano* and chorizo.

Pollo Campero and the Cult of Fried Chicken

If, like most people traveling home from Guatemala, you fly out on a commercial airline, don't be surprised by the distinct smell of fried chicken onboard your aircraft. One look at the overhead bins will quickly reveal that they are crammed tight with boxes of fried chicken. Meet Pollo Campero, which, along with coffee and bananas, may be one of Guatemala's main exports.

Guatemalans have always had an affinity for the stuff. It's actually quite good, though I've never taken it along as a carry-on. Many travelers take a box home for homesick relatives craving a taste of the land they left behind. Although Pollo Campero has opened up shop in recent years in several U.S. cities, expatriate Guatemalans still make a point of stopping at the store in La Aurora Airport to pick up a box. To illustrate the utter hold it has on the Guatemalan masses, the airport shop operated out of a streetside trailer during the airport's recent renovation at a time when all other businesses were simply closed.

You may be asked by U.S. Customs if you're carrying food, and this question might specifically address your smuggling of Pollo Campero. Rest assured, customs officials are happy to let the cooked chicken cross the American threshold after applying the requisite X-rays. Some Newark Airport customs officers even claim to have the uncanny ability to distinguish chicken from a Guatemalan Pollo Campero versus that of a San Salvador outlet, though I've never taken them up on offers to verify their claims.

Pollo Campero is becoming more than just a Guatemalan phenomenon, however. An aggressive company expansion includes the opening of numerous new locations throughout North America, Europe, and even Asia in the coming years. In 2007, Campero opened outlets in Jakarta, Indonesia, and Shanghai, China, with ambitious goals to open 500 more restaurants in China by 2012. Campero already operates 220 restaurants in 10 countries, including 38 in the United States. It employs more than 7,000 people and is the largest fast-food chain in Latin America. With such aggressive expansion plans, Pollo Campero may be headed for a location near you, and I don't mean seat 25F.

STEAKHOUSES

You'll find a variety of excellent steakhouses in Guatemala City, including **Hacienda Real** (5a Avenida 14-67 Zona 10, tel. 2380-8383, www.hacienda-real.com, lunch and dinner daily, $10-20), where the meals are served with tasty tortillas and savory side sauces. Try the peppered steak. There are other locations at Condado Concepción and Las Majadas. For absolutely astounding views of the city from its perch along Carretera a El Salvador, you can't top **El Portal del Ángel** (Km. 11.2 Carretera a El Salvador, tel. 2322-7300, www.elportaldelangel.net, noon-9pm Mon.-Thurs., noon-10pm Fri.-Sun., $8-35). The food is just as good as the views and the tasteful decor, with walls in vivid hues adorned with cool paintings of Catholic saints, make this place truly heavenly. It is also in Zona 11 at Paseo Miraflores and Zona 10 at Plaza Fontabella,

minus the city views. ★ **Don Emiliano** (4a Ave. 12-70 Zona 10, Oakland Mall; tel. 2475-5957, www.donemiliano.com.gt, noon-9pm Mon.-Thurs., noon-10pm Sun., $25) is another fine steakhouse with additional locations at Miraflores and the Mercado de Artesanías in Zona 13. It scores big points for its modern atmosphere and the beautiful presentation of its dishes. Try the tasty steak salads.

MEXICAN

Los Cebollines (6a Avenida 9-75 Zona 1, tel. 2232-7750 and Condado Concepción, at Km. 15.5 Carretera a El Salvador, tel. 6634-5405; www.cebollines.com, 7am-11pm Mon.-Thurs., 7am-midnight Fri.-Sat., 7am-10pm Sun.) serves tasty grilled meats, enchiladas, and tacos you can wash down with refreshing lemonades, smoothies, or cocktails. Try the delicious *tacos de pollo pibil*. Along with its branch in Antigua, **Fridas** (3a Avenida 14-60 Zona 10, tel. 2367-1611/13, lunch and dinner daily) serves Mexican dishes that include tasty fajitas and flautas at fairly reasonable prices ($5-10). The chicken in mango sauce is delectable, and the bar makes excellent margaritas. Pick your poison from the long list of tequilas ($4-12). The most casual of all the Mexican food options is **Ta'contento** (14 Calle 1-42 Zona 10, tel. 2444-4080, www.tacontento. com, 11am-midnight Tues.-Sun., $3-7), where you can eat tasty tacos alfresco fronting a lively Zona Viva street.

FRENCH

There has always been considerable French influence on Guatemalan culture, which is also evident in the city's culinary offerings. Among the excellent options are **Saint-Honoré** (14 Calle 2-51 Zona 10, tel. 2379-4548, 11:30am-11pm daily), inside the InterContinental hotel, a typical French bakery serving cakes and some of Guatemala's best coffee. Also in the hotel lobby is the excellent **Café de la Paix** (6am-11pm daily), the only franchise of the famous Parisian brasserie chain outside of France, serving heavier meals, including entrecôte and onion soup ($12-25).

★ **Jean Francois** (Diagonal 6, 13-63

Zona 10, tel. 2333-4785, www.grupoculinario. com, noon-3pm and 7pm-10:30pm Mon.-Fri., noon-3pm Sat., $8-25) is a longtime favorite with Guatemala's wealthy elite and arguably one of the finest restaurants in Latin America. The atmosphere is elegant with tablecloths and flowers adorning the tables and antique colonial furniture in the lounge. Entrées include snook in a cream and lemon sauce with fine herbs and steak *bondelaise* with porcini mushrooms. Try the fantastic cold lemon soufflé with caramel sauce for dessert.

A more casual and yet very tasty French dining option is **Enchanté** (20 Calle 25-96 Zona 10, Centro Comercial La Plaza, Local 15A, tel. 2366-9000). With pleasant indoor and outdoor seating at Plaza Fontabella, ★ **Clio's** (4a Avenida 12-59 Zona 10, tel. 2336-6949, www.cliosbistro.com, 12:30pm-3:30pm and 6:30pm-10:30pm Mon.-Sat., 12:30pm-3:30pm Sun., $25) serves classic French cuisine in a tasteful atmosphere with excellent service.

GUATEMALAN

For gourmet Guatemalan cuisine served in a wonderful atmosphere accented by a high-roofed thatch ceiling, head to ★ **Kacao** (2a Avenida between 13 and 14 Calle, Zona 10,

Señora Pu at work in her kitchen

tel. 2337-4188/89, www.kacao.com.gt, lunch and dinner daily, $7-13). You can try a variety of traditional Guatemalan dishes, including spicy beef and chicken dishes in *pepián* and *jocón* sauces as well as corn-based delicacies such as *chuchitos* and tamales. In the downtown area, another popular place for Guatemalan cuisine is **Arrin Cuan** (5a Avenida 3-27 Zona 1, tel. 2238-0242, or 5a Avenida 10-22 Zona 9, tel. 2366-2660, www.arrincuan.com, 7am-10pm daily, $5-10), with many dishes from the Cobán region, including *kakik* stew, but also some less adventurous recipes such as chicken in apple sauce. The atmosphere is charmingly simple. Another good place for hearty Guatemalan fare is **Casa Chapina** (1a Avenida 13-42 Zona 10, tel. 2367-6688 or 2368-0663, www.restaurantecasachapina.com, lunch and dinner daily, $8-20), serving well-presented Guatemalan dishes such as *pollo en salsa de loroco* accompanied by fresh avocado and corn on the cob. An awesome new discovery is ★ **La Cocina de la Señora Pu** (6a Avenida "A" 10-16 Zona 1, tel. 5055-6480, www.senorapu.com, lunch daily, $7-15), where you'll find a modern take on traditional Mayan fare. Señora Pu hails from Quiché department, and you can watch her lovingly prepare dishes before your very eyes in the cozy open-air kitchen. There are beef, lamb, pork, chicken, and even duck dishes cooked in a variety of traditional sauces. You can wash it all down with traditional cacao-based beverages.

ASIAN

Sushi places seem to have sprung up all over town recently—even the Holiday Inn and Radisson each have their own sushi restaurants in their respective lobbies. The best of the hotel lobby sushi places, however, is ★ **Tanoshii** (14 Calle 2-51 Zona 10, tel. 2379-4548, noon-3pm and 6:30pm-11pm Mon.-Sat., $10-25), inside the InterContinental hotel, also serving Japanese dishes in a hip, ultramodern setting. Also in Zona 10 is **Sushi Itto** (4a Avenida 16-01 Zona 10, tel. 2366-7676, www.sushi-itto.com, lunch and dinner daily). The

city's best Thai restaurant, ★ **Khawp Khun Kha** (13 Calle A y 7a Ave. Zona 10, Centro Comercial Plaza Tiffany, tel. 2367-1719, noon-3pm and 7pm-10:30pm Tues.-Sat., $7-15) features tasty pad thai but also has a number of other great dishes such as chicken satay, beef in coffee sauce, and hearty soups.

For Chinese food, downtown there's **Long Wah** (6a Calle 3-75 Zona 1, tel. 2232-6611, lunch and dinner daily) with reasonably priced staple dishes you can eat in or take out. It's the best of several Chinese places west of the central plaza. **China Town** (13 Calle and Avenida La Reforma Zona 10, tel. 2331-9574, lunch and dinner Mon.-Sat.) delivers to the Zona 10 hotels, or you can enjoy your meal in its pleasant atmosphere.

AMERICAN

You'll find a number of familiar restaurant chains in Guatemala City, including Applebee's, T.G.I. Friday's, Chili's, IHOP, and Tony Roma's. For a local take on American fare, check out **Frisco Grill** (4a Avenida 12-59 Zona 10, Plaza Fontabella; tel. 2336-7147/48, www.friscogrill.com.gt, 11am-11:30pm Mon.-Sat., 7am-10pm Sun., $15). There's outdoor patio seating and tasty American favorites such as nachos, burgers, steak sandwiches, fish-and-chips, and quesadillas. I'm a big fan of their margaritas. One of only three in Central America, **Hard Rock Café Guatemala City** (1a Avenida y 13 Calle Zona 10, Edificio Dubai Center, tel. 2332-3862, www.hardrock.com/cafes/guatemala-city, noon-12:30am Mon.-Sat., 11am-10pm Sun., $10-25) serves the usual HRC fare including nachos, burgers, and decent sandwiches. A chainwide menu revamp has brought tasty fish and steak dishes to the menu, which you can enjoy amidst a backdrop of rock 'n' roll memorabilia and loud music. The Rock Shop, on the ground floor, sells destination-themed souvenirs and opens an hour earlier.

ITALIAN

Pecorino (11 Calle 3-36 Zona 10, tel. 2360-3035, www.ristorantepecorino.com, noon-1am Mon.-Sat., $12-30) is an excellent choice for its authentic Italian food, including brick-oven pizza, seafood dishes, steak, pasta, salads, and panini served in an attractive old-world atmosphere. There's also a huge wine selection. ★ **Enoteca Toscana** (20 calle 12-84 Zona 10, Plaza Ferco, tel. 4739-6393, $15-40) is an authentic Italian restaurant with mouthwatering dishes lovingly made by its chef-owner Leonardo Nardini. Many of the ingredients used are imported from Italy, which is reflected in the prices. Worth it, if you ask me. In a modern, casual setting with attractive blue-and-white-checkered tablecloths, **Tre Fratelli** (2a Avenida 13-25 Zona 10, tel. 2420-5350, www.trefratelli.com.gt, noon-1am daily) serves ample portions of very good food in a lively atmosphere with prices in the $5-10 range. It's part of a growing chain of restaurants with locations in the United States, Mexico, and Central America. Other Guatemala City locations can be found in Zona 11 and Carretera a El Salvador. I love the country atmosphere and cool decor at ★ **L'Osteria** (4a Avenida 10-41 Zona 10, tel. 2278-9914, www.saulemendez.com, noon-10pm Mon.-Thurs., noon-midnight Fri./Sat., noon-6pm Sun., $10-16). The menu is actually a mix of Italian, Mediterranean, and Greek food. There's indoor seating (with open windows) in the remains of an old, tin-roofed farmhouse or outside on a patio under the shade of a 100-year-old avocado tree. You'll get 15 percent off your check if you ride your bike here.

My favorite pizza place is **Margherita** (Boulevard Vista Hermosa 23-41 Zona 15, tel. 2375-0000, margherita.gt, lunch and dinner daily, $10-20). There's phenomenal brick-oven pizza prepared New York-style, thin crust, Neapolitan, or Sicilian. There are tasty salads, antipasti, and calzone that you can wash down with beer or wine. The atmosphere is modern and casual with indoor or outdoor seating and electronica music on the stereo. You can dine in or carry out. Another good option for brick-oven pizza served in a casual atmosphere is **Pizzeria Vesuvio** (18 Calle 3-36 Zona 10 and three other locations, tel. 2323-2323, www.vesuvio.com.gt, lunch and dinner daily, $7-15). A trusted reader and in-the-know Guatemala City resident recommends **L'Apero** (Vía 5 2-24, Local 5, Zona 4, tel. 2360-2561, noon-3pm Mon.-Tues., noon-3pm and 6pm-10pm Wed.-Fri., noon-10pm Sat., $5-12), where there's tasty pizzas in an assortment of uncommon flavors. Try the scrumptious blue cheese and pear pizza.

colorful decor of L'Osteria

FUSION CUISINE AND FINE DINING

Many Guatemalan chefs study overseas early in their careers, which is clearly evident in the international influence permeating the city's excellent fusion cuisine. In other cases, talented chefs from New York and other international cities have set up shop in Guatemala, completely raising the bar for everyone else. Such is the case of ★ **Jake's** (17 Calle 10-40 Zona 10, tel. 2368-0351, www.restaurantejakes.com, noon-3pm and 7pm-10:30pm Mon.-Sat., noon-4pm Sun., $10-25), started by New York City artist-turned-chef Jake Denburg. Several unique features come together to make a visit to Jake's something truly special. For one, it has a wonderful atmosphere in a converted house with tile floors and wooden ceilings, interesting photography, and tables covered in butcher paper (crayons supplied). But nothing tops the eclectic menu and exquisite food. The wine list is also impressive, and rounding out your meal with one of the delectable homemade cheesecakes is a must.

A wonderful new addition to the city's already impressive list of restaurants is **Gracia, Cocina de Autor** (corner of 14 Calle and 4a Avenida Zona 10, tel. 2366-8699, noon-11pm Tues.-Sun., $8-20). Chef Pablo Novales has lived and worked in Spain, Switzerland, France, and England, gaining considerable culinary prowess evident in the dishes on the menu. The atmosphere is cozy, modern, and casual, with a small outdoor lounge next to the bar. I like the porcini mushroom risotto and Asian tuna avocado salad for starters, and the chicken kebabs in sesame seed sauce for the main course. The refreshing papaya sangria is a great way to get things started.

Also serving as a culinary school, **Camille** (9a Avenida 15-27 Zona 10, tel. 2368-0048 or 2367-1525, noon-3pm and 7pm-10pm Tues.-Fri., 7pm-10pm Sat., $10-15) serves creatively prepared fish, chicken, and seafood dishes. The steak in chipotle sauce served on a cheese *pupusa* (Salvadoran cheese-filled tortilla) is truly extraordinary. The atmosphere is pleasantly cozy with carbon sketches etched on the white plaster walls and also on ripped-out pages from spiral-bound notebooks framed and hung.

A longtime favorite is ★ **Tamarindos** (11 Calle 2-19A Zona 10, tel. 2360-5630, tamarindos.com.gt/en, noon-3pm and 7pm-10:30pm Mon.-Sat., 11am-3pm Sat. brunch; bar open 6pm-1am Mon.-Sat., $10-20), which makes some fine sushi and does an excellent job of

Tamarindos Bistro

combining Thai, Italian, and Guatemalan flavors into some irresistible dishes. There is pleasant indoor and outdoor garden patio seating and the hip ambience is set by postmodern decor and electronica music on the stereo. Try the crab-and-almond-stuffed mushrooms or the four-cheese gnocchi as an appetizer. The snook in banana sauce makes a fine main course. A spin-off of Tamarindos in a more casual environment is **Tamarindos Bistro** (Plaza Majadas ONCE, Zona 11, tel. 2473-7528, www.bistro.tamarindos.com.gt, 7am-10pm Mon.-Sat., 7am-8pm Sun., $8-20). There's a varied menu that includes delicious breakfasts, sushi, tasty sandwiches (try the Philly cheesesteak), and seafood.

Zona 14 also has some highly recommended restaurants. Amid spacious gardens is ★ **Ambia** (10a Avenida 5-49 Zona 14, tel. 2312-4690, www.fdg.com.gt, noon-midnight Mon.-Sat., $13-50), where the emphasis is on New Age cuisine consisting largely of Asian recipes, including Thai chicken and shrimp recipes, tuna tartare, flavorful soups, Italian pastas, and even gourmet burgers. There are decadent desserts, including black-and-white chocolate mousse and pears in red wine. The wine list, incidentally, is extensive and includes several fine malbecs and even a $700 bottle of Chilean Errazuriz Viñedo Chadwick Cabernet Sauvignon.

In the suburbs just east of the city, ★ **Tua** (Km. 14.5 Carretera a El Salvador, Centro Comercial Escala, tel. 6637-5443 or 6646-7038, $30) is a bistro serving wonderful cuisine that is on par with the fabulous volcano views off in the distance. It's definitely a place to choose outside seating, but the inside is modern and attractive as well, with dramatic high ceilings. I like the tuna tataki and coconut-breaded shrimp. The lamb chops and chipotle chicken are also fabulous.

In the city center and recommended more for the historical atmosphere than the somewhat overpriced, uninspired food is **Casa del Callejon Castillo Hermanos** (2a Ave. "A" 13-20 Zona 1, tel. 2366-5671, $15-35). Set in an old colonial home brimming with charm, the museum-like locale documents the life and times of the city's wealthy Castillo family, of Gallo beer fame. Interspersed with elegant dining areas are old photos, family heirlooms, and cool antique furniture on display. It makes a perfectly good place for a drink in a fancy, old-fashioned atmosphere. The best nights to visit are those featuring special performances of live jazz and tango, as dinner is often included in the admission price and tends to include better fare.

SEAFOOD

Donde Mikel (6a Ave. 13-32 Zona 10, tel. 2363-3308, lunch and dinner Mon.-Fri., lunch Sat.) serves some of the city's best seafood and grilled steak in a casual atmosphere. Its surf-and-turf plates are a popular favorite.

Information and Services

TOURIST INFORMATION

The main office of the **Guatemala Tourist Commission (INGUAT)** is at 7a Avenida 1-17 Zona 4, and it is open 8am-4pm Monday-Friday. Your best bet, however, is to stop by its kiosk in the airport arrivals area, which is open 6am-9pm. It also has smaller offices inside the **Palacio Nacional de la Cultura** (Parque Central, tel. 2253-0748), which keeps odd hours, and the historic **Palacio de**

Correos (Main Post Office, 7a Avenida 11-67 Zona 1, tel. 2251-1898, 9am-5pm Mon.-Fri.).

MAPS

The best maps of Guatemala are *Mapas de Guatemala* (tel. 2232-1850, www.mapas-deguatemala.com), a series of beautifully illustrated, full-color maps of Guatemala's main tourist regions that also include helpful information on local businesses. The free

Staying Safe in Guatemala City

Guatemala City can be a dodgy place, though some *zonas* are certainly more prone to crime than others. Most of the areas frequented by tourists are relatively safe, though the downtown area (Zona 1) is by far the country's purse-snatching and pickpocketing hub. Exercise common sense and caution when in public areas. Never leave valuables in a parked car and avoid flashing expensive items such as laptops and cell phones in public places.

Pay careful attention when using ATMs. Some thieves have been so ingenious as to set up fake keypads at the entrance to ATM kiosks asking cardholders to enter their PIN numbers in order to gain access to the machine. You should never enter your PIN number anywhere other than on the ATM keypad itself.

Riding public buses is not usually a good idea, though the new transit system, the Transmetro, has proven much safer. If driving, it's a good idea to keep the car doors locked and the windows rolled all the way up. (Make sure your car's air-conditioning system is working properly so as to avoid the temptation to roll down the windows when it gets hot out.) Avoid talking on a cell phone while driving; it will keep you alert to your surroundings and will not draw undue attention from potential thieves. Cell phones are a favorite target, as is flashy jewelry. Recently, some parts of the city have become prone to robberies whereby the perpetrators (usually on motorcycles) target cars stopped at traffic lights. In most cases, the victims have been talking on their cell phones or are women traveling alone and wearing expensive jewelry. For this reason, many Guatemalans tint their windows to keep prying eyes away from the contents of their car. If you are the victim of a robbery or witness one, dial 120 from any phone.

Watch out for a common scam, particularly in the vicinity of the airport, whereby a "Good Samaritan" informs you of a flat tire on your car. If you can confirm that you indeed have a flat, pull over in a well-lit, public place. Do not stop at the side of the road to change the tire. If you are able to make it to a public place such as a gas station, have someone in your party stay inside the car or keep an eye on it yourself while you a gas station attendant changes the tire for you. The important thing is not to lose sight of the inside of your vehicle for a moment. Thieves can be extremely crafty at distracting you and getting into your car; locked doors may be a deterrent but will not stop thieves if they've already targeted you. For information on other precautions and common scams while traveling in Guatemala, see the State Department's Consular Information Sheet online at http://travel.state.gov.

In November 2008, the U.S. Embassy issued safety warnings for certain Guatemalan roads. Among the areas mentioned was the road east of kilometer 13 of Carretera a El Salvador. Due to its popularity with the city's wealthy residents, it appears this sector has become the scene of several violent robberies, carjackings, and kidnappings. The embassy recommends avoiding travel beyond kilometer 13 between 9pm and 6am. The document also recommends avoiding travel on the following roads outside Guatemala City: Routes 4 and 11 in the vicinity of Lake Atitlán and Route 14 between Antigua and Escuintla.

For this and other pertinent information, visit http://guatemala.usembassy.gov.

maps are available at INGUAT and at tourist gift shops and restaurants seemingly everywhere. You can also find interactive versions on their website. **ITMB Publishing** (530 W. Broadway, Vancouver, BC, Canada, 604/879-3621, www.itmb.com) publishes an excellent *International Travel Map of Guatemala* ($10.95), which is weatherproof and can be found at well-known bookstores in the United States.

COMMUNICATIONS

The **main post office** (8:30am-5pm Mon.-Fri., 8:30am-1pm Sat.) is downtown at 7a Avenida 11-67 Zona 1. There are also branches at the airport and the corner of Avenida La Reforma and 14 Calle Zona 9 with the same hours. It's called El Correo. Now you can find post office locations and even track packages online via their website at www.elcorreo.com.gt.

For faster service, many people prefer to use one of the international couriers, including **FedEx** (14 Calle 3-51 Zona 10, Edificio Murano Center Local No. 1, tel. toll-free from Guatemala 1-801-00-333-39, www.fedex.com. gt), **UPS** (5a Avenida 7-92 Zona 14, Local 4, CC Euroshops, , tel. 2421-6000, www.ups. com), and **DHL** (12 Calle 5-12 Zona 10, tel. 2332-7547, www.dhl.com). For an all-in-one shipping locale, try **Fast Mail** (5a Avenida 7-42 Zona 14, tel. 2246-4646, www.fastmailcenter.com, 8:30am-5:30pm Mon.-Fri., 9am-1pm Sat.).

MONEY

You can exchange dollars and cash travelers checks at virtually all of the city's banks. ATMs linked to international networks can be found all over the city. Be especially careful when withdrawing money at ATMs in the downtown area. The safest places to hit up an ATM are the Guatemala City shopping malls and hotel lobbies. There are money exchange kiosks at La Aurora International Airport, though you'll get much better rates elsewhere.

You can search for Visa ATM locations online at www.visa.com/atmlocator and MasterCard ATMs at www.mastercard.com/ atm. A useful listing of Banco Industrial Visa ATM machines throughout Guatemala can be found at www.bi.com.gt.

The American Express agent in Guatemala City is **Clark Tours** (7a Avenida 14-76, Plaza Clark, Zona 9, tel. 2412-4700, www.clarktours. com). It also has offices in the Westin Camino Real and Barceló hotels.

LAUNDRY

Downtown there's **Lavandería El Siglo** (12 Calle 3-42 Zona 1, tel. 2230-0223, www. lavanderiaelsiglo.com, 8am-6pm Mon.-Fri., 8am-3pm Sat., $4 per load). There are other locations throughout the city. In Zona 10 is **Lavandería Obelisco** (20 Calle 2-16 Zona 10, tel. 2368-1469), where self-service laundry costs about $3 per load to wash and dry.

MEDICAL SERVICES

Guatemala City is becoming a destination for medical tourism, with many excellent private hospitals. Public clinics such as the **Clínica Cruz Roja** (Red Cross Clinic, 3a Calle 8-40 Zona 1, 8am-5:30pm Mon.-Fri., 8am-noon Sat.) offer free or low-cost consultations. Private clinics with doctors who speak English include the highly recommended 24-hour **Hospital Centro Medico** (6a Avenida 3-47 Zona 10, tel. 2279-4949, www.centromedico. com.gt) and the **Hospital Herrera Llerandi** (6a Avenida 8-71 Zona 10, tel. 2384-5959 or 2334-5955 emergencies, www.herrerallerandi. com). **Grupo Hospitalario Guatemala** (www.hospitalesdeguatemala.com) also has a good network of hospitals in the Guatemala City metro area.

EMERGENCY

Dial 120 from any phone for the police (6a Avenida and 14 Calle Zona 1). For emergency medical assistance, dial 125 for the Red Cross. For the fire department, dial 122 or 123.

IMMIGRATION

The offices of **Migración** (tel. 2361-8476, www.migracion.gob.gt) are on the second floor of the INGUAT building at 7a Avenida 1-17 Zona 4 and are open 8am-2:45pm Monday-Friday.

TRAVEL AGENTS

For booking plane tickets and onward travel within Guatemala, a good choice is **Viajes Tivoli** (6a Avenida 8-41 Zona 9, tel. 2386-4200, or 12 Calle 4-55 Zona 1, Edificio Herrera, tel. 2298-1050, www.tivoli.com.gt), as is **Clark Tours** (7a Avenida 14-76, Plaza Clark, Zona 9, tel. 2412-4700, www.clarktours.com). Clark Tours also has offices in the Westin Camino Real, Holiday Inn, and Barceló.

Transportation

GETTING THERE
Air

The once-wonky **La Aurora International Airport** (GUA, www.dgac.gob.gt), in Zona 13 six kilometers south of the city center, underwent a major expansion and renovation in 2007 and is now one of Central America's largest and most modern airports. Services include a bank, ATMs, various restaurants, excellent duty-free shopping, souvenir shops, and a post office. Members of United Airlines' United Club enjoy access to the airport's Copa Club, a lounge operated jointly with Copa Airlines and located next to gate 14. It's also open to First Class passengers traveling on United, Copa, or Star Alliance partners. Not traveling in first class? You can pay a day fee to visit ($50) if traveling on any of these airlines. Guests enjoy a TV lounge, free cocktails, wireless Internet, and space to relax before the flight.

Immigration, customs, and baggage claim are on the main building's first floor, while departures and check-in counters are on the third floor. There are technically two adjacent terminals, though they are merged into one large facility. The first area, known as *finger central*, consists of six gates for wide-body aircraft. It fronts the main terminal, which is all that remains of the original facility dating to the 1960s. The second terminal, known as *finger norte*, consists of gates 7 to 19 and is seamlessly integrated into the rest of the terminal building. There is a food court on the fourth floor of the main terminal building overlooking the check-in counters. Additional restaurants can be found past the security checkpoints leading to the two *fingers*, one floor down from the check-in lobby.

Immigration and customs procedures at La Aurora Airport are very straightforward. Customs (known as SAT) will look at your declaration paperwork (to be filled out on the airplane prior to arrival) and will either put you in a line where your bags will be searched and applicable duties (if any) collected or will simply wave you on. Most foreign travelers are waved on, as what they're mostly looking for are arriving Guatemalans with loot from stateside shopping sprees. A disproportionate number of bags per traveler are usually a sure tip-off.

Guatemala City's underutilized La Aurora International Airport

Taxis are easily booked from a kiosk inside the airport terminal, as are rental cars. A taxi from the airport costs $8-20 depending on what part of town you're going to. Avis, Budget, Hertz, and National have kiosks inside the airport terminal. Their lots are across the road fronting the airport's three-level parking garage. If you're arriving on a later flight and have never driven Guatemala City's chaotic streets before, it might make more sense to take advantage of free airport shuttles to Zona 10 hotels and have the rental car company drop off the vehicle at your hotel the next morning. You could also just as easily take a cab or shuttle from your hotel to the airport the following day and pick up the car at that time.

If most of your travel involves the Guatemala City and Antigua area, my advice is to forgo a car rental in favor of taxis and shuttle buses. You can also hire a driver to take you around for about US$75-100 a day. Local hotel concierges can usually recommend someone for you. Doing so will allow you to get a feel for the city without the stress of having to drive on its unfamiliar streets. It will also allow you to get acquainted with the particular style of Guatemalan urban driving you'll need to adopt if you do end up driving here.

If you're bypassing Guatemala City altogether, you'll find shuttle vans to Antigua (about $20) are easily booked upon arrival at the airport. There is also a very helpful INGUAT (Instituto Guatemalteco de Turismo) information desk just after passing customs. It's staffed by English-speaking agents who can help you get your bearings.

It's not a good idea to ride a public bus into the city, especially at night. The Transmetro is perfectly safe and efficient, but its coverage area is limited. It will not get you to or from the airport, though the newer *eje central* route can get you as close as Bulevar Liberacion, which fronts the airport runway's northern extreme.

Several U.S. and foreign carriers fly daily into Guatemala City. Most of these airlines have city ticket offices, including **American Airlines** (Barceló Guatemala City, 7a Avenida 15-45 Zona 9, tel. 2422-0000), **United Airlines** (18 Calle 5-56, Edificio Unicentro, Local 704, Zona 10, tel. 2385-9610 or 801/812-6684 toll-free), **Delta** (15 Calle 3-20 Zona 10, Centro Ejecutivo, Primer Nivel, tel. 2337-0642), **Avianca** (Avenida Hincapié 12-22, Zona 13, tel. 2470-8222), and **Iberia** (Avenida La Reforma 8-60 Zona 9, tel. 2332-0911). American Airlines and United Airlines passengers can check bags in the day before their flight at service centers in the Barceló Guatemala City hotel (7a Avenida 15-45 Zona 9).

The only **domestic service** is to Flores, near the ruins of Tikal, though other routes may open if government plans to revamp several smaller airports throughout the country ever come to fruition. The only airline leaving from the main terminal for domestic flights is Avianca, with several daily flights to Flores. Local carrier **TAG** (Ave. Hincapie y 18 Calle Zona 13, tel. 2380-9494, www.tag.com.gt) offers service from the other side of the runway at its private hangar.

The airport is located 6 km south of downtown Guatemala City and 25 km from Antigua.

Bus

Guatemala City's unattractive Zona 4 bus terminal is being phased out (at least in part) thanks to a long-overdue plan to bring order to the chaos traditionally characterizing the state of public transportation, both within and into and out of the city. Accounting for 80 percent of the bedlam are buses arriving from and departing to the Western Highlands and the Pacific Coast. Buses to and from both of these regions were to be based out of the **Central de Transferencias Sur (CENTRA Sur)** in Zona 12, on the southern outskirts of the city, though this was only partly implemented. From CENTRA Sur, a series of modern, bright green interconnected buses known as *buses articulados* take passengers on a new system called the **Transmetro** into the city center. **CENTRA Norte** (CA-9 Norte 40-26 Zona 17, Km 8.5, tel. 2500-9800, www.centranorte.com.gt) was unveiled in 2012 and serves as the hub for buses heading out along the highway leading east to Izabal, Las Verapaces, and Petén. It's open 24/7 and has a modern shopping center with stores and restaurants. The city's public transportation system, meanwhile, is being replaced almost entirely by the Transmetro, a sort of surface metro, which will cover the entire metropolitan area by 2020 (or so they tell us).

A number of the (mostly) **first-class buses** heading to the Highlands and the Pacific Coast still leave from their own depots spread throughout the city, and this will probably continue to be the case for some time. The consolidation of bus routes heading east to Izabal, Las Verapaces, and Petén has been more successful. Here is the information on some of the more popular first-class bus routes:

To Chiquimula (3.5 hours, $4, 170 km): **Rutas Orientales** (CENTRA Norte, tel. 2503-3100, www.rutasorientales.com), departures every half hour 4:30am-6pm, or **Transportes Guerra** (CENTRA Norte), every half hour 7am-6pm.

To Cobán (4.5 hours, $5, 213 km): **Transportes Escobar Monja Blanca** (CENTRA Norte) has hourly buses 4am-5pm, stopping at El Rancho and the Quetzal Biotope.

To Esquipulas (4.5 hours, $5, 222 km): **Rutas Orientales** (CENTRA Norte, tel. 2503-3100, www.rutasorientales.com), has departures every half hour 4:30am-6pm.

To Flores (eight hours, $10-30 depending on service level, 500 km): Options include **Línea Dorada** (CENTRA Norte, tel. 2415-8900,www.lineadorada.com.gt), with luxury buses departing at 10am and 9pm ($30), or a more economical overnight bus leaving at 10pm ($16). **Fuente del Norte** (CENTRA Norte, tel. 2251-3817) has about 20 daily departures ($10-20).

To Huehuetenango (five hours, 266 km): **Los Halcones** (7a Avenida 15-27 Zona 1, tel. 2238-1929, $5), departs at 4am, 7am, 10:15am, 2pm, and 5pm. **Transportes Velásquez** (20 Calle 1-37 Zona 1, tel. 2221-1084, $4) has nine buses daily. **Transportes Zaculeu Futura** (9a Calle 11-42 Zona 1, tel. 2232-2858, $5), has buses at 6am and 3pm.

To La Mesilla (seven hours, $6, 345 km): **Transportes Velásquez** (20 Calle 1-37 Zona 1, tel. 2221-1084, $5.50), every two hours 5:30am-1:30pm.

To Panajachel (three hours, 148 km): **Transportes Rebuli** (21 Calle and 4a Avenida Zona 1, $2) has hourly buses 5:30am-3:30pm.

To Puerto Barrios (five hours, 295 km): **Litegua** (CENTRA Norte, tel. 2220-8840, www.litegua.com) has 16 buses daily 4:30am-7pm.

To Quetzaltenango (four hours, $4.50, 205 km): **Transportes Álamo** (21 Calle 0-14 Zona 1, tel. 2251-4838) has six buses a day 8am-5:30pm. **Líneas América** (2a Avenida 18-47 Zona 1, tel. 2232-1432) has seven buses a day 5am-7:30pm. **Transportes Galgos** (7a Avenida 19-44 Zona 1, tel. 2253-4868) leaves seven times daily 5:30am-7pm. The newest option is a nonstop bus on an ultraluxurious coach aboard **Línea Dorada** (16 Calle 10-03 Zona 1, tel. 2220-7900 or 2232-9658, www.lineadorada.com.gt, $6) at 8am and 3pm.

To Río Dulce (six hours, $6-21, 280 km): **Línea Dorada** (CENTRA Norte, tel. 2415-8900, www.lineadorada.com.gt) has luxury buses departing at 10am and 9pm ($21), or a more economical bus leaving at 10pm ($11). Both continue to Flores. **Litegua** (CENTRA Norte, tel. 2220-8840, www.litegua.com) has buses at 6am, 9am, 11:30am, and 1pm.

To Zacapa (three hours, $3.50): **Rutas Orientales** (CENTRA Norte, tel. 2503-3100, www.rutasorientales.com) has 15 buses daily.

International Bus

To Copán, Honduras (five hours, 238 km, $35): **Hedman Alas** (2a Avenida 8-73 Zona 10, tel. 2362-5072, 2362-5073, or 2362-5074, www.hedmanalas.com) departs daily at 5am and 9am.

To San Salvador, El Salvador (five hours, 240 km): **Melva Internacional** (3a Avenida 1-38 Zona 9, tel. 2331-0874, $15) departs hourly 5am-4pm, with more expensive *especiales* ($20) leaving at 6:45am, 9am, and 3pm. **Tica Bus** (Calzada Aguilar Batres 22-55 Zona 12, tel. 2473-1639, www.ticabus.com, $20) leaves at 1pm. **King Quality** (18 Avenida 1-96 Zona 15, tel. 2369-0404, $30) has luxury buses departing at 6:30am, 8am, 2pm, and 3:30pm. **Pullmantur** (1a Avenida 13-22 Zona 10, Holiday Inn, tel. 2367-4746, www.pullmantur.com, $30-46) offers the most luxurious service on this route with double-decker buses and a choice of fare classes, departing at 7am and 3pm daily with additional buses Fridays at noon and Sundays at 4pm.

To Tapachula, Mexico (seven hours, 290 km): **Transportes Galgos** (7a Avenida 19-44 Zona 1, tel. 2253-4868, $22) has departures at 7:30am and 2pm. **Línea Dorada** (16 Calle 10-55 Zona 1, tel. 2232-5506, www.lineadorada.com.gt, $22) departs at 8am.

GETTING AROUND
Taxi

Getting around by taxi can be tricky, as there is really only one reliable taxicab company in the city and it requires you to call for a pickup if you wish to hire its services. **Taxis Amarillo Express** (tel. 2470-1515 or 1766, www.amarilloexpress.com) is also one of the only companies to use meters. Otherwise, the airport taxis and those at the Zona Viva hotels are generally reliable. It's not usually a good idea to hail a cab from the street, as some of these are gypsy cabs and robberies do sometimes occur. If you find a reliable cab driver, you can always ask for a business card and hire his services for the rest of your stay or ask him to refer you to another reputable driver.

Car Rental

Several car rental agencies operate out of the airport and nearby areas, including **Avis** (6a Calle 7-64 Zona 9, tel. 2324-9000 or 800/331-1212 U.S. toll-free, www.avis.com.gt), **Dollar** (Avenida La Reforma 8-33

Zona 10, tel. 2385-8728 or 800/800-4000 U.S. toll-free, www.dollar.com.gt), **Budget** (6a Avenida 11-24 Zona 9, tel. 2332-7744 or 800/472-3325 U.S. toll-free, www.budget.com), **Hertz** (7a Avenida 14-84 Zona 13, tel. 2314-4411 or 800/654-3001 U.S. toll-free, also with offices inside the Westin Camino Real, InterContinental, and Barceló, www.rent-autos.com.gt), **Alamo** (La Aurora Airport, tel. 2362-2701, www.alamoguatemala.com), and **Thrifty** (7a Avenida 14-28 Zona 13, Aeropuerto La Aurora, tel. 2379-8747 to 52, or 800/847-4389 U.S. toll-free, www.thrifty.com).

Public Buses

Guatemala City's chaotic public bus transportation is not recommended for international travelers, mainly for safety considerations, as armed robberies and purse snatchings are frequent. Buses are also particularly susceptible to the city's increasing gang-related violence, and drivers are often harassed and/or murdered for money by gang members.

Transmetro

A glimmer of hope for the city's mass transit system emerged in 2007 with the unveiling of the Transmetro, a completely revamped public transportation system, which should be in full operation by 2020. The first phase, including the first transfer center (in Zona 12) for buses coming in from other parts of Guatemala, is already up and running and a second branch was scheduled to go into service at time of publication. Bus service via long, train-like interconnected green units brings travelers from the transfer center to the downtown area. More transfer centers are in the works.

The system promises to provide Guatemalans (and foreign travelers) with a safe, comfortable, and fast option for getting around the city. Buses stop at designated locations, drivers no longer trundle the streets competing for passengers, a prepaid system eliminates onboard cash, and buses and stations are guarded by cameras and plainclothes police officers. It

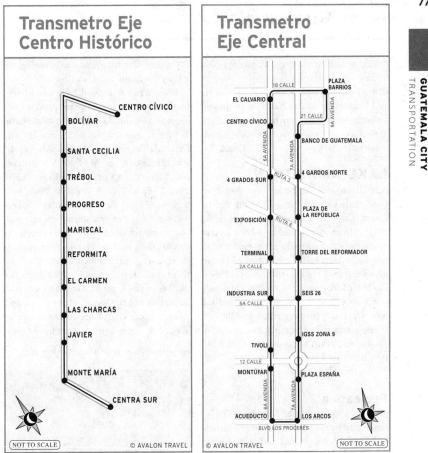

Transmetro Eje Centro Histórico

- CENTRO CÍVICO
- BOLÍVAR
- SANTA CECILIA
- TRÉBOL
- PROGRESO
- MARISCAL
- REFORMITA
- EL CARMEN
- LAS CHARCAS
- JAVIER
- MONTE MARÍA
- CENTRA SUR

NOT TO SCALE © AVALON TRAVEL

Transmetro Eje Central

- PLAZA BARRIOS
- 18 CALLE
- EL CALVARIO
- CENTRO CÍVICO
- 21 CALLE
- 9A AVENIDA
- BANCO DE GUATEMALA
- 6A AVENIDA
- 7A AVENIDA
- 4 GRADOS SUR
- RUTA 3
- 4 GARDOS NORTE
- PLAZA DE LA REPÚBLICA
- EXPOSICIÓN
- RUTA 6
- TERMINAL
- TORRE DEL REFORMADOR
- 2A CALLE
- INDUSTRIA SUR
- SEIS 26
- 5A CALLE
- IGSS ZONA 9
- TIVOLI
- 12 CALLE
- MONTÚFAR
- PLAZA ESPAÑA
- 6A AVENIDA
- 7A AVENIDA
- ACUEDUCTO
- LOS ARCOS
- BLVD LOS PROCERES

© AVALON TRAVEL   NOT TO SCALE

costs Q1 to ride the Transmetro and the system only accepts one-quetzal coins. Drop your coin in the slot, push past the turnstile, and wait for the next bus under a covered, raised platform.

For now, the Transmetro's routes include the *eje sur,* starting in Zona 12's CENTRA Sur and heading downtown to Zona 1's Plaza Amate, *corredor central,* and the newer *eje centro histórico.* The *eje sur* makes 12 stops along the way, including at the Centro Cívico (Plaza Municipal) and El Trébol. The *corredor central* route runs the length of 7a Avenida from Zona 1 to Zona 13's Avenida Las Américas all the way to Plaza Berlín, stopping at Zona 4's

bus terminal and Cuatro Grados Norte along the way. The bus terminal's status as the transportation hub for many bus lines will probably remain in place pending the gradual transition to the new system based on transfer centers. Direct Transmetro buses (no stops) heading from downtown to CENTRA leave from **Plaza Amate** (4a Avenida and 18 Calle Zona 1, 5am-9am and 4pm-9pm Mon.-Fri.). The *eje centro histórico* is quite convenient for visits to Guatemala's City's downtown sector, with a route that parallels Paseo de la Sexta and leaves you just one block from the central plaza at Parque Centenario.

Near Guatemala City

South of the city along Calzada Aguilar Batres, the sprawl continues into the adjacent district of Villa Nueva, a suburban housing and industrial area that has been swallowed up by the larger city. From here, the Carretera al Pacífico, or Pacific Highway (CA-9) leads south to Escuintla and the Pacific Coast.

LAKE AMATITLÁN

Amatitlán lies 30 kilometers south of Guatemala City on the road to the Pacific Coast. The lake is in the process of being rescued from what would have been certain ecological death caused by wastewater from nearby industry and uncontrolled urban growth. A new sewage treatment plant now filters the filthy waters of the Río Villalobos, which once flooded untreated sewage into the lake. Trees have been replanted, and the lake is being pumped with oxygen and cleaned of plants in an effort to reverse its eutrophication. It's still not possible to swim in the lake's waters, though it may be some day.

Recreation

The public beach of **Las Ninfas** was being remodeled by tourism authorities to include boat docks (for sailboats and motorboats), new food stalls, walkways, and landscaping, but like so many other projects in Guatemala it was never finished. The long-closed **Teleférico** (Aerial Tram, 9am-5pm Fri.-Sun., $2 adults, $0.85 children) was reopened in 2006, in an attempt to kick off the rebirth of one of Guatemala City's oldest recreational enclaves. The funicular climbs 350 meters up a mountainside along a 1.5-kilometer route. There's a lookout point at the top of the mountain where you can get out, appreciate the view of the lake and Guatemala City, and grab a bite to eat at a small cafeteria serving snacks. The Teleférico was unfortunately not operational

at the time of writing, and it's anyone's guess if it will be resuscitated any time soon.

If you'd rather just soak your weary bones in the warm waters of some pleasant hot springs, you can do that at **Kawilal Hotel & Spa** at Baños Termales Santa Teresita (Avenida Puente de la Gloria, Riveras del Río Michatoya, tel. 6644-1000, www.santateresita.com.gt, 9am-5:30pm Mon.-Thurs., 9am-7:30pm Fri., 8:30am-8:30pm Sat., 8:30am-6:30pm Sun. and holidays), where you can enjoy a private steam bath or a soak in a private tub filled with steaming hot water to your taste ($5). Several outdoor pools of varying temperatures are also available, and there's a restaurant serving grilled meats and chicken, salads, sandwiches, and seafood. Rounding out the list of offerings is a spa, where you can enjoy a one-hour massage for about $20. A modern, 18-room hotel (www.

aerial view of Lake Amatitlán, on the fringes of Guatemala City

kawilalhotel.com, $90 d) opened in 2013, with comfortable accommodations and its own swimming pool, restaurant, and bar.

Parque Nacional Naciones Unidas

This 491-hectare park near the lakeshore is managed by private conservation group **Defensores de la Naturaleza** (tel. 5651-4825 or 2310-2929, www.defensores.org.gt) and is open 8am-4pm Monday-Friday and 8am-5pm Saturday and Sunday. Admission is $3.50. Facilities include picnic areas with barbecue pits, hiking and mountain biking trails with hanging bridges and lookout points over the lake, basketball courts, and soccer fields. A five-platform, 400-meter canopy tour, and rappelling were added in 2008. There are miniature replicas of Guatemalan landmarks such as Tikal's Gran Jaguar temple and Antigua Guatemala in areas denominated "Plaza Guatemala" and "Plaza Antigua." The park is one of five original national parks dating back to 1955.

Getting There

You'll probably need to rent a car to get to Lake Amatitlán, though you could also hire a cab to take you there from Guatemala City for about $30. If you're driving, take the Pacific Highway (CA-9) south out of the city. The main entrance to the Amatitlán lakeshore is at Km. 26. You'll see signs. The exit veers off from the right side of the highway. From the exit ramp, you'll come to a Shell gas station, at which you turn left. Follow the road until it dead-ends just past the soccer fields on your left. Turn left at the dead end. You'll pass a bridge over the Río Michatoya on your right. The next left will take you to the Teleférico and farther up that same road is Parque Nacional Naciones Unidas. Turning right onto the bridge over the Río Michatoya followed by an immediate right will bring you to the Santa Teresita hot springs.

La Antigua Guatemala

ts name means "the old Guatemala," and this is in fact what it is. The former capital of Guatemala was destroyed by earthquakes in 1773. Rather than rebuild, the country's aristocracy opted for a fresh start in the neighboring Valley of the

Hermitage, the current site of Guatemala City. And so, by decree, the city and its inhabitants moved on. Still, some Antigueños stayed behind, choosing to live among the ruins, coffee farms, verdant hillsides, and sentinel volcanoes. The city's colonial architecture was maintained, as there were no plans to rebuild, and its ruined churches and convents remained just that. It is said the remaining residents of Antigua were so poor that they had to subsist on avocados, earning them the nickname Panzas Verdes (Green Bellies).

Today, Antigua (as it is more commonly referred to) is a UNESCO World Heritage Site and home to much of Guatemala's expatriate population along with scores of international students studying in its many Spanish schools. Its brightly colored houses and cobblestone streets harbor some of Guatemala's finest restaurants, shopping, and art galleries in a fantastic mountain setting that has inspired artists, writers, and wanderers for centuries. Antigua is a pleasant mixture of Mayan and Spanish colonial influences and makes an excellent base from which to explore other parts of the country.

Antigua lies 45 kilometers from Guatemala City via a good, paved highway. Its setting is spectacular, flanked on its southern extreme by the towering 3,750-meter (12,325-foot) Agua Volcano. The colossal 4,235-meter (13,044-foot) Acatenango and active Fuego Volcanoes lie to the west. The surrounding hillsides provide wonderful views of the valley and the volcanoes, and are excellent terrain for recreational pursuits such as hiking and mountain biking. The climate is similar to that of Guatemala City, as Antigua lies at about the same altitude, just over 1,500 meters. Days are warm and nights are pleasantly cool.

Previous: view of Antigua from Cerro de la Cruz, with Agua Volcano in the background; a flower-strewn Antigua street. **Above:** one of Antigua's many ruined churches.

Highlights

★ **Parque Central:** You can't miss the town's central plaza, easily Guatemala's loveliest, and the heart and soul of Antigua (page 86).

★ **Arco de Santa Catalina:** A beautiful colonial archway, which is also one of Antigua's most photographed landmarks, provides a suitable frame for views of Agua Volcano (page 87).

★ **Cerro de la Cruz:** This large stone cross on a hill overlooking the valley and volcanoes makes for a good afternoon stroll. Bring a camera (page 88).

★ **Iglesia y Convento de las Capuchinas:** One of Antigua's best-preserved colonial monuments has many interesting features, including a tower and 18 nuns' cells built around a patio (page 88).

★ **Centro Cultural Casa Santo Domingo:** The city's finest museum lies on the grounds of a fantastic restored monastery, which now functions as a five-star hotel (page 89).

★ **Casa Popenoe:** This fully restored colonial mansion offers a rare glimpse into the life of a royal official in 17th-century Antigua in addition to wonderful city views from the second-story terrace (page 91).

★ **Finca El Zapote:** Lush botanical gardens lie just outside of Antigua, with jaw-dropping views of Fuego Volcano to boot (page 97).

★ **Volcano Climbs:** Antigua's fantastic mountain scenery is dominated by the presence of Agua, Fuego, and Acatenango Volcanoes, affording excellent opportunities for mountaineering at a variety of difficulty levels. Active Pacaya Volcano is another popular day trip (page 98).

★ **Centro Cultural La Azotea:** This three-in-one coffee, music, and indigenous costume museum has excellent displays and offers an interesting glimpse into many aspects of modern-day Mayan culture (page 118).

HISTORY

The former capital of Guatemala, now known as Ciudad Vieja, was the first of Guatemala's capitals to suffer merciless destruction at the hands of nature. It was built on the slopes of Agua Volcano; an earthquake on the evening of September 10, 1541, unleashed a torrent of mud and water that came tumbling down the volcano's slopes and destroyed the city. The new Muy Leal y Muy Noble Ciudad de Santiago de los Caballeros de Goathemala, as it would officially come to be known, was established on March 10, 1543, in the Panchoy Valley. The new capital would be no stranger to the ravages of nature; its first earthquake occurred only 20 years after the city's founding.

An earthquake in 1717 spurred an unprecedented building boom, with the city reaching its peak in the mid-18th century. At that time, its population would number around 60,000. Antigua was the capital of the Audiencia de Guatemala, under the jurisdiction of the larger Viceroyalty of New Spain, which encompassed most of present-day Mexico and all of Central America as far south as Costa Rica. The Viceroyalty's capital was in Mexico City, which along with Lima, Peru, would be the only other New World cities exceeding Antigua's political, cultural, and economic importance. Antigua boasted Central America's first printing press and one of the hemisphere's first universities and was known as an important center of arts and education. Among its outstanding citizens were conquistador and historian Bernal Díaz del Castillo, Franciscan friar and indigenous peoples rights advocate Bartolomé de las Casas, bishop Francisco Marroquín, artist Tomás de Merlo, English priest/traveler Thomas Gage, and architect Juan Bautista Antonelli.

Antigua's prominence came crashing down in 1773. The city was rocked throughout most of the year by a series of earthquakes, which later came to be known as the Terremotos de Santa Marta. Two earthquakes occurred on July 29. The final blows would be delivered on September 7 and December 13. The city was officially moved the following year to its present location in modern-day Guatemala City.

Antigua lay in ruins occupied mainly by squatters, its monuments pillaged for building materials for the new capital. It wasn't until the mid-19th century that it became once again populated and its buildings restored, in part with the money from the region's newfound coffee wealth. The city was declared a national monument in 1944 and came under the protection of the National Council for the Protection of Antigua Guatemala in 1969. It was declared a UNESCO World Heritage Site in 1979. The council has done a fairly decent job at protecting and restoring the city's cultural and architectural heritage, though building code violations are not at all unheard of. Still, many power lines have gone underground and truck traffic has been effectively banned from the city's streets, greatly reducing noise pollution.

PLANNING YOUR TIME

A week in Antigua would give you ample time to explore the town, its ruins, museums, and churches, maybe climb a volcano, visit a coffee farm, and do some shopping. Depending on whether or not you plan to study Spanish, you could easily spend several weeks in Antigua. Some choose to study Spanish for a week just to brush up on their skills or get a very basic foundation before moving on to other parts of Guatemala. At the minimum, you should plan on spending two nights here. Some have even recommended Antigua as a long weekend getaway from cities such as Miami, Atlanta, Houston, and Dallas because of its proximity and ease of access. The Guatemala City international airport is about a 45-minute drive away.

ORIENTATION

Getting around Antigua is fairly straightforward. True to its colonial foundations, it was laid out in a grid pattern surrounding the central plaza with *calles* running east-west and *avenidas* running north-south. The plaza is bounded by 4a Calle and 5a Calle to the north

La Antigua Guatemala

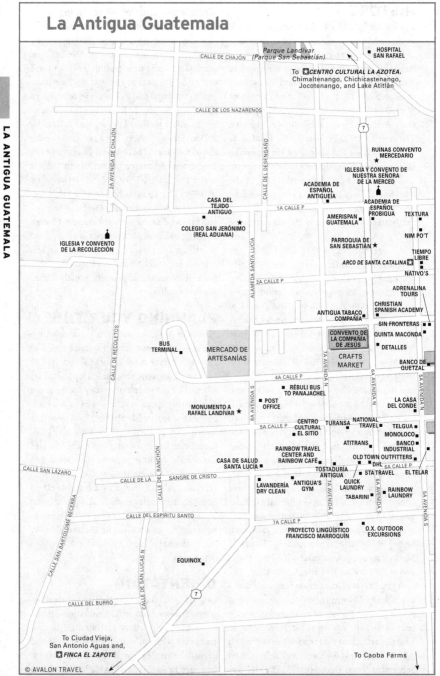

CALLE DE CHAJÓN

Parque Landívar (Parque San Sebastián)

HOSPITAL SAN RAFAEL

To ✪ *CENTRO CULTURAL LA AZOTEA*, Chimaltenango, Chichicastenango, Jocotenango, and Lake Atitlán

CALLE DE LOS NAZARENOS

2A AVENIDA DE CHAJÓN

CALLE DEL DESENGAÑO

RUINAS CONVENTO MERCEDARIO ★

IGLESIA Y CONVENTO DE NUESTRA SEÑORA DE LA MERCED

ACADEMIA DE ESPAÑOL ANTIGÜEÑA

ACADEMIA DE ESPAÑOL PROBIGUA

CASA DEL TEJIDO ANTIGUO

1A CALLE P.

AMERISPAN GUATEMALA

TEXTURA

NIM PO'T

COLEGIO SAN JERÓNIMO (REAL ADUANA) ★

ALAMEDA SANTA LUCÍA

PARROQUIA DE SAN SEBASTIÁN ★

TIEMPO LIBRE

IGLESIA Y CONVENTO DE LA RECOLECCIÓN

ARCO DE SANTA CATALINA ✪

NATIVO'S

CALLE DE RECOLETOS

2A CALLE P.

ADRENALINA TOURS

CHRISTIAN SPANISH ACADEMY

ANTIGUA TABACO COMPAÑÍA

SIN FRONTERAS

QUINTA MACONDA

BUS TERMINAL

MERCADO DE ARTESANÍAS

CONVENTO DE LA COMPAÑÍA DE JESÚS

DETALLES

7A AVENIDA N

6A AVENIDA N

CRAFTS MARKET

BANCO DE QUETZAL

4A CALLE P.

8A AVENIDA S

RÉBULI BUS TO PANAJACHEL

POST OFFICE

LA CASA DEL CONDE

MONUMENTO A RAFAEL LANDÍVAR ★

5A CALLE P.

CENTRO CULTURAL EL SITIO

TURANSA

NATIONAL TRAVEL

TELGUA

MONOLOCO

6A AVENIDA N

6A AVENIDA N

CALLE DEL RANCHÓN

ATITRANS

BANCO INDUSTRIAL

RAINBOW TRAVEL CENTER AND RAINBOW CAFÉ

OLD TOWN OUTFITTERS

CALLE SAN LÁZARO

CALLE DE LA SANGRE DE CRISTO

CASA DE SALUD SANTA LUCÍA

TOSTADURÍA ANTIGUA

STA TRAVEL

6A CALLE P.

EL TELAR

DHL

7A AVENIDA S

LAVANDERÍA DRY CLEAN

ANTIGUA'S GYM

QUICK LAUNDRY

6A AVENIDA S

5A AVENIDA S

RAINBOW LAUNDRY

TABARINI

CALLE DEL ESPÍRITU SANTO

CALLE SAN BARTOLOMÉ BECERRA

CALLE SAN LUCAS N

7A CALLE P.

PROYECTO LINGÜÍSTICO FRANCISCO MARROQUÍN

O.X. OUTDOOR EXCURSIONS

EQUINOX

CALLE DEL BURRO

To Ciudad Vieja, San Antonio Aguas and, ✪ *FINCA EL ZAPOTE*

To Caoba Farms

© AVALON TRAVEL

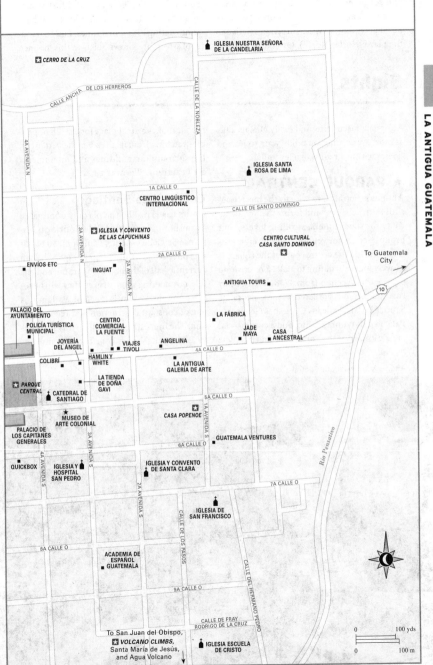

and south, and 4a Avenida and 5a Avenida to the east and west. Street addresses are labeled according to their direction relative to the plaza: Norte (North), Oriente (East), Sur (South), and Poniente (West). Most streets are known by this method, though all have names dating to colonial times. Only a handful of streets are known solely in this manner.

Sights

Antigua is fascinating and easily manageable, as most everything you might want to see and do lies within a radius of a few miles.

★ PARQUE CENTRAL

Antigua's central plaza is easily the most beautiful in the country and forms the hub of activity for shoe shiners, strolling lovers, tour groups, ice cream vendors, and foreign visitors. Gracing the central part of the square is a lovely fountain dating to 1936, a re-creation of an earlier version from 1738 destroyed by earthquakes. It is bordered by the Catedral de Santiago, Palacio de los Capitanes Generales, Palacio del Ayuntamiento, and a commercial arcade known as the Portal del Comercio. The *parque* makes a great place for a stroll or people-watching from its park benches. At night, the surrounding buildings and monuments are beautifully illuminated.

Catedral de Santiago

On its eastern side, the plaza is dominated by the beautiful **Catedral de Santiago** (entrance 5a Calle Oriente, 9am-5pm, $0.50). It was once wonderfully lit up at night, though currently half of the lightbulbs are out and one is left wondering when, if ever, they will be replaced. Its history, as is much of Antigua's, is one of constant destruction and reconstruction. The first cathedral built on this site dates to 1545, but its shoddy construction caused its

Antigua's lovely Parque Central

roof to come crashing down during an earth-quake in 1583. It was decided to build a new cathedral in 1670, a task that would require 11 years and the conscripted labor of indigenous Maya. The scale of the new structure was as-tounding, with 18 chapels, a huge dome, five naves, and a large central chamber measur-ing 90 meters by 20 meters. It was graced by paintings and artwork of renowned European and colonial artists; its altar was inlaid with silver, ivory, and mother-of-pearl. Although it withstood the earthquakes of 1689 and 1717, it finally succumbed to the earthquakes of 1773.

The current church is not really a cathe-dral in the strict sense of the word, as it con-sists of two restored chambers known as the Parroquia de San José. You can visit the in-teresting interior, where you'll find splen-did arches and towering columns. There is also a sculpted black Christ similar to the highly revered statue found in Esquipulas, both carved by Quirio Cataño. The remains of the rest of the colonial structure can also be seen here, a moss-covered mass of stones and rotting beams. The remains of some of the major players from colonial days are said to be buried beneath the church altar, including Don Pedro de Alvarado; his wife, Beatriz de la Cueva; Guatemala's first bishop, Francisco Marroquín; and conqueror/chronicler Bernal Díaz del Castillo. Steps behind the main altar lead to the former crypt, now a chapel, harbor-ing the black Christ statue.

Palacio del Ayuntamiento

Found on the north side of the plaza, this large structure functioned as the town hall, also known as the Casa del Cabildo. It has miraculously withstood the test of time, re-sisting damage from earthquakes until the most recent one in 1976, despite its construc-tion dating to 1740. Some fantastic views of the cathedral and Agua Volcano are framed by the **Palacio del Ayuntamiento**'s beau-tiful arches from its second-floor balconies. Perhaps a bigger draw than the historical building itself is the quite interesting colo-nial fountain embossed with the emblem of

Santiago (St. James), found in a quiet court-yard. Next door, the **Museo del Libro Antiguo** (Antique Book Museum, tel. 7832-5511, 9am-4pm Tues.-Fri., 9am-noon and 2pm-4pm Sat.-Sun., $1.50) features exhibits on colonial printing and binding processes. There's a replica of the country's first print-ing press, brought to Guatemala in 1660 from Puebla, Mexico.

Palacio de los Capitanes Generales

On the south end of the plaza, the **Palacio de los Capitanes Generales** or Palace of the Captains General dates to 1558 and was once the seat of government for the entire Central American territory from Chiapas to Costa Rica, of which Antigua was the capital, until 1773. Its imposing architecture is dominated by a row of 27 arches on both of its floors. It once housed colonial rulers, the royal mint, the judiciary, and tax offices, among other things. It has been recently restored and now houses a cultural center, after much debate about what its function would be. Among the attractions is **Museo de Armas de Santiago** (tel. 7832-2878, 9am-5pm Tues.-Sun., $4). It houses colonial artifacts, weap-ons (including cannons), historical paintings, and furnishings.

★ ARCO DE SANTA CATALINA

Three blocks north of the park along 5a Avenida Norte (also known as Calle del Arco) is one of Antigua's most recognizable landmarks, the **Arco de Santa Catalina.** The Santa Catalina archway is all that re-mains of a convent dating to 1613. As the convent grew, it expanded to include a structure across the street. The arch then was built to allow the nuns to cross to the other side while avoiding contact with the general populace in accordance with strict rules governing seclusion. Its current ver-sion with a clock tower is a reconstruction dating to the 19th century, as the original was destroyed in the 1773 earthquakes. The clock is a French model, which needed to be wound every three days. It stopped working after the 1976 earthquake but was repaired in 1991. Looking south through the archway, you'll find some nice framing for an unobstructed view of Agua Volcano. The archway is practically an Antigua icon and beautifully painted in a rich orange hue with white accents that have become delightfully aged.

★ CERRO DE LA CRUZ

In the hills north of the city stands this giant stone cross, from which there are sweeping views south over the city with Agua Volcano in the background. Robberies were once frequent here until the creation of the tourism police, which began escorting visitors to the site and pretty much put an end to these crimes. It's still a good idea to go along with a police escort and to visit during daylight hours. Escorts are available free from the tourism police near the central plaza. You'll want to bring along your camera and some water. It's about a 30-minute walk from the plaza to the **Cerro de la Cruz**. From the top of the hill, you can see the entire Antigua Valley and the cross makes for a nice foreground element.

CHURCHES AND MONASTERIES
★ Iglesia y Convento de las Capuchinas

The **Iglesia y Convento de las Capuchinas** (2a Avenida Norte and 2a Calle Oriente, 9am-5pm daily, $4) was abandoned after being destroyed in the earthquakes of 1773. Restoration began in 1943 and is still being carried out today; the convent now also serves as a museum. The convent's foundation dates to 1726, making it the city's fourth, and is the work of renowned Antigua architect Diego de Porres. There are beautiful fountains and courtyards flanked by sturdy stone pillars with stately arches and flowering bougainvillea. It is certainly the most elegant of Antigua's convents and well worth a look for those with even a casual interest in colonial

Arco de Santa Catalina

Latin American architecture. The convent was the haunt of the Capuchin nuns from Madrid, a rather strict order limiting its numbers to 28 and requiring the nuns to sleep on wooden beds with straw pillows and sever all ties to the outside world.

The church consists of a single nave lacking side aisles. There are two choir areas, one adjacent to the altar on the ground floor and another on the second floor at the end of the nave.

After the 1773 earthquakes and the subsequent transfer of the Guatemalan capital to its new location, many of the convent's historical artifacts were likewise transferred to their new home in the San Miguel de Capuchinas convent in modern-day Guatemala City.

Iglesia y Convento de Santa Clara

The **Iglesia y Convento de Santa Clara** (2a Avenida Sur #27, 9am-5pm daily, $4) originally dates to 1702, with its current incarnation having been inaugurated in 1734 and destroyed in 1773. The convent ruins are also pleasant for a stroll, and in front of its main entrance is **Parque La Unión** with several wash basins, known as *pilas*, where women gather to do their laundry. The park's other outstanding feature is a large stone cross, a gift from the city of Santiago de Compostela, Spain. The church is beautifully floodlit at night.

Iglesia de San Francisco

Southwest on 1a Avenida Sur, the **Iglesia de San Francisco** (8am-6pm daily) is one of Antigua's oldest, dating to 1579. It once harbored a hospital, school, printing press, and monastery, among other things. Its main claim to fame nowadays is the tomb of Central America's first saint, **Hermano Pedro de San José Betancur,** a Franciscan monk who came to Antigua from the Canary Islands and founded the Hospital de Belén. He is credited with miraculous healings. The **Museo del Hermano Pedro** (8am-5pm, $0.50) is found on the south side of the church along with

the ornate La Merced church

the ruins of the adjacent monastery. It houses church relics and some of Hermano Pedro's well-preserved personal belongings.

Iglesia y Convento de Nuestra Señora de la Merced

Known more commonly as **La Merced** (5a Avenida Norte and 1a Calle Poniente, 9am-6:30pm, $0.50), this is one of Antigua's most beautiful churches, painted in a bright yellow and adorned with white lily motifs on its columns. Inside are the ruins of its old monastery with the Fuente de Peces, said to be the largest fountain in Latin America and interestingly in the shape of a water lily. The pools were once used for breeding fish. The upper level affords some wonderful city views, and the fountain just outside the church is also worth a look.

Iglesia y Convento de la Recolección

On Avenida de la Recolección, the large **Iglesia y Convento de la Recolección** built between 1701 and 1715 was heavily damaged in 1717 in the same year it was inaugurated. The earthquakes of 1773 finished the job, and it has lain in ruins ever since.

MUSEUMS
Museo de Arte Colonial

On the former site of San Carlos University, the **Museo de Arte Colonial** (5a Calle Oriente #5, tel. 7832-0429, 9am-4pm Tues.-Fri., 9am-noon and 2pm-4pm Sat.-Sun., $3.50) harbors sculptures of saints, murals, furniture, and colonial paintings by Mexican artists. A beautiful Moorish courtyard dominates the surviving architecture.

★ Centro Cultural Casa Santo Domingo

Antigua's finest museum is housed inside the Casa Santo Domingo hotel: **Centro Cultural Casa Santo Domingo** (3a Calle Oriente #28, tel. 7832-0140 or 7820-1220, www.casa-santodomingo.com.gt, 9am-6pm Mon.-Sat., 11:15am-6pm Sun., $5). The site was once the city's largest and wealthiest monastery, with

Semana Santa in Antigua

Semana Santa, or Holy Week, runs from Palm Sunday to Easter Sunday and is one of the best times to visit Antigua for the elaborate Catholic pageantry surrounding these holy days. Visitors come from around the world to see the colorful, solemn processions in which life-sized images of Christ and other Catholic icons are paraded through the city's cobblestone streets. Before the processions pass through, Antigueños design and produce exquisite, though ephemeral, *alfombras,* or carpets made of colored sawdust and flowers. The parade floats, or *andas,* pass over the carpets, forever erasing their elaborate patterns under the feet of faithful *cucuruchos,* purple-clad bearers who carry the floats. The floats can weigh up to 3.5 tons and require 80 men to carry them. The bearers are accompanied by Roman soldiers and other robed figures who carry swaying, copal-laden incense burners. It can be quite a moving experience to see the swaying floats with images of a cross-bearing Christ bearing down on the men amid thick smoke.

A highlight of the week's festivities is a Good Friday event occurring at 3am in which Roman soldiers on horseback gallop through the streets proclaiming Christ's death sentence. Though several local churches participate in the festivities, the largest procession is the one leaving from La Merced on Good Friday with the 17th-century image of Jesús Nazareno (Jesus of Nazareth). Another well-known procession is that of the Escuela de Cristo, which features some striking images on its parade floats.

For specifics on Holy Week events, head to the **INGUAT office** (corner of 2a Calle Oriente and 2a Avenida Norte, 8am-12:30pm and 2:30pm-5pm Mon.-Fri., 9am-12:30pm and 2:30pm-5pm Sat.-Sun.) on the central plaza, where you'll find free maps and event schedules. If you plan to take in the festivities, book far in advance, as word about Antigua's Holy Week events has been out for quite some time and accommodations fill up several months ahead with foreign visitors and vacationing Guatemalans.

a church completed in 1666, but it was damaged and eventually destroyed by the 18th-century earthquakes. Several museums are housed within the same complex, including the **colonial museum** harboring Catholic relics, among them an old Roman coin found during the excavations for the hotel's construction. Other highlights of this wonderful historic complex include a gorgeous monastery church, cleared of rubble and restored in the early 1990s. It is now frequently used for weddings. Below this area are two crypts. The first of these, the **Cripta del Calvario,** has a well-preserved Crucifixion mural. The other crypt harbors two graves with human bones.

There is also a small archaeological museum, but the highlight here is the **Museo Vigua de Arte Precolombino y Vidrio Moderno,** a fantastic, well-presented juxtaposition of colonial and pre-Columbian artifacts mixed with glass art. Rounding out the impressive list of attractions is the Casa de la Cera, an elaborate candle shop.

★ Casa Popenoe

Authentically restored to recreate the living conditions of a 17th-century official, **Casa Popenoe** (1a Avenida Sur #2, tel. 2338-7959, www.casapopenoe.ufm.edu, by appointment only with a minimum of six people, 8am-4pm Mon.-Fri., 8am-11am Sat., $10) was originally built in 1762 by wealthy merchant Venancia López Marchán upon the ruins of two homes from 1650. Like much of Antigua, it was left abandoned after the 1773 earthquakes until Dr. Wilson Popenoe and his wife, Dorothy, bought it in 1929. Dr. Popenoe, an agricultural scientist, worked with the United Fruit Company for much of his career and had a long history of adventures in plant collecting and botany in addition to his painstaking restoration of this fantastic cultural monument. He died in 1975, but two of his daughters continued to live in the house, one the noted archaeologist Marion Popenoe Hatch. The house was eventually donated to Guatemala's Francisco Marroquín University. You'll see paintings of Bishop Francisco Marroquín and fierce conqueror Pedro de Alvarado. Also on display are the wonderfully restored servants' quarters and kitchen. A narrow staircase leads up to the roof terrace, from where there are gorgeous views of Antigua and the volcanoes off in the distance.

Entertainment

NIGHTLIFE

Antigua has a lively nightlife scene, particularly on weekends when wealthy youths from Guatemala City flood the city streets in search of a good time.

Bars

Always popular with the American expat crowd is **Café No Sé** (1a Avenida Sur #11C, tel. 7832-0563, www.cafenose.com, 6pm-1am daily), where you can enjoy drinks in a charmingly gritty setting, often with live music. There's also good pub grub, though the main attraction is the tequila/mezcal bar, featuring their very own brand, Ilegal Mezcal. The secondhand bookstore next door is open until 6pm. A welcome new addition to the town's pub scene is **The Snug** (6a Calle Poniente #14, tel. 4215-9601), where you'll find cheap beers and a fun, cozy atmosphere.

Monoloco (5a Avenida Sur #6, tel. 7832-4228, ext. 102, www.restaurantemonoloco.com, 11am-1am daily) is also wildly popular and lively. It's set on two floors, and you can drink alfresco on the second-floor terrace. Reasonably priced burgers, nachos, and pizzas are served, and there are sports on the downstairs TV.

An old standby for grabbing a drink and watching the sunset with nice volcano views is the rooftop bar at **Café Sky** (corner of 6a Calle and 1a Avenida, tel. 7832-7300, 8am-1am daily). In addition to the rooftop terrace café bar, there's the downstairs Sky Lounge and Bamboo Bar, where you can enjoy drinks and a full menu of tasty food that includes sandwiches, lasagnas, and quesadillas.

Another popular watering hole, **The Ocelot Bar** (4a Avenida Norte #3, tel. 7832-1339, 12:30pm-1am daily), enjoys a prime location near the central plaza. There's often live jazz and blues in addition to a weekly Sunday evening pub quiz. Upstairs and under the same ownership is **Lava Terrace Bar,** with nice views of the surroundings from shady patio umbrellas and scrumptious gourmet burgers made from imported Angus beef. Happy hour is at 5pm daily.

A few blocks south of the park, **La Sala** (6a Calle Poniente #9, tel. 7832-9524) hosts a fun mix of Guatemalans and foreigners. The ambience is modern with a splash of Guatemalan color. There's also a varied menu that runs the gamut from Indian chicken dishes to bangers 'n mash. Next door is the new incarnation of Antigua's original Irish pub, **Reilly's En La Esquina** (6a Calle Poniente #7, tel. 7832-6251).

Dancing

Antigua's most popular and dependably fun

disco is the two-story **La Casbah** (5a Avenida Norte #30, tel. 7832-2640, www.lacasbahantigua.com, 7pm-1am Thurs.-Sat., $4 cover), where you can dance the night away in a classy atmosphere popular with the wealthy Guatemala City crowd. The admission price includes one drink. **La Sin Ventura** (5a Avenida Sur #8, tel. 7832-0581) is a popular disco bar with mostly Latin music and dancing on weekend nights. There are a number of nightclubs in and around 6a Avenida Sur popular with the weekend crowds. Just follow the sound of music. Highly recommended is **Las Vibras** (Calle del Arco Casa #30, tel. 7832-3553, noon-1am daily) for its cool club vibe, dance floor, and very tasty food that make for a fun night out with friends. Down the street is **Sunset Terrace** (6a Avenida Norte #1C, tel. 5945-6640), which functions as a restaurant by day but gets increasingly more crowded (and raucous) as the night goes on. There are sometimes live dj sets.

Live Music

Restaurante Las Palmas (6a Avenida Norte #14, tel. 7832-9734, www.laspalmasantigua.com) has live Latin music on Friday and Saturday nights starting at 9:30pm. **Mesón Panza Verde** (5a Avenida Sur #19, tel.

The Ocelot Bar

7955-8282, www.panzaverde.com) features live jazz and Latin music nightly 8pm-10pm.

CINEMA

On the edge of town on the way to Santa Ana, **La Casa del Río** (Calle del Hermano Pedro #6, tel. 7832-5438) is a cultural center opened by two Guatemalan actors. There's a screening room where independent films and Guatemalan cinema are shown. It's worth checking out.

Shopping

Antigua is one of Guatemala's top places for shopping, with a wide assortment of excellent shops carrying quality items not found elsewhere in the country. You'll be hard-pressed to find the same variety of home decor, textiles, clothing, and jewelry anywhere else. Don't feel you have to confine your purchases to what you can fit in your checked airline baggage allotment, as there are a number of local companies that can help you ship your loot home.

HANDICRAFTS

Antigua's **Mercado de Artesanías** (4a Calle Poniente Final, 8am-7pm) is an attractive, safe place to shop for textiles, handicrafts, and souvenirs among several stalls. There is also an adjacent outdoor market selling fruits, vegetables, and wonderful fresh flowers. **Textura** (5a Avenida Norte #33, tel. 7832-5067, 10am-5:45pm Mon.-Wed., 10am-6:45pm Thurs.-Sat., 10am-5pm Sun.) sells stylish home furnishings in updated versions of Mayan textiles, including gorgeous hammocks and table dressings. Selling similarly exquisite indoor and outdoor home furnishings is **El Telar** (5a Avenida Sur #7, tel. 7832-3179, www.eltelarantigua.com).

Nim Po't (5a Avenida Norte #29, tel. 7832-2681, 9am-9pm daily) has a large selection of traditional Mayan dress items, including colorful *huipiles* (blouses), *cortes* (skirts), and *fajas* (belts). There is also a wide variety of artwork, souvenir T-shirts, tourist trinkets, masks, and other wooden carvings in the spacious warehouselike setting. Just down the street, **Nativo's** (5a Avenida Norte #25B, tel. 7832-6556, 10am-7pm daily) also sells textiles and has some extremely rare, beautiful, and no-longer-produced textiles in the $600 range. Ask to see them. **Quinta Maconda** (5a Avenida Norte #11, tel. 7832-1480 or 5309-1423, www.quintamaconda.com, 9:30am-1pm and 2pm-7pm daily) sells its own brand of high-quality handcrafted leather travel gear and handwoven Guatemalan brocades in beautiful muted hues and earth tones. It also has a fine collection of Southeast Asian antiques and wooden furniture in its by-appointment-only showroom. One of my favorite shops for high-quality (though somewhat expensive) crafts and textiles is **Colibrí** (4a Calle Oriente #3B, tel. 7832-0280, textilescolibri@turbonett.com, 9am-6pm daily). I particularly like their bedspreads, though a queen size will set you back about $200.

For gifts to bestow upon loved ones back home, head to **Atypical Treasures** (3a Calle and 4a Avenida #7A, tel. 7832-0467, 9am-7pm Mon.-Sat., noon-6pm Sun.), a well-curated selection of local handicrafts interwoven with hard-to-find items from regions like Cobán. There's also a fine assortment of beautiful women's clothing (original designs) and handbags made from reclaimed Guatemalan *huipiles* that you can purchase for a song. Mention *Moon Guatemala* (or better yet, bring in your copy) for a 10 percent discount off the already very reasonable prices.

JEWELRY

Guatemala produces some of the world's finest jade, including rare black jade, found only in this part of the world. You can buy fabulous jade jewelry here tax-free. The best store for perusing wonderful jade creations in colorful hues, including emerald, yellow, and lilac, is **Jade Maya** (4a Calle Oriente #34, tel. 7931-2400, www.jademaya.com, 9am-7pm daily), where you'll find a vast array of items varying from 18-karat gold/jade earrings to a unique $3,800 jade chess board. All of the jade found here is mined from a quarry in eastern Guatemala. The store doubles as a jade museum, and you can also visit the factory behind the shop. Guided tours are available in German, Spanish, English, French, and Italian. For fashionable and exotic jewelry, handbags, and sunglasses, visit **Joyería del Ángel** (4a Calle Oriente #5A, tel. 7832-3189, www.delangel.com, 9am-6pm daily). For silver jewelry, check out **Pablo's Silver Shop** (5a Calle Poniente #12C, tel. 7832-8960).

BOOKS

Hamlin y White (4a Calle Oriente #12A, tel. 7832-7075, 9am-6:30pm daily) has a good selection of books and international magazines. Under the same ownership is **Tiempo Libre** (5a Avenida Norte #25, tel. 7832-1816, 9am-7pm daily), with a wider assortment of books in English and Spanish, including Moon Handbooks. On the west side of the plaza in the Portal del Comercio, **La Casa del Conde** (5a Avenida Norte #4, tel. 7832-3322, 9am-7pm Mon.-Sat., 10am-7pm Sun.) sells an assortment of travel guides in addition to material specifically relating to Guatemala, Central America, and the Mayan world, mostly in English. **Dyslexia** (1a Avenida Sur #11, tel. 5162-4515, 1pm-6pm daily) has a good selection of secondhand books curated by its scribe owners who publish *La Cuadra* magazine.

ART, ANTIQUES, AND FURNITURE

Panza Verde (5a Avenida Sur #19, tel. 7955-8282, www.panzaverde.com) is a gallery housed inside its namesake restaurant/hotel; a new exhibit usually opens every second Wednesday of the month. **La Antigua Galería de Arte** (4a Calle Oriente #15, tel. 7832-2124, www.laantiguagaleria.com,

Colibrí's colorful coaster designs

9am-7pm Mon.-Sat.) exhibits the work of numerous local and international artists in a large building surrounding a pleasant courtyard. **Casa de Artes** (4a Avenida Sur #11, tel. 7832-0792 and 7832-1390, www.casadeartes.com.gt) is like a museum chock-full of textiles, masks, jewelry, and other wonderful finds where the items are available for purchase.

For antique furniture and architectural accents, a good bet is **Ritual** (7a Calle Poniente #30, tel. 7832-4767, www.ritualstyle.com). **Casa Chicob** (5a Avenida Norte #31, tel. 7832-0781, www.casachicob.com, 9am-6pm Mon.-Sat.) features a wonderful assortment of Guatemalan-inspired home decor and luxurious personal care products. **Uxibal** (Callejón del Sol Casa #9, tel. 7832-7417, www.uxibal. com) sells fashionable leather shoes, boots, handbags, and accessories incorporating Guatemalan textiles.

COFFEE AND TOBACCO

For coffee, head to **Tostaduría Antigua** (6a Calle Poniente #26, tel. 7832-5159, tostaduriaantigua.blogspot.com). You can buy Cuban and Honduran cigars, as well as enjoy them in a comfortable lounge, at **Antigua Tabaco Compañía** (3a Calle Poniente #12, tel. 7832-9420, 10am-10pm daily).

WELLNESS

One of Antigua's most interesting stores is **La Tienda de Doña Gavi** (3a Avenida Norte #2, tel. 7832-6514, noon-7pm daily), where you can pick up a number of natural remedies, including Jacameb, a powerful concoction created from the jacaranda flower that does the trick on amoebas and assorted other parasitic problems. (Friendly Doña Gavi also serves the tastiest mango ice cream I've ever had.) Organic groceries, natural foods, and eco-friendly products can be found at **Orgánica** (5a Calle Poniente #6, tel. 7832-6533, 8am-6pm daily).

Caoba Farms (5a Avenida Sur final, tel. 7758-9510 or 7832-9201, www.caobafarms. com, 8am-5pm Mon.-Fri., 8am-noon Sat., 9am-1pm Sun.) sells organic produce cultivated on several plots of land in the Antigua area. They also brew their own kombucha. Tours to the farms are available (see website for details) at a cost of $10 per person. Volunteer opportunities are available.

Caoba Farms

Recreation

HEALTH CLUBS

Antigua's Gym (6a Calle Poniente #31, tel. 7832-7554, 6am-9:30pm Mon.-Fri., 7am-3pm Sat., 8am-3pm Sun.) offers spinning, Tae Bo, cardiovascular equipment, free weights, and some weight-lifting machines. **La Fábrica** (1a Avenida Norte #7A, tel. 7832-9840) also has cardiovascular machines and weights in addition to aerobics and rock climbing. My gym of choice is **Equinox** (Carretera a Ciudad Vieja, tel. 7832-2957, 5am-9pm Mon.-Fri., 6am-3pm Sat., 8am-1pm Sun.). It's a somewhat large facility with plenty of equipment, classes, and parking out front.

SPAS AND YOGA

Casa Madeleine (Calle del Espíritu Santo #69, tel. 7832-9348, www.casamadeleine.com/spa) offers complete spa packages along with its swanky boutique hotel accommodations. Services include massage, reflexology, aromatherapy, mud therapy, pedicures, manicures, and deep facial treatments. **Healing Hands** (3a Avenida Norte #20A, tel. 7832-1648, www.healinghandsguatemala.com) is a well-run day spa offering the usual assortment of spa services in a pleasant environment. There are overnight accommodations and a yoga studio.

There are quality yoga classes by trained U.S. instructors available in Antigua. **YogAntigua** (tel. 5251-4809, www.yogantigua.com) offers classes every morning inside **Galería Panza Verde** (5a Avenida Sur #19) and afternoons at Calle del Hermano Pedro #16. Vinyasa and Hatha yoga classes start at $10 for drop-in or $32 for a five-class pass.

MOUNTAIN BIKING

Antigua's mountain terrain and the variety of trails traversing it make mountain biking a popular recreational activity. **Old Town Outfitters** (5a Avenida Sur #12, tel. 7832-4171, www.adventureguatemala.com, 9am-6pm daily) is a highly recommended outfitter offering rides for all skill levels. Half-day options include easy rides in the Almolonga Valley or in and around coffee plantations to edge-of-your-seat single-track rides careening down volcanic slopes or along narrow mountain ridges with fantastic views. Its equipment is top-notch and well cared for. **Guatemala Venture** (1a Avenida Sur #15, end of 6a Calle Oriente, tel. 7832-6264, www.guatemalaventure.com, 9am-6pm daily) is another recommended outfitter for tackling the rugged terrain around Antigua by mountain bike. It also rents out mountain bikes for $8 a day. Both companies also offer a lot of other recreational options in addition to mountain biking, as you'll see by the frequency with which they are mentioned here.

O.X. Outdoor Excursions (7a Calle Poniente #17, tel. 7832-0468, www.guatemalavolcano.com) has cornered the market on "cool" with the addition of mountain biking to its arsenal of adventurous offerings. Trip options range from cycling around Antigua's neighboring villages to adrenaline-inducing single-track careens down volcanic slopes. They also rent mountain bikes for $22 a day.

BIRD-WATCHING
Finca El Pilar

Just a 45-minute walk from Antigua's central park (or a 10-minute *tuk-tuk* ride), **Finca El Pilar** (tel. 7832-4937, fincaelpilar@live.com, 6am-6pm daily, $5) is a private reserve protecting a large area that includes dry forest, pine oak, and cloud forest. Among the bird species you can expect to find are numerous types of rare and endemic hummingbirds, emerald toucanet, golden-browed warbler, highland guans, and blue-throated motmot. There is a system of trails and observation platforms throughout the reserve and altitude ranges from 5,250 to 7,870 feet. To get here, walk south from the central plaza toward 7a Calle until you reach San Francisco

Church. Behind the church, you'll find the path leading to neighboring Santa Ana. Look for El Calvario church, where you'll turn left and continue all the way to the end of an uphill path, passing San Cristobal El Bajo church along the way. **Cayaya Birding** (tel. 5308-5160, www.cayaya-birding.com) does guided trips to the reserve. If you get tired of hiking, you can take a leisurely soak in the swimming pool ($1.50).

★ Finca El Zapote

Outside of town, along the road to Escuintla, is this Eden-like botanical garden situated on the slopes of active Fuego Volcano. **Finca El Zapote** (Aldea Guadalupe, Escuintla; tel. 5000-1899, www.fincazapote.com, $20 adults, $9 children) has been owned by the local Pettersen family since the late 1950s. Mr. Pettersen geared the farm toward quinine production, but Mrs. Pettersen, a renowned artist and author of *The Maya of Guatemala: Life and Dress,* used her considerable talents and British education to create Guatemala's most amazing botanical gardens. Birds naturally find this exotic locale, between the Pacific Coast lowlands and volcanic highlands, a very welcoming place, and there are numerous species in evidence including magpie jays,

several species of egret, herons, and woodpeckers. The views of Fuego Volcano alone are worth the price of admission, but the beautifully manicured lawns and 25 acres of luxuriant tropical foliage could easily be the envy of better-known European botanical gardens. There's a spring-fed swimming pool for refreshment and four lagoons for fishing.

Two different houses are available for rent if you choose to stay here (highly recommended). The **Estate House** ($575-800) sleeps up to 14 guests, while the more modest **Lake House** ($300-400) sleeps six. You'll need a high clearance vehicle to get here even in dry season, as it's a rough road that at times is impassible during the rainy season. Transfers from Antigua are sometimes available by request.

HIKING

There is no shortage of rugged hiking trails for enjoying the spectacular mountain scenery and peaceful mountain villages found near Antigua. The same recommended mountain biking outfitters can point you to the best hiking trails. A guide is highly recommended, as robberies of solo hikers along remote mountain footpaths is sometimes an issue in rural Guatemala. The bulk of the hiking done

the Lake House at Finca El Zapote

around Antigua involves one of the volcanoes towering ominously over its streets.

★ Volcano Climbs

At 3,750 meters (12,325 feet) **Agua Volcano** is one of Antigua's most visible volcanoes with its near-perfect crater that looms just south of Antigua. Unfortunately, its slopes have been plagued by safety issues for years. All of the local outfitters, tired from numerous instances of robberies, have ceased hikes up the volcano.

Just shy of 4,000 meters (13,044 feet), **Acatenango Volcano** is a safer and somewhat more interesting climb. It's an intense six-hour ascent through agricultural fields and cloud forests on sandy gravel. Most of the outfitters camp at a spot 500 meters from the summit. From there it's a grueling final push to the summit on the steepest part of the volcano (and the sandiest). It's worth the effort, however, as your reward is a spectacular view of active **Fuego Volcano** right next to it. You won't find better views of Fuego and the experience is quite unique, as no other volcano in Central America is quite like this. **Old Town Outfitters** (5a Avenida Sur #12, tel. 7832-4171, www.adventureguatemala.com, 9am-6pm daily) offers a one-day or

overnight trip to the volcano starting in the village of La Soledad, from where it's a 5-6-hour hike through cornfields and pine forests to the crater. A newer option is that of taking a 4x4 through private lands en route to a spot just two hours' hike from the summit. **Guatemala Venture** (tel. 7832-6264, www.guatemalaventure.com) also does this trip.

By far the most popular volcano trip is to active **Pacaya Volcano,** near Lake Amatitlán and closer to Guatemala City. There's no shortage of outfitters offering this trip, which generally leaves in the afternoon and costs $7-30 per person. Recommended companies include **Old Town Outfitters** (5a Avenida Sur #12, tel. 7832-4171, www.adventureguatemala.com, 9am-6pm daily), which leaves earlier than most other companies to avoid the crowds. **Adrenalina Tours** (3a Calle Poniente #2D, tel. 7882-4147 or 5308-1489, www.adrenalinatours.com) leaves daily at 6am and 2pm. The trip costs $10 and includes round-trip transportation and local Spanish-speaking guide. The more expensive VIP trip costs $75 and leaves whenever you want it to. The VIP tour includes bilingual and local guides, transportation, park admission, and breakfast.

Personally recommended for all of the

hikers running along the crater of Acatenango Volcano

Fire on the Mountain

Looming over Lake Amatitlán and the Guatemala City valley is the 2,552-meter-high active **Pacaya Volcano** (www.volcandepacaya.com) spewing lava and ash for the amazement of tourists and locals alike. Its current active phase began in 1965 and has barely ceased since. Activity varies from quiet gas, lava, and steam emissions to full-scale explosive eruptions hurtling rocks into the sky. It sometimes spews large ash clouds that prompt the closure of Guatemala City's La Aurora International Airport, as was the case when a 1998 eruption blanketed the airport runway in fine volcanic sand and again in May 2010.

Guatemala is one of few places in the world where you can get up close and personal with an active volcano in relative ease. While the climb is not for the faint of heart, adventurous types will find it to be a worthwhile endeavor. The volcano makes a convenient day trip from Guatemala City (45 minutes) or Antigua (1 hour). Logistically, it makes more sense from Guatemala City, but the tour operators offering the trip are almost entirely based in the old colonial city. It's possible to make the trip on your own, though going in a group with a local guide is highly recommended.

The volcano's national park status dates to 2001. A visitor's center and ticket booth can be found at the trailhead in the village of San Francisco de Sales. Admission to the park is $5. You can also hire a guide here. There is safe parking for vehicles in San Francisco de Sales, and the well-maintained trail has good signage, rest stops with trash receptacles, and outhouses. Park rangers patrol the trails and incidents of robbery, which once plagued this otherwise wonderful place, have become virtually unheard of since 2001.

From the town of San Francisco de Sales, the 3.7-kilometer trail up Pacaya Volcano (2-3 hours) climbs gradually through cornfields and secondary forest before arriving at a vast volcanic wasteland of old lava flows. After crossing a barren ridge, the trail then winds up the slopes of the volcanic crater itself. Hiking up the loose ash will give you the sensation of taking two steps forward and one step back. It's a good workout but worth the effort. At the summit, you're treated to a fine view of the main vent spewing lava, rocks, and ash. It may sometimes feel too close for comfort, as large chunks of lava rock often land nearby. Take a moment to glimpse Guatemala City, the Pacific Coast, and some of the neighboring volcanoes from here.

At the summit, avoid breathing in the clouds of sulfuric gases. Be especially careful where you step, as there are some hot zones and sometimes some slow-moving lava flows. The skilike descent down the same sandy ash can be tricky, and you should exercise due caution to avoid a nasty face-plant into the jagged lava rocks alongside the trail.

If hiking during the day, bring plenty of sunscreen along with a hat, preferably with a chin strap that will prevent it from blowing away at the windy summit. Water and some snacks are always a good idea. Try not to carry excessive amounts of cash, but just what you'll need for the park admission, guide tip, and a drink and/or snack when you arrive back at the base of the trail. Rain gear (depending on the season) and some good, sturdy boots are also important. You'll especially appreciate the latter because you'll need ankle support and it's easy to get rocks and sand in your shoes, which can be extremely uncomfortable, during the final ascent up the sandy crater.

To get here on your own steam, follow the CA-9 highway past Amatitlán to a signed turnoff at Km. 37.5. Head east eight kilometers to the village of San Vicente Pacaya, where you'll find the park entry station and information center. The road continues from here another 10 kilometers to San Francisco de Sales (turn left at the fork in the road just past San Vicente Pacaya). For an excellent map detailing the route of ascent, see the interactive map online at *Mapas de Guatemala* (www.mapasdeguatemala.com/mapas).

above trips is **O.X. Outdoor Excursions** (7a Calle Poniente #17, tel. 7832-0468, www.guatemalavolcano.com), offering well-guided trips to the Antigua area volcanoes. The Spires of Fire trip is a five-day adventure climbing Guatemala's three active volcanoes (Fuego, Pacaya, and Santiaguito); it costs $599. They also do a very challenging "Double Whammy" involving the ascent of Acatenango Volcano with a side trip to Fuego Volcano on the same day before arriving (exhausted) to Vista Camp for bed and the summit of Acatenango the next morning.

CANOPY TOURS

The zipline madness that seems to have gripped almost every tourist town in Central America has not bypassed Antigua. If you want to monkey around, zipping from tree to tree, your best bet is **Antigua Canopy Tours** (tel. 7728-0811, www.antiguacanopytours. com, $50-75). For the ultimate adventure, try its Canyon Express tour across a canyon in two stages (520 and 430 meters long) while dangling 500 feet above the ground. The zipline tour is located on the property of Finca Filadelfia, near Jocotenango.

HORSEBACK RIDING

In the nearby village of San Juan del Obispo, toward Agua Volcano, **Ravenscroft Riding Stables** (2a Avenida Sur #3, San Juan del Obispo, tel. 7830-6669) offers three-, four-, or five-hour rides in the hills and valleys near Antigua for $20 per person per hour.

CITY TOURS

Practically an Antigua institution, **Antigua Tours** (3a Calle Oriente #22, tel. 7832-5821 and 7832-2046, www.antiguatours.net) are guided by Elizabeth Bell (author of *Antigua Guatemala: The City and Its Heritage*) Tuesday, Wednesday, Friday, and Saturday at 9:30am. Tours on Monday and Thursday at 2pm are led by other experienced guides. All tours meet at the fountain in Antigua's central park and cost $25, including entrance fees to historical sites. There is also a guided tour of nearby villages, including San Antonio Aguas Calientes, San Pedro Las Huertas, and San Juan del Obispo, going out at 2pm Tuesday and Friday and lasting three hours. It costs $35 per person with a two-person minimum. Advance booking required.

Green Belly Adventure Co. (Callejón San Sebastián #2B, tel. 7832-1669, www.green-bellyadventure.com, $50-65 per person) offers tours of Antigua's historical sites and local coffee farms aboard off-road versions of Segways. It actually makes a great way to get around Antigua's narrow cobblestone streets.

GOLF

Antigua is home to Guatemala's newest—and nicest—golf course, the 18-hole Pete and Perry Dye-designed **Fuego Maya golf course** at **La Reunión Antigua Golf Resort** (RN-14 Km. 93, Alotenango, tel. 7873-1400, www.

Fuego Maya golf course at La Reunión Antigua Golf Resort

Chateau DeFay vineyards

to the 19th hole.) The golf course is 11 miles from Antigua and 40 miles from Guatemala City. Facilities include a driving range, putting green, chipping green, practice bunker, and pro shop.

WINE TASTING

Ever exciting and brimming with new leisure opportunities, Antigua Guatemala now boasts Guatemala's first winery. **Chateau DeFay** (tel. 2363-3858 or 5883-3911, www.fincadefay.com), on the slopes of Agua Volcano in neighboring Santa María de Jesús, is a 3,000-case winery and vineyard. Its owners, Jacques and Angie Defay, purchased a former coffee farm and converted part of the land into vineyards using plants brought in from Washington state. The farm also grows asparagus. Jacques, a former economist with the International Development Bank (IDB), retired to Guatemala from Falls Church, Virginia, in 2002 after numerous visits to the country.

The winery is open for tastings Saturday and Sunday 10am to 4pm. Chateau DeFay wines come in several varieties, including Angie's Blend, chardonnay, a moscato, a cabernet sauvignon/merlot blend, and Bruno's Favorite. The latter is named for resident winemaker Bruno Coppola.

The first year of wine production was 2008, but the 2009 vintage is substantially better. A bottle of wine costs between Q130 and Q190, or about $16-25.

lareunion.com.gt). The 72-par, 7,560-yard course is one of the country's most challenging and is the only golf course in the world with a view of four volcanoes (Agua, Fuego, Acatenango, and Pacaya). Its designers gleaned inspiration from the Mayan Solar Calendar, which consists of 18 20-day months; each of the course's 18 holes is named after the corresponding month. (The last month, Wayeb, is a five-day month and gives its name

Accommodations

UNDER $50

Antigua has a number of excellent hostels offering comfortable accommodations at budget prices. Most of them can help you arrange onward travel or book airport shuttle services if they don't offer it themselves. A favorite budget traveler hangout is friendly ★ **Terrace Hostel** (3a Calle Poniente #24B, tel. 7832-3463, www.terracehostel.com, $9 in shared-bath dorm to $30 d in room with shared bath). Included are the usual amenities found in most hostels such as luggage storage, laundry service, wireless Internet, TV, DVD collection and library, but Terrace Hostel goes the extra mile with a fun rooftop bar and restaurant. There's a nightly barbecue featuring hot dogs, burgers, nachos, and chili you can wash down with local microbrews. There are weekly pub crawls and occasional theme parties. **Jungle Party Hostel** (6a Avenida Norte #20, between 3a and 2a Calle Poniente, tel. 7832-8975, www.junglepartyhostal.com, $10-11 pp) is a lively backpacker hangout with clean dorm rooms and shared baths. There are fun communal areas that double as bar and lounge.

Conveniently located near some of the town's favorite watering holes, **El Hostal** (1a Avenida Sur #8, tel. 7832-0442, www.elhostal.hostel.com, $12-18) has cozy private rooms with shared bath ($18 d) or clean, shared-bath dormitories ($12 pp) in a remodeled colonial house that includes a pleasant little courtyard. Guests won't find electric water heaters here (yippee!), but rather the hot-water showers many visitors are used to. You can book and pay online in advance; wireless Internet is available throughout the house.

A rooftop chill-out area with wonderful views of Agua Volcano and a friendly, feel-good vibe make ★ **Holistico Hostal** (7a Avenida Sur #10, tel. 7832-4078, www.hostalholistico.com, $11 pp in dorm to 40 d with private bath) a popular choice. The nightly rate includes breakfast, served in its small café. There is free wireless Internet, a movie lounge, and laundry service for $2.50 per load. Tours to local attractions can be arranged. They also have decent hot-water showers.

Just one block from the central plaza, **Hotel Casa Rústica** (6a Avenida Norte #8, tel. 7832-0694, www.casarusticagt.com, $35-56 d) has comfortable rooms with shared bathroom ($39-45 d) or private bathroom ($49-56 d), with or without cable TV and garden view. There are apartments for rent starting at $250 per week. Rates include breakfast, filtered drinking water, and use of the kitchen. It also offers laundry service, bag storage, and wireless Internet. There are nice gardens and hammocks for lounging. The excellent-value ★ **Casa Cristina** (Callejón Camposeco #3A, between 6a and 7a Avenida, tel. 7832-0623, www.casa-cristina.com, $25-45 d) has beautifully decorated, colorful rooms with wrought-iron accents, Guatemalan bedspreads, tile

floors, and private hot-water bathroom. Pricier deluxe rooms have gorgeous volcano views and minifridges, in addition to cable TV. TVs are absent in the least expensive standard rooms. Room rates include unlimited use of wireless Internet, purified drinking water, coffee, and tea. The excellent-value **Hotel Posada San Pedro** (3a Avenida Sur #15, tel. 7832-3594, www.posadasanpedro.net, $41 d) is also stylish and comfortable, featuring 10 spotless rooms with firm beds, tile floors, wooden furnishings, attractive tile bathrooms, and cable TV. Guests also enjoy use of a living room and full kitchen. The staff here is friendly, and the place is well-run with a laid-back but efficient atmosphere. There's a second location at 7a Avenida Norte #29 (tel. 7832-0718, $46 d) with slightly higher rates for newer rooms.

$50-100

One of the city's best values is ★ **Chez Daniel** (Calle de San Luquitas #20, tel. 4264-1122, chezdanielantigua.blogspot.com, $59 d). It's seven blocks from the central square in a quiet neighborhood, in a large house fronting a green lawn. The comfortable, high-ceilinged rooms have flat-screen TVs and large bathrooms with shower tubs. They are wonderfully decorated with Guatemalan knickknacks and amazing photography depicting the country's vivid Maya culture. Amenities include a dining room, fully equipped communal kitchen, and rooftop terrace with volcano views. Featuring many of the fine decorative touches and amenities of its pricier boutique counterparts ★ **El Mesón de María** (3a Calle Poniente #8, tel. 7832-6068, www.hotelmesondemaria.com, $85-140 d on weekdays; $15-20 higher on weekends) is a good value. Its 20 brand-new, well-appointed rooms are attractively decorated with Guatemalan fabrics and beautifully carved wooden headboards. You'll feel the antique charm as soon as you enter the doorway of your room framed with antique wooden beams. Rooms on the second floor have skylights and some of the spacious tiled bathrooms have whirlpool tubs.

La Antigua Guatemala Accommodations

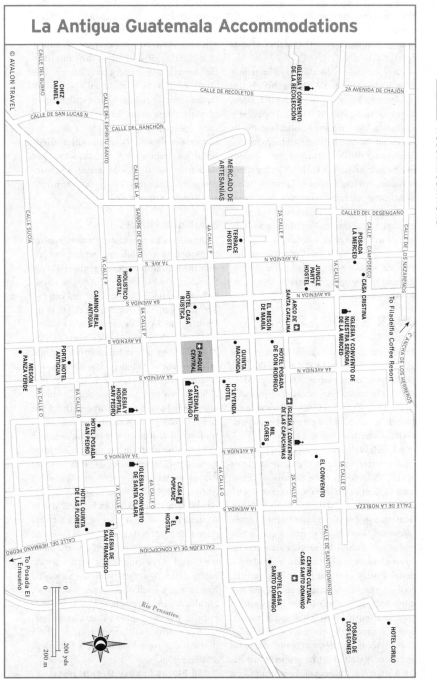

© AVALON TRAVEL

CALLE DEL BURRO
CALLE DEL ESPIRITU SANTO
CALLE DE SAN LUCAS N
CALLE DEL RANCHÓN
CALLE DE LA
SANGRE DE CRISTO
CALLE SUCIA
CALLE DEL HERMANO PEDRO

CHEZ DANIEL

CALLE DE RECOLETOS

2A AVENIDA DE CHAJÓN

IGLESIA Y CONVENTO DE LA RECOLECCIÓN

MERCADO DE ARTESANÍAS

TERRACE HOSTEL

CALLED DEL DESENGAÑO

CALLE CAMPOSECO

CALLE DE LOS NAZARENOS

POSADA LA MERCED

CASA CRISTINA

To Filadelfia Coffee Resort

CANCHA DE LOS HERREROS

JUNGLE PARTY HOSTEL

HOLISTICO HOSTAL

CAMINO REAL ANTIGUA

HOTEL CASA RUSTICA

ARCO DE SANTA CATALINA

EL MESÓN DE MARÍA

IGLESIA Y CONVENTO DE NUESTRA SEÑORA DE LA MERCED

7A CALLE P
7A AVE S
6A AVENIDA N
6A AVENIDA S
4A CALLE P
2A CALLE P
7A AVENIDA N
1A CALLE P

QUINTA MACONDA

HOTEL POSADA DE DON RODRIGO

PORTA HOTEL ANTIGUA

MESÓN PANZA VERDE

PARQUE CENTRAL

D'LEYENDA HOTEL

CATEDRAL DE SANTIAGO

IGLESIA Y HOSPITAL SAN PEDRO

IGLESIA Y CONVENTO DE LAS CAPUCHINAS

MIL FLORES

EL CONVENTO

HOTEL POSADA SAN PEDRO

CASA POPENOE

IGLESIA Y CONVENTO DE SANTA CLARA

HOTEL QUINTA DE LAS FLORES

EL HOSTAL

IGLESIA DE SAN FRANCISCO

CALLEJÓN DE LA CONCEPCIÓN

CENTRO CULTURAL CASA SANTO DOMINGO

CALLE DE SANTO DOMINGO

HOTEL CASA SANTO DOMINGO

CALLE DE LA NOBLEZA

POSADA DE LOS LEONES

HOTEL CIRILO

9A CALLE O
8A CALLE O
7A CALLE O
6A CALLE O
5A AVENIDA S
4A AVENIDA S
4A CALLE O
2A AVENIDA S
2A AVENIDA N
2A CALLE O
1A CALLE O

To Posada El Ensueño

Río Pensativo

0   200 yds
0   200 m

There are gorgeous views of the town and volcanoes from the delightful third-floor terrace. Rates include breakfast at the nearby La Fonda de la Calle Real.

For a phenomenal location at an incredible price, it's hard to beat ★ **D'Leyenda Hotel** (4a Avenida Norte #1, tel. 7832-6194, www.dleyendahotel.com, $90-110 d). The hotel is less than a block from the central square. Its somewhat smallish but comfortable rooms are named after different Antigua ghost legends and include flat-screen cable TV, safe deposit box, and wireless Internet. Three of its six rooms have bathtubs and fireplaces. A fountain graces the ground floor courtyard opposite a spiral staircase leading to a second-floor terrace with lounge chairs, tables, a hot tub, and volcano views. It bears mentioning that there's a popular watering hole next door, as that may or may not suit your style. Did I mention the staff is extremely friendly?

OVER $100
Resorts

Antigua's newest resort hotel is the ★ **Camino Real Antigua** (7a Calle Poniente #33B, www.caminorealantigua.com.gt, $145-210 d). The chain hotel has cozy rooms with high, wood-beamed ceilings and some of the most delicious beds I've ever slept on, as well as all the amenities you would expect.

A *Condé Nast Traveler* Gold List property, **Porta Hotel Antigua** (8a Calle Poniente #1, tel. 7931-0600, www.portahotels.com, from $125 d) has 77 sumptuous rooms with chimneys, colorful walls with faux finishes, Guatemalan decor, and charming stained hardwood floors in its standard and deluxe rooms and suites. It features a restaurant serving excellent Guatemalan and international dishes overlooking the swimming pool set amid tropical gardens, as well as a fully stocked, quaint wooden bar. Candles provide atmosphere at night and a colonial fountain graces the entrance to the hotel. The service is excellent, as is the courteous and friendly staff. Another property that has put Antigua on the map of the world's finest accommodations is the exquisite ★ **Hotel Casa Santo Domingo** (3a Calle Oriente #28, tel. 7820-1220, www.casasantodomingo. com.gt, $150-550 d), built in the ruins of an old Dominican monastery. Its 125 rooms have all the comforts you could wish for and effortlessly merge colonial charm with modern comfort. Some rooms have a chimney, and there are some newer rooms with chic glass and wooden showers. Other amenities include a charming swimming pool and a location just steps from the city's best museum and wonderful colonial ruins. The restaurant here is also highly recommended.

Boutique Hotels

Antigua has an astounding assortment of boutique properties offering comfort and privacy in an atmosphere of elegance and style. Spending a night in one of Antigua's boutique properties is the real deal and can feel like waking up in a museum chock-full of interesting knickknacks and artwork. **Posada de Don Rodrigo** (5a Avenida Norte #17, tel. 7832-9858, www.posadadedonrodrigo.com, $150 d) is one of Antigua's classic hotels, well situated near the Arco de Santa Catalina. Housed in a very old residence, the inviting rooms have been updated with all the comforts of a modern hotel. The staff wears traditional costumes and marimba music can often be heard in the main courtyard. President Clinton chose ★ **Posada del Ángel** (4a Avenida Sur #24A, tel. 7832-0260 Antigua or 305/677-2382 U.S., www.posadadelangel.com, from $195 d) for his 1999 visit to Antigua for a summit meeting with Central American leaders. If you'd like to follow in his footsteps, stay in the exquisite Rose Suite, the largest of the lodge's five, with a private balcony offering gorgeous volcano views and fine antiques. Each of the suites is different, but all are truly charming and include wood-burning fireplace, cable TV, and fresh flowers. Rates include a delicious breakfast served in the dining room looking out to the hotel's small lap pool.

Mil Flores Luxury Design Hotel (3a

El Convento boutique hotel

is sometimes the haunt of international celebrities. **El Convento** (2a Avenida Norte #11, tel. 7720-7272, www.elconventoantigua.com, from $169 d) is fabulously built on grounds across the street from Convento de las Capuchinas. All 26 of its well-appointed suites are unique and feature a magnificent melding of colonial and modern touches that include skylights, bathrooms with marble and glass accents, exposed stone walls, and charming courtyard patios. There is a wonderful second-floor terrace for enjoying cocktails (or Sunday breakfast buffet), and the vaulted-ceiling dining room at Elù Restaurant on the main floor serves gourmet Guatemalan fusion cuisine.

An excellent value in this category, ★ **Hotel Cirilo** (Calle de los Duelos #11, tel. 7832-6650, hotelcirilo.com, from $119 d) combines modern touches with the charm and history of La Antigua. Built on the grounds of an old hermitage, the property features spacious gardens, old ruins, and a wooden-decked swimming pool. Glass doors provide wonderful views of the grounds from the

the swimming pool at Hotel Cirilo

Calle Oriente #16A, tel. 7832-9715 or 7832-9716, www.hotelmilflores.com, from $175 d including breakfast) offers style with distinction, excellent service, and attention to detail. Each of the five luxurious suites is inspired after a different flower and features a fireplace, minibar, a private patio, and large bathroom.

One of Antigua's most elegant properties, ★ **Posada de los Leones** (Las Gravileas #1, tel. 7832-7371, www.posadadelosleones.com, $280-380 d) is set amid coffee trees and tropical gardens in a gated community just outside of town. Its six spacious, absolutely gorgeous rooms feature high ceilings, hardwood floors, and a delightful array of classy European and Guatemalan decorative touches. On the house's second floor is Antigua's loveliest terrace overlooking tropical gardens, the surrounding coffee plantation, and the volcanoes off in the distance. You can enjoy drinks on the terrace in addition to a lap pool, a comfortable living room, and library. There is wireless Internet throughout the house, which comfortable living room and breakfast areas. Some of the comfortable rooms are literally built around the old ruins, and you can have the old architecture all to yourself. Other room features include *retablo* headboards, a fireplace, and flat-screen TV. It's quietly outside of the town center.

OUTSIDE OF TOWN

On a working 40-acre avocado farm, **Earthlodge** (tel. 5664-0713 or 4980-2564, www.earthlodgeguatemala.com, dorms $8 pp to $45 d in cabin) is a sure bet for wonderful volcano views and the chance to get away from it all at a reasonable distance from town in the surrounding hillsides. Accommodations include a shared-bath, eight-bed dormitory, A-frame cabins, and tree houses. The private cabins and tree houses are wonderfully secluded in a grove of Spanish oaks and have fabulous views of the valley and surrounding mountains. There are shared or private bathroom options and queen or double beds.

Delicious vegetarian dinners are served family-style for $9, though carnivores need not despair as meat options are also available, including a fun weekend barbecue. Breakfast items include eggs, bacon, sausage, pancakes, and fresh fruit. Heaping sandwiches and salads are served for lunch. You can relax in a hammock and take in the valley views, hike nearby trails, or sweat out any remaining pre-vacation stress in the stone-and-mortar sauna. There are also books, movies, music, and games on hand should you need further entertainment. Spanish classes and massages are also available. The easiest way to get here is via the lodge-designated transfers from Antigua with a local driver. Rates start at $7 per person, one-way.

Also in the hills above Antigua in the area of El Hato is one of Guatemala's most unique hotels. **Hobbitenango** (tel. 5909-9106, camping $2.50, dorm $8 pp, $52 for 5-person cottage) takes its inspiration from J. R. R. Tolkien's fictional Hobbiton (of Lord of the Rings fame). It is still very much a work in progress, but its creators have focused their efforts on providing a place to get off the grid amid a spectacularly scenic location overlooking the Antigua valley. The property prides itself in environmentally sustainable practices, such as the use of recycled materials for construction, rainwater collection, organic farming, and wind/solar power generation. The accommodations mimic the homes of Tolkien's Shire-dwelling hobbits, and there's a restaurant/bar with wonderful views. A light menu is served weekdays, with a full menu on weekends. There are also shuttle transfers from downtown Antigua Friday through Sunday.

Outside the city center on the way to Santa Ana is **Hotel Quinta de las Flores** (Calle del Hermano Pedro #6, tel. 7832-3721/25, www.quintadelasflores.com, $75-140 d), another excellent value. The lodge was built on the site of what were once public baths, and you can still hear the soothing sounds of tinkling fountains throughout the property. The charming rooms, built around a peaceful and spacious garden, feature tile floors, chimneys, cable TV, Guatemalan bedspreads, and nice accents and furnishings along with a small porch with sitting area. Larger two-bedroom casitas comfortably sleep five and have living room, dining room, and fully equipped kitchen. There's a large outdoor swimming pool just next to the hotel's restaurant, which serves Guatemalan dishes, including delicious *chuchitos* and *tostadas,* or salads, steak, and chicken. It's a good choice for vacationing families. Also in Santa Ana, ★ **Posada El Ensueño** (Calle del Agua, Callejón La Ermita Final, Santa Ana, tel. 7832-7958, www.posadaensueno.com, $100-125 d) is a splendid bed-and-breakfast in a quiet setting. Run by American expatriate Carmen Herrerias, the lodge has three tastefully decorated rooms with garden showers, one of which is a suite. It's a great place to relax away from the action in Antigua. Breakfast and home-cooked meals are served poolside, and Carmen loves to cook for her guests. There's also a small heated lap pool and bikes to get around. It's about a 25-minute walk to Antigua's central park.

Just minutes from Antigua in neighboring San Felipe de Jesús, ★ **Filadelfia Coffee Resort and Spa** (150 meters north of the San Felipe de Jesús church, tel. 7728-0800, www.filadelfiaresort.com, $125-250 d including breakfast) is a working coffee farm where you can stay in a splendid neocolonial building harboring luxurious accommodations. The 20 spacious rooms have tile floors, king- or queen-size beds, classy Guatemalan furnishings, cable TV with DVD player, large two-sink bathrooms, glass showers with antique tiles, and pleasant patios with furniture. There are four standard rooms, 14 deluxe doubles, and two master suites with island kitchen and a living room with leather sofa and large desk. Coffee machinery and wooden carvings adorn the public areas, while the main building harbors a cozy lobby adorned with Persian rugs. An elegant restaurant in the main lodge serves international dishes with flair. Activities include daily coffee tours lasting two hours each at 9am, 11am, and 2pm ($18), mule riding ($15-40), paintball ($20-40), and a unimog ride to a lookout point ($20). There are free unimog transfers from Antigua's town center if you want to take a tour or just enjoy a meal here.

Opened in 2008, ★ **La Reunión Antigua Golf Resort** (Km. 91.5 Carretera CA-14, tel. 7873-1400, www.lareunion.com.gt, $220 d) lies 17 kilometers from Antigua in neighboring Alotenango on the road to the Pacific Coast. The hotel setting and its Pete Dye-designed 18-hole golf course is truly spectacular, flanked by four volcanoes and lush green fields. The larger suites are worth the splurge (an extra $50 over the deluxe rooms), for their private infinity-edge plunge pools and a hot tub with stunning volcano views (Agua and active Pacaya). The luxuriously well-furnished rooms have L'Occitane bath products, air-conditioning, and satellite TV. For dining, there's the resort's Mirador restaurant serving international fare, a snack bar, and Bar Wayeb. Plans call for the existing 26-room boutique hotel to be joined by a 125-room hotel managed by an international hotel chain. For now, La Reunión remains wonderfully peaceful. The only sounds you'll hear are the chirping of birds, the occasional roar of a distant lawnmower, and, once in a while, a landing helicopter announcing the arrival of Guatemala City's business elite coming in for a round of golf. It's all par for the course.

La Reunión Antigua Golf Resort

Food

Antigua's status as one of Guatemala's main tourist destinations is evident in the variety and number of excellent restaurants for every taste and budget. The mix here is rather eclectic, and restaurants can often be classified into more than one category. While the presence of a McDonald's in town hardly constitutes anything worth writing home about, Antigua's golden arches are the focus of some local lore completely in line with the magic seemingly everywhere in Guatemala. According to local urban legend, the Ronald McDonald sitting on the bench outside Antigua's McDonald's has at least on one occasion uncrossed its legs and come to life, scaring two employees sweeping the patio out of their wits.

CAFÉS AND LIGHT MEALS

★ **The Refuge** (7a Avenida Norte #18A, www.refugecoffeeroasters.com, 7:30am-7pm Mon.-Sat., $3) is an independent coffee shop serving phenomenal coffee and espresso beverages at very reasonable prices in a quaint, intimate atmosphere. Also recommended for its high-quality coffee is **Tretto Caffe** (1a Avenida Sur #4, tel. 4828-0692, 7:30am-8pm daily). For coffee on the go, **Café Barista** (on *parque central's* northwest corner) serves a variety of favorites, including caramel macchiato, mochas (hot or iced), and tasty pastries. It's part of a chain popular throughout Guatemala. One of Antigua's best-known cafés, **Doña Luisa Xicotencatl** (4a Calle Oriente #12, tel. 7832-2578, 7am-9:30pm daily) serves delicious breakfasts, snacks, pastries, and light meals in a delightful garden courtyard. There are fresh-baked breads and cakes available all day from the bakery at the front of the building. Next door, **La Fuente** (4a Calle Oriente #14, tel. 7832-4520, 7am-7pm daily) is a good place for breakfast and vegetarian fare as well as for a cup of coffee accompanied by an ever-so-sinfully delicious chocolate brownie topped with coffee ice cream and chocolate syrup.

On the west side of the central park, ★ **Café Condesa** (Portal del Comercio #4, tel. 7832-0038, 7am-8pm Sun.-Thurs., until 9pm Fri.-Sat.) is a great place to get some pep in your step with an early breakfast and coffee or to refuel later in the day. There are excellent cakes, pastries, sandwiches, and salads served in a pleasing garden atmosphere, or you can enjoy the all-day breakfasts. A Sunday brunch is served 10am-2pm and includes scrambled eggs, home-fried potatoes, silver-dollar pancakes, quiche, homemade bread, and muffins, just to name a few items. If you're on the go, grab a cup of the excellent coffee at the **Condesa Express** next door.

For fresh bagels, bagel sandwiches, and great coffee, stop at **The Bagel Barn** (5a Calle Poniente #2, tel. 7832-1224, www.thebagelbarn.com, 6am-9pm daily). There is wireless Internet if you're traveling with a laptop, and movies are shown in the afternoons and evenings. Another Antigua standby is the **Rainbow Café and Bookshop** (7a Avenida Sur #8, tel. 7832-1919, www.rainbowcafeantigua.com, all meals daily), serving delicious menu options including eggs Florentine, Israeli falafel, and the chocolate bomb for dessert. Try the outstanding Greek chicken fillet stuffed with spinach, bacon, raisins, feta cheese, and covered with a creamy oregano and lime sauce ($9). Live music, poetry readings, and other cultural events are held on-site. Under the same ownership as Café No Sé, ★ **Y Tu Piña También** (corner of 6a Calle Oriente and 1a Avenida Sur, www.ytupinatambien.com, $3-8) has evolved from its origins as a juice bar into a great all-day breakfast spot. There are awesome sandwiches, breakfast pizzas, salads, and of course, coffee. There's also no shortage of hangover-curing cocktails. Check out their Sunday brunch. Finally, a trip to Antigua wouldn't be complete without a stop for some *dulces típicos* (typical Guatemalan sweets) from **Doña**

La Antigua Guatemala Food and Nightlife

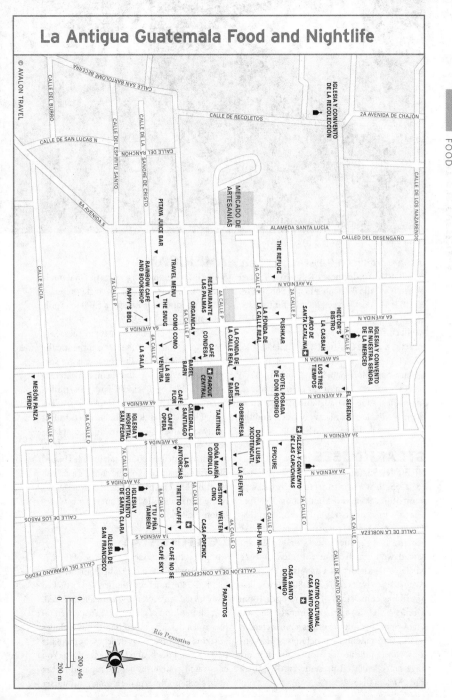

© AVALON TRAVEL

CALLE DEL BURRO

CALLE SAN BARTOLOMÉ BECERRA

CALLE DE SAN LUCAS N

CALLE DEL ESPÍRITU SANTO

CALLE DE LA SANGRE DE CRISTO

CALLE DEL RANCHÓN

CALLE DE RECOLETOS

IGLESIA Y CONVENTO DE LA RECOLECCIÓN

2A AVENIDA DE CHAJÓN

8A AVENIDA S

PITAYA JUICE BAR

MERCADO DE ARTESANÍAS

ALAMEDA SANTA LUCÍA

CALLED DEL DESENGAÑO

CALLE DE LOS NAZARENOS

7A CALLE P

RAINBOW CAFÉ AND BOOKSHOP

TRAVEL MENU

THE SNUG

ORGANICA

CAFÉ CONDESA

RESTAURANTE LAS PALMAS

4A CALLE P

5A CALLE P

THE REFUGE

3A CALLE P

PUSHKAR

LA FONDA DE LA CALLE REAL

7A AVENIDA N

2A AVENIDA N

ARCO DE SANTA CATALINA

HECTOR'S BISTRO

LA CASBAH

6A AVENIDA N

7A CALLE P

1A CALLE P

IGLESIA Y CONVENTO DE NUESTRA SEÑORA DE LA MERCED

CALLE SUCIA

7A CALLE P

PAPPY'S BBQ

COMO COMO

LA SIN VENTURA

LA SALA

6A CALLE P

6A AVENIDA S

BAGEL BARN

LA FONDA DE LA CALLE REAL

CAFÉ BARISTA

PARQUE CENTRAL

HOTEL POSADA DE DON RODRIGO

5A AVENIDA N

4A AVENIDA N

LOS TRES TIEMPOS

EL SERENO

MESÓN PANZA VERDE

9A CALLE O

8A CALLE O

CAFÉ FLOR

CAFÉ OPERA

CATEDRAL DE SANTIAGO

TARTINES

SOBREMESA

DOÑA LUISA XICOTENCATL

3A AVENIDA N

IGLESIA Y CONVENTO DE LAS CAPUCHINAS

EPICURE

5A AVENIDA S

4A AVENIDA S

IGLESIA Y HOSPITAL SAN PEDRO

3A AVENIDA S

LAS ANTORCHAS

DOÑA MARÍA GORDILLO

LA FUENTE

2A AVENIDA N

7A CALLE O

2A AVENIDA S

IGLESIA Y CONVENTO DE SANTA CLARA

8A CALLE O

7A CALLE O

6A CALLE O

TRETTO CAFFE

5A CALLE O

BISTROT CINQ

WELTEN

CASA POPENOE

CASA SANTO DOMINGO

4A CALLE O

NI-FU NI-FA

3A CALLE O

2A CALLE O

CALLE DE LA NOBLEZA

1A CALLE O

CALLE DE LOS PASOS

IGLESIA DE SAN FRANCISCO

CALLE DEL HERMANO PEDRO

1A AVENIDA S

CAFÉ TAMBIÉN

Y TU PIÑA

CAFÉ SKY

CAFÉ NO SE

CALLEJÓN DE LA CONCEPCIÓN

PAPAZITOS

CALLE DE SANTO DOMINGO

CENTRO CULTURAL CASA SANTO DOMINGO

CASA SANTO DOMINGO

Río Pensativo

0   200 yds
0   200 m

Pappy's BBQ

María Gordillo (4a Calle Oriente #11, tel. 7832-0403). Under new ownership, **Travel Menu** (6a Calle Poniente #14, tel. 5682-9648, $5-10) is a budget traveler favorite for its tasty, varied menu that runs the gamut from steak to Asian cuisine at affordable prices.

Pitaya Juice Bar (6a Calle Poniente #26, tel. 7832-1172, www.pitayajuicebar.com, 8:30am-6pm Mon.-Sat., 9am-4pm Sun., $2-5) serves a variety of natural blended juices, smoothies, soups, salads, and wraps. All of the ingredients are amazingly fresh, and the atmosphere is cheerful and bright.

STEAKHOUSES

Ni-Fu Ni-Fa (3a Calle Oriente #21, tel. 7832-6579, www.nifunifadeantigua.com, noon-10pm Sun. and Mon., noon-10:30pm Tues.-Thurs., noon-11pm Fri. and Sat., $5-22) is a genuine Argentinean steakhouse serving tasty grilled meats on a pleasant raised wooden deck surrounded by lush gardens. **Restaurant Las Antorchas** (3a Avenida Sur #1, tel. 7832-0806, www.las-antorchas.com, 11am-3pm and 6pm-10pm Mon.-Fri., 11am-4pm and 6pm-10pm Sat., 11am-5pm Sun., $8-31) offers a more elegant setting and a menu that includes grilled onions, cheese fondue, tortellini, salmon in orange sauce, and well-presented grilled steak and chicken dishes.

AMERICAN

Sometimes during long visits to Guatemala I get a little homesick for the taste of Texas. Thank goodness for **Pappy's BBQ** (6a Calle Poniente #21, tel. 7832-2768 or 5979-6771, www.bbqantigua.com, 11am-10pm Tues.-Sat., 11am-8pm Sun., $3-9), serving authentically tasty Texas barbecue. On the menu are several Texas favorites including mouthwatering coffee-rubbed beef brisket, pork ribs, pulled pork, smoked chicken, and smoked pork sausage. The latter, while on the menu, is in fact rarely available (which is my only complaint about this otherwise awesome dining option). Side dishes include potato salad, Texas baked beans, and spicy corn on the cob. It's a casual, friendly kind of place. There are delicious homemade sauces to bring out the meats' delicious flavors.

CONTINENTAL

Antigua is full of hidden gems. One of these is ★ **Hector's Bistro** (1a Calle Poniente #9A, tel. 7832-9867, lunch and dinner, $7-17), tucked away on the street fronting Iglesia La Merced. It's a simple kind of place with half a dozen tables and a bar. The menu rotates but includes amazing open-faced sandwiches, homemade pasta, seared duck, and beef tenderloin. You can watch your meal being prepared in the open kitchen. Olives make a wonderful starter to pair with a glass of wine. ★ **Como Como** (6a Calle Poniente #6, tel. 7832-0478, lunch and dinner Tues.-Sun., $5-20) specializes in Franco-Belgian cuisine and enjoys a loyal following thanks to consistently great food and a pleasant atmosphere that includes a lovely garden patio. **Sobremesa** (4a Calle Oriente #4A, tel. 7832-3231, www.alexferrar.com, $8-13) is a restaurant doubling as an art gallery. The art is fabulously eclectic, but the food is not to be outdone. Menu highlights include phenomenal croque-monsieur, delicious Unicorn Steak (tenderloin medallion in a wine and Dijon reduction), and yummy Japanese Plum Chicken. For dessert, savor exotic ice cream flavors the likes of strawberry merlot and jasmine blackberry. Antigua's finest delicatessen is **Epicure** (3a Avenida Norte #11 B, tel. 7832-5545, 10am-10pm daily, $5-12), serving phenomenal sandwiches and deli items. The owners prefer that patrons dine on-site rather than carry out, and the pleasant outdoor area centered around a lovely garden courtyard and the remains of an old aqueduct makes that request easy to accommodate. A second location (6a Avenida Norte #35 A, tel. 7832-1414) is only open until 7pm Monday-Saturday (until 6:30pm Sun.).

Extremely popular with Antigua's expat community for its wonderful views over town, laid-back vibe, and fresh farm-to-table vegetarian fare is **Cerro San Cristóbal** (tel. 7832-2681, 9am-9pm daily). The menu includes dishes such as stuffed mushrooms, quiche, and frittatas. You can tour the on-site organic farm and a lovely orchid nursery. There are frequent (and free) shuttle transfers from Nim Po't, located at 5a Avenida Norte #29.

Enjoying a new lease on life from its new location, **Caffé Opera Bistrot** (4a Avenida Sur #1, tel. 7832-9133, www.caffeoperabistrot.com, noon-3:30pm and 6:30pm-10pm Mon.-Tues. and Thurs., noon-11pm Fri.-Sat., noon-10pm Sun., $6-12) serves up tasty Italian food, including homemade pasta. For gourmet pizza, try **Papazitos** (4a Calle Oriente #39, tel. 7832-5209, 11am-10pm daily). It also serves nachos, panini, calzones, pastas, vegetarian dishes, wine, and beer. It offers free delivery with a minimum $7 purchase; 10- to 18-inch pizzas go for $9-16.

GUATEMALAN AND LATIN AMERICAN

One of Antigua's legendary restaurants is **La Fonda de la Calle Real** (3a Calle Poniente #7, tel. 7832-0507, www.lafondadelacallereal.com, noon-10pm daily; 5a Avenida Norte #5, tel. 7832-2696, noon-10pm daily; 5a Avenida

chips and salsa at Los Tres Tiempos

Norte #12, tel. 7832-0507, 8am-10pm daily, $5-12), with three branches, the nicest of which is the one on 3a Calle Poniente. There is a varied menu of Guatemalan favorites, including *chiles rellenos* as well as tasty grilled meats. If you can't decide, do as President Clinton did and order the filling sampler menu. For gourmet Guatemalan cuisine served in a stylish environment with modern Guatemalan decor, head to **Los Tres Tiempos** (5a Avenida Norte #21, tel. 7832-5161, www.lostrestiempos.com, 8am-10pm daily, $5-12). There are delicious enchiladas, *chuchitos,* and tacos to be enjoyed in a spacious second-floor patio with funky lounge chairs or inside in comfortable *huipil*-inspired seats. There's a cozy and equally stylish little downstairs bar if you're just stopping by for a cocktail.

ASIAN

Café Flor (4a Avenida Sur #1, tel. 7832-5274, www.cafeflorantigua.com, 11am-11pm daily, $6-12) does a reasonably good job with Thai food, though it won't taste familiar to die-hard fans of Asian cuisine. Offerings include Thai curries and rice dishes. For Indian food, check out **Pushkar** (6a Avenida Norte #18, tel. 7882-4098, lunch and dinner daily, $4-11). You'll find several of your Indian favorites on the menu, including meat or vegetable samosas, seafood curries, chicken tikka masala, and tandoori chicken. There's also pleasant outdoor patio seating. For decent Chinese food, head to **Restaurante La Estrella** (7a Avenida Norte #42, tel. 7832-4303). They also deliver.

FINE DINING

One of the city's most atmospheric restaurants, **El Tenedor del Cerro** (tel. 7832-3520, 7am-10pm Mon.-Sat., 7am-5pm Sun., $4-15) features fabulous views of the Antigua valley and its volcanic backdrop, along with a well-rounded menu that includes hearty breakfasts, salads, pasta, pizzas with an interesting array of international flavors, steaks, and decadent desserts. Many of the fresh ingredients come straight from the on-site garden. The views of Agua, Fuego, and Acatenango Volcanoes are fully appreciated with outdoor seating on a pleasant patio. There are a

the courtyard at Mesón Panza Verde

separate patio lounge, gift shop, aviary, and sculpture gardens to enjoy, along with rotating art exhibits. To get here, follow the winding road to the top of the hill. The entrance is just before Antigua's main entrance, on the left, on the road from Guatemala City. There are also free transfers from Hotel Casa Santo Domingo.

With a long tradition of excellence, **Welten** (4a Calle Oriente #21, tel. 7832-0630, www.weltenrestaurant.com, noon-10pm Mon.-Thurs. and Fri.-Sun. until 10:30pm, $13-22) is one of Antigua's well-established dining options serving an impressive menu of gourmet Guatemalan, French, and Italian specialties in an elegant atmosphere. Menu highlights include creamy peppered steak (filet au poivre), seafood fettuccine, and fish fillet in a traditional salsa. There are delicious homemade ice creams for dessert. ★ **Mesón Panza Verde** (5a Avenida Sur #19, tel. 7955-8282, www.panzaverde. com, lunch Tues.-Sun., dinner 7pm-10pm nightly, $10-30) is easily one of Guatemala's finest restaurants, with outstanding food and sophisticated European ambience. The mostly French cuisine is heavy on meat and fish dishes. The wine list is impressive, as are the desserts. Tapas are served 4pm-7pm Thursday-Saturday on the terrace. You can enjoy lunch and dinner in the main dining room surrounded by fine art under a vaulted ceiling or alfresco in La Cueva, a covered patio beneath baroque arches beside a gurgling fountain. *Chacun à son goût.*

The town's most authentic hotel restaurant can be found at ★ **Hotel Posada de Don Rodrigo** (5a Avenida Norte #17, tel. 7832-0291, all meals daily, $7-20), which is popular with Guatemalans who come here for its stellar service, wonderful ambience overlooking the hotel gardens, and consistently delicious Guatemalan and international cuisine. The tortillas are made fresh on the premises, and you can watch the dough being patted and placed on the *comal,* where it is cooked over a fire. There is sometimes live marimba music to complete the authentic Guatemalan feel.

A longtime favorite is ★ **El Sereno** (4a Avenida Norte #16, tel. 7832-0501, www. elserenoantigua.com, lunch and dinner daily, $9-25). The restaurant dates to 1980, but the wonderfully old colonial building in which it's housed dates to the 16th century and once housed the Spanish priests who built La Merced church. You can dine on gourmet international dishes in the elegant main dining room, in a romantic cavelike candlelit room, or alfresco either in a delightful covered garden patio or on the rooftop terrace.

Last but certainly not least of the fine dining options is ★ **Bistrot Cinq** (4a Calle Oriente #7, tel. 7832-5510, www.bistrotcinq. com, noon-10pm daily, until 11 Fri./Sat., $9-25). The emphasis is on French cuisine; dishes include chicken scaloppine and trout Armandine, but with take-out or delivery items such as scrumptious half-pound burgers and steak *frites* also on the menu. The bar is top-notch and includes absinthe.

Information and Services

TOURIST INFORMATION

The **INGUAT office** (5a Calle Oriente #11, tel. 7832-0787 or 2421-2951, 8am-5pm Mon.-Fri., 9am-5pm Sat.-Sun.), also known as Casa del Turista, has friendly, helpful staff who can help steer you in the right direction as well as provide free maps, bus schedules, and other useful information. A useful website with lots of information on hotels, restaurants, shops, and services is www. aroundantigua.com. Another useful publication is the monthly *Revue* magazine, available free at many hotels, restaurants, and shops. Another publication, *Qué pasa en Antigua,* has very complete information on all that's going on.

The Giant Kite Festival

If you're visiting the Antigua or Guatemala City area around November 1, you should certainly plan a trip to either of the highland Mayan towns of Santiago Sacatepéquez or Sumpango, home to the annual Giant Kite Festival. In addition to the lively atmosphere of a typical Mayan fiesta, you'll be treated to an awe-inspiring display of larger-than-life kites, typically 20-50 feet wide. The kites are painstakingly crafted from tissue paper and bamboo reeds incorporating colorful and elaborate designs. Preparations typically begin six weeks in advance, in mid-September, with teams working extended hours as the deadline for completion draws closer. Judges are on hand at the festival to name the best entries in a variety of categories.

Kites under 20 feet in diameter are flown over the town cemetery later in the day and are believed to be a vehicle for speaking with the souls of departed loved ones. The flying kites are representative of the floating spirits of the dead. Larger kites are only for show and typically carry a message or theme, sometimes overtly political in nature. The weather is typically windy during this time of year, with the surrounding hillsides still tinged with verdant hues thanks to the recently ended rainy season. The colorful cemetery structures and the typical native dress of the Mayan people cap off a Technicolor dream of a day.

The festival in Sumpango, the larger of the two towns, takes place in a broad field adjacent to the cemetery. Santiago Sacatepéquez has a somewhat more cramped setting, its cemetery being perched on the edge of a plateau and extending down a gently sloping hillside. Personally, I prefer Sumpango's version of the event. For a mere three dollars, you can purchase access to bleacher seating, which gets you some nice vantage points for photography. In the afternoon, around 3pm, the official festivities begin with a speech by the local mayor and other such pageantry. The highlight of the afternoon is watching the giant six-meter kites take flight as teams of kite fliers test their skills and the sturdiness of their creations. Only kites six meters across in diameter or smaller are able to take flight, though you'll find plenty of larger kites on display. The difficulty of getting these monstrosities to become airborne is exacerbated by the large crowds, which leave little room for participants to do the necessary running to get the kites going. As a result, you'll

COMMUNICATIONS

Antigua's **main post office** is near the bus terminal on the corner of 4a Calle Poniente and Calzada de Santa Lucía and is open 9am-5pm. There are also various international couriers with offices here, including **DHL** (Corner 6a Calle Poniente and 6a Avenida Sur #16, tel. 2339-8400, ext. 7515). A number of companies can also help you ship home any purchases you're unable to fit in your check-in baggage allotment. These include **Envíos Etc.** (3a Avenida Norte #26, tel. 7832-1212), which is also the local representative for FedEx.

MONEY

Banco Industrial (5a Avenida Sur #4), just south of the plaza, has a Visa/Plus ATM. There is also an ATM on the north side

of the plaza next to Café Barista. Another ATM may be found on the plaza's west side next to **Café Condesa** (Portal del Comercio #4). Avoid any and all BAC ATM machines, as there have been incidents of card cloning originating at their Antigua locations.

LAUNDRY

Detalles (6a Avenida Norte #3B, tel. 7832-5973, 7:30am-6:30pm Mon.-Sat., 8am-4pm Sun.) does dry cleaning and has coin-operated laundry machines. **Lavandería Dry Clean** (6a Calle Poniente #49, 7am-7pm Mon.-Sat., 9am-6pm Sun.) charges about $4 a load. **Quick Laundry** (6a Calle Poniente #14, tel. 7832-2937, 8am-5pm Mon.-Sat.) charges about $0.85 per pound.

often see the kites plunging quickly toward the crowd. It's all part of the fun, but it's also one more reason I prefer the bleacher seats off to the side. Many Antigua travel agencies offer special trips and shuttle transport to both towns on these days, or you can go by public bus. Santiago Sacatepéquez lies a few kilometers off the Pan-American Highway. You can take a direct bus from Antigua or get off from any Guatemala City-bound bus at the junction and continue from there. For Sumpango, your best bet is to get to Chimaltenango, also on the Pan-American Highway, and connect from there. Be prepared for huge crowds. If you drive your own vehicle, you'll likely need to park outside of town and walk uphill from the highway to the festival grounds.

EMERGENCY AND MEDICAL SERVICES

For the **Bomberos Municipales** (Municipal Fire Department), dial 7831-0049. **Casa de Salud Santa Lucía** (Calzada de Santa Lucía Sur #7, tel. 7832-3122) is a private medical hospital with 24-hour emergency services. **Hospital Nacional Pedro de Betancourt** is a public hospital two kilometers from town with emergency service. For serious issues, your best bet is to go to Guatemala City.

TRAVEL AGENCIES

Travel agencies are ubiquitous in Antigua. Among the recommended companies for shuttle buses is **Atitrans** (6a Avenida Sur #7, tel. 7832-3371, www.atitrans.net). For plane tickets and general travel needs, recommended travel agents include **National Travel** (6a Avenida Sur #1A, tel. 2247-4747), **Viajes Tivoli** (4a Calle Oriente #10, Edificio El Jaulón, tel. 7832-4274), and **Rainbow Travel Center** (7a Avenida Sur #8, tel. 7931-7878, www.rainbowtravelcenter.com).

Sin Fronteras (3a Avenida Sur #1A, tel. 7720-4400, www.sinfront.com) is another good all-around agency with package deals to Tikal in addition to local tours. It rents cars through Tabarini Rent A Car. **Bon Voyage Guatemala** (6a Avenida Norte #3A, tel. 7823-9209, www.bonvoyageguatemala.com) is a good source of travel information and acts as a booking agent for various transportation providers. The company also runs daily shuttles at 8am for El Salvador beaches. Also recommended for countrywide tours from Antigua is **Guinness Travel** (6a Avenida Norte #16, tel. 4623-6297, www.guinness-travel.com).

Choosing a Language School

Antigua has close to 100 language schools, and the task of choosing the right one can seem downright daunting. It really boils down to the quality of individual instructors, though some schools are definitely better than others. Look around and ask plenty of questions. If you decide midway through a weeklong course that you're just not jiving with the instructor, don't hesitate to pull out and ask for a new one. That being said, the following websites can help you out in your search: www.guatemala365.com and www.123teachme.com. Both have surveys and rankings of individual schools in Guatemala.

Among the recommended Antigua schools are **Academia de Español Antigueña** (1a Calle Poniente #10, tel. 7832-7241, www.spanishacademyantiguena.com), a small, well-run school with space for 10 students at a time. I've personally had the pleasure of working with **Spanish School La Unión** (1a. Avenida Sur #21, tel. 7832-7757, www.launion.edu.gt). They offer quality one-on-one instruction and are involved in a variety of social projects. **Escuela de Español San José El Viejo** (5a Avenida Sur #34, tel. 7832-3028, www.sanjoseelviejo.com) has its own very attractive campus where you can stay in comfortable accommodations with facilities that include a tennis court and swimming pool amid lovely gardens and coffee trees. A longtime student favorite is **Christian Spanish Academy** (6a Avenida Norte #15, tel. 7832-3922, www.learncsa.com), a very well-run school set in a pleasant colonial courtyard. Antigua's oldest language school is **Proyecto Lingüístico Francisco Marroquín** (7a Calle Poniente #31, tel. 7832-2886, www.plfm-antigua.org), run by a nonprofit foundation working toward the study and preservation of Mayan languages. It comes highly recommended. **Academia de Español Probigua** (6a Avenida Norte #41B, tel. 7832-2998, www.probigua.conexion.com) is run by a nonprofit group working to establish and maintain libraries in rural villages. Another good choice with comfortable accommodations across the street from the school is **Centro Lingüístico Internacional** (1a Calle Oriente #11, tel. 7832-0391, www.spanishcontact.com).

The recommended schools range in price $140-225 per week, including 20-35 hours of instruction and a stay with local family. While the schools provide everything you will need to learn the language, it might be a challenge to have a total language immersion experience because of the overwhelming presence of foreigners in Antigua. If this is an issue for you, consider taking Spanish classes in Cobán or Petén.

VOLUNTEER WORK

Although it's based in the city of Quetzaltenango, **EntreMundos** (www.entremundos.org) has a very useful database of volunteer projects throughout Guatemala. If you're interested in working with impoverished children, check out **The God's Child project** (U.S. tel. 612-351-8020, www.godschild.org).

COOKING SCHOOL

If you acquire a taste for traditional Guatemalan cuisine and want to re-create the country's myriad flavors at home, check out **El Frijol Feliz** (4a Avenida Sur #1, tel. 7832-5274, www.frijolfeliz.com, $30-45 per class). The school is open every day, and there are classes available in the morning or afternoon. The class includes instruction on the preparation of one main dish, two side dishes, and a dessert. More focused classes include instruction on the preparation of typical Guatemalan sauces such as mole and salsa verde. Dishes include *pepián*, *chiles rellenos*, and *chuchitos* (the author's favorite).

Transportation

BUS

The main **bus terminal** is found next to the market, three blocks west of the central plaza. It is separated from the heart of town by a broad, tree-lined street. There are connections to the highlands available by taking one of many frequent buses up to Chimaltenango (every 15 minutes, half-hour travel time) along the Pan-American Highway and a requisite stop for buses trundling along to the highlands from Guatemala City. You can also catch one of the slightly less frequent buses to San Lucas Sacatepéquez, which is closer to Guatemala City. There may be more seats available on the buses plying the same highway en route toward Chimaltenango. Buses for Guatemala City leave every 15 minutes or so 4am-7:30pm, taking about an hour and costing about $2. There is also a direct Rebuli bus to Panajachel at 7am leaving from the corner of Calzada Santa Lucía and 5a Calle Poniente (two hours, $5).

Otherwise, buses leave every 15 minutes for San Miguel Dueñas ("Dueñas," 30 minutes, $0.50) stopping along the way in Ciudad Vieja. There are also buses every 30 minutes for San Antonio Aguas Calientes and Santa María de Jesús.

SHUTTLE BUS

Many travelers opt for the comfort, convenience, safety, and hassle-free experience aboard one of the numerous shuttle buses. Destinations include frequent runs to the Guatemala City airport, at least one bus daily to Monterrico and Cobán, several daily to Panajachel and Quetzaltenango, and less frequently to Río Dulce. Recommended shuttle companies include **Atitrans** (6a Avenida Sur #7, tel. 7832-3371, www.atitrans.net) and **Adrenalina Tours** (3a Calle Poniente #2D, tel. 7882-4147, www.adrenalinatours.com).

the Antigua bus terminal

TAXI

Taxis can be found on the east side of the park next to the cathedral or by the bus terminal. The former is probably a safer place to board one. A ride to Guatemala City should cost around $30. You'll also see *tuk-tuks* (motorized rickshaws) throughout the city, costing considerably less and recommended for short distances.

CAR RENTAL

Hertz (7a Calle Poniente #33B, inside Camino Real Antigua hotel, tel. 3274-4420, www.rentautos.com.gt) has an office in Antigua, as does **Budget** (4a Avenida Sur #4, tel. 2203-2303, www.budget.com.gt). **Tabarini** (6a Avenida Sur #22, tel. 7832-8107) also rents cars.

BICYCLE RENTAL

O.X. Outdoor Excursions (7a Calle Poniente #17, tel. 7832-0468, www.guatemalavolcano.com) rents mountain bikes for $22 per day. You will need a passport and a valid credit card. Also for mountain bikes, check out **Old Town Outfitters** (5a Avenida Sur #12, tel. 7832-4171, www.adventureguatemala.com, 9am-6pm daily).

Near Antigua Guatemala

Antigua is surrounded by a number of picturesque towns and villages built in the midst of the Panchoy Valley and on the slopes of neighboring volcanoes. You'll find plenty of recreational opportunities in these parts—enjoy the region's natural backdrop, surrounded by coffee farms and even a winery.

JOCOTENANGO

Jocotenango lies just 3.5 kilometers northwest of Antigua. A pretty, pink stucco church adorns the main square. In colonial times, the town served as the official entry point into neighboring Antigua.

★ Centro Cultural La Azotea

The town's main attraction is **Centro Cultural La Azotea** (La Azotea Cultural Center, Calle del Cementerio, Final, tel. 7831-1486, www.centroazotea.com, 8:30am-4pm Mon.-Fri., 8:30am-2pm Sat., $4 adults, $0.85 children), which functions as a three-in-one coffee, costume, and music museum. The music museum, **Casa K'ojom** (www.kojom.org) features a wonderful assortment of traditional Mayan musical instruments, including *marimbas,* drums, a diatomic harp,

and flutes in addition to masks and paintings collected by its dedicated administrator, Samuel Franco. There is also an audiovisual room where you can watch a video on traditional music as it would be played in Mayan villages. Traditional costumes and crafts of the Antigua Valley are exhibited in a separate room dedicated to Sacatepéquez department.

The adjoining **Museo del Café** covers the history and evolution of coffee cultivation and is available as a self-guided or guided tour. You can see coffee beans in varying stages of production from recently harvested to fully roasted. The well-illustrated displays include information on wet and dry mills, some old roasters, and machinery. You can then tour an actual plantation on-site. There is also a shop where you can buy CDs, DVDs, handicrafts, and of course, coffee.

Also found here is the **Establo La Ronda** (tel. 7831-1120), where you can ride around the grounds on horseback for an hour in the mornings ($3). Call ahead.

You can get to Jocotenango by taking any Chimaltenango-bound bus leaving from Antigua's bus terminal. Buses leave every 20 minutes; you can also take a *tuk-tuk* or taxi.

The Western Highlands

Look for ★ to find recommended sights, activities, dining, and lodging.

Highlights

★ **Iximché:** Conveniently situated close to the Pan-American Highway about an hour outside of Guatemala City, the ruins of the former capital of the Kaqchikel kingdom are the most easily accessible of all the highland Mayan sites (page 125).

★ **Chichicastenango's Market:** Don't miss the chaos of this colorful Sunday and Thursday market at the center of a K'iche' town (page 154).

★ **Acul:** With pastoral scenery and Swiss ambience, Acul makes an excellent hike from Nebaj (page 162).

★ **Laguna Chicabal:** Mayan rituals still take place at this enchanting, bowl-shaped crater lake, which offers a worthy day hike (page 185).

Most visitors to Guatemala day-dream about the Western Highlands. The region is home to quaint and colorful mountain villages, highland lakes, pine forests, and the majority of Guatemala's indigenous peoples.

Although other parts of Central America offer attractions similar to those found elsewhere in Guatemala, nowhere else in the region are age-old traditions, exquisite Mayan culture, and a history both proud and painful so remarkably evident and incredibly alive. From the Indian markets in Chichicastenango and the Mayan practices of the *costumbristas* (shamans carrying out traditional Mayan rituals) in the hills just outside of town to the all-day November 1 horse races of Todos Santos, the region is steeped in rich culture.

In the Western Highlands, you'll find the ruined cities of the highland Mayan tribes encountered by Pedro de Alvarado and the Spanish when they arrived in 1524. The sites are still places of pilgrimage for the modern-day descendants of the various linguistic groups populating this part of the country. Traversing the pine tree-peppered mountain scenery, you'll also come across the region's spectacular volcanic chain, which runs like

a spine heading west from Antigua all the way to the Mexican border. The water-filled caldera of an extinct volcano forms the basis for one of the country's most outrageously beautiful natural attractions, the singular Lake Atitlán. In addition to water-based recreational activities, unlike any other lake in Central America, it offers the opportunity to observe and interact with the fascinating highland Mayan people inhabiting the dozen or so villages along its lakeshores. Farther west is Guatemala's second-largest city, Quetzaltenango, which has become a popular place for Spanish-language study as well as a hub of NGO activity in the aftermath of the civil war. It boasts some outstanding nearby natural attractions of its own and the cosmopolitan feel of a European city.

Throughout the highlands, you'll encounter the after-effects of Guatemala's bloody civil war, which affected this region more than any other. But, like a brilliant springtime

Previous: sunrise at Lake Atitlán; Chichicastenango's bustling market. **Above:** a Mayan weaver from Quiché department.

The Western Highlands

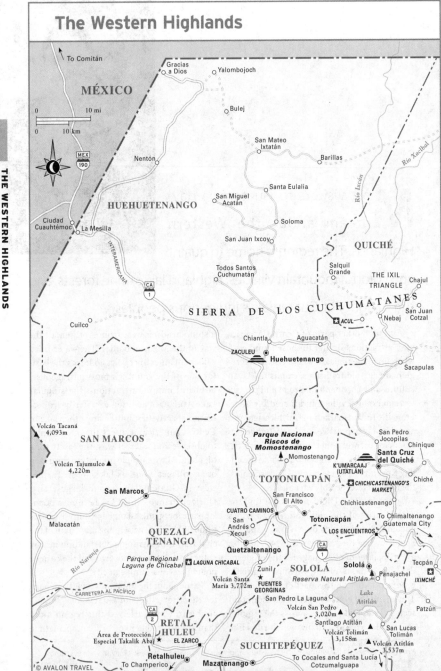

To Comitán

MÉXICO

Gracias a Dios
Yalombojoch

Bulej

0   10 mi
0   10 km

MEX
190

Nentón

San Mateo
Ixtatán

Barillas

Río Ixcán

Río Xacbal

HUEHUETENANGO

Santa Eulalia

San Miguel
Acatán

Ciudad
Cuauhtémoc   La Mesilla

Soloma

San Juan Ixcoy

QUICHÉ

INTERAMERICANA

CA
1

Todos Santos
Cuchumatán

Salquil
Grande

THE IXIL
TRIANGLE   Chajul

SIERRA   DE   LOS   CUCHUMATANES

ACUL   San Juan
Nebaj   Cotzal

Cuilco

Chiantla   Aguacatán

ZACULEU   Huehuetenango

Sacapulas

Volcán Tacaná
4,093m

SAN MARCOS

Parque Nacional
Riscos de
Momostenango

San Pedro
Jocopilas   Chinique

Momostenango   Santa Cruz
del Quiché

Volcán Tajumulco ▲
4,220m

K'UMARCAAJ
(UTATLÁN)

Chiché

San Marcos

TOTONICAPÁN   CHICHICASTENANGO'S
MARKET

San Francisco
El Alto   Chichicastenango

Malacatán

CUATRO CAMINOS
San
Andrés
Xecul   Totonicapán

To Chimaltenango
Guatemala City

QUEZAL-
TENANGO

LOS ENCUENTROS

CA
1

Quetzaltenango   Tecpán

Parque Regional
Laguna de Chicabal   LAGUNA CHICABAL

SOLOLÁ   Sololá   Panajachel

IXIMCHÉ

Río Naranjo

Zunil

Reserva Natural Atitlán

CARRETERA AL PACÍFICO

Volcán Santa
María 3,772m   FUENTES
GEORGINAS

Lake
Atitlán   Patzún

San Pedro La Laguna

CA
2

RETAL-
HULEU

Volcán San Pedro
3,020m

Santiago Atitlán

San Lucas
Tolimán

Área de Protección
Especial Takalik Abaj ★   EL ZARCO

Volcán Tolimán
3,158m

SUCHITEPÉQUEZ   Volcán Atitlán
3,537m

Retalhuleu

To Champerico   Mazatenango

To Cocales and Santa Lucía
Cotzumalguapa

© AVALON TRAVEL

flower emerging through fertile soil from winter's icy chill, the highlands and its people are fast changing and rising from the ashes of the armed conflict. There's a new feeling in the air. Where once there was fear and apprehension (and rightfully so) on the part of its Mayan inhabitants, there is now curiosity and a desire to build a new future while holding on to the culture that is their inheritance. You are a big part of this, as your presence in these parts is a catalyst to substantial progress along the lines of sustainable development with tourism at the forefront. There are many community-based tourism projects in this area, and your visit helps provide needed income but also positive interaction with the outside world.

It is so refreshing, years later, to be able to travel to areas that were once bombed out and cleared of vegetation but are now green and vibrant again. This painful legacy intertwined with optimism is most evident in the Ixil Triangle, which stands poised to become a mecca for cultural and ecotourism, overseen by and to the benefit of, its Ixil inhabitants. Despite having suffered some of the most horrendous atrocities during the civil war, still they smile, a testament to their fortitude. Farther west toward the Mexican border, the department of Huehuetenango boasts fascinating Mayan villages of its own in addition to some seldom-visited natural attractions along the Sierra de los Cuchumatanes mountain chain. It's only a matter of time before visitors to Guatemala put this vast wilderness on the map.

PLANNING YOUR TIME

The Western Highlands are home to many of Guatemala's main attractions, and there is plenty here worth seeing. Although distances on a map may be short, the rugged mountain terrain means getting to places that look close on a map will often take longer than expected because of twisting mountain roads, some of

which are not even paved. You could easily spend several weeks here or longer, as attested to by the sizable expat population living on the shores of Lake Atitlán. But, since most folks tend to be on a tighter schedule, you'll probably end up choosing among the many wonderful attractions.

The region is traversed in several parts by the Pan-American Highway, meaning that if you're on a limited schedule, you should stick to areas near this paved main road. Along this road, coming up from Guatemala City or Antigua, you may want to spend an hour or so at the ruins of Iximché, the former Kaqchikel capital, which also served as the first capital of Guatemala when the Spanish set up shop here after the conquest. If you have only a few days, you should certainly not miss a visit to Lake Atitlán, staying either in the large tourist and services hub of Panajachel or taking a boat across the lake to the village of your choice. Each has its own characteristics and tends to attract a certain crowd.

After the lake, you can continue along the Pan-American Highway to Quetzaltenango, Guatemala's second-largest city, where you can take in area villages or natural attractions, including the fantastic crater lake atop Chicabal Volcano. It's also a great place to sign up for a week (or more) of Spanish lessons if you have the time. If you can work it into your schedule, plan on visiting the market (Sundays and Thursdays) in the K'iche' town of Chichicastenango, which is easily accessible from Quetzaltenango and Panajachel. If you have more time, head north from Chichicastenango into the hills of Quiché department to the Ixil Triangle. You certainly won't be disappointed.

If you have still more time, consider heading west to Huehuetenango from the branch road in the town of Sacapulas (Quiché department) or east to Cobán and the Verapaces via a spectacularly scenic, and equally rugged, dirt road.

Chimaltenango Department and Vicinity

Although its namesake departmental capital is a collection of houses, bus depots, and businesses lining the side of the Pan-American Highway, the rest of the Chimaltenango department is nonetheless a worthy destination. Along the road traversing the region's highland plateaus, you'll find plenty of pine-studded landscapes, agricultural fields, and even some Mayan ruins of note.

CHIMALTENANGO

The departmental capital of Chimaltenango is a major transit point between Guatemala City/Antigua and the highlands. You may find yourself changing buses here if you're heading up from Antigua going east to Guatemala City or west to the highlands, including Chichicastenango, Lake Atitlán, Quetzaltenango, and Huehuetenango. There's little else to keep you in this busy commercial town and transportation hub.

TECPÁN TO LOS ENCUENTROS

A much more pleasant alternative to the noise and pollution of Chimaltenango is a stretch of the Pan-American Highway (CA-1) heading through the Western Highlands from the town of Tecpán, about an hour from Guatemala City, all the way west to the Los Encuentros Junction, from where a turnoff leads to a vertiginous drop down the sides of an extinct volcanic caldera to out-of-this-world Lake Atitlán. Another road leads north from Los Encuentros to the department of El Quiché, with its colorful markets and highland villages. Along the road from Tecpán to Los Encuentros, you'll find some interesting Mayan ruins and good eats, should you need to stop for sustenance or simply want a break from the drive to enjoy the wonderful sylvan settings.

Tecpán

The town of Tecpán proper is about half a kilometer from the main highway via a signed turnoff, though few people actually go into the town unless they're en route to the ruins of Iximché. You'll find plenty of roadside restaurants along this stretch of the highway, many with nearly identical menus. Some of these, such as ★ **Katok** (Km. 87.5, tel. 7840-3387, www.ahumadoskatok.com, 7am-10pm daily, $8-20) and **Kape Paulino's** (Km. 87.5, tel. 7840-3806, www.kapepaulinos.com, $8-20), are perennial favorites with Guatemalans and usually very busy, serving a variety of grilled steaks, chicken, Guatemalan dishes, and cured meats in a log cabin atmosphere.

At a turnoff from the main highway at Km. 90.5 heading to the village of Santa Apolonia, **El Pedregal** (tel. 7840-3055,

farm-to-table at El Pedregal, near Tecpán

$8-12) has pleasant grounds in a country setting away from the noise of the busy Pan-American Highway. It also makes a great place for kids, with ducks, cows, and other farm animals for them to enjoy. Delicious home-cooked meals including steaks, sandwiches, fresh bread, and cakes are served in a lovely covered patio fronting the gardens. The food here is homemade and tastes like it. It's worth getting off the main highway, just about one kilometer or so away. There is beer, but no wine. **La Cabaña de Don Robert** (Km. 93.5 Carretera Interamericana, tel. 7858-2181, $8-15) is another Guatemalan favorite, serving typical Guatemalan dishes in a wooden cabana surrounded by well-manicured gardens. Farther along the road at Km. 102, **Restaurant Chichoy** (tel. 5219-7092, also at Km. 78 in the village of Chirijuyú) is another good choice, serving breakfast, lunch, and dinner. It was originally started by a cooperative of widows from the civil war.

The nicest place to stay in the Tecpán area is undoubtedly ★ **Casa Xara** (tel. 2333-3926, www.casaxara.com, $17-30 pp). Set amidst the sprawling grounds of Molino Helvetia (an old flour mill), there are two lodging options to choose from. The larger Casa El Molino ($300, $200 for 10 people or $60 per room) is set in the original house and sleeps 17 guests. A creek runs behind the original house, and there's a network of small trails leading into the forest just past an old wooden chapel. Up the hill is newer Casa Xara ($275), which sleeps 9. The most recent addition, the smaller Casa del Bosque, is also my favorite part of the complex. Its more secluded hillside location overlooks the grounds of the old flour mill and has a lovely private patio where you can take in the view. All three houses are made of wood (a rarity in highland Guatemala) and are charmingly decorated with lovely old knickknacks. It's wonderfully peaceful here, though it can get cold at night. Space heaters are provided,

and the two larger houses have fireplaces. It makes a phenomenal weekend getaway. Food can be ordered from nearby El Pedregal restaurant and friendly manager Lucy Haase is on-site to cater to your wishes.

★ Iximché

Faced with the increasingly belligerent expansionist aims of their K'iche' rivals, the Kaqchikel moved their capital from present-day Chichicastenango to the more easily defended site of Iximché, surrounded on three sides by ravines, sometime around AD 1470. Like many other Mayan sites, it bore strong influence from present-day Mexico, an influence evident in its Nahua name, Cuauhtemallan, a derivative of which eventually gave the country its modern-day name meaning "land of many trees." Societal organization here was based on lineages, with evidence of bitter rivalry between different lineages including ritual cannibalism and human sacrifice. The new capital had been established for only about 50 years before the arrival of the Spanish, who would enlist the Kaqchikel as allies in their quest to conquer the K'iche' and other Mayan peoples of the Western Highlands.

After the highlands were fully conquered, the Spanish established the first capital of Guatemala here on July 25, 1524. Alvarado, however, began demanding excessive tribute and the Kaqchikel soon revolted, eventually fleeing the town after Alvarado finally burned it to the ground. From the surrounding countryside (demonstrating a remarkable symmetry to the country's more recent history), the Kaqchikel launched a guerrilla war against the Spanish that lasted until 1530.

Iximché (various transport, 10 minutes from Tecpán, 8am-5pm daily, $3.50) is the most easily accessible of Guatemala's highland Mayan ceremonial sites and makes an interesting stop for those with an interest in Mayan culture and history because of the differences it exhibits from the lowland Mayan sites of Petén, which date to much earlier times. Like many remoter highland counterparts (Mixco Viejo, K'umarcaaj, and Zaculeu), it was built on an isolated bluff surrounded and protected by ravines. Its smaller structures also exhibit much more of a Mexican influence, attesting to the population of the Guatemalan highlands by Toltec groups coming from the area near present-day Veracruz.

In March 2007, Iximché made a convenient stopover for President George W. Bush, the first lady, Laura Bush, and their Guatemalan hosts Oscar and Wendy Berger on their way back to Guatemala City from a visit to a nearby vegetable farming cooperative. They received a red carpet welcome of sorts, entering the ruins' main plaza on a specially made *alfombra* similar to the ones created for Antigua's Holy Week processions. They were also treated to a marimba band, an exhibition of the Mayan ball game, and a traditional dance performed by local children. In an impromptu display rarely seen in international protocol, Presidents Bush and Berger even attempted to play some ball of their own before members of the Secret Service rushed them on to the next order of business.

Of the ruined temple pyramids, only a few features stand out. The small altar at the base of Temple II, on Plaza A, has faint traces of murals. Other features include two ball courts and Plaza B, which housed royals. The museum has some interpretive displays predominantly on Pedro de Alvarado and the Kaqchikel uprisings. There's also a 1:200 scale model of Iximché based on an 1882 map created by Alfred Maudslay. To get here, turn off the main highway to Tecpán. From the town center there are buses, minibuses, and taxis heading out to the ruins, less than 10 minutes away.

Los Encuentros

The road diverting to El Quiché department is found at this junction and, about one kilometer farther down, is the turnoff for the road to Lake Atitlán. The Pan-American Highway (also known as the Interamericana) continues west to Quetzaltenango and Huehuetenango through lovely alpine scenery.

along the road to Panajachel from Los Encuentros

Lake Atitlán

From Los Encuentros, the road descends through beautiful agricultural fields tended by Maya, many of whom still wear traditional dress. After passing the departmental capital of Sololá, the road becomes steeper, descending to the Lake Atitlán shoreline with gorgeous views of the large, crescent moon-shaped lake bounded by three volcanoes on its southern shore. You'll also pass a waterfall or two along the way. For centuries the beauty of Lake Atitlán has captivated travelers, including Aldous Huxley, who compared it to Italy's Lake Como "with the additional embellishment of several immense volcanoes." Words cannot begin to describe the magic felt when seeing the lake for the first time, its waters shimmering in the afternoon light. Lake Como, as beautiful as it is, doesn't have volcanoes, tropical vegetation, and Mayan villages lining its shores.

Lake Atitlán's origins can be traced back 85,000 years to a volcanic eruption that created the collapsed caldera the lake now fills, also spreading ash over a 1,600-kilometer radius. The lake was created when drainage to the Pacific Ocean was blocked after the emergence of the more recent Tolimán and Atitlán Volcanoes. A third volcano, San Pedro, which is just about 3,000 meters (9,908 feet) high, is somewhat lower than the other two but still offers a challenging climb on a path straight up its slopes.

The lake covers about 130 square kilometers. Its maximum depth is more than 320 meters, though there are cyclical rises and falls in lake levels, leading to speculation that periodic seismic activity may block a drainage area somewhere. The lake has been rising steadily over the past few years. You'll see the remains of several buildings now partially submerged in many areas along the shoreline. Lake Atitlán has begun exhibiting signs of eutrophication, with a green gulag of cyanobacteria making its first widespread appearance on the water's surface in October 2009. A legacy of Hurricane Stan was the destruction of a wastewater treatment plant that was never rebuilt. Adding to the raw sewage streaming into the lake from

spectacular Lake Atitlán

Lake Atitlán

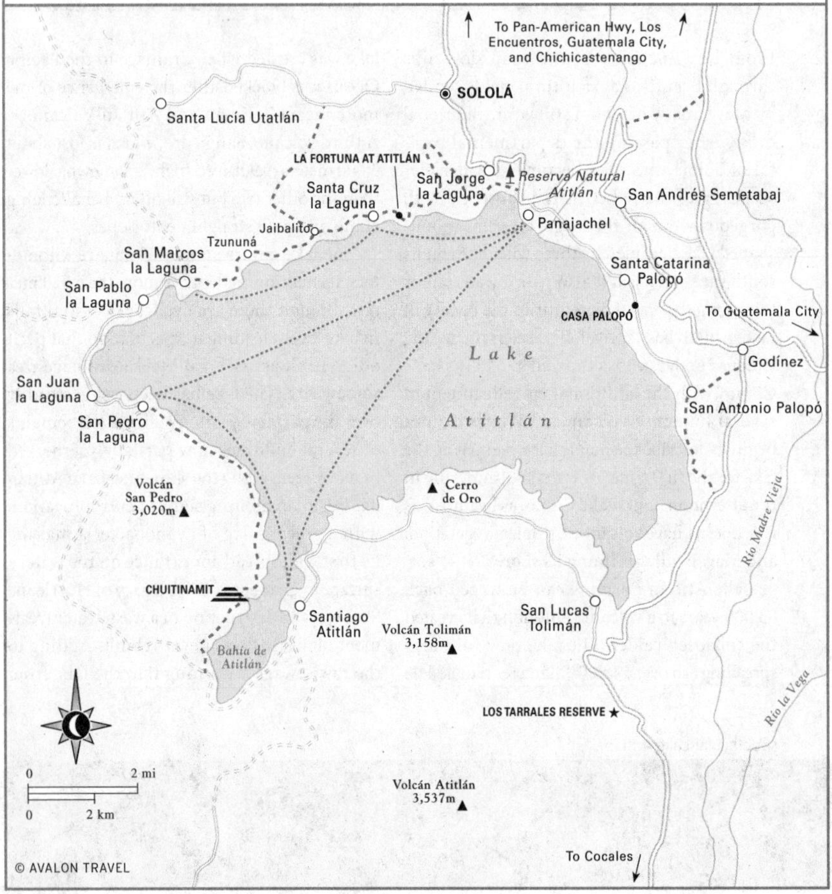

To Pan-American Hwy, Los
Encuentros, Guatemala City,
and Chichicastenango

SOLOLÁ

Santa Lucía Utatlán

LA FORTUNA AT ATITLÁN

Santa Cruz
la Laguna

San Jorge
la Laguna

*Reserva Natural
Atitlán*

San Andrés Semetabaj

Jaibalito

Tzununá

Panajachel

San Marcos
la Laguna

Santa Catarina
Palopó

San Pablo
la Laguna

CASA PALOPÓ

To Guatemala City

Lake

Godínez

San Juan
la Laguna

Atitlán

San Antonio Palopó

San Pedro
la Laguna

Volcán
San Pedro
3,020m ▲

▲ Cerro
de Oro

Río Madre Vieja

CHUITINAMIT

San Lucas
Tolimán

*Bahía de
Atitlán*

Santiago
Atitlán

Volcán Tolimán
3,158m ▲

Río la Vega

LOS TARRALES RESERVE ★

0   2 mi

0   2 km

Volcán Atitlán
3,537m ▲

© AVALON TRAVEL

To Cocales

the towns and villages on its shores are phosphates from agricultural fertilizers. The race to save Atitlán is on, with numerous grassroots organizations working hand-in-hand with government agencies to clean up algal blooms and cease the indiscriminate pollution of the lake's waters. Lake Atitlán is surrounded by a number of small villages, each with its own distinct feel. Across the lake, only San Pedro La Laguna rivals Panajachel in popularity with tourists. The other villages remain fairly quiet, though tourism has become a significant presence in almost all of them. Santiago Atitlán,

though one of the larger towns, remains very much traditional.

PANAJACHEL

The lake's main tourist town has always been Panajachel, once a requisite stop along the "Gringo Trail," as it was known in the 1960s, the path of American and European backpackers making their way down to South America. There are nice views across the lake from "Pana," as it's often referred to by locals, though in recent years several of the outlying villages have started receiving their own fair share of visitors. Many foreigners like the more peaceful atmosphere of the other villages surrounding the lake. As one expatriate living in San Pedro put it, "Twenty minutes in Panajachel is enough for me." Still, Pana is worth at least a night's stay if you like shopping its jam-packed stalls. Pana's main street is Calle Principal. Most buses coming in to town stop at the intersection of Calle Principal and Calle Santander, which leads directly to the lakeshore. Santander is lined with a plethora of banks, shops, restaurants, hotels, and other tourist services. You'll find that many of these don't use street addresses. The town hall, church, market, and a few other restaurants and hotels are found a half kilometer northeast along Calle Principal from the Calle Santander junction. East of Calle Santander and running parallel is Calle Rancho Grande, which also has some accommodations. Running roughly between the two along the lakeshore is Calle del Lago.

Sights

Museo Lacustre Atitlán (Atitlán Lake Museum, inside Hotel Posada de Don Rodrigo, Calle Santander, tel. 7762-2326, 8am-6pm Sun.-Fri., 8am-7pm Sat., $5 for nonguests) has well-displayed exhibits on the geological history of Lake Atitlán and its creation, along with sub-aquatic Mayan archaeology, including ceremonial urns and incense burners, mostly from Late Preclassic and Classic times. The museum has gained an added element of relevance with a 2014 documentary produced by *National Geographic* detailing the discovery and unearthing of a Mayan city submerged beneath the lake, known as Samabaj.

Casa Cakchiquel (Calle 14 de febrero, tel. 7762-0969, casadeche@gmail.com, 10am-6pm daily, free) is an arts and cultural center housed in a former hotel that once played home to Che Guevara. There are rotating exhibits on issues from women's rights to Mayan heritage and a permanent exhibit of historical photos of the lake and Panajachel. It makes a nice introduction to the local culture. A gift shop sells unique crafts made from recycled materials.

Just outside of town 200 meters past Hotel Atitlán, **Reserva Natural Atitlán** (tel. 7762-2565, www.atitlanreserva.com, 8am-5pm daily, $8 adults, $4.50 children under 12) is a wonderful nature preserve on the grounds of a former coffee farm. On offer are myriad attractions including a visitors center, a zipline between trees in the forest canopy, a butterfly farm, a lakeside beach, and well-designed nature trails with hanging bridges leading to waterfalls, where you can spot monkeys and coatis (*pizotes*) along the way. Spacious and attractive accommodations are available for up to six people with decks overlooking the surrounding forests. Rates vary from $81 to $93 d. You can also camp here for $8.50 per adult and $6 per child.

Nightlife

Pana is a popular weekend playground for folks from Guatemala City, and things are usually hopping on Friday and Saturday nights. There's a smattering of bars and dance places along Calle de los Arboles, which breaks off from Calle Principal just past its

Reserva Natural Atitlán

Panajachel

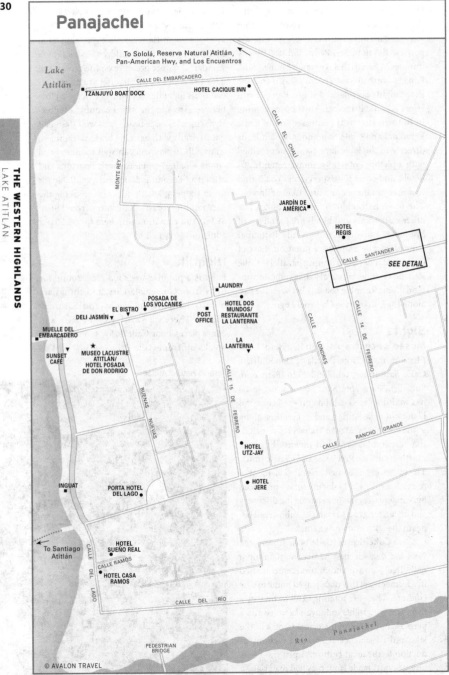

Lake Atitlán

To Sololá, Reserva Natural Atitlán, Pan-American Hwy, and Los Encuentros

CALLE DEL EMBARCADERO

TZANJUYÚ BOAT DOCK

HOTEL CACIQUE INN

CALLE EL CHALI

MONTE REY

JARDÍN DE AMÉRICA

HOTEL REGIS

CALLE SANTANDER

SEE DETAIL

LAUNDRY

POSADA DE LOS VOLCANES

EL BISTRO

DELI JASMÍN

POST OFFICE

HOTEL DOS MUNDOS/ RESTAURANTE LA LANTERNA

CALLE LONDRES

CALLE 14 DE FEBRERO

MUELLE DEL EMBARCADERO

SUNSET CAFÉ

MUSEO LACUSTRE ATITLÁN/ HOTEL POSADA DE DON RODRIGO

LA LANTERNA

BUENAS NUEVAS

CALLE 15 DE FEBRERO

HOTEL UTZ-JAY

CALLE RANCHO GRANDE

INGUAT

PORTA HOTEL DEL LAGO

HOTEL JERE

To Santiago Atitlán

HOTEL SUEÑO REAL

CALLE RAMOS

HOTEL CASA RAMOS

CALLE DEL LAGO

CALLE DEL RÍO

Río Panajachel

PEDESTRIAN BRIDGE

© AVALON TRAVEL

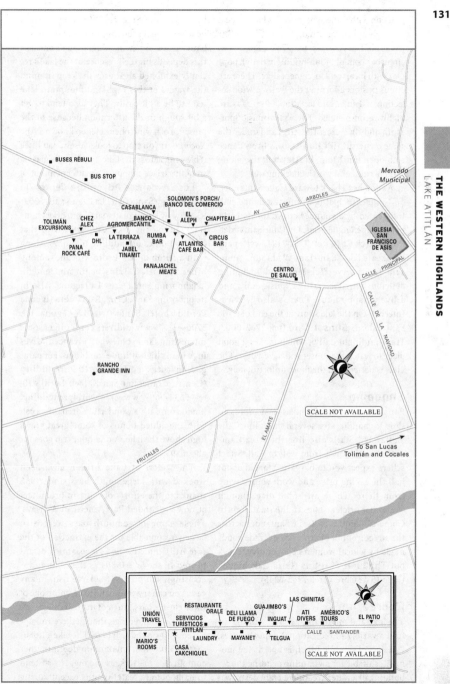

junction with Calle Santander. It's hard to beat the lively bohemian atmosphere at **Circus Bar** (Avenida Los Arboles, tel. 7762-2056, www. circusbar.com.gt, noon-midnight daily), popular with locals and foreigners alike. There are circus posters adorning the walls, a wide selection of drinks, and tasty food. Its pizzas are highly recommended. There's live music 8pm-11pm nightly. Across the street and under the same ownership is **Chapiteau,** a lively dance club open until 1am. **El Aleph** is also along this corridor and worth checking out.

As you head back toward Calle Santander, on Calle Principal is **Rumba,** a dance club frequented by a younger crowd for its Latin pop and merengue beats. On Calle Santander, **Pana Rock Café** (tel. 7762-2194, www.pan-arockcafe.com, 8am-1am Wed.-Sun., 4pm-1am Tues.) serves Tex-Mex food, including delicious burritos, has live music daily, and a lively happy hour. There's also wireless Internet. On the lakeshore at the end of Calle Santander is **Sunset Café** (tel. 7762-0003, 11am-midnight daily), which makes a good place to watch the sunset and have a beer. The view is better than the food, unfortunately.

Shopping

Pana is one of Guatemala's best places to shop for handicrafts; several shops line Calle Santander. Stalls also line the street jam-packed with goods from wall to wall. Street sellers expect you to bargain. Start at about half the asking price and work your way up from there. There are some nice, though somewhat pricier, shops in the small Centro Comercial Siquín on Calle Santander across the street from El Bistro. For fair trade goods made by a local women's cooperative, check out **Thirteen Threads** (Casa Cakchiquel, Calle 15 de febrero, tel. 7762-6245).

Recreation

The lake and mountainous surroundings afford a variety of recreational opportunities. Panajachel's public beach is not, at the moment, suitable for swimming pending the rebuilding of a water-treatment plant destroyed by Hurricane Stan in 2005. Some of the beaches in neighboring towns make much better places for swimming, though much of this depends on the presence of the lake's recently exhibited algal growth. Keep in mind the waters of this highland mountain lake tend to be a bit chilly. They also tend to get a bit rough in the afternoon because of the presence of a wind phenomenon known as the *Xocomil.* If you stop to look closely, you'll see it blowing across the lake, turning the glassy-smooth surface choppy in a matter of minutes.

Los Elementos Adventure Center (in neighboring Santa Cruz La Laguna, tel. 5359-8328, www.kayakguatemala.com) offers multiday, round-the-lake **kayaking** trips that cover 50 miles of paddling in 5 days, along with a climb of San Pedro Volcano, among other activities. Trips begin and end in neighboring Santa Cruz La Laguna. Also in neighboring Santa Cruz, **Ati Divers** (Iguana Perdida hotel, Santa Cruz La Laguna, tel. 5706-4117, www.atidivers.com) offers some interesting (and somewhat advanced) dives in Atitlán's high altitude conditions. For paragliding, check out **Realworld Paragliding** (Centro Comercial San Rafael, Local #10, tel. 5634-5699, www.realworldparagliding. jimdo.com). It's a wonderful adrenaline rush with the added bonus of some great views high above the lake. A one-hour trip goes for about $95.

The waters of Lake Atitlán have been stocked with largemouth bass since 1958 thanks to the efforts of tourism promoters at now-absconded Pan American Airways. These same largemouth bass were also largely responsible for the extinction of the rare Atitlán pied-billed grebe, which disappeared in the late 1980s as their young increasingly fell prey to the large fish. In any case, you can try your hand at catching one of these elusive bass. Most of the fish caught are in the five-pound range, though there are supposedly 20-pound fish here. The lake's 1,550-meter (5,100-foot) maximum depth further complicates matters, as the bigger fish tend to hang out at greater depths except during the annual spring spawn. Your best chance of landing "the big one" is between March and May, before and after the spawn. If you're interested in learning more about Lake Atitlán largemouth bass fishing, email the Atitlán Bass Club at bass@panajachel.com.

Accommodations

Mario's Rooms (Calle Santander, tel. 7762-1313, www.mariosroomsatitlan.com, $10-15 d) is the long-running budget favorite with basic but attractive clean rooms with shared bath. Rooms with private bathroom are just slightly more. Well-situated on a quiet side street near the lake and Calle Santander, ★ **Hotel Utz-Jay** (5a Calle 2-50 Zona 2, tel. 7762-0217, www.hotelutzjay.com, $35 d) has comfortable rooms housed in lovely adobe garden cottages decorated with traditional Guatemalan fabrics and equipped with fans and private hot-water bathrooms. There are good breakfasts (price not included) and the friendly, knowledgeable owners speak English, French, and Spanish. You can also enjoy a traditional Mayan sauna, or *chuj,* here. Internet access is available, and you can rent mountain bikes for getting around or go mountain biking along the lake on an organized trip.

★ **Rancho Grande Inn** (Calle Rancho Grande, tel. 7762-2255, www.ranchograndeinn.com, $80-90 d) dates to the 1940s and has 12 attractive rooms, suites, and cabins housed in faux-thatched-roof villas fronting a well-manicured lawn and tropical gardens. There's a nice kidney-shaped swimming pool with a partial wooden deck. Rates include a deliciously filling breakfast featuring pancakes, eggs, beans, and good, strong coffee to put some pep in your morning step. **Hotel Cacique Inn** (Calle El Chalí 3-82, tel. 7762-1205, www.caciqueinn.com, $75 d) fills up with vacationing Guatemalans during holidays and weekends. It has 34 rooms built around a garden swimming pool; rooms feature Guatemalan blankets, weavings, and fireplaces. **Hotel Regis** (Calle Santander 3-47, tel. 7762-1152, www.regisatitlan.com, $65 d) is set away from the street and has 25 comfortable rooms housed in a neocolonial building. The main attraction here is a hot spring set in the garden out back. **Hotel Dos Mundos** (Calle Santander, tel. 7762-2078, www.hoteldosmundos.com, $60 d) has comfortable rooms with tile floors and Guatemalan bedspreads set away from the street near a garden swimming pool. There's a recommended Italian restaurant on the premises as well as a streetside café and bar on Calle Santander.

Hotel Posada de Don Rodrigo (at the lakeside end of Calle Santander, tel. 7762-2326, www.posadadedonrodrigo.com, $130 d) has rooms in two separate areas, one of which is more modern and is worth the extra splurge for the splendid lake views. The rooms are comfortable and well furnished. The restaurant/bar serves excellent Guatemalan and international dishes in a pleasant dining room with views to the lake and the swimming pool below. The resort-style **Porta Hotel del Lago** (tel. 7762-1555, www.portahotels.com, $112 d) is housed in a modern five-story building overlooking the public beach. The recently renovated rooms have all the usual amenities, and there's a somewhat stark outdoor pool area.

Outside of town on a lovely and quiet lakeside plot, ★ **Hotel Atitlán** (tel. 7762-1441, www.hotelatitlan.com, $120-190 d) does a wonderful job of combining old-school charm with modern amenities in its well-furnished, tastefully decorated rooms featuring tile floors, antiques, and colorful textiles. All rooms have balconies with gorgeous lake views. There are extensive tropical gardens, an attractive swimming pool, and boat docks. The hotel's restaurant is a favorite with well-to-do Guatemalans.

Food

For morning coffee, your best bet is **Café Loco** (Calle Santander, near Pana Rock, 9am-8pm Tues.-Sun., 4pm-8pm Mon.). Another great option is **Cross Roads Café** (0-27 Calle del Campanario, www.crossroadscafepana.com, 9am-1pm and 2:30pm-6pm Tues.-Sun.).

In a pleasant garden patio decorated with

Asian-style spherical paper lamps, ★ **Deli Jasmín** (Calle Santander, close to the lakeshore, tel. 7762-2585, 7am-6pm Wed.-Mon.) serves delicious all-day breakfasts, including bagels and English muffins in addition to healthy fare such as tofu and vegetarian dishes. It sells teas, jams, whole wheat bread, and cookies for you to take away. Farther up Calle Santander and under the same management is **Deli Llama de Fuego** (tel. 7762-2586, 7am-10pm Thurs.-Tues.), with much the same menu and surroundings. Another good place for breakfast is **El Patio** (tel. 7762-2041, 8am-9:30pm daily), set in a sunny patio right next to the street about halfway down Calle Santander.

El Bistro (Calle Santander, closer to the lakeshore, tel. 7762-0508, 7am-10pm daily, $5-10) is a pleasant, shady café and bar serving steak, pasta dishes, and sandwiches in the $5-10 range. Try the fettuccine with spicy tomato sauce. For American-style deli sandwiches and imported items you might miss from home, check out **Pana Super** (Calle Principal, next to Casablanca, tel. 7762-0852, 8am-8pm Mon.-Sat., 8am-5pm Sun.). The meats and cheeses are imported, and the breads are baked fresh daily.

★ **Circus Bar** (Avenida Los Arboles, tel. 7762-2056, www.circusbar.com.gt, noon-midnight daily, $8-15) has the best pizza in town as well as excellent pasta and seafood. There's a relaxed vibe and colorful decor that conveys the feeling of being under the big top. For authentic Italian food, head to **Restaurante La Lanterna** (inside Hotel Dos Mundos, Calle Santander, tel. 7762-2078, www.hoteldosmundos.com/restaurant.htm), where there's excellent homemade pasta and a nice assortment of Italian wines. The large dining room has one of Panajachel's most pleasant atmospheres, and the service is impeccable.

For scrumptious Pan-Asian cuisine, check out **Las Chinitas** (Calle Santander, tel. 7762-2612, 8am-10pm daily), where you can savor Malaysian curries and Thai dishes, among other offerings, at moderate prices. It's a busy spot for dinner.

Halfway down Calle Santander, ★ **Guajimbo's** (tel. 7762-0063, 7am-10pm Fri.-Wed., $7-15) serves South American-style *parrilladas* (barbecued meats) including steaks, chicken, and sausage. There are also vegetarian dishes and good breakfasts. On Calle Principal, close to the intersection with Calle de los Arboles, **Atlantis Café Bar** (tel. 7762-1015) serves a good mix of international dishes, including decent burgers, pasta, pizza, and sandwiches along with a wide range of cocktails from its elegant wooden bar. The decor is eclectic and there are also some good desserts.

Duck, escargot, lamb chops, and Wiener schnitzel are on the menu at **Chez Alex** (halfway down Calle Santander, tel. 7762-0172, noon-3pm and 6pm-10pm daily) in a tasteful atmosphere with prices in the $10-12 range. **Casablanca** (at the intersection of Calle Principal and Calle Santander, tel. 7762-1015, www.panajachel.com/casablanca.htm, 11am-11pm daily, $8-22) serves delicious pastas, chicken, meat, and seafood dishes accompanied by Chilean wines in a sophisticated atmosphere. The dining room at the ★ **Hotel Atitlán** (tel. 7762-1441, www.hotelatitlan.com, 6:30am-10pm daily, $7-20) makes a fine place for a splurge, surrounded by pleasant gardens overlooking the lake and fabulous views. Patrons enjoy free use of the swimming pool, and there are Guatemalan and international dishes on the menu. There is a Sunday breakfast buffet for around $15. There are a number of eateries on Calle del Lago with similar seafood- and meat-based menus and outrageous decor, none of which I can bring myself to recommend.

Information and Services
TOURIST INFORMATION
The **INGUAT information office** (Calle Santander, tel. 7762-1392, 9am-5pm daily) has basic hotel information, transportation schedules, and friendly staff who can answer your questions. The main **post office** is on the corner of Calle Santander and Calle 15 de Febrero. **DHL** is in Edificio Rincón

Sai at the northern end of Calle Santander. **Telgua** (7am-midnight) is halfway down Calle Santander near the junction with Calle 15 de Febrero.

About halfway down Calle Santander, **Banco Industrial** has a Visa ATM and can cash U.S. dollars and travelers checks. There's a MasterCard ATM outside **Banco Agromercantil** on the corner of Calle Principal and Calle Santander. **Banco del Comercio** is on Calle Principal, also near the intersection with Santander. It has an ATM that accepts both Visa and MasterCard.

LAUNDRY

With Lake Atitlán's future at stake, it has become more important to choose environmentally friendly coin laundromats, where the detergents used are biodegradable. To that end, I highly recommend **Il Bucato** (Comercial El Dorado, at the junction of Santander and Calle Principal, 9am-6:30pm Mon.-Sat.), where you can wash up to 5 pounds for $4. They will also wash 6-12 pounds of laundry for you for $6. All the detergents used are nontoxic; hypoallergenic detergent is also available. Other options include **Lavandería Viajero** (Calle Santander, Edificio Rincón Sai, 8am-7pm); it

charges about $0.50 per pound. **Lavandería Automático** (Calle de los Arboles 0-15, 7:30am-6:30pm Mon.-Sat.) charges $4 for a full load.

MEDICAL SERVICES

Panamedic Centro Clínico Familiar (Calle Principal 0-72, tel. 7762-2174) has round-the-clock emergency medical attention. Doctors Francisco and Zulma Ordoñez both speak English. For an **ambulance,** dial 7762-4121.

TRAVEL AGENCIES

There are a number of travel agencies along Calle Santander that can book airline tickets, shuttles, and onward transport to other parts of Guatemala. Among the recommended agencies are **Atitrans** (Edificio Rincón Sai, tel. 7762-0146 or 7762-0152, www.atitranspanajachel.com) and **Servicios Turísticos Atitlán** (Comerciales Buenaventura, Calle 15 de febrero 2-81, tel. 7762-2075 or 5698-0030, www.transportatitlan.com).

Getting There and Around

Buses stop at the junction of Calle Santander and Calle Principal both leaving and arriving in Panajachel. Direct buses leave for Antigua ($5, 2.5 hours) at 10:45am daily except Sunday.

Boats are the preferred method for getting around Lake Atitlán.

You can also take a Guatemala City-bound bus ($4, 3.5 hours) and change at Chimaltenango. There are 10 daily buses to Guatemala City between 5am and 2:30pm. Six buses leave daily to Quetzaltenango ($4, 2.5 hours), and there are eight daily buses to Chichicastenango ($3, 1.5 hours).

The convenience and, most of all, safety of **shuttle buses** cannot be overstated. In the course of researching and writing this guide, it seemed that not a week went by without newspapers reporting some sort of incident aboard Guatemala's second-class buses, including armed robberies turning into shootouts between passengers and would-be thieves or tragic accidents on twisting mountain roads. That said, there are frequent shuttle buses to Antigua, Chichicastenango (on market days), Quetzaltenango, and Guatemala City. Recommended shuttle agencies include **Atitrans** (Edificio Rincón Sai, tel. 7762-0146 or 7762-0152, www.atitranspanajachel. com) and **Servicios Turísticos Atitlán** (Comerciales Buenaventura, Calle 15 de febrero 2-81, tel. 7762-2075 or 5698-0030, www. transportatitlan.com).

There are two different **boat docks** for getting around to the surrounding villages. The first of these, Tzanjuyú, is at the end of Calle del Embarcadero and is for boats to Santa Cruz (15 minutes), Jaibalito (25 minutes), Tzununá (30 minutes), and San Marcos (40 minutes). Some boats continue to San Pedro, across the lake (just under an hour, with stops), but there are also direct boats from Pana taking about 20 minutes. All of the aforementioned routes are serviced by small, fast *lanchas.* The second boat dock is at the end of Calle Rancho Grande and is for ferry (one hour) and *lancha* service (25 minutes) to Santiago Atitlán. Expect to pay anywhere between $1.50 and $3 for the ride. Locals pay less than visitors. Ask around for the time of the last boat back to Pana from the outlying villages. Some may be as early as 7:30pm. **Lake tours** ($12, full day) from Pana visiting San Pedro and Santiago also leave from the second pier and can be booked at any travel agency.

Tuk-tuks can get you anywhere in town for about $0.75. For longer trips to surrounding villages, such as Santa Catarina Palopó, expect to pay about $4 for the 20-minute ride.

SANTA CATARINA PALOPÓ

Five kilometers east of Panajachel is the quaint lakeside village of Santa Catarina Palopó, a collection of adobe houses with tin and thatched roofs built into the surrounding hillsides. The streets near the church and the road leading to the lakeside are excellent places to pick up some of the colorful textiles and handicrafts produced here. Many of the villagers still sport the traditional attire.

As elsewhere on Lake Atitlán, many well-to-do Guatemalans (and increasingly, foreigners) have bought property and built houses on the slopes just outside of town.

Accommodations and Food

Santa Catarina is the site of a few moderate to high-end hotels offering some of the lake's best accommodations. On the road between Panajachel and Santa Catarina, and under the same ownership as Antigua's Mesón Panza Verde, **Casa B'alam Ya** (tel. 7832-2925, www.panzaverde.com/villasbalamya, $150-350 d) encompasses four villas with one or two bedrooms and amenities such as a hot tub, spacious kitchen, and decks fronting the lake. There are kayaks for guests' use. You can arrange for a local chef to cook your meals or have the kitchen stocked with everything you need to cook your own. Just off the street leading from town to the lakeshore, the 36-room **Villa Santa Catarina** (tel. 7762-1291 or 7762-2827, www.villasdeguatemala.com, $68-104 d) has attractive rooms and junior suites with gorgeous lake views, tile floors, TV, hot-water private bathrooms, telephones, and some rooms with ceiling fans. There are lovely antique furnishings throughout the property, a swimming pool, and **Restaurante Las Playas** (7am-10pm daily, $5-10), serving Guatemalan and international dishes in an attractive dining room overlooking the swimming pool. Along the road leading out of town toward neighboring San Antonio Palopó, **Tzam Poc Resort** (tel. 7762-2680, www.atitlanresort.com, $85-170 d) has accommodations varying from standard and deluxe rooms in Mediterranean-style, thatched-roof villas to an entire, fully furnished villa for $400-1,000 per night. The beautiful rooms are nicely decorated. The resort's centerpiece is an exquisite infinity-edge swimming pool overlooking the lake below. There are tropical gardens throughout and some outrageous lake views. Other amenities include a tropical lounge, sauna, and solarium. ★ **La Casa Colibri** (Km 6.7 Via Rural a San Antonio Palopó, Entrada a Tzampoc Casa #4, tel. 5353-5823, www.lacasacolibri.com, $395-595 per night) is also among the area's fabulous villa offerings. The five-bedroom property is built in Mediterranean style with lovely tropical touches that include thatch-roof terraces, bamboo accent walls, and typical Guatemalan decor. Rooms have big wooden beds and awe-inspiring views of the lake and volcanoes. Amenities include a wooden-decked swimming pool, plenty of sun-lit patio space, a hammock deck, wireless Internet, flat-screen TVs, and a DVD player. A private chef is available at additional cost, though the room rate includes a light breakfast. For budget accommodations check out **Orion's Garden** (oriongarden@outlook.com, $35 d), where there are simple but attractive lakefront cabins and plenty of outdoor activities to keep you busy. It's near the main dock.

The most splendid of Santa Catarina's lakeside accommodations is ★ **Casa Palopó** (Km. 6.8 Carretera a San Antonio Palopó, tel. 7762-2270, www.casapalopo.com, $140-447 d), with rooms housed in a beautiful colonial-style villa featuring floor-to-ceiling windows with magnificent lake views. The rooms and common areas are loaded with antiques, brightly painted walls, exquisite furnishings, and wonderful extras such as Italian cotton sheets and L'Occitane bathroom products. There's also a wooden-decked swimming pool overlooking the lake. Farther up the hill is the even more alluring **Villa Palopó**, decorated with a tasteful mix of African tribal relics and Indonesian hardwood furnishings. There are hardwood floors and phenomenal lake views from each of the two suites ($206-447 d). You can rent the whole villa for $803-1,368, depending on

a suite at Casa Palopó in Santa Catarina Palopó

the season. The villa has its own lap pool, also overlooking the lake, and butler service.

Casa Palopó's restaurant, **6.8 Palopó,** is a bit on the expensive side ($15-30 for a typical meal), but the food is certainly some of the best you'll find on the shores of Lake Atitlán, with spectacular lake views from an airy terrace. If you're not staying there, it makes a great place to stop for a drink and watch the sunset or enjoy a romantic candlelit dinner.

SANTA CRUZ LA LAGUNA

West of Panajachel and accessible only by boat is the quiet village of Santa Cruz La Laguna, more commonly referred to simply as "Santa Cruz." There are a number of good accommodations here with a range of prices for every budget. It's understandably extremely popular with the backpacker crowd.

Recreation

Housed inside the Iguana Perdida lodge, **ATI Divers** (www.atidivers.com) is a PADI-certified **scuba diving** operation offering Altitude Specialty certifications for $90, fun dives for $35, or PADI open-water certifications for $240. Due to altitudinal pressure changes and the lake's location at just over 1,500 meters above sea level, you'll have to spend at least one night at lake altitude before your first dive to avoid decompression sickness. The lake offers a unique diving experience, including the chance to see underwater volcanic rock formations and a fault line where you can see and feel hot volcanic mud.

Los Elementos Adventure Center (tel. 5359-8328, www.kayakguatemala.com) provides myriad recreational options, including volcano climbs, a round-the-lake kayak trip, cliff jumping, and rock climbing using local guides. Proceeds from Los Elementos support nonprofit Amigos de Santa Cruz, focused on improving the nutrition and education of the local Maya. For utter relaxation and wonderful lakeside massages, check out their **Los Elementos Day Spa** (tel. 4095-3751).

Locally guided tours are also offered by

Tours Atitlan (tel. 5355-8849, www.tours-atitlan.com). Owned by a young Mayan couple, tours encompass the lake area and even involve treks to such far-away locales as the Ixil Triangle.

Options for exploring on your own include **hikes** up the hill to the village proper (20 minutes) to see the town church in addition to hiking along a trail skirting the lakeshore to the neighboring village of Jaibalito (45 minutes) or San Marcos (three hours).

Accommodations and Food

The first property you'll come across, on the outskirts of town, is ★ **La Fortuna at Atitlán** (Patsisotz Bay, between Santa Cruz and Panajachel, tel. 5203-1033, www.lafortunaatitlan.com, $79-123 d). It's also one of my new favorites thanks to its friendly Canadian ownership and wonderful design elements dripping with Asian influences (attesting to the owners' extensive travels on that continent). There are smaller petite bungalows and larger suites. All rooms have nice outdoor patios and outdoor showers, along with a loft that varies in size. The larger suites come with outdoor soaking tubs, bathrobes, and a selection of fruits and nuts in the room. The property does a fine job of being ecofriendly, incorporating would-be waste products into its design. Nice extras include an outdoor hot tub overlooking the lake, a wine cellar, and a cozy bar/dining area. It's all set on the grounds of a former coffee farm which is now a rather large private nature preserve. They grow their own coffee, and the food served is absolutely delicious.

Santa Cruz's original lakeside hotel, **El Arca de Noé** (tel. 4683-9015 or 5376-2849, www.hotelarcadenoeatitlan.com, $21-45 d) is still going strong. The delightful lodge has 10 rooms, half of them with private bathrooms. Three of the rooms are lovely stone-and-wood cottages. All of the rooms are rustic but nicely decorated with Guatemalan fabrics. Delicious breakfasts and lunches are served à la carte. Guests are treated to delicious meals consisting of Guatemalan and European specialties for around $10 (dinner), served family-style. The lodge is solar-powered.

Right next door is one of Guatemala's quintessential backpacker hideaways, **La Iguana Perdida** (tel. 5706-4117 or 7762-2621, www.laiguanaperdida.com, from $6 pp in dorms to $43 d with private bath), which has recently added some very attractive private rooms for those of us who have gotten just a bit older. There are three dormitories with a total of 22 beds and rooms with or without private bathrooms. Electricity was finally installed after years of making do without it, and I am happy to report that now hot showers and Internet access are available. Still, the electricity can be spotty, as in many lakeside communities, and kerosene lamps are on hand to provide agreeable ambient lighting after dark. Breakfast and lunch are served 8am-3pm, featuring delicious sandwiches, salads, crepes, and other yummy dishes prepared by a staff of indigenous women. Dinner is a family-style affair and is a three-course spread, including soup and homemade bread, a main course, and dessert. Vegetarian options are always available. The dinner atmosphere is lively, and it makes a great place to meet fellow travelers. The crowd is decidedly young. In addition to scuba diving, there are

Spanish lessons available for $160 per week with dorm accommodations (upgrades available), kayak and snorkeling equipment for rent, waterskiing, yoga, spa services, and tons of board games. On Saturdays, there's a fun dress-up barbecue party where you can eat chicken or veggie burgers and jam to a guitar and drums. If you get bored here, you should probably check your pulse.

Farther along the lakeshore heading back east toward Panajachel is **La Casa Rosa** (tel. 5803-2531, www.atitlanlacasarosa.com, $26-55 d), with modern, clean, and comfortable rooms with shared or private hot-water baths in addition to two suites housed in bungalows. An apartment with kitchen is available for rent for $250 per week. There are homemade jams and bread in addition to Guatemalan, international, and vegetarian dishes served in the main floor dining room. A wonderful more recent addition is that of a beautiful, airy wooden deck lounge overlooking the lake.

You might stumble upon a few private villas as you make your way farther east a few hundred meters to the lovely, American-owned ★ **Villa Sumaya** (tel. 4026-1390 or 4026-1455, www.villasumaya.com, $70-145

La Fortuna at Atitlán in Santa Cruz La Laguna

d). There are 19 beautiful rooms, all named after jungle animals and decorated with elements of Mayan and Asian style. Some are housed in a thatched-roof complex; others are farther up the hill in separate cabins. All of the spacious rooms have private hot-water bathrooms, warm Guatemalan wool blankets, and patios with furniture and lovely hammocks. The rooms up the hill have mosquito netting and larger bathrooms with tubs, one of which is impressively built into the side of the mountain with lava rock adorning the semi-outdoor shower. There's an impressive, hardwood-floor and thatched-roof yoga center, which is often booked months in advance by groups from the United States. Other amenities include a massage parlor, library, and two hot tubs. The restaurant here is correspondingly excellent, consisting of vegetarian selections as well as fish, meat, and chicken dishes prepared by two talented chefs. Delicious baked goods are also produced daily. Breakfast and lunch are à la carte. Dinner is a set menu served family-style. The outdoor café is housed in a pretty wooden patio overlooking the lake.

★ **Laguna Lodge** (tel. 7823-2529, www.lagunalodgeatitlan.com, $240-370 d), is also in this neck of the woods, built in ecofriendly style on the lakeshore on its very own 100-acre nature preserve. The beautiful though somewhat dark suites feature Guatemalan hardwoods and adobe walls, along with solar-heated showers and low-flow toilets. The Zotz Restaurant and Lava Bar have phenomenal lake views and feature a delightful array of vegetarian dishes ($35 set menu). A trail winds through the property's nature preserve and includes a lookout high atop a steep hill. There are several common areas at the lodge where you can laze the day away in a hammock or read a book. You can also enjoy a relaxing dip in a hot tub or sweat away your cares in a Mayan sauna. It was named one of the Top 25 Eco-lodges in the World by *National Geographic Traveler* in 2013.

From the main dock in Santa Cruz, heading west to Jaibalito, it's 400 meters to the private dock of ★ **Islaverde Hotel** (tel. 5760-2648 or 7823-5952, www.islaverde-atitlan.com, $43-55 d), with 11 comfortable, wooden A-frame cabins with wonderful lake views and shared or private bath. Two larger cabins ($75-125) with six beds apiece can accommodate families or groups. There are pretty gardens with plumeria flowers, a beautiful wooden deck, a restaurant, a lounge with books and games to keep you entertained in addition to a sauna, hot tub, and meditation and massage platform. All of the food served at the lodge is fresh and well prepared. The expanded beach includes a sitting area. The property is the culmination of 12 years of travel by a young Spanish and British couple, who have put many of the ideas found along the road into this splendid place they see less like a hotel and more like a garden of delights. It's all beautifully decorated, and there are plenty of places to hang out and enjoy the relaxing atmosphere.

Getting There

Santa Cruz is reached exclusively by boat. Boats leave from the Tzanjuyú dock at the end of Calle del Embarcadero in Panajachel. For the intrepid, there's a footpath from the departmental capital of Sololá.

JAIBALITO

West along the shoreline from Santa Cruz is the village of Jaibalito, which is even smaller than Santa Cruz and also accessible only by boat or foot trail. A number of lodges have sprouted here in recent years, taking advantage of the remote location to offer a comfortable stay in a quiet environment.

Accommodations and Food

Wildly popular, ★ **La Casa del Mundo** (tel. 5218-5332, www.lacasadelmundo.com, $37-83 d) is a charming inn built into the side of a rocky cliff. There are rooms with shared or private bathrooms, all housed in wonderful stone cottages with outrageous lake views and decorated with tasteful Guatemalan accents. There's excellent swimming in a rocky cove where the water is an exquisite shade of emerald. There are kayaks for rent ($4-7), and mountain biking can be arranged via Antigua-based Old Town Outfitters with at least two days' notice. The trail to Santa Cruz or San Marcos passes right outside the lodge's back door. Meals are served at set times in a small dining room on the ground floor of the main house. Dinner is served family-style and costs $13. The service here is excellent, and the Guatemalan American owners are very friendly. In the village proper and away from the lake, **Vulcano Lodge** (tel. 5744-0620, www.vulcanolodge.com, $45-90 d, including continental breakfast) is a Norwegian-owned lodge with five guest rooms, all smartly decorated and featuring private baths. The largest is a family-size villa, which sleeps five and has a living room, kitchen, and a nice big terrace with lake views. The restaurant serves tasty meals for breakfast and lunch, with dinner ($13 for four courses) served family-style. Many of the fresh ingredients, including bananas, avocados, and limes, come right from the on-site garden plot. Jaibalito's budget accommodations are at **Posada Jaibalito** (tel. 5192-4334, www.posadajaibalito.com, dorms $4.50 pp with use of kitchen, $12 d with private bath and kitchen), offering basic but pleasant rooms located in the heart of the village.

For utterly delectable food, refreshing cocktails, and killer lake views from its infinity-edge swimming pool, head to ★ **Club Ven Acá** (tel. 5122-6047, www.clubvenaca.com, 11am-5pm Wed.-Sun., $5-15). The fun staff will keep you entertained and fill your belly with delicious fish tacos, burgers, salads, barbecue sandwiches, and steaks. Try the signature beverage, the Jaibalito Mojito, made with basil instead of mint leaves. The pool has a swim-up bar.

TZUNUNÁ

West along the shore, the next village is Tzununá, home to the agreeable **Lomas de Tzununá** (tel. 5201-8272 or 5206-6215, www.lomasdetzununa.com, $90 d including

breakfast and tax), high atop a steep hill. You can call the lodge for a pickup from the hotel's pier or make the 100-meter trek up the slope. Run by a Belgian Uruguayan couple who discovered Guatemala while working with the United Nations, the lodge features 10 lovely stone-and-wood bungalows with tile floors and lake views greatly enhanced by their sheer height above the water. Amenities include Internet, a lap pool, library, board games, and a crafts shop. Meals are served alfresco on a wooden patio with superb lake views. Just the views of the volcanoes reflected in the placid swimming pool high above the lake are worth the price of admission. A more recent addition is **Maya Moon Lodge** (tel. 5533-2433, www.mayamoonlodgeatitlan.com, $12 pp to $70 d), which makes a great place to stay for those wanting seclusion in a scenic setting at a very affordable price. It's still a work in progress (there was construction taking place next to the restaurant during my visit), but it's shaping up to be a lovely property. The staff and

There are lovely lake views from Maya Moon Lodge in Tzununá.

owners are friendly and fun. The small on-site restaurant overlooks the water.

Tzununá is also home to **Atitlán Organics** (www.atitlanorganics.com), a large working organic farm. Its 2.2 acres are a fascinating study into the loss of precious topsoil in the Atitlán basin (and much of highland Guatemala) through outmoded corn-based agriculture, and the methods available for the recovery of fertile, arable land using sustainable practices. Weekly tours of the farm are available on Friday mornings (prior notice required) for $13 per person. It includes a waterfall hike and farm-to-table lunch. Surplus food is sold at the farm's weekly market activities in Santa Cruz, San Marcos, and Jaibalito. Atitlán Organics also offers workshops aimed at educating travelers in aspects of permaculture and sustainable living.

SAN MARCOS LA LAGUNA

San Marcos is a unique lake town in that it harbors a strangely esoteric vibe, aided by its prominence as Guatemala's New Age center. It's about a three-hour walk from Santa Cruz and two hours from San Pedro. Most visitors arrive at a boat dock beside Posada Schumann, though boats stop first at the main dock a few hundred meters east. A road runs beside the lodge into town, which together with a parallel street 100 meters west, form the main pedestrian arteries. When I first started coming to San Marcos, it was a dusty, makeshift, hybrid Maya-gringo village, complete with dirt paths. Nowadays, the main path into town from the Posada Schumann dock has been paved, and the whole place feels a lot cleaner and better organized.

Sights and Recreation

Among the spiritually inclined attractions is **Las Pirámides** (tel. 5202-4168 or 5205-7302, www.laspiramidesdelka.com), offering a variety of New Age alternative psychology courses, including a one-month "moon course" beginning with the full moon and culminating in a full week of fasting and silence.

With completion of the moon course there's further study, including a three-month sun course, featuring elements of Kabbalah, tarot reading, and lucid dreaming. Nonstudents can join in on hatha yoga sessions, classes on metaphysics, and meditation techniques. Sessions range $5-13. To get here, follow the path up the hill past Posada Schumann and then turn left along the signed pathway. It's about 200 meters on your left.

Back toward Posada Schumann is **San Marcos Holistic Cottage** (www.sanmholisticcottage.com, 10am-5pm Mon.-Sat.), offering a wide assortment of massages and holistic therapies. There are training courses in Reiki, shiatsu, massage, reflexology, and Bach flower remedies. English, Spanish, German, and French are spoken. A typical treatment costs $33.

It's not recommended, but you can **hike** from San Marcos east to Tzununá and Jaibalito. Check on the safety situation with local sources, as hiker robberies between here and Tzununá have been frequent in the past. Going west to Santa Clara La Laguna is a safer bet. If you do go, leave your valuables behind. Until recently, the waters here were excellent for swimming, when the lake was nice and clean. In the aftermath of Atitlán's recent cyanobacteria algal blooms, you may be hard-pressed to find a decent place to swim.

Kayaks are available for rent next door to the Lush Apartments and cost $4 per hour. The owners of **Tul y Sol restaurant** (tel. 5293-7997) can arrange **paragliding.**

Accommodations

Posada Schumann (tel. 5202-2216, $15-50 d) is the first place you'll come across if, like most people, you arrive into town at its dock. Most of the comfortable, well-furnished, and tastefully decorated rooms are housed in quaint stone-and-mortar cottages. An excellent value, room number 12 is a deluxe second-floor wooden bungalow ($25-36 d, depending on season) with its own deck. Numbers 8 and 10 have awesome volcano and lake views. The restaurant overlooking

the main street up from the dock at San Marcos La Laguna

the well-tended gardens serves sandwiches, smoothies, and Guatemalan fare for breakfast and lunch, though the service can be slow.

West along the lakeshore past Las Pirámides, ★ **Lush Apartments** (Formerly Aaculaax, tel. 4818-4258, www.lushatitlan.com, $15-65 d standard rooms, $100-150 d suites) is a work of art constructed out of recycled building materials, including glass, carved pumice stones, and colorful papier-mâché. Each of the rooms is unique, though all have private bathrooms with composting toilets and lovely terraces. There are five budget rooms costing $15 per person available on a first-come, first-served basis. The rooms are literally built around the rocks of the surrounding hillsides, which are prominently displayed in the architecture of some of the suites. The glasswork in evidence throughout the property is simply delicious, as is the lush landscaping. There's a small on-site store for basic sundries, laundry service, and a lending library.

The footpath continues farther west to

Hotel Jinava (tel. 5299-3311 or 5248-3052, www.hoteljinava.com, $22-40 d), on the edge of town right on the lake in a quiet bay with its own beach. The five rooms are housed in Spanish-style whitewashed, tiled-roof villas with private terraces and have private or shared bathroom and attractive decor with tile floors and colorful textiles. The restaurant serves decent meals, including Thai, Indian, Mexican, Greek, Italian, and Guatemalan dishes. There's also a full bar.

Up the path from Posada Schumann into the main part of town is **Posada del Bosque Encantado** (tel. 5208-5334, www.hotelposadaencantado.com, $20 d), with rooms housed in a charming adobe structure and surrounded by tranquil gardens. The rooms have Guatemalan furnishings and vaulted ceilings; some have an extra bed on a second floor loft.

In the heart of the tourist area is **Hotel y Restaurante Paco Real** (tel. 4688-3715, www.pacorealatitlan.com, $17-25 d), with simple but comfortable rooms and shared or private bath. The wooden, thatched-roof cabanas include Guatemalan furnishings and woven reed floor mats in a peaceful garden setting. There's a restaurant and bar on the premises where the highlights include Mexican dishes, seafood, and curried pineapple chicken. The town's newest accommodations are by the lakeshore near the town's easternmost dock. **El Dragon** (tel. 4147-7787, www.eldragonhotel.com) has comfortable rooms with attractive Guatemalan decor at a reasonable price.

Food

Among the decent eats in San Marcos is ★ **Fe** (tel. 3009-5537, 7:30am-midnight daily, $8-20), where you can feast on curries, pastas, meat, and fish dishes in a pleasant garden atmosphere accented with Guatemalan textiles. Enjoying a wonderful lakeside location west of Posada Schumann is French-owned **Tul y Sol** (tel. 5293-7997, www.eltulysolatitlan.jimdo.com, all meals daily) offering decent sandwiches served on thick slices of bread, grilled fish, and pasta. Try the homemade chocolate truffles for dessert. Up the path toward town from Posada Schumann, **Il Giardino** (tel. 7804-0186, 4pm-midnight Thurs.-Sun., $4-13) serves deliciously fresh, mostly vegetarian fare in a tranquil garden setting. Another good vegan/vegetarian option has moved up the hill from its former lakeside location. **Moonfish Cafe** (Calle Principal, tel. 5382-6312, 7:30am-8pm daily) serves large portions of tasty, locally grown organic food. I like their falafel.

Heading into the town center from the lakeshore and crossing the main road through town, you'll find ★ **Blind Lemon's** (tel. 5502-4450, www.blindlemons.com, 11am-10pm Mon.-Sat., $5-15), inspired by blues musician Lemon Jefferson and housed in a pleasant colonial-style courtyard. Tasty burgers, pizzas, steaks, chicken, and pasta are on the menu. There's live blues on Fridays starting at 8pm (or whenever friendly owner Carlos wants to play for you), and movies are shown on a big screen some nights. Also in this part of town (known as Barrio 3) is ★ **The Mojito House** (tel. 4069-2468, www.themojitohouse.com, 5pm-midnight Tues.-Sat., $5-15), where you'll find its namesake cocktail and tasty menu items that include goat cheese Waldorf salad, mango cilantro chicken, and fire-grilled filet mignon. The owners are in the process of building a green house and organic garden to supply not only their needs but also those of the local community.

On the lakeshore next to the soccer field, **El Dragon** (tel. 4147-7787, www.eldragonhotel.com) is a popular gathering place for its location and tasty food. You can hang out and enjoy drinks on the property's small sandy beach or have a meal on the covered patio overlooking the lake. The key lime pie is a town favorite.

Information and Services

Casa Verde Tours (tel. 5837-9092 or 7721-8344, www.casaverdetours.com), of San Pedro fame, also has an office in San Marcos and can arrange transport and local hikes. They are located at the top of the hill along the trail that leads straight into town from Posada Schumann. Another option is the newly formed **Jóvenes Mayas** (tel. 5787-7728), composed of local community guides offering English/Spanish guided hikes to local waterfalls, San Pedro, and the Pakachelaj forest reserve. They are on the path into town from Posada Schumann, near Posada del Bosque Encantado.

There are no banks or ATMs in San Marcos.

SAN JUAN LA LAGUNA

Serene San Juan La Laguna is a relative late-comer to the tourism scene and makes a good stop if you'd like to see a fairly sizable lakeside village that remains largely untouched by international tourism. It's accessible by boat or via a road that branches off from the Pan-American Highway, subsequently twisting and turning down the surrounding mountainside. If you'd like to stay here, **Uxlabil Ecohotel** (tel. 2366-9555, www.uxlabil.com, $48-72 d) has comfortable, tastefully rustic rooms housed in a large building overlooking the lake. There's a large dock for swimming among plentiful grass reeds dotting the lakeshore here as well as a sauna, whirlpool tub, kayaks for rent, and horseback riding available on request. A newer budget option is **Pa Muelle** (next to the municipal market, tel. 4141-0820, hotelpamuelle@turbonett.com, $13 d) with simple but attractive and clean rooms in a motel-style property with lake views. It's locally owned and operated.

If wine and cheese is your bag (like mine), you'll love **El Artesano Wine & Cheese Restaurant** (tel. 4555-4773, Tues.-Fri. lunch only). Owned by a Guatemalan couple with Swiss roots, the restaurant serves a curated collection of artisanal cheeses gathered from local farms throughout the Guatemalan highlands. The cheeses are served with cured meats, nuts, and dried fruits and paired with a fine selection of wines. As is often the case in Guatemala, you'll find it's a hidden gem in a very unlikely location. It's up the street from the main dock. Make the first right and follow the signs for about five minutes to this culinary oasis. *Tuk-tuk* drivers all know where it is.

SAN PEDRO LA LAGUNA

On the lake's southwest corner and accessible by frequent boats or road, San Pedro is second in popularity only to Panajachel and has a hip international atmosphere. The place has grown by leaps and bounds, from a once-scruffy village to a rather pleasant lakeside town with a solid international presence. You'll see signs in English, Spanish, French, and even Hebrew as you walk along the paths winding through town. The atmosphere in San Pedro embraces a simpler state of being, and you'll have no trouble slowing down to the local pace of life amidst the serene tropical foliage.

The town flanks the northern slopes of San Pedro Volcano, a popular climb for which the town is ideally suited as a base. It has increasingly become home to a number of language schools, some of dubious quality, collectively offering some of Guatemala's least expensive tuition rates. While it was originally a

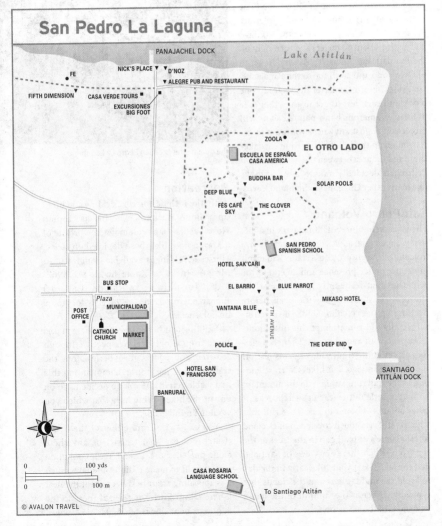

San Pedro La Laguna

PANAJACHEL DOCK

Lake Atitlán

NICK'S PLACE ▼ ▼ D'NOZ

FE ●

▼ ALEGRE PUB AND RESTAURANT

FIFTH DIMENSION ▼   CASA VERDE TOURS ■ ■

EXCURSIONES
BIG FOOT

ZOOLA ●

ESCUELA DE ESPAÑOL
CASA AMERICA

EL OTRO LADO

BUDDHA BAR

SOLAR POOLS ●

DEEP BLUE ▼

FÉS CAFÉ ▼ ■ THE CLOVER
SKY

SAN PEDRO
SPANISH SCHOOL

HOTEL SAK'CARI ▼

BUS STOP ■

EL BARRIO ▼ ▼ BLUE PARROT

Plaza

MIKASO HOTEL ●

POST
OFFICE ■

MUNICIPALIDAD

VANTANA BLUE ▼

7TH AVENUE

CATHOLIC
CHURCH   MARKET

POLICE ■

THE DEEP END ▼

HOTEL SAN
FRANCISCO ●

SANTIAGO
ATITLÁN DOCK

BANRURAL

0   100 yds

0   100 m

CASA ROSARIA
LANGUAGE SCHOOL

To Santiago Atitán

© AVALON TRAVEL

backpacker Shangri-La, there have been recent additions to the hotel infrastructure, making for suitable accommodations to house the non-backpacker crowd.

The bulk of the tourist hotels and services are between two docks, on the southeast and northwest sides of town, and in the areas adjacent to them. The first one serves boats to/from Panajachel and the rest of the lake towns; the other is for boats to Santiago Atitlán. They are about one kilometer apart. The area between them is known as El Otro Lado (The Other Side). Street numbers and names are not generally in use here. From the Santiago dock, go up about 50 meters and turn right on the footpath known as 7th Avenue to get to El Otro Lado and continue to the Panajachel boat dock. From the latter dock, go up one block and turn left to get to the other side of town. Numerous hand-painted signs will direct you almost anywhere you want to go. As you go up the hill, further from the lakeshore and the area between the two docks, San Pedro gets decidedly more Maya and looks like many other Guatemalan highland towns.

San Pedro Volcano

The volcano became a national park in 2006, so it is hoped that, as was the case with Pacaya Volcano, its newly protected status will result in greater police presence and an end to the robberies that frequently happen near the summit. For now, check with locals before heading up the volcano. Under no circumstances should you attempt this hike alone. Always go with a local guide. There is a visitors center at the trailhead, which is just off the road to Santiago. The hike is fairly strenuous, as the trail runs straight up the mountain with very little in the way of switchbacks. It takes about 4-5 hours to reach the summit, which is still very much covered in thick cloud forest. There's a small gap in the trees at the top from which there are views of Santiago and the lake. Start your hike early in the day to avoid the midday heat and the clouds that typically gather at the summit of the lake's volcanoes in the afternoon.

the quaint streets of San Pedro La Laguna

Recreation

Activities include horseback riding and hikes up a mountain known locally as "Indian Nose," as its shape resembles the profile of a Mayan nose like those depicted on stelae. Horseback riding is available from **Rancho Moisés** (next to Zoola hotel, tel. 5967-3235). **Tornado's Excursions** (Calle del Embarcadero, tel. 5633-3424) also does tours on horseback.

Walking to other villages from here makes sense from a logistical perspective, though too-frequent reports of robberies along the trails prevent me from recommending this as a viable activity. If you do decide to go on any of the hikes, bring only that which you wouldn't mind losing.

You can swim from either of the docks (watch out for boat traffic) or anywhere along the lakeshore, though recent pollution concerns have made a dip in the lake much less appealing. Your best bet to beat the heat is **The Deep End Bar & Pool** (next to the Santiago boat dock, tel. 5304-7357, www.

thedeependbar.com, 11am-dusk daily), where it costs $2.50 to swim (children $1.25) in a pleasant, clean swimming pool surrounded by tropical plants and mural art. A lively bar keeps things hopping. There's a weekly bocce ball tournament and southern-style barbecue on Saturdays starting at 1pm and costing about $8.

If you like your water bathtub-warm, you have at least two options for soaking in hot tubs. Both places feature concrete tubs filled with water that is solar-heated in black plastic tubing and pumped into reservoirs of various sizes. (You'll need to call ahead or visit with at least one hour's prior notice so they can draw the bath.) It costs $7 for one person, but you can split the cost with others sharing the same pool. The first of these, **Solar Pools** (7a Avenida 2-22, Zona 2, tel. 5770-5119, solarpools.blogspot.com, 8am-11pm daily), is on the main strip of El Otro Lado. Of the two, Solar Pools holds the slight edge in landscaping, and it has an adjacent snack bar, Tzan Saqarib'al, serving light fare. You can reserve by phone. Closer to the lakeshore and a short walk down a side path is **Los Termales** (8:30am-11:45pm daily), the town's self-proclaimed original hot tub operation. Its biggest draw is the sylvan lakeside setting. They prefer that you pre-book your tub in person.

Guide Companies

Excursiones Big Foot (tel. 7721-8202), on the main drag as you come up the hill from the Panajachel dock and turn left, is San Pedro's most reliable outfitter and has been in operation since 1995. It offers trips to San Pedro Volcano with knowledgeable guides and security for $14, including park admission. Big Foot can also guide you to Indian Nose with a four-person minimum for $5 pp. **Casa Verde Tours** (tel. 5837-9092 or 7721-8344, www.casaverdetours.com) just down the street from the Panajachel boat dock, is another recommended outfitter. They also have a variety of daily shuttle departures. **Tornado's Excursions** (Calle del Embarcadero, tel. 5633-3424) rounds out the list of possibilities.

Entertainment

San Pedro is a lively town harboring several bars where the party goes on until about 1am.

Just to the left of the dock and directly above Nick's Place, **D'Noz** is a lively bar with good food, including baguettes and croissants,

Lake Atitlán as seen from San Pedro La Laguna

where movies are shown nightly. In the center of town between the two docks, the ever-popular **Buddha Bar**, housed in a three-level building with a cool Asian atmosphere, has pool tables and dartboards on the first floor. The town's neighborhood bar is **El Barrio** (7th Ave., 5pm-1am daily) in the heart of the tourist zone. They have $2 mojitos all day every day. Right in the heart of the tourist area is **Fe's Sky Café**, a second-floor patio bar with happy hour from 5pm-7pm.

Accommodations

For budget accommodations, your best bet is **Fe** (tel. 5461-6625, www.hostelfe.com, $8 pp or $20 d including breakfast), where there are dorm beds and private rooms in a centric location overlooking the lakeshore near the Panajachel dock. It's a self-proclaimed party hostel and makes no apologies. Among the entertainment options is a dry season booze cruise on the lake Wednesday afternoons for $7.

Also on the list of the town's hip locales is **Zoola** (tel. 5847-4857 or 5534-3111, agmon2003@yahoo.com, $6 dorms, $15 d with private bath), found along the trail heading into El Otro Lado. It has eight rooms, half with private bathroom, and dorm beds. There is a movie lounge, book exchange, purified water from its own well, and a massage room, but the crowning achievement is the beautiful canvas-roof hammock lounge with comfortable pillows on woven floor mats. A heated swimming pool next to the lake is the latest addition. **Hotel Sak'cari** (7a Avenida 2-12 Zona 2, tel. 7721-8096, www.hotel-sakcari. com, $16 d) feels a bit like a motel, though the rooms on the second floor have nice lake views with hammocks out front. All rooms have a private bathroom. Furnished apartments were recently added to the mix. They've also added a swimming pool and a grassy area with hammocks.

The nicest place in town is ★ **Mikaso Hotel** (tel. 7721-8232, www.mikasohotel. com, $8 pp in dorm, $25-45 d) with 11 rooms and a dormitory housed in an attractive Spanish neocolonial-style building

fronting the lakeshore. Rooms have tile bathrooms, ceiling fans, tile floors, and tasteful decor. The rooftop restaurant here is also quite smart, serving Mediterranean food and yummy brick oven pizza. It's open 7am-10pm and has a pleasant patio overlooking San Pedro Volcano and the lake. The hotel also has a hot tub for guests' use.

Food

As you come up from the Panajachel boat dock, the first place worth mentioning is one block on the left as you head up the street into town. **Alegre Pub and Restaurant** (tel. 7721-8100, 5pm-1am Mon., 9am-1am Tues.-Sat., 9am-11pm Sun.) serves authentic pub grub, including Indian curry, Cajun fare, chili, baked potatoes, and fish 'n' chips. There's a nice rooftop patio area to take in the view of the street below.

Up the street from the Panajachel dock, if you make the first right, the first place of note is **Fe** (tel. 5273-6688, 7am-11pm daily, www. hostelfe.com, $4-7), popular for its wonderful wooden deck fronting the lake and a varied menu that includes wood-fired pizzas. Across the street, **The Fifth Dimension** (tel. 4965-2438, 10am-4:30pm Tues.-Sat., 6pm-10:30pm Sun., $3-9) is a vegetarian restaurant serving delicious smoothies, veggie burgers, homemade ginger ale, and flat bread pizzas. I'll pass on the vegemite, though. It's set on a pleasant patio overlooking the lake. Sunday is movie night.

There are a number of good eateries in the part of town inland between the two docks known as El Otro Lado. Among them is **The Buddha** (tel. 4466-3721, www.thebuddha-aguatemala.com, noon-1am daily, $5-10), housed in a three-level building with a pool table and darts on the first floor, a dining area and chill-out lounge on the second floor, and a rooftop terrace bar. The restaurant serves authentic Asian and Guatemalan fusion cuisine with a variety of rice, noodle, and curry dishes, sushi, soups, wraps, and tasty desserts at reasonable prices. There's a hookah water pipe smoking lounge.

San Pedro isn't without a decent chip shop to satisfy British palates. **Deep Blue Fish & Chips** (tel. 5984-0216, $4-6) serves up the real deal. Down the street, **The Clover** (7th Ave., tel. 4155-6654, 8:30am-midnight daily, $4-7) is a restaurant and bar on a nice patio overlooking the lake serving savory sandwiches and Pan-Asian inspired dishes such as scrumptious mango curry.

Ventana Blue (7th Avenue 1-21 Zona 2, tel. 5284-2406 or 4050-0500, 6pm-10pm Tues.-Sun.) features a small outdoor dining room painted in red hues and prides itself on creative Asian/Guatemalan cuisine. There are only a handful of tables in this tiny hidden gem, so get there early or call ahead. **Café La Puerta** (tel. 5098-1272, www.cafelapuerta. com) was once on the lakeside but has now moved uphill and attached itself to San Pedro Spanish School. The service seems to have gone with the move, though it's good for light meals *if* you can flag someone down. By contrast, the service at ★ **Blue Parrot Bar & Grill** (tel. 4106-5307, open seasonally 8am-10pm daily, $4-8) is phenomenal. They'll take good care of you while you imbibe well-crafted cocktails and North American favorites like mouthwatering biscuits with sausage, gravy, and eggs, tasty burgers, Philly cheesesteaks, nachos, and mozzarella sticks. You know; the healthy stuff. Its owners are the brains behind San Pedro's wildly successful **Smokin' Joe's BBQ** (noon-4pm Sun. at Café Chuasinayi, down the street from Mikaso Hotel). The weekly feast includes healthy favorites like baby back and spare ribs, bacon-wrapped steaks, mac & cheese, and potato salad. Get there early!

Information and Services

There's a **Banrural** (with ATM) in the heart of town, reached by heading straight up the street from the Panajachel dock for about a kilometer. You'll pass the town market on your right, two blocks before the bank, which will be on your left. From the Santiago dock, head up the street and turn left at the market. There's also an ATM just off the Panajachel dock.

For Internet and phone calls, **Casa Verde Tours** (tel. 5837-9092 or 7721-8344, www. casaverdetours.com) is your all-in-one stop for going online, laundry, international calls, and full-service travel agency including shuttle buses to Antigua, Guatemala City, and Xela. Recommended language schools include the following: **Casa Rosario** (Canton Sanjay, tel. 7613-6401, www.casarosario.com) and **Corazón Maya** (first left up the street from Santiago dock, tel. 7721-8160, corazonmaya. com). In the El Otro Lado sector between the two docks are **Mayab' Spanish School** (tel. 5979-7994, www.mayabspanishschool.com) and **San Pedro Spanish School** (tel. 5966-2072, www.sanpedrospanishschool.org).

Getting There

There are boats every half hour to Santiago (30 minutes, $2.50) from the dock at the northwest part of town starting at 6am. *Lanchas* also leave throughout the day for the lakeshore villages of San Marcos ($1.50), Jaibalito ($2), Santa Cruz ($2.50), and Panajachel ($3). All leave from the dock on the southeast side of town. The last boat going in either direction usually leaves around 5pm.

There are buses to Quetzaltenango ($3, 2.5 hours) leaving from in front of the church in the main part of town at 4:30am, 5am, 5:30am, 6am, 7am, 8am, 10:30am, and 11am Monday through Saturday. On Sundays these buses leave at 5am, 5:30am, 6am, 8am, and 11am. There are buses to Guatemala City from San Pedro departing Monday through Saturday at 3:30am, 4am, 5am, 5:30am, 6am, 8am, and 10am. Afternoon buses depart at noon and 2pm on the same days. Sunday departures for Guatemala City are at 6am and 7am and noon, 1, and 2pm. There are frequent pickups to the villages as far as the road goes to San Marcos and in the other direction to Santiago. Shuttle vans ($25) leave from San Pedro (Casa Verde) at 9am daily for Antigua and Xela.

Shuttle buses to Antigua and Xela depart multiple times daily and can be booked through any of the travel agencies in town.

SANTIAGO ATITLÁN

Santiago Atitlán is a more traditional sort of place and has a very different feel from San Pedro. It's spectacularly set in an inlet with gorgeous views of San Pedro Volcano just across this small body of water. Atitlán and Tolimán Volcanoes rise behind it. I personally think its setting is the most spectacular of all the Lake Atitlán villages. It is the main enclave of Guatemala's Tz'utujil-speaking Maya, whose wonderful painting and handicrafts can be seen along the main street coming up from the boat dock, which is lined with art galleries and craft shops. On display is a very distinct form of painting depicting various elements of indigenous life such as agricultural harvests and festivals.

Santiago suffered greatly during the civil war, as the area was a hotbed of activity for ORPA guerrillas, who established themselves in this strategic area between the highlands and the Pacific Coast. The Guatemalan military established a base here and began systematically searching for guerrilla sympathizers, killing hundreds. As the civil war waned, the military's presence became increasingly unnecessary, as was the case throughout much of Guatemala,

and villagers became increasingly resentful of its presence. The massacre of 12 unarmed villagers (including three children) in 1990 unleashed a flood of local and international pressure to close the military garrison. A petition presented to the Guatemalan government asking for the base's closure was soon granted.

More recently, Santiago made world headlines in October 2005 after a number of devastating mudslides in the wake of Hurricane Stan left close to 1,000 victims. The neighboring village of Panabaj was completely wiped out by the mudslides, and the scars can still be seen on the mountainside. Many international organizations are still working in the area, and Santiago has become a popular center for volunteer activities in the tragedy's aftermath.

Another Santiago curiosity is the presence of a highland Mayan deity known as Maximón, housed in the home of a different member of the local *cofradía*, or Catholic brotherhood, every year. The effigy is a wooden figure clad in colorful silk scarves and a Stetson hat, smoking a big cigar and receiving offerings of moonshine, cigarettes, and rum. Local village children will offer you their services to go see the idol, which you can

women doing laundry in Santiago Atitlán

photograph for a fee. It is not surprisingly a sore point between the Catholic syncretists and the increasingly prominent Evangelical Christian churches, which have won over many of Santiago's residents.

You will probably be approached by innocent-looking children as soon as you arrive from the boat dock offering any of a number of services, including a guided trip to see Maximón or assistance in finding accommodations. You have the right to politely refuse, but you might be surprised at the colorful language they can resort to (in English) if they're unhappy with you for not hiring their services or if you fail to provide an adequate tip. Internationally recognized finger gestures are also not out of the realm of possibility. As Guatemala becomes more popular with visitors, however, the desperate drive to secure tourist dollars seems less urgent as market conditions have finally seemed to establish critical mass. My latest visit seemed wonderfully absent of locals hawking their services.

Sights

Santiago's colorful market really gets going on Fridays and Sundays, when the town's streets are filled with vendors and Mayan women dressed in the town's spectacular purple costume. The men wear interesting striped shorts, though it seems in fewer numbers every year. Standing prominently in the central plaza, the Iglesia Parroquial Santiago Apóstol was built between 1572 and 1581. Inside lining the walls are wooden saints dressed in clothes made by local women and renewed yearly. At the far end of the church are three sacred colonial altarpieces refurbished with more Mayan-inspired motifs by two local brothers between 1976 and 1981. The altarpieces represent the three volcanoes in the vicinity of Santiago, which are believed to protect the village. Local creation myths distinguish them as the first dry land to emerge from the early seas. The wooden pulpit has interesting carvings, including corn and animal figures. The town's newest attraction is the **Museo Cojoyla** (9am-4pm Mon.-Fri.,

9am-1pm Sat., free), a block up the street from the main dock, on the left, with displays on Santiago's artful legacy of traditional back-strap weaving.

Recreation

Atitlán and Tolimán Volcanoes are tempting climbs from town but unfortunately have been the scene of robberies, a problem that unfortunately seems endemic in the Lake Atitlán area. Check with the local lodges on the security situation and for reliable guides who might be able to take you there, should you wish to venture on the path less traveled.

Accommodations and Food

Santiago's nicest accommodations are at the charming ★ **Posada de Santiago** (tel. 7721-7366 or 5784-9111, www.posadadesantiago.com, $50-115 d) with a variety of room types in comfortable stone cabins featuring tasteful Guatemalan decor. It has adjusted well to the recent influx of missionaries and volunteer groups, offering rooms for 4-5 people

Posada de Santiago in Santiago Atitlán

at budget prices. The lodge is run by Dave and Susie Glanville, a gracious American couple who have lived in Santiago for years. Ironically, the hotel originally opened just weeks before the installation of the defunct local military garrison. It was closed for 10 years and did not reopen until June of 1991. If you're interested in the hotel's interesting history be sure to ask for Dave's "Smart Aleck Interview," which should answer most of your questions. The restaurant here is one of the lake's finest. Breakfast, lunch, and dinner are served at set times throughout the day. Dinner costs $8-21 and includes Cajun, Asian, and continental cuisine. All of the sauces, breads, pastries, and ice cream served here are homemade, and the Glanvilles grow, process, and roast their own coffee. Activities include fishing or kayaking on the lake, Thai or deep tissue massages, lounging by the pool in a hammock overlooking the lake, and swimming. There is wireless Internet in the lodge.

Just outside of town, your backup plan is to stay at **Hotel and Restaurant Bambú** (Carretera San Lucas Tolimán, Km. 16, tel. 7721-7331, www.ecobambu.com, $55-65 d) with two bungalows, eight rooms, and a villa housed in pretty thatched-roof stone cottages with fantastic lake and volcano views fronting beautifully landscaped grounds. The rooms are cheerful and bright with beautiful Guatemalan furnishings. There are a very nice swimming pool, a private dock, and kayaks available for rent at $5 an hour. The restaurant serves tasty international and Spanish cuisine. Be sure to take a taxi or *tuk-tuk* if you decide to go into town at night, as robberies have been reported on the isolated paths from the hotel into town after dark.

For lake fish, snacks, sandwiches, and light fare, a good choice is **Restaurante El Pescador** (two blocks up the street from the dock, tel. 7721-7147, www.elpescadoratitlan.com, 8am-9pm Mon.-Sat., 9am-4pm Sun.).

Services
There's a **Banrural** right on the plaza where you can exchange dollars and travelers checks.

Getting There
Ferry service ($2.50) departs Santiago for Panajachel at 6am, 7am, and 11:45am, 12:30pm, 1:30pm, 2pm, and 4:30pm. The ferry crossing takes about an hour, and there is also faster *lancha* service. There are also frequent boats to San Pedro from here. There are seven daily buses leaving from the central plaza for Cocales and Guatemala City between 3am and 3pm.

SAN LUCAS TOLIMÁN AND VICINITY
San Lucas is probably the least attractive of the lakeside villages, though the adjacent area is as gorgeous as the rest of the lake. It makes a good place to get away from it all. If you're looking for comfortable accommodations to host your escape, you might want to check out **Hotel Tolimán** (6a Avenida 1-26, tel. 7722-0033, www.hoteltoliman.com, $50-95 d) on a sprawling lakeside ranch run by a wonderful Guatemalan couple. The 22 comfortable rooms, including some splendid suites, all have a private bathroom and a 17th-century hacienda ambience enhanced by numerous decorative touches that include delightful furniture and antiques. Hotel amenities include a swimming pool, wireless Internet, and a restaurant.

Just a few kilometers along Ruta Nacional 11, leading from San Lucas to the coastal town of Cocales, this is a gem of a place to stay. ★ **Los Tarrales** (Km. 164.2 RN-11, tel. 5919-8882 or 2478-4606, www.tarrales.com, $62-98 d) is a private reserve on the southern slopes of Atitlán Volcano named after the abundant bamboo trees that grow here. Altitudes range 700-3,000 meters (2,300-9,800 feet), providing for a wonderfully diverse array of ecosystems. Several locals are employed by the reserve, working on its coffee farm or in the ecotourism business, and the lodge runs a school for local children. Activities include hiking and bird-watching with naturalist guides, climbing Atitlán Volcano, mountain biking, canoeing, horseback riding, and visits to the working coffee farm. Accommodations include shared-bath rooms, beautiful rooms with private bathroom, or wonderful tree house cabins. Excellent, home-cooked meals are served ($10-12) for breakfast, lunch, and dinner including fresh salads, vegetarian and meat dishes, and bread from the on-site bakery. Buses heading to Cocales pass right by the entrance to the reserve, which is 15 minutes from San Lucas and about 45 minutes from Santiago.

Between San Lucas Tolimán and San Antonio Palopó, **Tosa La Laguna** (tel. 5198-3234, www.tosaspa.com, $175-295 d, including three vegetarian meals daily) bills itself as an all-inclusive, adults-only, holistic spa and retreat center. Its remote location (a 10-minute boat ride from San Lucas Tolimán) certainly helps in this regard. Readers have written in to rave about the wonderful accommodations and friendly staff found at this peaceful lakeside oasis. The hillside complex houses comfortable casitas painted in vivid hues and even

a dome-shaped suite. You can also visit here on a day spa package.

SAN ANTONIO PALOPÓ

Our round-the-lake circle is completed at the quiet village of San Antonio Palopó. It hasn't been greatly exploited by tourism (unlike its sister town Santa Catarina Palopó) and makes a great place to get away. Among the limited but quite lovely accommodations options is **Atitlán Villas** (Bahía Kachiman, tel. 3019-9822 or 2378-6921, atitlanvillas.com, $150-450 d). The modern rooms have anywhere from one to four bedrooms; all feature balconies with fabulous lake views. There's also a swimming pool. Please note that there is no parking on-site. You'll need to park your car in town with one of several reputable car parks the hotel can recommend and then take a boat (furnished by the lodge) to the property. It's a 10-minute ride.

Chichicastenango

Chichicastenango (Chichi, for short) will provide you with an opportunity to take in a unique highland market experience. There are certainly other, more authentic markets in highland Guatemala, at least one of which is larger, but Chichi's popular Sunday

and Thursday market is unique in that it includes allowances for the very strong foreign presence here. It is the only highland market where you'll see large tour buses packed with camera-toting tourists negotiating the hairpin, dizzying mountain switchbacks along the road from Antigua and Guatemala City. The road to Chichi diverts from the Pan-American Highway at the Los Encuentros Junction, along Km. 127.5.

The market, and Chichi's status as a bona fide tourist attraction, got their start in the 1930s when enterprising Alfred S. Clark opened the Mayan Inn and started busing folks in from the capital for a look at an authentic highland Mayan village. Chichicastenango, originally known as Chaviar, was an important Kaqchikel trading town long before the arrival of the Spanish. The Kaqchikel went to war with their K'iche' rivals based in K'umarcaaj (near present-day

Santa Cruz del Quiché, 20 miles north) in the 15th century, moving their capital to the more easily defended site of Iximché. Spanish conquistador Pedro de Alvarado would play the K'iche'-Kaqchikel rivalry to his advantage, using the latter as allies in his final push against the K'iche', who comprised the only real opposition to Spanish conquest. Chichicastenango got its name, meaning "place of the nettles," from Alvarado's Nahuatl-speaking Mexican allies after the town's reestablishment here after the defeat of the K'iche' capital in 1524.

Today, Chichi is still very much a K'iche' town with strong adherence to the old ways. Its traditional fiesta, the **Fiesta de Santo Tomás,** takes place December 14-21. There are plenty of loud fireworks, traditional dances, moonshine, and the fascinating *palo volador* ritual in which men spin from ropes attached to a 20-meter pole.

SIGHTS
★ Chichicastenango's Market
If you're a big fan of outdoor markets, you'll certainly enjoy this one. In addition to the crowds of vendors and potential buyers, you'll find a dizzying array of good-quality weavings, pottery, fabrics, gourds, and masks, to name just a few. On the stairs of the adjacent church of Santo Tomás, you'll see Mayans waving incense burners, filling the air with the pungent smell of *corozo* palm and adding an additional aura of mystique to this chaotic market that is a feast for the senses. There are certainly more authentic indigenous highland markets, but what makes Chichi unique is its accommodation of visitors' needs and desires for traditional handicrafts into a twice-weekly event (Sunday and Thursday) that would otherwise continue undeterred for the benefit of the locals it has always catered to.

Most of the better handicrafts are found in the central part of the plaza, but be prepared to rummage through piles of lesser-quality stuff, which is readily in abundance. In addition to the main part of the plaza, there are stalls peddling tourist-oriented trinkets along the streets to the north of it. The streets to the south and the *centro comercial* on the plaza's north side are home to the everyday items villagers come to market for, including fruits and vegetables, clothing, spices, household items, and baked goods. As in all of Guatemala's markets, haggling is in order. The best time to get a good deal on anything that might have caught your fancy is after 3pm, when the market starts to wind

Chichicastenango's market

The *Popol Vuh*

Believed to have been written by an unknown Mayan scribe in the 1560s, the *Popol Vuh* (Council Book), was found in the church archives in Chichicastenango early in the 18th century by parish priest Francisco Ximénez. Amazingly, it survived the burning and destruction most Mayan writings fell prey to at the hands of the Spanish and lives on as an important document recording K'iche' histories and legends. Ximénez painstakingly transcribed the document into Latin and then translated it into Spanish. This is now the only surviving copy of the Mayan text and resides in Chicago's Newberry Library.

The *Popol Vuh* contains the K'iche' peoples' creation myths as well as their history before the arrival of the Spanish. Although there are some striking similarities with Christian writings, including the Old Testament, scholars believe these are coincidences rather than evidence of overt Christian influence—this despite the fact that the text was written about 40 years after the conquest. It mentions Christianity only at its beginning and its end, framing the narration (as opposed to the events themselves) of the *Popol Vuh* as taking place within the context of the Christian era, for better or worse.

The book describes the moment of creation as having been spurred instantly by the words of the gods themselves describing the moments preceding creation with, "Whatever might be is simply not there: only murmurs, ripples, in the dark, in the night." It also describes how the gods attempt to create humans to give meaning to creation and have beings that can speak, praise, and keep the passing of time, first forming them out of earth and mud, which soon dissolves. The second version of humankind, the text relates, was created out of wood, but these beings were dull and could not speak in words. The gods decide to annihilate them by sending a flood and other devastations, including the revolt of the beings' own possessions, which turn and destroy their owners. The book explains that the remains of this previous version of humankind are the monkeys and humanlike creatures we see today. The gods finally create humankind using corn, which is not surprising given its importance as a Mayan subsistence crop to this day.

Other similarities shared with the Bible's book of Genesis include the explanation of astronomical features, including the Big Dipper, the assertion that woman was created after man, and the conclusion that man at one point had come too close to being like the divine, resulting in a confusion of languages to disperse humankind into different linguistic groups. The *Popol Vuh* is not without its own tales of heroics, the most prominent being the myth of the Hero Twins, who journey into the underworld (known as Xibalba), ruled by seven lords, and endure great hardships.

In addition to the interesting metaphysical speculation provided throughout the text, another fascinating feature of the *Popol Vuh* is that it may have served as a book of divination, with some hidden meaning if read in a certain way that allowed the reader to predict future events—hence its being referred to as the "Council Book." In a more literal sense, it also tells quite matter-of-factly of the impending difficulties that will arrive with the coming of "enemies, hidden behind mountains and hills," a possible allusion to the civil war and its atrocities. Despite the hardships, the book concludes that, "Our people will never be scattered. Our destiny will triumph over the ill-fated days which are coming at a time unknown. We will always be secure in the land we have occupied."

down. You can often score substantial price reductions simply by walking away and feigning disinterest. It's all a very complex game. For fair trade goods, visit **En Mi Salsa** (5a Avenida 5-24 Zona 1, local 21, www.enmisalsa.com, 1pm-5pm Wed., 9am-5pm Thurs./ Sun., 10am-5pm Sat.) where you'll find export-quality handmade goods.

Iglesia Santo Tomás

The town's oft-photographed church dates to 1540 and is the site of syncretic Catholic-Mayan rituals both inside and out. On the steps, you'll find *chuchkajaues*—indigenous people at prayer, swinging incense-laden censers (usually just metal cans punctured with holes) and reciting incantations. Take care to enter the church through the side door to the right, as the main entrance is reserved for religious officials and *chuchkajaues*. Inside you'll find an astounding number of lit candles lining the church floor along with pine boughs and offerings of liquor bottles wrapped in corn husks, flowers, and maize kernels in remembrance of departed relatives, some of whom are buried beneath the church floor. Photography is strictly prohibited inside the church.

Found beside the church is a monastery, where the *Popol Vuh* Mayan book was found among church archives by Spanish priest Francisco Ximénez in the early 18th century.

On the west side of the plaza is **Capilla del Calvario,** another whitewashed church somewhat like a miniature version of Santo Tomás and with much the same feel. There is a glass-encased Christ statue inside, which is paraded through town during Holy Week processions.

Museo Rossbach

The small **Museo Rossbach** (5a Avenida 4-47 Zona 1, 8am-noon and 2pm-5pm Tues., Wed., Fri., Sat., 8am-4pm Thurs., 8am-2pm Sun., $0.75) harbors a collection of jade objects, including necklaces and figurines in addition to historical objects such as ceremonial masks, obsidian spearheads, and incense burners. It's named after Hugo Rossbach, a German who served as the town's Catholic priest for many years until his death in 1944.

Pascual Abaj

On a hill just outside of town is this Mayan shrine dedicated to the earth god Huyup Tak'ah (Mountain Plain) where worshippers gather frequently to perform ceremonies. The idol is a blackened pre-Columbian sculpture standing about a meter tall and lined with stones, candles, and sacrificial offerings of booze. It has been around for centuries. Ceremonies performed by a Mayan shaman usually involve much incense, liquor-drinking, chanting, and offerings of candles, flowers, and maybe even a sacrificial chicken. If you happen to stumble upon one of these ceremonies during your visit, be sure to keep your distance and refrain from taking photographs. You can always ask for permission, but don't be surprised if the answer is a firm "no." To get to the shrine, walk down 5a Avenida from the main plaza turning right onto 9a Calle. At the bottom of the hill found along this street, head left onto a path through the signposted *morerías* (mask workshops) found there. The path continues uphill from there to

candles for sale in Chichicastenango

the hilltop site. It's best to go in a group and earlier in the day, as robberies of tourists along this route are not infrequent.

ACCOMMODATIONS

In the heart of town, ★ **Hotel Santo Tomás** (7a Avenida 5-32 Zona 1, tel. 5865-6453, www. hotelsantotomas.com.gt, $100 d) is a lovely colonial-style hotel with rooms centered around a graceful courtyard fountain complete with squawking macaws. There are a pool, hot tub, gift shop, a lively bar, and restaurant. A longtime favorite with travelers to Chichicastenango is the **Mayan Inn** (8a Calle "A" 1-91 Zona 1, tel. 2412-4753, www.maya-ninn.com.gt, $100 d), established by Alfred S. Clark, founder of Clark Tours, in 1932. The 30 rooms are beautifully decorated with antique furnishings and have fireplaces. Most of the bathrooms have tubs. Each room has its own attendant dressed in traditional village costume, as there are no locks on the doors from the outside. Rest assured, you can lock yourself in at night. There's a good restaurant here. The market is literally at your doorstep.

FOOD

Tziguan Tinamit (5a Avenida 5-67 Zona 1, tel. 7756-1144, 7am-10pm daily) serves a variety of light meals and has particularly tasty baked goods. **La Villa de los Cofrades** (Corredor Centro Comercial Santo Tomas, tel. 5510-6657, 9am-10pm Wed.-Sun.) serves tasty light meals, coffee, and crepes. There are delicious, large set-menu lunches and dinners for $5-7. **Restaurante Las Brasas** (6a Calle 4-52, Comercial Girón, tel. 7756-2226, 7am-9pm daily, $4-9) is a good-value steak house also serving decent breakfasts. Beside El Calvario church, ★ **Casa San Juan** (6a Calle 7-30 Zona 1, tel. 7756-2086, 9:30am-9:30pm Tues.-Sun., $8-13) serves creatively prepared sandwiches and Guatemalan food in a stylish environment that includes wrought-iron chairs and artwork. The town's most stylish eateries are at the restaurants housed inside the **Mayan Inn** and **Hotel Santo Tomás,** where a three-course meal runs in the vicinity of $15. The waiters at both places wear elaborate traditional costumes, though the food at Hotel Santo Tomás outshines that of its closest competitor, albeit slightly.

INFORMATION AND SERVICES
Communications

For post, you'll find **Correos** on 7a Avenida between 8a and 9a Calles.

a cocktail at Casa San Juan in Chichicastenango

Money

Conveniently, Chichi's banks stay open on Sundays. Among the options are **Banco Industrial** (6a Calle 6-05 Zona 1, 10am-2pm Mon., 10am-5pm Wed. and Fri., 9am-5pm Thurs. and Sun., 10am-3pm Sat.) with a VISA/Plus ATM. **Banrural** (6a Calle east of 5a Avenida, 9am-5pm Sun.-Fri., 9am-1pm Sat.) has a MasterCard/Cirrus ATM.

GETTING THERE
Bus

Chichi lacks a bus terminal, though bus arrivals and departures are centered around 5a Avenida and 5a Calle. There are buses to Guatemala City leaving every 30 minutes between 4am and 5pm (three hours, $2), eight daily buses to Panajachel (1.5 hours, $1.50)

between 5am and 2pm, and seven daily buses to Quetzaltenango (three hours, $1.75). Alternatively, you can take any of the above to the Los Encuentros Junction and change there for connecting service. If you're heading north, there are frequent buses to the departmental capital of Santa Cruz del Quiché leaving every 30 minutes.

Shuttle Bus

Adrenalina Tours (www.adrenalinatours.com), with offices in Quetzaltenango and Antigua, offers shuttle service from Chichi to Panajachel, Antigua, Quetzaltenango, and Guatemala City on market days. **Atitlan Tours** (tel. 5786-0227, www.atitlantour.com) offers shuttles on market days between Chichi and Panajachel, Guatemala City, and Antigua.

The Ixil Triangle

North of Chichicastenango, beyond the departmental capital of Quiché via a newly paved road, is the Ixil Triangle. The name was given to the area comprising the somewhat remote villages of Santa María Nebaj, San Juan Cotzal, and San Gaspar Chajul. The scenery here is spectacular, as are the weavings made by its Ixil-speaking inhabitants. Set in the foothills of the lush Cuchumatanes, the area was the scene of heavy fighting during the country's civil war. Its inhabitants suffered greatly during the violence, undoubtedly more than any other region in Guatemala. Peace has returned, but the region remains remote, drawing visitors with its colorful traditional Mayan culture, some of the country's best hiking, and breathtaking scenery.

HISTORY

The area populated by the Ixil-speaking peoples shows signs of having been inhabited since the latter part of the Classic period, between the 6th and 9th centuries AD, including various stelae, pyramids, and monuments unearthed in this region. The Ixil didn't come

under Spanish authority until 1530, having managed to successfully repel earlier invasions from their fortresses in Nebaj and Chajul with help from their neighbors and allies in Uspantán. When the Spanish did finally conquer the region, they burnt Nebaj to the ground and enslaved its people. After Spanish priests felt confident they had secured the souls of the newly conquered peoples, the region fell into a period of neglect until Dominican friars arrived on the scene in the 19th century seeking to convert the remaining outlying mountain villages. Guatemala's burgeoning coffee trade and its insatiable need for cheap labor had become fully established by this time, and the region's inhabitants were soon conscripted to work on the coastal plantations using debt peonage, among other tactics.

By the mid-20th century several wealthy families had firmly established themselves in the lower elevations of the Ixil region, owning huge cattle, coffee, cacao, and sugar plantations. Among the local landowning families, the Brol and Arenas families were notoriously cruel masters and the subject of eventual retribution during the civil war. The Brols owned thousands of acres as far as Uspantán, employing as many as 4,000 resident and seasonal workers at their Finca San Francisco in the northern lowlands near Cotzal. Many of its workers were held captive to debt peonage.

The Ejército Guerrillero de los Pobres, or EGP, moved into the region in 1972, crossing the border from Mexico and finding in the Ixil a populace willing to cooperate with them in the hopes of being finally liberated from the tyranny of the landowning elite. The swift acceptance of the EGP in the hearts and minds of the Ixil was further aided by weak government and military presence throughout the region. Eventually, the Guatemalan military moved into the region and began indiscriminately executing and "disappearing" suspected guerrilla sympathizers.

Although the EGP quickly displayed the ability to enlist thousands of peasants to its cause, the ideological momentum was not matched with a logistical capacity to arm or supply its followers. Villagers were soon caught in the middle of a scorched-earth campaign, with entire villages being massacred and destroyed, the guerrillas being largely unable to protect their followers.

An amnesty was declared under the subsequent government of Efraín Ríos Montt in 1982, bringing in thousands of refugees who had fled to the hinterlands trying to escape from the military. Between 1982 and 1984, 42,000 peasants turned themselves in. Other policies included the establishment of local Civil Defense Patrols, known as PACs, aimed at curtailing the influence of the guerrillas among the local population, and the rounding up of displaced citizens into so-called "model villages" closely guarded by the military.

By the time democratic rule finally returned to Guatemala in 1986, the guerrillas had been pushed back to the northern reaches of the El Quiché department. There were occasional skirmishes until the signing of the 1996 peace accords. Almost all the smaller villages and hamlets of the Ixil Triangle and neighboring Ixcán were destroyed during the 1970s and '80s, with 25,000 Ixil murdered or displaced during the atrocities.

NEBAJ

Nebaj is the largest of the three villages and has grown substantially through the last few years since the end of the civil war. I still have pleasant memories of my first visit to this enchanting town, at the ripe old age of 18, riding

pastoral scene in the Quiché highlands

on the roof rack of a crowded chicken bus on twisting mountain (dirt) roads. The location of this hamlet, nestled in a valley among the Cuchumatanes mountain chain, is superb, and you'll surely remember the first time you see its quaint houses and whitewashed church coming into view from the mountains above. As elsewhere, the town is centered round the plaza with the church and government offices built around it. A peek inside Nebaj's church reveals a multitude of small crosses as a memorial to civil war victims.

During the worst of the violence Nebaj was pretty much off-limits, with military checkpoints in Santa Cruz del Quiché, Sacapulas, and along the road north keeping close tabs on the activities of sojourners to these parts. Today it's become increasingly popular with foreign volunteers working with one of many NGOs helping out with postwar reconstruction and community development projects throughout the area. Despite its violent history, the region is remarkably safe, with reports of tourist robberies in these parts being virtually unheard of.

The women of Nebaj wear one of the most colorful and beautiful of Guatemala's indigenous costumes; they're imbued with animal and bird motifs and worn with an elaborate headdress adorned with purple, yellow, and green pom-poms. You can pick up colorful weavings with these motifs from several stalls along the plaza and at some of the local restaurants.

Hikes

The opportunities for hikes around Nebaj are virtually limitless. Two of the nicest hikes are to the villages of **Acul** and **Cocop.** One of the easiest hikes is along green pastures and meadows to some nearby waterfalls known as **Las Cataratas,** about 20 meters (60 feet) high. There are also several sites that are sacred to the Maya where you might witness ceremonies, though their locations are not well known and it's best to go with a guide. There are several multiday hikes offered by a number of outfitters

that afford you the opportunity to really get off the beaten path. These include a fantastic three-day hike over the Cuchumatanes mountain range to the village of **Todos Santos,** hikes across highland plateaus dotted with meadows and lagoons, and two- or three-day treks to the remote villages of **Xeo** and **Cotzal.**

Another nearby attraction of sorts is an old military landing strip still pockmarked with bomb holes that was a settlement for displaced war victims. Found four kilometers west of town, it's also known by its Ixil name **Ak'txumb'al,** meaning "New Mentality," certainly as a way of adding insult to injury by its military creators.

Guide Companies

Because of the remoteness of most of the locales mentioned here, as well as the chance to contribute directly to the well-being of local inhabitants, guides are strongly recommended. Among the local outfitters is **Guías Ixiles** (3a Calle Zona 1, tel. 5311-9100, www.nebaj.com/ixilguides.htm), housed inside El Descanso, which offers hikes to all of the above-mentioned locales. A share of the proceeds goes to finance community projects. Next door, **Pablo's Tours** (tel. 5416-8674) offers hikes to nearby waterfalls, a river cave near a magnificently pristine blue river, horseback riding ($5 per hour), and multiday hiking from Nebaj to Todos Santos. Quetzaltenango-based **Quetzaltrekkers** (Diagonal 12 8-43 Zona 1, inside Casa Argentinas, Quetzaltenango, tel. 7765-5895, www.quetzaltrekkers.com) is another recommended outfitter for the Nebaj-Todos Santos trek, with proceeds being donated to fund projects benefiting Quetzaltenango's street children. The six-day trip ($150) leaves from Quetzaltenango, though it might be possible to meet up with a group if you already happen to be in Nebaj. Trips leave every other Wednesday.

If you prefer to hike without a guide, pick up a copy of the very useful *Trekking en la Región Ixil* guide ($2) from Guías Ixiles.

Shopping

Nebaj's busy **market** is one block east of the church and sells basic items mostly of interest to local residents. It's substantially busier on Thursdays and Sundays, when merchants come from out of town peddling cheap developed-nation goods. For weaving and handicrafts, there are several stalls near the church. Another good spot is the **Centro Cultural Ixil y Mercado de Artesanías** (3a Avenida Zona 1, right off the park), where you can shop for handicrafts in a pretty neocolonial courtyard.

Accommodations

Nebaj's hostel is **MediaLuna MedioSol** (tel. 5749-7450, $5 pp in dorms or $7 pp in private room), half a block from El Descanso on 3a Calle, with several amenities, including wireless Internet, a comfortable DVD lounge, a dartboard, table tennis, and a Mayan sauna in addition to basic, clean rooms. Guests have use of the kitchen. **Hotel Turansa** (corner of 5a Calle and 6a Avenida, tel. 7755-8487, $18 d) has a secured parking lot around which are centered 16 clean rooms with private hot-water bathroom and cable TV. The nicest place in town is ★ **Hotel Villa Nebaj** (Avenida 15 de Septiembre 2-37 Zona 1, just north of the plaza, tel. 7756-0005 or 7755-8115, www.hotelvillanebaj.com, $30 d), where the comfortable rooms have big wooden beds with Nebaj quilts, private hot-water bathroom, cable TV, and tile floors. There's also plenty of parking. My other favorite option is ★ **Hotel Santa María** (Calle Real, two blocks from the park, tel. 4212-7927 or 4664-6094, www.hotelsantamarianebaj.com, $26 d), built in neocolonial style and harboring comfortable, clean rooms set round a small courtyard. The friendly innkeepers provide home-cooked meals for their guests and there is parking.

Food

Local specialties in Nebaj include *boxboles*, an Ixil dish of steamed corn dough served with lemon and either tomato or peanut sauce.

On the way out of town toward Chajul and Cotzal and one block from the courthouse, **La Quinta de los Reyes** (tel. 7755-8098 or 4067-7624, $5-8) serves hearty, all-you-can-eat, buffet-style meals, including Guatemalan and international fare, as well as dessert and a drink. For passable Guatemalan dishes and views overlooking the central plaza head to **Café Restaurante Maya Ixil** (tel. 7755-8168). It's also a good place for breakfast.

Nebaj's main gathering spot is ★ **El Descanso** (3a Calle Zona 1, tel. 5847-4747, 6:30am-10pm daily, $5-10) where there are good Guatemalan dishes, sandwiches, nachos, and pastries. There is seating upstairs on a covered patio as well as a bar/lounge with comfy couches on the lower level. Movies are sometimes shown here, and they serve *boxboles* on Thursdays. They also have free wireless Internet. For decent pizza, there's **Pizza del César** (2a Avenida 4-05 Zona 1, tel. 7755-8095). Just off the square is **Popi's** (5a Avenida 3-35 Zona 1, tel. 5906-5780), serving tasty baked goods.

Information and Services

Nebaj's de facto tourist information office is **El Descanso** (3a Calle Zona 1, tel. 5847-4747, 6:30am-10pm daily). It also serves as an all-in-one travel clearinghouse and services center providing Internet access ($1.50 per hour). Guías Ixiles is also based here, and they run the very informative website www.nebaj.com. The **post office** is at 5a Avenida 4-37, one block north of the central plaza.

For money, **Banrural,** on the north side of the plaza, has an ATM.

Established by the same folks who began El Descanso, **Nebaj Language School** (www.nebaj.com/nls.html) offers 20 hours of one-on-one teaching per week for $165, including homestay with a local family (includes two meals a day), two guided treks, and discounted Internet and food at El Descanso.

Getting There

Bus schedules in Nebaj, as in most small rural towns, are somewhat elastic. The bus depot is two blocks southeast of the plaza. There are several daily buses and minivans to the departmental capital of Santa Cruz del Quiché, with the last bus leaving sometime around 5pm. All of these stop in Sacapulas along the way. There are frequent buses and minivans to neighboring Chajul, Cotzal, and Acul.

★ ACUL

Originally established as one of the "model villages" under the authoritarian hand of Efraín Ríos Montt, Acul is starting to come into its own. It features friendly folk and a spectacular Swiss-like mountain setting enhanced by the presence of quaint dairy farms. There are fairly frequent buses and pickups heading out this way from Nebaj, though it seems most gringos prefer to walk out this way through the lovely countryside.

The hike from Nebaj to Acul takes about two hours and is fantastically scenic. The first half is a steep ascent to the top of a hill, then downhill into Acul. It's a fairly easy hike, aside from the hill climb.

Accommodations

If you'd like to stay in town, there's **Posada Doña Magdalena** (tel. 5782-0891, dorm $4 pp, private double room $7 pp). All of the simple rooms share a bathroom. The hostel is run by a friendly Nebajense woman who lived in Las Vegas and speaks English, Spanish, and Ixil. Meals here are served family-style. There are textiles for sale as well as a Mayan sauna, or *temascal,* out back.

Among the local dairy farms is **Hacienda San Antonio** (tel. 5702-1907, www.quesochancol.com), started in 1938 by Italian immigrant José Azzari, who died in 1999. The finca is a pleasant working farm run by Azzari's sons and grandsons and producing some delicious cheeses made using centuries-old methods brought over from the old country. They're happy to show you around and you're welcome to stay in the charming wooden cabanas featuring tile floors, simple but pleasing decorative touches, and shared ($13 pp) or private hot-water bathroom ($20 pp). One of the rooms upstairs has a deck with gorgeous views of the surrounding farmland. Activities include guided nature hikes and horseback riding in the surrounding countryside. Just next door along the road into town is ★ **Hacienda Mil Amores** (tel. 5704-4817 or 5774-5086, $50 d), also owned by members of the Azzari family. The four lovely, spacious tile-roofed cottages are a step above its neighbor's and are built of stone or wood. Each of the rooms is different and has elaborate

Hacienda Mil Amores in Acul

tree-trunk or terra-cotta floors and private bathroom, some with chimney. The property has several connections with well-known tour operators and has no trouble filling its rooms, so book well in advance if you wish to stay here. This is also a working farm where you can buy cheeses. Kids will love the opportunity to see farm animals and even milk cows if they're so inclined. Other activities include hikes to neighboring villages and horseback riding. Meals are served family-style in the main farmhouse, which is beautifully decorated with orchids grown on-site and has wonderful views of the surrounding pasturelands from a pleasant wooden deck.

SAN JUAN COTZAL

Cotzal was the Ixil Triangle's largest town until the road to Nebaj was built in the 1940s. It's now rather small, though its setting is (as everywhere else in these parts) gorgeous, surrounded by the imposing Cuchumatanes mountain chain. There's little to see in the town itself, though the weavings here are some of Guatemala's finest. Market days are Wednesdays and Saturdays. The **Iglesia San Juan** fronts a pretty plaza that has been remodeled and festooned with flowers and benches. The church's interior is not nearly as elaborate as that of neighboring Chajul, but its Christ statue curiously holds a staff with an Israeli flag. Jesus was a Jewish carpenter, after all.

Cotzal has been enhanced as of late by a community tourism project. **Tejidos Cotzal** (just behind the marketplace, tel. 4621-9725, www.tejidoscotzal.org) is a cooperative of 30 local weavers who retain traditional methods of weaving using natural dyes and backstrap looms. There are two-day guided tours to the weavers' homes, offering a wonderful opportunity to get out and meet the people who create these singular works of art. The trip costs $13 per person, with a minimum of two people, and can be combined with a visit to nearby waterfalls.

The paving of the road to Cotzal has opened it up to tourism, and there is now at least one decent hotel in town. **El Maguey** (tel. 7765-6199, $12 d), two blocks north of the plaza, has clean, basic rooms with TV and shared bathrooms. The hotel's eatery offers good set menus for about $2.50. Enterprising weavers may also offer you a place to stay.

Chimel and Santa Avelina Waterfalls

Some pretty waterfalls out this way make a good day hike, 10 and 12 kilometers from town. You can take pickups or minibuses to the villages of Chichel and Santa Avelina, from where it's a much shorter walk to the falls. The first waterfall, near Chichel, is Chimel, which cascades down a rocky cliff into a small river. There are some tables and benches in the surrounding grassy hillside beneath the falls, and it makes a pleasant place for a picnic. You can drive part of the way on a rugged dirt road, but you'll find yourself hiking the last half mile or so to the falls through beautiful pastureland.

The second waterfall is reached by going a further two kilometers along the main road out of Cotzal to the village of Santa Avelina. The town is built on a hillside, and if you go to the base of this hillside via the main road, you'll find the small Tienda Lux on the outskirts of town. You walk straight uphill from here on a very steep trail, turning left onto a smaller footpath, which eventually traverses cornfields for about 20 minutes to the falls. The water tumbles over a rock that is pitched just over the edge of the cliff and produces quite a bit of spray. There's a small tile-roofed changing room by the pool at the base of the falls and a friendly caretaker who will collect a $1 admission price. You can ask any of the locals how to get here and they can point you in the general direction.

CHAJUL

About 15 kilometers northeast of Nebaj, Chajul is a picturesque collection of quaint adobe houses with tiled roofs. Of the three Ixil Triangle towns, it certainly has the most traditional feel, though the paved road to Nebaj has many traditionalists fearing the end is near for one of the country's most pleasantly isolated villages. In any case, it still offers spectacular weavings you'll undoubtedly see everywhere. Market days are Tuesdays and Fridays, though on any given day sellers will most certainly find you to offer their wares in brilliant hues of red and blue embroidered with animals and plants.

The main attraction here is the town's church, **Iglesia de San Gaspar Los Reyes,** one of Guatemala's most ornate, with wooden doors containing finely carved depictions of animals. Inside, an elaborate goldleaf altar guarded by two figures dressed in traditional garb surrounds its Cristo de Golgotha statue. Check out the cool wool red coats, which are now rarely seen on the town's male inhabitants. The church is a major pilgrimage site on the second Friday of Lent.

Chajul's plaza was also the site of a grisly public execution of EGP guerrillas carried out by the Guatemalan military in retaliation for the 1979 murder of landowner Enrique Brol, an event which is narrated in Nobel Peace Prize winner Rigoberta Menchú's autobiography. While the basic facts of the army's extrajudicial murders have not come into question, Menchú's testimony certainly has. An investigation by author David Stoll has since revealed Menchú may not have been there at all and is also at odds with her claims that the prisoners were burned alive, claiming instead that they were mowed down with machine guns. The research and evidence supporting his claims and questioning much of Menchú's autobiography are presented in his book, *Rigoberta Menchú and the Story of All Poor Guatemalans.*

Practicalities

There's not much in the way of accommodations in Chajul, though there is now at least one decent place to stay. **Posada Vetz K'aol**

Chajul's ornate church

(tel. 7765-6114, $10 pp) lies about 300 meters south of the plaza down a dirt road turnoff from the main street. It's a bit hard to find, but any *tuk-tuk* driver can take you there for less than $1. Formerly housing a clinic, the building has large, clean rooms with bunk beds and wool blankets. There's also a pleasant sitting room with a fireplace and TV. Tasty meals cooked by the lodge's caretaker are available upon request.

You'll find a few simple eateries just off the plaza, the best of which is **Las Gemelitas,** two blocks downhill from the church. As in Cotzal, you will likely be approached by locals offering food and shelter in their homes.

There's a **Banrural** on the plaza for changing cash dollars.

Huehuetenango and Vicinity

Affectionately called "Huehue" (WAY-way) by locals, this somewhat busy coffee-trading town sits in a valley overlooking the glaciated peaks of the Sierra de los Cuchumatanes. Because of its location in the mountain chain's rain shadow, the town and surrounding areas are somewhat drier than the Quiché highlands to the east, which lie on the mountain chain's windward side. The departmental capital is busy with travelers heading to or from the western border with Mexico as well as with coffee farmers and traders heading to or from nearby farms. Since first coming here at the age of three, I watched the town grow up into a somewhat disorganized agglomeration of trade and commerce, though there has been a remarkable improvement in the level of its services. It makes a great jumping-off point for deeper explorations of the very diverse department of Huehuetenango and even includes a worthwhile site of its own, this being the ruins of Zaculeu just outside of town.

Access to Huehue is mainly via the Pan-American Highway, with the turnoff into town at Km. 264, from where it's another three kilometers to its center via a boulevard. A recently paved road now also leads east to Sacapulas, passing the town of Aguacatán (and wonderful mountain views) along the way.

SIGHTS

As always, the town is centered on the *parque central,* which is actually one of Guatemala's prettiest. At its center is a colonial fountain along with well-tended gardens and even a **relief map** of the department of Huehuetenango. On the plaza's southern end, facing 5a Avenida, is its neoclassical church, the **Catedral Templo de la Inmaculada Concepción.** It dates to 1874. The town's **Municipalidad** (City Hall) is on the west side of the plaza and curiously topped with an oyster-shaped band shell. On the park's eastern side, in early 20th-century architecture and notable for its clock tower, is the building housing **Gobernación Departamental,** the regional seat of government.

Zaculeu

Zaculeu (8am-6pm daily, $3.50) was the principal Mam ceremonial site. Dating to the Early Classic period (AD 400-700), it shows signs of having been occupied for more than 1,000 years until it was conquered by Gonzalo de Alvarado, brother of Guatemala's other infamous conquistador, in October 1525. It was starvation that eventually did the local population in, as Alvarado and his troops simply staked out the fortified city (surrounded by ravines) for two months, cutting off rescue attempts from neighboring Mam villages

Rivers run through the department of Huehuetenango.

with the help of the Spanish cavalry and 2,000 Mexica and K'iche' allies.

More than any of the other highland Mayan sites such as K'umarcaaj and Iximché, Zaculeu somehow manages to evoke the feel of the city as it might have looked in its heyday, thanks to a 1950s restoration project covering the restored temples in graying white plaster. At the same time, the temples lack the bright coloring they most certainly would have had and similarly lack any of their decorative details. The highest of its temple pyramids, **Structure I,** rises to about 12 meters. Another somewhat impressive structure is **Structure 13,** on the southeast corner of the main plaza. The site also has an interesting I-shaped ball court. There's an on-site museum with some interesting displays on the siege of the city as well as burial pieces found beneath Structure I.

Snacks and refreshments are available from a couple of simple eateries across from the main entrance to the park.

To get here, you can hire a cab from the central plaza for about $6, which includes about an hour at the ruins. Otherwise, there are frequent, cheap local buses heading out this way from 2a Calle and 7a Avenida near Hotel San Luis de la Sierra.

ACCOMMODATIONS

Half a block north of the plaza, **Hotel Zaculeu** (5a Avenida 1-14 Zona 1, tel. 7764-1086, www.hotelzaculeu.com, $28-35 d) has attractive ground-floor rooms with tile floors beside a garden courtyard. The top-floor rooms in a newer section have been upgraded with carpeting, accent lighting on the walls, and other pleasant decorative touches. All rooms have cable TV, great beds, and private hot-water bathroom. There's a dining room serving breakfast and dinner. **Hotel Casa Blanca** (7a Avenida 3-41 Zona 1, tel. 7769-0777, $37 d) has personal sentimental value, as it was once my grandfather's home and office. All mushiness aside, there's plenty here to recommend it, including attractive rooms

in the original house (with plenty of character) or beside the back patio (more modern and spacious). All 15 rooms have hot-water private bathroom, phone, and cable TV. There are two restaurants, each fronting one of the house's two patios. The town's newest option lies right beside the Interamerican highway, so you don't even need to go into town if you're passing through and just need a place to stay. ★ **Hotel Fuente Real** (tel. 4708-1514, www.fuenterealhotel.com, $46 d) is built in neocolonial motel style and has comfortably stylish rooms with plasma TVs, cable, and wireless Internet. The nicer rooms have hardwood floors and minifridges.

FOOD

Conveniently situated along the Interamerican highway adjacent to Hotel Fuente Real, ★ **Al Pomodoro Ristorante** (Km. 265.5 Carretera Interamericana, tel. 7768-1781, $8-20) serves scrumptious Italian dishes from an open-air kitchen. The spacious dining room is eclectically decorated and there's a full bar. A second location is in town at 4a Calle 8-40 Zona 1. You'll find tasty baked goods and good iced coffee at **Pastelería Monte Alto** (Corner 4a Avenida and 2a Calle, Zona 1, tel. 7764-9227). **Mi Tierra Café** (4a Calle 6-46 Zona 1, tel. 7764-1473, 7am-9pm Mon.-Sat., 2pm-9pm Sun.) is a friendly little restaurant that is ever-popular with locals, serving tasty nachos, pizza, and fajitas in addition to delicious breakfasts, including delectable croissant sandwiches. Try the "muffin ranchero," essentially a salsa-bathed egg sandwich with fried tortillas instead of bread. The strong coffee is locally grown and extraordinary. For steaks, seafood, and even some Chinese fare, check out **Restaurante Las Brasas** (corner of 2a Calle and 4a Avenida, tel. 7764-2339, 10am-11pm daily, $4-15). There's even duck on the menu. **Domino's Pizza** is at the corner of 7a Avenida and 5a Calle. Just down the street is one of the best places in town, ★ **Hotel Casa Blanca** (7a Avenida 3-41 Zona 1, tel. 7769-0777, 6am-10pm, $7-13), where you can dine alfresco in the backyard garden or inside facing the house's original courtyard. On the menu are steaks, grilled chicken, good soups, and salads as well as sandwiches.

INFORMATION AND SERVICES
Communications
The central **post office** is at 2a Calle 3-54 Zona 1 just east of the plaza. **Telgua** has pay phones and international calling right next door.

Money
The ATM at **G&T Banco Continental** on the north side of the plaza fronting 2a Calle works with both Visa and MasterCard. **Banco Industrial** (6a Avenida 1-26 Zona 1) has a Visa/Plus ATM. Both banks can change cash dollars and travelers checks.

GETTING THERE
The bus terminal is about two kilometers southwest of the city center, halfway along the boulevard leading out to the Pan-American Highway. There are frequent buses to many outlying towns and villages, most notably:

- **La Mesilla (Mexican border)** (two hours, $2): 20 daily buses 6am-6pm.
- **Nentón** (three hours, $2): six daily buses between 3:30am and 1pm.
- **Sacapulas, Quiché** (1.5 hours, $2): at 11:30am and 12:45pm.
- **Todos Santos Cuchumatán** (two hours, $2): leaving at 4:30am, 5am, 12:45pm, 1:30pm, 2:45pm, and 3:45pm. There may be others.

Frequent second-class bus departures also include **Guatemala City** (20 daily buses until 4pm, five hours, $5) and **Quetzaltenango** (16 daily buses until 2:30pm, two hours, $1.75).

Pullman bus service to Guatemala City is available via **Transportes Los Halcones** (10a Avenida 9-12 Zona 1, tel. 7765-7986, www.transportesloshalcones.com, $5) at 4:30am, 7am, and 2pm. **Transportes Zaculeu Futura** (3a Avenida 5-25 Zona 1, tel. 7764-1535) has departures at 6am and 3pm. **Transportes Velásquez,** operating from the main terminal, is another option, with buses every half hour or so between 8:30am and 3:30pm.

Huehuetenango Frontier

The road winds its way out of the departmental capital up the vertiginous face of the Cuchumatanes, with the superimposed quilt pattern of corn- and wheat fields upon the countryside transitioning to one of grasses and hearty maguey plants at about 2,700 meters (9,000 feet). At the top of the rise is a lookout point, **Mirador Dieguez Olaverri,** also known as **El Mirador** or La Cumbre (The Summit), from where there are views of Huehuetenango and Guatemala's impressive volcanic chain to the south.

A recent addition on par with the wonderful views is that of **Café del Cielo** (tel. 5316-6300, http://turismoruralguatemala.com/cafe-del-cielo, 8am-5pm daily, $5-7). Run by the same friendly folks who own nearby Unicornio Azul, the café serves excellent Huehuetenango coffees, pastries, chocolates, paninis, meat, fish, and pasta dishes. There are artisanal lamb sausages to-go and indoor/outdoor seating.

From the lookout, the road continues along the 3,300-meter (11,000-foot) Paquix plateau, characterized by smooth, rounded hills with scant vegetation that conjure images of the Peruvian Andes or Alaska. Windblown grasses, black granite rocks, sturdy maguey plants, and herds of sheep pepper the surrounding countryside with the occasional adobe house occupied by ruddy Maya more closely resembling their South American Inca relatives. The recent introduction of llamas to these areas adds further similarity.

About one kilometer north from the lookout, a dirt-road turnoff heads east to the village of Chancol and the **Unicornio Azul** equestrian center. Back along the main (paved) road another nine kilometers or so is the **Paquix Junction,** with its westbound turnoff heading to the village of **Todos Santos Cuchumatán.** Its northbound turnoff leads to the villages of San Juan Ixcoy, Soloma, Santa Eulalia, San Mateo Ixtatán, and, eventually, Barillas.

UNICORNIO AZUL

Not so much a hotel as a professionally run equestrian center, ★ Unicornio Azul (tel. 5205-9328, www.unicornioazul.com, $33 d) enjoys a spectacular location on the grassy plateau atop the rugged Cuchumatanes from where you can embark on horseback rides as short as one hour to as long as several days throughout the sprawling countryside. About 25 kilometers northeast of Huehuetenango, the operation consists of 11 well-cared-for horses, stables, and wonderful accommodations meticulously managed by its French Guatemalan owners. Prices for rides range from $80 for one day to $970 for nine days, though they vary depending on the number of riders in a group. The accommodations here are rustically beautiful, consisting of five rooms housed in two separate tiled-roof houses. All of the rooms are distinctly decorated and furnished with unique touches such as gorgeous lamps fashioned from Honduran Lenca pottery. At night, gas lamps provide wonderful ambience, though there is electricity for showers and cooking. Room rates include breakfast and one hour of horseback riding. Lunch and dinner are served family-style and cost $7 each. If you're not keen on riding, there are also mountain bikes for exploring the rugged roads and trails all around.

TODOS SANTOS CUCHUMATÁN

Todos Santos sits on the dry western slopes of the Cuchumatanes. Remote and largely retaining its traditions, it is a fine place to take in Mayan culture, do some hiking, and shop for unique weavings. It is one of only a few places in the highlands where you'll still see men wearing traditional attire, consisting of bright red pants with thin white stripes paired with a zany striped shirt featuring oversize,

Unicornio Azul

the church in Todos Santos

common sight throughout the highlands. As in the Ixil Triangle, the population here suffered greatly during the civil war. The army marched on the town in 1982 in the days following a brief occupation by EGP guerrillas, carrying out the torture, disappearance, and murder of suspected guerrilla sympathizers. Many villagers fled to the hillsides to wait out the troubles or went north to Mexico.

Todos Santos certainly remains very poor. Many of its residents have traditionally made ends meet by traveling to the Pacific lowlands to work in the annual harvests. Many Todosanteros now have family in the United States, a fact that becomes readily apparent as you walk the town's streets and see new construction funded with dollars sent from abroad by expatriate relatives. Despite its remoteness, it's not uncommon to see groups of villagers in their distinctive attire at Guatemala City's international airport waiting on the arrival of a returning family member. Statistics show Huehuetenango sends more of its inhabitants abroad than any other of Guatemala's departments.

As always, you should be careful not to photograph Mayan people (especially children) without permission, nor should you show undue interest. It can be tough at times, because Mayan children (and Maya in general) can provide some wonderful opportunities for portraiture. In 2000, a Japanese tourist and the Guatemalan tour bus driver who tried to protect him were lynched in Todos Santos by an angry mob after the tourist tried to photograph a child. The incident was certainly an isolated one and was attributed to a rumor about satanists who were supposedly in the area snatching local children at the time. If anything, it serves as a grim reminder that the old photographer's rule contending that it's easier to apologize (for taking a candid photo) than to ask permission doesn't really apply in Guatemala.

Sights

Museo Balam (tel. 5787-3598, fortunatopablomendoza@gmail.com, 6am-6pm, $1)

elaborately embroidered collars. The costume also includes a straw hat with a wide, blue, grommeted ribbon. The women wear equally stunning purple *huipiles* and embroider many items with the town's signature designs. Contributing to the remarkable preservation of local customs and dress is the intense local pride of Todos Santos's Mam-speaking residents, who stand a full head taller than most other Maya.

The village first gained notoriety after social scientist and world traveler Maud Oakes spent two years here starting in 1945 and wrote two books about her experiences, *The Two Crosses of Todos Santos* and *Beyond the Windy Place*. The local Mam hold four local mountain peaks sacred, and some of her neighbors reputedly believed the foreign-born female shaman to be the guardian of one of these.

The main market day here is Saturday. Don't be surprised to find inebriated men (mostly) stumbling through the streets or passed out on the sidewalk, an unfortunately is to the left 150 meters off the main street one block from the park. Run by a friendly local family, it features marimbas, costumes for traditional village dances, and old leather sandals, bags, plows, and saddles, affording a glimpse into the town's history and traditions.

Todos Santos is one of very few places in Guatemala that still largely adheres to the 260-day Mayan calendar known as the Tzolkin. There are frequent rituals, including animal sacrifices, performed at a small Mayan site just above town known either as **Cumanchúm** or **Tojcunenchén.** The ruins look out onto the 3,650-meter (12,000-foot) **Chemal** peak (also known as "La Torre" for the radio mast atop it), which is the highest nonvolcanic peak in Central America. To reach the summit, hike or take a bus east to the neighboring village of La Ventosa, from where a trail leads past adobe houses through sylvan settings to the top, a journey of about 1.5 hours. Your reward on a clear day is a breathtaking view of Guatemala's volcanic chain from Tacaná on the Mexican border all the way east to Agua and Acatenango, near Antigua.

Todos Santos is well known for its annual November 1 horse races capping off week-long festivities that include plenty of drinking, dancing, and general merriment.

Shopping

Housed in the Hotel Casa Familiar, **Artesanía Todosantera** (tel. 7783-0656) is a local weavers' cooperative displaying a fine array of handicrafts at reasonable prices. The gift shop is stocked with some of the region's most wonderful weavings and is almost an obligatory stop for anyone passing through.

Hiking

There are numerous opportunities for hikes. If you want a guide or printed information to make the most of your walk, head to either of the town's two language schools. One of the most popular walks is to the site of **Las Letras,** the town's equivalent of the "Hollywood" sign overlooking California's

highland scene on the road to Todos Santos

famous neighborhood. The Todos Santos version is a series of white painted rocks above town, with an arrangement that might be illegible depending on when they were last reassembled. It's about a two-hour hike round-trip. From there, you can continue another five hours to the villages of **Tuicoy** and **Tzichim. La Puerta del Cielo** is another amazing lookout point accessible via a detour from Tuicoy. A five-hour trek from Todos Santos is the village of **San Juan Atitán,** up the ridge looming over the village and down into a valley, crossing streams and verdant forests along the way.

Accommodations

Most of the town's accommodations can be found in a cluster up the hill about a block from the plaza. Only a few have phones to contact for reservations. A virtual Todos Santos institution, ★ **Hotel Casa Familiar** (tel. 7783-0656 or 5737-0112, $26 d) is a longtime favorite with travelers. Run by a local family, it has been remodeled to provide upgraded

All Saints' Day in Todos Santos

If you're in Todos Santos around November 1 (All Saints' Day) and love a good party, you won't want to miss the three-day annual town festival, at the center of which is a series of horse races. There's plenty of drinking, dancing, and marimba music during this time. The race begins with costumed riders galloping from one end of the 600-yard course, drinking *aguardiente* upon their arrival at the course's other extreme before heading back once again. The back-and-forth pattern is a competition of survival of the fittest; riders struggle to hang on as the race (and drunken stupor) reach a crescendo. Traditionally, the riders hit the horses with live chickens, though in recent years they have used whips. The races sometimes continue well into the afternoon.

By the end of the day, most people are lying passed out in the streets or in bars (if they're lucky) in a drunken spectacle rivaled in few places in Guatemala. There are always a few drunken brawls and some folks who wind up in the town jail. The next day is Day of the Dead, and the festivities transition to the local cemetery, where families visit departed relatives, marking their gravestones with candles and flowers. There's also more music and dance as part of the final day of celebration.

accommodations for visitors. Some of the new rooms have private bathrooms and patios; all have tasteful Maya-inspired decor. There is also a pleasant garden dining area. You can arrange guided hikes from here as well as reading lessons. Movies are shown daily at 4pm.

Another good choice is **Hotelito Todos Santos** (tel. 7783-0603 or 5327-9313, $12-17 d), also recently upgraded, with comfortable rooms with shared or private bath and typical Guatemalan decor. There's a pleasant living room area where guests like to congregate. It also has a dining room serving basic meals. Next door is the bare-bones **Hotel Mam** (tel. 5192-1794, $5 pp). All of the rooms are on a shared-bath basis. Turning right up the hill at the end of this same street, you'll find **Hotel El Viajero** (tel. 7783-0705 or 5789-3175, $4 pp), with basic rooms, one with private bath. The kitchen is available for use for about $1 a day and there's a nice view from the rooftop.

Food

There are a few decent places for food along the main street heading out from the plaza toward the main road and Huehuetenango. Among these is **Restaurante Cuchumatlán,** serving pizzas ($8 for a large pie), curry dishes, and fruit smoothies. It also has a book exchange. The patio dining area at **Casa**

Familiar (tel. 7783-0656, $3-7) is also a good place to grab a bite to eat.

Information and Services

For your banking needs, **Banrural** is on the trapezoidal plaza at the center of town. The post office and police are also here.

Todos Santos's two language schools charge about $130 per week for 4-5 hours of instruction per day plus homestay with a local family. Living conditions are very basic and most host families speak Mam, with a select few opportunities for homestay with Spanish-speaking families. Both schools also offer instruction in the local Mayan dialect. The two schools are **Academia Hispano Maya** (opposite Hotelito Todos Santos, www.hispanomaya. org) and **Nuevo Amanecer** (150 meters west of the plaza, escuela_linguistica@yahoo.com).

Getting There

There are seven daily buses to Huehuetenango (2.5 hours) that leave from the plaza, the last one leaving at 4:30pm.

WEST TO MEXICO
La Mesilla

Heading northwest from Huehuetenango, the Pan-American Highway leads to La Mesilla border and, beyond that, Mexico. Border formalities here are pretty straightforward, though the Mexican border crossing lies four kilometers away on the other side at Ciudad Cuauhtémoc, for which you'll need to take a collective taxi ($1) if you're not in your own car. There are basic services here, including banks, a post office, police station, and ubiquitous money changers.

Nentón to Gracias a Dios

A few kilometers east of La Mesilla along the Pan-American Highway, a turnoff branches north down a newly paved road to the town of Nentón and continues to a new border crossing at Gracias a Dios. Border formalities at Gracias a Dios are fairly straightforward, and the friendly immigration agents might grant you a day pass to cross into Mexico to see the spectacular **Lagunas de Montebello,** a national park with pristine emerald lagoons surrounded by luxuriant forests.

Along the road from Nentón to Gracias a Dios, you could stop to admire **El Cimarrón,** a cavernous, 300-meter-deep limestone sinkhole harboring a forest at its base that has only recently been descended and explored. From the main road about three kilometers from the village of **La Trinidad,** 35 kilometers north of Nentón, a network of trails leads through surrounding farmland and cattle pastures to the sinkhole. It's about a 30-minute walk from the road.

From La Trinidad, a dirt road leads east to the village of **Yalambojoch,** where you can grab a pickup heading east to San Mateo Ixtatán. It also serves as a transit point for visits to the wonderful **Laguna Yolnajab,** also known as Laguna Brava, five kilometers north of here. There are many returned refugees from Mexico living in these parts, and you should be aware that the activities of foreign mining companies here and in other parts of northern Huehuetenango have locals a bit on edge. (Even the local tourism committee in Yalambojoch was not exactly welcoming on a recent visit.) Exercise due caution. Better yet, go with the fun, friendly, and quite knowledgeable folks at Guatemala City-based **Expedición Extrema** (tel. 5655-3916 or 3003-2866, info.expedicion@gmail.com). They utilize the tourism services of the friendlier village of Aguacate, also close to the lagoon. Another option is to visit the lagoon via Mexico, just across the border. There is better road access and the northern part of the lagoon you'll have access to has some beautiful cenotes.

With help from local outfitter Unicornio Azul, a tourism initiative in the community

Posada Rural Finca Chaculá

of Chaculá began hosting visits to area attractions in 2009. Visitors stay at **Posada Rural Finca Chaculá** (tel. 5205-9328, www. turismochacula.com, $40 d), a revamped old farmhouse where there are basic but clean, comfortable accommodations. The posada runs trips to El Cimarrón and other nearby attractions, including the Cenotes de Candelaria, caves with interesting pictographs, and pristine Río Lagartero (also known as Río Azul), which is a dazzlingly exotic hue of blue.

Quetzaltenango (Xela) and Vicinity

Head southeast from Huehuetenango on the Pan-American Highway, some 80 kilometers toward Guatemala City, to the highland city of Quetzaltenango. The country's second-largest city is the main population center of the country's K'iche' Maya and an increasingly popular destination with language school students and NGO workers. Its original K'iche' name is Xelajú, still widely in use today, though in its abbreviated form, Xela. Set in a sprawling valley dominated by the near-perfect cone of 3,772-meter (12,375-foot) Santa María Volcano and the adjacent (active) Santiaguito, the city has a population of about 300,000. It sits at a rather high altitude of 2,400 meters (8,000 feet) and can be correspondingly chilly.

Xela is very cosmopolitan and has all the feel of a European highland city. It is considerably safe for a city of its size and has a lively cultural scene peppered by the presence of an ever-increasing number of foreign visitors. There are also good hotels and restaurants, along with interesting day trips to neighboring highland Mayan villages that still adhere strictly to the old ways. Nearby natural attractions include a wonderful crater lake, climbs to the surrounding volcanoes, and soaking in warm hot springs. If you really start to long for the warmer climates, the sweltering Pacific coastal lowlands are just about an hour away and beaches lie not much farther.

History
Quetzaltenango was originally a Mam-speaking Mayan town before coming under the influence of the K'iche'-speaking Maya of K'umarcaaj during their 14th-century expansionist wars. K'iche' leader Tecún Umán was defeated by Spanish conquistador Pedro de Alvarado in 1524 at a site known as Llanos del Pinal, southwest of town at the base of Santa María Volcano. The town became quite prosperous during the 19th-century coffee boom. Its newfound prosperity, coupled with the abatement of Spanish power in the aftermath of independence, contributed to strong separatist sentiments shared with highland areas to the west. Guatemala City would bring the renegade region back into the fold in the latter part of the century, though Quetzaltenango remains a strong focal point for regional identity.

Like other Guatemalan population centers, it is no stranger to earthquakes, having been rocked by an earthquake and a volcanic eruption courtesy of Santa María Volcano in 1902. It was subsequently rebuilt, largely in neoclassical style. Its strategic location at a crossroads for trade and transport between the highlands and agriculturally rich Pacific slope have continued to ensure the city's prosperity despite any setbacks along the way. A regional railway once connected Xela to the Pacific slope, but natural disasters and political manipulation from Guatemala City made the railway, known as the Ferrocarril de los Altos, extremely short-lived.

Orientation
Quetzaltenango lies a few kilometers south of the Cuatro Caminos Junction, found along the Pan-American Highway. Its Zona 1 downtown core houses most of its important monuments, as well as the bulk of its tourist

Quetzaltenango (Xela)

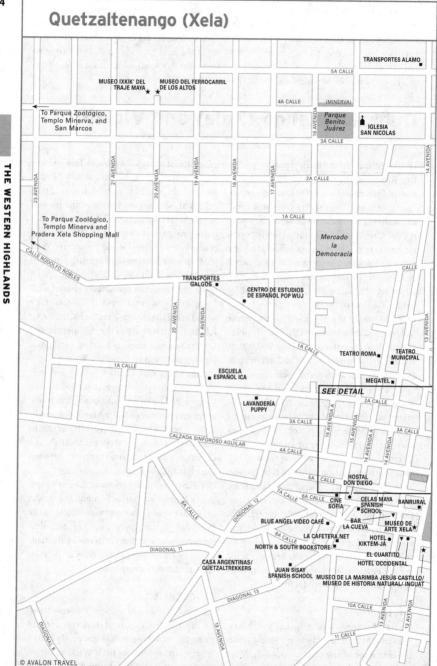

TRANSPORTES ALAMO ■

MUSEO IXKIK' DEL TRAJE MAYA ★

MUSEO DEL FERROCARRIL DE LOS ALTOS ★

5A CALLE

4A CALLE (MINERVA)

To Parque Zoológico, Templo Minerva, and San Marcos

16 AVENIDA

Parque Benito Juárez

IGLESIA SAN NICOLAS

3A CALLE

21 AVENIDA

20 AVENIDA

19 AVENIDA

18 AVENIDA

17 AVENIDA

2A CALLE

14 AVENIDA

23 AVENIDA

To Parque Zoológico, Templo Minerva and Pradera Xela Shopping Mall

1A CALLE

CALLE RODOLFO ROBLES

Mercado la Democracia

CALLE

TRANSPORTES GALGOS ■

CENTRO DE ESTUDIOS DE ESPAÑOL POP WUJ ■

20 AVENIDA

19 AVENIDA

1A CALLE

13 AVENIDA

TEATRO ROMA ■ TEATRO MUNICIPAL ■

ESCUELA ESPAÑOL ICA ■

MEGATEL ■

SEE DETAIL

2A CALLE

15 AVENIDA A

15 AVENIDA

14 AVENIDA A

14 AVENIDA

3A CALLE

LAVANDERÍA PUPPY ■

3A CALLE

CALZADA SINFOROSO AGUILAR

4A CALLE

5A CALLE

HOSTAL DON DIEGO ●

7A CALLE

6A CALLE

DIAGONAL 12

8A CALLE

CINE SOFIA ■

CELAS MAYA SPANISH SCHOOL BANRURAL

BAR LA CUEVA MUSEO DE ARTE XELA ▲

BLUE ANGEL VIDEO CAFÉ ■

8A CALLE

LA CAFETERA.NET ■

HOTEL KIKTEM-JÁ ●

NORTH & SOUTH BOOKSTORE ■

DIAGONAL 11

EL CUARTITO HOTEL OCCIDENTAL

CASA ARGENTINAS/ QUETZALTREKKERS ■

JUAN SISAY SPANISH SCHOOL

MUSEO DE LA MARIMBA JESÚS CASTILLO/ MUSEO DE HISTORIA NATURAL/ INGUAT

DIAGONAL 13

DIAGONAL 8

19 AVENIDA

10A CALLE

13 AVENIDA

12 AVENIDA

11 CALLE

© AVALON TRAVEL

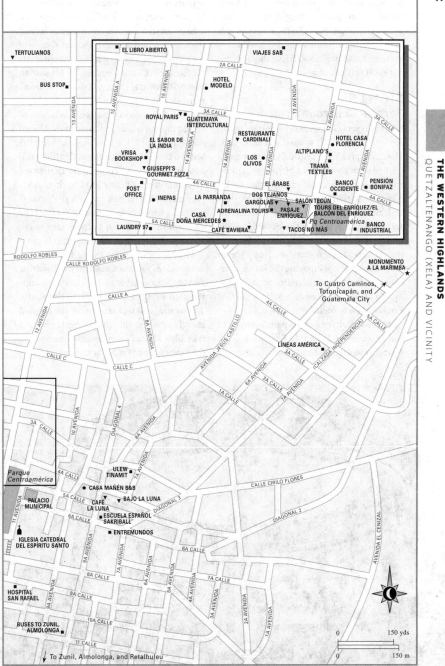

TERTULIANOS

BUS STOP

13 AVENIDA

EL LIBRO ABIERTO

VIAJES SAB

15 AVENIDA A

15 AVENIDA

2A AVENIDA

2A CALLE

HOTEL
MODELO

13 AVENIDA

12 AVENIDA

3A CALLE

ROYAL PARIS

3A CALLE

GUATEMAYA
INTERCULTURAL

14 AVENIDA A

14 AVENIDA

RESTAURANTE
CARDINALI

HOTEL CASA
FLORENCIA

EL SABOR DE
LA INDIA

ALTIPLANO'S

VRISA
BOOKSHOP

LOS
OLIVOS

13 AVENIDA

TRAMA
TEXTILES

11 AVENIDA

GIUSEPPI'S
GOURMET PIZZA

4A CALLE

EL ÁRABE

BANCO
OCCIDENTE

PENSIÓN
BONIFAZ

POST
OFFICE

INEPAS

LA PARRANDA

DOS TEJANOS

GARGOLAS

SALÓN TECÚN

4A CALLE

ADRENALINA TOURS

PASAJE
ENRIQUEZ

TOURS DEL ENRÍQUEZ/EL
BALCÓN DEL ENRÍQUEZ

CASA
DOÑA MERCEDES

5A CALLE

Pq Centroamérica

LAUNDRY 97

CAFÉ BAVIERA

TACOS NO MÁS

BANCO
INDUSTRIAL

RODOLFO ROBLES

CALLE RODOLFO ROBLES

MONUMENTO
A LA MARIMBA

CALLE A

To Cuatro Caminos,
Totonicapán, and
Guatemala City

4A CALLE

5A CALLE

12 AVENIDA

8A AVENIDA

AVENIDA JESÚS CASTILLO

LÍNEAS AMÉRICA

CALLE C

CALLE C

3A CALLE

CALZADA INDEPENDENCIA

10 AVENIDA

DIAGONAL 4

6A AVENIDA

2A CALLE

2A AVENIDA

1A CALLE

7A AVENIDA

8A AVENIDA

Parque
Centroamérica

3A CALLE

ULEW
TINAMIT

7A AVENIDA

CALLE CIRILO FLORES

4A CALLE

10 AVENIDA

CASA MAÑÉN B&B

DIAGONAL 3

PALACIO
MUNICIPAL

5A CALLE

CAFÉ
LA LUNA

BAJO LA LUNA

DIAGONAL 2

11 AVENIDA

6A CALLE

ESCUELA ESPAÑOL
SAKRIBALL

IGLESIA CATEDRAL
DEL ESPÍRITU SANTO

ENTREMUNDOS

AVENIDA EL CENIZAL

8A AVENIDA

6A AVENIDA

6A CALLE

5A AVENIDA

HOSPITAL
SAN RAFAEL

8A CALLE

9A CALLE

4A AVENIDA

7A CALLE

3A AVENIDA

2A AVENIDA

BUSES TO ZUNIL,
ALMOLONGA

9A AVENIDA

10A CALLE

1A AVENIDA

11 CALLE

To Zunil, Almolonga, and Retalhuleu

0   150 yds

0   150 m

services, and is laid out in the standard grid pattern. Avenidas run roughly north-south and calles run east-west. Zona 2 covers an area to the northeast, while Zona 3 sprawls to the north and northwest. You'll find the city's bus station at this end of town.

SIGHTS
Parque Centroamérica

Like the rest of Guatemala's important urban centers, Xela is built around a central park. The city's sprawling **Parque Centroamérica** is lined with government offices, museums, and a shopping arcade, among other buildings, and is itself splendidly shaded by trees and adorned by neoclassical monuments and flower beds. It gives the city a decidedly European feel, enhanced by the presence of several Greek columns, and is a fine place for people-watching or enjoying the warm afternoon sun amid the surrounding buzz of activity. An artisans' market is held here the first Sunday of every month.

At the western end of the park, between 12 and 13 Avenidas, is **Pasaje Enríquez,** a pedestrian thoroughfare and commercial arcade

originally built to house fine shops but now home to several good bars and restaurants. One of these, Salón Tecún, is on the second floor, from which there are wonderful views of the plaza below. On the park's southern end is the Casa de la Cultura, housing the **Museo de Historia Natural** (Natural History Museum, 8am-noon and 2pm-6pm Mon.-Fri., 9am-1pm Sat., $1). The museum is an odd collection of taxidermy and rooms dedicated to the Liberal Revolution of 1871 which, together with the **Museo de la Marimba Jesús Castillo** (also housed here), were collectively christened "Museum of the Kitchen Sink" by this guide's previous author for its antique dealer's garage sale feel. I have to concur, and unless you have a rainy afternoon with nothing else to do, you're probably better off skipping this one.

On the eastern end of the park is the original facade of **Iglesia Catedral del Espíritu Santo,** which dates to 1535 and was constructed by Bishop Francisco Marroquín. The facade is all that remains of the original church, as a new church was erected behind it in 1899 and was very heavily damaged in the earthquake of 1902. The current cathedral

Xela's Parque Centroamérica

building is the latest reconstruction. The neighboring Municipalidad (City Hall) was likewise reconstructed after the 1902 earthquake in grand neoclassical style.

Outside the City Center (Zona 3)

The legacy of maniacal dictator Manuel Estrada Cabrera's quest to emulate all things European, the neoclassical Templo Minerva is a monument to the Greek goddess of wisdom. It stands at the corner of Calle Minerva and Calle Rodolfo Robles. The temple looks over the city's bus terminal and busy market. Farther along, in Parque Minerva proper, is the Parque Zoológico Minerva (9am-5pm Tues.-Sun., free), where there's an unimpressive collection of animals housed in cages. Buses to this part of town leave from Pasaje Enríquez at 13 Avenida and 4a Calle Zona 1.

Formerly the Zona Militar 1715, the old building that once served as the train terminal for the defunct Ferrocarril de los Altos is now the city's train museum though it's not really anything to write home about. Also housed in this complex is the Museo Ixkik' del Traje Maya (4a Calle and 19 Avenida Zona 3, tel. 7761-6472, www.museoixkik.org, 9am-1pm and 3pm-6pm Mon.-Fri., $1), with a collection of indigenous costumes.

ENTERTAINMENT
Bars

Beer drinkers will want to try Cabro, an excellent local brew sold widely in Xela. As for watering holes, the ever-popular Salón Tecún (Pasaje Enríquez, on the west side of Parque Centroamérica, tel. 7761-2832 or 5630-2411, $5-20) is one of Xela's main gathering spots, with a great location, lively atmosphere, and funky decor. There's also outdoor seating fronting the attractive Pasaje Enríquez pedestrian thoroughfare. You can wash down your drink with menu items that include pizzas, pastas, and vegetarian dishes.

Gárgolas (4a Calle 12-49 Zona 1, Pasaje Enriquez, 5pm-1am daily) has a hip atmosphere and plays good music. You can drink at the bar or step into the stylish lounge areas to enjoy your evening under baroque, cathedral-like columns. A chill coffee bar also serving wine and cocktails is La Pequeña Fonda (15 Avenida 7-43 Zona 1, 3pm-10pm daily). There's live music some nights. The bar inside Pensión Bonifaz (4a Calle 10-50 Zona 1, tel. 7765-1111) is the place to go for high-brow socializing.

Nightlife

The town's local nightlife hot spots seem to change constantly, so you might be better off asking around. The city's so-called Zona Viva is centered between 12 and 15 Avenidas from 1a to 6a Calle in Zona 1. A walk around this part of town will surely yield some fun bar-hopping results. That said, La Parranda (14 Avenida 4-41 Zona 1, www.laparrandadisco.com, 8pm-1am Wed.-Sat.) is a solid choice for dancing. For salsa and merengue dancing, check out La Rumba (at the corner of 13 Avenida and 7a Calle Zona 1, 6pm-1am Mon.-Sat.).

Performing Arts

There are sometimes cultural performances at the elegant Teatro Municipal (1a Calle between 14 Avenida and 14 Avenida "A"), which dates from 1908.

Cinema

Blue Angel Video Café (7a Calle 15-79 Zona 1, 1pm-11pm Mon.-Sat., 3pm-10pm Sun., $1.30 for movie) shows two movies nightly starting at 8pm and serves vegetarian fare and smoothies. For the latest releases, head to Cines Pradera Xela (Avenida Las Américas y 7a Calle Zona 3, www.circuitoalba.com.gt, $5) inside its namesake shopping mall. Cinépolis (www.cinepolis.com.gt) was slated to open a new cinema at Utz Ulew Mall (19 Avenida 2-40 Zona 3) in early 2016.

SHOPPING

Compared to Panajachel and Antigua, Xela is not a big shopping destination. A standout in this regard is Trama Textiles (3a Calle 10-56 Zona 1, tel. 7765-8564, www.tramatextiles.org), a women's association that works with 17 cooperatives representing 400 women from five of Guatemala's highland regions. It sells high-quality products that are prewashed, preshrunk, and completely colorfast. There are scarves, purses, table runners, and some truly exquisite pillowcases for sale. Another good option is **Y'abal Handicrafts** (12 Avenida 3-35 Zona 1, tel. 4198-3615, www.yabal-handicrafts.com). For all your import shopping needs, **Pradera Xela Shopping Mall** (10am-9pm Mon.-Sat., 11am-8pm Sun.) is on Avenida Las Américas between 7a and 8a Calles Zona 3, outside the city center. Under construction at the time of writing was the gargantuan **Utz Ulew Mall** (19 Avenida 2-40 Zona 3, tel. 7930-4482, www.utzulewmall.com).

Books

North and South Bookstore (8a Calle and 15 Avenida 13-77 Zona 1, tel. 7761-0589, 9:30am-6pm Mon.-Fri., 9:30am-5pm Sat.) sells a good selection of books in English with subjects including Guatemalan politics and history, travel guides, birding manuals, maps, Spanish textbooks, and dictionaries. **Vrisa Bookshop** (15 Avenida 3-64 Zona 1, tel. 7761-3237, 9am-7pm Mon.-Sat.) sells mostly used books with some new titles, mostly in English. **El Libro Abierto** (15 Avenida "A" 1-56 Zona 1, tel. 7761-5195, 9:30am-5:30pm Mon.-Fri., 11am-5pm Sat.) has a wide selection of books in English and Spanish.

RECREATION
Volcano Climbs

Accessible from Xela are a variety of volcano hikes, including **Tajumulco Volcano,** which is Central America's highest volcano, in the neighboring department of San Marcos. Closer to Xela is **Santa María Volcano,** affording excellent views all the way to Lake Atitlán as well as over its active, much smaller neighbor **Santiaguito Volcano.**

It is very easy to get lost on these peaks so a guide is strongly recommended. (Hikers have gotten lost on the slopes of Volcán Santa María.) Several local companies offer trips. Highly recommended for volcano climbs as well as excellent tours to area attractions is **Adrenalina Tours** (13 Avenida and 4a Calle Zona 1, Pasaje Enríquez, tel. 7761-4509 or 7767-2474, www.adrenalinatours.com). Trips leave with a minimum of two people and include Santa María Volcano ($25-45 pp), Chicabal Lagoon ($25-50), the Santiaguito Volcano lookout ($25-50), Tajumulco Volcano ($50), and a rockin' three-day hike to Lake Atitlán ($85). Adrenalina Tours can also book plane tickets and Tikal tours. The company operates shuttle bus service to Antigua, Guatemala City, Panajachel, the Mexican border, and Chichicastenango.

Monte Verde Tours (13 Avenida 8-34 Zona 1, tel. 7761-6105, www.monte-verde-tours.com) offers guided hikes to all of the Xela area volcanoes as well as to Laguna Chicabal and multiday treks from Xela to Lake Atitlán ($85). Farther afield, they run treks from Nebaj to Todos Santos Cuchumatán (4 days, $120).

With excellent guides and proceeds that go directly to fund projects that benefit Xela's street children, **Quetzaltrekkers** (Diagonal 12 8-43 Zona 1, inside Casa Argentina, tel. 7765-5895, www.quetzaltrekkers.com) is highly recommended for its two-day volcano trips to Santiaguito and Tajumulco ($65), three-day treks to Lake Atitlán ($100), and a wonderful six-day highland trek between the villages of Nebaj and Todos Santos ($175). You can look at a calendar with scheduled trips on their website.

Other reliable options include **Altiplano's** (12 Avenida 3-35 Zona 1, tel. 7766-9614, www.altiplanos.com.gt) and **Icaro Tours** (6a Calle 14-55 Zona 1, tel. 7761-4342, www.icarotours.com). Upcoming trips are prominently displayed on their websites, taking some of the legwork out of trying to get a group together if you are traveling alone.

Rock Climbing

The **Cerro Quemado,** near Xela, offers good rock climbing on its 45-meter (150-foot) rock

Climbing Santa María Volcano

Santa María and Santiaguito Volcanoes

Santa María is one of the most popular volcano climbs from Xela, with spectacular views from its 3,772-meter summit. The trailhead is at the end of a paved road in the village of Llanos del Pinal. To get there, take one of the hourly pickups leaving from Xela's Cementerio General (General Cemetery) at 20 Avenida and 4a Calle 7am-5pm. Heading out of Llanos del Pinal, the road soon turns into a trail up the steep volcanic slopes, with painted arrows leading the way along this initial section of the footpath. About two hours from the starting point, you reach a flat grassy area known as "La Mesa," where the trail diverts to the right and then switchbacks up the mountainside through pine forests. This part of the climb is somewhat steeper, with the summit about three hours from this point. A few hundred meters from the summit, you'll see the end of the tree line and the summit itself, providing a much-needed mental boost for the end of your climb.

The best time to arrive at the summit is at sunrise, affording opportunities to take in the magnificent views before clouds start to roll in. From there, you can look southwest into the smoking crater of 2,500-meter Santiaguito Volcano, which has been belching out smoke and ash since its birth in 1902. To the east you'll see the cones of San Pedro, Tolimán, Atitlán, Acatenango, Agua, and Fuego. If you look west, you'll see the two highest volcanoes in Central America, Tajumulco and Tacaná, on the Mexican border.

Santa María's last major eruption took place October 24-25, 1902, when it coughed up 10 cubic kilometers of ash into the stratosphere, covering much of the Pacific Coast and destroying a large section of the volcano's south face. Ash from the eruption is reported to have reached as far north as California.

The safety situation on the volcanoes in Xela's vicinity is markedly better than on those around Lake Atitlán, though robberies are by no means unheard of. It's best to go with a guide. If after climbing Santa María and peering down into smoking Santiaguito you itch for more volcanic adventures, you'll be happy to know several outfitters run trips to the challenging, ashy slopes of this smaller active volcano.

faces known locally as "La Muela." Routes include traditional climbs as well as sport climbing and are rated 5.07 to 5.13. Antigua-based **Old Town Outfitters** (5a Avenida Sur #12C, Antigua, tel. 5339-0440, www.adventureguatemala.com) does a two-day trip, leaving from Antigua and staying overnight in a Xela hotel. Locally based **Quetzaltrekkers** (Diagonal 12 8-43 Zona 1, inside Casa Argentina, tel. 7765-5895, www.quetzaltrekkers.com) does a day trip for $39-46 pp including gear, transport, food, water, and guides.

ACCOMMODATIONS
Under $50

An excellent choice for budget travelers, **Hostal Don Diego** (6a Calle 15-12 Zona 1, tel. 5308-3616 and 5308-1489, www.hostaldondiegoxela.com, $8 pp dorm, $17 d) has clean rooms and a choice of twin- or queen size-beds in private rooms, some with wood paneling. **Casa Argentina** (Diagonal 12 8-43 Zona 1, tel. 7761-2470, $4 pp in dorms, $5 pp shared-bath room to $13 d with private bath) is a budget hotel with 27 rooms. Some have cable TV, and there are always tea, coffee, and purified water available. Guests have use of the kitchen. Quetzaltrekkers is housed here.

★ **Casa Doña Mercedes** (6a Calle and 14 Avenida 13-42 Zona 1, tel. 5687-3305, www.hostalcasadonamercedes.com.gt, $23-37 d) has excellent-value rooms with tile floors, wood ceilings, Guatemalan bedspreads gracing the firm beds, and spotless shared bathroom. It's well located.

★ **Hotel Modelo** (14 Avenida "A" 2-31 Zona 1, tel. 7761-2529, www.hotelmodelo1892.com, $45 d) is a well-situated, excellent-value hotel in an old colonial home run by a friendly Guatemalan family. The nicest rooms are in a section fronting the street and opening to a pleasant garden courtyard. All have private bathroom, hardwood floors and ceilings, cable TV, charming antique furniture, warm wool blankets to ward off the chill, and pleasantly hot showers. There's free wireless Internet, and the restaurant here serves good breakfasts. **Hotel Casa Florencia** (12

Avenida 3-61 Zona 1, tel. 7761-2326, $32 d) has nice, carpeted rooms with private bath, cable TV, wood paneling, tungsten reading lights, and nice extras such as shampoo and soap. The friendly innkeeper, Celeste, keeps it spotless. It's also really well situated with plenty of restaurants nearby.

$50-100

A gorgeous flower garden and rock waterfall set the mood as you enter Xela's most wonderfully atmospheric hotel, ★ **Casa Mañen B&B** (9a Avenida 4-11 Zona 1, tel. 7765-0786, www.comeseeit.com, $50-100 d), with nine tastefully decorated rooms featuring exquisite furnishings, wool blankets and throw rugs, terra-cotta floors, cable TV, and private bathroom. There's a rooftop terrace bar with wonderful city views. The delicious breakfast is served in a pleasant dining room looking out to the peaceful garden courtyard.

The haunt of Guatemala's oligarchy on visits to Xela, ★ **Pensión Bonifaz** (4a Calle 10-50 Zona 1, tel. 7723-1100, www.pensionbonifaz.com.gt, $65-100 d) is a beautiful old hotel. It has spacious, well-decorated rooms with private bathrooms, desks, and cable TV. There are a restaurant, small gift shop, and a heated swimming pool in a pretty garden courtyard under an opaque ceiling letting in just enough sunlight. There's wireless Internet on the first floor, and the rooms just above it (numbers 123-130) get a signal. More modern rooms are housed in a newer section, but those in the original building harbor all the charm. Be aware the rooms are spread out over five floors and there is no elevator. The parking garage connects to the fourth floor.

FOOD
Cafés and Light Meals

★ **Café Baviera** (5a Calle 13-14 Zona 1, tel. 7761-5018, 7am-10am daily, $4-10) is a breakfast spot with a decidedly German atmosphere chock-full of antiques where you can enjoy scrumptious pastries, sandwiches, crepes, and shakes in addition to some of the best coffee in town. **Café La Luna** (8a Avenida 4-11 Zona

lunch at El Sabor de la India in Xela

1, tel. 7761-2242 or 5174-6769, 9:30am-9pm Mon.-Fri., 4pm-9pm Sat.-Sun.) is wonderfully decorated with an eclectic mix of antiques, including old signs, gas lamps, cash registers, and even pre-Columbian artifacts. Menu options include great coffee, snacks, and desserts, and there are daily specials of various Guatemalan dishes, including delicious enchiladas on Sundays. Try the scrumptious chocolate cake.

Around the corner and under the same ownership is **Bajo La Luna** (tel. 7763-0125, 7pm-11pm Tues.-Sat.), a cozy wine cellar with a charming old-world feel where there's a good mix of bottled wines ranging in price $9-50. There are also various cheeses on offer. With wonderful views of Parque Centroamérica from its second-floor terrace, **El Balcón del Enríquez** (12 Avenida 4-40 Zona 1, tel. 7765-2296, all meals daily) is a good place to start the day or wind it down with a cup of coffee or cocktail while people-watching over the plaza below. There are good sandwiches, breakfasts, and pastries. For a quaint coffee-bar atmosphere, check out **El Cuartito** (13 Avenida 7-09 Zona 1, 11am-11pm Wed.-Mon.), serving organically grown fair trade coffee, tea, and chocolate beverages in addition to tempting cookies and baked goods. There are books and board games to keep you entertained, free wireless Internet, and live music some nights. You'll find tasty pizzas, salads, crepes, and pastas at **Sabe Delis** (14 Avenida "A" 3-38 Zona 1, tel. 7761-2635). The atmosphere is warm and cozy.

Mediterranean

El Árabe (4a Calle 12-22 Zona 1, tel. 7761-7889, noon-midnight daily, $4-10) serves delicious Middle Eastern fare, including fresh hummus and tasty falafel. It's conveniently situated just off the plaza and can also be a lively place at night.

Asian

Still going strong, ★ **El Sabor de la India** (15 Avenida 3-64 Zona 1, tel. 7765-2555, noon-10pm Tues.-Sun., $4-12) serves delicious vegetarian and nonvegetarian Indian dishes in generous portions. For mouthwateringly delicious Chinese food, head to **Sublime Café** (23 Avenida 1-87 Zona 1, tel. 4162-7380, $4-12). I love the dim sum sampler, which is a selection of eight dishes including noodles, wontons, pork buns, and egg rolls.

Tex-Mex

Xela boasts an excellent Tex-Mex restaurant in **Dos Tejanos** (4a Calle 12-33, Pasaje Enríquez, tel. 7765-4360, 7am-11pm daily), where you can dig into authentic Texas barbecue ribs, chicken, and brisket.

Italian

For authentic Italian food in a wonderful old-world family atmosphere, head to ★ **Restaurante Cardinali** (14 Avenida 3-25 Zona 1, tel. 7761-0922, 11:30am-10pm daily, $9). There's a large wine selection. **Giuseppe's Gourmet Pizza** (15 Avenida 3-68 Zona 1, Edificio Santa Rita Segundo Nivel, tel. 7761-2521 or 7761-9439,

11am-9:30pm) has fairly decent hand-tossed pizza and pastas.

Fine Dining

The dining room at the upscale **Pensión Bonifaz** (4a Calle 10-50 Zona 1, tel. 7723-1100, all meals daily) is a good place for a splurge with a variety of Guatemalan and international dishes served in a classy atmosphere frequented by the city's elite. **Royal Paris** (14 Avenida "A" 3-06 Zona 1, tel. 7761-1942, noon-11pm Tues.-Sun., 6pm-11pm Mon., $5-15) is a very popular, highly authentic French bistro with dishes that include crepes, baked camembert, and onion soup, as well as meat, chicken, fish, and pasta that you can enjoy accompanied by excellent wines. There's live music on Friday and Saturday nights, and French or Italian movies are shown on Tuesdays at 8pm. Housed in a charming century-old mansion, ★ **Tertulianos** (14 Avenida 5-26 Zona 3, tel. 7767-4202, www.tertulianos.com.gt, 7am-10pm Mon.-Sat., 7am-5pm Sun., $6-15) serves a varied menu that includes meats, seafood, pasta and various types of fondue. Its quaint wine cellar is best reserved for a romantic dinner.

INFORMATION AND SERVICES
Tourist Information

The **INGUAT tourism information center** (7a Calle 11-35 Zona 1, tel. 7761-4931, 9am-5pm Mon.-Fri.) is on the southern end of Parque Centroamérica next to Casa de la Cultura, though you might have better luck getting information from local travel agencies such as Adrenalina Tours just a few steps away in Pasaje Enríquez.

Useful websites with some helpful information include www.xelapages.com, www.xelapages.net, www.xelawho.com, and Spanish-language www.xelaenlinea.com.

Communications

The main **post office** is at 4a Calle 15-07 Zona 1. Couriers include **DHL** (4a Calle 23-27 Zona 3, Centro Comercial Plaza La Villa, tel. 2339-8400 ext. 7520). Some travelers have complained of incorrect import duties for packages shipped to Guatemala via DHL.

Money

There are several banks, some with ATMs, on Parque Centroamérica, including **Banco de Occidente,** on the north end of the park, where you can change cash dollars and travelers checks. **Banco Industrial,** on the east side of the plaza, has a Visa ATM, while **Banrural,** on its west side, has both a Visa and MasterCard ATM.

Laundry

Lavandería Pilas (7a Avenida 5-48 Zona 1, tel. 7767-4608, 8am-6pm Mon.-Sat.) charges $3 for a four-kilogram load, washed and dried.

Medical Services

Private hospitals include **Hospital Privado Quetzaltenango** (Calle Rodolfo Robles 25-31 Zona 3, tel. 7761-4381/82), **Hospital La Democracia** (13 Avenida 6-51 Zona 3, tel. 7763-6760/62), and **Hospital San Rafael** (9a Calle 10-41 Zona 1, tel. 7761-4414 or 7761-2956), with 24-hour emergency service.

Emergency

For the firefighters (*bomberos*), dial 122 or 7761-2002. For the Red Cross (Cruz Roja), dial 125 or 7761-2746. The Policía Nacional Civil (National Civil Police) can be reached at 120, 110, 7765-4991, or 7765-4992. The number for the Municipal Police (Policía Municipal) is 7761-5805.

Language Schools

Xela has become increasingly popular as a place to learn Spanish, even rivaling Antigua, and the days when Xela hosted few foreigners are long gone. Still, it's a much larger city than any other in Guatemala, save the capital, and affords an opportunity for the foreign population to more easily blend into their surroundings, providing an adequate Spanish-language immersion experience. Schools in Xela were charging between $150 and $225 per week for 25 hours of instruction and room and board with a local host family at the time of writing. Xela also tends to attract a rather humane crowd and so there are plenty of operations that allow you to combine your language instruction with some time working with charitable organizations. The following schools are recommended for their consistently good marks on student evaluations. If you're a college student, you may be able to get college credit with several of these language schools. Ultimately, you'll have to check the schools out to see which one works best for you. This is just one of the many things to consider when visiting potential schools. Rates go up between June and August, when college students come down in droves. Useful websites for checking out schools include www.123teachme.com and www.guatemala365.com.

Proyecto Lingüistico Quetzalteco de Español (5a Calle 2-40 Zona 1, tel. 7765-2140, www.plqe.org) is an extremely popular school often booked months in advance. Students have the opportunity to volunteer with the school's Luis Cardoza y Aragon Popular Culture Center, next door, providing art, music, and computer skill instruction to underprivileged local children. There are also opportunities to work in reforestation projects and meet with human rights workers, former guerrilla combatants, and union leaders. **Celas Maya** (6a Calle 14-55 Zona 1, tel. 7765-8205, www.celasmaya.edu.gt) is another fairly popular school and set around a pleasant garden courtyard. There's an adjacent Internet café.

Run by a cooperative of experienced teachers who are very active in social projects, **Centro de Estudios de Español Pop Wuj** (1a Calle 17-72 Zona 1, tel. 7761-8286, www.pop-wuj.org) is another highly recommended school. **Escuela de Español Sakribal** (6a Calle 7-42 Zona 1, tel. 7763-0717, www.sakribal.com), a school founded and run by women, has a project benefiting civil war widows and orphans. **Inepas** (15 Avenida 4-59 Zona 1, tel. 7765-1308, www.inepas.org)

combines quality language instruction with a widely recognized service-learning program.

In business for more than 30 years, **Escuela de Español ICA** (19 Avenida 1-47 Zona 1, tel. 7763-1871, www.guatemalaspanish.com) runs social welfare projects that include a medical clinic, adult literacy education, and reforestation. **Juan Sisay Spanish School** (15 Avenida 8-38 Zona 1, tel. 7765-1318 or 7765-5343, www.juansisayspanishschool.org) is named after a self-taught indigenous *primitivista* painter who was massacred in his home village on the shores of Lake Atitlán in 1989. It's run by a teachers' collective involved in numerous social projects. **Ulew Tinimit** (4a Calle 15-23 Zona 1, tel. 7763-0516, www.spanishguatemala.org) is a good setup, allowing plenty of one-on-one instruction time with your individual teacher. Also recommended is **Madre Tierra Spanish School** (13 Avenida 8-34, Zona 1, tel. 7761-6105 or 5296-1275, www.madre-tierra.org/english).

Volunteer Opportunities

There are several volunteer opportunities available in and around Xela, as there's plenty of work to be done in Guatemala's impoverished Western Highlands. Any of the town's language schools can help you get plugged in to volunteer projects. A particularly helpful organization for volunteer opportunities is **EntreMundos** (El Espacio, 6a Calle 7-31 Zona 1, tel. 5606-9070 or 7761-2179, www.entremundos.org), which publishes a widely available free publication (*EntreMundos*) and has several resources on its website, including a database with contact information and descriptions for more than 150 NGOs in Xela and vicinity.

GETTING THERE AND AROUND
Air

Xela's airport terminal was upgraded a few years back as part of a Guatemalan governmental plan to revamp several domestic airports. It's anyone's guess as to whether scheduled flights will ever get off the ground.

Bus

Xela is a transportation hub for many buses heading to and from highland destinations. Upon arriving in town, you can avoid ending up at the Minerva bus terminal, which is well outside the city center, by getting off at a stop at 7a Avenida and 7a Calle. You'll see a giant monument to the marimba with a Mayan woman atop it at a traffic circle on Avenida de la Independencia. Most buses stop here, and you can grab a taxi or minibus to the city center. If you do end up at the terminal, you can grab a taxi or bus into town from the south side of 4a Calle. Look for the bus labeled "Parque." As elsewhere, Pullman, or first-class buses, leave from their own stations throughout town. Second-class bus routes include the following:

- **To Antigua:** Take any bus heading to Chimaltenango (including first-class buses to Guatemala City) and change buses there.

- **To Chichicastenango:** 10 daily buses, 2.5 hours, $1.50.

- **To Guatemala City:** Frequent buses from 3am-4:30pm, $5.

- **To Huehuetenango:** Buses every 30 minutes 5am-5:30pm, 1.5 hours, $1.

- **To La Mesilla (Mexican border):** Six daily buses, 3.5 hours, $2.

- **To Panajachel:** Buses at 5am, 6am, 8am, 10am, noon, and 3pm, 2.5 hours, $2.

- **To Retalhuleu:** Every 30 minutes 4:30am-6pm, one hour, $1. The bus will most likely read "Reu."

- **To San Pedro La Laguna (Lake Atitlán):** Six daily buses, 2.25 hours, $2.

- **To Tecún Umán (Mexican border):** Buses leave hourly 5am-2pm, 3.5 hours, $2.50.

- **To Zunil:** Every 30 minutes 7am-7pm, 30 minutes, $0.35.

First-class bus lines with service to Guatemala City include the following: **Líneas Américas** (7a Avenida 3-33 Zona 2, tel. 7761-2063), with six daily buses; **Transportes Alamo** (14 Avenida 5-15 Zona 3, tel. 7761-7117), six daily buses; **Transportes Galgos** (21 Calle 0-14 Zona 1, tel. 7761-2248), seven daily; and the ultraluxe, nonstop service of **Línea Dorada** (5a Calle 12-44 Zona 3, tel. 7767-5198 or 7761-4509), with departures at 4pm.

Shuttle Buses

There are also a number of companies running shuttle buses to destinations that include Guatemala City, Antigua, Panajachel, the Mexican border, Chichicastenango, and Huehuetenango. **Adrenalina Tours** (13 Avenida and 4a Calle Zona 1, Pasaje Enríquez, tel. 7761-4509 or 7767-2474, www.adrenalina-tours.com) is recommended for dependable shuttle-bus service, as is **Monte Verde Tours** (13 Avenida 8-34 Zona 1, tel. 7761-6105, www.monte-verdetours.com).

Car Rental

Adrenalina Tours (13 Avenida and 4a Calle Zona 1, Pasaje Enríquez, tel. 7761-4509 or 7767-2474, www.adrenalinatours.com) rents vehicles, as does **Tabarini** (9a Calle 9-21 Zona 1, tel. 7763-0418, www.tabarini.com).

Bike Rental

For bike rentals, head to **Vrisa Bookshop** (15 Avenida 3-64 Zona 1, tel. 7761-3237, 9am-7pm Mon.-Sat., $6/14/27 for daily/weekly/monthly rentals). **Monte Verde Tours** (13 Avenida 8-34, Zona 1, tel. 7761-6105, www.monte-verdetours.com) rents bicycles for $10 a week and offers guided bike trips ($20) to San Andrés Xecul, Zunil, and the Fuentes Georginas hot springs.

NEAR QUETZALTENANGO

The towns and villages surrounding Quetzaltenango make for some interesting day trips. Found nearby are the Santa María and Santiaguito Volcanoes, hot springs, Indian markets, colorful churches, and an exquisite crater lake.

Zunil

About 15 kilometers southeast of Xela is the spectacularly set town of Zunil. You'll see the white Iglesia de Santa Catarina gleaming from a distance as it towers above the tiled-and tin-roofed houses around it. Lovely mountains flank its surroundings. Zunil is one of a handful of towns in Guatemala where there is still strong adherence to the worship of the Maximón idol, as in Santiago Atitlán. The idol's location is rotated yearly, but it's easy to find out its whereabouts from any local resident, assuming the local children don't first intercept you and offer their guiding services for a small tip. It's known locally as San Simón and, unlike elsewhere, visitors here can actually pour liquor offerings down the effigy's throat. You'll probably be charged around $1 to see it, more if you want to take photographs. Zunil's annual fiesta takes place on November 25.

Las Cumbres

About half a kilometer south of town is ★ Las Cumbres (tel. 5399-0029 or 5304-2102, www.lascumbres.com.gt, 7am-7pm daily), a superb establishment harboring steam baths, beautiful accommodations housed in quaint red-tiled-roof cottages with mountain views, and a restaurant (all meals daily) serving mostly Guatemalan dishes but also sandwiches and wine. Its 11 rooms range $33-50 d and have nice wooden furnishings with warm wool blankets, private bathrooms, cable TV, CD player, and plenty of rustic charm. Some have their own in-room hot tubs. If you don't want to stay but just want a steam bath, you can have a private sauna for $5. Room rates include sauna access. There are also a squash court, pool table, and a small gym.

Fuentes Georginas

A popular day trip from Xela with locals as well as visitors, the Fuentes Georginas hot springs (office in Xela at 5a Calle 14-08 Zona 1, tel. 5704-2959 or 7761-6547, www.lasfuentesgeorginas.com, 8am-6:30pm Mon.-Sat., 7am-5pm Sun., $7) were hit hard by

Hurricanes Mitch and Stan but it was 2010's Agatha that dealt them the final blow. The first of these wiped out a Hellenic statue that once gazed upon the pools. The site reopened in March 2011 and is again up and running, though the large main pool now has water so hot it's better suited for cooking lobster than for soaking. A medium-sized and small pool offer slightly more comfortable water temperatures. In addition to the wonderfully warm thermal pools you can enjoy a fairly decent restaurant serving cocktails overlooking the emerald-green waters surrounded by tropical ferns and flowers. There are also sheltered picnic areas with barbecue pits for which you'll need to bring your own fuel. Trails lead to the Zunil and Santo Tomás Volcanoes with guides available at the restaurant for about $15. The hikes require about 3-5 hours one-way. There are accommodations available ($40 d), but they are very basic and not recommendable.

To get here, you can first take a bus to Zunil leaving frequently from Xela's Minerva bus terminal and then take a pickup the rest of the way (eight kilometers) to the hot springs. You can also walk from Zunil in about two hours. Head out from the plaza going uphill to the Cantel road (about 60 meters), turning right, and then going downhill to where you'll see a sign for the hot springs indicating their distance eight kilometers away. The easy way to get here is to book a trip through any of the local guide companies, including Adrenalina Tours, which runs transfers to the site at 8am and 2pm for $16. Fuentes Georginas also shuttles visitors from its office in Xela for $16 departing at 9am and 2:30pm. The price includes entry fee.

★ Laguna Chicabal

From the nearby village of San Martín Sacatepéquez, 15 kilometers west of Xela, it's a two-hour hike to the magical Laguna Chicabal (www.lagunadechicabal.com), ringed by lush cloud forest in a spectacular volcanic crater at an altitude of 2,700 meters (8,900 feet). The lagoon can be reached by taking the signed path on the side of the road from where the bus drops you off heading into town. From there you'll go uphill through fields, cresting and descending a hill. You'll soon see the rangers' station, where you pay a $2 park entrance fee. If you've driven out this way, parking costs an additional $1.30. There's a rustic visitors center here where you can get food. There are also some very basic bungalows with a (cold-water) shared bathroom. Bring your own sleeping bag if you're thinking of staying here. You can camp on the shore of the lagoon for $1.30, though most folks end up camping at the visitors center.

From the visitors center it's about 45 minutes to an hour, uphill, to a wonderful lookout point where you might catch a glimpse of the fantastic crater lake ringed by verdant cloud forest. Most of the time, however, the clouds have the view completely socked in. Opposite of the lagoon lookout is another lookout toward Santa María and Santiaguito Volcanoes; both have covered observation platforms. From the lookout, a trail of stairs descends to the lakeshore and the gorgeous lagoon, which is caressed by wisps of cloud just barely glancing the waters' surface. You'll soon realize why it's considered sacred by

modern-day Maya and a central element of their creation myths. An annual event includes 40 continuous days of prayers for rain and healing, ending on May 3. During the last few days culminating on this date, the lagoon is essentially off-limits to outsiders so as to allow the ceremonies to proceed undisturbed. Bathing in the lagoon's waters is strictly off-limits at all times and, as always, you should be careful to respect the native culture by not photographing any ceremonies that might be in progress throughout the year. You'll find the locals extremely friendly and willing to answer your questions if you put forth the effort to inquire amicably. As always, a smile goes a long way.

San Andrés Xecul

A road branches off to the west from a crossroads between Salcajá and the Pan-American Highway junction at Cuatro Caminos leading to San Andrés Xecul, home to a stunning Technicolor dream of a church festooned with vines, saints, and assorted other characters. It's easily one of Guatemala's most photographed churches, and certainly one of its most bizarre. It's certainly worth a look.

Laguna Chicabal is a beautiful crater lake.

The Pacific Coast

Look for ★ to find recommended sights, activities, dining, and lodging.

Highlights

★ **Xocomil Water Park and Xetulul Amusement Park:** This amazing recreational center has quickly become Guatemala's top tourism draw. It's a must-see if you're traveling to Guatemala with children—or if you just need to indulge your inner child (page 193).

★ **Takalik Abaj:** This site spread over a series of terraces and coffee farms reveals interesting elements of Olmec influence in early Mayan culture. Adding to its allure is a wonderful lodge on its ninth terrace (page 196).

★ **Manchón Guamuchal Wetland Preserve:** These important protected wetlands are an excellent spot for bird-watching. The clean, gently sloping dark-sand beaches are also among Guatemala's best-kept secrets (page 197).

★ **Iztapa:** Guatemala is undoubtedly the sail-fishing capital of the world, with several world records for single-day catch-and-release in the waters just off the coast of Iztapa (page 203).

★ **Biotopo Monterrico-Hawaii:** Here is one of Guatemala's most popular, accessible beaches. In season, you'll have the rare chance to spot nesting sea turtles before their initial voyage out to sea (page 209).

Guatemala's identity as a mostly mountainous country of cool lakes, evergreen forests, and wandering rivers means the coasts (Caribbean and Pacific) have often been overlooked.

Very few of the Pacific Coast's black-sand beaches are inhabited, the chief economic activities along the seaboard being fishing, shrimp farming, and loofah production. The actual sand beaches are on a barrier island separated, along much of the coast, from mainland Guatemala by a narrow channel known as the Canal de Chiquimulilla, running the length of the coast from the town of Sipacate east to Las Lisas, near the Salvadoran border, traversing Puerto San José, Iztapa, and Monterrico along the way.

Things have started to change in recent years with the growth of Guatemala's tourism industry, as visitors and foreign residents seek new places to explore beyond the well-trod path. The Pacific port of San José has always been popular with Guatemala City residents as a place for sun and surf, though foreign visitors will find more acceptable places to visit elsewhere along the Pacific seaboard; it's just 90 minutes from the capital via a four-lane toll road. Adjacent to Puerto San José is the newer Puerto Quetzal, best known for its cruise ship terminal hosting an increasing number of seafaring visitors to Guatemala. The Pacific Coast plains are bisected by Highway CA-2, which runs west to east from the Mexican border all the way to El Salvador.

The beaches found in and around the area of Monterrico and its namesake sea turtle preserve have become the site of vacation homes and resort hotels. Nestled in between these two poles lies Iztapa, Guatemala's original colonial seaport, which in recent years has gained notoriety as word gets out about the world-class sailfishing in Guatemala's Pacific waters.

Guatemala is also Central America's surfing frontier, with some excellent breaks on many of the coast's empty beaches, particularly around the village of Sipacate and farther west toward Mexico. Retalhuleu, a haunt of the Pacific Coast's farming and

Previous: fishing in Iztapa; the beach in Monterrico. **Above:** Paredón Surf House in El Paredón Buena Vista.

The Pacific Coast

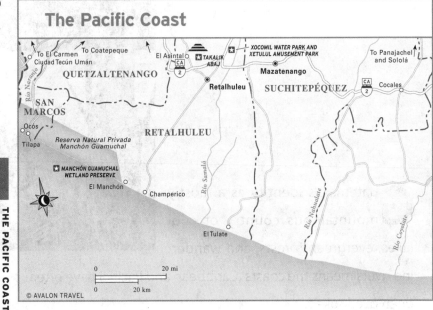

To El Carmen
Ciudad Tecún Umán
To Coatepeque
QUETZALTENANGO
El Asintal
TAKALIK ABAJ
XOCOMIL WATER PARK AND XETULUL AMUSEMENT PARK
To Panajachel and Sololá
Mazatenango
Retalhuleu
SUCHITEPÉQUEZ
Cocales
SAN MARCOS
Río Naranjo
Ocós
Tilapa
Reserva Natural Privada Manchón Guamuchal
RETALHULEU
Río Samalá
MANCHÓN GUAMUCHAL WETLAND PRESERVE
El Manchón
Champerico
Río Nahualate
El Tulate
Río Coyolate

0   20 mi
0   20 km

© AVALON TRAVEL

ranching community, is the site of the large-scale Xocomil and Xetulul amusement parks that are collectively Guatemala's most-visited tourist attraction.

While many of the Pacific Coast beaches are not particularly good for swimming because of riptides, they are noteworthy because of their dark sand, the product of

Dos Mundos Pacific Resort in Monterrico

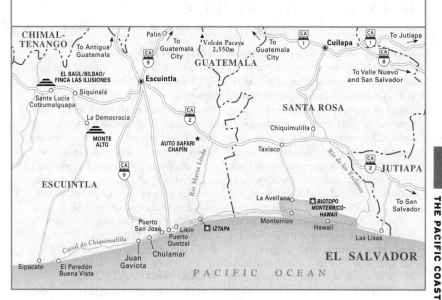

nearby volcanoes, which can be seen in the distance on a clear day. At the very least, the Pacific Coast offers the chance to enjoy a holiday in warm tropical weather, relaxing in a hammock strung between graceful coconut palms. This can be a welcome respite from an extended stay in the more temperate (and sometimes chilly) Guatemalan highlands.

Border towns, beginning with El Carmen and then moving south and east from the Mexican border, are generally unattractive and increasingly unsafe. There is no reason to linger in these parts.

PLANNING YOUR TIME

Two nights would be optimal to explore and enjoy the twin parks of Xetulul and Xocomil. A few hours is enough time to explore the ruins of Takalik Abaj, but the excellent accommodations at Takalik Maya Lodge might keep you busy for another two days. Retalhuleu also makes an excellent base for exploring some of the surrounding countryside by bike, thanks to the presence of an excellent outfitter based here.

If you are in search of sand and sun, you might find yourself spending several nights at Monterrico. If your interest lies in surfing, you'll certainly want to spend a few days in Sipacate or Iztapa. For sailfishing, Iztapa is the place to go and you'll probably spend at least three days here. The 25-kilometer road between Iztapa and Monterrico is shaping up to be the closest thing to a Guatemalan Riviera and will certainly undergo some drastic changes in the next few years. For now, it's still a sleepy seaside area largely dedicated to the production of loofah.

Retalhuleu and Vicinity

East from the Mexican border, the first town of any real interest to visitors is a rather pleasant place with a newfound importance as the gateway to some increasingly popular attractions. The most prominent of these are also Retalhuleu's newest: the twin amusement parks of Xocomil and Xetulul, just a few minutes outside of town. Adding to its prominence as the southern coastal region's new recreational hub is the proximity of the ruins of Takalik Abaj and some decent stretches of beach within a relatively short distance.

Commonly referred to as "Reu" by locals, the town has always been the playground of local coffee and sugarcane farmers, a fact that will be readily apparent by the prevalence of roadside hotels with sparkling swimming pools and pleasant outdoor restaurants. The weather here is warm year-round, but you can always find shelter from the scorching sun under the abundant palm trees, as you will see from the palm-lined boulevard leading to the town center from the main highway.

Reu is becoming increasingly attractive as a hub for exploring this side of Guatemala. Even if amusement parks aren't your thing, there is plenty to keep you busy here and very comfortable accommodations from which to base your explorations. At least one local outfitter has begun to unravel the beauties of this pleasant sun-kissed stretch of the Pacific lowlands.

SIGHTS

Downtown Retalhuleu's main attraction, aside from the central square, is the Museo de Arqueología y Etnología (6a Avenida 5-68 Zona 1, tel. 7771-0557, 8am-5:30pm Tues.-Sat., 9am-noon Sun., $1.50) featuring archaeological relics on the ground floor and a collection of historical photographs from various stages of the city's past on the second floor.

SHOPPING

Retalhuleu's impressive outdoor shopping mall, Centro Comercial La Trinidad (www. latrinidad.com.gt, 10am-9pm Mon.-Thurs., 10am-10pm Fri.-Sat., 11am-7pm Sun.), is near the bus depot at 1a Calle and 5a Avenida "A" Zona 5, and has a modern La Torre grocery store, cell phone stores, banks, ATMs, and a Carrion department store. There's also a large condominium complex attached, attesting to the town's prosperity and its status as an enclave of the agricultural elite. Another option is Paseo las Palmas (Avenida Circunvalación 8-30 Zona 6, tel. 7771-5156), with several shops and restaurants.

ACCOMMODATIONS

There are several motel-style places lining the main highway just outside of town where Guatemalan families like to stop and visit while en route from chillier locales in the highlands. These places tend to get a bit noisy on weekends, but during the week they tend to be quite silent. Hotel La Colonia (at Km. 178, Carretera al Pacífico, tel. 7955-5600, www. hlacoloniareu.com, duplex bungalows $48-52 d) is an old standby with spotless, comfortable, air-conditioned rooms. There is a swimming pool with a pleasant restaurant and bar. The higher prices are for recently renovated rooms. You can use the pool for the day at a cost of $1.50.

In the heart of town, Hotel La Quinta B&B (Corner of 5a Avenida and 5a Calle, Edificio Moran, 2nd floor, tel. 7771-0267 or 7771-4182, www.hotellaquintaguatemala. com, $34 d including breakfast) has comfortable, modern rooms with nice extras like flat-screen cable TV and free wireless Internet. Another fine place to lay your head is the friendly ★ Posada de Don José (5a Calle 3-67 Zona 1, tel. 7962-2900, www.posadadedonjose.com, $50-65 d), in an attractive two-story building centered around a small swimming pool and courtyard. Standard rooms are spotless and have good beds, cable TV, air-conditioning, ceiling fan, phone, and private hot-water bath. The larger suites have a sitting area and some nice furniture. The hotel's restaurant, managed by Don José's wife, serves some of the town's tastiest food. The Mexican consulate is also based here. The well-furnished rooms in **Hotel Astor** (5a Calle 4-60 Zona 1, tel. 7957-8300, www.hotelastorguatemala.com, $55 d), are set in a colonial building and centered around a pretty garden courtyard and swimming pool. All rooms have air-conditioning, ceiling fan, and cable TV in addition to private hot-water bath. There is a restaurant in the lobby and a small sports bar.

FOOD

A variety of decent restaurants are downtown. An excellent choice is the restaurant at ★ **Posada de Don José** (5a Calle 3-67 Zona 1, tel. 7771-0180 or 7771-0841, 8am-10pm daily), serving international cuisine with Guatemalan flair. **Restaurante La Luna** (5a Avenida 4-97 Zona 1, tel. 7771-0194, all meals daily), just off the plaza's west corner, is a local favorite serving inexpensive Guatemalan fare.

At Paseo las Palmas, you'll find **Puro Rollo** (Avenida Circunvalación 8-30 Zona 6, tel. 7771-0776, $2-5), which is Guatemala's answer to Chipotle. They serve up deliciously fresh burritos made with corn or flour tortillas. You can accompany your meal with plantain chips, beer, soda, or a slushy.

SERVICES

Banco Industrial has Visa ATMs at its locations on the central plaza (6a Calle 5-17 Zona 1) and at Centro Comercial La Trinidad (1a Calle and 5a Avenida "A" Zona 5). **Banco Agromercantil**, also on 5a Avenida facing the plaza, has a MasterCard ATM. Both banks change U.S. dollars and travelers checks.

GETTING THERE

Most buses plying the Pacific Coast Highway (Carretera al Pacífico) stop in Retalhuleu's main bus depot at 7a Avenida and 10a Calle. There are regular buses to Guatemala City, Quetzaltenango, the Mexican border, Champerico, and El Tulate.

NORTH AND WEST OF RETALHULEU
★ Xocomil Water Park and Xetulul Amusement Park

The first of these, **Parque Acuático Xocomil** (Km. 180.5 on the road to Quetzaltenango, tel. 7772-5780, www.irtra.org.gt, 9am-5pm Thurs.-Sun. Jan. 8-Oct. 31, Wed.-Sun. Nov. 1-Dec. 15, daily Dec. 15-Jan. 7, $13 adult, $7 children and seniors), is a wonderful water park on par with the world's best and a must-see if you are traveling with children. Among the attractions are 14 waterslides, a wave pool, and a lazy river meandering through the complex of re-created Mayan ruins and monuments. The main restaurant showcases a Mayan pyramid painted in ocher, green, and yellow, as it would have looked in the Classic period. Additional food stands are scattered throughout the park.

replica of Tikal's Gran Jaguar Temple at Xetulul

The second phase of an eventual four-park plan is **Parque de Diversiones Xetulul** (tel. 7722-9450, www.irtra.org.gt, 10am-6pm Thurs.-Sun. Jan. 8-Oct. 31, Wed.-Sun. Nov. 1-Dec. 15, daily Dec. 15-Jan. 7, $13 adult, $7 children and seniors; admission to both parks $19 adults, $10 for children and seniors), where a variety of amusement park rides are spread out among seven plazas, each with its own restaurant and gift shop showcasing a variety of replicated world monuments. Among the highlights are Paris's Moulin Rouge, Rome's Trevi Fountain, and Guatemala's own Gran Jaguar Temple from Tikal. The park is also home to Central America's largest roller coaster.

A new convention center and 18-hole golf course were in the planning stages at the time of writing.

Hostales del IRTRA

Just across the road from the two theme parks are the lodgings created specifically to house visitors. The **Hostales del IRTRA** (Km 180.5 Carretera a Quetzaltenango por la Costa Sur, tel. 7722-9100, www.irtra.org.gt) encompass a virtual leisure city with various lodges, restaurants, bars, swimming pools, and a minigolf course. There are four separate lodging concepts ranging in price from $53 a night in the simplest accommodations without air-conditioning to $355 a night for a suite. The newest of the four *hostales,* ★ **Hostal Palajunoj,** was inspired by the cultures inhabiting the world's tropical rainforests and is a favorite of guests. The five buildings in this complex each have a different theme: African, Polynesian, Thai, Indonesian, and Mayan. All rooms have air-conditioning, cable TV, a private bathroom, and wonderful wooden furnishings. The buildings housing the rooms at Palajunoj are worth a look for their unique architecture. The *hostales* outside this complex feature Spanish colonial, Greek, and rustic cabana architecture.

There are three restaurants, the nicest of which is **Restaurante Kapa Hapa,** inspired by the cultures of Asia and the Pacific. A beautifully luminescent Polynesian sailboat graces the

well-designed architecture of Restaurante Kapa Hapa at Hostales del IRTRA

entrance as you make your way up the stairs to the second-floor dining room. Try the chicken satay and wash it down with a mai tai. Main dishes cost $7-12. Outdoor seating overlooking the Moana swimming pools is also available and a great place for breakfast, which includes a delicious menu of croissant sandwiches or lighter fare such as yogurt and pancakes.

A newer addition is that of **Los Corozos Spa,** offering a variety of spa treatments and massage therapy. Athletic facilities include tennis and squash courts. Racquets are available for rent ($2).

Any bus traveling along the Quetzaltenango-Retalhuleu road can drop you off here.

Dino Park (Parque Xulik)

Hollywood's fictional Jurassic Park may have Costa Rica as its setting, but the closest thing to a real-world incarnation may be here in Guatemala. The **Dino Park** features animatronic versions of 12 different dinosaur species scattered among the grounds of a lush,

25,000-square-meter jungle area, complete with replicas of the jeeps and SUVs used in the aforementioned movie. It's part of the larger **Parque Xulik** (Km. 175.5 Carretera a Quetzaltenango, 6am-6pm daily, $7 adults, $4 children), which is a toy museum dedicated in large part to action heroes.

Reserva Patrocinio

Farther north along the road heading to Quetzaltenango, in the area known as Las Palmas, lies ★ **Reserva Patrocinio** (tel. 7771-4393 or 5203-5701, www.reservapatrocinio.com), an agro-ecological tourism destination with a variety of recreation options for à la carte fees (advanced reservations required). So-called "agritourism" is an increasingly popular form of recreation in Guatemala and encompasses natural areas adjacent to farms. The main attraction at El Patrocinio is bird-watching in and around its 25-hectare forest reserve. Other areas are dedicated to the cultivation of coffee, cacao, macadamia nuts, and exotic flowers, among others, which visitors are free to check out. There are three rooms in a comfortable, well-equipped farmhouse, each renting for $100 d with shared bath. The house has a kitchen and there is a separate and very pleasant open-sided dining room that fronts the coffee fields; meals can be prepared for you with advance notice.

The farm itself is on the slopes of Santiaguito Volcano and has outstanding views of its smoldering cone. It's a great place to get away from it all. For the best views of the surrounding coffee fields, mountains, and volcanoes, climb atop the platform near the farmhouse. You can call the owner, Mario Aguilar, for a pickup ($12) or for directions from the Cuatro Caminos crossroads just outside of Retalhuleu; from there, it's another 14 kilometers to the farm. A detailed map is available on the website.

Birding packages can be arranged by booking in advance directly through Reserva Patrocinio or through **Cayaya Birding** (tel. 5308-5160, www.cayaya-birding.com).

Comunidad Nueva Alianza

About 45 minutes north of Retalhuleu, **Comunidad Nueva Alianza** (tel. 5348-5290, www.comunidadnuevaalianza.org) is a 300-acre organic coffee and macadamia plantation owned and operated by a cooperative of 40 Guatemalan families. Large tracts of tropical forest have been preserved on the property. A walk through the plantation will bring you to cascading waterfalls and wonderful views of Santa María and Santiaguito

Reserva Patrocinio

Volcanoes. The community received legal title to the land in 2004 after a drawn-out conflict with the farm's former owner who failed to pay workers' wages for 18 months and subsequently declared bankruptcy. The community received a loan to purchase the land and is actively making efforts to fund repayment of the loan via numerous activities. These include ecotourism, production of bamboo furniture, sustainable energy production, and coffee and macadamia nut production.

Tours can be arranged via Quetzaltenango travel agencies or directly through the cooperative. You can stay in the community's comfortable lodgings in a dorm-style room with shared bath for $9 pp or in a private room with shared bath for $30 d. Meals cost $4-8 each. The community accepts volunteers for hostel maintenance, agricultural work, and community development. See the website for detailed instructions on how to get here.

★ Takalik Abaj

The site of **Takalik Abaj** (7am-5pm daily, $3.50), meaning "standing stones," is particularly interesting because it reveals elements of Olmec influence in early Mayan culture. It made headlines as recently as 2002 with the discovery of an intact royal burial tomb thought to be that of the site's last Mayan ruler, a discovery featured in the May 2004 issue of *National Geographic*.

Formerly known as Abaj Takalik because of an error in translation, the site is spread out over 6.5 square kilometers along nine terraces. Its ceremonial center, at the city's core, is open to visitors but the remains of the city's outskirts are now on lands occupied by five coffee farms. One of these, on the ninth terrace, is home to an ecolodge.

In its heyday, between 800 BC and AD 200, Takalik Abaj was an important commercial and political center at the heart of a far-ranging trade network in which cacao and salt were exchanged for obsidian, quetzal feathers, pyrite, and jade.

More than 275 structures have been unearthed here. Now being restored in an area once belonging to a private coffee and banana plantation is Structure 5, the tallest structure at 16 meters high. It occupies Terrace 3. East of here is Structure 7, thought to have been an astronomical observatory. Structure 4 contains some very clear engraving in Mayan style. There are many sculptures scattered throughout the site. Among them are smaller versions of the giant Olmecoid heads seen elsewhere, as well as the potbellied *barrigones* that are also typical of Olmec influence. Also noteworthy is Structure 12, the largest structure with a base measuring 56 by 42 meters and dating to AD 300. Standing before it are seven carved monuments, including Altar 8, and Stela 5, which shows two kings presiding over bound captives. Olmecoid heads and zoomorphs compose the other finely carved monuments at this structure. Structure 11 is similar, also with seven monuments before it.

Takalik Abaj was sacked sometime around AD 300 and its Mayan-style monuments were ritualistically defaced. Some were rebuilt after AD 600. The location is still an important ceremonial site and many highland Maya perform ceremonies there.

To get to Takalik Abaj, drive or take a bus heading out from Retalhuleu to the town of El Asintal, 12 kilometers northwest of Reu and 5 kilometers north of the Carretera al Pacífico (Pacific Coast Highway, CA-2). The turnoff is at Km. 190.5. Buses leave from 5a Avenida "A" southwest of the town plaza about every half hour during daylight hours. From El Asintal, pickups cover the remaining four kilometers to the site. You can also take a taxi from Reu's main plaza for about $30 round-trip, including waiting time.

Takalik Maya Lodge

Just two kilometers up the road, on the site's ninth terrace, is the exquisite ★ **Takalik Maya Lodge** (Terraza 9 del Sitio Arqueologico Takalik Abaj, Km. 190.5 Carretera al Pacífico, tel. 4055-9831 or 2506-4716, www.takalik.com, $32-62), where you have your choice between two different concepts, both on lands occupied by the working

A Guatemalan Take on Disney World

The twin theme parks of Xocomil and Xetulul sprouted seemingly out of nowhere just a few years ago on the outskirts of Retalhuleu along the road to Quetzaltenango. The first of these, Xocomil, opened its doors in 1997, with Xetulul being added in 2002. Both parks are operated by IRTRA, the Institute for the Recreation of Guatemalan Private Industry Workers, a private entity created by the Guatemalan congress. This organization operates three other parks near Guatemala City.

Xocomil and Xetulul opened to much fanfare and are beloved by Guatemalans and foreigners alike for the quality of the parks' attractions, their cleanliness, and the friendliness of the staff. By any standard, the parks are impressive, and they are special because they showcase the excellent quality and amazing potential of the Guatemalan service sector. The theme parks and the accommodations built to house their guests truly have nothing to envy in similar attractions in developed nations. If you are traveling in this part of Guatemala with children, a stop at Xocomil or Xetulul is almost obligatory.

Xocomil and Xetulul receive more than one million visitors annually, making them Guatemala's top tourist draw. There are plans to build two more parks in the lands adjacent to them. Retalhuleu itself has already begun a transformation inspired by the parks' creation. Though it has always been a regional recreational center, the arrival of more visitors to the area has vastly improved the quality of local hotels, though prices have likewise increased. In addition to its popularity with Guatemalans, visitors from southern Mexico, El Salvador, and Honduras also flock to the parks in droves. There are plans to build an airport, allowing those visitors to arrive by plane on package tours.

Montes Eliseos coffee farm. The Kacike Maya concept is built in a heavily forested area near the lodge's restaurant. There are two beautiful and comfortable rooms, each with unique interior paint and decor. Both have a winding staircase leading to a second-floor balcony, where you can lounge away soothed by the sounds of the surrounding jungle. The rooms are truly a work of art, and the walls are painted with motifs inspired by the natural beauty all around. Indigenous bedspreads, gas lamps, and tile floors complete the ambience. You can stay at the Kacike Maya for $47-62 per person, including breakfast.

At the Paseo del Café, just up the road, you can stay in the heart of a 19th-century coffee farm in comfortable wooden buildings with charming red tin roofs centered around a small plaza. The seven rooms here have electricity and share a bathroom. They are also just steps from a refreshing swimming pool surrounded by lush jungle and coffee bushes. Rooms here range from $32-42 per person and include breakfast. The restaurant, on the Kacike side

of the lodge, serves a somewhat limited menu, though the food is quite good, with entrées in the $6-9 range that include kebabs and salads. The homemade lemonade is particularly thirst-quenching after a visit to the ruins.

Numerous nature trails wind their way through the farm and there is a small but refreshing waterfall just a 10-minute hike away. In addition to Takalik Abaj tours, the lodge can also arrange bird-watching, horseback riding, and visits to the Manchón Guamuchal Wetland Preserve and Chicabal Lagoon.

★ Manchón Guamuchal Wetland Preserve

This wild, 13,500-hectare private wetland reserve harbors the last remaining undisturbed mangrove swamps in the country. The Manchón Guamuchal is included in the Ramsar Convention on Wetlands, encompassing a list of globally important sites, particularly those that provide habitat for aquatic birds. The convention was adopted in 1971 and signed by more than 100 countries. Guatemala ratified the convention in June 1990, and in 1998 the Manchón Guamuchal was added to the list of sites with international importance.

According to a recent study by a Brazilian biologist, the wetlands are an important stop along the path of migratory birds coming from Canada and the United States. Among the varied birdlife are 14 duck species, 12 of which are migratory, sparrow hawks, buzzards, falcons, and 20 species of egrets. Birds arrive sometime in October to November, leaving in March after wintering in the lagoons. In addition to birds, there are crocodiles, iguanas, and an abundance of fish.

The reserve is just now being made accessible to tourism, and ingress to the park is fairly straightforward. Along the road from Retalhuleu to the port of Champerico, a turnoff at kilometer 215 veers right (west) through Aldea Acapán and then 17 kilometers to the village of El Manchón. There is one daily bus leaving for Retalhuleu at 5am and making the return journey to El Manchón at 3pm.

Your best bet for staying here is **Casa Mar Azul** (tel. 2438-3934 or 4686-0940, www.casamarazulguate.com), where there are comfortable seaside accommodations and good food at decent prices. Facilities include a swimming pool with plenty of room to lounge and kayaks for exploring the mangrove-laden canals.

EAST TO ESCUINTLA

East of Retalhuleu along the Pacific Coast Highway to the department of Escuintla is **Mazatenango,** a coffee and sugarcane hub with little of interest for the international traveler. If you need to stop for a bite to eat your best bet is Plaza Americas, a modern shopping center conveniently situated just off the Pacific Coast Highway outside the town center. Choose from Pollo Campero, Sarita, Pizza Hut, and Burger King. There's even a movie theater.

Escuintla Department

Escuintla department is in many ways the gateway to the Pacific Coast, as it is easily accessed from Guatemala City and La Antigua. The departmental capital is a somewhat shady agglomeration of dilapidated houses and businesses serving mostly as a stopping point on the way elsewhere. (A toll road circumvents the departmental capital, so it's no longer even necessary to pass through it.) The department itself harbors the Pacific Coast's main ports, cruise ship terminal, and several seaside attractions.

SIPACATE

Sipacate is Guatemala's surfing capital. Nowhere near as popular as in Costa Rica or even neighboring El Salvador, surfing nonetheless has some aficionados in this neck of the woods, and there are some perfectly surfworthy waves on the Guatemalan shores. International travelers are just now starting to get a clue, but in the meantime, a lucky few surfers can still ride these waves undisturbed by throngs of fellow wave enthusiasts, despite international travel magazines' best attempts to make these sites more widely known.

The drive south to Sipacate is almost as pretty as the beaches, with palmettos lining the road on either side of the well-paved, fast highway. Once in town, it should cost you about $1.40 to cross the Canal de Chiquimulilla over to the beaches. Sipacate's recommended accommodation, **Rancho Carrillo** (tel. 4730-7024 or 5413-9395, www.marmaya.com, $50-130) is on a clean stretch of private beach. Rancho Carrillo offers a restaurant, pool, and bungalows with air-conditioning, private baths, minifridges, and cable TV. The bungalows house six or eight people and cost $110 or $130-156 regardless of occupancy. A family-sized unit for up to eight people costs $130. Smaller, more basic rooms with air-conditioning, outdoor hammocks, and decks fronting the beach cost $50 d. There are deals available if you're here Sunday-Thursday.

Surf Guatemala!

While neighboring countries such as Costa Rica, Nicaragua, and even El Salvador have acquired relative status as Central American surf spots, Guatemala has remained somewhat obscure in this regard. Although the country's Pacific shores have perfectly surfworthy breaks, the coast has always taken a backseat to the scenic and cultural wonders of the highlands, among other areas. A relative lack of tourism infrastructure in this region has also contributed to keeping the Pacific Coast on the periphery of Guatemala's emerging status as a destination for outdoor-loving, adventurous travelers.

The newfound popularity of beach destinations such as Monterrico and Iztapa has resulted in the corresponding development of coastal areas near these beach towns. As more and more people visit, locals and foreigners alike are discovering that you can, in fact, surf in Guatemala. The Guatemalan surfing community can be found mostly in small villages along the coast and numbers only about 100 people, according to local estimates. Surfing Guatemala's breaks means

Surfing has become increasingly popular in Guatemala.

you won't have to share a wave with 20 other people, as is the case with other, more popular regions along the Central American coast. The best surfing beaches in Guatemala can be found at Iztapa and Sipacate, both of which have more-than-adequate accommodations.

U.S. travel magazines have put the word out concerning **El Paredón Surf Camp** (tel. 4593-2490, www.surf-guatemala.com), a bare-bones surfing paradise on one of Guatemala's best breaks. Still, you wouldn't know it cruising around the sandy streets of this quiet village where chickens roam freely. You can still show up on almost any given day with nary another surfer in sight.

The biggest waves can be found during swells occurring between mid-March and late October with wave faces sometimes as large as 18 feet. During other times of the year, waves average 3-6 feet with the occasional 10-foot swell.

If you want to check out the surfing scene in Guatemala, a useful website is www.surfinguatemala.com, established by Pedro Pablo Vergara, a local surfer who costarted Maya Extreme Surf School and offers trips to Guatemala's surf spots. The site lists about 20 breaks along the Pacific Coast with area maps to help you find them, along with information on accommodations ranging from budget surf camps to stays in private villas. The school can also arrange transportation for you and your surfboards to various surf spots from Guatemala City.

Along with Maripaz Fernandez, Vergara started **Maya Extreme Surf School** (www.mayaextreme.com) in 2001 and **Maya Extreme Surf Shop** (Centro Comercial Pradera Concepción Local 308, tel. 6637-9593) in 2005. The shop sells the company's own brand of "G-land surfboards" and is based in one of Guatemala City's nicest shopping malls. A one-day "learn to surf" package costs $125, including transfers, food, equipment, and instruction.

In 2006, Robert August (of *Endless Summer* fame) traveled to Guatemala with his crew to surf the Pacific Coast waves. The result was *The Endless Journey Continues*, a movie chronicling their trip to Guatemala.

El Paredón Buena Vista

East from Sipacate about five kilometers is the village of **El Paredón Buena Vista,** home to Guatemala's surfing mecca. El Paredón is inside **Sipacate-Naranjo National Park,** home to large extensions of mangrove forests. Little has been done to make the park an authentic ecotourism attraction. The emphasis at El Paredón is decidedly on the surfing aspects, though local lodges can arrange kayaking in the neighboring lagoons. El Paredón is accessible by boat from Sipacate or along a dirt road leading to the village. The turnoff for the final 14-kilometer journey is just past the luxury Juan Gaviota condominium complex.

Volunteer opportunities are now available working with **La Choza Chula** (www.lachozachula.org), which is busy building a school and has already put together a library. They've also helped locals build relationships with international retailers for which they produce yoga mat bags and surfboard socks. You can get your surf on *and* help out the local community.

Featured in *National Geographic Adventure* and *Outside* but still very much off the radar, **El Paredón Surf Camp** (tel. 4593-2490, www.surf-guatemala.com, $3.75-40) is the Pacific Coast's surfing hideaway. Rates range from $3.75 sleeping in your own tent to $40 in an equipped double-occupancy apartment. Other options include bunk beds ($6 pp) and private rooms ($20 d). Meals ($3-5) are provided by a local family and are heavy on seafood. Surfboards are available for rent at $15 a day, though there is a $50 deposit. You can put them to good use on the sea, which dishes out 1.5- to 2-meter (5- to 6-foot) rollers opposite the lovely beach at your doorstep. The owners insist you book in advance. Transport from Antigua or Guatemala City takes two hours and costs $50-60 per person with a two-person minimum. It is highly recommended, as getting here by public bus involves changing buses four times.

Another option is ★ **Paredón Surf House** (tel. 5691-3096 or 4994-1842, www.paredonsurf.com, $11 pp in loft to $100 d in casita with private bath and beachfront porch). It's a stylish and yet simple seaside retreat perfect for surfers looking to be right on the beach in more private surroundings or anyone just looking to get off the grid for a bit. The raised-platform beachfront bungalows ($47 d) share a communal bathroom with the lofts. Spring for one of the private-bath seaview suites, a good value at $75 d. The new casitas are great for couples or those traveling

Boats take passengers from Sipacate across the Canal de Chiquimulilla to El Paredón.

with friends, as they have a downstairs bar area and breezy bedrooms with sea views upstairs. This place just keeps getting better. There are boogie boards and surfboards for rent; surfing lessons are also available. A full restaurant and bar serves up good food and cocktails. A three-course dinner is about $11. Transport from Antigua (starting at $15 pp) and the Guatemala City airport are available.

ESCUINTLA

The departmental capital of Escuintla is a sweltering, busy place and mainly a pit stop along the road to the coast from Guatemala City, or if you're heading east-west along the Pacific Coast Highway. A four-lane *autopista* starts just outside of Guatemala City and leads from Palín to Escuintla, with inspiring views of Agua, Fuego, and Acatenango Volcanoes along the way. Another four-lane highway continues south from Escuintla to Puerto San José, Puerto Quetzal, and Iztapa. A bypass means you don't need to even pass through town unless it's absolutely necessary.

Auto Safari Chapín

East on the road from Escuintla to Taxisco is one of the most unusual attractions in Guatemala and indeed all of Central America,

the **Auto Safari Chapin** (Km. 87.5 Carretera a Taxisco, tel. 2222-5858, www.autosafarichapin.com, 9:30am-5pm Tues.-Sun., $8 adults, $7 children), where you can drive through grounds harboring a variety of animals, including zebras, hippos, rhinos, giraffes, and a lion. There are also local species such as macaws and monkeys, which you can see in a small zoo, and an aviary. There is a rest area partway through the drive where you can get up close and personal with the park's giraffes. A swimming pool and restaurant round out the list of amenities.

Chulamar

West of the dilapidated, grungy port town of Puerto San José, **Chulamar** is home to many of the weekend vacation homes of wealthy folks from Guatemala City. Here you'll find one of the Pacific Coast's most luxurious lodging options, built to satisfy the demands of the Guatemalan elite. The ★ **Soleil Pacífico** (tel. 7879-3131, www.hotelessoleilguatemala.com, $80-122 d), formerly a Radisson property, is a huge resort complex on a clean private beach with all the feel of an Acapulco beachside megaresort. Although it's popular on weekends, you may just have the place all to yourself if you visit during the middle

a seaview casita at Paredón Surf House in El Paredón Buena Vista

Juan Gaviota:
Guatemala's Planned Paradise

While Guatemala's Pacific Coast hasn't yet attracted the attention of foreign investors, this doesn't mean the region lacks infrastructure comparable to that of its better-known neighbors. Local investors, as they always do in Guatemala, have stepped in to fill the void. The planned community of Juan Gaviota began in the late 1990s as the dream of a group of five Guatemalan investors who purchased a sizable land plot with 15 kilometers of beachfront.

The development essentially sprang up out of nowhere. A trail crisscrossing the property was upgraded to a serviceable road, a canal was dredged (and a bridge to cross it built), and electricity had to be brought in. The latter, at a cost of over $4 million, now benefits nearby communities in addition to residents of Marina del Sur. Wave breakers were installed in order to provide a safe haven for boats and facilitate the construction of the marina. Several thousand tons of rock were also brought in. The first phase of Marina del Sur alone is estimated to have cost over $130 million.

The project has a 20-year master plan, made in conjunction with a local consulting firm. The next phase encompasses a golf course and three hotels, opening Juan Gaviota to foreign investors and visitors. It is rumored the hotels are being built by a U.S. investment firm.

of the week. There are two swimming pools and a variety of dining options. You can get a day pass to enjoy the swimming pool and the hotel grounds for $50 per person, a popular option with cruise ship passengers. Many of the sailfishing outfits also accommodate their clients here. Transport to the hotel is available from Guatemala City and Antigua with prior arrangement.

Juan Gaviota

Juan Gaviota (www.juangaviota.com), a huge planned community spanning 15 kilometers of beachfront located 12 kilometers west of Puerto San José, is the newest enclave of Guatemala's elite and has all the feel of a Miami subdivision. The first of several construction phases encompassing this ambitious project is Marina del Sur, which features a central clubhouse with a restaurant fronting the Pacific Ocean, in addition to swimming pools, tennis courts, soccer fields, and beach volleyball courts. Juan Gaviota is equipped with a boat marina, and future plans call for a golf course, time-share condos, and hotels. A few homes are available for rent. The best place to look for beach villa rentals in this neck of the woods is on the website of Antigua-based **Century 21 Casa Nova**

(www.vacationrentalsguatemala.com). Homes here rent for about $700 a week, or $400 for a weekend. This is a self-contained, gated community, and you won't find much outside of the private homes in the community.

PUERTO QUETZAL

The main attraction here is the **Puerto Quetzal Cruise Ship Terminal,** where an increasing number of boats calling on Guatemala's Pacific Coast make landfall. Within the larger terminal area is the **Marina Pez Vela** (tel. 2379-5790), harboring boats for sailfishing adventures. You can also book sailfishing trips from here. **Guatemala Sport Fishing** (tel. 5709-8697) has a charter desk that operates out of the marina. Cruise ship passengers will find several amenities, including Internet access, telephone communications, and stands selling a variety of local handicrafts. There's also an excellent restaurant, **7 Caldos del Mar** (Seven Soups of the Sea, tel. 2361-8176, $10-30), run by the amiable Dimitris Moliviatis. You'll find more than seven soups on the menu—including *tapado*, *sancocho*, and *kakik*—as well as a variety of meat and seafood dishes, and a fully stocked bar. Order a Cuba Libre (rum and coke) with Guatemala's famous Zacapa Centenario rum.

★ IZTAPA

Farther west along the coastline are the lovely beaches of **Iztapa,** which are remarkably clean, wide, and sandy. Although the town itself is a dilapidated old port town, it is becoming increasingly popular as the jumping-off point for some of the world's best sailfishing. Iztapa is Guatemala's original port, used by the Spanish conqueror Pedro de Alvarado to build boats and set sail for his onward journey to Peru. Anglers will find first-class accommodations to complement the world-class fishing just off the coast. Surfers will find plenty of waves to ride here, as there is a fairly decent break. A newer recreational offering is that of whale-watching tours during the winter months. All beach access in Iztapa is private and visitors have to cross the canal to get to the beaches. Your best bet is to stay at an area lodge.

Sailfishing Outfitters

A five-night fishing package (includes boat, captain, meals, transport from Guatemala City airport, accommodation in Iztapa and Antigua/Guatemala City hotels) generally starts at $1,550 per person, based on a group of four. Add-ons include golfing in Guatemala City or La Antigua. Tips for the boat captain generally run about $100 per day per group.

Among the recommended outfitters is the American-owned and operated **Sailfish Bay Lodge** (tel. 2426-3909 direct or 800/638-7405 U.S. reservations, www.sailfishbay. com). Packages include food and accommodations at a beautiful eight-room lodge right on the beach across the canal in Iztapa. Under the same ownership, **Pacific Fins Resort & Marina** (tel. 888/700-3467 U.S., www.pacificfins.com.gt) operates out of its very attractive namesake lodge and restaurant fronting the Canal de Chiquimulilla. Another option is **Buena Vista Sportfishing Lodge** (Calle Baja Mar, Aldea Buena Vista, tel. 7880-4203/04 or 866/699-3277 U.S., www.buenavistasportfishing.com, $100 d), owned by an American expatriate. Its developer sees huge potential along the Guatemalan coast after having drifted here from Costa Rica.

Based in Antigua, and a joint Guatemalan-American venture, is **The Great Sailfishing Company** (tel. 7934-6220, Antigua or 877/763-0851 U.S., www.greatsailfishing. com). You can fish using conventional methods as well as fly-fishing, and the company's informative website can point you in the right direction when planning a sailfishing trip

THE PACIFIC COAST
ESCUINTLA DEPARTMENT

the shoreline at Iztapa

to Guatemala. Guests stay at Soleil Pacífico resort or a private villa within the same compound.

Based in Florida and operating out of its namesake lodge one mile west of Puerto San José, **Casa Vieja Lodge** (tel. 800/882-4665 U.S., www.casaviejalodge.com) is one of the larger outfitters. Many of its staff members worked for Iztapa's original sailfishing lodge, Fins 'N Feathers. The lodge is in an old wood house (as its name implies) that has been wonderfully restored to afford anglers a comfortable place to come back to after a day of fishing. Also recommended is **Blue Bayou Sailfishing** (tel. 5208-0098 Guatemala, 810/516-0578 U.S., www.bluebayouguatemala.com), run by a Michigan transplant. Sailfishing trips include accommodations in a comfortable poolside villa inside a private compound near Marina Pez Vela.

A good value-priced option is **Big Buoy Fishing** (tel. 3215-9312 Guatemala, 850/226-2608 U.S., www.bigbuoyfishing.com). It operates out of a somewhat less ostentatious villa fronting the canal. Last but not least is **Sailfish Oasis** (tel. 5251-4809 in Guatemala, www.sailfishoasissportfishing.com) operating out of its namesake (and very attractive) lodge on the banks of the Canal de Chiquimulilla.

Whale-Watching

Whale Watching Guatemala (tel. 2366-1026, www.whalewatchingguatemala.com, $235 per person adults, $210 per child) operates a six-hour tour. In addition to whales (humpback, short-finned pilot, finback, and whale sharks), you can expect to see bottlenose dolphins, sea turtles, and manta rays. Trips leave on weekends from December through April (at 7am from Aldea Buena Vista), and the cost includes breakfast, lunch, and drinks onboard the boat. You can also charter a boat with a minimum of eight people on weekdays. **Guatemala Fishing Tours & Whale Watching** (tel. 5707-1710, www.guatemalafishingtours.com, $800-1,350 for boat charter) also does whale-watching tours. They charge for the boat charter, including fuel but nothing else. Maximum capacity is six. It's an alright setup if you want to put a group together and take care of your own food and beverage.

Accommodations and Food

In town, adequate accommodations can be found at **Sol y Playa Tropical** (1a Calle 5-48 Zona 1, tel. 7867-3847, $40 d), which has rooms with private baths and ceiling fans or air-conditioning, situated around a nicely

landing a sailfish on Guatemala's Pacific coast

The Sailfish Capital of the World

A unique swirling of ocean currents between Mexico and El Salvador creates an eddy unusually rich in pelagic fish (such as herring and mackerel) right on Guatemala's doorstep, where billfish, including sailfish and marlin, gather to feed along with large concentrations of dorado, yellowfin tuna, and wahoo. The result is some of the world's best sailfishing waters.

Enthusiasts of Guatemala's emerging sailfishing scene are quick to point out that it is the true "Sailfish Capital of the World" and have the numbers to back up their claims. The world records for conventional and fly-fishing single-day catches have been set here, at 75 and 23 respectively. In March 2006, a single vessel carrying five anglers caught and released a whopping 124 sailfish. While the records are indeed impressive, anglers plying the Guatemalan Pacific Coast need not worry about any "feast or famine" phenomenon, as catch-and-release numbers are quite consistent. In terms of billfish releases per angler, Guatemala ranks at the top (a statistic compiled by The Southwest Fisheries Science Center in California). Its catch per unit of effort (CPUE) for Pacific sailfish in 2005 was 5.83 compared to Costa Rica's 2.57 and Panama's 2.25. On average, you can expect to catch 15-20 fish per boat per day, but catches of 25 fish aren't uncommon.

Guatemala's strength is certainly in its numbers. Unlike most of its competitors, Guatemala's not known as a beach destination with impressive resort accommodations. All that is starting to change, however, and there are now some very comfortable accommodations where you can stay right on the beach and relax after a long day at sea. Some outfitters accommodate anglers in their own lodges; otherwise there are private luxury villas on the beach or the large Soleil Pacífico resort. Many outfits combine fishing packages with a round of golf on one of Guatemala City's excellent golf courses. All of the outfitters listed practice catch-and-release and use circle hooks, as mandated by Guatemalan law.

Fishing is active year-round, but most anglers come between November and May seeking a respite from colder climates. Prices for fishing packages vary by the size of the boat used and can be fairly expensive in Guatemala; boats generally travel 40-80 kilometers (25-50 miles) offshore to a deep, 600-meter (2,000-foot) basin where sailfish tend to congregate around its rim, translating into higher fuel costs. Boats heading out this way are usually in the 28-foot range, but there are also a few 42- and 43-foot boats. Expect to pay about $2,100 per person for two people on a two-day and three-night fishing package on a 28-foot boat. Most packages include food and drink, accommodations, boat and captain, gear, and transfers to and from the Guatemala City airport. Anglers often spend their last night in Antigua or Guatemala City.

landscaped swimming pool area. A nicer option is **Hotel Suites Mar y Sol** (Km. 104.5 Carretera a Iztapa, tel. 7934-2364, www.hotelmarysol.com, $78 d). Its spacious suites include a kitchen with microwave oven and refrigerator; rooms have cable TV and air-conditioning. There are two swimming pools and a swim-up bar. Across the Canal de Chiquimulilla and right on the beach, Iztapa's nicest accommodations are at the ★ **Sailfish Bay Lodge** (tel. 2426-3909 direct or 800/638-7405 U.S. reservations, www.sailfishbay.com, $175 d). Accommodations here are usually sold as part of a sailfishing package, but you are more than welcome to stay on your own. The Guatemalan Pacific Coast's best-kept secret is a modern, well-designed lodge featuring a thatched-roof seaside bar and swimming pool with whirlpool bath, comfortable ocean-view rooms with all the usual amenities, and an excellent restaurant fronting the canal. You can enjoy phenomenal views of three volcanoes rising above the surrounding mangroves while you dine. The outstanding feature of this place is that it's the only lodge sitting right on the broad, black-sand beach. A number of luxurious beach villas are the only neighbors. There are surfboards for guests' use. Transportation to the lodge from Guatemala City or Antigua is also available.

Another option is **Buena Vista Sportfishing Lodge** (Calle Baja Mar, Aldea

Buena Vista, tel. 7880-4203/04 or 866/699-3277 U.S., www.buenavistasportfishing.com), housed in a large yellow villa fronting the Chiquimulilla canal. Boats dock right in front of the property, so it's a quick trip to your shower or the lodge's swimming pool. The large somewhat spartan rooms feature air-conditioning and private baths.

Iztapa's best-known restaurant is popular with anglers and locals alike. **El Capitán** (tel. 7881-4403 or 3036-7333, 7am-9pm daily) serves large portions of tasty seafood and meat dishes under a thatched-roof *palapa* facing the lagoon. It also has a lively bar.

Next door to El Capitán, the ★ **Pacific Fins Resort & Marina** (tel. 888/700-3467 U.S., www.pacificfins.com.gt, $150-250 d) is an attractive lodge with six two-bedroom/two-bath villas with kitchenette and living room. Rooms include satellite flat-screen televisions, hardwood accents, wireless Internet, and brand-new furniture. All rooms have air-conditioning. The bar and restaurant, facing the lodge's swimming pool, offer a varied menu that includes sandwiches, pasta, grilled, sautéed, or breaded fish, chicken Florentine, and Argentinean-style *parrilladas*. Stays at the resort are usually part of a multiday fishing package, but hosts are also open to receiving guests just looking for a place to relax in the tropical swelter. If you're not in Guatemala to fish and just want to stay here, your best chance of scoring a room is during the off-season (May-Oct.).

Getting There

The same buses that leave Guatemala City's bus terminal for Puerto San José more often than not continue to Iztapa. Most anglers arrive on all-inclusive packages booked directly through their operation of choice, covering transportation logistics.

ALONG THE IZTAPA-MONTERRICO ROAD

Heading east from Iztapa, a smooth paved road travels along the coastline for about 25 kilometers to Monterrico. A bridge from Iztapa's *Colonia 20 de Octubre* ($3 per vehicle) transports you across the canal to Puerto Viejo, from where the road begins. You'll see loofah farms lining the side of the road and the occasional turnoff toward the beach, where numerous small hotels have begun to spring up on what is probably the finest stretch of sand on Guatemala's Pacific shores. There are rumors of a luxurious 18-hole golf course planned somewhere along this route in the not-too-distant future.

Accommodations and Food

★ **Cayman Suites** (Km. 10.5, tel. 5529-6518/19 lodge; 2332-7161 reservations, www.caymansuites.com.gt, $85-155 d) is set on a spectacular beach flanked by a kidney-shaped swimming pool and open-air *palapa*-roofed restaurant and bar. Its 22 rooms feature all the usual amenities, some with gorgeous sea views, and include deluxe rooms, junior suites, and spacious, fully furnished suites. All rooms have wireless Internet, DirecTV, and fine hardwood accents. The restaurant serves good international cuisine and seafood. ATVs are available for rent. Just one kilometer away, at kilometer 11.5, is the also stylish ★ **Villa Los Cabos** (tel. 2363-4325, www.villaloscabos.com.gt, $300-325). Although a private community, villa number 12C has been kept open for rentals. The horseshoe-shaped complex comprises three-story units built around a sprawling swimming pool overlooking the sea. The beautiful villa includes three bedrooms, two bathrooms, air-conditioning, a private patio with hot tub, and a living room, dining room, and full kitchen. It sleeps eight and comes fully equipped.

Should you need to fill up, there is a gas station at kilometer 17. A good place to stop for a snack or pick up any needed groceries is **Las Garzas** (Km. 17.5, tel. 4073-1399, 7:30am-9pm daily). The owners of this friendly roadside minimart can help you get your bearings. They also serve snacks, including pizza and sandwiches, which you can enjoy in a pleasant outdoor patio setting.

oceanfront Cayman Suites, along the road from Iztapa to Monterrico

The last place you'll come across on this road is **Utz Tzaba** (Km. 21.8, tel. 5318-9452, www.utz-tzaba.com, $95 d, $200 bungalow for up to 6 people), which has 10 rooms in a large main building as well as four bungalows. All rooms have tile floors, private hot-water bathrooms, wireless Internet, air-conditioning, and ceiling fans. The bungalows include two bedrooms and a living room and come fully furnished with minifridge, gas range, kitchen sink, and dining room table. There is a bar by the infinity-edge swimming pool, along with whirlpool tub. The hotel's restaurant serves excellent meals, including sandwiches, pasta, and seafood in the $6-10 range. The lodge is closed yearly on Christmas Eve and Christmas Day. Call ahead, as it's also closed for fumigation about every two months.

Monterrico and Hawaii

Monterrico, once a sleepy fishing village with one hotel run by an ex-Peace Corps volunteer is fast becoming popular with foreigners looking to get some time by the beach on their trip to Guatemala. The village has grown considerably in the last few years, as has the quality of its accommodations. It is a popular weekend destination with folks from Guatemala City and students from Antigua's Spanish schools. The same architects who gave Xocomil and Xetulul Parks their outstanding visual appeal were hired by INGUAT and local tourism authorities to provide Monterrico with an urban face-lift—complete with a tree-lined entrance to the main beach, pedestrian walkway, and a boat marina fronting Canal de Chiquimulilla. The pedestrian thoroughfare, officially dubbed Paseo de Don Pedro (after Pedro Cofiño Kepfer, a key player in masterminding Monterrico's urban face-lift, who died in a tragic accident in 2007), has yet to attract the upscale businesses it seems to have been designed for. Nonetheless, it is a pleasant way to get from town to the beach.

Although it's easy to see Monterrico as a beach destination, it should be noted that it

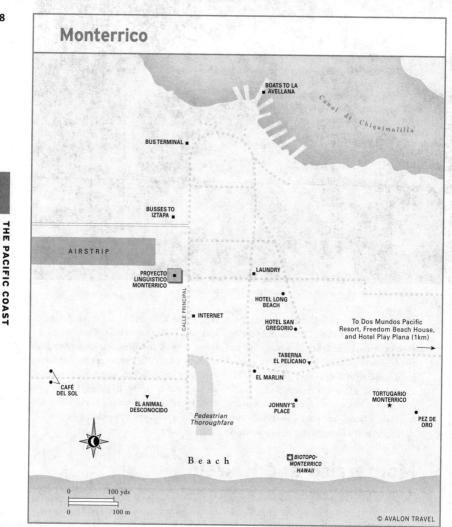

Monterrico

BOATS TO LA
AVELLANA

Canal de Chiquimulilla

BUS TERMINAL

BUSSES TO
IZTAPA

AIRSTRIP

PROYECTO
LINGÜÍSTICO
MONTERRICO

LAUNDRY

CALLE PRINCIPAL

INTERNET

HOTEL LONG
BEACH

HOTEL SAN
GREGORIO

To Dos Mundos Pacific
Resort, Freedom Beach House,
and Hotel Play Plana (1km)

TABERNA
EL PELICANO

EL MARLIN

CAFÉ
DEL SOL

EL ANIMAL
DESCONOCIDO

Pedestrian
Thoroughfare

JOHNNY'S
PLACE

TORTUGARIO
MONTERRICO

PEZ DE
ORO

B e a c h

BIOTOPO-
MONTERRICO
HAWAII

0   100 yds

0   100 m

© AVALON TRAVEL

was a protected sea turtle nesting site long before it became the haunt of beach-seeking vacationers. Visitors can contribute to the conservation efforts of the local sea turtle conservation site via their paid admission to tour its grounds. As for the beaches in Monterrico, there are, in all honesty, better and cleaner stretches elsewhere along Guatemala's Pacific seaboard. The waves break very close to the sand here and the beaches slope dramatically downward, which means you don't have a particularly wide stretch of beach, unlike at Iztapa or Tilapa farther west. The undertow, as along much of the Pacific Coast, is severe, and drownings are not uncommon. Exercise due caution.

In addition to the beaches, Monterrico offers the opportunity to interact with nature in some unique ways, whether it's touring the mangrove canals, holding a baby sea turtle in your hand before its maiden voyage out to sea, or watching a mother turtle come ashore to lay eggs in total darkness. Try to engage in at least one of these ecologically responsible activities while keeping in mind the ecological significance of this site. The sea turtles here have a fighting chance, though they are being wiped out elsewhere by the indiscriminate harvesting of their eggs. A newer threat to Guatemala's coastal ecosystems comes from Canadian and Australian mining interests, as its black-sand beaches are said to harbor 12 percent of the world's iron reserves.

Eight kilometers east along the sandy shoreline is **Parque Hawaii,** a remoter turtle nesting and iguana and crocodile breeding site on a pretty beach marked by the presence of sand dunes. **The Wildlife Rescue and Conservation Association** (ARCAS, www.arcasguatemala.com) has a sea turtle, crocodile, and mangrove conservation project here. Volunteers are welcome for a minimum one-week commitment ($90 per week for accommodations only) and assist in various projects, including animal care, construction projects, mangrove reforestation, environmental education, and turtle egg collection and hatchery management. Volunteers are also needed for another project in the neighboring village of El Rosario, six kilometers east. Turtle nesting season runs June-November with the peak of the action in August and September.

Hawaii is host to a few weekend homes for Guatemala's elite but has also added some recommended hotels of late. It has an online presence at www.hawaiiguatemala.com. You can get to Hawaii from Monterrico via public bus ($0.50), pickup ($4), or a 20-minute boat ride through the canals ($12). Buses leave at 6am, 11am, 1:30pm, and 3:30pm.

SIGHTS
★ Biotopo Monterrico-Hawaii

The protected biotope of **Biotopo Monterrico-Hawaii** (www.visitmonterrico.com) encompasses the beaches and mangrove swamps of Monterrico and those of adjacent Hawaii, which are the prime nesting sites for sea turtles on Guatemala's Pacific seaboard, including the giant leatherback and smaller olive ridley turtles. Residents are involved in a conservation project with the local turtle hatchery whereby they are allowed to keep half of the eggs they collect from nests and turn in the other half to the hatchery. Sadly, leatherback turtle arrivals have declined dramatically in recent years.

In the heart of town and run by the San Carlos University Center for Conservation Studies (CECON), the **Tortugario Monterrico** (on the sandy street just behind Johnny's Place, tel. 5978-3588, www.tortugamarina.info/monte-rico, 8am-noon and 2pm-5pm daily, $1) encompasses a turtle hatchery right on the beach, where collected eggs are reburied and allowed to hatch under protected conditions. There's also a visitors center. In

a baby sea turtle in Monterrico

Monterrico-Hawaii and Its Sea Turtles

If you're traveling to the Monterrico-Hawaii area between June and December, you might have the opportunity to witness a sea turtle coming ashore to lay its eggs or watch baby sea turtles making their maiden voyage out to sea.

Turtle nesting peaks during August and September, when you might be able to glimpse a large leatherback (*baule*) or the smaller olive ridley (*parlama*) coming ashore to lay eggs. Unfortunately, locals are also on the lookout for egg-laying sea turtles to snatch up the eggs and sell them, but under an agreement with the CECON monitoring station at Monterrico and ARCAS in Hawaii, they donate part of their stash toward conservation efforts. Your best bet for seeing a nesting turtle is to go with one of the CECON-trained guides or volunteer with ARCAS.

Volunteers are welcome at both stations. Among the duties are the collection of turtle eggs after the mothers have come ashore and moving them to a protected nesting site, where they are reburied and allowed to hatch. The typical incubation period for olive ridley eggs is 50 days, 72 for leatherbacks. After a few days in a holding pen, the young turtles are released, either at sunrise or sunset, and make their way across the sand and into the ocean. As the young turtles scamper across the sand, they are being imprinted with the unique details of the beach and its sand, where they will return and nest when they are adults. All this assumes they make it to adulthood, a big assumption when taking into account that only one turtle in 100 lives that long. Sea turtles are threatened not just by the collection of their eggs but also by fishing activities, where they often end up in nets, and sea pollution. Plastic bags, for example, are often mistaken for jellyfish by hungry sea turtles. The **CECON station at Monterrico** (www.visitmonterrico.com) releases about 5,000 sea turtle hatchlings per year.

Turtle eggs are incubated in designated areas at the *tortugario*. Upon hatching, the baby sea turtles crawl through the sand to the surface. They are placed in large cement tanks and held for release the same day. Turtle releases happen at sunset (in season) and you can donate to the *tortugario* in exchange for a baby sea turtle for release on its maiden voyage to the sea. There's nothing quite like watching these cute little critters crawling toward the ocean as the sun sets behind the waves. A newer initiative is the annual **Festival de la Tortuga Marina,** which takes place sometime during October or November. It features turtle releases, live music, and a surfing competition.

The ARCAS turtle hatchery in Hawaii also releases sea turtles. Visitors are allowed to witness turtle releases in limited numbers for a donation of about $3.25 (includes admission to the hatchery). If you're interested in volunteering with sea turtle conservation efforts, check out local grassroots turtle conservation group **Akazul** (http://akazul.org).

addition to baby sea turtles, the hatchery has enclosures housing green iguanas, crocodiles, and freshwater turtles bred on-site for release into the wild. The staff at CECON is always on the lookout for Spanish-speaking volunteers.

NIGHTLIFE

For a Central American beach town, the nightlife scene in Monterrico is pretty tame (weekends aside). This is certainly not your average spring break destination. Most places close at 10pm, with only a few exceptions. The liveliest spot in town is **Johnny's Place** (right on the beach, tel. 4369-6900, www.johnnysplace-hotel.com), where the party goes until 1am on weekends. Another hot spot is the beachfront **El Animal Desconocido** (tel. 4661-9255, 5pm-2am Fri.-Sat.), where you can chill out to an eclectic mix of dance and rock music in a colorful atmosphere. Behind Johnny's Place is **Taberna El Pelícano** (tel. 4001-5885), but it also closes early. The poolside bar at **El Marlin** (tel. 5715-4934) is another popular watering hole. It sometimes closes late.

RECREATION

You won't find a whole lot to do around here other than the beaches. Whether from a lack of entrepreneurial initiative or what have you, the recreational options aside from sunbathing and walking along the shore are pretty limited. Boat tours of the mangrove-lined canals are offered by ARCAS and CECON. They can often be arranged via the local hotels. You'll see plenty of birds and, with some luck, iguanas and anteaters. Antigua-based **Old Town Outfitters** (www.adventureguatemala.com) offers kayaking in the canals with prior arrangement. Monterrico's riptides and huge waves that literally crash onshore make swimming a perilous option.

ACCOMMODATIONS
Under $50

A good value can be found at **Hotel Long Beach** (tel. 7848-1577 or 5867-3732, www.hotellongbeach.galeon.com, $10 pp), down the street from Taberna El Pelícano, with spotless rooms with firm beds built next to a pool. There are hammocks for lounging outside your door. Another recommended budget hotel is **Hotel El Delfin** (tel. 4187-7260, www.hotel-el-delfin.com, shared bath $5 pp, private bath $15 pp). There are basic but clean rooms with shared bath or rooms with two king-size beds and private bath. All of the beds, as in most Monterrico budget hotels, consist of a foam mattress on a concrete slab. There's a clean swimming pool, a bar and restaurant, and plenty of hammocks to lounge on.

An old standby enjoying a new lease on life, thanks to savvy web marketing and good management, is **Johnny's Place** (tel. 5812-0409 or 4369-6900, www.johnnysplacehotel.com, $6 pp in dorm to $150 for 6-person bungalow) set right on the beach. The rooms are built so as to share a swimming pool with the unit next door and run the gamut from basic backpacker accommodations to souped-up bungalows sleeping up to eight. The basic shared-bath dorm rooms have foam beds and some spartan furnishings under a thatched roof. Room rates for weekend stays are about 20 percent higher. There's a restaurant and bar on the beach and a sand volleyball court. Johnny's is popular with the backpacking crowd. A few doors down, I like the quirkiness of **Hotel El Mangle** (tel. 5514-6517, www.hotelelmangle.com, $26-39 d), with its pseudo-colonial architecture reminiscent of Antigua. Some of the rooms on upper floors have nice sea views, and there are pleasant lounging areas with hammocks. It has a nice, family-friendly atmosphere that makes a good alternative to the budget backpacker hotels. There's a restaurant and a small swimming pool. The degree of comfort varies greatly here from room to room, so be sure to check out the various room types to find one that suits your needs.

Along the beach heading east from Johnny's Place, you'll find ★ **Hotel Pez de Oro** (tel. 2368-3684 or 5232-9534, www.pezdeoro.com, $40-52 d), an excellent choice with tastefully decorated rooms built around a swimming pool with wooden deck. The 11 attractive bungalows, all with private baths, feature terra-cotta floors, nice decorative accents, and firm beds. Rates are $40 on weekdays and $52 on weekends. The cost is the same for equally well-decorated and furnished raised-platform bungalows with nice decks (or patios) and hammocks in a separate area with its own swimming pool. The restaurant here is recommended.

West of Calle Principal along the beach you'll find pleasant ★ **Café del Sol** (tel. 5810-0821 or 5050-9173, www.cafe-del-sol.com, $40-74 d), where double rooms in the original building with warm-water showers in private bath, fan, and mosquito netting cost $40-67. There's a newer section behind the hotel across the street where slightly nicer rooms painted in cheerful yellows and equipped with air conditioning cost $74 d. These rooms also have a small patio fronting the street. The restaurant here is quite good.

A welcome addition to the options in Hawaii is ★ **Freedom Beach House** (Km. 159, tel. 5308-3018 or 5716-6988, www.freedombeachhouse.com, $39-110 d). All the rooms are cheerfully painted in green and white tones and have private bathroom and either fan or a/c. The deluxe private room also has a balcony with sea views. Room rates are discounted $7 Monday through Thursday nights. Breakfast (featuring banana pancakes) is included in the room rate, and there is a full restaurant and bar, along with a swimming pool.

$50-100

Heading east toward Hawaii are a number of slightly more expensive beach hotels. **Hotel Honolulu** (tel. 4005-0500, www.hotelhonolulu.com.gt, $80 d) is a comfortable beachfront hotel housed in quaint wooden cottages built round a pleasant swimming pool. It has a restaurant and bar serving mostly seafood dishes. My favorite of Hawaii's accommodations is also a good value. ★ **Hotel Playa Plana** (Km. 161, Aldea Los Limones; tel. 5628-0379 or 5417-6860, www.playaplana.com, $78-94 d with breakfast) enjoys a wonderful seaside location. The modern rooms are nicely decorated and set round a swimming pool. There's a restaurant and poolside bar.

Over $100

Monterrico's most stylish beachside digs are at the Italian-owned ★ **Dos Mundos Pacific Resort** (tel. 7823-0820, www.hotelsdosmundos.com/monterrico, $122 d weekends, $90 d weekdays), about one kilometer east of Monterrico, along the beach. This fabulous property features 14 luxurious beachfront villas with terra-cotta floors, hot-water showers, and air-conditioning housed in ecochic thatched-roof structures with private patios. The bathrooms feature artsy ceramic sinks and oversized "rain" showerheads. The fine restaurant serves excellent Italian cuisine overlooking an infinity-edge swimming pool and the sea.

Another option in this pricier domain is east of Monterrico in Hawaii. **Casa Bella** (tel. 7821-3088 or 5907-2522, www.casabellamonterrico.com, from $150 per bungalow) offers spacious one- or two-story bungalows (two or four bedrooms) with cable TV, full kitchens, and sitting areas featuring tropical rattan furniture. Each bungalow has a covered private patio with sea views. A pool and a restaurant are also on the premises. Also in Hawaii, **Hawaian Paradise** (tel. 5361-3011, www.hawaianparadise.com, $127 d) is another welcome addition to the area's hotel infrastructure. Comfortable air-conditioned rooms are housed in a cheerful yellow

Dos Mundos Pacific Resort in Monterrico

structure topped with a *palapa*-roofed terrace. Spacious apartments with comfortable living room area ($300-450) sleep up to seven guests. The hotel fronts a swimming pool and the ocean. There are a restaurant/bar, hammock lounges, and a pool table. It's a good alternative if you're not into Monterrico's somewhat raucous weekend atmosphere and just want to get away from it all.

FOOD

Most of Monterrico's hotels, particularly those that are on the beach, serve food. The following are the best of the hotel restaurants, along with a few non-hotel eateries serving decent food. ★ **Café del Sol** (tel. 5810-0821, www.cafe-del-sol.com, all meals daily) serves excellent seafood dishes ($4-8) under an airy *palapa* or on a pleasant beachside patio. For Italian fare at affordable prices, you can't beat the atmosphere at **Pez de Oro** (tel. 2368-3684, www.pezdeoro.com, $5-7). On the pricier side, the restaurant at ★ **Dos Mundos Pacific Resort** (tel. 7823-0820, www.hotelsdos-mundos.com/monterrico, 8am-10pm daily, $10-35), overlooking both the sea and an infinity-edge swimming pool, is simply wonderful. Accompany your meal with a selection from the decent wine list.

Hotels aside, there are also a few decent stand-alone eateries in town. Behind Johnny's Place, on the sandy street parallel to the shore, is **Taberna El Pelícano** (noon-2pm and 6:30pm-9:30pm Mon.-Fri., 6:30pm-10pm Sat., noon-3pm and 7pm-9:30pm Sun.), where there are good pasta dishes and seafood ($8-20) and a fully stocked bar.

Dining options are limited in Hawaii outside of the aforementioned hotels, though **Lahaina East** (on the main street, tel. 3320-0949, open weekends, $8-20) plays off the town's Hawaiian name and serves tasty American comfort and Asian fusion cuisine in a seaside setting. Among the options are summer rolls, burgers, artisanal pizzas, fish tacos, and Korean barbecue. It also doubles as the town's main sports bar.

SERVICES

There is an ATM at Banrural, right in the heart of town. Monterrico's post office is on Calle Principal. You'll also find a nameless Internet communications center on this street.

Language Schools

If you want to learn Spanish at the beach, head to **Proyecto Lingüistico Monterrico** (Calle Principal, tel. 5619-8200, www.proyectolin-guisticomonterrico.com), where 20 hours of one-on-one instruction per week cost $100. Accommodations with a local family are available for $70 per week for room and board.

GETTING THERE

There are two ways to get to Monterrico. The first of these is via the 25-kilometer road from Puerto Viejo (Iztapa). The other option is via the town of Taxisco, from which you continue south for 17 kilometers to La Avellana. At La Avellana you make a ferry crossing ($7 per vehicle), traveling for about 20 minutes through the mangrove swamps. Most people seem to prefer the route via Iztapa, as the road is smooth and fast and there are some new, enticing accommodations options along the way. Buses leave from Guatemala City's Zona 4 bus terminal every 30 minutes for Taxisco on their way to Chiquimulilla between 5am and 6pm. Connecting buses make the trip down to La Avellana. **Transportes Cubanita** leaves the Zona 4 bus terminal directly for La Avellana at 10:30am, 12:30pm, and 2:30pm. There are five buses a day from Puerto Viejo (Iztapa) to Monterrico leaving at 8am, 10am, noon, 1:30pm, and 4pm. As always, there's the occasional pickup truck heading this way. There are now also direct buses from Guatemala City ($5) and La Antigua ($6) a few times daily.

Increasingly popular are daily shuttle buses from Antigua costing about $20 and departing at 8am. The return trip departs Monterrico at 4pm. Any of the Antigua travel agencies can book it for you.

El Oriente and Izabal

Look for ★ to find recommended sights, activities, dining, and lodging.

Highlights

★ **The Ruins of Copán:** This wonderful Mayan city just across the border in Honduras is home to some of the finest carved stelae in the Mayan world (page 224).

★ **The Ruins of Quiriguá:** Harboring beautifully carved stelae set amid luxuriant banana plantations and jungle, this small Mayan site is one of only three UNESCO World Heritage Sites in Guatemala (page 235).

★ **Cerro San Gil and Río Las Escobas:** This fantastic rainforest preserve harbors waterfalls and pristine pools—just minutes away from the cruise-ship terminal at Puerto Santo Tomás de Castilla (page 239).

★ **Playa Blanca:** My favorite beach on Guatemala's Caribbean Coast makes a pleasant day trip from Lívingston. Relax on its clean, palm-fringed, white sands and bathe in clear, cool water (page 248).

★ **Río Tatín:** This jungle-clad tributary of the larger Río Dulce makes a fine base for enjoying and exploring the area's tropical terrain (page 250).

These two very different geographical regions comprise the part of Guatemala east of Guatemala City all the way to the Honduran border and the Caribbean Sea.

Izabal is a sweltering jungle coastland with rainforests and beaches sharing some similarities with Belize to its north. The region known as El Oriente, meanwhile, is a mix of temperate mountains and semiarid plains. As you head east from Guatemala City on the Carretera al Atlántico (CA-9), the road descends into this region of dusty plains and cactus-studded hills. Farther along, in the department of Izabal, the terrain becomes lush and green before ending at Puerto Barrios, on the Caribbean Sea, just about 300 kilometers from the capital.

The Izabal region features a unique kind of Caribbean experience not at all like Cancún or the West Indies but nonetheless beautiful. Tourism promoters have labeled this, "A different Caribbean." Cruise ships regularly dock at Puerto Santo Tomás de Castilla, just across the bay from Puerto Barrios. Its new cruise-ship terminal is fast becoming a motor for the tourism development of this long-overlooked Caribbean coastal region. Cruise-ship day-trippers can explore a rainforest and pristine

jungle river with waterfalls and pools in the lush green mountains looming over the port. From Puerto Barrios, it's just a quick hop to the intriguing Caribbean town of Lívingston or the exotic jungle canyon of the Río Dulce.

Lívingston is a standout for its unique Garífuna culture brought to coastal Guatemala from the Caribbean island of St. Vincent by way of Roatán, Honduras. This Black Carib influence provides a fascinating contrast to Guatemala's largely Mayan heritage with rhythmic dancing and musical customs that complete the Caribbean experience. The Río Dulce canyon connects Lívingston (and the Caribbean Sea) to Lake Izabal, Guatemala's largest lake. Along the Río Dulce, you'll find lush jungle canyons, hot springs, and side streams offering unique options for jungle accommodations. In the town of Río Dulce, at the mouth of Lake Izabal, you'll find a variety of tourist services and boat marinas, as it's become a popular shelter for boats sailing the Western Caribbean.

Back on Highway CA-9 closer to Guatemala

Previous: Rancho Corozal; colorful scene from a street in Lívingston. **Above:** the beautiful beach at Playa Blanca.

El Oriente and Izabal

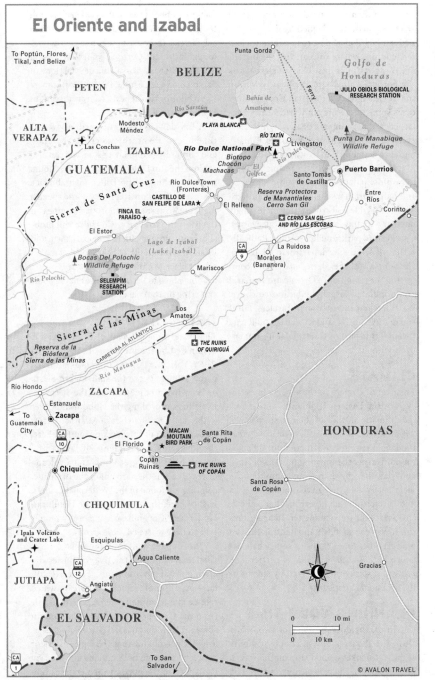

To Poptún, Flores, Tikal, and Belize

PETEN

ALTA VERAPAZ

Las Conchas

GUATEMALA

Sierra de Santa Cruz

El Estor

Bocas Del Polochic Wildlife Refuge

Río Polochic

SELEMPÍM RESEARCH STATION

IZABAL

Modesto Méndez

Río Sarstún

BELIZE

Punta Gorda

Golfo de Honduras

JULIO OBIOLS BIOLOGICAL RESEARCH STATION

Bahía de Amatique

PLAYA BLANCA

RÍO TATÍN

Río Dulce National Park

Biotopo Chocón Machacas

El Golfete

Livingston

Río Dulce

Punta De Manabique Wildlife Refuge

Ferry

Santo Tomás de Castilla

Puerto Barrios

Entre Ríos

Corinto

Río Dulce Town (Fronteras)

CASTILLO DE SAN FELIPE DE LARA ★

FINCA EL PARAÍSO ★

El Relleno

Reserva Protectora de Manantiales Cerro San Gil

CERRO SAN GIL AND RÍO LAS ESCOBAS

Lago de Izabal (Lake Izabal)

CA 9

Mariscos

La Ruidosa

Morales (Bananera)

Sierra de las Minas

Los Amates

Reserva de la Biósfera Sierra de las Minas

CARRETERA AL ATLÁNTICO

Río Motagua

THE RUINS OF QUIRIGUÁ

Río Hondo

ZACAPA

Estanzuela

To Guatemala City

Zacapa

CA 10

El Florido

MACAW MOUTAIN BIRD PARK

Santa Rita de Copán

HONDURAS

Copán Ruinas

THE RUINS OF COPÁN

Chiquimula

Santa Rosa de Copán

CHIQUIMULA

Ipala Volcano and Crater Lake

Esquipulas

Agua Caliente

Santa Rosa de Copán

Gracias

JUTIAPA

CA 12

Angiatú

EL SALVADOR

CA 1

To San Salvador

0   10 mi
0   10 km

© AVALON TRAVEL

City, a branch road heads southeast to El Oriente, partially occupied by Guatemala's Eastern Highlands. The road continues east to Honduras, where you can visit the incredible ruins of Copán, just 12 kilometers across the border. Along with the nearby Mayan site of Quiriguá (Guatemala), Copán showcases some of the Mayan world's finest stelae, carved monuments depicting historical events in the life of Mayan dynasties. Copán's museum is among the finest attractions in the Mayan world, along with its restored temple pyramids, palaces, hieroglyphic stairway, and ball court. The surrounding mountainous countryside is also becoming increasingly popular with travelers exploring coffee farms, a jungle bird park, and hot springs. Radically different from the department of Izabal, Guatemala's other eastern departments comprising the region of El Oriente are semiarid and populated largely by ladino cowboys. It attracts few international travelers, but if you're traveling by land to Izabal, you'll pass through this part of Guatemala. It's not entirely without its charms.

CLIMATE

The overall climate in these parts is warm, even in the Eastern Highlands, which lack the dramatic altitude of their western counterparts. The Motagua Valley is arid, whereas the Izabal region is warm and humid year-round. During the warmest months of April and May, the temperature and humidity can seem unbearable, though coastal regions get a lightly refreshing sea breeze that helps alleviate some of the tropical swelter. Temperatures can hover round 100°F during this time of year. At other times, it hovers somewhere between 85°F and 95°F. Izabal is particularly rainy and sometimes battered by storms or the occasional hurricane.

PLANNING YOUR TIME

Copán can be done in a day or two, while Quiriguá requires only a couple of hours at most. It makes a good stop on the way to Puerto Barrios. There is plenty to see and do

on the Caribbean Coast. Puerto Barrios is not the most pleasant town, but there's no need to stay here as there are now better alternatives for exploring the Cerro San Gil Reserve and Río Las Escobas across Bahía de Amatique in Santo Tomás de Castilla. Puerto Barrios merits an hour or two at best as a transit point to Lívingston or Río Dulce.

A few days in Lívingston will allow you time to explore nearby waterfalls, beaches, and rainforests. From Lívingston, you can also explore the Río Dulce canyon in a few hours while traveling to Río Dulce town, but it's also possible to stop over midway and spend a night or two at some comfortable lodgings on the Río Tatín tributary. Río Dulce will probably captivate you with its tropical charm and location at the mouth of Lake Izabal. It makes a great place to chill out for a few days before heading north to Petén or before or after some exploring on the coast.

ORIENTATION

The eastern department of El Progreso is dominated by the presence of the Motagua River Valley, a region of cactus-studded plains lying between the rain-soaked Sierra de las Minas to the north and the Sierra del Espíritu Santo, along the Honduran border to the east. The Carretera al Atlántico passes through much of this terrain. South of here, the low-lying departments of Jalapa and Jutiapa have some green hills and a volcano or two, though they are not of the dramatic, conical kind found in the Western Highlands. East of here, the areas along the Honduran border near Copán have some pretty mountain scenery where coffee is grown.

The department of Izabal is one of Guatemala's most attractive for those who enjoy coastal environments. There are still large expanses of tropical rainforests, which receive ample rainfall when warm, moist air from the Caribbean Sea rises on mountain slopes. The Montañas del Mico stand as silent sentinels dominating a biological corridor between the Bahía de Amatique and the lazy Río Dulce to the north, which empties into the Caribbean. Guatemala's Caribbean coastline lacks the aquamarine beaches of Cancún and Belize, but there is at least one white-sand beach worthy of mention near Lívingston.

Farther out to sea are the tail end of the Belize Barrier Reef and some easily accessible cayes. Inland, Lake Izabal is a huge body of water harboring some impressive wetlands.

Río Hondo to Zacapa

The town of Río Hondo is an oasis of fun, featuring excellent restaurants, refreshing swimming pools, and even a water park. Many travelers heading between Guatemala City and Puerto Barrios like to break up their journey here. Heading south from the Río Hondo Junction, the road passes through the hot lowland towns of Zacapa and Chiquimula.

RÍO HONDO JUNCTION

The hotels and restaurants lining CA-9 (the road to the Atlantic Coast) at Río Hondo are popular places to stop and eat for travelers heading to or from faraway Puerto Barrios. The dry, warm climate lends itself marvelously to swimming and other water-centered activities.

Accommodations and Food

All of the options listed here are found at Km. 126 and offer comfortable air-conditioned rooms with private bathroom and cable TV. All have swimming pools. Among the options is old standby **Hotel Longarone** (tel. 7933-0488, www.hotel-longarone.com, $59-81 d). Its large swimming pool has diving boards and a waterslide. Some of the rooms are more dimly lit than others. The restaurant and bar serves international food ($6-20) with excellent service and cleanliness. In addition to a large, attractive palm-trimmed swimming pool, **Hotel El Atlantico** (tel. 7933-0598, www.hotelatlanticoguate.com, $65 d) boasts lovely gardens, a gym, and children's play areas.

Valle Dorado Water Park

Another 23 kilometers east from Río Hondo along CA-9 is **Valle Dorado Water Park** (Km. 149, tel. 7790-2121, www.hotelvalledorado.com, 6am-6pm Tues.-Sun., $7 adults, $5 children), well worth the wait if you can curb your appetite, as there are a variety of food options inside the park and tons of fun stuff for the kids (or the kid in you). The large theme park has a variety of pools and waterslides as well as a very comfortable hotel with room rates starting at $70 (d).

ESTANZUELA

Continuing southeast about six kilometers from Río Hondo along Highway CA-10 (the junction is at Km. 135), the first town you'll come across is Estanzuela. The terrain here is decidedly dry, resembling parts of Arizona, making for an excellent environment for the preservation of fossils. Sure enough, you can see some dinosaur bones, including the skeleton of a 50,000-year-old mastodon and that of a prehistoric whale at **Museo de Paleontología Robert Woolfolk Saravia** (tel. 7941-4981, 9am-5pm daily, free). To get here, go through the town and follow the blue signs to the *museo*.

ZACAPA

The next stop along CA-10 is the departmental capital of Zacapa. Its redeeming quality is the award-winning **Ron Zacapa Centenario,** sold in a festive woven-straw bottle holder. You don't have to go all the way to Zacapa to pick up a bottle, as it's available from its own duty-free shop at Guatemala City's international airport. You can pick up a bottle (or two) before your flight home.

Copán Archaeological Site (Honduras)

The Mayan site of Copán, just 13 kilometers across the border in Honduras, features some of the Mayan world's greatest artistic treasures, including numerous stelae and a hieroglyphic stairway that is the longest known Mayan inscription. Whereas Tikal has been likened to the Manhattan of Mayan cities for its grand scale and a population once thought to have numbered 100,000, Copán is likened to Paris for the exquisite quality of its artwork, unmatched in the Mayan world. It is thought to have harbored 25,000 inhabitants in its heyday.

Archaeologists are still busy excavating and restoring this site in addition to deciphering the jumbled mess of a hieroglyphic stairway (found tumbled and out of order). In recent years, they have undertaken the ambitious enterprise of digging tunnels beneath existing structures to uncover previous constructions. Among the magnificent finds are the well-preserved Rosalila (Rose-lilac) Temple and the tombs of several of Copán's rulers. You can see a wonderful reconstruction of the temple in all its Technicolor glory at Copán's excellent Sculpture Museum, in addition to several of the original finely carved stelae and monuments found in situ.

In addition to the ruins, the nearby town of **Copán Ruinas** has become increasingly popular as a destination unto itself for its excellent restaurants and accommodations. From here, you can explore the ruins and the surrounding countryside with ease.

CROSSING THE BORDER

The bare-bones border crossing at **El Florido** (open 6am-6pm) includes some basic services but little else. There are some snack and soda stands and a Banrural which changes dollars and travelers checks. Ubiquitous money changers are also on hand to help you change your quetzales for Honduran lempiras.

However, note that many tourist places in Copán take quetzales.

Crossing the border is fairly straightforward. If you're driving a rental car, you'll need to present a written letter from your rental-car agency allowing you to take the vehicle into Honduras. Otherwise, you'll have to leave it at the border. Most Western nationalities, including U.S. citizens, need only a passport to get into Honduras; no visas are required. You can either get a three-day permit to enter and visit Copán and vicinity only or request a 30-day or 90-day entry permit by filling out an official request form. It all depends on your nationality what length of stay you're allowed. If on a three-day permit, you can still use your original entry stamp into Guatemala upon your return to continue traveling for the rest of your stay in the country. On the Guatemalan side, there is a $1.25 (Q10) exit tax. There is a $3 customs fee on the Honduran side (for entry only).

As this guide was being researched, Guatemala and Honduras were embarking on a process of customs integration similar to agreements Guatemala has with El Salvador. If it's anything like the latter, border procedures and red tape should be greatly reduced. The new measures were set to take effect on January 1, 2016, but details at writing were still sketchy. Check locally for the latest.

Once in Honduras, there are onward buses from the border to Copán Ruinas every 30 minutes or so ($2). Heading back, the last bus from El Florido to Chiquimula leaves at 4:30pm, but you are exhorted to cross the border much earlier in the day. To call Honduras, the country code is 504. Phone numbers are eight digits long. As in Guatemala, there are no area codes or city codes.

HISTORY
Early Copán

Although the fertile Copán Valley is thought

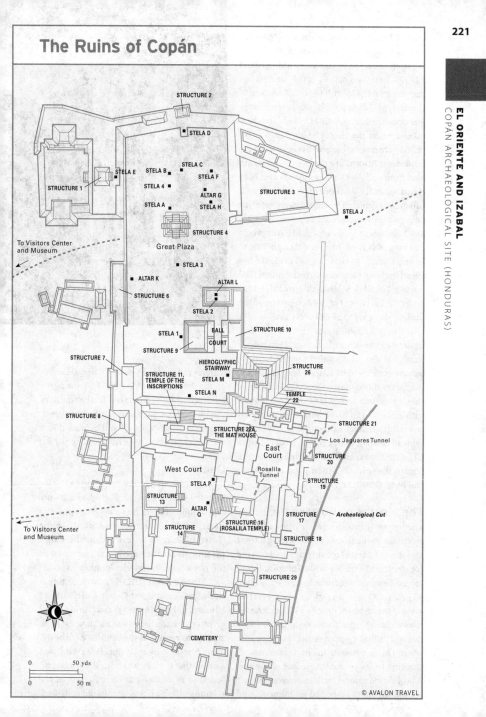

The Ruins of Copán

STRUCTURE 2

STELA D

STRUCTURE 1

STELA E

STELA B
STELA 4
STELA A

STELA C
STELA F
ALTAR G
STELA H

STRUCTURE 3

STELA J

STRUCTURE 4

To Visitors Center
and Museum

Great Plaza

STELA 3

ALTAR K

ALTAR L

STRUCTURE 6

STELA 2

STELA 1
STRUCTURE 9

BALL
COURT

STRUCTURE 10

STRUCTURE 7

HIEROGLYPHIC
STAIRWAY

STRUCTURE
26

STRUCTURE 11,
TEMPLE OF THE
INSCRIPTIONS

STELA M

STELA N

TEMPLE
22

STRUCTURE 8

STRUCTURE 22A,
THE MAT HOUSE

STRUCTURE 21

Los Jaguares Tunnel

East
Court

STRUCTURE
20

West Court

STELA P

Rosalila
Tunnel

STRUCTURE
19

STRUCTURE
13

ALTAR
Q

STRUCTURE
17

Archeological Cut

To Visitors Center
and Museum

STRUCTURE
14

STRUCTURE 16
(ROSALILA TEMPLE)

STRUCTURE 18

STRUCTURE 29

CEMETERY

0   50 yds

0   50 m

© AVALON TRAVEL

to have been inhabited as early as 1400 BC, archaeological evidence points to its not having been occupied by the Maya until around AD 100. Recorded history at the site does not begin until AD 426 with the establishment of Copán's royal dynasty. The site's early history was unearthed as recently as 1989, when excavations under the Hieroglyphic Stairway revealed a chamber subsequently nicknamed the **Founder's Room.** The chamber is thought to have been built by Copán's second ruler, **Mat Head** (after the odd-looking headdress with which he is depicted on stelae) in honor of his father, Copán's first ruler, in power AD 426-435. Subsequent kings appear to have revered this king, **Yax K'uk'Mo'**, and thought him to be semidivine. Archaeological evidence has found that he was indeed a great shaman. The tomb of Yax K'uk'Mo' was discovered in 1993 under the East Court of the Acropolis, and the findings have yet to be fully revealed.

Little is known about the next several leaders in the dynastic line established by Yax K'uk'Mo', which ruled Copán throughout the entirety of its Classic Mayan history. It appears this dynasty was consolidating its rule at this time and establishing trade routes within the Mayan world and farther afield to powerful cities such as Teotihuacán. We know some of the names of Copán's leaders before AD 628: Cu Ix, the fourth king; Waterlily Jaguar, the seventh; Moon Jaguar, the 10th; and Butz' Chan, the 11th.

The Height of Power

The height of Copán's power came with the ascension to the throne of **Moon Jaguar** on May 26, 553. Moon Jaguar is credited with the construction of the **Rosalila Temple,** found buried beneath Structure 16 in 1993. Ruling AD 628-695 was one of Copán's greatest kings, **Smoke Imix,** the city's 12th ruler, who consolidated Copán into a regional commercial and military power. A stela at the nearby site of Quiriguá bears his name and image, attesting to his probable takeover of the site. A prolific monument builder, Smoke Imix left behind the most inscribed monuments and

one of Copán's magnificently carved stelae

temples out of all of Copán's rulers. His successor, **18 Rabbit** (AD 695-738), was also a prolific builder and pursued further military conquest. He came to a very unfortunate end, however, being captured and beheaded in a war with Quiriguá by its ruler, Cauac Sky.

Decline

Next in line was **Smoke Monkey** (AD 738-749), the 14th ruler of Copán, who built only one temple and erected no self-promoting stelae. The crushing blow suffered against Quiriguá may have resulted in the king's sharing power with a council composed of the city's nobility. Smoke Monkey's successor, **Smoke Shell** (AD 749-763), commissioned the creation of Copán's magnificent **Hieroglyphic Stairway,** containing 2,500 glyphs narrating the city's glorious past in an attempt to recapture the brilliance of the dynasty's heyday. By this time, however, it was evident that the city was in decline, a fact attested to by the subpar construction of the monument, which was later found collapsed, its narrative left scattered and out of order like a messy game of Jenga.

Yax Pac (AD 763-820) was Copán's 16th ruler, who continued along the same lines of beautifying the city. He left behind a fantastic monument known as **Altar Q,** depicting the city's 16 kings carved around a four-sided square monument with Copán's first king, Yax K'uk'Mo', passing the baton of leadership on to Yax Pac, thus legitimizing his rule.

Copán's 17th and final leader was **U Cit Tok',** assuming the throne in AD 822. His only legacy is the unfinished Altar L, of rather lackluster quality. Some believe this to be evidence of a sudden abandonment of Copán rather than a gradual collapse. As elsewhere in the Mayan world, Copán's collapse is thought to have been at least partially the result of exhausting the local ecosystem's carrying capacity, with a population thought to have reached 25,000 at its zenith. Agricultural areas were forced from the central part of the valley by urban expansion and the surrounding, less fertile hillsides eventually came under heavy cultivation. Soil erosion, droughts, deforestation, and rainy season flooding became the inevitable result. Though the city's core was abandoned, the valley was still somewhat heavily populated after this time. Archaeological evidence suggests another drop in population around 1200, after which the settlement patterns reverted to the small villages found by the Spanish in 1524. The ruins were left to be reclaimed by the jungle.

Rediscovery

The first known European to lay eyes on the ruined city was Diego García de Palacios, a representative of Spanish King Felipe II living in Guatemala and traveling through the Copán Valley. He described the ruins in a letter written to the king on March 8, 1576, and related that there were only five families living in the valley at the time, knowing nothing of the ruins' history or the people who built them. A Spanish colonel by the name of Juan Galindo would be the first to map the ruins almost 300 years later. Inspired by Galindo's report, John L. Stephens and Frederick Catherwood included a stop in Copán in 1839 during their famous journey to Mayan lands chronicled in *Incidents of Travel in Central America, Chiapas and Yucatán,* published two years later. Inspired by this book, British archaeologist Alfred P. Maudslay would make his way down to Copán in 1881. He returned four years later to fully map, excavate, photograph, and reconstruct the site off and on until 1902. Other scholars, among them Sylvanus Morley and J. Eric Thompson, would follow on his heels.

Present Day

In 1975, Harvard's Peabody Museum continued the investigations it had previously supported through Maudsley. Among its goals was the excavation of temples lying beneath existing structures, a product of the customary manner in which the Mayans built atop existing temples and pyramids. They embarked on a project to tunnel through Copán's numerous layers of construction and so have a glimpse into the city's history. Among the fascinating discoveries was the 1989 unearthing of the Rosalila Temple by Honduran archaeologist Ricardo Agurcia. An even earlier temple, Margarita, lies beneath it. Rosalila was found with its vivid ocher paint still visible. You can visit the excavation tunnel nowadays and see a replica of Rosalila in the Sculpture Museum.

Tunneling farther into the East Court, archaeologists came across a glyph panel paying homage to Copán's original ruler, Yax K'uk'Mo'. His tomb was found buried far below the East Court in 1993 by a team led by Robert Sharer of the University of Pennsylvania. This area remains closed to the public. Teams from Harvard, Tulane, and the University of Pennsylvania continue to work in different areas of the site.

EXPLORING THE PARK

The ruins of Copán lie about 1.5 kilometers from the town of Copán Ruinas, a 20-minute walk along a footpath running parallel to the highway. The **visitors center** houses the ticket office, where you pay a $15 admission fee for entry to the park (8am-4pm daily), including entry to the neighboring site of Las Sepulturas. Another $15 gets you admission to two underground tunnels where, among other attractions, you can see the Rosalila Temple in its original context. The tunnels are recommended for serious Mayan archaeology buffs, but not so much for the casual visitor. You can also buy your $7 ticket for admission to Copán's excellent Sculpture Museum which is well worth the price of admission. There's a small exhibit placing Copán's importance in the context of the larger Mayan world at the visitors center.

Also at the visitors center are registered **guides** for hire, costing about $40 for a two-hour tour. There are English-speaking guides, though their skill levels vary, so be sure to assess their mastery of the English language before sealing the deal. Across the parking lot in front of the visitors center is a small **eatery** serving drinks and basic meals. There's also a small gift shop.

It's a few hundred meters' walk from the visitors center to the ticket checkpoint where you enter the ruins. A short **nature trail** winding its way through the surrounding forest diverts from the main path just before this checkpoint. A few semidomesticated scarlet macaws sometimes hang out in this area. Try to visit the site right at opening time, as the crowds tend to get larger as the day goes on, especially on weekends. You'll also have better-angled light for photography.

★ THE RUINS OF COPÁN

Enthusiasts of Mayan archaeology will find some of the best hieroglyphic carvings in the whole of the Mayan world along with well-restored structures, including palaces, temple pyramids, and a ball court. The Hieroglyphic Stairway alone is worth the price of admission, not to mention the chance to see the buried section of temple pyramids from tunnels

A carved head lies among the ruins of Copán.

(Rosalila and Los Jaguares) originally used by archaeologists excavating the ruins.

Great Plaza

The first place you'll come to as you walk along the forest path from the main entrance to the park is the **Great Plaza.** You'll see a variety of stelae in a spacious grassy area, which was once paved. Traces of red paint (created by mixing mercury sulfate and tree resins) can still be seen on **Stela C,** which dates to AD 730. Most of the stelae date to the rule of Smoke Imix (AD 628-695) and 18 Rabbit (AD 695-738). The latter ruler is depicted on Stelae 1, 2, 3, 10, 12, 13, and 19. The plaza's standout is **Stela A** (AD 731). Among its 52 glyphs are the emblem glyphs of Palenque, Tikal, Calakmul, and Copán, establishing Copán's position as one of the great cities of the Mayan world. As with many other important monuments, the original now resides in the Sculpture Museum. Another beautifully carved monument is **Stela H,** depicting what looks to be a woman wearing a skirt with a leopard skin underneath, wrists weighed down with jewelry, and an intricate headdress. This may be an image of 18 Rabbit's wife.

Copán's **ball court** is south of the Great Plaza after you cross what is known as the Central Plaza (Plaza Central). Completed in AD 738, it was the third ball court to have been erected at the site. There are three elaborate macaw heads on each side. It is one of the most often-photographed buildings in Copán.

Hieroglyphic Stairway

Farther south from the Great Plaza is the **Hieroglyphic Stairway,** which rises up the southeast corner of the plaza up the side of the neighboring Acropolis. The impressive structure, now covered with a roof for protection from the elements, contains 2,500 glyphs on its 72 steps and is the longest known hieroglyphic inscription found anywhere in the Mayan world. Commissioned in AD 753 by Smoke Shell, its substandard construction was evident in that it collapsed and was found by archaeologists as a jumbled mess, which they reassembled in 1940. Only about 15 steps, primarily on the bottom section, are thought to be in the correct order. Archaeologists are working on getting the correct order and deciphering the long message encoded on the steps. Its construction came at a time when Copán's rulers were attempting to once again instill confidence in their city's power and glorious history after the gruesome death of 18 Rabbit at the hands of neighboring Quiriguá.

At the base of the Hieroglyphic Stairway is **Stela M** (AD 756), with a figure presumed to be Smoke Shell dressed in a feathered cloak along with glyphs telling of a solar eclipse in that year. An altar in front depicts a feathered serpent with a human head emanating from its jaws.

A tomb thought to belong to a royal scribe and possibly one of the sons of Smoke Imix was discovered underneath the Hieroglyphic Stairway in 1989. It was laden with painted pottery and well-carved jade objects. Digging ever deeper below the stairway, in 1993 archaeologists uncovered an earlier temple called **Papagayo,** erected by Mat Head. Farther below was a chamber dedicated to Yax K'uk'Mo', the city's original king. Archaeologists called it the **Founder's Room** and believe it was used as a place of reverence for the shaman king believed by subsequent kings to have been semidivine.

The Acropolis

Copán's dominating architectural feature is the massive **Acropolis,** which rises about 30 meters above the ground south of the Great Plaza. It is here that some of the more interesting archaeological finds have been unearthed in recent years by digging tunnels under existing structures to reveal what was originally beneath them.

South of the Hieroglyphic Stairway is a flight of steps running along the **Temple of the Inscriptions.** Walls atop the stairway are carved with various glyphs. Toward the top of the Hieroglyphic Stairway is a temple curiously adorned with engravings resembling woven mats and appropriately named the **Mat House,** also known as Structure 22A. It was built in AD 746 by Smoke Monkey shortly after the death of his predecessor, 18 Rabbit, and provides further evidence of the new power-sharing arrangement with the city's nobility after the shocking defeat at the hands of Quiriguá. It was thought to have operated as a council house, the mats being a symbol for authority and community. South of here is the **East Court,** the city's original plaza, underneath which were found the tombs of Yax K'uk'Mo' and his wife. It is also known as the "Patio de los Jaguares." Also buried in the East Court, below **Structure 18,** was Yax Pac, though it was unfortunately discovered and looted long before the arrival of archaeologists.

Between the East Court and nearby West

Court lies **Structure 16,** which was dedicated to the themes of death, war, and veneration of past rulers. The well-preserved **Rosalila Temple** was found buried here in 1989.

In the **West Court** at the base of Structure 16 is a replica of the magnificently carved square monument known as **Altar Q,** depicting Yax Pac receiving the baton of rulership from Yax K'uk'Mo' himself. The altar is adorned with four kings on each side, giving us a complete line of succession for Copán's ruling dynasty of 16 kings from Yax K'uk'Mo' to Yax Pac, who commissioned its carving in AD 776. It was once thought to have portrayed a gathering of astronomers, but recent advances in glyph decipherment have shed light on its true meaning. The original can be seen in the Sculpture Museum. Behind the altar is a sacrificial vault, which contained the remains of 15 jaguars and several macaws sacrificed in honor of Yax Pac and his royal lineage.

Túnel Rosalila and Túnel de los Jaguares

Opened in 1999 to much fanfare, the original excavation tunnels used by archaeologists to discover the hidden gems of Copán are available for visitors to explore. The first of these, **Túnel Rosalila,** brings you to the **Rosalila Temple** found buried under Structure 16, still with some of its original brilliant hues. Only about 25 meters of the tunnel are open to visitors. Sheltered behind windows to protect it from the elements and human touch, you'll find small patches of the temple peeking out from underneath the outer layers of newer structures. Considered by some to be the best-preserved stucco structure in the Mayan world, the carvings are surprisingly crisp. To fully appreciate the scale, magnificence, and brilliant hue of this temple, you'll have to go to the Sculpture Museum, where it dominates the edifice and is beautifully lit from above by opaque sunlight.

The second tunnel, **Túnel de los Jaguares,** brings you to the **Tumba Galindo** beneath Structure 17 in the southern part of the East Plaza. About 95 meters of this tunnel, fully comprising 700 meters, are open to visitors. It is somewhat less dramatic than the Rosalila Tunnel, comprising burial tombs and niches for offerings, though there is also a nice macaw mask to be seen. The tomb's discovery dates to 1834.

At $15, admission to the tunnels is a bit on the pricey side and is recommended for serious enthusiasts of archaeology but less so for the casual visitor.

Las Sepulturas

This smaller residential complex is connected to the main group by a *sacbe,* or elevated causeway, running through the forest. This path is closed to visitors, and so you must exit the archaeological site and head up the main road for two kilometers toward San Pedro Sula. You'll see a sign on the right (bring your admission ticket, as you'll need it to get in).

Las Sepulturas was ignored by archaeologists earlier in Copán's history but recent work here has revealed some information about the daily lives of the city's ancient inhabitants. Meaning "the tombs," the complex was named by local farmers who uncovered the remains of long-departed Mayan nobles who had been buried here.

This area is not of much interest to the casual visitor, though you might like walking along the quiet forest trails. Little remains of the original structures. An exception is the **Hieroglyphic Wall** found on Structure 83, comprising a group of 16 glyphs telling about events in the rule of Yax Pac and dating to AD 786. This site contains the remains of the **Palacio de los Bacabs** (Palace of the Officials), which is thought to have once housed 250 nobles. Only 18 of about 40 residential compounds have been excavated. In Las Sepulturas's Plaza A, archaeologists uncovered the tomb of a shaman from about AD 450, which can be seen in the town's Museo Regional de Arqueología. Traces of human settlement have been found here dating to 1000 BC, long before the Copán dynasty's rise to power.

Los Sapos

An outlying part of Copán even farther away is **Los Sapos,** in the hills opposite the main site. A rock outcrop carved in the form of a frog gives it its name, though the years have worn it down considerably. An even more badly degraded carving is thought to depict a woman with her legs spread and possibly giving birth. The site is believed to have been a birthing center. The hillside setting overlooking the valley is more dramatic than the carvings, which are set on the grounds of the fabulous **Hacienda San Lucas.** The property harbors a fantastic upscale farmhouse lodge, and the owner has built a network of trails through the farm leading to the site. Admission is $2. If you're worn out from the walk, stop in for a drink or lunch at the friendly hacienda or, better yet, spend the night.

THE SCULPTURE MUSEUM

Copán's on-site **Sculpture Museum** (8am-3:45pm daily, $7) is surely the best museum of its kind in the Mayan world. Other sites would do well to follow its lead for the sheer variety of original monuments well presented in a spacious and airy environment. Dominating the large, two-story building is a full-scale replica of the outrageously colorful Rosalila Temple, decorated in hues of red, green, and yellow, and offering the visitor a rare opportunity to admire the full grandeur of what the ancient Mayan temples may have looked like during the fullness of the civilization's splendor.

Entrance to the museum is via the mouth of a serpent. Winding through a dark cave-like tunnel, you are greeted at once as you emerge from the darkness by the arresting view of the Rosalila Temple lit from above by a giant opaque skylight. On the first floor are various sculptures of skulls, bats, and assorted images of death and violence. Also found here is the splendidly carved **Altar Q,** showing Yax Pac receiving the ceremonial ruler's baton from the highly revered first king of the Copán dynasty Yax K'uk'Mo'. The second floor contains original building facades, stelae, and other carved monuments. A reconstruction of Structure 22A, with its curious woven mat facade, should be open by the time you read this.

Copán's wonderful Sculpture Museum

Copán Ruinas Town (Honduras)

Set amid the lush hills of the Río Copán Valley, this pleasant town of cobblestone streets serves as the perfect gateway for exploring the nearby archaeological site and some natural attractions, which include hot springs, a bird park, and coffee farms. The range of accommodations and places to eat here is excellent.

The Copán Valley is also the site of tobacco plantations, some of which supply the well-known Flor de Copán factory in Santa Rosa de Copán, east of here. The hillsides surrounding the Copán Valley grow good-quality coffee and cardamom. If you're visiting the ruins of Copán, try to spend at least one night in Copán Ruinas.

SIGHTS

As elsewhere in Central America, the town is built around its *parque central,* recently remodeled in questionable pseudo-Mayan architectural style, but with a pretty colonial church. **Museo Casa K'inich** (up the hill north of town in the old fort, 8am-noon and 1pm-5pm Mon.-Sat., adults $1) is an interactive children's museum on Mayan subjects such as music and the Mayan number system. Few museums in the Mayan world live up to Copán's on-site museum, though the **Museo Regional de Arqueología** (tel. 651-4437, 8am-noon and 1pm-4pm daily, $3), on the southwest corner of the plaza, is worth a look. There are exhibits of carved jade, painted pottery, and figurines. The museum's highlight is the Tumba del Brujo, the tomb of a Mayan shaman said to have died around AD 700 and found buried under the Plaza de los Jaguares.

The town hall is the site of a wonderful photographic exhibit, titled "Fragile Memories," gleaned from a series of 19th-century glass plate negatives belonging to the Peabody Museum archives. The photos show the early days of Copán's excavation and restoration and provide new insights into Copán's history.

The exhibit is open during normal business hours. Ask to see the exhibit (usually locked) at the information center.

ENTERTAINMENT

A popular watering hole is **Twisted Tanya's** (tel. 2651-4182, www.twistedtanyas.com), with its happy hour 4pm-6pm. A popular after-dark option is **Café Via Via** (tel. 2651-4652), where you'll find plenty of fellow travelers.

For weekend movies, head to **Hacienda El Jaral** (tel. 2656-7091), a few kilometers outside of town on the road to San Pedro Sula. You'll see signs around town with current shows and schedules.

GUIDE COMPANIES

Locally owned **Yaragua Tours** (inside Hotel Yaragua, tel. 2651-4147, www.yaragua.com), under the same ownership of its namesake hotel, offers a variety of active tours, including caving, visits to hot springs, horseback riding, river tubing, waterfall hikes, and coffee farm visits at prices ranging $15-45 per person with a two-person minimum. Another option is **Basecamp Outdoor Adventures** (tel. 2651-4695, www.basecamphonduras.com), which is under the same management as the Via Via across the street and offers a variety of alternative recreational options, including 2- to 6-hour hikes in and around the hills surrounding Copán Ruinas, motorcycle riding, and three- or five-hour horseback rides. It also runs daily shuttle buses to Antigua ($12) and Río Dulce ($20) with a 40-minute stop in Quiriguá along the way to the latter.

ACCOMMODATIONS

You'll have to walk a few blocks southwest of the plaza to find the ★ **Iguana Azul** (tel. 2651-4620, www.iguanaazulcopan.com, $8 dorm bed, $18 d in private room), but it will be well worth it. There are excellent-value dorm

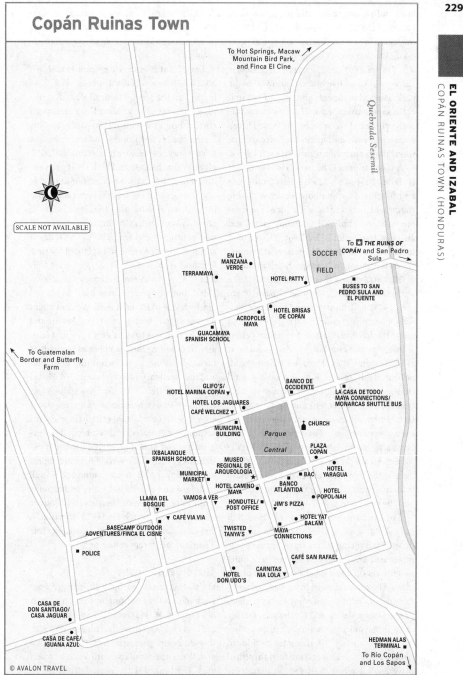

Copán Ruinas Town

To Hot Springs, Macaw Mountain Bird Park, and Finca El Cine

Quebrada Sesemil

SCALE NOT AVAILABLE

SOCCER FIELD

To ★ THE RUINS OF COPÁN and San Pedro Sula

EN LA MANZANA VERDE

TERRAMAYA

HOTEL PATTY

BUSES TO SAN PEDRO SULA AND EL PUENTE

HOTEL BRISAS DE COPÁN

ACROPOLIS MAYA

GUACAMAYA SPANISH SCHOOL

To Guatemalan Border and Butterfly Farm

GLIFO'S/ HOTEL MARINA COPÁN

BANCO DE OCCIDENTE

LA CASA DE TODO/ MAYA CONNECTIONS/ MONARCAS SHUTTLE BUS

HOTEL LOS JAGUARES

CAFÉ WELCHEZ

MUNICIPAL BUILDING

✝ CHURCH

Parque Central

PLAZA COPÁN

IXBALANQUE SPANISH SCHOOL

MUSEO REGIONAL DE ARQUEOLOGÍA

HOTEL YARAGUA

MUNICIPAL MARKET

HOTEL CAMINO MAYA

BANCO ATLÁNTIDA

BAC

HOTEL POPOL-NAH

LLAMA DEL BOSQUE

VAMOS A VER

HONDUTEL/ POST OFFICE

JIM'S PIZZA

CAFÉ VIA VIA

HOTEL YAT BALAM

BASECAMP OUTDOOR ADVENTURES/FINCA EL CISNE

TWISTED TANYA'S

MAYA CONNECTIONS

POLICE

CAFÉ SAN RAFAEL

HOTEL DON UDO'S

CARNITAS NIA LOLA

CASA DE DON SANTIAGO/ CASA JAGUAR

CASA DE CAFÉ/ IGUANA AZUL

HEDMAN ALAS TERMINAL

To Río Copán and Los Sapos

© AVALON TRAVEL

beds and private rooms sharing a hot-water bathroom. The same Honduran American owners run the beautiful La Casa de Café next door. Another decent budget option is **Hotel Via Via** (tel. 2651-4652, www.viaviacafe.com/en/copan, $16 d), two blocks southwest of the park. Housed in the café and traveler hot spot of the same name, the hotel has spotless rooms with private hot-water baths and fans. There's a thatched-roof lounge on the second floor where movies are shown amid tropical foliage.

A block south of the park, **Hotel Popol-Nah** (tel. 2651-4095, $25-45) is a comfortable and modern 12-room hotel that has double rooms with fans and cable TV for $25 or double upstairs rooms with balcony views and air-conditioning for $45. All rooms have good mattresses and private hot-water bathrooms.

My favorite of the boutique hotels in Copán is ★ **Terramaya** (2.5 blocks north of the park, tel. 2651-4623, www.terramayacopan.com, $90-110 d). It's stylish and contemporary, with a beautiful outdoor patio and tables to enjoy the free breakfast and excellent coffee. A lovely garden overlooks a wonderful view of the Copán Valley. There are six rooms, all beautifully decorated. Rooms on the ground floor are slightly noisier on account of their fronting a busy street. The four upstairs rooms feature high ceilings that make the rooms feel even more spacious. They also have ceiling fans, air-conditioning, cable TV, and DVD player. All rooms have private patios or balconies; the two most expensive rooms have balconies overlooking the rear of the property and the best view.

The enchanting **La Casa de Café** (tel. 2651-4620, www.casadecafecopan.com, $58 d, breakfast included) is Copán Ruinas's premiere bed-and-breakfast inn, set in a quiet neighborhood a few blocks southwest of the plaza. The rooms are well furnished and tastefully decorated. You can enjoy fantastic views of the Copán Valley and Guatemala, farther west, from your patio hammock in a wonderful garden setting. The friendly Honduran American owners also rent out fully furnished private villas across the street, including the

Casa Jaguar (www.casajaguarcopan.com, $90 per night) and **Casa de Don Santiago** (www.casadedonsantiagocopan.com, $110 per night).

Lovely **Yat B'alam Boutique Hotel** (tel. 2651-4338, www.yatbalam.com, $75 d) is housed on the second floor of a small shopping complex. The ground floor features a coffee shop and handicrafts store. Rooms are on the second floor, some with pleasant street views, and feature nice extras like DVD players, minifridges, and high ceilings in addition to ceiling fans, air-conditioning, cable TV, and plenty of hot water. There's also a nice little sitting area fronting the street from the second floor. Decorative knickknacks give it that boutique hotel feel. The town's fanciest accommodations are found at **Hotel Marina Copán** (tel. 2651-4070/71, 877/893-9131 toll-free U.S., www.hotelmarinacopan.com, $95-150 d, including breakfast), built in the old family home of Doña Marina Welchez about 65 years ago. There are standard rooms and suites; all rooms have cable TV, ceiling fans, air-conditioning, and telephones. Amenities include a sauna, gym, swimming pool, bar, and the excellent Glifos restaurant. ★ **Hotel Don Udo's** (tel. 2651-4533, www.donudos.com, $40-80 d) scores major points for atmosphere with comfortable tiled-floor rooms tastefully decorated with Guatemalan furnishings and accents centered around a delightful garden courtyard. There are rooms with or without air-conditioning and TV; all have fans and private hot-water baths. Some bathrooms have a tub. There's a lobby lounge where you can watch DVDs. Alternatively, you can relax in a sauna or the whirlpool tub. There's also a decent restaurant.

Outside of Town

On the outskirts of Copán Ruinas are a variety of excellent lodging options. You may hear about ★ **Hacienda San Lucas** (tel. 2651-4495, www.haciendasanlucas.com, $100 d) even before your arrival in town, as it has a well-earned reputation for excellent service. The beautiful accommodations are set

Hacienda San Lucas overlooks the Copán Valley.

own), and tasty food you can wash down with beer and wine. It enjoys a pleasant garden setting with nice mountain views. **La Casa de Todo** (tel. 2651-4185, www.casadetodo.com, 7am-9pm daily, $4-10) serves delicious snacks all day, including tasty *baleadas,* flour tortillas filled with beans and cheese, or scrumptious homemade yogurt with granola and fruit. The breakfasts here are excellent with good, potent coffee. Enjoy your meal in the sunny garden courtyard. Right on the plaza next to the Hotel Marina Copán, **Café Welchez** (7am-9pm daily) serves up espresso drinks and delicious cakes, pastries, and assorted other baked goods.

Italian

Jim's Pizza (tel. 2651-4381, 11am-9pm daily), a block south of the plaza, makes tasty pizzas ($6-10) and pasta.

Honduran

Popular with locals is **Restaurant Llama del Bosque** (tel. 2651-4431, 6am-10pm), across from the Via Via, where the varied menu includes steak and seafood entrées for around $7. Go here for traditional breakfasts of eggs and beans or fondue cooked in a clay pot with beans and sausage ($5).

International

There are a variety of good choices for international fare. ★ **Twisted Tanya's** (tel. 2651-4182, www.twistedtanyas.com, 3pm-10pm Mon.-Sat.) manages to be classy yet casual in a pleasant, second-story balcony setting overlooking the street. For $20, you get a soup or salad starter, main course, and dessert. Typical dishes include such creations as curry shrimp, Chinese dumplings with wasabi, fish fillet with sautéed vegetables, and seafood pasta with crab. The desserts are equally creative and appetizing. It's a block west and then half a block south of the plaza. Stop in for happy hour 4pm-6pm.

Café Via Via (tel. 2651-4652, 7am-midnight daily) is a popular watering hole with travelers that doubles as a hip and trendy café. You can substitute vegetarian options for

on a renovated 100-year-old hacienda oozing with atmosphere, the brainchild of Honduran Flavia Cueva. The lodge's eight rooms, spread about the beautifully landscaped grounds, manage to be comfortable and yet stylishly rustic at the same time, with adobe walls, wooden furniture, and Guatemalan fabrics. At night, candles provide additional atmosphere. Enjoy a drink and watch the sunset over the Copán Valley before settling down to a delicious five-course dinner ($35) served in a gorgeous garden patio.

FOOD
Cafés and Light Meals

Avoid drinking beverages with ice cubes while in Copán's restaurants, as they seem to be of dubious origin.

★ **Café San Rafael** (Avenida Centroamerica, across from Carnitas Nia Lola, www.cafesanrafael.com, tel. 2651-4546, 7:30am-8pm daily, $5-15) is more a delicatessen than a simple café, with a fine selection of artisanal cheeses, coffee from the family farm (they roast their many of its dishes, including veggie burgers ($6). It also makes a good stab at Thai curry ($8). There are tables overlooking the street where you can enjoy the wonderful organically grown coffee.

Fine Dining

One of the finest restaurants in town can be found inside the Hotel Marina Copán. ★ **Glifo's** (tel. 2651-4070, www.hotelmarinacopan.com, 6:30am-9:30pm daily, $8-16) serves a variety of international dishes with a distinctly Mayan slant in a pleasing blue and yellow dining room. For a local treat, try the Pollo al Loroco, cooked in a savory sauce of pungent edible flowers. The house specialty is Glifo's Traditional Chicken, cooked in a sauce of roasted, ground sesame and squash seeds flavorfully seasoned with Mayan herbs. International dishes include curry chicken, steak in mushroom wine sauce, and tarragon fish. **Don Udo's** (tel. 2651-4533, www.donudos.com, $6-13) has a stylish restaurant to accompany the hotel's tasteful atmosphere. Among the excellent dishes are steak and seafood dishes, homemade pastas, and Mayan cuisine. Outside of town, the delightful restaurant at ★ **Hacienda San Lucas** (tel. 2651-4106, www.haciendasanlucas.com) is the perfect place to catch the sunset from a perch overlooking the Copán Valley before digging into a scrumptious five-course dinner ($35). Much of the produce used in preparing the meals comes right from the farm. Typical dishes include cream of corn soup, tamales, chicken in adobo sauce, and flan for dessert. Reservations are required for dinner, though you can drop in for breakfast or lunch anytime. Even if you're not staying here, you should aim to eat at least one meal (preferably dinner) at Hacienda San Lucas during your visit to Copán. It's *that* good.

INFORMATION AND SERVICES

Copán Ruinas's tourist office (tel. 2651-4394, 8am-7pm daily) is just east of the plaza on the same street as La Casa de Todo.

Communications

The **post office** (8am-noon and 1pm-5pm Mon.-Fri., 8am-noon Sat.) is half a block west of the plaza.

For Internet, the most popular spot is **Maya Connections** (tel. 2651-4077, 8am-8pm daily, $1.75 for one hour) at La Casa de Todo a block east of the park and near Jim's Pizza a block south of the park. Another option is **Copán Net** (one block south and one block west of the park, tel. 2651-4460, 9am-9pm), where a lightning-fast connection costs $1.50 an hour.

For phone calls, **Hondutel** (7am-9pm Mon.-Fri., 7am-noon and 2pm-5pm weekends) can be found just south of the square but you can also make phone calls from the Internet hotspots.

Money

On the south side of the park, **Banco Atlántida** and **BAC** both have Visa ATMs and cash travelers checks, dollars, and quetzales. **Banco de Occidente,** on the park's northeast corner, exchanges dollars and quetzales as well as cashing travelers checks and issuing cash advances on Visa cards. Many hotels and restaurants accept Guatemalan quetzales as payment.

Laundry

For laundry, head to **Casa de Todo** (tel. 2651-4185, www.casadetodo.com), where a load costs about $1.

Language Schools

Spanish instruction is slightly more expensive here than in Guatemala, with two schools to choose from. **Ixbalanque Spanish School** (tel. 2651-4432, www.ixbalanque.com) offers five days of one-on-one instruction for $125 or $185 including homestay with a local family. The other option is **Guacamaya Spanish Academy** (tel. 2651-4360, www.guacamaya.com), where a week's worth of instruction costs $130 alone or $200 including room and board with a local family.

GETTING THERE

Minibuses to the El Florido border leave town from the corner next to the market about every half hour for the 20-minute, 12-kilometer trip. There are hourly onward buses from there to Chiquimula, taking about an hour. A much more comfortable and increasingly popular option is to book a shuttle bus. **Hedman Alas** (tel. 2651-4037, www.hedmanalas.com) operates twice daily direct first-class bus service to Guatemala City ($35, four hours) and Antigua ($41, five hours) from its terminal on the road south of town heading toward the river. There are also onward buses to Tegucigalpa and San Pedro Sula. Shuttle buses to Guatemala City ($20), La Antigua ($20), and further into Honduras can be booked from **Café Via Via** (tel. 2651-4652).

If driving a rental car to Copán from Guatemala, be aware that you'll need written permission from your car-rental agency.

In March of 2015 authorities inaugurated Copán's new **airport**, located 18 miles along the road to San Pedro Sula. Although scheduled service has not yet been announced, flights will probably begin to arrive from Tegucigalpa and Roatán, Honduras, in the near future. It's entirely possible to see direct service from Guatemala City (GUA) and Flores/Tikal (FRS) further down the line.

NEAR COPÁN RUINAS
Macaw Mountain Bird Park

A few kilometers outside of town in the surrounding hillsides, **Macaw Mountain Bird Park** (tel. 2651-4245, www.macawmountain.org, 9am-5pm daily, $10 pp) has a phenomenal collection of birds, including macaws, parrots, and toucans, housed mostly in large cages found alongside a trail with wooden walkways winding through the park's splendidly sylvan riverside setting. In one area, you can interact freely with domesticated birds outside of their cages. There's a restaurant at the main entrance serving mostly meat and seafood dishes ($5-8) as well as a café along the trail. There's also a gift shop.

Luna Jaguar Hot Springs

About 22 kilometers from town along this same road are a series of pleasant hot springs known as **Luna Jaguar Hot Springs** ($3), where you can soak in a synthetic pool or take a series of trails to several hot springs that get cooler as you go downhill. A nice mix of cool river water blends with boiling hot water from

horseback riding at Finca El Cisne

the springs to make the water perfect for a soak. The jungle setting is also very relaxing. It's not quite as nice as Costa Rica's Tabacón hot springs, but it's certainly worth a visit. You can catch a pickup here from town, but a better way to get here is to combine a visit to the springs with a trip out to Finca El Cisne, preferably overnight, when you can use the springs after they have closed to other visitors.

Finca El Cisne

Farther along this same road and a 45-minute drive from Copán Ruinas is **Finca El Cisne** (www.fincaelcisne.com), a century-old, 1,000-hectare coffee farm where you can ride horseback, tour the coffee and cardamom plantations, and bathe in warm jungle hot springs. Cowboy Carlos Castejón, whose family owns the farm, leads most trips and speaks good English. He can show you around the farm and show you everything you ever wanted to know about coffee cultivation. The farm also produces breadfruit, beans, avocados, corn, plantains, and oranges, among other crops. Riding on horseback through the extensive plantation affords the opportunity to really appreciate the surrounding countryside.

Day trips (leaving at 8am and returning at 6pm, $82) include horseback riding, visits to the cardamom and coffee fields, a home-cooked lunch, and a visit to the nearby hot springs. You can also stay overnight in a cozy solar-powered cabin with all of the above plus breakfast and dinner for $95. The booking and information office is inside the Via Via in a shared office with **Basecamp Outdoor Adventures** (tel. 2651-4695, www.basecamphonduras.com, 8am-noon and 4pm-8pm Mon.-Sat.).

Quiriguá to Puerto Barrios

Quiriguá, a Mayan site that once rivaled Copán (in present-day Honduras) as the regional center of power, is still home to the region's tallest stelae. It makes a good excursion on the way to Puerto Barrios when traveling along CA-9.

QUIRIGUÁ

Set amid banana plantations, the Mayan site of Quiriguá is smaller but somewhat similar to Copán, particularly in regard to its inhabitants' skill and propensity in the carving of stelae. It's just 50 kilometers from Copán as the macaw flies, back on the Guatemalan side, though getting here from Copán is a bit more complicated than it looks on a map because the roads are structured so as to make you loop west, north, and then finally east on the highway leading to the Caribbean Coast (CA-9). Coming from Guatemala City, it's just a few kilometers down a dirt road turnoff from the main highway (CA-9), making it a worthy side trip along the road to Puerto Barrios or Río Dulce. Restoration of the site was conducted by the University of Pennsylvania in the 1930s, and in 1981 Quiriguá was declared a UNESCO World Heritage Site. The only other sites of this kind in Guatemala are Tikal and Antigua. It boasts the tallest known Mayan stela.

History

Quiriguá's history largely mirrors that of Copán, of which it was a vassal state for much of its history. In AD 653, for example, Copán's very own king Smoke Jaguar erected Altar L in Quiriguá's Great Plaza in his own honor after installing the city's new ruler. Quiriguá's stelae were carved with help from Copán's artisans using beds of brown sandstone brought from the nearby Río Motagua. The sandstone was soft when first cut, allowing the artisans to create the excellent-quality carvings, which hardened through time and can still be seen today.

Quiriguá's subservient status changed

dramatically under the leadership of its king Cauac Sky with the capture and subsequent beheading of Copán's ruler 18 Rabbit in AD 737, an event which would mark the beginning of Copán's gradual downward slide. Cauac Sky quickly embarked on his own plan to expand the greatness of Quiriguá, carving most of the stelae in evidence there today. He can be seen on Stelae A, C, D, E, F, H, and J. Cauac Sky was succeeded by his son, Sky Xul (784-800), who lost his throne to Jade Sky, Quiriguá's last great king, who embarked on his own grand-scale reconstruction of the city's Acropolis. Quiriguá managed to remain independent of Copán for the remainder of its history until its own silent and mysterious demise in the middle of the 9th century.

Like Copán, Quiriguá captured the attention and fascination of John L. Stephens, who compared it to "the rock-built city of Edom, unvisited, unsought and utterly unknown." Stephens even attempted to buy the site in 1840 and cart it off to New York City via the Río Motagua and out to sea. Assuming that Stephens was negotiating on behalf of the U.S. government, the landowner quoted an exorbitant price and the deal was never made. The noted archaeologist Alfred Maudsley followed up with his own visit and excavations between 1881 and 1894, making some fine illustrations of the site's stelae and zoomorphic rock figures. In the early 1900s, the site and surrounding lands became the property of the United Fruit Company, which preserved the ruins and the area in its vicinity. The rest of the land was converted to banana plantations, miles and miles of them.

★ The Ruins of Quiriguá

What is left of Quiriguá is limited to its ceremonial center. As you enter the park from the main entrance, you'll see the **Acropolis** straight ahead and the various stelae and zoomorphs (stone sculptures depicting animals and hybrid human-animal forms) in the **Great Plaza** to your left. The stelae are housed under thatched-roof structures to protect them from further deterioration from the elements. It can be somewhat difficult to view the carvings and even more difficult to get a good photograph. The most impressive is **Stela E,** standing almost 11 meters high, making it the tallest known Mayan stela. Noteworthy features in the carvings include their bearded subjects with elaborate headdresses, the staffs of authority clutched in their hands, and glyphs running up and down the monuments' sides. The various

one of the carvings at the ruins of Quiriguá

zoomorphs can also be seen here, depicting turtles, jaguars, frogs, and serpents. Near the Acropolis, **Altar P** depicts a figure seated in a strange, Buddhalike pose. The Acropolis itself is rather unimpressive, failing to rise in height above the treetops of the surrounding jungle, though it is somewhat spread out. There's a small ball court on its western side.

Practicalities

The park is open 7:30am-5pm daily. Admission is $4. There's a small museum housing displays on the site's significance in relation to Mayan history and geopolitics along with a model showing the extent of the site's boundaries and unexcavated sections.

The site lies four kilometers from the main road with frequent transport heading up and down thanks to the activities of the nearby banana plantations. At the entrance to the site are a ticket office, the museum, and a few simple soda stands as well as some folks selling coconuts. The turnoff to the park from the main road (CA-9) is between Km. 204 and Km. 205, about 70 kilometers northeast of the Río Hondo Junction. Any bus heading along CA-9 can drop you off at the junction to the road leading to the park.

JARDÍN BOTÁNICO Y RESTAURANTE ECOLÓGICO EL HIBISCUS

Near Puerto Barrios, at Km. 284 of CA-9, is the **Jardín Botánico y Restaurante Ecológico El Hibiscus** (tel. 5294-0397 or 5514-9525, 6am-5:30pm Mon.-Sat.), a pleasant restaurant tastefully furnished with tropical wicker furniture and Mayan textiles that serves excellent breakfasts ($3-4), seafood, steaks, sandwiches, salads, and Guatemalan dishes. A tasty *caldo de gallina criolla* (chicken soup) is served on Saturdays. You can enjoy your meal in a pleasant wooden dining room or outside on one of two patios. Visitors can also enjoy a stroll through the botanical gardens housing a wide variety of flowers and tropical plants. It makes a pleasant stop on the way to Puerto Barrios or a good place to eat outside of town if you're staying there. The restaurant also serves as an information center for the Cerro San Gil and Punta de Manabique protected areas.

Puerto Barrios and Vicinity

This hot, humid port city holds little of interest for travelers except as a jumping-off point to surrounding attractions such as Lívingston and resorts across the Bahía de Amatique. It was once Guatemala's main Caribbean shipping port but has been replaced by Puerto Santo Tomás de Castilla across the bay. It may be one of the main beneficiaries of a new $7 billion "dry canal" due to begin construction in 2012 but which still hasn't taken off. The project is a joint venture between the public and private sectors and encompasses the construction of two new ports, a railroad, a four-lane highway, and a gas pipeline that will supposedly someday link Guatemala's Caribbean and Pacific Coasts.

Construction of the port that now bears his name was initiated by reformist president Justo Rufino Barrios in the 1880s and was linked to Guatemala City via a railroad completed in 1908. Puerto Barrios was important during the long-past glory days of the United Fruit Company. The company financed much of the railroad's completion and linked its banana plantations to Puerto Barrios, which served as the company-controlled shipping center for produce bound for New Orleans and New York. United Fruit was sold to Del Monte in the 1970s, and Puerto Barrios sank into a tropical slumber.

ACCOMMODATIONS

Many of the ultra-low-budget accommodations in this town are used for prostitution, which is rampant in this sweltering coastal town, so backpackers beware. For Caribbean atmosphere and antique charm, you can't beat the 100-year-old **Hotel del Norte** (7a Calle and 1a Avenida, tel. 7948-2116, $25-35 d). Its quaint, crooked wooden floors evoke another time and have a certain dilapidated charm. Double-occupancy rooms in the original building cost $25 and have cold water, fans, and fluorescent lighting. Newer double rooms in a separate building cost $35 and have hot water, ceiling fans, warmer tungsten lighting, air-conditioning, and hot water. The restaurant, housed in a pleasant open-air thatched-roof building overlooking the hotel pool and sea, serves seafood, grilled meats, pasta, and other international dishes for $5-10.

On the outskirts of town are some pricier options that are conveniently near the main highway should you not want to stay in the heart of town. **Hotel Marbrissa** (25 Calle y 20 Avenida, Colonia Virginia, tel. 7948-1450, www.marbrissa.com, $85-140 d) has comfortable rooms centered around the hotel's large swimming pool with all the amenities you would expect in this price range, including air-conditioning and minifridge. There are also larger suites with kitchenettes and living and dining rooms. The open-air *palapa*-style restaurant here is one of the nicest in town for its tranquil atmosphere overlooking the swimming pool.

Outside of town just past the airstrip on tropical grounds bordering the sea is the sprawling ★ **Amatique Bay Resort and Marina** (tel. 7931-0000, www.amatiquebay. net, $120-250 per room), where comfortable accommodations are housed in neocolonial villas. There are standard rooms and larger suites with full kitchens; the largest of these have additional sofa beds and a living room. All have air-conditioning and the usual amenities. There's an artificially constructed white-sand beach on the tranquil waters of the Bahía de Amatique and a swimming pool complete with a Spanish galleon, though at last visit the tile looked like it needed some work. Three restaurants keep vacationers happy, including one that's right beside the swimming pool, serving lighter fare and sandwiches. The other two are more formal and serve a variety of international dishes. All in all, this complex is a self-contained leisure city built in colonial style somewhat resembling a seaside version of Antigua,

Amatique Bay Resort and Marina

complete with a whitewashed church. It is a popular day trip amongst cruise-ship passengers docking at nearby Puerto Santo Tomás de Castilla. Activities include a zipline with multiple platforms, kayaking, and horseback riding. The hotel is affiliated with Interval International.

FOOD

Local dishes include *tapado,* a seafood stew made from prawns, fish, and shellfish, seasoned with plantains, yucca, and coriander, and cooked in coconut milk. *Tortillas de harina* are flour tortillas stuffed with cheese, or anything else for that matter.

As for restaurants, ★ Safari (5a Avenida and 1a Calle, tel. 7948-0563, 10am-9pm, $4-10) is popular with locals for its large portions of excellent seafood dishes served in style on an open air, thatched-roofed platform over the sea. It also does excellent chicken and meat dishes. The best steakhouse in town is the Rincón Uruguayo (7a Avenida and 16 Calle, closed Mon.), serving excellent *parrilladas* (grilled meats South American-style), *papas asadas,* and *cebollines* (grilled spring onions). If you're staying at the Hotel Marbrissa (25 Calle y 20 Avenida, Colonia Virginia, tel. 7948-1450, www.marbrissa.com) or nearby, try its excellent restaurant and bar set on the second floor of a large *palapa*-style building above the hotel lobby and overlooking the swimming pool. Parrots roam the premises while you dine on excellent seafood, grilled steaks, pasta, and other international dishes. You can also enjoy use of a pool table and a large flat-screen TV.

SERVICES
Communications

The post office is on the corner of 8a Avenida and 6a Calle. Telgua is at 8a Avenida and 10a Calle.

Money

Banco Industrial (7a Avenida Norte #73) has a Visa ATM and changes U.S. cash dollars and travelers checks. Banrural (8a Avenida and 9a Calle) has a MasterCard ATM and also changes dollars and travelers checks. Just outside of town at the junction of the roads leading to Guatemala City and Puerto Santo Tomás is La Pradera Puerto Barrios shopping mall, with various ATMs.

Immigration

The offices of *migración* are on the corner of 12 Calle and 3a Avenida, a block from the municipal docks. This is where you get your entry or exit stamp when arriving from or heading to Belize. There is a $10 departure tax. The offices are open 7am-8pm.

GETTING THERE
Air

Puerto Barrios's long, paved runway has been inaugurated several times and even supported frequent flights to Guatemala City at one time. That service is suspended for the moment, but the airport remains one of the main landing strips in a nascent network of domestic airports. The runway is equipped to receive jet aircraft, including Boeing 737s.

Bus

Most of the transport in and out of Puerto Barrios is via the excellent Transportes Litegua (6a Avenida and 9a Calle, tel. 7948-1172, www.litegua.com), which operates comfortable, modern buses departing every half hour to and from Guatemala City. Some buses stop in Morales en route, where you get off for Río Dulce.

Boat

Boats leave from the municipal dock at the end of 12 Calle. There is ferry service to Lívingston ($1.50, 1.5 hours) Monday-Saturday at 10am and 5pm. Try to get there at least 30 minutes prior to departure time to secure your seat. *Lanchas,* taking 30 minutes to make the journey, depart when they have a dozen people or so and cost about $5 one-way. Most of the traffic heading to Lívingston is in the morning hours.

There are also departures to Punta Gorda,

Belize ($20 one-way), via **Transportes El Chato** (1a Avenida between 10a and 11a Calles, tel. 7948-5525 or 7948-8787) leaving Puerto Barrios at 10am daily and taking about an hour. You'll need to stop by the immigration office to get your passport stamped prior to getting on the boat.

PUERTO SANTO TOMÁS DE CASTILLA

Cruise ships dock in Santo Tomás de Castilla, just across the bay from Puerto Barrios, where those wishing to go ashore will find some of the country's best bird-watching, lush tropical rainforests, and refreshing jungle rivers. Local tourism authorities in nearby Lívingston and Río Dulce are improving the quality of their services to cater to arriving visitors.

The history of Santo Tomás de Castilla actually dates to 1604, when it was founded as the coast's original colonial port. It was abandoned within a few years but later became the site of an ill-fated Belgian colony in 1843 after Guatemala's independence from Spain.

A paved road from Puerto Barrios leads to the main shipping center. From there, a dirt road continues along the coast to some of the area's natural attractions. For cruise ship daytrippers, a recommended travel company is **Go with Gus** (tel. 7947-0694, www.gowithgus.com), which runs tours of the Río Dulce canyon with stops at area attractions along the way.

★ Cerro San Gil and Río Las Escobas

This idyllic park, centered around the Cerro San Gil mountain, comprises more than 7,700 hectares (19,000 acres) of lush rainforest. Bathed in rainfall throughout most of the year (averaging 255 inches) as warm, humid air rises over the mountains from the sea to elevations in excess of 1,100 meters (3,900 feet), the preserve harbors an astounding level of biodiversity. Among the wildlife protected here are 56 species of mammals, including tapir and jaguars, 50 species of reptiles and amphibians, and more than 350 species of birds, including toucans, black-and-white hawk-eagles, and keel-billed motmots. More than 90 neotropical migrants winter in the area and include the blue-winged warbler and wood thrush.

The park also protects the important watershed of the Río Las Escobas, which supplies water to Puerto Barrios. Part of the watershed is open to visitors ($10, including guided tour), who can bathe in Las Escobas's cool, clear waters and hike a series of nature trails winding through the park. The park is administered by the private conservation group **FUNDAECO** (tel. 2314-1900, www.fundaeco.org.gt), which in partnership with The Nature Conservancy has been able to buy large tracts of this rainforest ecosystem for preservation.

Facilities for visitors are found at **Las Pozas** (tel. 5708-0744 and 5004-1143, http://riolasescobasizabal.com, 9am-6pm daily) and include a visitors center, tropical gardens, a snack bar (open on weekends and when cruise ships are in town), and picnic areas. An excellent system of **trails** winds through the river and waterfalls and includes wooden bridges

Río Las Escobas

The Guatemala-Belize Border Dispute

During your travels, you might be surprised to find the neighboring country of Belize included as part of Guatemala on many maps produced in-country. It would seem that Belize is just another Guatemalan *departamento* despite its status as an independent nation since 1981. Guatemala did not in fact recognize its neighbor's independence until 10 years later in a highly criticized and unconstitutional move by then-president Jorge Serrano Elías. Guatemala's constitution clearly states that any decision regarding the independence or territorial integrity of Belize must be submitted to a public referendum. And so the debate continues over the "Belize question." It seems to be one of those issues that just won't go away, with succeeding governments always promising a final solution to this centuries-old problem.

Several governments have used the issue as a diversionary tactic during times of civil unrest, particularly during the military regimes of the 1970s. Matters came to a head in 1977 when Great Britain sent 6,000 troops to the border in anticipation of an invasion by Guatemalan troops during the presidency of military strongman Romeo Lucas García. Today, there are occasional reports of incidents along the northern Petén region's eastern border with Belize when Guatemalan peasants are forcefully evicted from the "no-man's land" along the border in clashes with Belizean security forces. The border is often referred to as a *zona de adyacencia,* or "imaginary border" area. Guatemalan newspapers love to publicize these incidents of supposed injustice against unarmed peasants, calling for a final solution to the long-standing problem.

The dispute dates to colonial times, when Spain officially claimed all of the Central American coast but was unable in practice to enforce its claim. English privateers and traders established a beachhead along the southern coast of Belize and extracted valuable timber products, including mahogany. The English presence was officially recognized by Spain in 1763, granting the British the right to extract forest products but refusing them the right of permanent settlement. The first permanent settlements came soon after Central American independence from Spain, the British clearly taking advantage of the power vacuum created in the aftermath of Spanish rule. The weakness of Guatemala's early governments was evident in an 1859 treaty, which officially recognized the British presence and "lent" the Belize territory to them for further resource extraction in exchange for a payment of £50,000 and the construction of a road from Belize to Guatemala City. Great Britain never held up its end of the bargain on either point and so the treaty was rendered null and void. British occupation of the lands continued, however, and the land eventually became known as the colony of British Honduras, which was granted its independence from England in 1981.

In recent years, Guatemala has limited its claims to the southern half of Belize, from the Río Sibún to the Río Sarstún, arguing that historical documents support its claims and include this territory as part of the region of "Las Verapaces." Some Guatemalan analysts believe there might be a case here, though the reasons for Guatemala's insistence in this matter remain a mystery. The current government has expressed its interest in getting its case settled once and for all by international arbitration, which would mean bringing it to the International Court in The Hague if all other avenues fail. Belize has tried to get the matter resolved in the Organization of American States (OAS), so far unsuccessfully, and has repeatedly stated that it will not cede "a single inch of its territory."

It's doubtful Guatemala will ever be able to recover its full claim, though the possibility for comanagement of the Sapodilla Cayes Marine Park (also claimed by Honduras) as a trinational park might be the most realistic outcome of any internationally mediated settlement on this matter. It would give Guatemala the one thing its geography and tourist offerings lack: white-sand Caribbean beaches with clear, turquoise waters. A referendum to decide whether the case goes to arbitration at the International Court in The Hague was to be celebrated simultaneously in both countries on October 6, 2013, but never came to pass.

with stops along the way for swimming in stunning turquoise pools.

The park is an increasingly popular day trip with cruise-ship passengers, many of whom reportedly state this to be their favorite stop after the crass commercialism of places such as Cancún and beaches that all pretty much look the same. The park lies just off the road, hugging the coastline from Puerto Santo Tomás de Castilla to the beach of Punta de Palma.

Green Bay Hotel

Farther along this same road is the 50-room **Green Bay Hotel** (tel. 7948-2361 or 2410-5000, $80 d room-only or $150 d all-inclusive), which was built far ahead of its time in the early 1990s but now seems perfectly situated to cater to cruise-ship day-trippers. The comfortable thatched-roof duplex bungalows are built into the side of a beautifully forested hillside near the water's edge and have all the comforts, including air-conditioning, TV, private hot-water bathroom, and bay windows that look out to the jungle. Although the exteriors are thatched-roof, it's really only for show, as the room interiors pretty much look like any standard modern hotel room. There is an airy, thatched-roof restaurant and bar overlooking the swimming pool and Bahía de Amatique. In addition to seafood, the restaurant serves international dishes including pasta, sandwiches, and grilled steaks. It's a bit overpriced at about $8 for a basic pasta dish.

Out front is a dock from where you can book a tour of the bay or a motorboat transfer to Punta de Palma, Punta de Manabique, Livingston, or Río Dulce. Otherwise, you can catch some rays on the lagoon-front beach or explore the waters in a kayak. Two small mangrove islets, known as the Cayos del Diablo, lie just off the coast. Mountain bikes are also available for rent and there's a sandy beach

volleyball court. As at most of Guatemala's Caribbean beaches, the water here is not clear like that along the Yucatán Peninsula, but more emerald in color. It's what the tourism promoters have called "a different Caribbean."

Punta de Palma Beach

The road continues north from here to the beaches of Punta de Palma, a popular weekend getaway for folks from Puerto Barrios and where a sliver of sand meets the Caribbean Sea. There are some refreshment stands but little else here. Although locals might try to talk it up, you'll probably be very disappointed, as the Riviera Maya this is not. If you really want to hit the beach, there are some better options near Livingston and across the bay at Punta de Manabique.

On the up side, there are some new accommodations in this neck of the woods that now actually make this place worth a visit (and a stay). **Darangilaü** (www.darangilau.com) is a glamping hideaway tucked into the hills overlooking the beach and the Caribbean Sea that is somewhat reminiscent of the early days of ecotourism in Costa Rica. There are large, airy safari tents on raised wooden platforms with thatch roof, a/c, and wooden deck for $55 d. Simpler accommodations include smaller tents with a shaded sitting area for $40 d with a/c or $25 d without a/c but with fan (and minus the shaded sitting area). All of the tents are on a shared-bath basis. Amenities on the eight-acre-property include a swimming pool overlooking the ocean, hiking and mountain biking trails, and the quaint wood-and-stone main lodge with cool spaces for lounging. The main lodge also has a restaurant and bar. It makes a good base for trips to nearby Río Las Escobas. Day trips to Playa Blanca, Livingston, and other area attractions can be organized. Access is via boat from Puerto Barrios or a decent dirt road that continues 14 kilometers from Puerto Santo Tomás de Castilla.

Lívingston

A bit of an anomaly in Mayan and ladino Guatemala, Lívingston is an interesting Caribbean enclave of Garífuna culture and completes Guatemala's list of offerings with the authentic feel of a West Indian coastal town. This characteristic is made even more poignant by the fact that it's accessible only by boat. The

town's setting is as exotic as its culture, splendidly situated at the mouth of the Río Dulce on the shores of the Bahía de Amatique. It makes a great base for upstream explorations of the Río Dulce canyon as well as nearby beaches, waterfalls, and pools, or the outlying Zapotillo cayes. The sounds of *punta* rock and reggae drifting

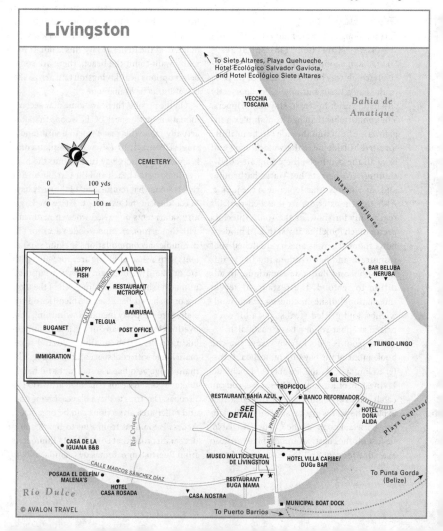

Lívingston

To Siete Altares, Playa Quehueche,
Hotel Ecológico Salvador Gaviota,
and Hotel Ecológico Siete Altares

VECCHIA TOSCANA

Bahía de Amatique

CEMETERY

0   100 yds
0   100 m

Playa Barique

HAPPY FISH   LA BUGA
                    RESTAURANT MCTROPIC
                    BANRURAL
BUGANET   TELGUA
                    POST OFFICE
IMMIGRATION

BAR BELUBA NERUBA

TILINGO-LINGO

GIL RESORT

TROPICOOL
RESTAURANT BAHÍA AZUL   BANCO REFORMADOR
SEE DETAIL   HOTEL DOÑA ALIDA

Río Crique

Playa Capitan

CASA DE LA IGUANA B&B

MUSEO MULTICULTURAL DE LÍVINGSTON

HOTEL VILLA CARIBE/ DUGu BAR

To Punta Gorda (Belize)

CALLE MARCOS SÁNCHEZ DÍAZ
POSADA EL DELFÍN/ MALENA'S
HOTEL CASA ROSADA
Río Dulce
RESTAURANT BUGA MAMA
CASA NOSTRA

MUNICIPAL BOAT DOCK

© AVALON TRAVEL

To Puerto Barrios

out from the town's numerous restaurants and bars complete the Caribbean atmosphere. You can find some useful information on the town at www.livingston.com.gt.

As for orientation, it's hard to get lost here. The main street, known as Calle Principal, goes up the hill from the boat dock all the way to the shoreline at the other end of town. The other main street, Calle Marcos Sánchez Díaz, veers left from the dock.

SIGHTS
Museo Multicultural de Lívingston
The **Museo Multicultural de Lívingston** (tel. 7947-0944, 9am-5pm Tues.-Sun., $2) is just to the left of the municipal docks on a second story and features displays on the local Garífuna, Q'eqchi', Hindu, and Cagey cultures in addition to the local flora and fauna. There are some interesting old fishing nets as well as some old and new photographs on display. It's worth a quick stop, and the friendly staff will be happy to answer your questions.

Los Siete Altares
A side stream forms this series of seven waterfalls and emerald-green pools known as **Los Siete Altares** (Seven Altars, $2.60) lying five

kilometers northwest of town. You'll likely be disappointed if you visit here after visiting Rio Las Escobas. The water's flow at Siete Altares has declined in recent years due to increased consumption upstream and there's now very little water actually making it into the pools. Robberies have also been reported here in the past. I'd skip it, as there are better options for exploration.

Beaches
Lívingston has some acceptable beaches nearby, though the ones adjacent to town are generally not the cleanest and have had some security issues in the past. Locals insist the group perpetrating past robberies has been caught, with at least one of them having met an unfortunate end. The nicest beach close to town is that of **Playa Quehueche,** about two kilometers northwest along Bahía de Amatique. There are a couple of comfortable hotels here, allowing you the opportunity to stay right on the beach. Both have nice wooden docks for swimming in the placid Caribbean waters. Playa Quehueche becomes **Playa Bariques** as you get closer to town. A standout among the beaches bordering Lívingston is **Playa Capitanía,** on the town's southeast fringes.

Playa Capitanía

Lívingston's Garífuna Culture

Lívingston is one of Guatemala's most culturally diverse regions, with Garífuna, Hindu, Q'eqchi', and ladino cultures peacefully coexisting here. Of these, the Garífuna and Hindu influences are particularly interesting because they are not found elsewhere in Guatemala, giving this region a unique flavor. Guatemalans are often surprised to see Afro-Caribbean people when they visit the Atlantic Coast, as they are not readily in evidence elsewhere in the country, looking upon them with a certain sense of wonder simultaneously fueled by a form of racism familiar to the country's Mayan people. A number of far-fetched myths have been affixed to the Garífuna, including the belief that seeing an Afro-Caribbean person on the street (outside of Lívingston) means you will soon come in contact with a long-lost acquaintance. Also common is the general suspicion of widespread practice of voodoo and cannibalism by Garífuna peoples.

Guatemala's Garífuna population numbers about 4,000 and traces its history to the Caribbean island of St. Vincent. Ethnically, they are a mix of Amerindian and African peoples, and their language comes from the Brazilian Arawakan language family. These Arawak-speaking peoples migrated from northern Brazil long before the arrival of Europeans in the New World and lived peacefully on the island until they were subdued by Carib speakers from the South American mainland. The African element of their bloodline came about after intermingling with the survivors from the wreck of a Spanish ship carrying Nigerian slaves just off the coast of St. Vincent. These people eventually became known to the British as Black Caribs—in their own language, Garinagu. Garífuna is the Spanish translation of this word. In the 1760s, the British tried to take St. Vincent but were driven off by the Caribs with help from the French. The Caribs would continue to oppose the British on and off for several years until finally being defeated in 1796, when they surrendered. The Garífuna were subsequently captured and imprisoned by the British before being shipped off to the island of Roatán, off the coast of Honduras. One of the ships transporting the prisoners was captured by Spanish forces and sent to the Honduran mainland. Only 2,000 Garífuna made it to Roatán, as many died during their imprisonment on St. Vincent or along the subsequent journey.

Pleas for help from the Garífuna stranded on the tiny island of Roatán were answered by the Spanish forces who arrived some time later to take survivors to Trujillo (Honduras), where they were conscripted to serve in the armed forces or work in agricultural fields. The Garífuna continued to move along the coast, eventually settling other parts of Honduras as well as Nicaragua.

The beaches in and around Lívingston are of white or grayish brown sand, unlike the volcanic sands on the Pacific Coast. It's not the talcum-powder white typically found on Caribbean shores elsewhere, and the water is not turquoise as in the Belize cayes, mostly because silt from the surrounding jungle rivers flowing into the bay conspires to keep the waters a greenish-brown color. But they're still perfectly nice for lounging. A boat ride from Lívingston to Playa Quehueche costs about $5.

NIGHTLIFE

If you're the kind of person who likes to spike the punch at the party, you might want to try a *coco loco,* a rather fun concoction consisting of a coconut with the top chopped off and enhanced with a generous helping of rum. The bars along Calle Principal as you come up the street from the municipal docks, including **La Buga** and **McTropic,** can usually satiate your thirst should the fancy take you.

Lívingston has a fairly vibrant nightlife scene befitting of its tropical location by the sea. Down by the beach on the northern end of town (Playa Bariques) is **Bar Beluba Neruba** with a small dance floor and tables right on the sand. It can be reached by heading west along the beach at the end of Calle Principal.

The classiest place in town is part of the

Some were taken to southern Belize to work in logging operations, from where they spread to Guatemala, establishing Lívingston in 1806. Today, the largest population of Garífuna can be found along the coast of Honduras (100,000), but there are also sizable populations in New York (50,000), New Orleans, and Los Angeles. Like other ethnic groups in Central America, they have been emigrating to the United States in increasing numbers since the 1970s.

Modern Garífuna speak Spanish, English, and the Garífuna language, which melds French, Arawak, Yuroba, Swahili, and Banti. Central to their culture are music and dance, namely *punta*, a form of musical expression with obvious West African influences incorporating ritual chanting, mesmerizing drumbeats, and rhythmic dancing. A traditional Garífuna band consists of three large drums, a turtle shell, a large conch shell, and maracas. You will probably hear live *punta* music at least once during your visit to Lívingston. Also common is *punta* rock,

a more modern version of popular Garífuna music. Another fascinating traditional dance is the *yancunu* New Year's dance, similar to those of indigenous South American rainforest peoples with distinctly West African musical origins. Lívingston's annual Garífuna festival is a weeklong event held during the third week of November.

Villa Caribe hotel. **Dugu Bar** (5pm-midnight daily) is housed in a cheerful, yellow wooden house on the town's main street opposite the Immigration office. The interior is decorated with tons of old pictures, and there's a full bar. The poolside bar at **Vecchia Toscana** (Barrio París, tel. 7947-0883 or 7947-0884, www.livingston-vecchiatoscana.com) is also a good bet.

EXCURSIONS

Hotel Casa Rosada (tel. 7947-0303, www. hotelcasarosada.com), **Happy Fish** (tel. 7947-0661 or 7947-0268, www.happyfish-travel.com, $5-25), and **Hotel Río Dulce** (tel.

7947-0764) do trips to Siete Altares ($13) or Playa Blanca ($15) , stopping at Siete Altares along the way, with a minimum of six people. **Hotel Posada El Delfín** (tel. 7947-0056, www.posadaeldelfin.com) offers a number of adventurous itineraries, including a full day of deep-sea fishing, an overnight scuba-diving trip to San Nicolás caye (in the Belize cayes), and a hike up a nearby mountain for an overnight stay in a jungle villa.

ACCOMMODATIONS

Despite its location right on the Caribbean Sea, Lívingston lacks beachside resort properties, as the beaches in the immediate vicinity are somewhat lacking. There are, however, some midrange accommodations on a serviceable beach just north of town. Most of the listed accommodations are found in the heart of town.

Under $50

The most pleasant budget accommodations are found at the rustically charming ★ **Casa de la Iguana B&B** (tel. 7947-0064, www.casadelaiguana.com, $8-20 per person), about one kilometer from the center of town along Calle Marcos Sánchez Díaz, where you can choose between staying in the dorm, private room with shared bath, or a spacious bungalow with private bathroom. Breakfast ($4) is served 7am-10am in a thatched-roof dining room overlooking a pleasant tropical garden and includes a choice of scrambled eggs, pancakes, or cereal. There's also a book exchange. Budget travelers can camp or sleep in a hammock for $3.50.

Along Calle Marcos Sánchez Díaz, about 400 meters west of the boat docks, is ★ **Hotel Casa Rosada** (tel. 7947-0303, www.hotelcasarosada.com, $20 s/d), a delightful place to stay with 10 rooms housed in attractive wood-and-thatch bungalows, all with shared bath and two single beds, centered around a pretty pink wooden house on the shores of the Río Dulce. The rooms have nice furnishings and hand-painted accents. Amenities include ceiling fans and mosquito netting. Some rooms are brighter than others. There is a dock leading out to the river where you can get dropped off. The restaurant here is also highly recommended.

Out of town northwest toward Siete Altares is Playa Quehueche, a sliver of a beach that holds a few comfortable lodgings. The first of these is **Hotel Ecológico Salvador Gaviota** (tel. 7947-0874 or 4011-9722, www.hotelsalvadorgaviota.com), which has simple rooms in thatched-roof cabins, including shared-bath doubles ($20), rooms with private bath ($13 pp), and bungalows sleeping up to five for $60. There is a simple seaside café serving local fare and there's a pier out front over the ocean

a *coco loco* in Livingston

where you can swim or lounge in a hammock. A boat ride into town costs about $5.

$50-100

Right at the entrance to town near the main dock, **Hotel Villa Caribe** (tel. 7947-0072 or 2223-5000, www.villasdeguatemala.com, $79-110 d) is a large white building with a commanding presence over the waterfront. Standard rooms have tile floors, fan, and private hot-water bath, while three attractively furnished suites housed in separate bungalows come with air-conditioning, TV, minibar, and lovely sea views. There's a large swimming pool and a restaurant that serves bland international fare. Splurge for the suite.

About 500 meters west of town along Calle Marcos Sánchez Díaz is the ★ **Posada El Delfín** (tel. 7947-0694 or 7947-0056, www.posadaeldelfin.com, $75-150 d), where the modern, comfortable rooms have air-conditioning, private bath, ceiling fan, phone, and wooden furniture. All upstairs rooms have carpeting. There are also larger suites,

Hotel Villa Caribe

including the wonderful honeymoon suite on the end of the two-story dock with a balcony overlooking the river below. It comes equipped with fridge, TV, and a CD player. Guests can relax in a lounge on the second floor, in the small swimming pool, or in hammocks on the dock over the river. For overall comfort and relaxing riverside ambience amid refreshing breezes, this place can't be beat.

On the street parallel to Playa Capitanía is **Gil Resort** (tel. 7947-0039 or 5206-8124, $60 d), housed in an airy, two-floor wooden building. The comfortable rooms have wood paneling, TV, and a/c. There's a nice sitting area with sea views and a Jacuzzi. The most atmospheric of the town's accommodations is ★ **Vecchia Toscana** (Barrio París, tel. 7947-0883 or 7947-0884, www.livingston-vecchiatoscana.com, $61 d to $183 for six-person bungalow). The tastefully decorated rooms feature mosquito netting and a fan or a/c and are built on well-manicured grounds surrounding a swimming pool. The star attraction is the beachfront bungalow, with a

private roof terrace, Jacuzzi, minibar, and comfortable lounge chairs.

FOOD

The specialty here and elsewhere in Izabal is a dish known as *tapado,* a seafood stew prepared using coconut milk and bananas.

On par with the wonderful accommodations at **Hotel Casa Rosada** (tel. 7947-0303, www.hotelcasarosada.com, 6:30am-9pm daily) is its excellent restaurant, where delicious meals are served on charming hand-painted tables in a thatched-roof covered patio overlooking the Río Dulce. Dinner is a three-course set menu, including fresh salad and coconut bread, main course, and dessert costing about $13. Typical entrées include lobster, shrimp, filet mignon, Thai curry, and fish. Lunch and breakfast are served à la carte and include sandwiches, fruit salads, and quesadillas. Try the banana pancakes for breakfast. Excellent coffee and espresso drinks are also served here.

A few doors down Calle Marcos Sánchez Díaz, heading west, ★ **Malena's** (inside the Hotel Posada El Delfín, tel. 7947-0694, www.posadaeldelfin.com, 6am-9:30pm daily) is one of Lívingston's finest restaurants, serving a varied menu of international dishes at reasonable prices, including vegetarian nachos with Provençal sauce, chicken, burgers, and veggie burgers. Seafood entrées include *tapado,* ceviche, fish chowder, and sea bass. There are delicious homemade desserts, coffee, and espresso beverages to top off your meal. The restaurant is on the second floor of a two-story dock jutting over the Río Dulce with pleasant modern decor, sea breezes, and the unmistakable feel of the tropics.

Along this same street close to the municipal dock, ★ **Restaurant Buga Mama** (tel. 7947-0891, www.bugamama.org, noon-10pm Mon., 10am-10pm Tues.-Sun., $5-25) is a good place for reasonably priced fish, shrimp, and pasta dishes. The restaurant, housed in a bright-blue wooden building, is wonderfully staffed by tourism industry students from a local school run by grassroots development organization Ak' Tenamit. On the riverbank, ★ **Casa Nostra** (Calle Marcos Sánchez Díaz, tel. 7947-0842, www.casanostralivingston.com, $5-15) is highly recommended for its delicious pizzas and excellent service. Its friendly owner, Stuart, is also a wealth of information on local attractions and transport logistics. Other menu items include yummy smoothies, chai tea, Spanish tapas, seafood and meat dishes, pasta, and quesadillas. There are rooms for rent and more are being built.

Calle Principal has a number of eateries. One of the first places you'll see as you come up the hill from the main dock is **Happy Fish** (tel. 7947-0661 or 7947-0268, www.happyfishtravel.com, 7am-10pm daily), serving reliable seafood and salads in a pleasant patio setting just off the street. It's a good bet for breakfast. Across the street is **Restaurante McTropic** (tel. 5558-5656, 7am-10pm daily, $4-15), where the specialty is Cantonese food, including chop suey and fried rice. A few doors down and across the street is the popular **Restaurante Bahía Azul** (tel. 7947-0151, 7am-10pm daily), where meals are also served on a patio overlooking the street. The creative menu includes curry, sweet and sour or soy sauce chicken. There is live music some nights. It's also a good bet for breakfast. Try the "Gangster" breakfast sandwich with ham, cheese, hotcakes, and honey—a bit like a McGriddle. If you crave authentic Italian cuisine, head to ★ **Vecchia Toscana** (tel. 7947-0883/84, www.livingston-vecchiatoscana.com, 8am-1am daily, $4-9), in Barrio París on the beach north of town toward Playa Quehueche. There are delicious pastas and wood-fired-oven pizzas.

SERVICES

For money, **Banrural** is on Calle Principal, just past Villa Caribe, with an ATM. Farther up the street is **Banco Reformador,** also with an ATM.

The **immigration office** (tel. 7947-0081, 6am-7pm daily) is also on Calle Principal across the street from the Villa Caribe. You'll need to stop here first if heading out to or

arriving from Belize. **Telgua** and the **post office** are right next to each other just up the street on the right side.

GETTING THERE

The only access to and from Lívingston is by water, either from the Caribbean Sea to Puerto Barrios, Belize, or Honduras or via the Río Dulce. There is Monday-Saturday ferry service to Puerto Barrios at 5am and 2pm (1.5 hours, $1.50), along with motorboats ($5) leaving all day when they have a full load of people. From Puerto Barrios, there are departures to Lívingston Monday to Saturday at 11am and 5pm. There is also service to Punta Gorda, Belize, Monday through Friday at 7am (one hour, $26). Any of the town's travel agencies can book tickets for you, but you must have the confirmed ticket the night before, along with your exit stamp from the immigration office. There's a $10 departure tax when leaving Guatemala by sea. From Punta Gorda to Lívingston, the boat leaves weekdays at 12:30pm. **Exotic Travel** also runs shuttle transport directly to Placencia for $50 per person with a six-person minimum. If you're heading to Honduras and have at least four people, it can also take you to La Ceiba for $75 per person, including boat to Puerto Barrios and then a minibus for the rest of the way.

ASOCOLMORAN, the water taxi association, runs transfers to Río Dulce (2.5 hours, $13 one-way or $24 round-trip) leaving at 9am and 1:30pm, but these stop along the way at the Río Dulce hot springs. Boat transfers to Río Dulce are also available from **Ríos Tropicales** (tel. 7947-0158, www.mctropic.com, $16).

NEAR LÍVINGSTON
★ Playa Blanca

About 13 kilometers along the coast northwest from Lívingston is my favorite Guatemalan beach, **Playa Blanca** ($2.60), with a pretty stretch of white sand and palm trees on the tranquil Caribbean Sea. The private beach is under the same ownership as the Villa Caribe. It's becoming increasingly popular as a day

Playa Blanca

beach along the bay. Trips leave around 9am and return in the afternoon around 5pm. If you're looking to hook up with a group, try Exotic Travel first, as it seems to be the popular favorite and might have a group already going out. Most of the outfitters provide beach chairs, beach umbrellas, and hammocks for people going on the trip.

Río Sarstún

As you continue northwest along the Caribbean Coast past the beaches of Playa Blanca, the last stop along the Guatemalan Caribbean shores is the Río Sarstún, which forms the border between Belize and Guatemala. This beautiful jungle river has just recently become a viable option for exploration now that it is fully protected as a park administered by conservation group **FUNDAECO** (www.fundaeco.org.gt). The park ($20) protects 2,000 hectares of tropical rainforest, flooded forest, wetlands, and mangroves. You can kayak and explore wetland canals, see the recently discovered Cerro Sarstún cenote, swim in the emerald-green waters of a small lagoon, or hike along well-maintained nature trails, all of which are included in the price of admission.

Accommodations are in the **Eco-Albergue Lagunita Creek** (tel. 2253-4991 and 5241-9342, www.fundaeco.org.gt), a modern facility with clean, shared-bath dormitories with bunk beds for $10 and double rooms with private baths, queen-size beds, and balconies overlooking the river for $35. You can buy meals from the local community for $7-10. There's also a biological station here.

trip from Lívingston. There is now a little restaurant and small *palapas* fronting the quiet beach. New, rustic beachside accommodations are in the works. There are also bathrooms and showers here.

Several outfitters including La Casa Rosada, Happy Fish, and Exotic Travel do trips to Playa Blanca for $13 per person with a six-person minimum and including a box lunch. The Exotic Travel tour stops at the waterfalls of **Siete Altares** and the **Río Cocolí** along the way. The river is a pleasant side stream suitable for swimming with a small sliver of

Río Dulce National Park

One of Guatemala's oldest parks, the waterway connecting the Caribbean Sea with Lake Izabal is protected as Río Dulce National Park, covering 7,200 hectares along the river's 30 kilometer (19-mile) course. Much of the riverbank is shrouded in dense tropical forest punctuated at its most dramatic point by a large jungle canyon with hundred-meter rock faces known as **La Cueva de la Vaca.** The canyon is a 15-minute boat ride upstream from Lívingston. Along this route you'll also come across a graffiti-covered rock escarpment known as **La Pintada** with the earliest painting in evidence dating to the 1950s.

Just after the canyon (heading upstream from Lívingston), you'll come across the first of Río Dulce's many accommodations. **The Round House** (tel. 4294-9730, www.round-houseguatemala.com, $7 pp in dorm, $15 d in shared-bath private room) is a well-run, fun sort of place with dorms and private rooms. There's a swimming pool and a Sunday afternoon pool volleyball game that includes lunch and drink specials. Kayaks are available for rent. Meals are served family-style in the open-sided dining room.

★ RÍO TATÍN

This small tributary diverts north from the Río Dulce just upstream from the canyon. Along its course, you'll find some excellent accommodations built into the surrounding jungle and in complete harmony with their environment. It showcases the region's wonderful seclusion while at the same time providing a comfortable base from which to explore the area.

Finca Tatín

★ **Finca Tatín** (tel. 4148-3332 www.fincatatin.com, $7-52) is a wonderfully secluded jungle camp and backpackers' haven about half a kilometer up the river where you'll find a variety of accommodations, including shared-bath dormitory beds for $7 per person, shared-bath doubles for $17, and bungalows for $26-52. Some of the bungalows are in the jungle area to the rear of the property, but the nicest ones are riverside and have patios. All rooms have mosquito netting and fan. The lodge gets major props for ecological consciousness. Water for the showers comes from the river, while water for the bathroom sinks is collected rainwater. All the bungalows have their own septic tanks with all waste material being buried.

Excellent meals are served in the lodge's open-air restaurant housed under a thatched roof. Dinner is a family-style affair, allowing

Río Dulce canyon

for opportunities to meet fellow travelers. Breakfast, lunch, and dinner cost $5, $7, and $10. The menu is a varied palette of creative vegetarian, Guatemalan, and international dishes.

Activities include bird-watching in the surrounding forests, hikes lasting from 30 minutes to four hours all the way to Lívingston, day and overnight trips to the Belize cayes, and kayaking in the Biotopo Chocón Machacas or down the Río Dulce to Lívingston. A two-person kayak rental costs $10 per day. The lodge is run by a friendly Argentine. Italian, English, and French are spoken.

Rancho Corozal

A little farther down the Río Tatín is ★ **Rancho Corozal** (tel. 5309-1423 in Guatemala, 866/621-4032 toll-free U.S., www.quintamaconda.com/rio_dulce.htm), an absolutely astounding private villa that can be yours for $250 per night for the entire villa for 2 people, or $82 per person per night for 9-10 people, including breakfast. The owners

Rancho Corozal, a private hideaway on the Río Tatín

are quick to point out that it's not a hotel but rather a private hideaway. It can sleep up to 10 people in five double beds with stylish safari netting. The beautiful house, designed with soaring thatched roofs and attractive ceramic and stucco accents, is set right beside the river on its own 20-acre forest reserve. There are tastefully landscaped tropical gardens, a short nature trail, open-air living and dining rooms, and a hammock patio. The house is wonderfully watched over by its live-in caretaker, Sabino, who can show you around and take you to area attractions aboard the house skiff ($125 per day). At night, the villa is lit by the warm glow of gas lamps and torches. There is no electricity, but you won't even miss it. Food can be arranged at the house or at one of a few local eateries. Try the freshwater crab cooked in coconut milk at neighboring Doña Lola's.

Ak' Tenamit

Heading back downstream toward the Río Tatín's confluence with the Río Dulce, you'll find **Ak' Tenamit** (tel. 5908-3392 or 5908-4358, www.aktenamit.org), a grassroots health and development organization helping to provide a better living for the local Q'eqchi' Maya who inhabit the area in several villages. Thanks to this organization's efforts, these extremely impoverished communities now have access to health care and education, among other basic necessities. There is a women's handicraft cooperative, a 24-hour clinic, primary and secondary schools (including curricula in tourism and social welfare), and an ecotourism center. At the visitors center you can buy locally made crafts and enjoy light meals in a pleasant *palapa*-style café, which is open 7am-4:30pm. Volunteer doctors, dentists, and nurses who can commit for at least one month are always welcome.

RÍO LÁMPARA

Continuing upstream, on the south bank of the Río Dulce, is another tributary known as the Río Lámpara. You'll see a small island known as Cayo Quemado at the mouth of this small river. This area is seldom explored, though a new jungle camp has put this remote area on the map.

Accommodations

The exquisite little jungle lodge **El Hotelito Perdido** (tel. 5725-1576 or 5785-5022, www. hotelitoperdido.com, dorm beds $7-8 pp, rooms with shared bath $20 d, bungalows with private bath $27-33 d) lies on the quiet banks of the Río Lámpara hidden away (as its name implies) from civilization. If you're looking for an exotic, affordable escape to the outer limits of civilization, El Hotelito Perdido might just do the trick. The accommodations are built in typical thatched-roof jungle style and include a dorm and shared or private bath bungalows with typical Guatemalan fabric accents. The two-story bungalows have sleeping areas upstairs and a living area on the ground floor. Solar panels provide electricity, while rainwater is collected for showers. Breakfast, lunch, and dinner ($3-9) are available at the hotel's restaurant and include a variety of dishes including vegetarian fare. There's a nearby waterfall for exploring in addition to gorgeous views of the Río Dulce canyon from the grounds, kayaks for rent, hammocks for lounging and a swimming dock. Other activities include full-moon kayaking trips to nearby hot springs, jungle hikes, and bird-watching.

To get here, hitch a ride on any of the boats heading in either direction between Río Dulce town and Lívingston. They should have no problem dropping you off here. The lodge also offers a pickup service for $7 per person (two-person minimum) from the Lívingston municipal dock.

EL GOLFETE

Back along the Río Dulce, another kilometer or so upstream, is a spot where warm sulfurous waters bubble from the base of a cliff, providing a pleasant place to swim. The local community has banded together to provide

the hot springs on the Río Dulce at Centro Turístico Agua Caliente

quality tourism infrastructure for visitors in the form of **Centro Turístico Agua Caliente** (tel. 5375-0496, www.turismocomunitarioguatemala.com, $1.50). Among the facilities are a thatched-roof bar and snack stand, a gift shop selling locally made handicrafts, and a dock from which to swim in the river or soak in the warm waters. Heading inland, you'll find a series of caves with an interesting array of rock formations and even a large central chamber.

Shortly after the hot springs, the river widens into a lake known as El Golfete. The lake is home to a dwindling population of manatees protected on its northern shore by the **Biotopo Chocón Machacas** (7am-4pm daily, $5). The large, slow-moving aquatic mammals (also known as sea cows) are extremely elusive creatures, and fewer than 100 are thought to inhabit these waters. The walrus-like animals are threatened throughout their range by long reproductive cycles (they reach sexual maturity late in life) and collisions with motorboats. The 186-square-kilometer (72-square-mile) park is run by CECON, and there are aquatic routes through several jungle lagoons as well as a nature trail running through the park and its protected forests.

A comfortable base for exploring the area is the community tourism project at **Lagunita Salvador** and its **Hotel Q'ana Itz'am** (tel. 5992-1843 or 4059-3836, www.lagunitasalvador.com). There are rustic but clean and comfortable accommodations in thatched-roof structures fronting jungle wetlands. There are dormitory-style rooms with shared bathrooms ($10 pp) or bungalows with private bathrooms ($37 for up to six people). The restaurant serves tasty seafood dishes, fried chicken, fruit plates, and cold beer and soda. There are guided tours to the reserve and surrounding areas (including several lush, little-known lagoons) in addition to kayaks for rent. You can even witness a traditional Dance of the Deer performance.

Heading west from here, the river

Lagunita Salvador

continues its course upstream past the expensive villas of Guatemala's oligarchy to the town of Río Dulce, at the confluence of the river and Lake Izabal. A long bridge connects both shores along Highway CA-13, which continues north to Petén.

Río Dulce Town (Fronteras)

The town of Río Dulce is the community centered around a long bridge crossing over the river near its meeting point with Lake Izabal. You'll find most of the town's accommodations on the north side of the bridge, also known as Fronteras.

SIGHTS AND RECREATION

Although the river and jungle are all around you, exploring this area may not be so easy on your own. It's always possible to hire a *lanchero* to take you around. Bargain hard. A more viable alternative is to stay at one of the more ecologically oriented lodges, which usually offer a full range of options for exploring. The two best places to stay in this regard are **Hacienda Tijax** (tel. 7930-5505, 7930-5506, VHF channel 09, www.tijax.com) and **Tortugal** (tel. 5306-6432, VHF channel 68, www.tortugal.com),

which both do an excellent job of providing engaging nature hikes as well as supplying equipment (kayaks, for example) to explore on your own.

Castillo de San Felipe de Lara

More commonly known as "El Castillo de San Felipe," **Castillo de San Felipe de Lara** (8am-5pm, $1.50) also gives its name to a small community on the northern shores of Lake Izabal. The castle was originally built by the Spanish in 1652 in an attempt to deter the activities of pirates, who would come up the Río Dulce to raid supplies. It would later serve as a prison but was finally abandoned and left to deteriorate. The present fortress was reconstructed in 1956. It's worth a look around for its thick walls enclosing a maze of small rooms as well as its old cannons. There are some nice lake views, a picnic area, and green grounds. Castillo de San Felipe is three kilometers along the lakeshore from Río Dulce or four kilometers by road, which you can walk in about an hour. Heading north out of town on the main road, turn left after the Banco Industrial. After a few kilometers, you'll pass the turnoff for El Estor on the right. Continue straight on the main road for another kilometer or so from here to the castle. Minivans ($0.50) leave every 30 minutes from the north end of the bridge, or you can hire a water taxi ($5).

Finca El Paraíso

On Lake Izabal's northern shore, between El Estor and Río Dulce, is the wonderful waterfall hot springs of **Finca El Paraíso** (tel. 7949-7122), a working farm easily accessible from either town. Here a wide, 12-meter-high warm-water fall plunges into a clear pool cooled by flows from surrounding streams. If you think soaking in warm water in a tropical climate wouldn't be inviting, think again. Above the falls are some caves worth exploring, for which you'll need to bring a flashlight. Two kilometers west from the falls is a comfortable lodge and restaurant. The wooden bungalows have private bathrooms, and you can catch the cool lake breezes from a hammock on your very own patio. The restaurant is housed in a bamboo-and-thatch open-air structure with a menu that includes pasta and meat dishes.

The farm lies along the Río Dulce-El Estor bus route, about an hour from Río Dulce and 40 minutes from El Estor. Buses and pickups go by about every hour in both directions, with the last of these around 4:30pm. Hacienda Tijax and Tortugal, in Río Dulce, can also bring you here on a tour.

Sailing to the Belize Cayes

Aventuras Vacacionales (tel. 7832-6056, www.sailing-diving-guatemala.com, $200-440 pp) offers year-round sailing trips up the Río Dulce and out to the Belize cayes on a 46-foot Polynesian sailboat. You can see set departure dates on a calendar through their website.

Castillo de San Felipe de Lara

ACCOMMODATIONS

Most of Río Dulce's accommodations can be found on the north side of the bridge, starting from there and spreading east and west a few kilometers along the riverbank. Directly underneath the bridge is **Bruno's Hotel and Marina** (tel. 7930-5174, www.mayaparadise.com/brunoe), a popular establishment with the sailing set containing rooms in shared-bathroom dormitories for $7 per bed, double rooms with shared bath for $25; or double rooms with air-conditioning, hot-water private baths, and porches overlooking the gardens and river for $50. There's a small swimming pool next to the river, which makes a great place to hang out.

About one kilometer farther east along the river is ★ **Hacienda Tijax** (tel. 7930-5505, 7930-5506, VHF channel 09, www.tijax.com, $29-88), one of Guatemala's most enjoyable places to stay. The quaint little A-frame cabins on the riverfront are what this place is all about. Double-occupancy cabins with shared baths go for $29, or $49 d with private

one of the hanging bridges at Hacienda Tijax

bathroom. There are six private-bath cabins with air-conditioning available for $73 d. Spacious bungalows cost $88 d. All rooms have comfortable beds with mosquito netting and fan. There is an excellent restaurant housed under a large *palapa* structure, an inviting swimming pool, and Internet access. Activities include a guided tour around the hacienda's working rubber plantation to a lookout tower with gorgeous views of the river and El Golfete, passing a hanging bridge over the forest along the way, two-hour horseback riding tours around the farm, kayaking, and sailing. Tours cost $10-25 per person. There's a boat marina here.

Farther east along the river, the next place over is the fancier, 35-room ★ **Catamaran Island Hotel** (tel. 7930-5494, www.catamaranisland.com), set on a splendid private island. Rooms are housed in comfortable wooden cabins with ceiling fan, air-conditioning, and private bath. There are double rooms on land for $85 including breakfast or set over the water for $91 d, also including breakfast.

There's a fancy restaurant serving seafood and international dishes, a tennis court, and a poolside bar with a happy hour 4pm-7pm. There are sports on its DirecTV-equipped units. There's also a marina here.

Casa Perico (tel. 7930-5666 or 5909-0721, www.casa-perico.com, VHF channel 68) lies another few kilometers farther east. Situated beside the Río Bravo, a small tributary of the Río Dulce, the lodge offers rooms in a dormitory above the restaurant and bar for $8 per person, private rooms for $18 d, or wooden cabins with private baths for $26. It's a bit out of the way, which is precisely what brings most guests here. The Swiss owners cook good meals (dinner is about $5-6) and will pick you up from Río Dulce for free and drop you off at the end of your stay.

Back near the bridge, on its south side, is **Hotel Backpackers** (tel. 7930-5480, www.hotelbackpackers.com). Another budget travelers' hideout, it has rooms in shared-bath dorms for $7 per person, double rooms with shared bath for $20, or doubles with private bath for $20-35. Air-conditioned rooms are priced between $39 and $70 d. It's run by Casa Guatemala, a nonprofit that manages a center on El Golfete for abandoned and malnourished children. There's a restaurant and bar here serving inexpensive international dishes, beers, sodas, and cocktails. Services include laundry, phone, fax, and email. You can inquire here about volunteer opportunities with Casa Guatemala. If arriving on the bus from Guatemala City, get off before crossing the bridge so as to avoid a long walk back from its other end.

On the right side of the bridge, southwest about one kilometer from the bridge toward Castillo de San Felipe is ★ **Tortugal** (tel. 5306-6432, VHF channel 68, www.tortugal.com, $10 pp to $50 d), where a splendid setting, beautiful accommodations, and attention to details make this one of the best places to stay in Río Dulce. You'll fall in love with this place as soon as you step off the boat and onto its private dock. Spacious rooms with lovely terraces and shared bath go for $44 d. My favorite accommodation is La Casita Elegante ($56 d), with a king-sized bed, antique furnishings, private bath, and airy terrace overlooking the jungle. There's an excellent restaurant serving vegetarian fare and Guatemalan takes on international dishes in a soaring thatched-roof structure built on a platform over the water. Activities include catching some rays on the docks, kayaking (free for guests), sailing, and Rover tours to the jungle hot springs of nearby Finca El Paraíso.

FOOD

Bruno's Hotel and Marina (tel. 7930-5174, www.mayaparadise.com/brunoe, 7am-10pm daily) is especially popular with boaters for its varied menu of international dishes and snacks in the $5-10 range as well as its TV news and sports in an open-air dining room right beside the water. There are pancakes, omelets, and hash browns for breakfast; burgers and ribs for lunch and dinner. Just up the street, ★ **Sundog Café** (tel. 5529-0829, $3-9) has a nice riverside location and serves delicious hot sandwiches, including an avocado melt, baguettes, and pastrami sandwiches. They also do decent pizzas. It's lively at night.

Serving authentic Mexican food is **Las Mexicanas** (at Hotel Kangaroo, tel. 5363-6716, www.hotelkangaroo.com, 8am-8pm daily, $5-8), which has quickly become a town favorite with locals and visitors alike. There's an airy screened-in dining room next to the water and a full bar. It's on the opposite side of the river across from Castillo de San Felipe. You can call them for a pickup. Also near Castillo de San Felipe, **Restaurante Rosita** (tel. 4812-2114 or 5902-0275, 9am-9:30pm daily, $5-15) serves large portions of amazingly tasty seafood in an airy open-sided dining room next to the river. Try the out-of-this-world vodka melon sangria.

Whether or not you're staying at **Hacienda Tijax** (tel. 7930-5505, 7930-5506, VHF channel 09, www.tijax.com), it makes a great place to eat for its rugged jungle ambience and delicious sandwiches, seafood, salads, pasta, and

steak dishes in the $5-13 range served in an airy high-ceilinged *palapa* structure. It brews excellent coffee and has a full bar. Farther out this way, about two kilometers downstream from Río Dulce, is **Mario's Marina** (tel. 7930-5560, www.mariosontherio.com), which has a restaurant and bar that is popular with the sailing crowd and serves a variety of seafood and international dishes. Bar patrons can browse the book exchange or enjoy a game of darts.

West from the Río Dulce bridge toward the Castillo de San Felipe, the restaurant at ★ **Tortugal** (tel. 5306-6432, VHF channel 68, www.tortugal.com, 7am-10pm) is worth a stop for its deliciously prepared, creative menu options and superb location right on the water away from the noise and traffic closer to town. Prepared using fresh ingredients, the menu harmoniously blends authentic Guatemalan cuisine with American and European flourishes. Dinner options range $5-12 for items varying from a quarter-pound barbecue burger to seafood stew. It's also a great place for breakfast ($3-6) or lunch ($4-7). The bar here serves some excellent cocktails that you can enjoy along with the gorgeous jungle river scenery. There's always something on special for $2.50, served in a large cocktail glass.

INFORMATION AND SERVICES

An excellent source of information on all things Río Dulce is the *Río Dulce Chisme-Vindicator* (http://riodulcechisme.com).

Money

All of the banks are on the main road on the north side of the bridge. **Banco Industrial** has a visa ATM and **Banrural** has Visa and MasterCard ATMs.

Travel Agencies

You can book shuttle buses, sailing trips, and boat transfers from three very similar travel agencies on a small alleyway just north of Bruno's along the main road. These are **Otitours** (tel. 7930-7674), **Atitrans** (tel.

by changing buses at La Ruidosa Junction near Morales. From there you can catch a westbound bus to Guatemala City or east to Puerto Barrios. All of these companies have offices in Río Dulce. There are shuttle buses to Guatemala City ($30), Antigua ($37), and Copán Ruinas ($37) that can be booked through the local travel agencies.

Boat

Boats to Lívingston leave from underneath the north side of the bridge via **ASOCOLMORAN** (tel. 5561-9657), the local water taxi association, at 9am and 1:30pm, taking about 90 minutes and costing $13 one-way or $24 round-trip.

MARINAS

Several of the aforementioned hotels and restaurants also operate full-service marinas. Among these are Tijax, Tortugal, Bruno's, Catamaran Island Hotel, and Mario's Marina. Other options include **Monkey Bay Marina** (www.monkeybaymarina.com) and **Mar Marine** (www.marmarine.com.gt). A full listing of other available options can be found online at http://riodulcechisme.com.

the marina at Hacienda Tijax

7832-0644 or 5218-5950), and **Tijax Express/ Gray Line Tours** (tel. 7930-5196/97, www. graylineguatemala.com).

GETTING THERE
Bus

The north end of the bridge, also known as Fronteras, is a hub for transport heading out in several directions from here. Buses heading north to Petén all stop here before continuing to Poptún and Flores ($7, four hours). The same is true for the return trip south from Flores to Guatemala City ($6, six hours). Bus lines covering this route include Línea Dorada and Fuente del Norte. Both companies also have some more expensive luxury coaches plying this route. **Litegua** buses can take you to and from Puerto Barrios directly or

SAFETY

Sailing vessels should take care to anchor in protected private marinas and not out in the middle of the open water where they may fall prey to local pirates. In June 2008, an American citizen was murdered while attempting to resist an armed robbery aboard his yacht anchored in the waters near Río Dulce town. In the aftermath, several of the town's marinas and local tourism authorities contracted the services of an overnight boat patrol to make the rounds at several of the better-known marinas. These include Hacienda Tijax, Bruno's, and Tortugal, among others.

Las Verapaces

Collectively known as "Las Verapaces," the departments of Alta and Baja Verapaz are mostly mountainous, remote, and clothed in verdant forests. Guatemala's national bird, the resplendent quetzal, and its national flower, a rare orchid known as the *monja blanca*, inhabit the cool cloud forests of this region.

This is probably Guatemala's most overlooked area in terms of tourism potential, as it sees surprisingly few visitors. The recreational opportunities and natural attractions are boundless and include spectacular waterfalls, cool mountain forests, mysterious caves, Mayan ruins, turquoise lagoons, and whitewater rivers. Perhaps because Guatemala has always had more fame as a cultural destination, its equally splendid natural attractions have been overlooked. This tendency seems to be changing.

Although it might seem the Verapaz Highlands are a continuation of the rugged Western Highlands, they are unique in a number of ways, including their settlement patterns, history, climate, geology, and population. You won't find much traditional attire being worn in these parts, particularly among the men. The women tend to wear traditional skirts with loose white blouses not nearly as colorful or intriguing as those worn elsewhere in the highlands. Still, Mayan culture is very much alive and well in the mountain towns and villages of the Verapaz Highlands. The stunning mountain scenery is on par with that found in the Western Highlands.

Perhaps most exciting for the visitor is the palpable sense of Las Verapaces being a well-kept secret just waiting to be told. It's easy to fall in love with all that this wonderful area has to offer. New and increasingly comfortable accommodations with greater sophistication in services make this Guatemala's ecotourism frontier.

CLIMATE

As elsewhere in Guatemala, the main determinant of climate is the altitude. As both Alta and Baja Verapaz are largely dominated by the presence of mountain chains, you can expect to find some chilly weather at high

---

Previous: the Río Cahabón; on the road to Lanquín. **Above:** Semuc Champey.

Look for ★ to find recommended sights, activities, dining, and lodging.

Highlights

★ **Biotopo Mario Dary Rivera:** Also known as the Quetzal Biotope, this beautiful mountain park conveniently situated along the road to Cobán is the easiest way to explore the cloud forests and spot the resplendent quetzal (page 267).

★ **Rafting the Río Cahabón:** Battle rapids with names such as Rock and Roll, Sex Machine, and Corkscrew Falls. You can also explore caves and thermal hot springs along the forested riverbanks (page 276).

★ **Semuc Champey Natural Monument:** The turquoise limestone pools and waterfalls of Semuc Champey are among Guatemala's most exquisite natural attractions (page 278).

★ **Parque Ecológico Hun Nal Ye:** One of Guatemala's best-kept secrets is this private 135-hectare nature reserve where you can swim in pristine rivers, visit a limestone sinkhole, ride horses, and zip across the forest canopy (page 281).

★ **Laguna Lachuá National Park:** This exquisite and remote lagoon is thought to have been the site of a prehistoric meteor impact. The surrounding forests and azure Río Ikbolay are worth some exploration (page 282).

altitudes. The Sierra de las Minas reaches altitudes of 2,375 meters (7,800 feet), while Cobán displays similar temperatures to those in Guatemala City, which sits at the same altitude. It is considerably damper in these parts, as much of the year sees the *chipi-chipi*, a misty drizzle that often dampens the atmosphere for entire days. Farther north, toward Chisec and the jungle flatlands extending northward, the temperature is substantially warmer, and it can be extremely humid. All of these conditions are further influenced by the seasons (rainy and dry) dominating the entire country, though this area tends to see much more rainfall throughout the year with a shorter dry season (Feb.-Apr.) than elsewhere in Guatemala.

HISTORY

The history of the Verapaces is also quite different from elsewhere in Guatemala. The region was populated by the Achi' Maya, who were historically at war with the K'iche' of the Western Highlands before the Spanish conquest. The Spanish themselves were unable to conquer the Achi' and eventually gave up on this task, declaring the area a *tierra de guerra*, or "land of war." The church eventually succeeded where the conquerors had failed. Convinced by Fray Bartolomé de las Casas, the Spanish military forces agreed to leave the region for five years to give de las Casas and his companions a chance to pacify and convert the Indians. De las Casas and three friars set out for the Verapaz Highlands in 1537, quickly befriending the Achi' chiefs and learning the local dialects. New converts were made, and the Maya living in scattered hamlets were convinced to move into Spanish-style settlements. After this five-year term, the Achi' were officially recognized as subjects of the Spanish crown, partially as a result of the passing of the New Laws in 1542 granting Indians basic rights and prohibiting their enslavement. The Spanish crown renamed the region Verapaz, or "true peace."

The region began to grow and develop with the arrival of coffee cultivation in Guatemala, aided by its proximity to the Caribbean port via the Río Polochic and across Lake Izabal. A railroad would eventually be built along this corridor. In the early 1900s, a flood of German immigrants snapped up large pieces of land and began cultivating coffee and cardamom, thus further altering the regional demographics. By 1915, half of all Guatemalan coffee was grown on land owned by these German immigrants, who sold a large percentage of the harvest to their fatherland. Cobán in particular was greatly altered by this demographic shift, as it took on the appearance of a German mountain town. The vestiges of this old-world influence can still be seen here and there. German economic and cultural dominion over the region was abruptly put to an end during World War II, when the United States prevailed upon Guatemala to deport the German farm owners, many of whom were unabashed in their support for the Nazis.

Today, the Achi' still inhabit Baja Verapaz in the area around Rabinal, with a largely Q'eqchi' and Poqomchi' population inhabiting the lands of Alta Verapaz. The region is still very much rural, much like the rest of Guatemala. Coffee and cardamom cultivation are still at the heart of the economy, with tourism beginning to make some significant inroads.

PLANNING YOUR TIME

You could easily spend your entire Guatemalan holiday in Las Verapaces, and it would be entirely worth it. But, time being the finite entity that it is, you'll probably have to narrow your stay to your particular interests. North along Highway CA-14, the newly established **Cloud Forest Biological Corridor** is shaping up as a wonderful spot to explore a variety of natural attractions along the road to Cobán. Among these are the well-preserved cloud forests of the **Sierra de las Minas Biosphere Reserve.** Cobán still serves as the most convenient base for exploring all that the region has to offer and has some

Las Verapaces

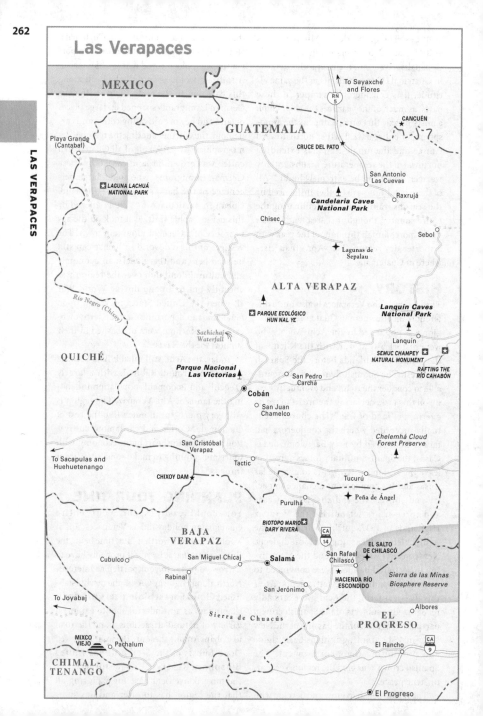

MEXICO

GUATEMALA

To Sayaxché
and Flores

RN
5

CANCUÉN

Playa Grande
(Cantabal)

CRUCE DEL PATO

San Antonio
Las Cuevas

Raxrujá

LAGUNA LACHUÁ
NATIONAL PARK

Candelaria Caves
National Park

Chisec

Sebol

Lagunas de
Sepalau

ALTA VERAPAZ

Río Negro (Chixoy)

Parque Ecológico
HUN NAL YE

Lanquín Caves
National Park

Sachichaj
Waterfall

Lanquín

QUICHÉ

Parque Nacional
Las Victorias

SEMUC CHAMPEY
NATURAL MONUMENT

RAFTING THE
RÍO CAHABÓN

San Pedro
Carchá

Cobán

San Juan
Chamelco

Chelemhá Cloud
Forest Preserve

San Cristóbal
Verapaz

To Sacapulas and
Huehuetenango

Tactic

Tucurú

CHIXOY DAM

Peña de Ángel

Purulhá

BIOTOPO MARIO
DARY RIVERA

CA
14

BAJA
VERAPAZ

EL SALTO
DE CHILASCÓ

Cubulco

San Miguel Chicaj

Salamá

San Rafael
Chilascó

Sierra de las Minas
Biosphere Reserve

Rabinal

HACIENDA RÍO
ESCONDIDO

To Joyabaj

San Jerónimo

Albores

Sierra de Chuacús

EL
PROGRESO

MIXCO
VIEJO

Pachalum

El Rancho

CA
9

CHIMAL-
TENANGO

El Progreso

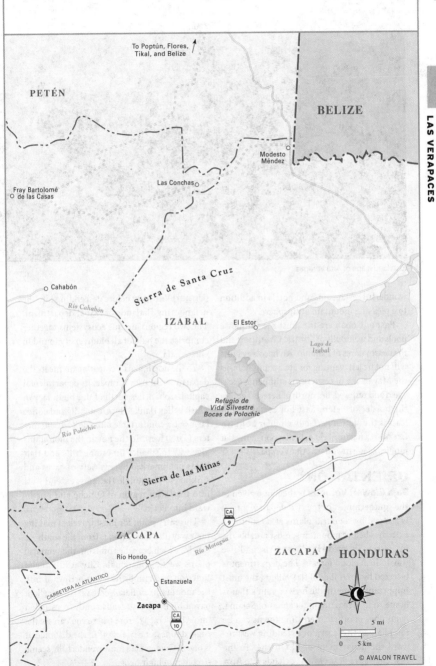

lush landscape of Alta Verapaz

wonderful restaurants and hotels in addition to a pleasing mountain atmosphere.

East of Cobán are the must-see turquoise pools and waterfalls of **Semuc Champey** and the nearby caves of Lanquín. Archaeology buffs will not be left wanting for attractions here, as the Mayan site of **Cancuén,** still being excavated and restored, lies north of here just across the border of Petén. Last but certainly not least is the almost perfectly circular **Laguna Lachuá,** a magnificent azure lagoon in the flat jungles of northwestern Alta Verapaz.

ORIENTATION

Baja (Lower) Verapaz is the name given to the southernmost of the two departments. It is fringed by semiarid plains at its southern extremes before mountains, most notably the impressive **Sierra de las Minas,** rise and give way to lush cloud forests. The department is bisected by a number of flat valleys, the most important being the lush river valley that is home to its departmental capital of Salamá. A number of other interesting towns can be found along this corridor extending west toward the department of El Quiché. To the east, the Sierra de las Minas extends into **Alta**

(Upper) Verapaz before descending into the neighboring flatlands of Izabal department. The two regions' unique ecosystems together comprise the bulk of all biodiversity found in Guatemala.

To the north, Baja Verapaz again meets the department of Alta Verapaz. Its departmental capital, Cobán, lies north of this boundary in a lush valley flanked by green hills and coffee farms at a comfortable altitude of 1,500 meters (5,000 feet). To the north, the mountains give way to smaller limestone hills and flatlands pockmarked by a variety of caves and sinkholes. The jungle flatlands extend west into the Ixcán region of Quiché and northward into Petén.

The entry point for most travelers making their way into this region is from the south via CA-14, which branches off from the semiarid plains west of Guatemala City at El Rancho Junction and climbs its way northward into the mountains of Baja Verapaz. An excellent paved highway also leads south from Petén into Alta Verapaz, from where you can see the rugged limestone peaks off in the distance. It is one of Guatemala's most wonderfully scenic stretches of highway.

Along the Cloud Forest Biological Corridor

The **Cloud Forest Biological Corridor** (Corredor Biológico del Bosque Nuboso, tel. 5918-5581 or 5322-8264, www.corredorbosquenuboso.com) is a relatively new creation that encompasses a forested area bisecting the Quetzal Biotope and Sierra de las Minas Biosphere Reserve. Its purpose is to provide a buffer zone for a biological corridor protecting many species of animals living in these cloud forests. The area along the road to Cobán (CA-14) between Km. 142 and Km. 172 is part of this corridor, and it is clearly marked at its beginning and end. The corridor covers 28,640 hectares and includes nine communities and eight private reserves. A number of these private reserves are part of local hotels and restaurants that have begun catering to visitors interested in exploring all that this exuberant highland forest ecosystem has to offer. The result is an emerging ecotourism

Hacienda Río Escondido

development area, which may serve as a model for other areas in Guatemala with roads adjacent to protected areas.

The initiative is managed by an association based at Restaurante Montebello, at Km. 164 in the vicinity of Purulhá, which can provide additional resources and information.

HACIENDA RÍO ESCONDIDO

The first stop along this ecotourism corridor is **Hacienda Río Escondido** (Km. 144, tel. 5308-2440 or 5208-1407, www.rioescondido.net, $25 per person), where you'll find pleasant wooden cabins on a private nature reserve bisected by the cool, clear waters of the Río San Isidro. There are several kilometers of nature trails, horseback riding, and inner tubing to keep you busy should you not want to just relax and unwind. The best of the cabins are set along the creek. The restaurant here does barbecued meats, pastas, and smoothies you can enjoy in an open-air patio.

SIERRA DE LAS MINAS BIOSPHERE RESERVE

The Sierra de las Minas is a vast, 242,642-hectare mountain park harboring an astounding diversity of plant and animal life and encompassing a motley assortment of ecosystems, including cloud forests harboring several species of endemic conifers, as well as tropical moist forests and rainforests. The park extends 130 kilometers eastward (it's 30 kilometers wide) into the neighboring department of Izabal, where it meets with the lowland forests and grasslands of the Río Polochic delta. The biosphere reserve ranges in elevation from 400 to 2,400 meters and is composed mainly of cloud forests throughout its mountainous core in Baja Verapaz. Sixty-two permanent streams have their source in the upper slopes of the biosphere reserve, making it an

What Is a Cloud Forest?

a cloud forest in the Alta Verapaz highlands

Cloud forests are essentially high-altitude rainforests, though the biological characteristics and corresponding classification are much more complicated than a matter of mere altitude. In Guatemala, cloud forests average an annual precipitation of between 2,000 and 6,000 millimeters and are found at altitudes between 1,000 and 2,500 meters. The forests essentially serve as a large sponge, retaining water that is later distributed to surrounding areas by means of evaporation or the formation of small streams. More than 60 small streams originate in Guatemala's Sierra de las Minas, for example.

A distinct characteristic of these forests is the presence of low-lying cloud banks forming on the mountains, under which the forest is immersed for much of the time. Large amounts of water are deposited directly onto vegetation from the clouds and mist, with the leaves of trees at higher elevations often dripping water. Cloud forests serve as the habitat for many species of plants and animals, including epiphytes, which grow on other plants. You'll see tree branches thick with bromeliads, orchids, and tree ferns. As for wildlife, the forests support an abundance of rare and endangered species, including quetzals, howler monkeys, jaguars, and wild boars.

The Verapaz Highlands still contain many of these forests, including the largest protected cloud forest in Central America, the Sierra de las Minas Biosphere Reserve. The cloud forests that once covered much of the Western Highlands have been largely lost to subsistence agriculture by indigenous people who seek to make a living by clearing the forests and cultivating crops on steep hillsides. Outside of the Verapaces, there are still some patches of cloud forest left in the Sierra de los Cuchumatanes as well as on the slopes of Guatemala's volcanoes.

important watershed supplying the Motagua and Polochic Rivers. It is home to healthy populations of quetzals and jaguars, among other exotic species. Together with the adjacent Bocas del Polochic Wildlife Refuge, the parks account for 80 percent of Guatemala's biodiversity. The biosphere reserve is privately administered by **Defensores de la Naturaleza,** a well-known local conservation group with ties to The Nature Conservancy, among others.

San Rafael Chilascó

San Rafael Chilascó is a small agricultural settlement that serves as a gateway for visits into the biosphere reserve. The town has unfortunately been the site of land conflicts (as elsewhere in Guatemala), and its Chilascó

Community Tourism Organization has all but dissolved and is no longer the best way to arrange visits to the reserve. Likewise, the trail leading to one of Guatemala's highest waterfalls is badly deteriorated, along with the signage that once guided hikers. A local landowner has closed off access to the park.

San Rafael Chilascó is reached via a 12-kilometer dirt road branching east from the main highway heading northward toward Cobán (CA-14). The turnoff is at Km. 144, just past Hacienda Río Escondido. There are daily buses to Salamá leaving at 5:45am, 8:30am, 12:30pm, and 3pm, all of which pass by the CA-14 turnoff ($1). You can flag down a northbound bus to Cobán or southbound to Guatemala City from the turnoff.

Albores

A five-hour hike from San Rafael Chilascó deep into the heart of the reserve brings you to the farming community of Albores, on the southeastern side of the mountain range. **Defensores de la Naturaleza** (tel. 2440-8138 or 2471-7942, sminas@defensores.org.gt or info@defensores.org.gt, www.defensores.org) has built comfortable **cabins** ($30 per person) to house visitors at its **biological research station** nearby. You can also stay in the community with a local family for $5 per person. There are about 70 families living in Albores, most of which have traditionally made a living from cultivating coffee, cardamom, and vegetables. Ecotourism is a relatively new source of income for them, and they welcome visitors with open arms. They can provide you with meals for about $5. There are cooking facilities at the research station and solar panels for electricity.

A park admission fee of $5 applies for exploring this part of the reserve. From Albores, there are two trails into the surrounding cloud forest. The first trail takes you to the magnificent **Peña del Angel**, an igneous rock formation at an altitude of 2,400 meters, from where you have an incredible view of the surrounding cloud forest and the Polochic and Motagua River Valleys. The rock gets its name from its appearance, like that of two extended angelic wings, thanks to the 1976 earthquake, which broke the rock in two. The second trail takes you to a lookout point built by Defensores to monitor forest fires, from which there are also fabulous views.

Albores is also accessible from the road leading east from Guatemala City to Izabal department (Hwy. CA-9). At Km. 89, a dirt-road turnoff (4x4 vehicles only) in San Agustín Acasaguastlan heads north for 22 kilometers to Finca Trinidad in Los Albores. From there, it's a 5 kilometer hike to the biological station.

★ BIOTOPO MARIO DARY RIVERA

Also known as the Quetzal Biotope, **Biotopo Mario Dary Rivera** (tel. 5333-6947, biotopo-cecon@gmail.com, 7am-4pm daily, $5) is a 1,044-hectare protected area and one of several biotopes administered by University of San Carlos's Center for Conservation Studies (CECON). It is conveniently situated along CA-14 at Km. 160.5, about an hour from Cobán. Though quetzals are easier to spot in Sierra de las Minas, the elusive birds are said to frequent the yard of some local eating establishments (Biotopín Restaurant and Ranchitos del Quetzal), where they like to feast on the fruits of the *aguacatillo* tree. The Quetzal Biotope's convenient roadside location means that if you're on your way to or from Cobán, you should at least stop in for a look. You might just get lucky and see one of Guatemala's most beloved national symbols, with its exotic green plumage, long tail feathers, and bright red breast. Your best chances are between February and September. Plan on being up early if you want to see them.

Exploring the Park

Only a small part of the reserve is open to visitors, though there is plenty to keep you busy. There are two trails beginning at the visitors center, winding their way through the exuberant vegetation. The shorter **Los Helechos** (The Ferns) trail is two kilometers long, while

Mario Dary Rivera

Considered by many to be the patriarch of Guatemala's environmental movement, Mario Dary Rivera was a biologist who served as rector of the University of San Carlos in 1981, the same year in which he was assassinated. Dary succeeded in getting the municipality of Salamá to donate part of the land for the creation of the Quetzal Biotope, which was subsequently named after him; he served as the new park's director from 1977 to 1981. Dary also founded the university's Center for Conservation Studies (CECON) in 1981, along with its system of protected areas known as biotopes, set aside for the protection and scientific study of endangered plants and animals.

Today there are at least half a dozen of these biotopes throughout Guatemala. Among the animals being protected and studied are quetzals, sea turtles, jaguars, bats, deer, and Petén turkey.

Although the urban militant wing of the leftist Guatemalan Workers Party (PGT) has been attributed with Dary's assassination, some believe his conservation activities stirred the waters with local logging interests, who may have also played a part. Unlike most political killings at the height of the violent civil war, Dary's stands out because he was generally perceived to be right of center in his political inclinations.

Los Musgos (The Mosses) trail is twice as long. While you may or may not see a quetzal, you'll certainly see a dense growth of epiphytes, mosses, ferns, and orchids along the well-maintained trails. Both trails pass by some nice waterfalls where you can swim.

Trail maps are available for $1 at the visitors center, where there is also an exhibit. A small shop sells snacks and drinks, and there are camping and barbecue areas. Camping is allowed with prior arrangement only.

Accommodations and Food

A number of comfortable lodgings are alongside the road in the vicinity of the biotope. The first place you'll find, coming from Cobán, is **Ranchitos del Quetzal** (Km. 160.5, tel. 4130-9456 or 5368-6397, www.ranchitos-delquetzal.com, $33 d), where there are eight comfortable rooms in concrete structures with electric hot-water heater. The restaurant here serves basic, inexpensive meals ($3-6), and there is a trail to a waterfall and swimming hole 40 minutes away. Quetzals are sometimes seen here. Admission to the trail costs $5 for nonguests. It's also known as Parque Ecológico Gucumatz. Across the street from the biotope is **Restaurante Biotopín** (tel. 4587-9155, 7am-5pm Fri.-Sun.), serving snacks, barbecued meats, burgers, hot dogs,

and other picnic fare in an open-air dining room facing the woods. There are basic accommodations ($7 pp) and a trail leading to a swimming hole ($2.50 admission). Farther along the highway at Km. 158.5 is ★ **Hotel y Restaurante Ram Tzul** (tel. 5908-4066, www.ramtzul.com, $48 d), with comfortable accommodations in wooden cabins, all with private bath. A large restaurant tastefully constructed using 3,500 bamboo shoots serves good food three meals a day. The lodge is on a private 150-hectare forest preserve. A 45-minute hike leads to a pretty waterfall. Another lodge on a private forest reserve is **Posada Montaña del Quetzal** (Km. 156.5 on the road to Cobán, tel. 5800-0454, www.hposadaquetzal.com, $36-46 d), where you have a choice of staying in standard rooms or family-size bungalows. There are firm beds and an on-demand hot-water heater. The rooms can be moldy, which is common in these cold, humid parts. There are two swimming pools, table tennis, and a trail leading to a waterfall 30 minutes away.

Getting There

Any bus heading along the Cobán-Guatemala Highway can let you off at the biotope, though be sure to let the driver know you're getting off here. The entrance is at Km. 160.5.

Maya Cloud Forest Lodge

a quaint family-run inn and café. The delicious homemade food includes sandwiches, breads, cookies, and cakes. There are also smoked meats for sale. Double rooms in the main house with tiled floor, cable TV, large, firm beds, tasteful decor, and private hot-water bath go for $45. Bungalows range from $30 for a unit accommodating two people to $100 for a large, six-bed cabin. Camping in a covered area with cooking facilities, shower, bathroom, and a common area with table tennis, foosball, and a swimming pool is a great value at $7 per person. Bonfires and nighttime lightning bug shows between April and June are among the fun activities available.

The restaurant and lodge are on Country Delight's own private reserve, but there are also other reserves adjacent to the property: **Reserva Natural Privada Llano Largo** and **Reserva Privada Santa Rosa.** Combined, they are roughly the same size as the Quetzal Biotope. The lodge can arrange visits to both.

PURULHÁ AND VICINITY

As you continue along the road toward Cobán, the next sizable town is Purulhá. Though the town itself is unremarkable, there are several important stops on the biological corridor along the road in the vicinity of town and farther east from the town itself.

Reserva Natural Privada Montebello

The private nature reserve and restaurant known as **Reserva Natural Privada Montebello** (tel. 7953-9234 or 7953-9215) sits along Km. 164 of CA-14. The specialties are a tasty chicken stew and traditional pastries. A small shop sells locally made handicrafts, and there are nature trails for hiking amid several pleasant streams crisscrossing the property.

Accommodations

At Km. 166.5, ★ **Reserva Natural Privada Country Delight** (tel. 5514-0955, countrydelight@hotmail.com, 7am-7pm daily) is

CHELEMHÁ CLOUD FOREST PRESERVE

A turnoff at CA-14's Km. 180 heads east for 22 kilometers to the town of Tucurú, from where it's another 26 kilometers via a rugged dirt road passable only in a four-wheel-drive vehicle to the fantastic **Chelemhá Cloud Forest Preserve.** This privately managed protected area comprises 500 hectares of primary cloud forest and is part of the **Sierra Yalijux mountain range,** said to harbor Guatemala's highest density of quetzal populations. The reserve forms part of an important migratory corridor to and from the Sierra de las Minas.

On the outskirts of the reserve, the ★ **Maya Cloud Forest Lodge** (tel. 5308-5160 or 5303-8708, www.chelemha.org, 2-night package deal for 2 people $367) is a comfortable, well-equipped wooden cabin built right into the side of the mountain in an environmentally friendly manner. Each of its four rooms comes with private hot-water bath and two beds. There are a lounge, dining area, and an observation deck with outrageous views of the forest-clad mountains in the vicinity. Its Swiss-born manager serves delicious European and international dishes for breakfast, lunch, and dinner. Activities include hikes through the reserve along trails with local Q'eqchi' guides, visits to a local village, wildlife-viewing, and, of course, bird-watching. This is one of the best places in the country to spot a quetzal.

Volunteer opportunities in the reserve are available through **Unión Para Proteger el Bosque Nuboso** (UPROBON, uprobon@chelemha.org), which manages the park. It also offers opportunities for scientific study and research.

Cobán

Pleasant Cobán sits amid evergreen forests and coffee-studded mountains, making an excellent gateway for exploring nearby natural attractions. It has good hotels and food, as well as a tranquil country atmosphere. A small national park lies square in the middle of town. Though it is no stranger to urban sprawl and noise, the tranquility of this small town quickly reveals itself to you as you walk down its quieter side streets away from the noisy central area.

Cobán can sometimes feel a bit dreary, as much of the year sees the presence of a rainy mist known as *chipi-chipi,* though it's not nearly as prominent nowadays because of local climate change from deforestation. Still, there's something upbeat about this place and the abundance of nearby natural wonders gives it an entirely different feel from towns in the Western Highlands.

The town and its surroundings are an important gourmet coffee-growing center and also produce cardamom and allspice for export. The town is often referred to as the "Imperial City," owing to its charter by Emperor Charles V in 1538. More recently, in the 19th century Cobán saw an influx of German families, who came to dominate the local culture and economy owing to their fortunes made growing coffee for export. The United States pressured the Guatemalan government to remove the Germans from the country during World War II. There are still bits of German influence here and there, giving the city its distinctive air.

Cobán is home to a yearly folklore festival taking place in late July or early August known as **Rabin Ajau,** in which a Mayan beauty queen is selected from among various hopefuls. Another important event is the annual **orchid show** held here in December.

A number of excellent outfitters have regular departures for the Lanquín caves and Semuc Champey as well as the Quetzal Biotope and points farther afield. Cobán makes a great place to regroup and get information before heading out on deeper explorations of all that Las Verapaces have to offer.

An excellent resource for planning a trip can be found online at www.cobanav.net.

SIGHTS
Parque Central
Cobán's triangular central park is interesting in that it is on a hilltop from which the rest of the town drops off in all directions. The cathedral contains the remains of a large, cracked church bell. A block behind the cathedral is the town's market.

Templo El Calvario
For many, this whitewashed church dating to 1810 holds greater significance than the town's cathedral because of its prominence as a site for Q'eqchi' religious rituals on altars lining the long staircase leading up to it. Among the themes represented at its different altars are the granting of wishes for love and health, among others. The inside of the temple is virtually covered with votive candles, while

hundreds of corncobs hang from the roof. Outside, there are fantastic views of Cobán and the rolling green hillsides all around. To the southeast is Mount Xucaneb, the highest point in Alta Verapaz. To get there, head west from the main plaza up 1a Calle and then north two blocks on 7a Avenida. You'll see the long, winding staircase heading up to the temple.

Museo El Príncipe Maya

The excellent private Museo El Príncipe Maya (6a Avenida 4-26 Zona 3, tel. 7952-1541, museoprincipemaya@yahoo.es, 9am-6pm Mon.-Sat., $2) harbors an impressive collection of artifacts, including carvings in mother-of-pearl and jade, polychromatic pottery, ceremonial objects, tools, and weapons. Among the highlights is a Classic-period hieroglyphic panel from Cancuén and an Olmec crystal figurine with decidedly Asian features. The museum gets its name from a figurine of a Mayan prince dressed in full regalia, including a quetzal-feather headdress.

Finca Santa Margarita

Cobán has some of Guatemala's best coffee, so it's only fitting that you might have the opportunity to go behind the scenes and see the process of how the morning elixir makes it from a bush to your Bodum. The Dieseldorff family's Finca Santa Margarita (3a Calle 4-12 Zona 2, tel. 7951-3067, 8am-12:30pm and 1:30pm-5pm Mon.-Fri., 8am-noon Sat., $5) is a working coffee farm where excellent, 45-minute guided tours are available in English or Spanish. You will get up close and personal with the process governing the planting, picking, roasting, packaging, and exporting of these wonderful beans. At the end of the tour, you're treated to a cup (or two) of coffee fresh from the roaster and can buy a bag (or several) of the farm's excellent coffee. The more exclusive "special" selection is a steal at just $5 per pound. You can also enjoy their coffee in a very pleasant café at Plaza Magdalena Shopping Mall.

Vivero Verapaz

Lovers of orchids will find nirvana at Vivero Verapaz (Carretera Antigua de Entrada a Cobán, tel. 7952-1133, 9am-noon and 2pm-4pm daily, $1.50). This wonderful nursery is just outside of town and has several hundred species of orchids on display. The best time of year to visit is between October and February, when many of the flowers are in bloom. The national orchid show is held here in December and is reportedly magnificent. A guide is on hand to show you around and will lend you a magnifying glass for viewing miniature orchids. Guatemala's national flower, the rare *monja blanca,* can be seen here in season. Otto Mittelstaedt, the original collector of the nursery's orchids, has died, but the nursery lives on. Vivero Verapaz is about a 40-minute walk from the central plaza, two kilometers southwest. A taxi costs about $4.

Orquigonia

Orchid enthusiasts will also love Orquigonia (Km. 206 on the road to Cobán, tel. 4740-2224, www.orquigonia.com, 9am-5pm daily, $4). A guided tour takes visitors along a 1-kilometer trail where they can view over 200 species of orchids, birds, tree frogs, butterflies, and ferns while learning about the history of orchid cultivation in Guatemala as far back as the Maya.

SHOPPING

Plaza Magdalena Shopping Mall (1a Calle 15-20 Zona 2, tel. 7952-2124, www.plazamagdalena.com) is where you can go to find goods from industrialized nations you might need while on the road or catch a movie. Its pleasant architecture pays homage to the city's German roots. Run by a handicrafts cooperative, Aj K'uubanel (Diagonal 4, 5-13 Zona 2, tel. 7951-4152) has a variety of textiles, maize and wax art, and silver jewelry for sale.

RECREATION

Cobán has a variety of nearby attractions that can be visited in one day as well as numerous outfitters that can get you there. Popular day trips include the Semuc Champey pools and the **Lanquín caves.** Although these can certainly be done in a day, they are worth a stay of at least one night, as there are comfortable accommodations and plenty to see and do. If you have the time, stay overnight in Lanquín.

Another day-trip option includes the **Quetzal Biotope,** about one hour south of Cobán.

North of town, along Km. 24 on the road heading to Chisec, is the **Sachichaj waterfall,** another increasingly popular attraction. Most of the following tour operators can get you there.

Guide Companies

Since the last edition of this guide, it seems the level of service provided by several local tour operators has gone downhill. Common complaints included issues with punctuality, unsafe driving practices, and involuntary bumping from full shuttles. One reputable company that is recommended is **Cobán Travels** (5a Avenida 2-28 Zona 1, tel. 7951-3528, www.cobantravels.com), offering day trips to Semuc Champey and the Lanquín caves in comfortable vans with breakfast, lunch, and park admissions included ($45). You can also book transport-only options to Semuc Champey ending up in Lanquín. Other options include trips to the Quetzal Biotope, Laguna Lachuá, and adventure activities like white-water rafting and rappelling. They're also the best option for shuttle transport.

Proyecto Ecológico Quetzal (2a Calle 14-36 Zona 1, tel. 7952-1047, www.ecoquetzal.org) is a local NGO working with indigenous people in two communities near well-preserved areas of cloud and rainforest in Chicacnab (southeastern Alta Verapaz) and Rokjá Pomtilá (near Laguna Lachuá) to offer economic alternatives to deforestation via sustainable tourism. Guides are rural Q'eqchi' Maya who know the forest intimately and have received thorough training as nature guides. Trekkers to these remote parts stay in the guides' homes, which have been fitted with beds, toilets, and boiled drinking water, among other basic comforts. It allows

for a true cross-cultural experience as well as a means for providing locals with a viable alternative to the destruction of the fragile ecosystem they call home. Your chances of spotting a rare quetzal are also fairly good. A two-night trip to Chicacnab costs about $55 per person, including guide, food, and accommodations with additional nights available for about $15 apiece. A two-night stay at Rokjá Pomtilá also costs $55.

ACCOMMODATIONS

In the budget range is **Casa Luna** (5a Avenida 2-28 Zona 1, tel. 7951-2922, www.cobantravels.com/casaluna, $7 pp in bunk bed to $16 d), where there are clean rooms, pleasant public areas for lounging, and nice extras like laundry service and free wireless Internet.

West of the central plaza and being renovated at the time of my most recent visit is **Hotel La Posada** (1a Calle 4-12 Zona 2, tel. 7951-0588, www.laposadacoban.com.gt, $60 d), in a 400-year-old colonial mansion with tiled floors, Guatemalan accents, and attractively tiled private hot-water bathrooms. The main drawback here is its location right in between the town's two busiest roads. Under the same management as the bare-bones Hostal de Doña Victoria, **Alcazar de Doña Victoria** (1a Avenida 5-34 Zona 1, tel. 7952-1388, www.hotelescoban.com/alcazar.htm, $40 d) is a much larger, 50-room operation. The spacious rooms centered around a courtyard have firm beds and private hot-water bathroom, though rooms on the first floor can be a bit damp. All have tile floors and cable TV. There are a café and bar as well as banquet halls (which can be noisy). Beautiful ★ **Casa Duranta** (3a Calle 4-46 Zona 3, tel. 7951-4188, info@casaduranta.com, www.casaduranta.com, $60 d) has 10 tastefully decorated, well-appointed rooms—all with private baths—with Guatemalan indigenous blankets, tiled floors, and wrought-ironworks inside and outside the rooms. There are a TV lounge, a reading area, and wireless Internet throughout the colonial house centered round an appealing courtyard. An on-site café is open for three meals daily.

Outside of town and in a class all by itself on the road into Cobán from Guatemala City is Italian-owned ★ **Park Hotel** (Km. 196.5 Carretera a Cobán, Santa Cruz Verapaz, tel. 7955-3600, www.parkhotelresort.com, $40-65). It's situated on its own 15-acre forest preserve and has many excellent amenities, including a gym, tennis courts, nature trails, and even a small zoo. Its 96 comfortable and well-decorated rooms are an excellent value starting at $40 for a standard double room with all the usual amenities, though they are near the road and tend to be noisy. A better option is a junior suite ($60 d). Try to book one in the Firenze building, where odd-numbered rooms have a view of sprawling gardens and a fishpond under a quaint wooden bridge. Suites with a living room and chimney are also available ($65 d), but these tend to feel smaller than the junior suites. Italian food is the specialty at one of its restaurants, while the other is a Uruguayan steakhouse. The gift shop sells orchids. On the way in to town at Km. 204.5, **Casa Kirvá** (tel. 4693-4800, www.casakirva.com, $80 d) is set back far enough from the highway so as to be quiet and peaceful. A neocolonial building houses comfortable rooms on two floors overlooking the area's sylvan landscape. There are flat-screen cable TVs in the rooms and wireless Internet access in the lobby. A restaurant serves three meals daily. A swimming pool rounds out its decent list of amenities. Also outside of town is ★ **Guatefriends Cobán** (Km. 205, Aldea Chicuxab, tel. 4013-4687, $15 pp in dorm to $40 d). You're essentially staying in someone's home, but the location 10 minutes outside of town overlooking forested mountains, and the host family itself, couldn't be friendlier. The gorgeous house is made entirely of wood, brick, and stone and quite cozy. You'll feel right at home.

FOOD

Arguably offering the best food in town, ★ **Casa D'Acuña** (4a Calle 3-11 Zona 2, tel. 7951-0482 or 7951-0484, www.casadeacuna.com, 6:30am-10pm daily) is a bistro-style restaurant in a pleasant garden courtyard. It serves a variety of excellent international dishes, including great pasta ($5-6), pizzas, meat dishes, homemade breads and pastries, salads, and sandwiches. The orchid collection here is exquisite, and there's a small shop selling farm-fresh eggs and pastries. Another good dining option can be found at **Café and Restaurant La Posada** (1a Calle 4-12 Zona 2, tel. 7952-1495 or 7951-0588,

Casa Kirvá

one of the many orchids adorning Casa D'Acuña

www.laposadacoban.com.gt), inside the Hotel La Posada. The café (1pm-8:30pm Wed.-Mon.) is at the far end of the building and looks out onto the plaza. The fancier restaurant (7am-9:30pm Mon.-Sat., 7am-11am Sun.) is set in an attractive dining room with a fireplace and two terraces facing a garden. The food at both is excellent, though the service is notoriously slow. The menu includes Guatemalan and international dishes.

Another popular dining option is Venezuelan-owned ★ **La Abadia** (Calle Belice 3-98 Zona 3, tel. 7952-1782 or 5788-6532, www.abadiacafe.com/gt, $7-13). Set in a cozy colonial-style house, the restaurant serves a unique fusion of Guatemalan and Venezuelan flavors. There's a good selection of wines to pair with your meal. **El Peñascal** (5a Avenida 2-61 Zona 1, tel. 7951-2102, 7am-11pm daily, $7-13) is the place to go for regional specialties, including tasty *kakik,* but the more original cardamom steak steals the show.

There are a variety of decent cafés in

Cobán, among them the café at **Casa Duranta** (3a Calle 4-46 Zona 3, tel. 7951-4188, www.casaduranta.com, 7am-10am and 3pm-8pm daily), where the specialty is crepes (sweet and salty) as well as sandwiches and pastas. **Xkape Kob'an** (Diagonal 4, 5-13 Zona 2, tel. 7951-4152) does a variety of coffee drinks but specializes in local dishes such as chicken stew, tamales, and *kakik* in addition to pastries in a pleasant atmosphere with rustic wooden tables in a garden setting. There is artwork for sale and the café is managed by the Artisans' Association of Verapaz. Finca Santa Margarita has a very pleasant coffee house at Plaza Magdalena Shopping Mall. **Diesseldorf Kaffee** (1a Calle 15-20 Zona 2, tel. 2381-9393, 7am-9pm daily) serves wonderful coffee, espresso beverages, and pastries in a modern atmosphere.

There are several cheap eats lining the central plaza, the best (and safest) of which is **Empanadas Argentinas,** on the north end next to Telgua, where you can savor a tasty chicken empanada for just $1.

INFORMATION AND SERVICES
Tourist Information
Cobán has an **INGUAT office** (1a Calle 3-13 Zona 1, info-coban@inguat.gob.gt, 8am-4pm Mon.-Fri., 9am-1pm Sun.) on the north end of the plaza.

Communications
The **post office** is on the corner of 2a Avenida and 3a Calle one block southeast of the main plaza. **Telgua** is right on the plaza, on the north side, with card phones outside.

Money
Banco Industrial has a Visa ATM at 1a Calle and 7a Avenida, Zona 1. **Banco G&T Continental** has a branch at 1a Calle and 4a Avenida, across the street from Hotel La Posada, with a versatile 5B ATM. There's another branch at 1a Calle and 2a Avenida, Zona 3. You can change travelers checks and dollars at all of these.

Laundry
Lavandería La Providencia (8am-noon and 2pm-5pm Mon.-Sat.) is on the south side of the plaza. It costs about $3.50 to wash and dry a load.

GETTING THERE
Bus
The situation with public bus transport in Cobán is rather chaotic, as different buses heading for different places leave from various parts of town despite the presence of (in theory) a central bus terminal. (You can find complete bus schedules for virtually any place you might want to go from Cobán at www.cobanav.net/bus.php.) That being said, buses to Guatemala City via **Transportes Escobar Monja Blanca** (tel. 7951-1793) depart from a bus station at 2a Calle 3-77 Zona 4 every 30 minutes between 2am and 5pm. Departures from the so-called "Terminal Nueva" (New Terminal) near the soccer stadium are limited to Tactic (every 30 minutes), the Quetzal Biotope (every 30 minutes), El Estor (six buses daily), and Fray Bartolomé de las Casas via Pajal (five buses daily).

Microbuses to Lanquín leave from 3a Calle near the Posada de Don Juan Matalbatz. Buses for San Juan Chamelco (4a Calle and 4a Avenida Zona 3) and San Pedro Carchá (2a Calle and 4a Avenida Zona 4) leave every 20 minutes. Buses to San Juan Chamelco also reputedly leave from the Wasen Bridge, Diagonal 15, Zona 7, every half hour.

Shuttle Bus
Cobán Travels (5a Avenida 2-28 Zona 1, tel. 7951-3528, www.cobantravels.com) runs shuttle service to Antigua, the Guatemala City airport, Lake Atitlán, Quetzaltenango, and Flores.

Car Rental
Several car-rental companies (though none of international stature) have offices in Cobán. The best of these is **Tabarini Rent A Car** (8a Avenida 2-27 Zona 2, tel. 7952-1504, www.tabarini.com).

Lanquín and Semuc Champey

Lanquín and its caves, along with the turquoise pools of Semuc Champey, are quickly becoming requisite stops for travelers making their way through Guatemala. Recreational opportunities abound, and you may find yourself spending more time here than you had originally planned. Whether it's exploring caves, white-water rafting, river tubing, or swimming that suits your fancy, you'll find plenty to see and do in these parts.

LANQUÍN
From Cobán, a paved road diverts northeast through coffee and cardamom plantations to

El Pajal Junction, where there is a turnoff for a dirt road that twists and turns for another 12 kilometers to the small town of Lanquín. Lanquín is home to some interesting caves and has some comfortable accommodations to use as a base for exploring the nearby countryside.

Lanquín Caves National Park

The **Lanquín Caves National Park** (8am-6pm daily, $4) lie one kilometer northwest of town. They are several kilometers long, though only a small part is open to visitors. Although there are diesel generator-powered lights, these sometimes fail, so bring a flashlight and good shoes for navigating the slippery, guano-laden surfaces inside. The entire cave system has yet to be fully explored or mapped, so don't wander too far into the cavern's core. There are some interesting stalactites to be found here.

Another highlight of a visit to these caves is the thousands of bats flying out from the cavern at dusk. The Río Lanquín also flows out of this cave and forms a turquoise ribbon meandering through the surrounding jungle. It's perfect for a refreshing swim.

★ Rafting the Río Cahabón

In addition to the caves, Lanquín serves as a departure point for white-water rafting trips down the Class III-IV Río Cahabón. **Maya Expeditions** (tel. 2366-9950, www.mayaexpeditions.com) pioneered white-water rafting in Guatemala starting in 1987 and was named one of the "Top 20 Eco-Outfitters in the World" by *Condé Nast Traveler*. The outfit takes groups to both the upper and lower gorges as day trips ($115/155), but it also has various options for 3-to 6-day adventures ($210-678). The complete six-day adventure begins in Guatemala City and includes stops at the Quetzal Biotope, Cobán, Lanquín, Semuc Champey, and the Candelaria caves in addition to rafting both the upper and lower gorges of the Cahabón. A newer option is **Rafting Guatemala** (tel. 5069-3518, www.guaterafting.com), offering 12-kilometer and

along the road to Lanquín

19-kilometer river trips on the Río Cahabón ($35/45). Both trips end in the village of Tamax. They work with a four-person minimum. It's a community tourism initiative based in the village of Saquijá that employs local guides.

Both outfitters provide basics such as food, transport, and equipment.

Accommodations and Food

One of the hippest backpacker hotels in all of Central America lies 500 meters along the road from Lanquín toward the village of Cahabón. ★ **El Retiro** (tel. 3225-9251, www.elretirolanquin.com, $4-46) offers a variety of accommodations for all budgets in a splendid setting beside the Río Lanquín. The new suites are tastefully decorated with private baths and electric hot-water heater ($46 d with a/c). There are hammocks out front for taking in the wonderful vistas toward the river and surrounding hillsides. A bed in one of the four-person dormitories costs $7. Rooms with shared bath are also available, and range $13-20 for a double. You can camp here or sleep in a hammock for $4. The *palapa*-style bar plays great music and is lined with rope-swing bar seats. The restaurant's creative lunch menu includes tuna melts, *chiles rellenos,* and Thai eggplant curry, with dinner being a nightly communal buffet experience. The lodge can arrange a variety of activities for you, including inner tubing on the river for $7 (includes beer and guide), transport to Semuc Champey, and white-water rafting.

Also in this neck of the woods is wonderful ★ **Zephyr Lodge** (tel. 5168-2441, www.zephyrlodgelanquin.com, $10 pp in dorm-33 d). The beautiful lodge is housed in several thatched-roof structures and has a fun, feel-good atmosphere along with some amazing views of the surrounding countryside. Shared-bath dorm rooms start at $10 per person but there are also rooms with private bathroom and a deck overlooking the splendid scenery. There's great food, including delicious pizza made in a wood-fired oven, and a well-stocked bar. Tours include Semuc Champey, the Lanquín caves, river tubing,

and a zipline. A swimming pool overlooking the grand landscape rounds out the lodge's list of wonderful amenities.

On the other end of town as you come in to Lanquín from the El Pajal Junction is **Hotel El Recreo** (tel. 7823-4069, $20-31), with rooms in a wooden main house or in an adjacent concrete structure. The main house has a lower-level section with shared-bath rooms for $20 (d). The lighting is fluorescent. Nicer rooms with private bath are $31 (d). This lodge is usually empty unless there's a tour group in town. There's a restaurant here, too.

Other options for food include **Comedor Shalom,** near the Hotel Rabin Itzam, with set-menu lunches and dinners comprised of mostly meat and rice dishes for around $2.

El Muro Lanquín (tel. 5413-6442 or 4904-0671, www.elmurolanquin.com, $3 pp in hammock, $6 pp in dorm, $20 d in private room) is a lively hostel that is well located in the heart of town. The restaurant/bar here is a good place to grab a drink or a bite to eat and there's a nice open-air terrace for taking in the natural surroundings.

a Class IV rapid on the Río Cahabón

The Raging Rapids of the Río Cahabón

Guatemala's best white-water river is the Class III-IV Río Cahabón. In addition to the exhilarating rapids, the traverse downstream on its emerald waters is interspersed with more tranquil stretches that afford opportunities to view several species of birds and explore caves, waterfalls, and hot springs along its forested banks.

The Cahabón is the same river that flows into a cave under the limestone pools of Semuc Champey, reemerging several hundred meters downstream. Most river trips begin at a put-in point near Lanquín. There are some rather menacing rapids along this stretch of the Upper Cahabón, including Rock and Roll, Entonces, and Las Tres Hermanas, making for an adrenaline-filled ride. The Middle Gorge has some nice jungle scenery and continuous Class III rapids. There are a few more challenging rapids after passing the bridge at a place called Oxec before reaching an obligatory takeout point at Takinkó to portage the Class VI (not possible to run) Chulac Falls. A dam was once planned here, but dam builders seem to have gone cold on the idea after discovering a fault line running right beneath the proposed site. The two-day river trip camps here.

The Lower Gorge is a boatload of fun with titillating rapids such as Saca Corchos (Corkscrew) and Saca Caca. There are stops along the way to explore caves and enjoy lunch at "El Pequeño Paraíso," a small sidestream with delightful waterfalls and hot springs flowing into the Cahabón. The next rapid is appropriately named Lose Your Lunch, shortly after which the river widens and you are treated to a serene stretch of river with mountainous jungle-clad banks. The takeout is at Cahaboncito, where the intrepid can take a plunge into the river from a 30-foot bridge.

Rafting the Cahabón affords the opportunity to see some remote natural attractions and come in contact with the local people inhabiting the area. As is often the case in Guatemala, the beauty coexists with a sobering reality. In addition to still-forested areas you will see some steep, badly deforested slopes given over to corn cultivation, shedding light on the desperate plight of peasants willing to live and grow their crops anywhere they can.

Cuevas de K'an Ba

Along the road from Lanquín to Semuc Champey, in the vicinity of **Posada Las Marías** (tel. 4068-3399, www.posadalasmarias.com), you'll find these rather interesting caves on the lodge's private property. There are wonderful opportunities for exploring the **Cuevas de K'an Ba** by floating through on inner tubes ($5 for hotel guests, $7.50 for nonguests). You'll see several formations and underground waterfalls before emerging onto the clear, turquoise waters of the Río Cahabón. The trek through the caves involves climbing waterfalls with the aid of a rope or ladder and jumping into pools in virtual darkness. It's not for the faint of heart. El Retiro and Zephyr Lodge also organize trips to the caves.

★ SEMUC CHAMPEY NATURAL MONUMENT

The gorgeous limestone pools of the **Semuc Champey Natural Monument** (6am-6pm daily, $7) lie at the end of a rough dirt road nine kilometers from Lanquín. Although they were once considered a remote attraction far off the beaten path, they are now one of Las Verapaces's top tourist draws. Accordingly, infrastructure has improved to keep up with the rising numbers of visitors, though the rough road to get here still makes it an adventure. Try not to visit on a weekend, as there are daytrippers in droves from Cobán and vicinity.

A giant, 300-meter-long limestone bridge forms the backbone for the descending series of pools and small waterfalls that make up Semuc Champey. The water that fills the pools is the product of runoff from the Río Cahabón, churning as it plunges into an underground chasm from where it reemerges downstream at the end of this massive limestone overpass.

Recreation

In addition to **swimming** in the perfectly

Semuc Champey in moonlight

There are a few hotels just minutes away from the park entrance. Up the road just 400 meters past the entrance to Semuc Champey is the friendly, Israeli-owned **Greengo's Hotel** (tel. 4002-0066, www.greengoshotel.com). There are two sets of dorms ($7 pp) or you can stay in brightly-painted, A-frame wooden cottages next to a rushing river for $33 d. All are on a shared-bath basis, but they do get bonus points for hot-water-showers. There's a decent restaurant and even a sand volleyball court. One quirk is that you'll need to leave a cash deposit for towels and sheets upon check-in. Heading back toward Lanquín from Semuc Champey, the first place you'll come across is **Hostal El Portal de Champey** (tel. 4091-7878, www.elportaldechampey.com, $7 pp to $30 d) where there are also A-frame cottages set on a hillside overlooking the Río Cahabón. Bring mosquito netting if you're staying in the dorms, as the cabins housing them are open-ended. An on-site restaurant serves passable fare.

A better option lies about one kilometer from Semuc Champey. **Posada Las Marías** (tel. 4068-3399, www.posadalasmarias.com) enjoys a wonderful riverside location and offers accommodations in dorms with shared bath ($7 pp), rooms with shared bath ($10 d), or rooms with private bath ($20 d). The restaurant serves three meals a day ($4-7) and the menu includes sandwiches, nachos, and barbecued steak. Activities include inner tubing on the Río Cahabón and visits to the nearby caves of K'an Ba ($5 for guests), where you can explore an underwater river.

Utopia Eco Hotel (tel. 3135-8329 or 3056-9178, www.utopiaecohotel.com, $4 pp in hammock, $7 pp in dorms, $20 d in shared-bath private room, $49 d in riverfront cabin with private bathroom and hot-water shower) is three kilometers from Semuc Champey and enjoys a splendid location on the banks of the Río Cahabón. Accommodations run the gamut from a hammock lounge to riverfront cabins and include camping or dorm rooms in between. It's a good place for outdoor

placid pools, you can travel a series of **trails** and hanging wooden bridges to the sites where the river makes its underground plunge and where it reemerges downstream. It is truly awe inspiring to see the force of nature as the raging river is crammed into an underground cavern. A longer, 1.2-kilometer trail heads straight up the side of a mountain to a fantastic **lookout point,** where you can see the pools from above. It's worth the substantial effort required to climb on the steep mountainside, sometimes with the help of vines and tree roots. Closer to the park entrance is a walkway that will take you to an **observation platform** where you can see a pretty waterfall gushing into the Río Cahabón over the point where it reemerges from its cave.

Across from the parking lot and park entry booth, you'll find a nearly abandoned visitors center with bathroom facilities. Vehicle parking costs $1.30. Guides are available here to take you around, as are plenty of local children looking to sell you trinkets.

adventures, including overnight hikes and camping trips ($30) and extreme inner tubing on the river ($8). More serene options include 700 feet of riverside to enjoy, along with a rope swing and sundeck. There's a full restaurant and bar. Spanish lessons start at $75 per week.

Getting There

Most of the local lodges in Lanquín and Semuc Champey offer transportation and guided tours to the park. There are also several tour companies in Cobán operating day and overnight trips to Lanquín and Semuc Champey. Shuttle-only options are available and highly recommended as the best way to get here. From Cobán, **Cobán Travels** (5a Avenida 2-28 Zona 1, tel. 7951-3528, www.cobantravels.com) runs shuttle transfers and overnight tours. They can also get you there from Antigua.

If you're driving, you'll need a four-wheel-drive vehicle for the road from El Pajal to Lanquín. The road onward to Semuc Champey deteriorates badly in the rainy season.

Hourly buses (5am-5pm) from Lanquín to Cobán cost $4. There are six microbuses and at least two shuttles a day to Cobán.

Northern Alta Verapaz

Northern Alta Verapaz is quickly gaining momentum as the site for a varied assortment of ecotourism options thanks to its location along the corridor connecting Alta Verapaz and Petén on a good paved road. Among the highlights in this neck of the woods is Laguna Lachuá National Park. It will be interesting to see how this area grows and develops during the next several years with the ever-increasing presence of international tourism. For now, the scene here is very low-key, but it won't be that way forever. Get out and explore this part of Guatemala, where there are relatively few visitors, while you can.

LAS CONCHAS POOLS

Near the nondescript town of Fray Bartolomé de las Casas lies Las Conchas, a series of limestone pools and waterfalls on the Río Chiyú, 50 kilometers east toward Izabal. The pools are rather large and great for swimming, though the water is not of the sweet emerald color found at Semuc Champey. There is a small picnic area.

The falls' remote location means you may find yourself needing to spend the night in the area. This is also an increasingly popular backdoor route to Izabal and Río Dulce. You can easily combine a trip to the waterfalls with a stay at a nearby jungle camp. **Oasis Chiyú** (tel. 4668-3519 or 4826-5247, www.naturetoursguatemala.com, $20 d) is a 10-hectare (25-acre) working farm and lodge owned by a transplanted American, beautifully situated at the confluence of two jungle rivers. The gorgeous views of the surrounding jungle, rivers, and waterfalls alone are worth the price of admission. The lodge serves delicious vegetarian fare ($5-9). Meals are prepared on a wood-burning stove using fresh ingredients and include vegetarian specialties such as fried rice, pastas, curries, hummus, sandwiches, and salads. Bikes and kayaks are available to explore the surroundings, and guided hikes can take you to nearby waterfalls, mysterious caves, sultry jungles, and cool rivers. This is your chance to really become one with nature: no phones, fax, email, or electricity—truly an oasis of tranquility. The lodge was recently remodeled after 10 years in business.

CHAHAL

The closest settlement near Las Conchas is Chahal, which is fairly unremarkable but nonetheless offers at least one hotel worthy of mention. **Hotel Villa Santa Elena** (Franja

Transversal del Norte Km. 365, tel. 4011-6472 or 4032-4053, www.hotelvse.com, $39 d) offers basic, clean rooms with hot water, plastic furniture, and good beds housed in a neocolonial building built around a patio. Some of the rooms have air-conditioning and most have private bathroom. The restaurant here serves very good food.

★ PARQUE ECOLÓGICO HUN NAL YE

This eco-amusement park and museum lies down a dirt road turn-off from Km. 259.5 along the road from Cobán to Chisec (RD-09). **Parque Ecológico Hun Nal Ye** (tel. 7951-5921, www.hunalye.com, 8am-6pm Wed.-Sun., $13 adults, $7 children) is a private reserve sprawling across 135 hectares of tropical rainforest with an abundance of plant and animal life and bisected by emerald green rivers and lagoons. Activities include bird-watching (over 200 species of birds have been recorded), fishing, tubing, kayaking, snorkeling, and scuba diving. There's a cave, an eight-meter (26-foot) waterfall, a limestone sinkhole (*cenote*), observation towers, a canopy zipline, and trails for horseback riding, all-terrain vehicles, and mountain bikes. Facilities include a restaurant, archaeology museum, picnic areas,

changing rooms, and a swimming pool. You can stay at the comfortable on-site accommodations consisting of five neocolonial tile-roofed cabins ($79 d) with private baths.

Lest Hun Nal Ye strike you as just another theme park, you should know that it lays claim to the very important discovery of an ancient Mayan box engraved with exquisite hieroglyphs and dating to Early Classic times. It was discovered in 2005 by landowner Leonidas Javier and is thought to have once harbored a Maya codex, or book. The box made headlines when it was stolen by looters in 2006 and returned anonymously about a month after it was reported missing from the cave. The item had been purchased on the black market by a collector who, in an apparent attack of conscience, shipped the item to the Ministry of Culture in Guatemala City after realizing the priceless value of his purchase from widespread publicity of the heist. A replica of the box is housed in the park's museum; the original is now in Guatemala City's Museo Nacional de Arqueología in Zona 13.

To get to the park, take the dirt road turn-off heading east from RD-09 at Km. 259.5. From there, it's about six kilometers to the village of Samanzana, where you'll head south

a river at Hun Nal Ye

for one kilometer and then continue east another five kilometers to San Vicente Chicatal. From there, follow the signs another 500 meters to the park entrance. If you don't have a car, there are buses and pickup trucks heading from the Cobán-Chisec road to San Vicente Chicatal.

PLAYA GRANDE (CANTABAL)

This remote outpost in the northwest corner of Alta Verapaz was once the scene of intense fighting during the civil war, with regular military operations in the neighboring Ixcán jungles, where URNG rebels hid out. All that is now in the past, opening some wonderful attractions that were once off-limits. Heading northwest from Chisec, it's a 62-mile journey down a rough dirt road to the town of Playa Grande, also known as Cantabal or Ixcán. There is little to see or do here, but nearby is a remarkable natural attraction.

★ Laguna Lachuá National Park

This almost perfectly circular turquoise lagoon is its own ecological island, like a square patch of forest floating on a surrounding sea of deforestation. To see it from the air is to get a crash course in tropical forest management and the significance of ecological islands. The razor-sharp park boundaries stand out from the quiltlike fields all around this giant mirror in the middle of nowhere. You'll probably arrive by land, but this description at least gives you some appreciation for the natural beauty of this park and the need to protect it from those who might further encroach upon its boundaries. Already, logging operations have unscrupulously harvested some of the forest's giant mahoganies with reckless disregard for what is, on paper at least, a national park. In 2013, indigenous peasants cut down over 3,000 trees in the park next to an adjacent road. But I digress.

Laguna Lachuá

The 14,500-hectare **Laguna Lachuá National Park** (tel. 4084-1706, $7) is still one of the most beautiful places on earth, despite its challenges. Here you can enjoy the refreshing waters and the dense forest all around in an atmosphere of utter tranquility. From the banks of the lagoon, you can see the forested peak of La Sultana. There are more than 300 species of birds found here, including mealy parrots and keel-billed toucans. Jaguars still roam the park, and you can sometimes see their footprints. The lagoon's Caribbean-like waters contain calcium deposits and high levels of sulfur, indicating the probable presence of petroleum beneath its waters. The lake lies partially below sea level, at an altitude of 173 meters above sea level but also 222 meters deep. One of the more exciting theories concerning the lake's formation contends the lakebed is an old meteor crater, with the rest of the meteor that created it having fallen near Cobán in an area known as the Nim Tak'a depression.

There's a visitors center where you'll find cooking facilities, a campground, a shelter with bunk beds ($7 pp), showers, hiking trails, and canoes for rent ($3). You can string a hammock or pitch your own tent for $3.50.

The park's main entrance is a few kilometers before Playa Grande as you come along the road from the east. From there it's a four-kilometer walk to the lakeside through some very nice forest trails. After the first 2.4 kilometers, you'll come to a pier. The second pier and swimming area (also where the accommodations are) is another 1.8 kilometers away.

Petén

G uatemala's northernmost department conjures images of a remote
wilderness, dense forests, and lost
Mayan cities.

Today, that image is only partly true, as much of the Ohio-sized Petén has been cleared by settlers for subsistence agriculture and cattle ranching. In an attempt to save the remaining forest and the still unexcavated Mayan ruins they harbor, roughly a third of Petén has been protected since 1990 in the form of several national parks collectively known as the Maya Biosphere Reserve. It is one of the largest remaining continuous tracts of tropical forest in Central America. Recreational opportunities inside and outside the reserve are boundless and the region is slowly becoming a magnet for adventure and ecotourism, thanks in large part to the filming of *Survivor Guatemala* here in 2005.

Among the attractions are the enigmatic Mayan ruins of Tikal, one of the largest cities ever populated by the Mayans and certainly a must-see for any visitor to the area. Not only are the restored ruins impressive, to say the least, but the abundant wildlife found in the lush rainforests protected within the adjacent national park makes this a prime spot

for birders and wildlife enthusiasts. Along the paved road to Tikal, you'll pass the spectacular Lake Petén Itzá, one of Guatemala's largest, surrounded by jungles and characterized by its luminescent turquoise-blue waters. The village of El Remate has sprung up along the highway and is quickly becoming a destination unto itself with a number of very comfortable accommodations and plenty of activities for the outdoor enthusiast. Many travelers now spend an extra day here after exploring the ruins.

Southeast of Tikal, the remote ruins of Yaxhá, overlooking the site's namesake lagoon, remain a remote jungle outpost despite their prime-time TV fame, and you can still have the place all to yourself on a typical afternoon. But that probably won't last too much longer.

Petén is without a doubt the cradle of Mayan civilization, as it lays claim to some of the oldest known Mayan sites along with the earliest evidence of the writing and royal dynastic rule characterizing the civilization

Previous: Lake Petén Itzá; atop Tikal's Temple IV. **Above:** a colorful detail in Flores.

Look for ★ to find recommended
sights, activities, dining, and lodging.

Highlights

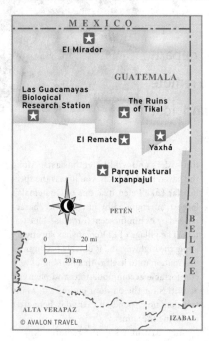

★ Parque Natural Ixpanpajul: The hanging bridges and nature trail here provide a toucan's-eye view of the Petén forests (page 303).

★ El Remate: Once a sleepy lakeside fishing village, El Remate provides access to beautiful Lake Petén Itzá and a variety of recreational opportunities such as kayaking, swimming, birdwatching, and horseback riding (page 308).

★ The Ruins of Tikal: No trip to Guatemala would be complete without a visit to the enigmatic ruins of one of the largest cities ever built and inhabited by the Maya (page 318).

★ Yaxhá: Featured in *Survivor Guatemala,* the ruins of Yaxhá enjoy a spectacular location beside the site's namesake lagoon and provide commanding views of the surrounding forests (page 329).

★ El Mirador: Deep in the northern recesses of the Maya Biosphere Reserve, the ruins of El Mirador offer world-class adventure in an arduous two-day journey through swampy forests (page 332).

★ Las Guacamayas Biological Research Station: Observe nesting scarlet macaws with the knowledge that the money you spend is going directly toward their survival (page 339).

that flourished here. At the remote site of El Mirador, on the northern fringes of Petén near the Mexican border, you can gaze in awe at the massive temple pyramids of El Tigre and La Danta, which were erected centuries earlier than most other well-known Mayan sites but nonetheless show much the same level of sophistication. All of these sites are harbored within the Maya Biosphere Reserve and its seemingly interminable expanses of mostly undisturbed tropical forests. Hikers will appreciate the numerous opportunities for trekking to remote Mayan ruins along jungle paths, creating the potential for adventures not unlike those of the early explorers.

HISTORY

During colonial times, Petén remained a backwater, the only Spanish settlement being the island city of Flores, a pleasant town of pastel-colored houses that remains the region's main tourist services hub. In 1840, Guatemalan President Rafael Carrera dispatched a small platoon of soldiers to officially claim the Petén region as part of the country. Mexico decided the territory was not worth the trouble of contesting. The region has been a backwater ever since, officially the poorest of Guatemala's departments, which is especially evident to travelers coming in from Belize along an unpaved highway lined with cattle ranches and simple thatched-roof huts.

Petén harbors 550,000 of Guatemala's inhabitants, making it the country's most sparsely populated region, though its rate of population increase from immigration is the highest in the country. Much of this unprecedented growth is the product of an ill-conceived 1960s government program to colonize Petén, meant as a safety valve to relieve pressures for land reform. A battle is being waged to save this valuable natural and cultural heritage, and visitors to Guatemala's northern parks can derive some satisfaction from the knowledge that their visit lends importance, justification, and the financial means for the continued preservation of what remains.

PLANNING YOUR TIME

Petén is one of Guatemala's most fascinating regions, particularly for lovers of archaeology and outdoor activities. The parks encompassing the Maya Biosphere Reserve could keep you busy for weeks, in addition to the requisite visit to Tikal National Park. Some people make day trips to Tikal, coming across the border from Belize or flying in from Guatemala City. This will certainly serve only to whet your appetite for more Petén explorations. Visitors on one of these short stints should at least consider spending the night at Tikal or nearby Lake Petén Itzá. Another increasingly popular destination is the archaeological site of Yaxhá, site of *Survivor Guatemala.* There is a comfortable jungle lodge right on the shores of Yaxhá Lagoon where you can spend the night, a good idea if you want to take in all that this site has to offer, given its remote location.

El Mirador, deep in the jungle near the Mexican border, involves an arduous journey of two days from the nearest village but is well worth it for the opportunity to visit one of the largest and earliest Mayan cities in existence. The tallest, and some of the largest, manufactured pre-Columbian structures can also be found here in the form of the massive La Danta and El Tigre pyramids, with bases the size of three football fields. A typical round-trip itinerary to El Mirador takes 5-7 days, depending on how long you want to stay at the ruins and if you want to stop at other nearby sites on the way back.

The most natural starting point and hub for any in-depth Petén explorations is the island city of Flores, with its pretty pastel-colored houses and quiet streets; it's unlike any other town in Guatemala. Its sister city of Santa Elena, on the mainland shores of Lake Petén Itzá, is an equally logical choice for a base, though it's not nearly as attractive. Many conservation organizations and adventure travel outfitters are based in Flores/Santa Elena. Air and ground service connects Flores/Santa Elena to most of Petén, other parts of Guatemala, and Belize.

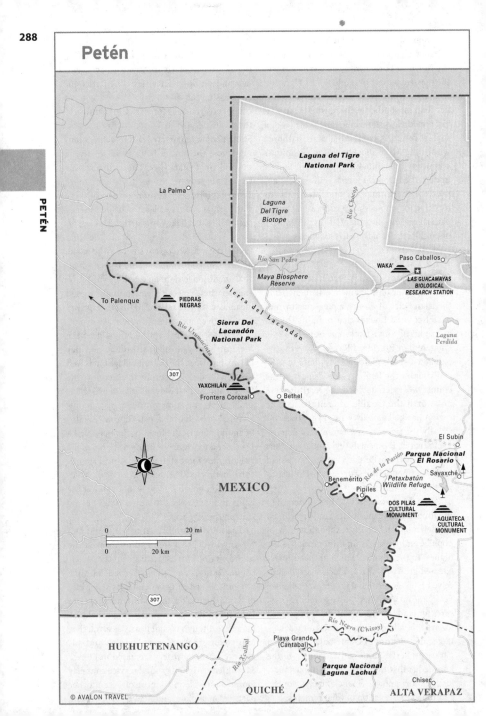

Petén

Laguna del Tigre
National Park

Laguna
Del Tigre
Biotope

La Palma

Río Chocop

Río San Pedro

Paso Caballos

WAKA'

LAS GUACAMAYAS
BIOLOGICAL
RESEARCH STATION

Maya Biosphere
Reserve

To Palenque

PIEDRAS
NEGRAS

Sierra del Lacandón

Laguna
Perdida

Río Usumacinta

Sierra Del
Lacandón
National Park

307

YAXCHILÁN

Frontera Corozal   Bethel

El Subín

Parque Nacional
El Rosario

Río de la Pasión

Sayaxché

MEXICO

Benemérito

Petexbatún
Wildlife Refuge

Pipiles

DOS PILAS
CULTURAL
MONUMENT

AGUATECA
CULTURAL
MONUMENT

0   20 mi

0   20 km

307

Río Negro (Chixoy)

HUEHUETENANGO

Playa Grande
(Cantabal)

Río Xcalbal

Parque Nacional
Laguna Lachuá

Chisec

© AVALON TRAVEL

QUICHÉ   ALTA VERAPAZ

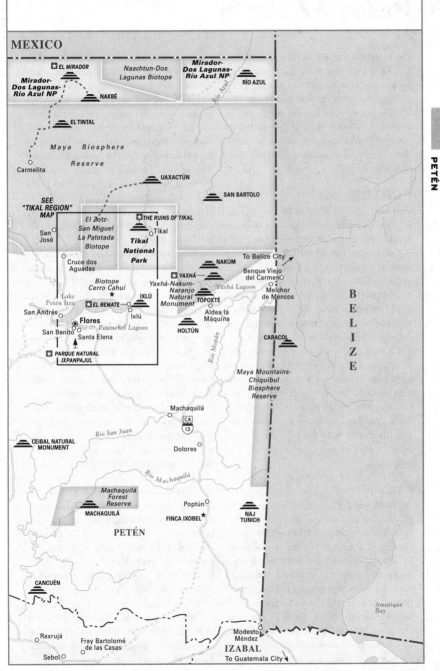

Poptún and Vicinity

The small town of Poptún is unremarkable in and of itself, but there are a number of good recreational opportunities in the vicinity. Travelers coming from Guatemala City often break up their journey with a stay in Poptún's landmark Finca Ixobel. In the vicinity of Poptún are numerous caves, jungle rivers, and forests easily explored with help from area lodges.

POPTÚN

Halfway between Río Dulce and Flores, Poptún has always been a favorite stopping point, particularly before the road to Flores was paved and travelers needed to split up the grueling journey on a rutted dirt road. Nestled in the foothills of the Maya Mountains, which extend into neighboring Belize, the area is unlike the rest of Petén in that it is cooler by virtue of its altitude at more than 600 meters (2,000 feet) and features a largely pine-forested, karst landscape. There are many relatively unexplored Mayan sites here as well as some small expanses of tropical forest, which have survived the expansion of the agricultural frontier to which most of southern Petén has succumbed. A military base once operated in this area, but it has been closed down since the 1996 peace accords, as elsewhere in Guatemala.

Recreation

Poptún's wonderful setting at a comfortably higher altitude and its pine-studded, karst landscape make exploring this part of Guatemala a delight. You can choose from, among others, treks to remote Mayan sites, jungle hikes, caving, or tubing down lazy stretches of jungle river. All of these activities can be arranged at area lodges, particularly Finca Ixobel (on the road from Río Dulce, tel. 5410-4307, www.fincaixobel.com), which pioneered ecotourism in this neck of the woods and is always interested in new offerings. You can choose from a number of caves, which can take two hours, a half day, or a full day of exploring. The full-day trip takes you to Cueva del Río, an underground river with rapids and waterfalls where you can swim and leap into the river in total darkness. There are also trips twice a day to Ixobel Cave, with its rim stone walls, stalactites, and stalagmites a 45-minute walk from the farm. Just 25 minutes' walk from Finca Ixobel, Echo Cave offers a fun adventure exploring the cave's hidden chambers and caverns, and it is a good option if you have only two hours' time.

Horseback riding is also available at the Finca Ixobel with trips lasting as little as two hours or as much as two days ($53). A full day of horseback riding costs $23.

Finca Ixobel also runs a number of excellent multiday jungle adventures lasting a minimum of three days, with a two-person minimum. The treks take you to remote Mayan sites such as Ixcún, a replica of the caves of Naj Tunich, and waterfalls on the Río Mopán. All trips are on horseback.

Inner tubing on the Machaquilá River from Finca Ixobel ($25, including lunch and transportation) is possible in June and July, when the water is high enough but before the summer rains are in full swing.

Accommodations and Food

There is at least one good place to stay in Poptún proper, though you are probably better off staying at one of the local, highly recommended jungle lodges. Should you get stuck in town, Hotel Posada de los Castellanos (tel. 7927-7222, corner of 4a Calle and 7a Avenida, $10 d) is your best bet with basic, clean rooms with fan and private hot-water bath. For eating, La Fonda Ixobel (Avenida 15 de Septiembre, tel. 7927-7363) has tasty baked goods, sandwiches, and meat dishes. There's also a full bar.

Naj Tunich

The **Naj Tunich caves** have long been a local attraction and were even featured in the August 1981 issue of *National Geographic*. The caves, which are more than one kilometer long, are famous for their intricate murals and hieroglyphic text. Naj Tunich appears to have been one of the most highly revered sites in the Mayan world, and it is known that several of the glyphs were painted by scribes from such faraway cities as Calakmul, in present-day Mexico.

The caves were defaced some years ago, and the site was closed to visitors. A replica of the caves showcasing some of the best of the Naj Tunich cave paintings is located just 400 meters from the original caves. Check with the staff at **Finca Ixobel** (tel. 5892-3188, www.fincaixobel.com) for details.

Services

Banrural (5a Calle, 8:30am-5pm Mon.-Fri., 9am-1pm Sat.) has a MasterCard ATM and changes U.S. dollars and American Express travelers checks.

Getting There

The Poptún area is accessible via several buses and minivans leaving Flores daily at half-hour intervals during daylight hours. **Línea Dorada** (Avenida 15 de Septiembre 9-71 Zona 2, tel. 7924-8434, www.lineadorada.com.gt, $15-30 one-way) has buses from Guatemala City (10am and 9pm daily), stopping in Río Dulce and Poptún along the way. Buses arrive and depart on Playa Sur in Flores.

Buses heading north from Guatemala City via Río Dulce also come this way and stop at Finca Ixobel, Poptún, and Machaquilá.

NEAR POPTÚN
Finca Ixobel

Just south of Poptún, on the road from Río Dulce, ★ **Finca Ixobel** (tel. 5410-4307, www.fincaixobel.com, $3-49) has long drawn travelers coming overland to Petén for its wonderful accommodations and excellent food

at moderate prices in an attractive jungle setting. Its wide-ranging activities allow guests the chance to explore myriad attractions nestled in the surrounding cool pine forests and rolling green hills. There are accommodations to suit every taste and budget, including hammocks ($3), clean, comfortable dorms for $6 per person, double rooms with shared bath for $18, and rooms with private bath for $41 d. There are more luxurious bungalows and a suite for $41 and $49 d. The latest addition to Finca Ixobel's offerings is a series of tree houses set amid spacious grounds. Some have electricity; others are candlelit. Prices range from $18 d with candlelight to $32 d with electricity. Only one of the so-called tree houses is actually in a tree, but all are attractive, quite comfortable, and set above the ground.

The restaurant here serves delicious, inexpensive meals, largely using ingredients grown in the finca's vegetable garden. Breakfast and lunch are à la carte, while dinner is served buffet style ($5-10). Breakfast items include homemade yogurt and granola, pancakes, and eggs, with plenty of vegetarian options for lunch and dinner. There is also a bar set beside a swimming pond where you can chill out in a hammock or play a game of "Twister" with your new friends and fellow travelers.

Any bus traveling the Río Dulce-Flores Highway will drop you off at the turnoff to Finca Ixobel. From there, it's just a short 15-minute walk to the lodge. You can arrange minibus transport to Flores and book bus tickets to Guatemala City from Finca Ixobel. Minibuses go by every half hour 8am-5pm and cost $7 one-way. Transport to Guatemala City on Linea Dorada bus lines ranges $13-20 one-way. If you are arriving at Finca Ixobel after nightfall, your best bet is to go to La Fonda Ixobel in Poptún town and get a cab from there to the farm.

DOLORES

At first glance, Dolores, north of Poptún, appears to be just another roadside town in rural Petén. But closer inspection reveals it harbors a decent archaeology museum and several lesser-known Mayan sites in its vicinity. Set on a hill in the heart of town, **Museo Regional del Sureste de Petén** (museodolores@mcd.gob.gt, 8am-5pm daily, $4) holds an impressive collection of artifacts and stone sculptures excavated from sites in the southeastern portion of the Petén lowlands. The displays are well presented and include descriptions in Spanish and English. Most of the items on display are ceramic pottery. There are wonderful views of the town and its jungle surroundings from the museum's courtyard.

Ixcún and Ixtontón

Ixcún is a large Mayan site showing signs of occupation from Preclassic times on through the Postclassic period. It is believed to have been the most important of four cities located in the upper Mopán Valley and subservient to the larger kingdom of Caracol, lying 35 kilometers northeast in present-day Belize. Ixcún is just 6 kilometers north of Dolores via a rough dirt road. It's about an hour's walk, or you can take a cab for $5. The site itself occupies about 16 square kilometers and includes a ball court, palaces, stepped pyramids, and several stelae (including the second-largest stela in the Mayan world). Most of the site remains unexcavated, consisting of overgrown temple mounds, and was most recently excavated by the Atlas Arqueológico de Guatemala, which runs the Museo Regional. It enjoys a peaceful park-like setting, with a splendid jungle location. The Mopán River flows just 4 kilometers

sculpture at Museo Regional del Sureste de Petén

from here. There are ranger facilities and a covered pavilion for camping. Admission is $4 and it's open 8am-5pm.

Ixtontón is a smaller Mayan site that once rivaled Ixcún. It's along the banks of the Mopán River, 2 kilometers east of Dolores and about 6 kilometers from Ixcún. Although it wasn't officially discovered until 1985, it had already been looted of artifacts prior to that. Only two of its stelae survived and are on display in the Museo Regional.

Flores

In the heart of Petén, the twin towns of Flores and Santa Elena are often referred to simply and collectively as "Flores." The latter is actually limited to a small island on Lake Petén Itzá connected to Santa Elena, on the mainland, by a causeway. Flores is a pleasant island town unlike any other in Guatemala with pastel-colored houses and quiet streets. Santa Elena is a bit noisier and more chaotic because of its prominence as Petén's main commercial center. Farther west, Santa Elena runs into the downright ugly town of San Benito.

Flores is the natural starting point for a visit to Petén's wild interior, as it is the region's transportation and services hub. Many NGOs are based here, and the quiet streets are

Flores and Santa Elena

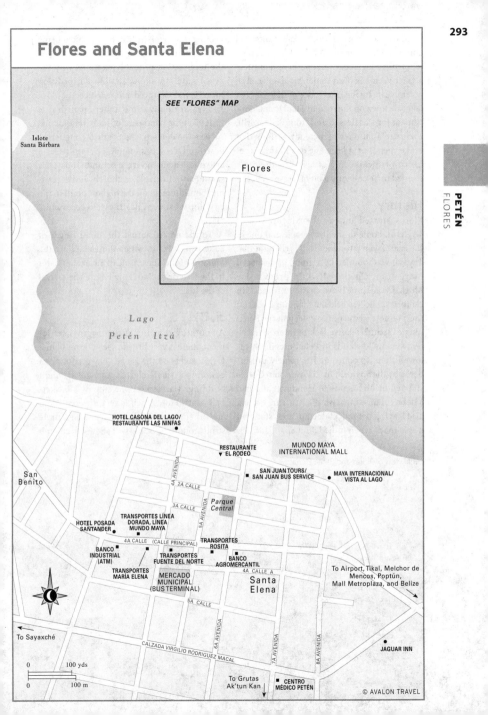

Islote
Santa Bárbara

SEE "FLORES" MAP

Flores

Lago
Petén Itzá

HOTEL CASONA DEL LAGO/
RESTAURANTE LAS NINFAS

RESTAURANTE
▼ EL RODEO

MUNDO MAYA
INTERNATIONAL MALL

■ SAN JUAN TOURS/
■ SAN JUAN BUS SERVICE

MAYA INTERNACIONAL/
VISTA AL LAGO

San
Benito

4A AVENIDA

2A CALLE

3A CALLE

5A AVENIDA

Parque
Central

HOTEL POSADA
SANTANDER ●

TRANSPORTES LÍNEA
DORADA, LÍNEA
MUNDO MAYA

TRANSPORTES
ROSITA

4A CALLE   (CALLE PRINCIPAL)

BANCO
INDUSTRIAL
(ATM) ■

TRANSPORTES
FUENTE DEL NORTE

■ BANCO
AGROMERCANTIL

TRANSPORTES
MARÍA ELENA

MERCADO
MUNICIPAL
(BUS TERMINAL)

4A CALLE A

Santa
Elena

To Airport, Tikal, Melchor de
Mencos, Poptún,
Mall Metroplaza, and Belize

5A CALLE

6A AVENIDA

7A AVENIDA

8A AVENIDA

←
To Sayaxché

CALZADA VIRGILIO RODRÍGUEZ MACAL

0   100 yds

0   100 m

JAGUAR INN ●

To Grutas
Ak'tun Kan ↓

■ CENTRO
MÉDICO PETÉN

© AVALON TRAVEL

lined with a variety of shops, restaurants, and comfortable lodgings. While Flores is excellent from a logistical standpoint and entirely attractive, it has been somewhat displaced in recent years by the emergence of El Remate, a lakeside town on the road to Tikal that is convenient for travelers to and from Belize. Still, there are a number of local attractions that make spending at least one day in the Flores area worthwhile, and at last visit the town seemed to be enjoying a bit of a resurgence.

History

Flores started out as the Mayan site of **Tayasal,** home to the Itzá people and one of the last Mayan strongholds. It is thought that Tayasal was founded by a group of displaced Maya from Chichén Itzá, in present-day Mexico, sometime between the 13th and 15th centuries. The Itzá held out for quite a while in their remote island outpost deep in the Petén jungle. Spain's relative lack of interest in the hot, steamy lowlands of Petén inevitably allowed them to continue life largely unhindered by the Spanish. In 1525, Hernán Cortés stopped by on his way to Honduras and had a peaceful meeting with the Itzá king Canek, also leaving behind a lame horse. A statue of it was made when it died, and Spanish friars

visiting the region in 1618 would find it being worshipped by the Itzá. The friars destroyed the idol, which probably explains why the next round of visitors, a military expedition in 1622, was captured and sacrificed.

Tayasal finally came under Spanish rule in 1697 at the command of Martín de Ursúa. As was the custom, the Spanish conquerors destroyed the city's temples, pyramids, and artwork, leaving no trace behind. Today, the small Flores town plaza, church, and government buildings sit on the highest point in the city atop what was once Tayasal's ceremonial plaza.

To the north, across the small finger of Lake Petén Itzá in which Flores lies, are the remains of the Mayan site of Tayazal. It dates to the Classic period, long before the arrival of the Itzá.

SIGHTS

As nothing remains of the original settlement, there is very little to see in terms of historical sights on the island. The quaint plaza contains a small church and government buildings flanked on one side by a basketball court. Flores itself is very different from any other town in Guatemala, and a leisurely stroll around the island will allow you enough

aerial view of Flores and Santa Elena

Flores

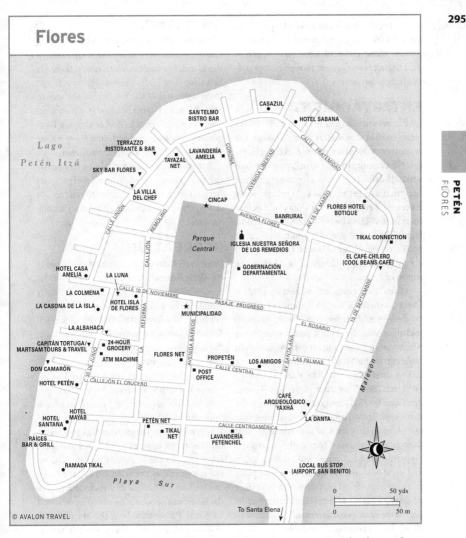

Lago
Petén Itzá

SAN TELMO
BISTRO BAR
CASAZUL
HOTEL SABANA
TERRAZZO
RISTORANTE & BAR
LAVANDERÍA
AMELIA
CALLE FRATERNIDAD
TAYAZAL
NET
CORONA
AVENIDA LIBERTAD
SKY BAR FLORES
LA VILLA
DEL CHEF
CINCAP
REMOLINO
AVENIDA FLORES
FLORES HOTEL
BOTIQUE
AV 15 DE MARZO
CALLE UNIÓN
BANRURAL
Parque
Central
IGLESIA NUESTRA SEÑORA
DE LOS REMEDIOS
TIKAL CONNECTION
CALLEJÓN
EL CAFÉ CHILERO
(COOL BEANS CAFÉ)
HOTEL CASA
AMELIA
LA LUNA
GOBERNACIÓN
DEPARTAMENTAL
CALLE 10 DE NOVIEMBRE
LA COLMENA
HOTEL ISLA
DE FLORES
PASAJE PROGRESO
15 DE SEPTIEMBRE
LA CASONA DE LA ISLA
REFORMA
LA ALBAHACA
MUNICIPALIDAD
EL ROSARIO
CAPITÁN TORTUGA/
MARTSAM TOURS & TRAVEL
24-HOUR
GROCERY
AVENIDA BARRIOS
FLORES NET
PROPETÉN
LOS AMIGOS
AV SANTA ANA
LAS PALMAS
ATM MACHINE
30 DE JUNIO
AV LA
DON CAMARÓN
CALLE CENTRAL
POST
OFFICE
Malecón
HOTEL PETÉN
C. CALLEJÓN EL CRUCERO
CAFÉ
ARQUEOLÓGICO
YAXHÁ
HOTEL
MAYAB
PETÉN NET
LA DANTA
HOTEL
SANTANA
TIKAL
NET
CALLE CENTROAMÉRICA
RAÍCES
BAR & GRILL
LAVANDERÍA
PETENCHEL
RAMADA TIKAL
Playa Sur
LOCAL BUS STOP
(AIRPORT, SAN BENITO)

0   50 yds
0   50 m

To Santa Elena

© AVALON TRAVEL

time to take in the funky pastel architecture and the quiet streets. One addition to Flores's infrastructure is the *malecón,* or waterfront walkway, spanning the entire island. Parts of the *malecón* are prone to periodic flooding due to rising lake levels.

CINCAP (Centro de Información sobre la Naturaleza, Cultura, y Artesanía de Petén, tel. 7926-0718, 10am-noon and 2pm-8pm Mon.-Fri.) is housed in the Castillo de Arismendi on the north side of the park. It serves as an

information center on Petén's culture and natural history and holds a small gift shop.

If you're really into caves and won't have time to explore the areas of southern Petén or Las Verapaces, you might want to check out **Ak'tun Kan** (8am-5pm daily, $1.50), also known as the *cueva de la serpiente* for the large snake said to inhabit it. To get there, follow 7a Avenida south out of Santa Elena until you get to the power plant. Turn left to get to its east side, and continue south another kilometer. A *tuk-tuk* can also take you there for just a few quetzales. There's a museum on a small island just across the main boat hub next to Raíces restaurant, though it's not particularly impressive.

ENTERTAINMENT

Like many small towns in Guatemala, Flores tends to shut down after dark. Though the restaurants mentioned here are perfectly fine for stopping in for a drink, you may find yourself drinking alone. Depending on the season, it can get very quiet here, and some places may even shut their doors well before their posted 1am closing time. On weekends, locals like to party, and if you are up for it, you can certainly mingle with them at any of a number of establishments. Just follow the sound of music.

Aside from being a fine restaurant, **La Luna** (corner of Calle 30 de Junio and Calle 10 de Noviembre, tel. 7867-5443, noon to midnight Mon.-Sat.) has a pretty swanky bar where you can enjoy the very atmospheric old building in which it's housed under a whirring ceiling fan. Right on the lake, **Raíces Bar and Grill** (tel. 7867-5743, 2pm-10pm Sun.-Thurs., 2pm-1am Fri.-Sat.) is a great place to catch the sunset while you enjoy your favorite cocktail. Also in this neck of the woods is **Don Camarón** (11:30am-11pm daily), a seafood restaurant and bar with chill lakeside vibes and good beats on the stereo. It's a nice place to enjoy some fried shrimp and a cold beer while enjoying the lake breezes. A classy addition to the island's bar offerings is **Cantina El Remolino** (corner of Calle 10 de Noviembre and Avenida La Reforma, inside Hotel Isla de Flores; tel. 7867-5176, www.hotelisladeflores. com, 2pm-11pm daily), housed in a wonderfully restored old hotel that evokes feelings of Havana or Panama City's restored Casco Antiguo. Its second-floor rooftop terrace affords **Sky Bar** (Calle Unión, tel. 5522-0318, 5pm-1am daily) some of the best sunset views around. It's a fun, friendly place with great cocktails. There are tasty pizzas for when you get hungry.

SHOPPING

There are several handicrafts stores lining Calle Centroamérica, on the south side of the island. For more modern needs, there are two shopping malls nearby. **Mundo Maya International Mall,** just across the way in Santa Elena and immediately east of the causeway, has a modern selection of shops, a large grocery store and a movie theater. Burger King and Pollo Campero outlets are adjacent.

Metroplaza (9am-8pm daily) lies across the road from Mundo Maya International Airport and has a Pizza Hut, electronics stores, a travel agency, and a pharmacy among its stores.

RECREATION

You can rent **kayaks** and **mountain bikes** at **Re-Cicle Rentals** (Playa Sur, tel. 4770-4908, 8am-6pm Tues.-Sun.) for $26 for a 24-hour rental, $20 for a full day (business hours) or $4 per hour. The **Ramada Tikal** (Playa Sur, tel. 7867-5549, www.ramadatikal.com) just down the street also rents both for $5 per hour for guests and nonguests.

The other main recreational option involves **lake tours** offered by various boat operators congregating at the embarcaderos opposite Hotel Santana and on Playa Sur. Direct *colectivo* boats ($1) can take you across the lake to the town of San Miguel and leave from a dock next to Posada de Don José on the north end of the island. The lake tours can be had for $20-25 and include a trip to the lakeshore opposite the island's northwest corner to **Petencito Zoo,** the Mayan ruins of **Tayazal,** and **ARCAS,** a wildlife rescue center.

Guide Companies

Flores makes a natural starting point for trips into the wilderness because of its central location within Petén and its proximity to roads leading from here in all directions. The following recommended outfitters can hook you up with one day or multiday adventures to Petén's increasingly popular parks and archaeological sites.

Highly recommended, **The Mayan Adventure** (tel. 5830-2060www.the-mayan-adventure.com) is run by the owners of Café Yaxhá, who are very knowledgeable about the region. Trip options include the usual sites such as Tikal and Yaxhá, but also some lesser-known communities they work with. They can also organize trips to El Mirador, which is no easy task. **Tikal Connection** (Mundo Maya International Airport, tel. 5575-4335, www.tikalcnx.com) works with local communities to involve them in the business of sustainable tourism in and around several of Petén's protected areas. Tikal Connection offers multiday treks from the site of El Zotz to Tikal, rigorous journeys to El Mirador, and the "Scarlet Macaw Trail," in Laguna del Tigre National Park near the Mayan site of Waka'.

Martsam Tours and Travel (Calle 30 de Junio in the lobby of Capitán Tortuga restaurant, tel. 7926-0346 or 7832-2742, www.traveltoursguatemala.com) has an excellent reputation and offers a variety of trips throughout Petén. In addition to El Zotz-Tikal, Waka', and El Mirador, it offers day trips to Tikal and multiday adventures involving hikes from Tikal to Yaxhá, stopping in Nakum along the way.

ACCOMMODATIONS

For the best value in town head to Flores's hostel, ★ **Los Amigos** (Calle Central next to ProPetén, tel. 7867-5075, www.amigoshostel.com). This backpacker's paradise features a restaurant/bar, security lockers, broadband Internet, and laundry service among its well-rounded list of amenities. The friendly Guatemalan and Dutch owners can also help you plan your travels to other parts of Guatemala. For the ultimate in affordable lodging, you can sleep in a hammock for $5. Other options include dorm beds ($7), private rooms with shared bath ($20 d) or with private bath ($39 d). Best of all, the showers are nice and hot.

On Calle 30 de Junio, a good choice in the budget category is friendly **Green World Hotel** (tel. 7867-5662, $26 d), offering basic but pleasant rooms with hot-water private bathroom, ceiling fan, and comfortable beds. The clean rooms are painted a pleasant light green, evoking tranquility and space. Some upstairs rooms have balconies with lake views for the same price, and there are nice chill spaces upstairs and downstairs. **Hotel Petén** (Calle 30 de Junio, tel. 7867-5203 or 2366-2841, www.hotelesdepeten.com, $56-60 d depending on season) is said to be the island's oldest hotel, dating to 1960. You have a choice of air-conditioning and/or ceiling fan in its smallish but comfortable rooms with private bath and cable TV, some of which have balconies overlooking the lake. A small swimming pool and a dining room are on the ground floor just opposite the lobby. One of my perennial favorites is sister property ★ **La Casona de la Isla** (Calle 30 de Junio, tel. 7867-5200 or 2366-2841, www.hotelesdepeten.com, $60-65 d depending on season), an attractive lakeside house painted in bright yellow and orange hues housing 26 rooms with air-conditioning, cable TV, and private bath. There is a nice outdoor swimming pool, around which the rooms are centered, as well as a whirlpool. The hotel's Isla Bonita restaurant and bar serves three delicious meals a day at reasonable prices.

Casazul (Calle Unión, tel. 7867-5451 or 2366-2841, $46-50 d depending on season) has pleasant rooms with air-conditioning, cable TV, private bath, and minifridge housed in a pretty blue house, as its name would indicate. It has a nice balcony with wonderful lake views. Nearby, ★ **Flores Hotel Boutique** (Calle Fraternidad, tel. 7867-5768, www.floreshotelboutique.com, $127 d) is a great option for those seeking space, privacy, and apartment-like sleeping arrangements. The large suites have fully furnished living rooms and fully stocked kitchens. The four units share a garden patio with a nice fountain, and there's an upstairs patio with a hammock and tables where you can enjoy breakfast or an afternoon cocktail.

An excellent value is **Hotel Casa Amelia** (Calle Unión, tel. 7867-5430, www.hotelcasamelia.com, $53 d). It offers attractive, spotless double rooms with original decor incorporating burlap bags for curtains, wooden furnishings, firm beds, ceiling fans, air-conditioning, and large hot-water bathrooms. Six of the 12 rooms have nice lake views. All have large cable TVs. There's a nice restaurant with very decent food served on an airy patio fronting the *malecón*.

An impressive makeover has transformed the once-lackluster ★ **Hotel Isla de Flores** (Corner of Calle 10 de Noviembre and Avenida La Reforma, tel. 7867-5176, www.hotelisladeflores.com, $78-90 d) into Flores's most fabulous property. I'm a big fan of the architecture and the tasteful use of color throughout. The restoration was done keeping in mind the island's history and architectural heritage. Room amenities include a/c, ceiling fan, and flat-screen cable TV. There are street or lake views from the rooms' blue-shuttered windows. The more expensive suites have minibars and in-room coffeemaker, a nice touch you won't often find in Guatemala. There's a rooftop swimming pool and lounge area, though the pool is somewhat on the small side. The lobby has

a cool restaurant, a very nice little gift shop, and a fun streetside bar.

The island's sole chain hotel is the confusingly named **Ramada Tikal** (Playa Sur, tel. 7867-5549, www.ramadatikal.com, $109 d with breakfast buffet), near the causeway as you come into town on the shore facing Santa Elena. The multistory property is a large building that seems somewhat out of place in mostly low-rise Flores. Rooms include all the usual comforts of its price range such as private bath, air-conditioning, cable TV, and attractive furnishings. There is a good restaurant and bar with an outdoor patio fronting the lake. There are two swimming pools, one of which is under cover. Wireless Internet is freely available in the lobby. Nice extras include a fitness center and kayaks and bikes for rent.

Santa Elena

There's really no reason to stay in Santa Elena unless everything on the island of Flores is booked for some reason. That being said, there are several pleasant accommodations along the lakeshore with wonderful views of Flores. Among the budget accommodations is

the restaurant inside Hotel Isla de Flores

the **Jaguar Inn** (Calzada Virgilio Rodriguez Macal 8-79, tel. 7926-2411, www.jaguartikal.com, $40-54 d), where tastefully decorated rooms are centered around a courtyard and the helpful staff can assist you plan your onward travel. They have free airport and/or bus station transfers. The owners also have a hotel at Tikal National Park by the same name.

Along the lakeshore, as you approach town from the airport, is the **Maya Internacional** (Calle Litoral del lago, Zona 1, tel. 2223-5000 central reservations or 7926-2083 direct, www.villasdeguatemala.com, $70-100), with 24 standard rooms and two junior suites. The rooms differ in newness and decor, so be sure to check them out before committing. The more tastefully decorated rooms have balconies overlooking the lake, tiled floors, ceiling fans, air-conditioning, and cable TV. The lodge's **Vista al Lago Restaurant** offers gorgeous lake views and a varied menu. A swimming pool, wireless Internet, and lovely open-air *palapa* lobby round out the list of features. The property's proximity to a shopping mall and the airport may or may not suit you.

Farther along the lakeshore near the causeway connecting Santa Elena to Flores are a number of newer options, including the 62-room **Petén Espléndido** (tel. 2360-8140, www.petenesplendido.com, $90 d), with the feel is that of a U.S. chain hotel with all the usual amenities. The standout in this part of town is the ★ **Hotel Casona del Lago** (tel. 7952-8700 or 2366-2841, www.hotelesdepeten.com, $90-100 d), a beautiful blue house that could just as easily fit in to the seaside landscape of Cape May, New Jersey. The large, bright rooms have spacious bathrooms, tasteful decor, and the usual comforts, including cable TV. Some have lake views; all are centered around a pretty swimming pool with a whirlpool. The hotel's **Restaurante Las Ninfas** serves varied international cuisine for breakfast, lunch, and dinner in a pleasant dining room overlooking the pool and lake. The lobby is decorated with classic photos from Petén's past dating to the 1920s, 1930s, and 1940s, along with some more modern scenes.

FOOD

Flores has a small grocery store. **La Colmena** (corner Calle 30 de Junio and Avenida 10 de Septiembre, tel. 7926-1268) has a variety of local and imported favorites. It also takes credit cards. There is also a minimart (with an ATM machine) across the street from Capitán Tortuga restaurant on Calle 30 de Junio. The larger La Torre grocery store is across the causeway in Santa Elena's Mundo Maya Mall.

Cafés and Light Meals

Flores has no shortage of coffee shops and cafés, most of which offer something different and equally pleasing, depending on what you're in the mood for.

El Café Chilero (Cool Beans Café) (Calle 15 de Septiembre, tel. 5571-9240, 8am-10pm daily except Tues.) has a wide assortment of hot and cold coffee beverages using gourmet beans from a very well-known coffee farm in Alta Verapaz. It also serves smoothies and light meals in a relaxing jungle garden atmosphere and makes a great place for breakfast.

If you're looking for inspiration before an adventure to one of Petén's numerous archaeological sites, head to ★ **Café Arqueológico Yaxhá** (Avenida 15 de Septiembre, tel. 5830-2060 or 4934-6353, www.cafeyaxha.com, 7am-10pm daily), where you can dine in a pleasant atmosphere featuring colorful Guatemalan tablecloths and photo montages of various Mayan sites, including Tikal, Yaxhá, and Nakum. Although it does a variety of dishes, including steak, chicken, seafood, pasta, and even curry, it specializes in what it calls "pre-Columbian" fare (a variety of Petén-Yucatec dishes), which are highly original and recommended.

For street tacos, check out **Taco Taco** (adjacent to Hotel Santana, lunch and dinner on weekends, $2-3), where you can enjoy your food in a festive Mexican atmosphere.

Steakhouses

On the island's western shore is ★ **Raíces Bar and Grill** (tel. 7867-5743, 2pm-10pm Sun.-Thurs., 2pm-1am Fri.-Sat., $10-20), serving large portions of grilled steak, chicken, and fish with scrumptious side dishes in a hip semioutdoor setting featuring a deck built over the lake. If you're lucky, you might catch a thunderstorm here during the rainy season for a spectacular lakeside lightning show. Alternatively, it makes a great place for a sunset cocktail. Order the kebabs and share with a friend.

Continental

Housed in a tastefully decorated old building festooned with overhanging bougainvillea blossoms and painted in bright shades of green and blue, the finest restaurant in Flores is undoubtedly ★ **La Luna** (corner of Calle 30 de Junio and Calle 10 de Noviembre, tel. 7867-5443, noon to midnight Mon.-Sat., $6-14). Culinary highlights include stuffed peppers, steak in a black pepper cream sauce, boneless chicken breast in wine sauce, pastas, and vegetarian dishes, including falafel. Also on Calle 30 de Junio is **Capitán Tortuga** (tel. 7867-5089, www.capitantortuga.com, 7am-10pm daily). The spacious dining room housed under a large *palapa* structure has lake views, and you can enjoy pasta, tacos, sandwiches, chicken quesadillas, grilled meats, and tasty pizzas in addition to a fully stocked bar. For snacks, try the burritos for about $5. Across the street is ★ **La Albahaca** (tel. 7867-5449, 6pm-11pm Tues.-Sun.), a cozy little place with a quiet atmosphere serving delicious fish, beef, and chicken recipes as well as scrumptious homemade pasta and homebaked bread at reasonable prices. There is a nice assortment of Chilean wines.

On the southern end of Avenida 15 de Septiembre, **La Danta** (tel. 7867-5707, www.ladantarestaurante.com, noon-10pm Tues.-Sun., $5-15) prides itself in delicious fusion cuisine made from fresh ingredients and flavors gleaned from the area's Mayan heritage. They also have tasty crepes for dessert.

There are a number of good choices along Calle Unión, on the island's northwest corner. **La Villa del Chef** (tel. 4211-3849, noon-11pm daily, $4-15) serves a wide variety of

San Telmo Bistro Bar

sandwiches, pasta, chicken, and seafood dishes in an attractive lakeside atmosphere atop a small wooden deck. The *parrillada petenera* ($13) is a good option for sharing, and their new specialty is a tasty, locally sourced rabbit burger. Just down the street, ★ **Terrazzo Ristorante & Bar** (tel. 7867-5479, 7:30am-10pm Mon.-Sat., $5-12) is one of Flores's finest restaurant offerings. The owners have plenty of restaurant experience, having worked as chefs in some of the country's best restaurants. There are delicious panini, pastas, tagliatelle, oven-baked fish fillet in potato, as well as smoothies and a full bar. The ambience is also quite pleasant, set in an airy second-floor terrace overlooking the lake. Chill music plays on the stereo. Also in this area is **San Telmo Bistro Bar** (Calle Unión, tel. 7867-5751, 7am-11pm daily), which scores big points for originality with a varied menu and whimsical decor. It's a hippy-esque kind of place with New Age music on the stereo. There are pizzas, panini, veggie burgers, meat, seafood, Asian noodle dishes, falafel, smoothies, and even kombucha on the menu.

INFORMATION AND SERVICES

Tourist Information

INGUAT has a desk at the airport arrivals area, where staff can answer your questions and help you get your bearings. There is also an office in Flores on **Calle Centroamérica** (tel. 2421-2957, 8am-4pm Mon.-Fri.). Another option for getting tourist information is **Café Arqueológico Yaxhá** (Avenida 15 de Septiembre, tel. 5830-2060, www.cafeyaxha. com, 7am-10pm daily). Its German owner knows a lot about the local Mayan sites and has even authored a guidebook to the Mayan region in his native tongue. It's a great place to learn about Petén's archaeological sites and is often a meeting place for folks working on archaeological digs or environmental projects.

Money

The only bank in Flores is **Banrural**, about a block east of the plaza. There's an ATM inside the minimart across from Capitán Tortuga restaurant on Calle 30 de Junio.

In Santa Elena, three blocks up 6a Avenida from the Flores causeway on the corner of 4a Calle is **Banco Agromercantil** with a MasterCard ATM. Three blocks west, also on 4a Calle, is **Banco Industrial,** with a Visa ATM.

Laundry

The **Laundry Room,** on Calle Central next to ProPetén, is a full-service laundry place. There's also **Lavandería Petenchel,** on Calle Centroamérica, and **Lavandería Amelia,** behind CINCAP.

Emergency and Medical Services

For the **police,** dial 7926-1365. The closest hospital is **Hospital San Benito** (tel. 7926-1459).

Volunteer Work

Volunteer opportunities are available with several of the NGOs working in town. Among the options is the opportunity to volunteer at the **Las Guacamayas Biological Research Station** (tel. 7867-5296, www.propeten.org) in Laguna del Tigre National Park. Another option is working with the local **Wildlife Rescue and Conservation Association, or ARCAS** (tel. 5208-0968, www.arcasguate-mala.com), at its site on the other end of the lake opposite Flores's north shore.

Spanish School

Dos Mundos Spanish School (Calle Fraternidad, tel. 5830-2060, www.thespan-ishschooltikal.com) offers 30 hours of language instruction for $170 per week, plus a $35 enrollment fee. Accommodations options with host family, including meals, start at $100 per week.

GETTING THERE

Air

Flights arrive at **Mundo Maya International Airport** (FRS), a few kilometers outside of Santa Elena east on the road to Tikal. In 2008, the airport underwent a substantial renovation and the facilities are vastly improved (including badly needed air-conditioning). Most flights to the Flores/Santa Elena airport arrive from Guatemala City, with two daily on **Avianca** (tel. 800/400-8222, www.avianca. com) and a handful of smaller local carriers, among them **TAG** (www.tag.com.gt). From Belize City, **Tropic Air** (tel. 800/422-3435, www.tropicair.com) flies to Flores daily. Among the flights to/from Guatemala City, Avianca operates larger, 68-seat ATR-72 turboprop aircraft. TAG's airplanes are substantially smaller. Flights between Guatemala City and Flores are usually in the vicinity of $275 for a round-trip flight.

The only direct service to FRS from the United States, a Saturday-only flight via Houston on Continental Express, was dropped in November 2006 after 18 months in operation. Flights to Cancún, Mexico, were rather inexplicably dropped by Avianca, leaving a potentially large market without air service.

Bus

Linea Dorada (tel. 7926-1788, www.lineado-rada.com.gt, $15-30 one-way) has buses from Guatemala City at 10am and 9pm daily, stopping in Río Dulce and Poptún along the way. There are also daily buses to and from Belize City ($28 one-way), leaving at 7am. Buses arrive and depart from the main bus terminal along 4a Calle in Santa Elena as well as from another office on Playa Sur in Flores (tel. 7926-3649).

You'll find minibuses to Melchor de Mencos, Poptún, and Sayaxché west of the market in Santa Elena on 4a Calle. Buses and minibuses to San José and San Andrés ($2, 40 minutes) leave from 5a Calle, west of the market.

Fuente del Norte (www.grupofuente-delnorte.com) buses make the trip to Belize City daily at 5am. The trip costs $28 one-way. There are 15 daily departures to Guatemala City.

GETTING AROUND
Taxis and *Tuk-Tuks*

You'll find taxis at the larger hotels in Santa Elena and at the Mundo Maya International Airport. A taxi from the airport to Flores should cost no more than $3. More popular and much less expensive are the *tuk-tuks* (Asian-style motorized rickshaws) you'll find seemingly everywhere. Short trips of about a kilometer or two within the Flores and Santa Elena area on *tuk-tuks* are usually in the range of $1.

Shuttle Buses

Shuttle buses and minivans ply the road between Flores and Tikal. **Onca Travel Agency** (Calle Unión, Flores; tel. 5930-1661, oncatravel.wix.com/onca, $20 pp) has hourly shuttles beginning at 4:30am until 10am. Another option with similar scheduling is **Crasborn Travel** (tel. 4637-2411 or 5589-9249, www.crasborntravel.com). Their Tikal sunrise tour leaves at 3am. *Colectivo* buses also ply the road between Flores and Tikal. If arriving at the airport, your best bet is to negotiate a ride with a bus taking a tour group (if not booked in advance) or go across the street to the shopping mall, where roadside pickup on cheap *colectivo* buses is facilitated. Once-frequent *colectivo* buses leaving straight for Tikal from the airport seem to have disappeared with fewer flights flying into FRS utilizing smaller aircraft.

Mundo Maya International Airport

Car Rentals

You'll find several options at the airport upon your arrival. Among them are a few local operations I can't bring myself to recommend. Stick with **Hertz** (tel. 3274-4424 Mundo Maya International Airport or 800/654-3001 U.S., www.rentautos.com.gt).

NEAR FLORES AND SANTA ELENA

There are a variety of attractions in and around Flores and Santa Elena that work well if you have a day or half a day while awaiting connecting flights or onward travel. Several of these attractions—**ARCAS, Petencito Zoo,** and **Tayazal**—are a five-minute boat ride across the lake from Flores's north shore near the village of San Miguel. A road also goes this way along the shoreline and is useful in this discussion for orientation only, as most visitors find themselves catching a boat when heading out in this direction. You can take in 2-3 of these destinations as part of a lake tour leaving from Flores, which should cost between $20 and $25. *Colectivo* boats ($1) leave from a dock beside Calle Fraternidad, on the north shore of Flores, as they fill up.

★ Parque Natural Ixpanpajul

Covering an area of nine square kilometers and conveniently just off the highway toward Guatemala City, the main attraction at **Parque Natural Ixpanpajul** (tel. 2336-0576 or 4062-9812, www.ixpanpajul.com, 7am-6pm daily) is a series of six suspension bridges built over the forest canopy, giving you a toucan's-eye view of the forest. The trip along the forest trail takes a little more than an hour and includes a stop at a lookout point to take in the astounding view from the top of the mountain. Other activities include a Tarzan Canopy Tour (zipline), Spot Lighting (nighttime wildlife-viewing), horseback riding, mountain biking, tractor rides, and ATV rentals. You can tour the hanging bridges (Skyway) for $22 per adult or $13 per child. You also have a choice of mountain biking, tractor rides, or horseback riding, ranging

from $5 to $25. Packages allow you to combine the Skyway with the Tarzan Canopy Tour and/or the Spot Lighting tour for a full day of adventure.

There is a campsite on the premises ($5) and you can rent tents ($10) and other equipment, but you have to book at least one of the main activities. There are also accommodations consisting of comfortable cabins with bunk beds and private bathrooms sleeping up to five people. The park can provide transportation from Flores or Tikal if you call in advance. A taxi from Flores should cost about $7.

Cooperativa Nuevo Horizonte

Seventeen kilometers south of Santa Elena on the road to Guatemala City lies **Cooperativa Nuevo Horizonte** (www.coopnuevohorizonte.org/en), a community of returned refugees and former combatants from the Guatemalan civil war. The cooperative was formed in 1998, when the community was resettled near the town of Santa Ana following the 1996 peace accords.

Nuevo Horizonte offers a fascinating glimpse into Guatemala's sociopolitics. Although each family retains individual ownership of a house and farm plot, the pasturelands, a 250-acre forest preserve, a lake, and plantations of pineapple, pine, and lime trees are collectively owned. The co-op provides free day care, primary and secondary education, adult vocational training, and operates a pharmacy and clinic. The community also keeps two pickups and a minivan for anyone's use. Additional infrastructure includes a welding shop and two corn mills. In an effort to minimize dependence on outside sources, the community maintains its own seed bank.

Many of the community's residents lived in the Petén rainforests during the war years, on the run from Guatemalan government forces. In time, the jungle became a source of food, shelter, and safety, and these experiences provided insights into uses for medicinal plants and food.

Among the cooperative's initiatives is community-based tourism. They are happy to show you around the village and share their stories, and also take great pride in their forest preserve and reforestation program. Rustic cabins and meals from the community are available for visitors.

Las Lagunas Boutique Hotel

As you head east along the road from the airport to Tikal, a dirt road turnoff cuts north toward the Petenchel Lagoon. Just two kilometers down the road you'll find ★ **Las Lagunas Boutique Hotel** (Carretera a San Miguel, tel. 7790-0300, www.laslagunashotel.com, $325-375 d), an absolutely beautiful place on the edge of Quexil lagoon. The very comfortable wooden bungalows are set over the water and include some nice extras like large soaking hot tubs. There's an infinity-edge swimming pool with an adjacent bar for cooling off. The restaurant inside the main building serves delicious international cuisine prepared by its Dutch chef. There's a collection of pre-Hispanic artifacts on display in a room with some interesting taxidermy in addition to a nice gift shop with local crafts. You can tour the property's expansive, 200-acre private reserve, including an island in the lagoon

inhabited by playful spider monkeys. Other activities include kayaking, bird-watching, and four-wheeling.

Hotel Villa Maya

About four kilometers in, along the road to San Miguel, is the excellent **Hotel Villa Maya** (tel. 2223-5000, www.villasdeguatemala.com, $85 d), with its 56 comfortable, tastefully decorated rooms equipped with air-conditioning, hot water, and balconies overlooking the placid lagoon. There are also a swimming pool and an excellent restaurant. It's a bit out of the way, but the exclusive feel of this jungle outpost only adds to its allure.

Petencito Zoo

Farther west along this same road leading to the village of San Miguel is **Petencito Zoo** (8am-5pm, $5), housing a collection of local wildlife, including jaguars, monkeys, and macaws. The concrete waterslides (only recommended for the intrepid and/or foolhardy) were closed at last visit. It's not my favorite place in these parts and part of me wonders if it should be shut down, as it has a derelict feel to it these days. Come here only if you have lots of time to spare.

a room at Las Lagunas Boutique Hotel

ARCAS

Continuing west, the road again connects the larger Lake Petén Itzá to **ARCAS** (tel. 5208-0968, www.arcasguatemala.com), the Wildlife Rescue and Conservation Association, where an animal rehabilitation center harbors animals captured from poachers, including jaguars, macaws, monkeys, and coatis. Although the animal rehabilitation area is not open to outsiders, an **Environmental Education and Interpretation Center** caters to the casual visitor. There is a nature trail showcasing a variety of medicinal plants, a beach, a bird observation platform, and an area for observing animals that cannot be reintroduced to the wild. Captive breeding programs for scarlet macaw populations have been very successful, and they are also a key player in the fight to save emblematic species such as jaguars and spider monkeys.

Tayazal

Not to be confused with Tayasal, which once occupied the same territory as present-day Flores, the remains of this small site of **Tayazal** can be found up a hill near the village of San Miguel. Although the ruins themselves are not overly impressive, there is a wonderful lookout, known as a mirador, built into a tree atop a temple mound from where you have an exceptional view of Flores. The lookout is about two kilometers outside of town. Follow the signs for the "mirador."

Lake Petén Itzá

Once a pit stop for travel between Flores and Tikal, Lake Petén Itzá is quickly becoming a destination in its own right. The area around El Remate is home to some of Petén's fanciest accommodations, the 72-room Camino Real Tikal and the smaller, more rustic, but exclusive, La Lancha. Other luxury options have sprouted up elsewhere along the lakeshore in recent years, including the very classy Bolontiku Hotel Boutique. There are also simpler accommodations, allowing you to take in the serene beauty of this large lake without busting your budget.

On the western shores of the lake, the towns of San Andrés and San José offer pleasant lakeside atmosphere and are an excellent place to learn Spanish or just get away. Language instruction here is combined with the opportunity to experience Petén's rich ecology and even contribute to its preservation while helping to meet the needs of local people. The Itzá culture has largely survived the onslaught of modernity, and its people are more than willing to share their proud heritage with visitors.

SAN ANDRÉS AND SAN JOSÉ

The road from Flores heads west before cutting north along the lakeside to the small town of San Andrés on its shores. You'll find the people here and in neighboring San José extremely friendly and laid-back. Many of the villagers still make their living from harvesting forest products such as chicle, allspice, and *xate* palm. The NGOs have been particularly active here since the creation of the Maya Biosphere Reserve and have found the communities very amenable to their conservation goals. The creation of a Spanish school was done in partnership with Conservation International several years ago, providing a viable alternative for income along the lines of sustainable development. The successful model has been emulated elsewhere, and there are now four Spanish schools operating in this area. They offer a unique alternative to more typical language school destinations, where a large presence of foreigners sometimes works against the immersion experience.

Although the towns are accessible from Flores by boat, the high cost of motorboat fuel and the ease of access from the road have made this a less popular option for getting here. Still, boats sometimes leave from the boat dock near Hotel Santana, and this is still the best option if you're staying at the wonderful Ni'tun Lodge near San Andrés.

San Andrés

Most travelers in these parts are almost certainly studying Spanish or helping out with one of the local NGOs in conservation or community development projects. Rates at all the area schools are comparable, somewhere between $150 and $175 per week, including 20 hours of one-on-one instruction and room and board with a local host family. The original San Andrés language school, **Eco-Escuela de Español** (tel. 3099-4846, www.ecoescuelaespanol.org), is still going strong and is the area's largest.

For comfortable budget accommodations in San Andrés, head to **Villa Benjamin** (Barrio Buena Vista, tel. 5099-9474 or 4500-8930, www.villa-benjamin.com, $25-45 d). There are clean, comfortable rooms with private bath and balconies overlooking the lake. There's also a restaurant on an airy terrace.

Three kilometers east of San Andrés along the road from Flores and then a few kilometers down a rugged dirt road accessible only by four-wheel-drive vehicles, is charmingly rustic ★ **Ni'tun Lodge** (tel. 5201-0759 or 5414-5780, www.nitun.com, $144-176 d). Its somewhat rustic yet comfortable cabins are made from stone, stick, and mortar and set on a hill overlooking the lakeshore. Inside you'll find wooden tree-trunk floors and typically Guatemalan accents, including Mayan blankets, rugs, and wooden furniture. All rooms have private hot-water bathroom. Room rates include breakfast. Gourmet meals, including a choice between 2-3 main courses, cost $25-30 for lunch or dinner. Live-in chef Lorena takes great pride in her culinary prowess and serves up some of the lake's best cuisine. Most of the lodge's high-end clientele arrives by boat from Flores on all-inclusive packages, which you can book directly through the lodge. The

a room at Ni'tun Lodge

lodge's creator and live-in manager, Bernie, has explored Petén extensively and is also the inspiration behind **Monkey Eco Tours** (tel. 5201-0759 or 5414-5780, www.nitun.com), which can take you to many of Petén's remoter sites in relative comfort and style with accordingly expensive prices. A five-day trek to El Mirador, for example, costs $185 per person per day for a five- or six-day trip with 4-6 people.

The area's newest accommodations are also its most elegant. ★ **Bolontiku Hotel Boutique** (tel. 7963-0909, www.bolontikuhotel.com, $216-260 d) enjoys a splendid location overlooking the lake. The beautiful rooms are tastefully decorated with fine fabrics that work well with the sylvan surroundings. Amenities include air-conditioning, minibar, and safe deposit boxes. There is a gourmet restaurant facing a large swimming pool with lovely views of Lake Petén Itzá. Recreational options include stand-up paddleboarding, kayaking, pedal boating, and a sunset boat tour.

arriving by boat at Bolontiku Hotel Boutique

dance in which a young girl and a horse skip together through the town streets. The second annual festival takes place on October 31 and November 1. It begins with a solemn Mass in the town's Catholic church, which houses three skulls in a glass case thought to belong to Spanish missionaries or the town's founders, depending on whom you believe. One of these skulls is removed from its resting place and put on the church altar during the service; it is then carried through town on a velvet pillow by black-clad devotees, followed closely by children in traditional village costume and townsfolk. The procession stops along the way in several homes, where cane liquor, along with traditional food, are consumed and prayers and chants are offered. At the end, the skull is returned to its glass case in the town church, where it remains on display throughout the year.

The first of the town's two Spanish schools, **Escuela Bio Itzá** (tel. 7928-8056, bioitza@yahoo.com), works with the Bio Itzá's women's cooperative, which runs a botanical garden for the production of natural products such as soap. San José's other language school is the more recently established **Mundo Maya Ecological Spanish School** (tel. 4663-3856, www.mundomaya.edu.gt). They offer homestays with a local family or accommodations in their student guesthouse.

For food, there's pleasant **El Búngalo** serving reasonably priced Guatemalan fare right at the lakeside.

For accommodations, there's splendid ★ **Bahía Taitzá** (along the road into town in Barrio El Porvenir, tel. 7928-8125 or 5402-1961, www.taitza.com, $55 d), set along the lakeshore on one of Lake Petén Itzá's prettiest beaches. Its eight comfortable rooms are housed in a large building. All have high wooden ceilings and come equipped with fans, tiled floors, comfortable beds, and private hot-water baths. A patio out front offers nice views of the manicured lawns toward the lake. There are lakeside hammocks and a restaurant and bar serving good food and wonderful cocktails.

San José

San José is a surprisingly pleasant town complete with a municipal recreation area on the lakeshore. Its somewhat steep streets meander into the surrounding hillside, affording stunning views of the pretty bay below. Adding to the town's intrigue is a Mayan cultural revival of the Itzá people. You'll see signs in this Mayan dialect around town. A community organization, the **Bio Itzá,** has its own language school and also manages a private forest preserve north of town along the fringes of El Zotz-San Miguel La Palotada Biotope.

According to local lore, the Itzá people came to San José from the Yucatán site of Chichén Itzá, led by the mythical figure Taitzá along a pathway known as the Camino Real 100 years before the arrival of the Spanish in the New World. Another unique aspect of the local culture is the town's two main annual **fiestas.** The first of these takes place between March 10 and 19 and includes a parade and fireworks, capped off by an unusual costumed

★ EL REMATE

El Remate starts about one kilometer past the turnoff to Yaxhá and the Belize border on the road from Santa Elena to Tikal. Once considered a stopping point along this road, El Remate has come into its own in recent years and has begun to pull its fair share of the Petén travel market. Its proximity to Tikal, fabulous lakeside setting, and variety of accommodations make it a wonderful alternative to staying at Tikal or Flores, or better yet, a destination unto itself worthy of at least one night's stay.

Sights

The turnoff for the road heading west toward Belize, about two kilometers south of El Remate, was once known as "El Cruce," though the small settlement here is now known as **Ixlú**. Just off the road, about 200 meters down a signed path, are the ruins of **Ixlú** on the shores of **Laguna Salpetén**. There is a basic campsite where you can rent canoes to take on the lake, but there is otherwise little else to do. A small information center can be found under a thatched-roof shelter by the road, with toilets and a map of the site.

Along the shores of Lake Petén Itzá, three kilometers down a dirt road heading west from the main Tikal-bound branch, is the **Biotopo Cerro Cahuí** (7am-4pm daily, $5). This 650-hectare mountainside park is particularly good for **bird-watching** and was initially set aside for the protection of Petén's ocellated turkey. It encompasses part of the lake's watershed and ranges in elevation 100-360 meters above sea level. You'll find several lowland rainforest species of birds, including toucans, parrots, and trogons. Two trails (2.75 miles or 3.75 miles long) take you up the hill into the surrounding forest to lookout points where there are wonderful views of the lake below. Maps and information are available at the entrance kiosk. A swimming dock near the entrance juts to a splendidly clear expanse of turquoise water and is a great place for a swim.

Shopping

El Remate is also a great place to pick up local crafts, consisting of some very attractive wood carvings made from fallen logs and providing a sustainable alternative to wide-scale forest destruction for agriculture. You'll find several handicrafts shops on the main strip along the road to Tikal.

Recreation

Bird-watching tours with knowledgeable, English-speaking local guides can be arranged from **La Casa de Don David** (tel. 7928-8469 or 5306-2190, www.lacasadedon-david.com) and cost between $40 and $75 for a 3- to 6-hour tour. In addition to Biotopo Cerro Cahuí, trips are available across the lake to roosting sites and other birding areas up the Río Ixpop and Río Ixlú.

Most of the area lodges can arrange **horseback riding** to Ixlú and Laguna Salpetén for about $20 per person. **Casa Mobego** (tel. 5909-6999) does **walking tours** to Laguna Salpetén for $10 per person and rents double **kayaks** for about $4 for one hour or $8 for four. **Casa de Doña Tonita** (tel. 5701-7114) also rents kayaks for about $2 an hour and **mountain bikes** for $5 a day. Alternatively, La Casa de Don David can arrange almost anything you can think of and also sells discount tickets to area **canopy tours.**

There are some wonderful **swimming** docks around the lake, the best of these at Restaurante El Muelle along the main road, in front of the Cerro Cahuí Biotope, and in front of Casa Mobego.

Accommodations

You'll find plenty of accommodations along the town's main drag beside the northbound Tikal road as well as along the dirt road diverting west that hugs the lakeshore.

On the dirt road running alongside the Lake Petén Itzá shore toward Cerro Cahuí Biotope are a number of very pleasant budget accommodations set far off from the noise of the main highway. **Hostal Casa Mobego** (tel. 7909-6999) is a popular place, also known as Casa Roja. Rooms with shared bath are housed in attractive stone and wood cottages; beds on a concrete base with squishy foam mattress and mosquito netting cost $7 per person. There is a nicely decorated main house where breakfast is served ($5) and dinner ($7) can be arranged with a bit of notice. There's also a book exchange, kayaks for rent, and the staff can arrange minibus transportation anywhere you may need to go.

Farther down the road as you approach the entrance to Cerro Cahuí is **Hotel y Restaurante Mon Ami** (tel. 3010-0284 or 4919-1690, www.hotelmonami.com), with a variety of accommodations from a six-bed dormitory with shared bath at $10 per person to bungalows with private hot-water bath costing $20-26 d. The lodge is owned by ecologist Santiago Billy, a pioneer of Petén's environmental movement who has fought for many years for the preservation of the Maya Biosphere Reserve. Near the entrance to the Biotopo Cerro Cahuí preserve, my favorite of El Remate's hotels is ★ **Posada del Cerro** (tel. 5376-8722, www.posadadelcerro.com, $13 pp in dorm, $40-64 d). It's an excellent value and a great place to get away from it all. The comfortably rustic rooms lack nothing in style; some feature cool stonework, while others have angled thatched-roof ceilings. There are also more modern apartments with full kitchens available. There's a small restaurant where guests can enjoy meals or simply hang out under the *palapa* roof. The lake is right in front of the property. and there's a nice swimming area.

Also in this area is the **Hotel Gringo Perdido** (tel. 2334-2305, www.hotelgringo-perdido.com, $90 d), which started several years ago as a budget accommodation but has gradually worked its way into pricier domains. Rates include a tasty four-course dinner and breakfast. The lodge's setting is right on the lakeshore within the boundaries of the Cerro Cahuí preserve. The rooms have private baths and are semi-open with roll-up blinds and private patio. There's mosquito netting. A newer concept is the boutique hotel ★ **Piramide Paraiso** (tel. 2334-2305, www.hotelgringo-perdido.com), on the adjacent grounds, where stylish and spacious villas housed in more modern concrete constructions with hardwood and Mayan textile accents go for $200 d, breakfast and dinner included. The rooms also have ceiling fans, air-conditioning, and plasma TVs.

Along the main street is the friendly **Hotel y Restaurant Sun Breeze** (tel. 7928-8044 or 5898-2665), where clean, simple double rooms with mosquito netting and fans go for $20 with shared-bath accommodations or $25 with private bathrooms. The helpful staff can do your laundry and also arrange reasonably priced transport or guided tours to area attractions such as Tikal and Yaxhá. Also on the main Flores-Tikal highway, midway through town, you'll find **El Muelle** (Km. 30, tel. 5581-8087, www.hotelelmuelle.com, $50-60 d) along with its namesake dock on the lake. The comfortable rooms are housed in an airy wooden building, and there's a nice swimming pool to cool off in. Charming ★ **La Mansión del Pájaro Serpiente** (tel. 5702-9434, www.30minutesfromtikal.com, $44-55 d) is another fine choice. Owned by a Guatemalan American family, the lodge sits along the main road to Tikal at the southbound entrance to El Remate. Set on a hillside overlooking the lake are 11 stylish guest rooms housed in stone and thatched-roof exteriors with Guatemalan furnishings and stone, tile, and hardwood accents; they have fans or air-conditioning and private hot-water bathrooms inside. The restaurant serves three meals a day, and there is a swimming pool amid the tropical landscape.

Along the lakeside road toward Cerro Cahuí, at the junction with the road leading to Tikal, is ★ **La Casa de Don David** (tel. 5306-2190, www.lacasadedondavid.com, $46-56), a highly recommended establishment owned by a native Floridian transplanted to Guatemala in the late 1970s. His friendly wife and daughter help run the lodge, consisting of 15 rooms with private hot-water bathrooms set amid nicely landscaped grounds that include a ceiba tree. Eleven of the rooms have air-conditioning; all have fans. Rates account for slightly noisier double rooms with fans or a/c and shared or private bath under the restaurant to quieter double rooms with air-conditioning set farther back from the main house. All prices include one free meal per day (breakfast or dinner). The restaurant serves delicious international dishes ranging $5-10 for lunch or dinner. The friendly staff can help you book transportation to virtually anywhere and can answer your travel questions. You can also snag discounted tickets for area canopy tours at the attractive gift shop in the main lobby. The hotel's very informative website is well worth checking out before visiting Petén.

Straight out of a West Texas cowboy's dream is **Palomino Ranch Hotel** (tel. 3075-4189, www.hotelpalominoranch.com, $50 d), with quirky antiques and cool Western-inspired decor that's tastefully done. There's even an old jukebox. Rooms are housed in a large hacienda-style building centered round a swimming pool and have hot water and air-conditioning. The lodge organizes horseback-riding trips to area attractions, and there is sometimes a horse show in the large pen. The lodge is on the Cerro Cahuí road about 500 meters from the junction with the main Tikal-bound highway.

Lake Petén Itzá is not without a large resort. The **Camino Real Tikal** (tel. 7926-0204 or 2410-5299, www.caminorealtikal. com.gt, $120 d) is a 72-room complex that has been in operation for over 25 years. The Camino Real has all the comforts you would expect from an international resort chain. The modern rooms are housed in concrete structures topped with thatched-roof exteriors. There are two restaurants, a bar, a coffee shop, and a swimming pool. Recreational activities available to guests include sailing, kayaking, and sailboarding. A large ship does lake tours on weekends, and transfers from the Mundo Maya International Airport can be arranged before arrival via a free shuttle service. Discounted accommodation packages are often available by calling directly or booking via a travel agency.

the hotel El Muelle's namesake dock

For Petén's ultimate in rustic jungle luxe, head to fabulous ★ **La Lancha** (tel. 7928-8331 Guatemala or 855/670-4817 U.S., www.coppolaresorts.com/lalancha), farther west along the lakeshore in the village of Jobompiche. Part of movie director Francis Ford Coppola's impressive portfolio of properties, including two other hotels in Belize, La Lancha is Petén's best-kept secret. Its 10 comfortable rooms are housed in lake-view casitas ($259 d) or rainforest casitas ($179 d). All rooms have exquisite Guatemalan fabrics and Balinese hardwood furniture. The rooms' wooden decks are graced with hammocks in which you can lounge the day away watching the sky's reflection on placid Lake Petén Itzá or order drinks from the bar via your in-room "shell phone." Outdoor patios are shared with the unit next door. Rates include a continental breakfast, and the restaurant serves gourmet Guatemalan dishes for lunch and dinner for about $25 per person.

There is a swimming pool, but if you wish to cool off in the lake, a short downhill walk leads to the water's edge. Kayaks and mountain bikes are available for exploring at your leisure, and you can book day trips to Tikal. Other activities include sightseeing in El Remate and Flores, fishing on the lake, and bird-watching at Cerro Cahuí.

Food

Most of the hotels have their own restaurant. There are also a number of more-than-adequate restaurants in El Remate. Along the road to Tikal, **El Muelle** (tel. 5514-9785, all meals daily) serves daily specials for about $10. The menu is heavy on meat dishes and lake fish, but it also serves pasta, vegetarian fare, and a wide assortment of desserts. The atmosphere is quite pleasant with views of the lake and the establishment's attractive namesake dock from which you can take a refreshing plunge into the turquoise waters. There is also a small gift shop selling books, wood carvings, and other knickknacks. Nearby is **La Piazza** (tel. 5956-4103, 5am-9pm daily), a well-established place with a covered, open-air dining room where tasty sandwiches and pasta dishes are served.

Along the road fringing the lake shore, you'll come across ★ **Las Orquídeas** (tel.

the pool at Francis Ford Coppola's hotel, La Lancha

5701-9022, lasorquideasremate@yahoo.com, 6am-10pm Tues.-Sun.), serving decent pizza, pasta, and sandwiches. Just down the road, **Mon Ami** (tel. 3010-0284, all meals daily) serves tasty French and Guatemalan fare.

For a splurge, head to ★ **La Lancha** (tel. 7928-8331, all meals daily) for gourmet Guatemalan cuisine for about $25 per person for lunch and dinner. You can enjoy an assortment of flavors from the Francis Ford Coppola wineries or your favorite drink from the bar while dining in an airy *palapa*-style building high above the lake. It's housed in its namesake lodge west of El Remate in Jobompiche.

Getting There and Around

El Remate is extremely easy to get to and from, as there is plenty of traffic heading up and down the road between Tikal and Flores. A local transport cooperative also operates minivans for trips to local attractions. Check with **Hotel y Restaurant Sun Breeze** (tel. 7928-8044 or 5898-2665) for availability and prices.

La Lancha's bar

East to Belize

The road heading east to Belize is (mostly) paved nowadays. There are some interesting sites along the way, the most important being the ruins of Yaxhá, 11 kilometers north from the main road. (The ruins are covered in the section on *The Maya Biosphere Reserve*, of which the site is a part.) Encouragingly, some of the lagoons and surrounding forest just north of this road are being opened to ecotourism by forward-thinking entrepreneurs, thus providing an alternative to the ecological destruction that has characterized the traditional northward advance of the agricultural frontier into protected lands.

LAGUNA SALPETÉN

Just one kilometer from the Ixlú turnoff (where there is a small settlement by the same name) on the road heading east to Belize is Laguna Salpetén. Although most of the forest around this beautiful emerald-colored lagoon was cleared for agriculture long ago, a small patch remains on a spit of land jutting into the body of water. This is also the well-chosen location of **Maya Zacpetén Lodge** (tel. 7823-5843, mayazacpetenjunglelodge.com, $140 d). The rooms are housed in comfortable concrete cottages with thatched-roof exteriors. Activities include bird-watching, hiking the jungle trails, horseback riding, boat tours of the lagoon, and nighttime crocodile sighting. Access is via a lake-bound turnoff from the main road heading east to Belize and then a short boat ride across the lagoon.

HOLTÚN

This small, unrestored Mayan site lies 30 kilometers from Ixlú and then a 20-minute walk south from the main road. It features small temple mounds and is really suitable only for the die-hard fan of Mayan ruins.

MELCHOR DE MENCOS

This small border town sits on the edge of the Río Mopán and is fairly pleasant as far as border towns go. The border crossing with Belize is fairly straightforward, though you'll probably be asked to pay the local equivalent of about $1.50 to exit or arrive in Guatemala, which is technically illegal. Some travelers have asked for a receipt in an attempt to dissuade the collection of the token bribe, but border officials sometimes issue you a deposit stub stamped with an official-looking immigration seal. The account most likely belongs to the bribe's collector.

Many people cross the border from Belize on day trips to Tikal or Yaxhá from one of the Belize jungle lodges. Daily shuttle vans make the trip to the border from Flores continuing to Belize City, and there is also public transport to the border from the bus depot in Santa Elena.

On the Belize side, there are buses leaving from the border every half hour. You can also take a taxi ride three kilometers to Benque Viejo del Carmen, the first sizable settlement, from where there are more frequent services. Another 13 kilometers east is San Ignacio, a pleasant town with much to see and do.

Accommodations and Food

There is little reason to linger here, as at most border crossings in Guatemala, but there are at least two serviceable hotels should you need to spend the night here. Right at the border overlooking the Río Mopán is the aptly named Río Mopán Lodge (tel. 7926-5196, $25 d). Its Swiss owner organizes various nature tours to local attractions—including remote archaeological sites such as Holmul—and is a great source for local information. Other activities include canoeing or tubing on the river. The lodge has a restaurant specializing in Mediterranean food. Another option is Hotel La Cabaña (Barrio El Centro, tel. 7926-5205, $40 d), with comfortable rooms including air-conditioning, private hot-water bathrooms, and cable TV. There are also a swimming pool and a restaurant serving local and international dishes. Aside from a few snack and drink stands on the road leading to the border crossing, these two hotels are your best (and really, your only) options for food.

Tikal National Park

Tikal National Park, the oldest and best known of Guatemala's national parks, was created in 1956. It encompasses 575 square kilometers (222 square miles) of primary tropical forest and protects a vast array of wildlife, as well as harboring the remains of one of the Mayan civilization's greatest cities. Tikal is understandably high on the list of priorities for any visitor to Guatemala and shouldn't be missed, as it affords the unique opportunity to combine a visit to a site of mammoth historical importance both in terms of natural and human heritage. Owing to its singular importance in the spheres of natural and human history,

UNESCO declared Tikal National Park a World Heritage Site in 1979.

Tikal's towering Temple I dominates the city's Great Plaza and is an icon for Guatemala itself, much like the Eiffel Tower and Paris. Perhaps not as readily apparent, Tikal National Park also represents the ongoing effort to protect what remains of Petén's tropical forest ecosystem. The park is at the edge, geographically speaking, of the Maya Biosphere Reserve, but at the very heart and soul of what conservationists and archaeologists are trying to protect. The conservation of Petén's rich archaeological and natural treasures has the potential to provide a livelihood to a

Tikal Region

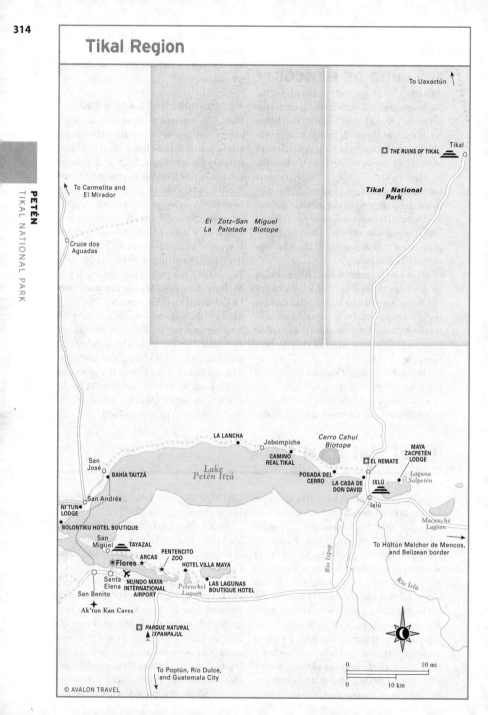

To Uaxactún

THE RUINS OF TIKAL

Tikal

Tikal National Park

To Carmelita and
El Mirador

Cruce dos
Aguadas

*El Zotz–San Miguel
La Palotada Biotope*

*Cerro Cahui
Biotope*

LA LANCHA

Jobompiche

CAMINO
REAL TIKAL

San
José

BAHÍA TAITZÁ

*Lake
Petén Itzá*

POSADA DEL
CERRO

EL REMATE

MAYA
ZACPETÉN
LODGE

*Laguna
Salpetén*

LA CASA DE
DON DAVID

IXLÚ

San Andrés

NI'TUN
LODGE

Ixlú

*Macanché
Lagoon*

BOLONTIKU HOTEL BOUTIQUE

San
Miguel

TAYAZAL

To Holtún Melchor de Mencos,
and Belizean border

ARCAS

PENTENCITO
ZOO

Flores

Río Ixpop

Río Ixlú

HOTEL VILLA MAYA

Santa
Elena

MUNDO MAYA
INTERNATIONAL
AIRPORT

*Petenchel
Lagoon*

LAS LAGUNAS
BOUTIQUE HOTEL

San Benito

Ak'tun Kan Caves

PARQUE NATURAL
IXPANPAJUL

To Poptún, Río Dulce,
and Guatemala City

0   10 mi

0   10 km

© AVALON TRAVEL

growing population of Peteneros long after any perceived benefits from clearing the forests for short-term gain. The lessons learned from Tikal's 50-plus-year existence can help conservationists better manage newer parks deeper inside the forest reserve, which will eventually be open to increasing numbers of visitors. Whatever the approach to managing these newer parks, what is certain is that Petén's vast wealth as the heartland of the Mayan civilization remains largely untapped.

If you are fortunate enough to visit Tikal, go home with the knowledge that you have been afforded a glimpse into the vast wilderness that remains mostly untouched north of this complex. In the forests beyond Tikal are countless other sites, some still undiscovered, which deserve as much protection and require the vigilance of international travelers and activists to ensure their continued preservation.

HISTORY

Tikal was settled somewhere between 900 and 700 BC on a site undoubtedly selected because of its position above seasonal swamps that characterize much of the terrain in this part of Petén, as well as the availability of flint for trade and the manufacture of tools and weapons. It remained little more than a small settlement for at least 200 years. By 500 BC the first stone temple was erected and later used as the basis for the large Preclassic pyramid dominating the complex now known as El Mundo Perdido. Tikal continued its steady progress during the late Preclassic period, sometime around 200 BC, with the construction of ceremonial buildings found in the North Acropolis and the completion of the pyramid at El Mundo Perdido.

Classic Period

By the time of Christ, Tikal's Great Plaza had begun to take shape and by the Early Classic period, around AD 250, Tikal was an important religious, commercial, and cultural center with a sprawling population. King Yax Ehb' Xoc established his dynasty at this time, one which was recognized by the 33 subsequent rulers of Tikal until recorded history at the site goes silent in AD 869.

The history of Tikal is closely tied to the emergence of Teotihuacán, a powerful city-state to the north in central Mexico, which it should be noted was completely non-Mayan in origin. Its influence began to be felt during the middle of the 4th century AD, when Teotihuacán dispatched a warrior by the name of Siyak K'ak' (Born of Fire) to aid Tikal in its war against the neighboring city of Uaxactún. Siyak K'ak' introduced the use of the atlatl, a wooden sling that allowed Tikal's warriors to defeat their enemy by firing arrows without having to engage in hand-to-hand combat. The aid from the north, according to recorded texts chronicling the execution of Tikal's Jaguar Paw I, amounted to a military takeover with the installation of Yax Nuun Ayin I (Curl Nose or First Crocodile), of Teotihuacán royalty, who later married into Tikal's dynasty.

With Teotihuacán hegemony now firmly established, Tikal dominated central Petén for most of the next 500 years. It grew to become one of the richest and most powerful Mayan city-states, aided by its dominance of strategic lowland trade routes. Tikal's influence reached as far south as Copán and as far west as Yaxchilán.

At the same time, the city-state of Calakmul, just north of the Guatemalan border in present-day Mexico, began its assent toward regional dominance. As the power and influence of Teotihuacán waned in the 5th century AD, Calakmul emerged as a geopolitical force to be reckoned with, incorporating a number of vassal states surrounding Tikal and contesting its dominion over the Mayan lowlands. A key alliance was forged between Calakmul and Caracol, in present-day Belize. Tikal launched a preemptive strike against Caracol in AD 556. With backing from Calakmul, Caracol launched a counter-attack on Tikal in AD 562; the latter suffered a crushing defeat. Desecration of Tikal's stelae and ritual burials, in addition to the destruction of many of its written records, followed. After this defeat, Tikal underwent a

130-year hiatus from erecting inscribed monuments, though it has recently been discovered that Temple V was constructed during this period. Mayanists now believe Tikal was never completely broken, despite defeat at the hands of its bitter rival.

Height of Power and Decline

Tikal reemerged as a dominant power beginning in AD 682 under the new leadership of Hasaw Chan K'awil (Heavenly Standard Bearer), whose 52-year reign was marked by the definitive defeat of Calakmul in AD 695 with reassertion of control over regional satellite cities such as Río Azul and Waka' as well as a frenzy of new temple construction. The six great temples dominating Tikal's ceremonial center were reconstructed between AD 670 and 810 by Hasaw Chan K'awil and his successors.

At the height of the Classic period, Tikal covered an area of about 30 square kilometers and had a population of at least 100,000, though some Mayanists believe it may have been much greater.

By the beginning of the 9th century AD, conditions worsened for many city-states across the Mayan lowlands with the Classic Mayan collapse in full swing. Tikal was no exception. The city-state's last inscription is recorded on Stela 24, which dates to AD 869. Tikal, like Petén's other Mayan cities, was completely abandoned by the late 10th century. The city would be reclaimed by the jungle and largely forgotten until its rediscovery in the late 17th century.

Rediscovery

The Itzá who occupied the present-day island of Flores probably knew about Tikal and may have worshipped here. Spanish missionary friars passing through Petén after the conquest mention the existence of cities buried beneath the jungle, but it wasn't until 1848 that the Guatemalan government commissioned explorers Modesto Méndez and Ambrosio Tut to visit the site. The pair brought along an artist, Eusebio Lara, to record their discoveries. In 1877, Swiss explorer Dr. Gustav Bernoulli visited Tikal and removed the carved wooden lintels from Temples I and IV. He shipped them to Basel, where they remain on display at the Museum für Völkerkunde.

Scientific study of the site would begin in 1881 with the arrival of British archaeologist Alfred P. Maudslay. His work was subsequently continued by Teobert Maler, Alfred M. Tozzer, and R. E. Merwin, among others. The inscriptions at Tikal owe their decipherment

view of Tikal from Temple V

Howler monkeys are a frequent sight at Tikal National Park.

to the work of Sylvanus G. Morley. In the mid-1950s, an airstrip was built, making access to the site much easier. The University of Pennsylvania carried out excavations between 1956 and 1969, along with Guatemala's Institute of Anthropology and History. With help from Spanish Cooperation, Temples I and V have been restored as part of a project begun in 1991.

A relatively small part of Tikal has been officially discovered and excavated. New discoveries await, along with new information that will undoubtedly continue to shed light on the turbulent history of the Mayan civilization. Among the more recent discoveries are the 1996 unearthing of a stela from AD 468 in the Great Plaza and the location of Temple V inscriptions challenging the notion of Tikal's 130-year hiatus after its defeat against Calakmul.

FLORA AND FAUNA

Tikal's abundant wildlife is most active early and late in the day, with birds and forest creatures more easily seen at these times. The summit of Temple IV, Tikal's highest structure, is a particularly popular place at sunrise and sunset. From your position high above the forest canopy, you can watch the sun dip below (or rise above) the horizon of unbroken tropical forest as far as the eye can see, while the chatter of myriad birds and forest creatures permeates the air. The roof combs of the Great Plaza pyramids pop out from the jungle canopy as toucans dart from tree to tree with their curious yellow beaks, like bananas with big black wings. More than 400 species of birds have been recorded at Tikal. *The Birds of Tikal*, by Frank Smythe, is a useful guide in this regard.

Other animals you may come across during your visit include coatis, which you should refrain from feeding. If you spend the night here, don't be afraid if you awake to the raucousness of a howling roar emanating from the forest. Sometimes confused with wildcats by first-time visitors, the sounds come from the locally abundant howler monkeys. During your explorations in Tikal, you will probably come across the smaller and ever-more-playful spider monkeys, which swing from tree to tree in the forest surrounding the ruins.

Among the park's most fascinating creatures are jaguars. Recent studies done over a two-month span have revealed the confirmed existence of seven of these large spotted cats within the national park's boundaries, and it is thought that at least nine roam its 575-square-kilometer (222-square-mile) confines.

EXPLORING THE PARK

Many visitors come to Tikal on day trips from Belize, Flores, and Guatemala City. While a day at the ruins is adequate for seeing some of the archaeological highlights, staying at the park allows you to enjoy its equally splendid natural setting. After the crowds have departed, you'll be free to wander about the ruins unhurried, and at times you may feel as if you have the site all to yourself. The sunset from the top of Temple IV is truly inspiring, but is now only an option in the winter months when the sun sets earlier as park rangers make sure everyone is out by 6pm. For movie buffs, the view from Tikal's Temple IV can be appreciated in *Star Wars: Episode IV,* as the site of the rebels' secret base. The Great Plaza also made an appearance in the movie *2012.*

The park's main gate is found along the road from Flores and El Remate, where there's a checkpoint. From here, it's another 17 kilometers to the main entrance, parking lot, and visitors center. Entrance to the park costs $19 ($3.50 for Guatemalan nationals) and is collected at the booth just opposite the parking lot. The park is open 6am-6pm daily. If you arrive after 3pm, your ticket should be stamped with the next day's date, allowing you to enter the ruins the next day at no additional cost. Tickets are checked at a second booth on the trail between the first gate and the entrance to the ruins proper, opposite an oft-photographed ceiba tree gracing the side of the road. There are no ATMs at the park and entrance fees must be paid in cash.

The visitors center is at the main entrance to the park on your left. There are a scale model of the site, the Museo Lítico, an overpriced eatery, and a few small shops selling books, souvenirs, snacks, and sundries, including bug spray and sunscreen. Nearby are the park campsite, police substation, and a post office. The Museo Tikal is farther along, near the airstrip next to the hotels.

The park website is www.tikalpark.com and has lots of very useful information for planning your visit. A modern center for research and conservation of cultural heritage was built opposite the visitors center with a donation from Japan.

Guided Tours

Guided tours of Tikal are best arranged with one of the recommended Flores travel agencies, though you can also hire the services of a certified freelance guide at the visitors center near the park entrance for $50 for up to four people, plus $5 for each additional person.

★ THE RUINS OF TIKAL

There is plenty to explore in this vast Mayan city that once harbored thousands of people, and you could easily spend several days here taking it all in. The ruins in evidence today are representative of the latter years of Tikal's existence, as the Maya built on top of existing temples and palaces. Most of the major structures you'll see were built after the time of Tikal's resurgence in the late 7th century.

The Great Plaza

Most visitors to Tikal head straight from the park entrance to the Great Plaza, and if you are crunched for time, this is probably the best approach. A path from the ticket control booth leads you to the plaza in about 20 minutes. You'll gain an appreciation for the site's elevated setting as you walk uphill toward the heart of the ceremonial center. The view from the back of Temple I as you approach the Great Plaza is always impressive at first sight, as it gives you an idea of the sheer size of the monuments erected by the Maya. Tourist brochures and posters can never adequately convey just how large and impressive Tikal's temples are.

The path continues alongside the temple, and you are at once greeted by the magnificent Temple II, which faces Temple I, as you enter the large, grassy plaza. Also known as "El Gran Jaguar" (The Great Jaguar), Temple I rises to a height of 44 meters (144 feet). The imposing structure was erected to honor Hasaw Chan K'awil (Heavenly Standard Bearer), the ruler who successfully led Tikal to victory against Calakmul. It was built to harbor his remains and was completed shortly after his death in AD 721 by son and successor Yik'in Chan K'awil, probably with instructions from his father.

The tomb was situated at the temple's core and contained the ruler's remains surrounded by jade, stingray spines, seashells, and pearls, which were typical of Mayan burials. It was believed the instruments would aid the person in his journey into the underworld. This journey is depicted on a bone fragment, also found

The Ruins of Tikal

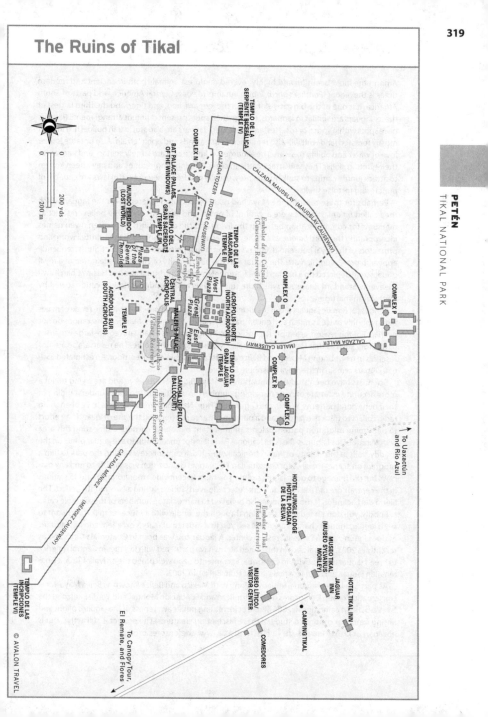

TEMPLO DE LA SERPIENTE BICÉFALICA (TEMPLE IV)

COMPLEX N

BAT PALACE (PALACE OF THE WINDOWS)

MUNDO PERDIDO (LOST WORLD)

TEMPLO DEL GRAN SACERDOTE (TEMPLE III)

Plaza of the Seven Temples

CALZADA TOZZER (TOZZER CAUSEWAY)

CALZADA MAUDSLAY (MAUDSLAY CAUSEWAY)

Embalse de la Calzada (Causeway Reservoir)

TEMPLO DE LAS MÁSCARAS (TEMPLE II)

Embalse del Templo (Temple Reservoir)

West Plaza

ACRÓPOLIS NORTE (NORTH ACROPOLIS)

COMPLEX O

COMPLEX P

CENTRAL ACRÓPOLIS

Gran Plaza

East Plaza

ACRÓPOLIS SUR (SOUTH ACROPOLIS)

TEMPLE V

MALER'S PALACE

Embalse del Palacio (Palace Reservoir)

TEMPLO DEL GRAN JAGUAR (TEMPLE I)

CALZADA MALER (MALER CAUSEWAY)

CALZADA MALER

COMPLEX R

COMPLEX Q

CANCHA DE PELOTA (BALLCOURT)

Embalse Secreto (Hidden Reservoir)

To Uaxactún and Río Azul

CALZADA MÉNDEZ (MÉNDEZ CAUSEWAY)

Embalse Tikal (Tikal Reservoir)

HOTEL JUNGLE LODGE (HOTEL POSADA DE LA SELVA)

MUSEO TIKAL (MUSEO SYLVANUS MORLEY)

JAGUAR INN

HOTEL TIKAL INN

MUSEO LÍTICO/ VISITOR CENTER

CAMPING TIKAL

COMEDORES

TEMPLO DE LAS INSCRIPCIONES (TEMPLE VI)

To Canopy Tour, El Remate, and Flores

© AVALON TRAVEL

0
200 yds

0
200 m

Balam: Jaguars in Guatemala

Among the most beautiful and highly revered rainforest animals both in ancient and modern times is the jaguar (*Panthera onca*), which inhabits Mexico, Central America, and parts of South America. It is one of the big cats, along with the leopard, lion, and tiger, and the third largest of these. Jaguars are similar to leopards, though their spots present different arrangements (jaguars have spots within spots, or rosettes, and are larger). Jaguars are also stockier in build. They inhabit mostly forested lands but will also range across grasslands and open terrain. Also notable is their love of water and ability to swim. These gorgeous jungle cats are largely solitary and known for their hunting skills. They will attack cattle in areas fringing jungle zones and have been known to attack jungle camps to stalk human prey, usually children. Their powerful jaws are capable of puncturing tortoise shells.

Perhaps for these reasons, the Maya had great respect and reverence for the jaguar, which they called *balam.* Jaguars were a symbol of power and strength and were believed to act as mediums for communication between the living and the dead. Kings were often given names incorporating the word *balam,* which they viewed as their companions in the spiritual world and protectors of the royal household. Rulers wearing jaguar pelts and man-jaguar figures frequently appear in pre-Columbian art. The jaguar was the patron deity of Tikal and is featured in a royal burial scene depicted on a human bone fragment found in the burial tomb of Hasaw Chan K'awil (Heavenly Standard Bearer) in which the ruler travels to the underworld in a canoe rowed by mythical animal figures.

Ranges for female jaguars are in the vicinity of 25-40 square kilometers, with the range of males being roughly twice as much and encompassing that of 2-3 females. Male jaguars' ranges do not overlap. For this reason, attempts to conserve existing numbers of jaguars require large expanses of territory such as that found in Guatemala's Maya Biosphere Reserve. The reserve also adjoins reserves in neighboring Mexico and Belize as part of a vast biological corridor. An estimated 550-650 jaguars remain in the Maya Biosphere Reserve.

Scientists have been studying jaguars in the Maya Biosphere Reserve and are trying to get a more accurate estimate of their remaining numbers in addition to a greater understanding of their behavioral patterns. Within the Laguna del Tigre National Park, biologists have been using radio collars to track five jaguars and a puma in the area surrounding the site of Waka' in an effort to determine migration patterns along an important biological corridor connecting this area with Mirador-Dos Lagunas-Río Azul National Park. It is not uncommon to see jaguar prints on the muddy trails in the vicinity of Waka'. Ironically, in 2006, a camera crew visiting the park to film a program on scarlet macaws for Guatemalan TV channel Guatevisión was unable to find any macaws but did manage to get a jaguar sighting on tape. Recent video monitoring along 15 stations in the central core of Tikal National Park detected seven jaguars during a two-month period. The Sierra del Lacandón National Park is also believed to harbor large numbers of these jungle cats.

Luckily, you don't need to go traipsing through the jungle with a saucer of milk if you want to see a jaguar, though chances are it will see you first. Guatemala City's excellent zoo has jaguars, as does Petén's ARCAS wildlife rescue center. A jaguar cub was born in Guatemala City's zoo as recently as 2003. Several zoos in the United States have partnered with facilities in Central America to breed jaguars in captivity. In California, Sacramento's zoo welcomed the arrival of Tina, a Guatemalan jaguar, and Mulac, a male jaguar from Belize, in 2002.

As part of a larger regional initiative along with Mexico and Belize known as Selva Maya, local conservation group Defensores de la Naturaleza and Fundación Monte Carlo Verde launched the SalvaBalam campaign in 2006 aimed at increasing public awareness of the jaguar's plight and raising funds for continued study of these fascinating creatures. The project is still active, but is now part of Defensores de la Naturaleza (www.defensores.org.gt).

Temple I at sunrise

as the Temple of the Masks for the large, severely eroded masks flanking its central staircase, it is thought to predate Temple I by a few years. About 10 years ago, a staircase was constructed on its side to allow access to the top, though you could once climb directly up its central staircase. The view from the top is still as good as ever, with a frontal view of Temple I and the North Acropolis off to the side. Temple II probably once stood at the same height as its counterpart when its roof comb was intact, though its restored height is 38 meters (125 feet).

The North Acropolis

Occupying the Great Plaza's northern end is the aptly named North Acropolis, its foundations dating as far back as 100 BC, though the 12 temples sitting atop this large structure are part of a later rebuilding effort dating to AD 250. Some of these earlier structures can be seen today thanks to a tunnel excavated by archaeologists that provides a glimpse of two giant masks from Early Classic times guarding the entrance to a still-buried temple. The remains of Yax Nuun Ayin I, the first of Tikal's rulers under Teotihuacán hegemony, were found buried here in 1959 and revealed many details of Teotihuacán influence, including ceramics and the dreaded atlatl.

Some much-eroded stelae line the front of the North Acropolis. These depicted Tikal's ruling elite, and many have been subjected to ritual defacement at the hands of invaders from neighboring states such as Calakmul.

The Central Acropolis

Commonly referred to as palaces, this complex of interconnecting rooms and stairways built around courtyards probably housed administrative offices and residences for Tikal's elite, though their exact use is uncertain. The Central Acropolis occupies the south end of the Great Plaza. It is known that the configuration of the various rooms was altered frequently, lending credence to the idea that it served as a royal dwelling place for the ruling elite. One part of the acropolis housed

in the tomb, showing a royal figure in a canoe rowed by mythical animal figures. Tikal's museum harbors a reconstruction of the tomb, known as Tumba 116. Carried off to a museum in Basel, Switzerland, is the door lintel found at the top of the pyramid depicting a jaguar from which the temple gets its name.

It was once possible to climb Temple I, but this has not been allowed for several years now. The view from the top was truly spectacular, with Temple II in the foreground and the roof combs of Temples III and IV protruding from the jungle behind it. The structure was closed to climbers partly because of damage caused by a chain aiding in this activity, though the death of at least two visitors after tumbling down its steep steps certainly put the final nail in the coffin. The view from the top was popular in tourism posters and brochures from the early 1980s, and you can still sometimes see them in unexpected places.

Across the plaza stands the slightly smaller **Temple II,** built to honor Hasaw Chan K'awil's wife, Lady 12 Macaw. Also known archaeologist Teobert Maler in 1895 and 1904, subsequently coming to be known as **Maler's Palace.**

The West Plaza and Temple III

The West Plaza, or Plaza Oeste, lies north of Temple II. Its main features include the presence of a large Late Classic temple on its north end and the unrestored **Temple III,** across the Tozzer Causeway, to the southwest. Temple III, which is 60 meters high, gives you a good idea of what Tikal's temples looked like to the early explorers when they were still covered in jungle vegetation. That's about all you'll be able to admire of it, as it is closed to visitors.

Some believe Temple III was built to honor the last of Tikal's great rulers, Dark Sun, and he may in fact be the figure depicted in the structure's badly eroded lintels. Behind the temple is a large palace complex. One of them, known as the **Bat Palace,** has been restored. It is also known as Palacio de las Ventanas.

Temple IV and Complex N

Continuing along the Tozzer Causeway, which is one of the original elevated walkways connecting various parts of the city, you'll come across Complex N on the left. Complex N is a twin-temple complex of the variety frequently constructed by Tikal's Late Classic rulers, supposedly to commemorate the passing of a *katun,* or 20-year cycle in the Mayan calendar. Found here is the beautifully carved **Stela 16,** showing Hasaw Chan K'awil in a plumed headdress. The complex was built in AD 711 to mark the 14th *katun* of *baktun* 9, a *baktun* being 400 years. **Altar 5,** also found here, depicts Hasaw victoriously presiding over sacrificial skull and bones with a lord from one of Calakmul's former vassal states. The corresponding text also mentions the death of Lady 12 Macaw, Hasaw's wife.

Farther along, you'll come to the colossal Temple IV, the tallest of Tikal's temples at 65 meters (212 feet). Like the Great Plaza's temples, it was completed in AD 741 by Yik'in Chan K'awil and may have served as his burial monument, though there is no concrete

Temple V

evidence as of yet. In addition to offering the best views of the site from its summit, it is also known as the origin of some excellent lintels depicting a victorious king surrounded by glyphs. As in the case of the lintels from Temple I, you'll now have to travel to Basel if you want to see the originals. A replica of Lintel 3 is in Guatemala City's archaeology museum.

The climb to the top of the temple up a series of wooden ladders attached to its side can be described as simply breathtaking, both for the effort required and for the spectacular views of the forest on all sides. The base of the temple is currently being restored and affords the opportunity to more fully appreciate the massive scale of these impressive constructions.

Temple V and the South Acropolis

The South Acropolis, due south of the Great Plaza, is the site of some excavations that are just beginning to unravel its significance. Its top layers are from Late Classic times, much like elsewhere in Tikal. Temple V lies just east of the South Acropolis. Standing to a height of 58 meters, it may be the original of Tikal's six temples dating to AD 600. A wooden staircase providing access to the somewhat cramped area below the roof comb and an interesting side view of the Great Plaza was closed during my last visit.

Plaza of the Seven Temples

This small plaza can be found to the west of the South Acropolis and contains a series of seven temples arranged in a straight line dating to Preclassic times. There is a triple ball court on the plaza's north side similar to a larger one just south of Temple I. It's one of the least visited areas and yet one of the most visually interesting.

The Lost World Complex

Known in Spanish as El Mundo Perdido, this complex is strikingly different from the rest of the site owing to its Preclassic origins, which may help to shed light on Tikal's early history. The area is dominated by the presence of a 32-meter pyramid, its foundation dating as far back as 500 BC, when it served as an astronomical observatory similar to the one found at Uaxactún. The structure now in evidence marks the top of four layers of construction. There are fabulous views of the Great Plaza and Temple IV from the top, though the stone central staircase on the temple's steep face can be slippery after it rains. Exercise due caution.

Temple of the Inscriptions (Temple VI)

The most remote of Tikal's temples, Temple VI lies about one kilometer southeast of the Central Acropolis along the **Mendez Causeway,** where it stands all by itself. Rediscovered in 1957, this temple is unique because it contains inscriptions much like the temples found at Quiriguá and Copán but unlike Tikal's other temples. On the back side of the temple's 12-meter roof comb are a series of 180 glyphs, barely visible today, charting

the history of Tikal's ruling dynasty AD 200-766. They also chart Tikal's early history as far back as 1139 BC, which the Maya probably guessed at. Still, ceramic evidence at Tikal has corroborated other dates found at the site. The temple is most likely the work of Yik'in Chan K'awil. Stela 21 and Altar 9 adorn the front of the temple at its base and date to AD 736.

The temple's relative isolation makes it an excellent location for spotting wildlife. Robberies, none of them recent, have been reported here. That said, you should probably not wander off to these parts unaccompanied.

Complexes Q and R

Two other areas deserve mention in this discussion of Tikal's archaeological highlights. You'll find them shortly after entering the park, on a path bearing right after passing the ticket control booth. Complex Q and Complex R comprise two sets of Tikal's twin-temple complexes built by Yax Ain II to commemorate the passing of a *katun*. One of the pyramids at Complex Q has been restored with its corresponding stelae repositioned in front of it. The best of these, **Stela 22,** can be seen at the **Museo Lítico** and depicts Yax Ain II's ascension to the throne. The temple here dates to AD 771.

Farther west, as you approach the Maler Causeway, is Complex R, another twin-pyramid complex dating to AD 790.

MUSEUMS

Tikal's two museums are oddly in different parts of the park. The first of these is the **Museo Lítico** (9am-noon and 1pm-4:30pm Mon.-Fri., 9am-4pm Sat. and Sun., $2.50 for both museums), housing stelae and carved stones from the archaeological site with a scale model outside showing what the city probably looked like around AD 800. There are some interesting photos taken by explorers Alfred Maudslay and Teobert Maler showing Tikal's temples overgrown by a tangle of jungle vines and branches as they looked when they were first discovered.

The **Museo Tikal** (also known as

Sylvanus G. Morley Museum, 9am-5pm Mon.-Fri., 9am-4pm Sat. and Sun., $2.50), across the way next to the Jaguar Inn, has some interesting exhibits, including the burial tomb of Hasaw Chan K'awil found inside Temple I. Some of the ceramics from this museum have been moved to the newly completed Center for Conservation and Investigation of Cultural Heritage, across from the visitors center.

RECREATION

In addition to exploring the ruins, there are a variety of recreational opportunities in and around Tikal National Park.

Canopy Tour

You have a choice of two zipline trajectories between raised platforms in the jungle at **Canopy Tours Tikal** (tel. 5615-4988 or 4262-0813, www.tikalcanopy.com, 7am-5pm daily, $30, at the national park entrance). The first of these includes 11 platforms with ziplines ranging in length 75-150 meters while you dangle 25 meters over the forest floor. The second, more adrenaline-inducing option, includes ziplines up to 200 meters long hovering 40 meters above the safety of ground level. There are also 400 meters of hanging bridges for a more leisurely look at the forest canopy, or there's horseback riding if you prefer to explore from the ground level.

Bird-Watching

Specialty tours for bird-watchers can be arranged by contacting **La Casa de Don David** (tel. 7928-8469 or 5306-2190, www.lacasadedondavid.com) in El Remate. The lodge's knowledgeable staff can connect you with good English-speaking local guides who know the park and its birds. Another recommended outfitter is Guatemala City-based **Cayaya Birding** (tel. 5308-5160, www.cayaya-birding.com).

ACCOMMODATIONS

Lodging at Tikal National Park is limited by law to three lodges and a campground.

An increasing amount of competition from accommodations at nearby El Remate has spurred the Tikal hotels toward higher standards while keeping prices relatively reasonable. There are few places in the world where you can stay in a comfortable jungle lodge inside a national park just minutes away from a UNESCO World Heritage Site. That being said, the Tikal hotels do feel somewhat overpriced in terms of what you get for your money.

Electricity at the park is sporadic, with accommodations and other facilities having to limit the hours during which this convenience is available. Power is usually turned on in the morning for 2-3 hours and then again in the evening shortly after sunset for another three hours. If you need to use a computer provided by one of these facilities for checking email or need to recharge camera batteries or cell phones, you should plan accordingly. If you absolutely need a fan to cool your room while you sleep overnight in the humid Petén jungle, you may want to stay outside the park, as ceiling fans go silent once the electricity turns off. It can get very hot here, even at night. None of the lodges have air-conditioning. More recently, the Jaguar Inn has begun providing electricity round-the-clock and this seals the deal for many a traveler.

Beware if booking online, as at least two of the three lodges have lower-priced accommodations mysteriously missing from their online price lists. If you call the hotels looking for one of the less expensive shared-bath rooms, you'll most likely need to ask for one specifically, as they'll automatically try to sell you one of their premium rooms.

Coming from the ruins, the first place you'll come across is the **Jungle Lodge** (tel. 2476-8775, www.junglelodgetikal.com, $45-100 d), offering decent bungalows with private hot-water baths, ceiling fans, and two double beds as well as a few very basic, less expensive rooms with shared bathrooms. All are set amid a pleasant tropical garden atmosphere and there is a swimming pool.

The restaurant here serves breakfast ($7), lunch, and dinner ($8-12). Be advised the lodge is closed every year during September. As you head toward the old airstrip just past the museums, you'll reach the friendly **Jaguar Inn** (tel. 7926-2411, www.jaguartikal.com), where you can choose from nine comfortable bungalows with small front patios with hammock ($80 d), a dormitory ($13 pp), hammocks with mosquito netting ($5), or camping in a supplied tent ($15 pp). The restaurant here is a safe bet, serving adequate portions of good food (though the service can be very slow). Dinner is about $10. There are laptops available for Internet surfing and checking email ($5/hour). The electricity here stays on round-the-clock, thanks to a generator. Next door, **Tikal Inn** (tel. 7926-0065, www.tikalinn.com, $45-100 d) gets consistent praise for its good service and large, comfortable rooms centered round the swimming pool just behind the hotel's restaurant. You can choose from standard rooms or pricier, more private bungalows; all have ceiling fan and private bath. The restaurant serves three meals a day.

Tikal's **campground** is opposite the visitors center with a spacious grassy area for tents as well as *palapa* structures for stringing hammocks. There are showering stalls among the bathroom facilities. Hammocks and mosquito netting are available for rent ($10), and a two-person tent costs $14 for the night.

FOOD

Your best bet for food is at one of the three on-site lodges, but there are a number of *comedores* here serving basic yet passable fare in adequate portions for about $7 for a full meal and a drink. The menus are virtually indistinguishable from one another and are heavy on local staples such as beans, eggs, and tortillas but also feature some international fare like burgers and pasta. The *comedores* are across from the visitors center on the right-hand side as you enter the park from the main road. They include **Comedor Tikal, Restaurant Imperio Maya,** and **Comedor Ixim K'ua,** all of which open early for breakfast and close at 9pm daily. **El Meson** (tel. 7952-8700, lunch only) is a simple, open-air, thatched-roof eatery that serves tasty set menus that include soup, chicken or beef, rice, vegetables, and fruit. It's located at the end of a short trail to the right of the main entrance to the park (if you're coming from the parking lot). The trail is a few meters past the oft-photographed ceiba tree at the junction with the road leading to Uaxactún.

You can get your morning coffee fix right at the visitors center at **Caffé Ital-Espresso**. Its Italian owner uses some fine Guatemalan beans for his espresso beverages. There are also sandwiches to go.

As for the hotel restaurants, the large dining room at the **Jungle Lodge** is a popular stop for lunch with tour groups. As such, it tends to offer dependable set-menu lunches of meat or chicken dishes accompanied by rice and salad for about $9. Dinner options include a varied assortment of meat dishes, pasta, and sandwiches. The **Jaguar Inn** caters largely to the international backpacker crowd and makes a particularly decent place for good-value dinners, including tasty pastas and desserts. The **Tikal Inn** gets props for its hearty breakfasts with good, strong coffee.

GETTING THERE

Most people arrive here from Flores, El Remate, or Belize. See the corresponding sections for information on how to get here. Minibuses leave Tikal from the airstrip fairly frequently, particularly after about noon, heading south toward El Remate, Ixlú, and Flores. Change buses at Ixlú if you're heading east to Belize. If all else fails, a taxi to Flores should cost about $50.

The Maya Biosphere Reserve

The largest protected tropical forest in North America, this 1.7 million-hectare (4.3 million-acre) reserve is Guatemala's last chance for preserving a significant part of the forests that once covered all of Petén. It is gradually gaining notoriety among international travelers for its vast expanses of tropical forest and the remote Mayan ruins that lie buried within. It is hoped that ecotourism here will take hold as a major industry, providing jobs and a viable alternative to ecological destruction, as in neighboring protected areas in Belize and Costa Rica. A cursory glance at a map of Guatemala reveals that the northern third of Petén is a sparsely populated region harboring an unusually high concentration of Mayan sites, remote jungle wetlands, rivers, and lagoons. Those with a strong sense of adventure will find plenty to see and do in one of Central America's last ecological frontiers.

Although the biosphere reserve has been in existence since 1990, many of the parks that compose it remain little more than "paper parks," as the government entities charged with enforcing protection of these areas are woefully underfunded and understaffed. Several of the parks are now being administered jointly between Guatemala's National Protected Areas Council (CONAP) and local conservation organizations. Foreign NGOs have also joined the battle to preserve the Maya Biosphere for future generations against seemingly insurmountable odds. Threatening the continued existence of this unique area are traditional factors common to tropical forests in developing countries, including the expansion of the agricultural frontier by land-hungry peasants and changes in land use such as cattle grazing. But there are also more sinister forces at work here, and the reserve is under serious assault by wildlife and timber poachers, both from within Guatemala and neighboring Mexico, as well as from the activities of drug smugglers occupying large extensions of the park to move their product.

Guatemalan authorities have stepped up their efforts to regain control of this vast wilderness area, and it should be noted that not all of the above-mentioned forces are in operation throughout the park. There are many areas within this vast biosphere reserve that are easily and safely explored, combining the splendors of some of the Mayan civilization's most spectacular ruins with the wonders of a largely intact tropical forest all around. In some cases, these are not so easily accessible, but the rewards for those putting forth the effort to reach some of Guatemala's least-visited attractions are well worth it.

Among the highlights of the reserve are the **Mirador-Dos Lagunas-Río Azul National Park,** which is home to the largest manufactured pre-Columbian structures in the Americas, found at **El Mirador,** and at least 25 other smaller Mayan sites. Some, such as Wakná, have been discovered only as recently as 1998, and many more undoubtedly await discovery. At the site of **San Bartolo,** archaeologists uncovered the earliest evidence of Mayan writing in a wall mural discovered in 2001. The area is also home to the last remaining undisturbed tropical forests in Guatemala and is being considered for special protection as the **Mirador Basin National Park.**

Much of the western part of the reserve, particularly **Laguna del Tigre National Park,** has unfortunately been lost due to population pressures. Still, the area around the Mayan site of **Waka'** (also known as El Perú or Waka'-Perú) remains well preserved and is the home of a biological research station and a project to help conserve Petén's last remaining populations of scarlet macaws.

The Maya Biosphere was also featured on U.S. television with the filming of *Survivor Guatemala* at the Mayan ruins of Yaxhá. The spectacular ruined city is rivaled in

chicle tapping in Uaxactún

leaves. In 2000, Guatemala's Protected Areas Council (CONAP) granted the community a sustainable forestry concession to selectively harvest timber from surrounding multiple-use zones of the Maya Biosphere Reserve. While it's yet to be seen how sustainable it is in practice, the logging concession has already been partially nullified in areas approaching the subsequently created Mirador Basin archaeological zone and could be completely eliminated with the eventual creation of a proposed Mirador Basin National Park. Locals also guide visits from here to remote sites such as Río Azul and El Zotz, which may be their best hope for earning income without harming the fragile tropical forest ecosystem they inhabit.

The ruins themselves might seem a bit unimpressive after a visit to their better-known neighbor to the south, as they are smaller and not nearly as well preserved, though Uaxactún's main claim to fame is the presence of a fairly elaborate astronomical observatory. Sylvanus G. Morley is credited with rediscovering Uaxactún in 1916. Its original name has subsequently been deciphered as Siaan K'aan (Born in Heaven), though Morley is said to have chosen the name Uaxatún (Eight Stone) as a reference to a stone dating to the 8th *baktun* in the Mayan calendar, then the earliest-known Mayan inscription. It is also speculated that his choice of name was a play on words for "Washington," the U.S. capital and home of the Carnegie Institute that funded his explorations. Morley's initial investigations focused on the site's inscriptions. Uaxactún's structures would have to await being mapped and more closely inspected until the arrival of Frans Blom in 1924. The Carnegie Institute excavated the site between 1926 and 1937.

History

Uaxactún is a Middle Preclassic site dating to about 600 BC that came into its own in the Late Preclassic sometime between 350 BC and AD 250 with the appearance of its first ceremonial plazas in the areas now known as Groups A and E. Its earliest stelae date to

magnificence only by Tikal and El Mirador, and its splendid setting next to a tropical lagoon complete with hungry crocodiles is second to none.

Survivor Guatemala certainly catapulted Guatemala and Yaxhá into the collective consciousness, and many people believe it is just a matter of time before the treasures hidden in the Petén forest gain greater notoriety and become an engine for the preservation of this incredible but often-overlooked adventure-travel destination.

UAXACTÚN

The remote site of Uaxactún lies just 23 kilometers north of Tikal on an unpaved road through the jungle passable by four-wheel-drive vehicle. The Wrigley Company once had a busy chicle extraction operation here, complete with an airstrip. Today the airstrip lies in disuse, with the ruins and small community built around it. Many of Uaxactún's residents make their living from gathering forest products such as chicle, allspice, and *xate* palm

The Murals of San Bartolo

Fascinating discoveries at the newly famous site of San Bartolo have rocked the world of Mayan scholars, completely shattering long-held beliefs about the origin of elaborate Mayan art and writing that narrates the stories of ruling monarchies. It is now clear that Preclassic Mayan societies had achieved a degree of sophistication in art, writing, and government once thought to have been attained only several centuries later. San Bartolo, deep in the jungle near Río Azul, has yielded the earliest known Mayan mural and the oldest known Mayan burial tomb. The murals are impressive not only for their early date (AD 100-200), but also for their quality. The best-known Mayan murals, at the site of Bonampak (Mexico), date to the late 8th century AD. San Bartolo's location, while no longer secret, is known only to a few in the archaeological community. Visitors are not welcome, but there are plans to make a replica of the murals available to tourists in the future. The Mayan site of San Bartolo encompasses more than 100 structures, among them temple pyramids (at least two of which are more than 25 meters high), a palace, and ball court, and is still being excavated.

The mural was discovered in 2001 by Harvard University's William Saturno when, in search of shade from the midday sun, he ducked into a trench hacked by looters under an unexcavated pyramid. What followed were two years of planning the painstaking excavation, and the mural depicting creation mythology was reclaimed from the soil beneath the temple structure. It is similar to one found in the *Dresden Codex,* one of three Mayan books to survive the wide-scale destruction of ancient Mayan texts by Spanish priests in the 16th century (the other two are the *Madrid Codex* and the *Paris Codex*).

Among the themes depicted are the establishment of order to the world, the latter portrayed as upheld by trees with roots leading to the underworld and branches holding up the sky. Stationed at each tree are four deities providing a blood sacrifice and an offering.

In another section, the mural shows the maize god setting up the tree at the center of the world and crowning himself king. This section of the panel traces the maize god's birth, death, and resurrection. In the final scene, a historic coronation of an actual Mayan king is depicted with his name and title written in hieroglyphics.

Project iconographer Karl Taube believes the writing style differs from that evidenced in later periods of Mayan history, but it is nonetheless sophisticated. He also points to the appearance of similar scenes in the *Dresden Codex.* Saturno speculates the king depicted in the mural likely claimed the right to rule from the gods themselves and not merely from lineage, as did kings in later times.

The second major discovery is the tomb of an early Mayan king dating to 150 BC found in 2005 by Guatemalan archaeologist Mónica Pellecer Alecio about a mile away from the mural, also under a small temple pyramid. The find provides further evidence of early monarchic rule.

A full-length feature on these amazing discoveries can be found in the January 2006 edition of *National Geographic* magazine and online at www.sanbartolo.org.

---

around AD 328. More complex architecture and several other plazas also make their appearance at this time.

After the decline of El Mirador in the 2nd century AD, Uaxactún and Tikal became embroiled in a great political and military rivalry for local supremacy until the site was conquered by Tikal in AD 378. Tikal was aided in its takeover of Uaxactún by its newly formed alliance with Teotihuacán and the introduction of a spear-throwing apparatus imported from the central Mexican city-state. Uaxactún remained a subordinate state for the remainder of its history.

The Ruins

The most impressive set of ruins lies a 15-minute walk southeast of the airstrip and is called **Group E.** A series of small, partially restored temples, Structures E-I, E-II, and E-III, are arranged side by side, going north to south, and designed as an astronomical observatory.

The structures are arranged in such a manner as to coincide with the sunrise on key dates. When viewed from the top of nearby Temple E-VII-Sub, the sun rises over E-1 on the summer solstice and over the southernmost E-III on the winter solstice. Temple E-VII-Sub's foundations date to about 2000 BC, and there are some much-deteriorated jaguar and snake heads flanking the temple's side.

Northeast of the airstrip are Groups A and B, which were less carefully excavated but include several altars and stelae found mostly fallen among the remains of the larger temple palaces.

Accommodations and Food

Lodging and dining options in Uaxactún are extremely basic, as it is a remote forest community literally in the middle of nowhere. The settlement's best accommodations are at **Campamento El Chiclero** (tel. 7926-1095, $8 pp) on the north end of the airstrip with 10 basic rooms with shared bath and mosquito-netted windows. You can also camp or string a hammock here for $4. The restaurant serves large portions of good, basic food ($5 per meal), and there is a small on-site museum (free) with local artifacts. The friendly owners can arrange trips to some of the remoter places in the biosphere reserve, including El Zotz, Río Azul, Naachtun, and El Mirador. A less expensive alternative is **Aldana's Lodge,** just off the street leading to Groups A and B, where simple thatched-roof cabanas are $7 per person, or you can camp for $4 per person. Aldana's can also arrange visits to area sites.

You can eat at your choice of three simple *comedores* in town: **Comedor Uaxactún, Comedor La Bendición,** and **Comedor Imperial Okanarin.**

Getting There

A Pinita bus leaves Santa Elena at 1pm daily, stopping in Tikal at about 3pm. From there it's about 1.5 hours to Uaxactún. These times are not set in stone, as with most schedules in Guatemala, and the bus can arrive in Uaxactún as late as 6pm sometimes. The return trip to Santa Elena leaves Uaxactún at 6am. (There is sometimes a minivan leaving Uaxactún for Tikal at 8am with the inbound minivan from Tikal arriving at 6pm, but it's sporadic and doesn't always operate.)

If you're driving, be aware that the road is passable only in a four-wheel-drive vehicle at any time of year. If you're unable to fill your gas tank in Flores, the last gas station en route is at Ixlú, south of El Remate.

YAXHÁ-NAKUM-NARANJO NATURAL MONUMENT

This park encompasses the Mayan sites of Yaxhá, Topoxté, Nakum, and El Naranjo. Most prominent of these is Yaxhá, which gained international fame in 2005 with the filming of *Survivor Guatemala*. The park was closed for two months, during which time contestants lived among the ruins eating corn, plotting ways not to get voted off, and fighting off mosquitoes. Only El Mirador and Tikal are bigger than Yaxhá, and its isolated setting on a limestone ridge overlooking the lagoons of Yaxhá and Sacnab is simply splendid. Despite its TV fame, you can still wander the site with nary another visitor in sight. Don't even think of swimming in the lakes here, as they have a healthy population of rather large crocodiles.

★ Yaxhá

The relative lack of inscribed monuments found at **Yaxhá** (8am-5pm daily, $10 admission includes entrance to Nakum) has made tracking its history a bit of a challenge, though it appears it was a major player during the Classic period. It is believed Yaxhá was locked into an ongoing power struggle during much of this time with its smaller neighbor, Naranjo, about 20 kilometers northeast. Yaxhá's sphere of influence was almost certainly limited by the proximity of Tikal, and the architecture here shows many similarities to that of the latter site. Naranjo eventually overran Yaxhá in AD 799. Spanish friars passed through here in 1618, and Austrian explorer Teobert Maler visited in 1904. Much of the site remained unexcavated until recently. A German-Guatemalan effort is conducting the site's ongoing excavation and restoration.

Yaxhá's highest structure is **Structure 216,** offering wonderful views of the lagoons and forests from its summit. Watchers of *Survivor Guatemala* will probably recognize the temple from numerous aerial shots shown during the program's run. It features a broad central staircase and rises to a height of about 30 meters. Access is via a wooden staircase built into the temple's side.

The temples at Yaxhá appear constructed from a very light-colored limestone markedly different from the stones used elsewhere in the Mayan world, giving the ruins a very different feel. You'll find the ruins spread out over nine plazas with 500 mapped structures, including temples, ball courts, and palaces. Other highlights include the recently restored **North Acropolis,** surrounded by three temples, two of which are fairly large. A path known as **Calzada Blom** leads almost one kilometer north from here to the **Maler Group,** a complex featuring twin temples facing each other across a plaza similar to the setup at Tikal. A

number of weathered stelae and the broken remains of a large circular altar further adorn the complex. Another great location affording wonderful views closer to the heart of the ruined city is the top of an unnamed astronomical observation pyramid between Plaza F and Structure 116.

The parking lot and restrooms are on the east side of the park near Plaza C, along with a small museum. There are two boat docks here, one below the parking lot and one at the western end of the site.

You can camp for free at **Campamento Yaxhá,** a designated lakeside campsite below the ruins proper. A more comfortable option is the friendly **Campamento Ecológico El Sombrero** (tel. 7926-5229, www.ecosombreroinicio.tripod.com), about 200 meters from the main road before you come to the park entry post. Its 13 comfortable rooms are housed in thatched-roof bungalows fronting the lake. There's a dock, but it's not recommended for swimming because of the crocodiles. A restaurant serves adequate food, with the variety of menu items on offer heavily dependent on whether or not there's a group

view of Yaxhá from atop Structure 216

staying at the lodge. The lodge arranges boat trips to **Topoxté** and guided tours of Yaxhá.

A series of roads leads to Yaxhá. About 31 kilometers east of Ixlú, on the road toward the Belize border, a well-marked turn-off leads a further 11 kilometers north to the Yaxhá guard post, where you pay admission and sign in to the park. It's another three kilometers from here to the actual ruins of Yaxhá. The road is in good condition, even during the rainy season. If traveling by bus, you can get off at the junction to Yaxhá and hitch a ride with an occasional passing pickup truck or fellow travelers. There is some traffic along this route because of the presence of the small village of La Máquina, about two kilometers from the park guard post.

Several of the Flores tour operators now do Yaxhá with certain frequency. You can also get a minivan from El Remate to the site, but expect to pay about $60 round-trip. Try to find people to share the ride.

Topoxté

This smaller site is situated on an island close to the southwest shore of Yaxhá Lagoon near the Reserva Natural Privada Yaxhá and dates to Preclassic times, though the structures in evidence are mostly from the Late Postclassic period. Plazas and temples are being restored, though nothing is of the scale found at Yaxhá. Topoxté was one of the last strongholds of the Itzá people.

The site was surveyed on several different occasions throughout the 20th century starting in 1904, though restoration and preservation would have to wait until the early 1990s. The most notable structure here is **Temple Pyramid C,** the only Postclassic building remaining in Petén. Similar to structures in the Yucatán and Guatemala's highlands, it has three levels crowned by a portal supported by two pillars.

The only feasible way of getting here is to catch a boat ride from Campamento Ecológico El Sombrero or via boats docked at Yaxhá.

Nakum

North of Yaxhá on a road suitable only for dry-season driving is the Late Classic site of Nakum, now being excavated. Near the site lies the marshy swampland of **Bajo La**

on the road from Yaxhá to Nakum

Justa, which was under intense cultivation during Mayan times. You'll pass through it on your way there. Nakum features the usual assortment of pyramids, plazas, and temples, though there are some unique arches found here along with stelae dating from AD 771-849. Noted archaeologist Alfred Tozzer passed though here in 1909-1910, working for the Peabody Museum; he recorded his findings in a work titled, *A Preliminary Study of the Prehistoric Ruins of Nakum, Guatemala.*

MIRADOR-DOS LAGUNAS-RÍO AZUL NATIONAL PARK

This vast wilderness area encompasses the ruins of El Mirador, one of the earliest and largest Mayan cities to emerge from Petén's jungles, as well as several other Preclassic Mayan sites. It abuts Mexico's Calakmul Biosphere Reserve to the north, which protects another important archaeological site and a large tract of forest in its vicinity. The protected status along the southern border of Guatemala's northern neighbor, and the lack of road access, have allowed this park to remain a largely untrammeled wilderness. Access is difficult and best attempted during the dry season, as seasonal flooding of swamps known as *bajos* turns forest paths into knee-deep mud for much of the year. The other major Mayan site giving its name to this park is Río Azul, which lies deep in the jungle near the western border with Belize.

Archaeologists and environmentalists are lobbying for the creation of the Mirador Basin National Park, and the Guatemalan government has shown interest in preserving this wilderness area harboring Mayan ruins of at least equal importance to that of Tikal.

★ El Mirador

This massive city, rediscovered in 1926 and photographed from the air in 1930, but only recently the focus of ongoing excavations, holds great promise both as a tourism destination rivaling the magnitude of Tikal and as an important piece in the puzzle concerning the advancements of Preclassic Mayan society. El Mirador flourished between 200 BC and AD 150 (about 1,000 years before Tikal) and has revealed a greater level of sophistication than once thought concerning early Mayan society. It is thought to have been home to 80,000 people at the height of its occupation. Its sheer size and the earliness of its development have earned it accolades, such as the "Cradle of Mayan Civilization."

The site sits on a series of limestone hills at an altitude of just over 240 meters (800 feet) and occupies about 16 square kilometers. El Mirador's dominating feature is the presence of two large pyramid complexes, El Tigre and La Danta, running east to west and facing each other. The architecture is characterized by triadic structures composed of one large temple pyramid flanked on either side by two smaller pyramids, a pattern that is repeated elsewhere in the Preclassic sites of the Mirador basin.

The base of the **El Tigre Complex** is as large as three football fields, while the large temple dominating the structure reaches 55 meters (180 feet) in height. The lower flanking pyramids contain gigantic stucco jaguar masks.

The city's **Central Acropolis** takes the form of a narrow plaza bordered on one side by a series of small buildings. Moving south from the El Tigre Complex, you come to the **Monos Complex,** another triadic structure named after the howler monkeys tending to congregate in this area.

The colossal **La Danta Complex** lies to the east of the main plaza and Central Acropolis. Although technically lower than El Tigre, it rises to a height of 70 meters (230 feet) thanks to its elevated location on a hillside, making it the tallest structure in the Mayan world. Its base is equally impressive. There are jaguar and vulture heads built into the sides of the smaller temples here and the spectacular views from the top of the pyramid afford views of nearby Mayan sites, including Nakbé and Calakmul.

Other interesting site features include the

The Mirador Basin Project

Deep in the untouched forests of northern Petén in what archaeologists call the Mirador Basin, far from the throngs of tourists at other Mayan sites, lie the overgrown remains of the most fascinating cities ever built in Preclassic times. The Mirador Basin, as defined by its geographical characteristics, is an elevated basin dominated by low-lying swamps known as *bajos* surrounded by karst limestone hills to the south, east, and west, forming a triangular trench covering roughly 2,100 square kilometers. Some of its sites, including El Mirador and Nakbé, are being excavated and have yielded many clues concerning the advanced nature of early Mayan civilization. As the excavations continue to bring fascinating new discoveries, archaeologists, conservationists, and local residents remain at odds about how best to preserve the remaining Petén forests and the important monuments they harbor.

At the heart of the controversy is the proposal for a Mirador Basin National Park, spearheaded by UCLA's Dr. Richard Hansen, who heads the excavation project at El Mirador. The park would stretch clear to the Mexican border at its northernmost points, encompassing parts of Mirador-Dos Lagunas-Río Azul National Park. At its southern tip, it would stretch all the way down to El Zotz-San Miguel La Palotada Biotope. The area is home to Petén's last remaining expanses of well-preserved forests.

Hansen envisions a large national park guarded by armed rangers similar to those of the U.S. National Park Service. There would be several luxurious ecolodges, visitors centers, an airstrip, a narrow-gauge railroad, and hiking trails linking the various restored Mayan sites within the basin. The proposed park would be roughly four times the size of Tikal National Park and would be largely based upon the same management model. Hansen sees the potential to accommodate up to 80,000 visitors per year.

Hansen's plans, though well-intentioned, have met substantial opposition from local communities and Petén's powerful environmental groups, who have spent many years and millions of dollars developing relationships with local communities to encourage the sustainable extraction of forest products. The sustainable forestry programs have received support from The Nature Conservancy and the U.S. Agency for International Development, among others.

Some believe the communities could receive greater economic benefit from sustainable forestry than from working as staff in tourist hotels and restaurants. The community of Uaxactún, for example, was awarded a sustainable forestry concession in 2000 by CONAP, and villagers there have made a living from collecting forest products for decades.

Although the park itself will supposedly be without roads, new infrastructure would have to be built to make the region more accessible to visitors, raising the specter of a much-talked-about road connecting Tikal to Mexico's Calakmul. Along these lines, Mexico has been insisting on the construction of a road from Chetumal to Tikal in an attempt to integrate the two countries' archaeological sites as part of the Plan Puebla-Panama, an idea vehemently opposed by local conservationists because it would bisect some of the best-conserved areas of the Maya Biosphere Reserve.

For more information on the Mirador Basin project, check out the FARES website at www.miradorbasin.com.

León Pyramid, at the northern edge of the city, and Structure 34—a Preclassic building with the oldest known Mayan standing wall.

Excavations are being done under the direction of UCLA's Dr. Richard Hansen, who has led a larger project aiming to protect the entire Mirador basin as an ecoarchaeological preserve. The preservation of its delicate monuments is being aided by technological advances, including housing structures under polycarbonate roofs designed by Hansen and his associates, so as to protect them from rain and ultraviolet light.

In 2009, Hansen and Guatemalan authorities unveiled the discovery of a frieze at El Mirador depicting a scene from a Mayan sacred book, the *Popol Vuh,* in which the mythical "Hero Twins" visit the underworld. According to Hansen, the frieze lends further credence to the *Popol Vuh*'s creation myth and its authenticity as a Mayan document, despite its first translation well into the Christian era in the 1700s. The frieze took three months to excavate and was found while archaeologists were looking for water reservoirs at the site.

GETTING TO EL MIRADOR

Getting to El Mirador is not an easy task, though you wouldn't know it judging by the readiness of certain Flores tour operators to book you on a trip even at the height of the rainy season. The trek to El Mirador is not for the faint of heart and should not be attempted July-November, when the mud is knee-deep throughout most of the trail. In the worst of places, a rope is tied to the end of a tree and trekkers must pull themselves through shoulder-deep mud. This is, after all, a tropi-cal forest and the terrain is characterized by swamplands. Add to this the incessant buzz of hungry mosquitoes, extreme heat and humid-ity, and you start to realize why so few people make it to this remote site. Your best bet is to attempt the trek at the height of the dry sea-son between February and April. Mel Gibson has visited on several occasions. He arrives by helicopter.

Treks begin in the village of **Carmelita,** in-side the biosphere reserve at the end of the line for the road from Flores. Carmelita consists of a small cluster of houses grouped alongside the road with a few basic services such as a *comedor,* a small general store, and simple ac-commodations. The journey usually lasts five days. The first night is spent at El Tintal, and the next day is a grueling hike that puts you at El Mirador close to nightfall. You spend two nights at the ruins before the two-day hike back to Carmelita. Trip prices vary, but expect to pay about $250 per person for two people. Some outfitters do the trip in seven days, al-lowing more time at El Mirador and stopping en route at Nakbé and Wakná. Mules carry the supplies, but you can also rent additional

the La Danta Complex at El Mirador

mules or horses for riding. This is particularly recommended if you make the journey in the wet season. Expect to pay an extra $13 per day for riding horses.

Be very careful in your selection of an out-fitter to get you to El Mirador. The commu-nity of Carmelita, with help from NGOs, has trained and licensed guides to take visitors on the hike as part of a sustainable tourism initia-tive contributing to the ecologically friendly livelihood of local residents. While it's a nice idea in theory, it may not always be the best way to go. Not all of the local guides have the same skills or experience in running the trek, and you run the risk of getting one of these lesser-experienced guides if you book your trip directly through the community. The task invariably falls on whoever is available to take you at that particular time. Further complicating the scenario is the presence of "gypsy" guides falsely claiming to be part of the local tourism committee.

That being said, you can save some money by taking public transport to Carmelita and then hooking up with the local **Comité de Turismo Comunitario—Cooperativa Carmelita** (tel. 7861-2639 or 7861-2640, www.turismocooperativacarmelita.com, expedicionmirador@yahoo.com). The trip should cost about $250 per person for two people. Book at least a few days in advance, as the supplies and food must be brought in from Flores and the guides must go into town to get them. If you do go this route, make sure the guide buys adequate amounts of food for the duration of the trip. A common complaint is that food runs low halfway through the trek. You should also verify that there is enough water. Have the guide unpack all the supplies and show you exactly what you're taking. Don't hesitate to tell the guide if the food supply is inadequate for the trip's duration. In the worst of cases, you might buy a chicken to eat from the guards at the site, though it won't be cheap and there's no guarantee they'll have one to sell to you.

A final consideration if booking directly through the community is that the guide will want money up front so as to buy food and supplies. This may or may not be an inconvenience to you, but it bears mentioning nonetheless. The more established Flores tour operators take credit cards and arrange everything for you in advance.

This leads us to your second option, that of booking the trip from Flores through one of several recommended outfitters. Although any Flores travel agency will claim to offer the trip, the quality of the service often differs, and you run the risk of getting set up with an inferior guide at premium prices. These outfitters may or may not contract the services of the local Carmelita guides. Matthias, one of the friendly owners of **Los Amigos Hostel** (tel. 7867-5075, www.amigoshostel.com) in Flores, organizes trips using local guides for $225 per person for two people and says he is happy with his current selection of guides after much trial and error. On the high end of the spectrum (and highly recommended) is **Monkey Eco Tours** (tel. 5201-0759 or 5414-5780, www.nitun.com, $185 per person per

picnic lunch on a tour with Monkey Eco Tours

PETÉN
THE MAYA BIOSPHERE RESERVE

Lost and Found: The Mystery of Site Q

For much of the 20th century, looters worked Petén's remote sites undisturbed, raiding tombs and extracting precious artifacts before archaeologists had a chance to study and document them. At the height of the looting, in the 1960s, archaeologists marveled at a series of magnificent glyphs making their way into a number of private collections and museums from an unknown site. Archaeologists dubbed the pieces' origin "Site Q" and the search to find the mysterious producer of the wonderful glyphs was on.

The glyphs made repeated references to a place deciphered as *kan,* or "snake head," which was eventually deduced to be Calakmul, and recorded several events in its history. It was once thought that this might be Site Q, but the badly eroded stelae at Calakmul were not of the same high-quality limestone.

The identity of Site Q would remain a mystery for more than four decades. The mystery first began to unravel in 1997 when an expedition headed by Ian Graham of Harvard University and David Stuart, now at the University of Texas at Austin, found evidence at remote La Corona leading them to suggest the possibility that it was Site Q. Then, in 2005, a 1 by 0.5 meter limestone panel containing 144 hieroglyphs was unearthed when an anthropologist working at the site followed a looter's trench into a small chamber.

Marcello A. Canuto, of Yale University, made the amazing discovery, which matches the Site Q pieces geologically. The translated text of the La Corona glyph panel, meanwhile, is consistent with the writings on the other Site Q pieces.

Although archaeologists are satisfied with finally putting to rest one of the longest-running searches for a lost Mayan city, they still have some unanswered questions. Among the Site Q glyph panels in private collections is one known as the "Dallas panel," which archaeologists believe was cut from a throne room. No such room has yet been found at La Corona.

day for a five- or six-day trip with 4-6 people), with multiday treks done in style and with wonderful camp cuisine.

Part of the Guatemalan government's plan to bring more visitors to El Mirador has involved the construction of visitor facilities. These include two new tent platforms, a kitchen, eating area, hammock lounge, showers, and toilets. Facilities at Carmelita have likewise been improved with a visitor information center, a gift shop selling maps and souvenirs, and toilets.

The most expensive option (but also the easiest) is to make like a celebrity and take a helicopter. This isn't as difficult to arrange as you might think, now that at least one recommended outfitter has begun offering these trips on a fairly regular basis. Guatemala City-based **Expedición Extrema** (tel. 5655-3916 or 3003-2866, info.expedicion@gmail.com) coordinates overnight chopper rides to El Mirador for about $2,000 per person, including transport from Guatemala City with a pit stop in Flores, camping and park entrance fees, and guided hikes around the site and nearby complexes. The fee does not include food, beverages, or overnight camping equipment such as tent, sleeping bag, and sleeping pad. Trips operate with a five-person minimum and are subject to favorable weather conditions. They often post future dates for this and other trips on their Facebook page.

Nakbé, El Tintal, and Wakná

Part of the proposed Mirador Basin park, the smaller sites of Nakbé, El Tintal, and Wakná are important links in the chain unveiling the mysteries of early Mayan civilization. **Nakbé** is thought to be the earliest of Petén's Mayan cities with settlement as early as 1000 BC and several thousand inhabitants by 400 BC. Its layout is much like that of El Mirador, with triadic temple structures in two groups separated by a causeway. Its tallest structure, the Western Temple, reaches a height of just under 46 meters (150 feet), making it about as tall as

Tikal's Temple I. It was completed in 500 BC. A large stucco mask has also been unearthed here, on the side of one of the temples, much like at El Mirador. The excavations here, under the direction of Richard Hansen, are still in their early stages, but more finds are sure to follow.

On the trek to El Mirador, 21 kilometers south, you'll pass by the site of **El Tintal,** which is also similar in construction to the larger city to the north. It has been badly looted, and the temples here remain unrestored. There are excellent views of the surrounding forest from the top of its highest temple, including a glimpse of El Mirador far off in the distance. It's sure to motivate you to continue the second leg of the journey. Trekkers usually camp here the first night en route to El Mirador.

Rediscovered by Landsat imagery as recently as 1998, **Wakná** is another Preclassic site buried under the forest cover of the Mirador Basin. A ground crew led by Dr. Hansen confirmed the site's existence but unfortunately also found evidence of looting. A deep trench had been dug into a tomb allowing looters to cart off the priceless artifacts found therein. Hansen's plans to restore and protect the Mirador Basin's sites may prevent further plunder of Wakná and other sites within the proposed park.

LAGUNA DEL TIGRE NATIONAL PARK

This vast park on the northwestern corner of Petén encompasses important wetlands, the largest in Central America. It also contains the only remaining populations of scarlet macaws in Guatemala, which are being protected via ongoing conservation efforts at a biological research station. Oil drilling, present before the park's creation, continues in the western part of the reserve, despite protests from environmental groups and their having been declared a violation of the park's intended use. In 2006, the Guatemalan government granted further oil exploration concessions in the park's multiple-use zone.

Visitors to this park should limit their activities to those centered around the Scarlet Macaw Biological Research Station and the site of Waka', as the security conditions and the loss of much of the local habitat prevent me from recommending more in-depth explorations of this wild frontier.

Within the larger national park is the **Biotopo Laguna del Tigre Río-Escondido,** which has two biological stations open to researchers. It has been badly fragmented by seasonal forest fires and the encroachment of communities illegally settled inside park boundaries.

Sights

Unlike other parts of Petén, Laguna del Tigre has not been widely explored for the presence of archaeological sites or in terms of its biological diversity. Among the few archaeological discoveries is the site of **Waka',** now being excavated by archaeologists from Southern Methodist University under the direction of David Freidel and Héctor Escobedo. Waka' has yielded some amazing finds, including the 2004 discovery of the royal burial tomb of a queen dating to about AD 620. The find is especially significant because there are only a handful of known tombs pertaining to women in the entire Mayan world. The location of yet another royal tomb was announced in May 2006.

Waka' is thought to have been an important commercial and political center because of its location on a tributary of the Río San Pedro, giving it direct access to the sites of central Petén, the Southern Highlands, and Mexico. It flourished between AD 400 and 800, apparently coming under the dominion of Calakmul in its protracted power struggle with Tikal. It was later invaded by a resurgent Tikal in AD 743. There are several well-preserved stelae here, including Stela 16, which tells of the visit of a Tikal-bound Teotihuacán warrior in AD 378.

Nearby, the rediscovery of **La Corona** has solved the decades-old mystery of the location of a long-sought Mayan city. The limited

Saving Guatemala's Scarlet Macaws

Among Petén's most beautiful creatures are the brightly colored scarlet macaws that once roamed freely throughout Petén. You'll probably run into these large parrots throughout your travels in Guatemala; they are popular pets in hotel courtyards on account of their colorful red, blue, and yellow plumage—including two beautiful red tail feathers—in addition to their boisterous squawking and ability to mimic human speech. Unfortunately, their populations have been decimated by habitat loss and wildlife poaching for the international pet trade. Still, there remain pockets where macaws continue to nest, and local scientists have taken it upon themselves to help protect what's left of Guatemala's dwindling numbers of these exotic birds.

In the dense forests that still surround the site of Waka', biologists from several agencies working in Petén, including **ProPetén** (www.propeten.org) and **Wildlife Conservation Society** (www.wcs.org), have established protected nesting grounds. There are 21 nests in hollow forest trees and additional "artificial" nests are being created. The latter involve creating hollowed-out tree trunks, which are then placed high in the treetops. Biologists report success with this new method. Like most parrots, scarlet macaws lay 2-4 white eggs in a tree cavity, with their young hatching after about 25 days. The hatchlings fly about 105 days later and leave their parents as late as one year.

The nests at Waka' enjoy year-round protection by a joint military-police force charged with safeguarding Guatemala's natural resources.

Volunteers are welcome at the site, giving visitors an exciting opportunity to help out in the conservation of Guatemala's exotic creatures while helping to fund the biological station's efforts.

amount of exploration in this part of Petén inevitably leads you to wonder what else may be lying undiscovered in this vast park of wetlands and jungle.

The park enjoys on-site protection by armed guards that are part of a joint task force involving the Civilian National Police (PNC) and SEPRONA, a specially trained unit of the military created to guard and protect nature preserves. You will see the guards at the site's ranger station, about a 25-minute walk from the riverbank. You are welcome to camp here. Many travelers visit Waka' as part of a tour known as the **Scarlet Macaw Trail,** which can be booked from a number of travel agencies in Flores and costs anywhere between $200 and $300 per person. The duration of the trip, as well as the places to visit, can be adjusted to suit your preferences. Most visitors combine the site of Waka' with hikes into the surrounding pristine forests to see the nesting sites of scarlet macaws, which local scientists here are working to protect.

★ Las Guacamayas Biological Research Station

Las Guacamayas Biological Research Station (tel. 7867-5048 or 5699-3669, www. lasguacamayas.org) is owned by ProPetén and welcomes visitors. The biological station sits amid verdant jungle on the shores of the Río San Pedro, a 20-minute boat ride from the village of Paso Caballos. It is one of the best places in Petén to combine wildlife-viewing and rainforest trekking while staying in relative comfort, offering easy access to the ruins of Waka' and the surrounding forests. The current facility is the second incarnation of the biological station; the first was burned to the ground by angry villagers from Paso Caballos in the 1990s. ProPetén has since worked on strengthening ties to local communities and educating them about conservation.

There are basic dorm rooms with somewhat stiff mattresses, shared bath, mosquito netting, and screened-in rooms accommodating up to 20 people. For extended stays, try packing a sleeping pad for extra cushioning. Nice views of the river and a series of nature trails round out the list of amenities. The shortest trail leads to an observation tower, where you have a sweeping view of the Río San Pedro and the wetlands of Laguna del Tigre National Park west to the foothills of the Sierra del Lacandón. There is a six-kilometer-long network of trails.

In the evening, you can go out on the river in search of crocodiles with the station's staff. Bird-watching is available in the mornings.

There are observation platforms inside the site of Waka' where the scarlet macaw project operates. The staff may offer photo safaris whereby you can watch and photograph macaws from a platform sometime in the near future. The best time to visit for a glimpse at nesting macaws is during February and March, though the macaws can usually be seen between November and April.

A two-day, three-night package including meals, accommodation, round-trip transport from Flores, bird-watching, and a tour of El Perú costs about $300 each for two people. There are different itineraries, all with a certain amount of flexibility, which can be tailored to particular interests such as archaeology or bird-watching, for example. Some travelers extend their stay to include a hike to the impressive cliffs of **Buena Vista,** which stand out from the surrounding jungle and afford wonderful views from the top.

Volunteers are also welcome at the biological station. During one of my last visits, two Spanish women were busy on a two-week tour of duty recollecting animal droppings for scientific investigation as to the health of local populations of certain species. Volunteers provide their own food and pay an average of $10 per day. The station prefers a two-week minimum commitment. Other activities you may be asked to assist with include wildlife monitoring and trail building and maintenance.

Getting There

Access to the park and, more specifically, Waka', is via a dirt road heading northwest from Flores to the village of Paso Caballos (two hours). From there, it's a 20-minute motorboat ride up the Río Sacluc to the biological station and another five minutes to the entrance to Waka'.

Background

The Landscape

GEOGRAPHY

Guatemala is the third-largest country in Central America. It occupies 42,042 square miles, making it about the size of Tennessee. The country shares borders with Mexico, Belize, Honduras, and El Salvador. Within Guatemala's relatively small area are 14 distinct ecosystems found at elevations varying from sea level to higher than 4,200 meters (13,780 feet). Many people think of Guatemala as a sweltering tropical country, which is only partially true. While it does feature warm tropical coastal environments and hot lowland jungles, a rugged spine of mountains and volcanoes runs through the country's center. In the tropics, elevation mostly determines climate, and this is certainly the case in Guatemala. Temperatures drop dramatically the higher you go in elevation, and precipitation varies greatly depending on what side of a mountain chain you're on. All of this translates into a dizzying array of landscapes, making Guatemala a delight to explore.

The country divides rather neatly into various geographical zones. The volcanic highlands run through the country's center going west to east from Mexico to El Salvador. Elevation tends to get lower closer to the Salvadoran border. The eastern areas of Alta and Baja Verapaz are largely mountainous but also largely composed of limestone. A curious feature of this area, found in its northern limits, is the presence of small, forested limestone hills much like those found in parts of China. East from Guatemala City toward Honduras, the terrain is largely dominated by semiarid flatlands covered in cactus.

Closer to the Caribbean Coast in the department of Izabal, the terrain once again becomes lush and largely filled with banana plantations. A small sliver of Caribbean coastline runs between the Honduran border and Belize but features white-sand beaches, swamplands, and some impressive tropical rainforests. Small mountains are interspersed throughout parts of the Caribbean coastal region.

Running roughly parallel to the highlands, to the south, are the Pacific Coast flatlands. This is a rich agricultural area once covered in tropical forest but now home to vast sugarcane and coffee plantations, the latter being on the slopes of the highland zones as they descend into the coastal plain. The Pacific Coast is also home to wetlands, mangrove swamps, and beaches of curiously dark color because of their proximity to the country's volcanic chain.

The northern third of Guatemala is a vast Ohio-sized limestone flatland known as Petén. Once covered entirely in tropical forests, it has increasingly become deforested in its southern parts with only the northern third retaining large unbroken swaths of forest.

Here is a brief discussion of some of Guatemala's outstanding geographic features and why they might be of interest to the visitor.

Mountains

The highest of Guatemala's mountains are actually volcanic peaks. There are 33 of them in total with a handful now active. Volcán Tajumulco, at 4,220 meters (13,845 feet), is the highest point in all of Central America, followed closely by nearby Volcán Tacaná, at 4,110 meters (13,484 feet). The most frequently climbed volcanoes include the active Pacaya near Guatemala City, the three volcanoes

---

Previous: the crater of 12,000-foot Agua Volcano; African palm plantation in Petén.

on the shores of Lake Atitlán, Agua, and Acatenango near Antigua. Some volcanoes, such as Chicabal and Ipala, feature turquoise lagoons, which fill their craters. Other active volcanoes include Fuego and Santiaguito.

Among the nonvolcanic mountains, the Sierra de los Cuchumatanes, near the border with Mexico, is Guatemala's, and Central America's, highest mountain chain. It stands 3,837 meters (12,588 feet) at its highest point. Its smooth, rounded peaks attest to years of erosion from being glaciated thousands of years ago. Other noteworthy mountain chains include the Sierra de las Minas, in the eastern part of the country. Protected as a private forest reserve, it still contains large stands of virgin cloud forest. Farther east near the Caribbean Coast are the Cerro San Gil and Montañas del Mico, which are still covered in dense tropical rainforest. Petén has relatively few mountains, but the foothills of the Maya Mountains of neighboring Belize run into the department's southeastern corner with an elevation of over 1,000 meters (3,300 feet) at Petén's highest point. Petén's other noteworthy mountain range is the remote and mostly forested Sierra del Lacandón, at the far western edge of the department bordering Mexico and exceeding 600 meters (2,000 feet) at its highest point.

Guatemala's mountain scenery comes largely as a product of its geographic location at the intersection of the North American, Cocos, and Caribbean plates, making it one of the most seismically and volcanically active places in the world. Indeed, Guatemala is no stranger to earthquakes. Among the many fault lines running through the country are the parallel Chixoy-Polochic and Motagua faults. The latter is responsible for the most recent major earthquake to rock Guatemala, a magnitude-7.5 whopper in February 1976 killing thousands and wiping entire villages off the face of the map. A series of massive earthquakes in 1773 resulted in the relocation of the Guatemalan capital from the Panchoy Valley (Antigua Guatemala) to the Valley of the Hermitage, where it remains today, better known as Guatemala City.

Rivers

Guatemala has several rivers worthy of mention. The greatest of these is the Usumacinta, which is formed by the confluence of the Chixoy and Pasión Rivers, making it Central America's most voluminous river. Guatemalan author Virgilio Rodríguez Macal, in his novel *Guayacán,* calls it the "father and lord of the Central American rivers." The

Acatenango Volcano is a popular climb.

Usumacinta forms much of Guatemala's border with Mexico and continues its northwesterly flow all the way to the Gulf of Mexico. On the Guatemalan side, the Usumacinta borders the relatively untouched Sierra del Lacandón National Park, which harbors dense tropical rainforests. The Usumacinta is a wild frontier and an active waterway for drug smuggling, contraband logging, and boats carrying illegal immigrants on their journey north.

The Pasión, an Usumacinta tributary, meanders through southern Petén. Much like the larger Usumacinta, its watershed was extremely important in Mayan times. Several Mayan sites lie near the river. In the arid southeastern part of the country, the Río Motagua connects the highlands to the Caribbean Sea and forms a dry river valley of agricultural importance since Mayan times. Other notable rivers include the Río San Pedro, also in Petén; the Verapaces-area Río Cahabón, which has excellent white-water runs year-round; and the Río Dulce, a lazy tropical river connecting Lake Izabal to the Caribbean.

Lakes and Lagoons

Guatemala has several lakes noteworthy for their size, recreational opportunities, and sheer natural beauty. Foremost among these is highland Lake Atitlán, called "the most beautiful lake in the world" by author Aldous Huxley during his travels through the region. The lake's spectacular mountain scenery is punctuated by the sentinel presence of three towering volcanoes along its southern shores. Near Guatemala City, Lake Amatitlán has been a weekend getaway for city dwellers since time immemorial but industrial pollution has spoiled the once-clear waters. Still, Guatemalans have taken on the onerous task of rescuing its waters with foreign help, and the lake may soon be safe again for swimming. An aerial tram operating on surrounding hillsides has recently reopened the area to visitors, making a side trip to this tranquil spot increasingly alluring for wonderful views of the rugged mountain terrain. The largest of Guatemala's lakes, Lake Izabal, is a tropical lake connected to the Caribbean by the Río Dulce. The Río Polochic delta, on Izabal's southwestern shore, is becoming increasingly popular as a bird-watcher's paradise. Petén's Lake Petén Itzá is also a tropical flatland lake with the added bonus of tropical forests, crystal-clear waters, and a variety of accommodations from which to enjoy all of these. As much of Petén is limestone, the lake's waters have a distinct turquoise color near the shores and from the air look very much like those of the Mexican Caribbean. Farther east toward Belize is Yaxhá Lagoon, near the ruins of the same name. The lagoon, and its aggressive crocodiles, was made famous by the *Survivor Guatemala* television series filmed here in the summer of 2005.

There are many beautiful lagoons in the Guatemalan highlands. Some, atop volcanoes such as Ipala and Chicabal, are believed by the Maya to harbor mystical powers and are the site of rituals. Laguna Lachuá is a beautiful, almost perfectly round lagoon in the Ixcán jungle region just north of the highlands. The surrounding rainforest has been preserved, but unfortunately it is an ecological island, a green square in a surrounding sea of deforestation.

The Coasts

Guatemala has a significant amount of coastline along the Pacific Ocean, though there are few beaches to speak of. Still, there are a few places with surf-worthy waves, and the Pacific Coast beaches are exotic because of their dark sands, which are due to the proximity of active volcanoes. Among the best places to hit the beach are Monterrico and Las Lisas. Guatemala is gaining international fame among anglers for the quality of its deep-sea fishing. On the Caribbean side, there are a few pleasant white-sand beaches on the remote peninsula of Punta de Manabique as well as closer to the towns of Puerto Barrios and Lívingston. There is excellent scuba diving in the outlying Belize cayes and around Punta de Manabique.

CLIMATE

Guatemala has a tropical climate, though temperatures vary greatly between regions because of differences in altitude. The coastal plains and lowlands have an average yearly temperature of about 27°C (80°F), with little seasonal change. Mountain valleys 1,200-1,800 meters (4,000-6,000 feet) high are usually comfortably mild. Major cities such as Guatemala City, Antigua, and Quetzaltenango all lie at these altitudes, meaning they have mostly pleasant year-round spring-like temperatures of 16°C-21°C (60°F-70°F). Higher mountain peaks and valleys sometimes have frost and average 4°C (40°F). Keep in mind that these are averages and certain times of year are markedly warmer than others. The North American winter solstice often brings the arrival of cold fronts, which make temperatures in the highlands dip below freezing on mountain summits but also in highland cities such as Quetzaltenango. If you're traveling to Guatemala November-February, bring a warm sweater or two for the chilly highlands and a heavy jacket if you plan to climb some volcanoes. At the other extreme, March and April, coinciding with the spring equinox, is the warmest time of year. Temperatures in the Petén lowlands, Izabal, and Pacific Coast

plain routinely hover around 38°C (100°F) during these months. Guatemala City and Antigua hover at around 29°C (85°F).

There are distinct dry and rainy seasons in Guatemala. The dry season runs from November to the beginning of May. If you are a photographer interested in capturing images of Guatemala's fantastic mountain scenery, you may want to avoid visiting during March and April, when haze from dust and agricultural burning tends to obliterate any views of surrounding scenery. The volcanoes around Antigua and Lake Atitlán become extremely difficult to spot during this time of year.

The rainy season generally lasts May-November with daily showers during most of this period, usually in the afternoon. Mornings are usually sunny and clear, with a gradual buildup of giant rain clouds throughout the day, culminating in a torrential downpour. The latter months tend to be the rainiest with deluges sometimes lasting entire days. The rainy season is sometimes referred to as *invierno,* meaning winter, though it is officially summer in the Northern Hemisphere, where Guatemala lies. *Verano,* or summer, refers to the tail end of the dry season.

The Pacific coastal plain and Western Highlands receive 76-150 centimeters

Lake Petén Itzá is one of Guatemala's largest lakes.

(30-60 inches) of rain a year, and the Eastern Highlands average 51-76 centimeters (20-30 inches). Again, these figures vary greatly from place to place depending on factors such as altitude and what side of the mountain chain you're on. An example of this is the presence of ample rainfall and lush cloud forests on the forested slopes of the Sierra de las Minas in contrast to semiarid plains in the mountain's rain shadow along the neighboring Motagua Valley. Petén receives 200-381 centimeters (80-150 inches) of rain annually, which falls throughout most of the year. The rainiest place in Guatemala is said to be the Cerro San Gil rainforest, on the Caribbean Coast, where warm, moist air rises from the ocean and dumps precipitation on this small mountain chain. There is really no dry season to speak of in this area.

There are sometimes breaks in the rainfall, known as *canícula,* for a week or two in July and/or August. Rainfall can vary substantially from year to year, which is due to factors such as the presence of El Niño or La Niña. El Niño often means a prolonged dry season, which can lead to intense wildfires in forested areas such as Petén.

Hurricanes and tropical storms sometimes hit Guatemala during the latter months of the rainy season, causing widespread damage. Much of this is due to soil saturation on deforested and waterlogged hillsides, which give way to devastating mudslides, as occurred in parts of the Lake Atitlán basin after Hurricane Stan in 2005. Hurricane Mitch also left a trail of devastation along the Caribbean Coast in 1998, obliterating much of the banana harvest and destroying thousands of homes.

ENVIRONMENTAL ISSUES

Guatemala's environmental issues, particularly in regard to tropical deforestation, can seem daunting at times. The country and its people appear to be caught in a vicious cycle that will end only when the environmental degradation reaches its peak and the consequences are fully reaped. It seems greed, apathy, poverty, corruption, ignorance, and neglect have all conspired against Guatemala's precious natural resources. I do not mean to sound pessimistic in my introduction to this subject. I just think I've had the opportunity to see what's at stake, having explored much of Guatemala during my teenage years and seeing firsthand the gradual encroachment of the agricultural frontier into what was once virgin forest. It is hoped that visitors to Guatemala, much like those to Belize and Costa Rica, will play a pivotal role in raising awareness of the abundant natural heritage with which Guatemalans been blessed, enabling the conservation of these resources to become a source of economic and moral value.

There is a long way to go to make environmental awareness a matter of national consciousness, as demonstrated by how frequently one sees garbage by the roadside or car and bus passengers casually throwing refuse out their windows. The problem of raising this consciousness is exacerbated when one takes into account the overwhelming lack of education of the general populace, with its alarming levels of illiteracy, and the fact that environmental protection always takes a backseat when it comes down to a question of preserving the forest or cutting it down to plant subsistence crops.

At the same time, there is much to be hopeful about, particularly in the three decades since Guatemala established its democracy, during which time the country has been governed by civilian presidents interested in environmental matters. In addition to establishing the Maya Biosphere Reserve, Vinicio Cerezo Arévalo pushed through congress much of the legislation serving as a basis for the protection of Guatemala's natural heritage. Many valiant Guatemalans have likewise done their part to establish a genuine environmental movement in their country. Their courage is underscored by the fact that, in Guatemala, environmental activism necessarily entails standing firm in the face of death threats and intimidations. Environmental protection often conflicts with the interests of the still-powerful agricultural elites, among these: lumber barons; drug cartels using remote parks for illicit activities; cattle ranchers, some of whom have military ties; and land-hungry peasants. Environmental martyrs are many in Guatemala, much the same as the legacy of those campaigning for greater respect for human rights and better socioeconomic conditions. In these ways, environmental issues in Guatemala are largely circumscribed within the larger social issues of endemic poverty, power politics, and the rule of law.

Deforestation

In 2005, about 37 percent of Guatemala was still forested, down from 40 percent in 2001. Most of the country was at one time covered by forests, a fact attested to by Guatemala's ancient Mayan-Toltec name meaning "land of the trees." The once-forested Pacific plains have given way largely to sugarcane and coffee plantations while the forests of the Caribbean slope have been turned largely over to banana plantations. The highlands, for their part, have been under intense cultivation since preconquest times, though there are still substantial forests left in remote corners of Quiché and Huehuetenango. Most of the loss of forest cover in the past 40 years has been due to

government incentives aimed at colonizing the northern department of Petén in an attempt to ease pressure for land by an ever-increasing population. The Petén thus became an escape valve from pressures for land reform historically thwarted by Guatemala's agricultural elites. It is here that a modern-day battle is being waged over Guatemala's remaining forests.

It is hoped that history will not repeat itself, as the ancient Maya have a valuable lesson to teach about what happens when the forests are cut down. It is speculated that among the reasons for the Classic Mayan collapse is widespread drought caused by the overwhelming deforestation of the tropical lowlands the Maya inhabited. This may have, in turn, led to widespread warfare among Mayan city-states as populations scrambled to assert dominance over dwindling resources. The southern and central sections of Petén have been almost completely deforested, leading to local declines in annual rainfall marked by prolonged and warmer dry seasons. The northern third of Petén remains mostly intact, for now, protected as the Maya Biosphere Reserve. Pressures against the reserve continue to mount, however, with illegal land grabs and clandestine logging continuing to

tropical deforestation in Alta Verapaz

make inroads. There is no guarantee that the reserve's borders will remain inviolate or that they will stave off the advance of the agricultural frontier.

In addition to the activities of peasant farmers steadily encroaching on virgin forests, the activities of contraband loggers, looters of unexcavated archaeological sites, and wildlife poachers inside park boundaries constitute an additional threat to the forests. Adding insult to injury, contraband loggers, wildlife poachers, and peasants from neighboring Mexico have been scuttling the border separating their country from Guatemala to burn forest, kill wildlife, and plant crops in cleared lands. A now-famous Landsat image appearing in the October 1989 issue of *National Geographic* shows the once razor-sharp border between Mexico and Guatemala's Laguna del Tigre National Park. The border is now dotted with burned-out land parcels along much of this boundary marker as a curious extension of the wide-scale deforestation in Mexico.

A recent development is the clearing of forest to build clandestine landing strips for drug-laden aircraft coming in from South America. With the virtual absence of local law enforcement and the aid of poor peasants eager for extra income, drug lords have found a haven for their illicit activities in Guatemala's remote parks. They have even gone so far as to acquire property by buying lands from settlers and then registering them illegally in their own names. Whether through bribes or the falsification of documents, *narcos* have infiltrated Guatemala's protected lands to suit their illicit operations.

Water Resources

Access to safe drinking water is a widespread problem throughout most of Guatemala. According to figures from the United Nations Development Program, roughly a quarter of Guatemalans still lack this basic necessity. This figure becomes even more dramatic in rural areas, where it is actually closer to 50 percent. The lack of potable water in turn leads to many illnesses, including intestinal parasites and amoebic dysentery, among others. Although most cities have sewer systems, wastewater treatment is virtually nonexistent—raw sewage often flows into rivers, lakes, and oceans. Guatemala City's sewage, for example, is responsible for polluting the nearby Motagua River with human excrement, solvents, and metallic waste. Adding to Guatemala's water woes is pollution from petroleum-based fertilizers used in commercial coffee, banana, and sugar plantations, which openly dump wastewater into nearby rivers and streams.

Air Quality

Guatemala City is notoriously polluted by old, recycled U.S. school buses, the basis of its public transportation network, which belch out diesel fumes in the form of black clouds. A promising recent development is a revamping of the city's public transportation system to include newer vehicles and stop older buses from circulating in the city center. In addition to auto exhaust, pollution from industrial facilities and burning garbage from the city dump combine to form a thick haze often hanging over the city. The worst days occur when thermal inversions cause the haze to hang in a low-altitude pollution gulag, much like a pineapple-upside-down cake. Concentrations of particulates, ozone, and nitrogen dioxide often exceed World Health Organization safety standards, particularly on these days. During the rainy season, the haze is washed away by the afternoon rains, after which the atmosphere is amazingly free of pollutants.

Elsewhere, smoke and ash from occasional volcanic eruptions can make the atmosphere somewhat hazy, though the worst pollution comes from dry-season agricultural burning and forest fires. When one considers that more than half of all energy consumption comes from burning firewood, the reasons behind the thick haze hanging over much of the country during March and April begin to emerge.

Resource Extraction

Mining activities have made Guatemalan newspaper headlines in recent years, as mining interests have cast an interested eye upon Guatemalan lands. Although environmental-impact studies are required by law, these often fall prey to government corruption in the form of payoffs in exchange for a favorable assessment. Threats and intimidation against environmental groups often attempt to quell any opposition to these projects.

Residents of the Western Highlands town of Sipacapa have demonstrated vehement opposition to the opening of a strip mine in the vicinity of their town, bringing the case directly to the president of the World Bank and officials of the International Finance Corporation (IFC), the World Bank's private-sector lending arm. Among the arguments against the installation of mining activities is the conflict of an open-pit mine with Mayan belief in the sacredness of the Earth.

Residents of Sipacapa held a referendum overwhelmingly rejecting the presence of a mine on community lands. In early 2005, protests against the mine's establishment, including roadblocks, were broken up by military forces, resulting in 11 people being injured and one killed.

More than 550 mining concessions now cover 10 percent of the country. Almost 20 percent of these are for open-pit mining of minerals such as gold, silver, nickel, and copper. A gold mine operating in Huehuetenango has been the subject of particularly harsh criticism by local environmentalists and an object of contention with indigenous residents.

Petroleum extraction continues in the northern Petén lowlands and parts of Alta Verapaz, including the Laguna del Tigre National Park, although ecological organizations have long denounced its negative effects upon the environment. Oil exploration and extraction were present before the creation of the Maya Biosphere Reserve and have thus been allowed to continue, mostly in parts of the buffer and multiple-use zones. During the civil war, oil pipelines became a frequent

Sugarcane harvesting involves agricultural burning and is a major polluter.

target for guerrillas sabotaging the activities of multinationals involved in resource extraction. Occupations of oil-drilling facilities were also frequent. In addition to creating roads through sparsely populated areas, the oil extraction activities have come under fire because of oil spills in protected lands.

In 2005, the Guatemalan government opened new concessions in an area along the Petén-Alta Verapaz border said to harbor an estimated 200 million barrels of oil. Guatemala's total estimated reserves amount to about 2 billion barrels. Guatemalan oil's high sulfur content prevents it from being used in the production of diesel or gasoline, relegating it to use in the production of asphalt.

Soil Erosion

Unbridled deforestation on steep hillsides is responsible for much of the erosion of Guatemala's soil. Already about one-third of all land cover is considered eroded or seriously degraded, a significant amount when one considers the high degree of susceptibility to erosion of Guatemala's soil, which is composed largely of unconsolidated volcanic ash. Deforestation and soil erosion work hand in hand and are responsible for many of the tragic mudslides in the aftermath of tropical storms such as Hurricanes Mitch and Stan. Soil erosion has also contributed to greatly shortening the useful life of Chixoy Dam, which supplies about 15 percent of Guatemala's electricity, through siltation of the dam's reservoir.

Conservation Groups

Many grassroots environmental organizations operate in Guatemala in partnership with international conservation organizations. Among the best-known groups is **Fundación Defensores de la Naturaleza** (7a Avenida 7-09 Zona 13, Guatemala City, tel. 2310-2929, www.defensores.org.gt), which administers Sierra del Lacandón National Park, Sierra de las Minas Biosphere Reserve, Bocas del Polochic Wildlife Refuge, and the United Nations National Park just outside of Guatemala City. Through private land purchases, Defensores has been able to acquire large tracts of land in Sierra de las Minas and Sierra del Lacandón with help from The Nature Conservancy.

The Nature Conservancy also works locally with the Fundación para el Desarrollo y la Conservación (Foundation for Development and Conservation), or **FUNDAECO** (7a Calle "A" 20-53 Zona 11, Colonia Mirador, Guatemala City, tel. 2474-3645, www.fundaeco.org.gt). Together, they have bought more than 9,000 acres of tropical rainforest in the Caribbean coastal mountain chain of Cerro San Gil.

The forests of Petén are understandably the center of much attention from local and international organizations. **ProPetén** (Calle Central, Flores, Petén, tel. 7867-5296, www.propeten.org), an offshoot of Conservation International, began operating shortly after the creation of the Maya Biosphere Reserve and is credited with implementing innovative approaches to bridge the gap between the need for environmental conservation and the needs of communities living in or near the reserve. Among its successful programs are the establishment of a research station for the protection of scarlet macaws, forestry concessions with local communities in the Maya Biosphere Reserve's buffer zone, and two Spanish-language schools owned and operated by local villagers.

Another important organization is the Asociacion de Rescate y Conservacion de Vida Silvestre (Wildlife Rescue and Conservation Association), or **ARCAS** (Km.30, Calle Hillary, Lote 6, Casa Villa Conchita, San Lucas Sacatepéquez, Guatemala, tel. 7830-1374, www.arcasguatemala.com). It works to protect and rehabilitate wildlife, including sea turtles on the Pacific Coast and animals falling prey to poaching for the lucrative pet trade in Petén, including cats, monkeys, and birds.

Several organizations operate in Guatemala's eastern Verapaces and Izabal regions. Finally, **Tropico Verde** (Vía 6 4-25 Zona 4, Edificio Castañeda, Oficina 41, Guatemala City, tel. 2339-4225, www.tropicoverde.org) is a watchdog organization monitoring the state of Guatemala's parks via field studies. In addition to local monitoring, it helps bring awareness of local repercussions of international environmental issues such as Guatemala's participation in international conventions on whaling, to name just one example.

Plants and Animals

Guatemala harbors an astounding degree of biodiversity due greatly to the variety of ecosystems found within its borders. Its location in the Central American land bridge between North and South America means it is the southernmost range for certain North American species as well as the northernmost range for certain Southern Hemisphere species. Fourteen of the 38 Holdridge Life Zones are represented in Guatemala.

PLANTS

Among the cornucopia of plantlife are 8,000 varieties of plants, including more than 600 types of orchids. Of these, nearly 200 are unique to Guatemala. The rugged cloud forests of Sierra de las Minas, meanwhile, boast the presence of 17 distinct species of pine trees found nowhere else on earth. Endemic orchid species include Guatemala's national flower, the rare *monja blanca,* or "white nun." It is found in the cloud forests of the Verapaces region.

Guatemala means "land of the trees" in the ancient Mayan-Toltec language. According to 2005 figures, 37 percent of Guatemala remained covered in forest in 2005, down from 40 percent in 2001. Among the different types of forests present in Guatemala's varied climate zones are tropical rainforest, tropical dry forests, evergreen forests, and cloud forests. In some cold, mountainous parts of Guatemala there are temperate forests whose broadleaf trees' leaves briefly change color before falling to the ground, though not at all to the extent of the displays of fall foliage present in parts of North America.

The forests of Petén are officially classified mostly as tropical moist and tropical wet forests. Guatemala's only true rainforests, strictly speaking, are found in the Cerro San Gil along the Caribbean Coast.

Most of Guatemala's remaining forest cover is found in Petén, especially the northern third

of the department in a huge park known as the Maya Biosphere Reserve. The Verapaces, Izabal, Quiché, and Huehuetenango also have significant amounts of forest cover remaining. Many of these forests are on remote mountains that have remained inaccessible and have therefore escaped the ravages of the advance of the agricultural frontier. Significant wetlands, including four of international importance, are found in Petén, Izabal, and the western section of the Pacific Coast plains near the Mexican border. Mangrove forests are found on the Pacific and Caribbean Coasts.

Among the plants you'll find in Guatemala's tropical forests is the towering ceiba (*Ceiba pentandra*), which is Guatemala's national tree and was considered sacred by the ancient Maya. It has a wide trunk and buttressed roots with branches found only at the very top. The ceiba can reach heights of 60 meters. You will often find them in cleared fields—one of only a few trees left standing amid grazing cattle. The most famous example is along the footpath at the entrance to Tikal National Park, where visitors are often photographed standing next to the tree's colossal trunk.

Another common tropical forest tree is the *chicozapote,* from which chicle is extracted for use in the manufacture of chewing gum. *Chicleros* cut V-shaped notches in the tree's trunk, allowing the sap to drip down the tree to a receptacle placed there for its collection. These days chicle goes to Japan, which still favors the traditional base for making gum. During the early 20th century, most of Guatemala's chicle went to the Wrigley Company.

The *ramón,* or breadnut tree, is found throughout the tropical flatlands and was widely used during Mayan times for making tortillas and drinks, among other things. Archaeologists have linked the increasing consumption of ramón seeds to decreasing food-production cycles during Mayan times, speculating that it served as a replacement to more traditional staples during periods of drought.

One of the most curious plants found in the tropical forests is the strangler fig, or *mata palo* (*Ficus obtusifolia*), which wraps itself around its host, eventually killing it. It has thick roots and looks much like a wooden rope wrapped around a tree. It's easy to spot; you'll recognize it when you see it.

Guatemala's forests contain excellent hardwoods, the most prominent of these being cedar (*Cedrela angustifolia*) and mahogany (*Swientenia alicastrum*). Much of the Petén forest has been logged, legally and illegally. Peasant forestry cooperatives operate in the multiple-use zone of the Maya Biosphere Reserve sustainably harvesting eco-certified hardwoods. Guatemalan mahogany is highly prized in the making of furniture. The cabinets of the Four Seasons resort on Costa Rica's Pacific Coast, for example, are made from Guatemalan mahogany. Also important as a forest product is *xate* palm (*Chamaedorea spp.*), which is harvested in the forests using sustainable methods, though overcutting is entirely possible. The bright green palm leaves are used in floral arrangements throughout the United States and Europe.

ANIMALS
Birds

Guatemala's abundant birdlife includes more than 700 different species. Although not nearly as popular a bird-watching destination as Belize or Costa Rica, Guatemala has become increasingly well known among birders now that pristine areas conducive to the activity are no longer the site of skirmishes between army and guerrilla forces, as was the case during the civil war. This has opened new areas to bird-watching and Guatemalans are quickly taking steps to gain some ground in catering to this very lucrative tourism market.

Among the highlights of a visit to Guatemala is the opportunity to spot its rare, endangered national emblem, the resplendent quetzal (*Pharomacrus mocino*). The quetzal gives its name to the national currency and was revered by the Maya for its long green tail feathers used in ceremonial headdresses. Quetzals have become increasingly rare because of the loss of their cloud forest habitat, but they still survive on the slopes of the Lake Atitlán volcanoes, parts of the Sierra de

Guatemala's exuberant vegetation

los Cuchumatanes, and particularly in the Sierra de las Minas. A forest preserve in Baja Verapaz, known as the Quetzal Biotope, has been set aside specifically to protect the quetzal. It can often be seen on the grounds of one of the area lodges feeding on the *aguacatillo* trees. The larger, nearby Sierra de las Minas Biosphere Reserve is also a safe bet. Among endemic species is the flightless Atitlán grebe (*Podilymbus gigas*), commonly known as *poc,* which was officially declared extinct in 1989. The introduction of nonnative large- and smallmouth bass into the lake seems to have precipitated its drastic decline in numbers from about 200 in 1960 to only 32 in 1983. The bass ate the young grebes as well as the crabs and fish species on which *poc* fed.

Endemic to the northern Petén region is the Petén ocellated turkey (*Meleagris ocellata*), readily seen strutting around Tikal. It is smaller but much more colorful than its northern relatives, somewhat resembling a peacock. Other interesting birds found in Guatemala's tropical forests include the keel-billed toucan (*Ramphastos sulfuratus*), a perennial jungle favorite because of its large, colorful, bananalike beak. Many of these can be seen at Tikal around sunrise and sunset flying among the temples peeking from the forest canopy. A large variety of parrots also inhabit the Petén forests. The most impressive of these is the scarlet macaw (*Ara macao*), which once inhabited large parts of Petén as well as the Pacific coastal plain. It now inhabits only very remote parts of the Petén forests. Conservationists are fighting to save the birds from local extinction and protected nesting sites have been established in the Maya Biosphere Reserve, specifically in Laguna del Tigre National Park. Rounding out the list of noteworthy birds is the harpy eagle (*Harpia harpyja*), a large, powerful raptor that also enjoys healthy populations at Tikal National Park.

Toucans are a frequent sight in Guatemala's tropical forests.

Land Mammals

Guatemala's list of native land mammals is impressive, with a large variety of exotic cats, primates, and other furry creatures. The largest of Guatemala's cats is the jaguar (*Panthera onca*), found in lowland parts of Petén, Izabal, and the Verapaces. Referred to as *tigre* by locals, it is known to sometimes wander into *chiclero* camps as well as kill livestock in cattle ranches that have encroached on remote areas. Sightings of this beautiful spotted cat are rare, so consider yourself lucky if you are able to glimpse one in the wild. Its tracks are more likely to be seen on travels to the remote forests of the Maya Biosphere Reserve, which can be exciting enough. Other cats include the jaguarundi (*Herpailurus yaguarondi*), puma (*Puma concolor*), and their smaller relatives the margay (*Leopardus wiedii*) and ocelot (*Leopardus pardalis*).

Among the most widely seen mammals are monkeys. You are likely to hear the roar of howler monkeys (*Alouatta pigra*) during the early morning hours if camping overnight in Petén. Less aggressive, smaller, and ever more playful, are spider monkeys (*Ateles geoffroyi*).

The gray fox (*Urocyon cinereoargenteus*)

can often be seen in the early morning and evening among Tikal's temples. More exotic forest dwellers include the piglike collared peccary (*Tayassu tajacu*) and white-lipped peccary (*Tayasu pecari*) as well as the hefty Baird's tapir (*Tapirus bairdii*), and the tamandua anteater (*Tamandua mexicana*).

Also easy to spot are some of the smaller mammals, particularly in parks such as Tikal and Yaxhá. Among these are the raccoon-like white-nosed coati (*Nasua narica*), which practically walk up to you at Tikal; mouselike agoutis (*Dasyprocta punctata*); and kinkajous (*Potos flavus*).

If you happen to like bats, you'll be pleased to know Guatemala harbors more than 100 species of the flying critters. Many of these are found in the limestone caves of Petén and the Verapaces. Most of these are harmless to humans, feeding on fruits and insects. There are blood-sucking vampire bats (*Desmodus rotundus*) flying about, though these feed mostly on cattle.

Sealife

Five species of sea turtles can be seen on Guatemala's Atlantic and Pacific Coasts, where they also come ashore to lay their eggs. These are olive ridley, hawksbill, leatherback, green, and loggerhead. Of these, olive ridley, leatherback, and hawksbill turtles nest on the Pacific shores and can be seen at the Monterrico-Hawaii Biotope. Between September and January, visitors to this park have the rare opportunity to hold baby sea turtles in their hands before releasing them to begin their mad dash across the sand and a lifetime at sea. If they survive to adulthood, the females will return to very same beach to lay their eggs and begin a new life cycle. All of these turtle species are endangered because of the harvesting of their eggs by poor coastal dwellers in search of food and a means to supplement their incomes.

Guatemala's Pacific sailfish have become the object of widespread praise in the angling circuit with blue marlin, Pacific sailfish, and yellowfin tuna just waiting to be caught. Humpback whales can also be seen breaching in the Pacific waters. As for the Caribbean Coast, Guatemala just missed out on the Belize Barrier Reef, as it ends right at the doorstep of the Punta de Manabique peninsula. The barrier reef is easily accessible, however, along with the wonders of its corals and exotic fish. Although lacking the barrier reef per se, the waters off Guatemala's Atlantic Coast are certainly not devoid of exotic sealife. Bottlenose dolphins readily follow motorboats as they make their way along the Caribbean Coast. The endangered manatee (*Trichechus manatus*), or sea cow, has become increasingly rare as the large, slow, sea grass-eating mammal has fallen prey to hunting, motorboats, and drowning in fishing nets. A small reserve in Izabal's El Golfete is attempting to protect the few that remain in Guatemalan waters.

Amphibians

There are 112 species of amphibians represented in Guatemala. Guatemala is out of range for some of the colorful miniature frogs, such as poison arrow frogs, found farther south in Costa Rica and Panama, but there are still some interesting frogs to be found in Guatemala's tropical forests; among these are the red-eyed tree frog (*Agalychnis callidryas*) and the similar Morelet's tree frog (*Agalychnis moreletti*). Fleischmann's glass frog (*Hyalinobatrachium fleischmanni*) is translucent and lime green with small yellow spots and yellowish hands. Its organs and bones are visible through the abdominal skin. All three of these prefer vegetation near rivers and streams.

Reptiles

With 214 species of reptiles, Guatemala has no shortage of snakes. Among the little critters to watch out for are the fer-de-lance (*Bothrops asper*), known locally as *barba amarilla*. The aggressive pit viper is found in abundant quantities in the tropical forests of Petén, Izabal, and the Verapaces, though you are not likely to see one. Baby fer-de-lance can be especially dangerous as they are yet unable to control the amount of poison they inject into a bite.

Other snakes include tropical rattlesnakes (*Crotalus durissus*), several species of colorful coral snakes, and nonvenomous boa constrictors.

If you watched the *Survivor* TV series, you probably noticed there are crocodiles in Guatemala, particularly in and around Lake Yaxhá. The crocodiles seen on *Survivor* are Morelet's crocodiles (*Crocodylus moreleti*). The larger American crocodile (*Crocodylus acutus*) can be found in coastal areas, swamps, and larger rivers in Petén and Izabal. Many species of river turtles inhabit the tropical lowlands. Basilisk lizards and at least two species of iguana round out the highlighted list of Guatemala's reptiles.

Insects

This subject might give some readers "the itchies," but in addition to the myriad species of arachnids, such as tarantulas and scorpions, or plentiful amounts of mosquitoes in some places, Guatemalan lands are host to many other and more beautiful creatures. Among these are thousands of species of butterflies, including the beautiful blue morpho, which you might see flitting about the forest in an iridescent flash of blue. While hiking Guatemala's forests, keep an eye out for the industrious leaf-cutter ants, which cut pathways through the forest and carry small pieces of bright green leaves to their nests, where they are used as compost for underground fungus farms. Butterflies and leaf-cutters are virtually guaranteed favorites among the youngest of travelers to these parts.

History

Guatemala's history is complicated and fascinating, though it often reads like a tragic novel. A basic understanding of its history is a crucial element for the well-informed traveler hoping to get the most out of a visit to this mystifying land of culture and contrasts. This section will familiarize you with the basics of Guatemala's past and what it means in relation to its present, with an emphasis on Guatemalan history in the years since the end of its civil war.

PREHISTORY

It is generally accepted that the first inhabitants of the North American continent came in waves by way of a land bridge across the Bering Strait connecting Siberia to Alaska, some 25,000 years ago. The migrants continued to make their way southward, possibly using boats to assist them, and eventually came to populate, albeit thinly, large portions of the Americas occupying a diverse range of climates. It is believed passage via the Bering Strait was intermittently open until about

10,000 years ago when the last Ice Age ended, submerging the land bridge with rising sea levels.

MAYAN CIVILIZATION

The people that settled the New World eventually grew in population and transitioned from hunter-gatherers to nascent agricultural societies. The developing civilizations then made a clear transition from hillside swidden agriculture to more intensive forms of cultivation, including terrace farming, the construction of drainage ditches, and the development of fertilizers, which in turn produced large food surpluses. With greater food security, the population gradually became more specialized in its individual occupations, paving the way for advances in writing, art, architecture, and mathematics. A common language and universal belief system are thought to have existed throughout the Mayan region, providing a necessary social cohesion that served as a catalyst for the development of a larger civilization.

not the case. The Mayan civilization proper indeed came crashing down for reasons that are becoming increasingly evident, and the Maya simply dispersed into other parts of present-day Mexico, Guatemala, Belize, and Honduras while falling prey to increasing cultural and military dominance from invading central Mexican Toltecs.

The site of modern-day Guatemala City was originally occupied by Kaminaljuyú, whose commercial dominance was established largely on the strength of its strategic location for the trading of obsidian and jade.

THE PRECONQUEST PICTURE

Toltec-Mayan Yucatán cities, such as Chichén Itzá and Uxmal, finally gave out sometime in the late 13th century and were abruptly abandoned. At about the same time, the Guatemalan highlands were invaded by groups of Toltec-Maya, though it is uncertain whether they are the product of a mass exodus from the Yucatán cities or a new group from the Toltec heartland in the Gulf of Mexico. In any case, their arrival in the Guatemalan highlands signaled a transition from the existence of relatively peaceful, religious village societies to ones increasingly secular and warlike.

Quickly establishing themselves as a ruling elite, the Toltec invaders founded a series of competing empires including the K'iche', Kaqchikel, Tz'utujil, Mam, Ixil, Achi', and Q'eqchi', among others. Interestingly, these and other tribes encompassing the highland indigenous groups continue to form the basis for today's cultural landscape, with differentiation based on their individual dialects.

Among these tribes, the K'iche' and Kaqchikel emerged as dominant forces, a rivalry the conquering Spanish would later use to their advantage. Prior to the arrival of the Spanish, the highland region was engulfed in a widespread power struggle between rival groups for cultivable land to feed an increasing population.

beautifully carved Mayan glyphs

Today, the remains of this civilization can be seen throughout northern Guatemala's Petén region at sites such as Tikal, Uaxactún, Yaxhá, Piedras Negras, and El Mirador. The inhabitants of these Mayan cities, now lying in ruins, spent their time trading, stargazing, and fighting wars before abandoning their cities, which were later reclaimed by the surrounding jungle.

Our knowledge of the Maya comes largely from the edification of large carved monuments, or stelae, which document the lives of the individual city-states' rulers and include historical events associated with their reign, such as battles, marriage alliances, and successions. The Maya built their temples and palaces atop previous constructions; what we see today is literally the pinnacle of their progress.

Of particular note is what is sometimes referred to as the Classic Mayan collapse, giving the impression that the civilization collapsed and vanished into thin air. This is certainly

THE SPANISH CONQUEST

After the Spanish conquered the Aztec empire and captured its capital at Tenochtitlán in 1521, the K'iche' sent ambassadors north to Mexico informing Hernán Cortés of their desire to be vassals of the newly established power structure. In 1523 Cortés dispatched Pedro de Alvarado to Guatemala on a fact-finding mission meant to establish the veracity of the tribe's claim. If indeed Cortés's intentions were limited to fact-finding, he could have done better than to choose Alvarado for the job. Alvarado is described as handsome, athletic, distinguished, eloquent, and graceful, among other things, from Spanish accounts of the conquest. He was also extremely cruel.

Alvarado arrived in Guatemala along the Pacific Coast flatlands accompanied by 120 horsemen, 173 horses, 300 soldiers, and 200 Mexican warriors from the allied Tlaxcalan armies. He made his way up to the highlands, where he met the K'iche' in battle near present-day Quetzaltenango, also known as Xelajú. An estimated 30,000 K'iche' were unable to forge alliances with neighboring tribes to repel the Spanish invasion and faced the Spanish alone. Legend has it Alvarado met Tecún Umán, grandson of the K'iche' ruler, in hand-to-hand combat, cutting him down.

Following these events, the K'iche' invited the Spanish to their capital at Utatlán for the signing of a formal surrender but secretly planned to ambush them from the safety of their mountain fortress. Alvarado knew an ambush when he saw one, and so he withdrew to the city's outskirts, followed by the K'iche' rulers, whom he seized and later had burned at the stake. Eight days of fighting followed, with the Spanish enlisting the help of the rival Kaqchikel to finally gain the upper hand against the K'iche'. Utatlán was then burned to the ground.

The Kaqchikel alliance with the Spanish stuck for a time, with the Spanish establishing the first capital of Guatemala alongside the Kaqchikel capital of Iximché, from which they launched raids to conquer Guatemala's remaining highland tribal groups. The campaign would last several years and was made increasingly difficult when the Kaqchikel severed their alliance with the Spanish in 1526 in response to demands for tribute. They abandoned their capital at Iximché and took refuge in the mountains, launching a guerrilla war. The Spanish then moved the Guatemalan capital, establishing the city of Santiago de los Caballeros on November 22, 1527. Now known as Ciudad Vieja, it lies near present-day Antigua.

Indigenous uprisings and resistance would continue throughout Guatemala's history into the present day, as various groups responded to repressive policies imposed by those in power. The recent civil war has been likened by scholars, human rights activists, and journalists to a kind of "second conquest" aimed at eliminating the indigenous population through genocidal extermination attempts.

A final aspect of the conquest that bears mentioning is the work of European diseases and their hand in greatly reducing the population of the indigenous peoples who had no resistance to smallpox, plague, typhus, and measles. These diseases were responsible for the loss of more than three-quarters of Guatemala's two million inhabitants in the first 30 years following contact with the Spanish. It is thought that a third of the population died before Alvarado's invading army even set foot in the indigenous peoples' Guatemalan homeland.

COLONIAL GUATEMALA

The Guatemalan capital required 10 years from its founding to complete and included a cathedral, town hall, and Alvarado's palace. Alvarado died in 1541 while in Mexico attempting to subdue an uprising. The city was destroyed shortly thereafter by a mudslide that rolled down Agua Volcano after an earthquake and heavy rains combined to unleash the contents of the flooded crater.

Guatemala's capital was then moved a few miles away to present-day Antigua. It

Guatemala's rich colonial legacy is evident in Antigua's ruined churches.

more recent tragedies to befall its people lies in understanding the significance of earlier events dating back to just before the conquest.

At the center of Guatemala's new power structure was the Catholic Church, which arrived with the conquistadors and included various sects such as Franciscans, Mercedarians, Dominicans, and Jesuits. These were granted large concessions of land and indigenous people, allowing them to amass huge fortunes from the cultivation of cash crops including sugar, indigo, and wheat. This power structure was held in place by institutions established by the Spanish crown, namely the *encomienda* and *repartimiento.*

The *encomienda* was a grant of indigenous labor and tribute, though not necessarily of land, over a geographical area. The *encomenderos* holding such a grant were allowed to tax the peoples under their care and to conscript them for labor in exchange for their promise to maintain order and educate the indigenous populace in the Spanish language and Catholicism.

The *repartimiento,* which is essentially indistinguishable from its predecessor, is a reformed version of the *encomienda* system, at least on paper. It put control of the distribution of workers into the hands of local magistrates and called for the donation of a percentage of laborers from populations close to Spanish settlements, between 2 and 4 percent of the indigenous population.

Further adding to the transformation of community organization in the conquered territories was the establishment of *reducciones,* part of the larger process of *congregación,* consisting of towns founded in the Spanish vein with the purpose of congregating indigenous populations into manageable settlements and assimilating them into the dominant culture and religion. They would also serve as a handy nearby source from which to pool labor.

would serve as the administrative headquarters of the newly established Audiencia de Guatemala, which included the provinces of San Salvador, Nicaragua, Honduras, Costa Rica, Chiapas, and Guatemala. The city of Santiago de los Caballeros, as it was officially known, would grow to become the third-largest city in Spanish colonial America, surpassed only by Mexico City and Lima. In 1776, a series of devastating earthquakes destroyed most of the city's buildings and churches, leading to a final move of the Guatemalan capital to the Valley of the Hermitage, just over a mountain to the east, where it has resided ever since.

The colonial period is significant in that it completely transformed Guatemala's physical and cultural landscape, establishing new cities and institutionalizing new economic and religious systems that would come to form the basis for a racist hierarchy persisting largely unaltered to this day. Guatemala's history displays a striking symmetry throughout the years. The key to understanding many of the

INDEPENDENCE

Guatemalan, and indeed Central American, independence came more as a result of pressures from without than from a genuine internal uprising demanding freedom from Spanish rule. This is not to say that all was well with Spanish colonial rule, as there were policies and social stratifications in place contributing to unrest among the lower strata of society. Spanish policies kept wealth and power in the hands of Spanish-born elites, or *chapetones*. *Criollos,* or those born in the New World of Spanish descent, were the next rung down the ladder, with the lowest standings reserved for mixed-blood *mestizos* and full-blooded Indians.

Napoleon's invasion of Spain in 1808 led to the imposition of a liberal constitution on Spain in 1812. When Mexican general Agustán Iturbide declared his own country's independence from Spain, Guatemala followed suit. The reigning Captain General Gabino Gaínza bowed to demands for independence but hoped to maintain the existent power structure with the support of the church and landowning elites. The declaration of independence essentially maintained the old power structure under new management. Mexico quickly dispatched troops to annex Guatemala, and all of Central America, to establish Iturbide's new empire.

Iturbide was dethroned in 1823, and Central America, minus the state of Chiapas, declared its independence from Mexico. This second declaration joined the remaining states in a loose federation and adopted many U.S.-modeled liberal reforms, such as the abolition of slavery. A protracted power struggle between liberals advocating a secular, more egalitarian state and conservatives wanting to maintain the church-dominated political and economic structures marked the early years of independence. The Central American Federation was weakened not only by inner power struggles within individual member states, but also by a struggle to determine regional leadership over neighboring states.

JUSTO RUFINO BARRIOS AND THE LIBERAL REFORMS

The liberals would finally succeed in 1871 under the leadership of General Justo Rufino Barrios, who, along with Miguel García Granados, set out from Mexico with a force of just 45 soldiers, gaining numbers as their approach to the capital grew closer. The capital was taken on June 30, 1871, and Granados was installed as the leader of the new liberal government. Granados made only limited reforms, and by 1872 a frustrated Barrios

the Guatemalan flag, designed to emulate the country's blue sky

marched to the capital with his troops and demanded elections, which he won overwhelmingly.

Among the reforms quickly instituted by Barrios, who would go down in Guatemalan history as "The Reformer," were educational reform and separation of church and state. Barrios was the first of the *caudillos*, military strongmen who ruled the country with an iron fist and sense of absolute omnipotence, mostly uninterrupted, until the revolution of 1944. He masterfully strengthened his power over the entire country with links to local strongmen in rural areas wielding power on his behalf but unable to challenge his hold because of the restricted development of secondary market centers and the overwhelming economic dominance of Guatemala City.

To further exercise his dominion, Barrios professionalized the military, creating a new military academy, the Escuela Politecnica, still in existence today. The addition of rural militia further strengthened national control over the rural hinterlands. Barrios was decidedly pro-Western and sought to impose a European worldview to suppress what he saw as a vastly inferior Indian culture. Liberal economic policies ensured minimal protection of village lands, Indian culture, or the welfare of peasant villages.

During this time, coffee came to dominate the Guatemalan economy and Barrios's economic policies ensured the availability of a peasant workforce to supply the labor-intensive coffee harvest with its share of needed workers. Furthermore, the increasingly racist attitudes of Guatemala's coffee elites toward the Indians served to justify the coercive means used to secure this labor force. The Indians were seen as lazy, making forced labor and the submission of the indigenous masses both necessary and morally justified. In this regard, the *mandamiento*, which came to replace the *repartimiento*, was increasingly enforced in the last two decades of the 19th century, requiring villages to supply a specified number of laborers per year.

Increasingly, however, elites found more coercive ways to exact labor from the Indians by way of debt peonage. Rural workers were required to carry a *libreto*, a record containing an individual's labor and debt figures. *Habilitadores*, or labor contractors, were charged with advancing money to peasants in exchange for labor contracts. The contractors often used alcohol as an added incentive and took advantage of widespread peasant illiteracy to ensure many of them contracted debts they would never be able to repay. In this way, depressed rural wages from debt peonage and low-cost labor increased the wealth of agricultural elites while making the rural peasantry even poorer.

MANUEL ESTRADA CABRERA

Justo Rufino Barrios died in battle in 1885 while fighting to create a reunified Central America under Guatemalan leadership. He was succeeded by a string of short-lived *caudillo* presidents. The next to hold power for any significant time was Manuel Estrada Cabrera, whose legacy included undivided support for big business and crackdowns on labor organization. He ruled from 1898 until his overthrow in 1920, having been declared insane. Among Cabrera's many peculiarities was the construction of several temples to honor Minerva, the Roman goddess of wisdom. Cabrera's legacy includes gross corruption, a beefed-up military, and a neglected educational system.

Export agriculture continued its unprecedented growth under Cabrera, thus paving the way for the dominance of two foreign groups that would come to control much of Guatemala's economy in later years. The first of these were German coffee planters who settled in the region of Las Verapaces. By 1913 this German enclave owned 170 of the country's coffee plantations, with about half of them in the vicinity of Cobán. The other significant foreign presence in Guatemala during this time was the U.S.-owned United Fruit Company (UFCo), aptly nicknamed "El Pulpo" (The Octopus), and its tentacles consisting of International Railways of Central America (IRCA) and the UFCo Steamship Lines. Its vast control of land, rail, and steamship transportation, in addition to Guatemala's sole Caribbean port, Puerto Barrios, made it a political and economic powerhouse. Its political clout would be seen in the mid-20th century when, together with the CIA, it would be directly responsible for ousting Guatemala's president, Jacobo Árbenz Guzmán, from power when land reform policies interfered with the company's vast land holdings.

JORGE UBICO

After the overthrow of Estrada Cabrera in 1920, the country entered a period of instability and power struggles culminating in the rise to power of Jorge Ubico. Continuing in the now well-established pattern of megalomaniacal, heavy-handed leadership that would come to characterize many of Guatemala's presidents, Ubico continued the unconditional support for U.S. agribusiness and the local oligarchy. By 1940, 90 percent of Guatemala's exports were sold to the United States. Ubico caved in to U.S demands for the expulsion of the German coffee planters from Guatemala during World War II, evidencing the increasing U.S. hold on Guatemalan domestic policy.

Within Guatemala, Ubico embarked on various reforms, including ambitious roadbuilding projects, as well as improvements in health care and social welfare. Debt peonage was also outlawed but was replaced by a vagrancy law enforcing compulsory labor contributions of 150 days upon landless peasants in either rural plantations or in the government road-building programs. Ubico's reforms always had in mind the modernization of the state economy. Far from an attempt to free the indigenous peoples from coercive labor practices, the vagrancy law asserted centralized control over the national labor force while keeping the political power of the oligarchy firmly in check.

Ubico's palace in Guatemala City, now the Palacio Nacional de la Cultura

Ubico was also obsessed with internal security. He saw himself as a reincarnated Napoleon and became increasingly paranoid, creating a network of spies and informers used to repress opposition to his increasingly tyrannical rule. Much of this opposition came from the indigenous peasant population, whom Ubico ignored and regarded as retrograde and inferior. This led to numerous revolts in the late 1930s and early 1940s. The discovery of an assassination plot in 1934 led to the execution of 300 suspected conspirators within 48 hours.

THE OCTOBER REVOLUTION OF 1944

Opposition finally reached a head in June 1944 when widespread discontent erupted in violent street protests by large portions of the urban middle class demanding democratic opportunities and new economic policies. Ubico was forced to resign after 14 years in office. When his interim replacement signaled to be more of the same, young students, professionals, and forward-thinking military officers orchestrated a widespread social movement culminating in his overthrow in what has been dubbed "The October Revolution." Elections were called for in December of that same year. In a radio address, then front-running presidential candidate Juan José Arévalo, an exiled professor living in Argentina, described the transcendental nature of the recent events: "What has occurred in Guatemala is not a *golpe de estado* (coup d'etat); it is something more profound and beneficial; it is a revolution.... It is a revolution that will go to the roots of the political system.... In a word: It is a revolution called to wash, to purify our political life, to quiet everyone, and to honor Guatemala."

Arévalo would go on to win the election with an overwhelming majority and take office on March 1, 1945.

A DECADE OF "SPIRITUAL SOCIALISM"

Guatemala made much progress under Arévalo, who quickly set out on the road to badly needed structural reform. Prominence was given to education and health care with the construction of new schools and hospitals, immunization programs, and literacy campaigns. A new national budget allowed for a third of government spending to go into these programs, which were further facilitated by a new constitution drafted prior to Arévalo's taking office. Ubico's hated vagrancy laws were abolished, and in their place a labor code was instituted establishing union representation and granting workers the right to strike. Many of the farms expropriated from German planters during World War II, now in state hands, were transformed into peasant cooperatives. Government policies provided technical assistance and credit for peasant farmers and protected their lands from usurpation by agricultural elites and foreign agribusiness.

The gains in social justice ruffled the feathers of many of Guatemala's traditional power elites, including the church, urban business elites, the landed aristocracy, and the politicians who defended their interests. They increasingly opposed much of the reformist legislation passed by Arévalo in congress. A divided military also became the source of much opposition, with Arévalo surviving 25 coup attempts originating from conservative sectors of the armed forces. Meanwhile, U.S. business interests became increasingly unsettled by the reforms. At the top of this list was the United Fruit Company. As opposition stiffened, Arévalo was unable to fully implement the social transformation of the country he had intended and passed on to his successor an increasingly polarized political landscape.

His successor, Jacobo Árbenz Guzmán, continued along the path of reform, concentrating on fomenting economic development and independence from foreign intervention in politics and the economy. At the core of his economic development program was the Agrarian Reform Law of 1952, intended to redistribute land ownership by breaking up large plantations and promoting high productivity on smaller, individually owned farms. The urgent need for land reform was historically evident in the nature and function of institutions that, over time, placed Guatemalan land in the hands of a wealthy few to the detriment of indigenous peasants. It is estimated that 2 percent of the country's population controlled 72 percent of all arable land in 1945, but only 12 percent of it was being utilized.

Central to the law were stipulations limiting expropriation to lands lying fallow. Árbenz himself was not immune to land expropriation, giving up 1,700 acres of his own land in the process. Also among the lands to be expropriated were extensive holdings by United Fruit ceded to the company under Estrada Cabrera and Ubico, which had made United Fruit Guatemala's largest landowner. Fully 85 percent of its holdings remained uncultivated. The Agrarian Reform Law allowed for the compensation of expropriated lands based on values declared for tax purposes, which United Fruit had, of course, grossly underreported.

Unfortunately for Árbenz and his reformist policies, UFCo had strong ties to the U.S. government and, more specifically, the CIA. Among United Fruit's shareholders were U.S. Secretary of State John Foster Dulles and his brother, CIA Director Allen Dulles.

On the home front, it was clear that Árbenz had incurred the wrath of the oligarchy and conservative military sectors. He faced increasing political fragmentation despite attempts to forge a functional revolutionary coalition of political parties to further his goals, and he looked to several dedicated, competent individuals for support in implementing the agrarian reform and labor organization. Many inside and outside of Guatemala conveniently labeled Árbenz and his supporters as communists, though how much influence the communists actually had in Guatemala is still hotly debated. In 1952 Guatemala's official communist party, the Partido Guatemalteco de los Trabajadores (PGT, the Guatemalan Labor Party), was legalized. Communists subsequently gained considerable minority influence over important peasant organizations and labor unions, but not over the governing political body, winning only 4 of 58 seats.

In any case, the country became increasingly unstable. This instability, combined with Árbenz's tolerance of the PGT and other communist and labor influences, caused Washington to grow increasingly alarmed. The CIA finally orchestrated the overthrow of Árbenz in 1954 in the form of a military invasion from Honduras dubbed "Operation Success," led by two exiled Guatemalan military officers. The invading forces established Colonel Carlos Castillo Armas, who had previously led a failed coup against Árbenz, as chief of state. A series of military governments supported by the nascent military oligarchy partnership and conservative elements of Guatemalan society followed. Thus began one of the most tragic chapters in Guatemala's already turbulent history.

THE CIVIL WAR (1960-1996)

With the professionalization of Guatemala's army now in place thanks to the policies of Barrios and Ubico, the military was now poised to become the country's dominating political force and would do so for the next 30 years. Further paving the way for military dominance over Guatemalan politics was the Cold War climate and the fight against communism. U.S. policy and military aid would assist the dictators' rise to power and facilitate their increasingly repressive nature, all in the name of defeating communist insurrection.

Among the new regime's first moves was the revocation of the 1945 constitution, with the consequent reversal of the reforms of the previous years. The rule of the oligarchy was firmly reestablished, and a wave of repression against peasants, labor unions, and agrarian reformers was unleashed.

Castillo Armas would only be in power until 1957, when he was shot by one of his own palace guards. Political turmoil ensued, followed by the rise to power of Miguel Ydígoras Fuentes, an army officer from the Ubico years now representing the National Democratic Renovation Party. His five years in office were characterized by incompetence, corruption, nepotism, patronage, and economic decline. Opposition to Ydígoras grew, with young army officers led by Marco Yon Sosa and Turcios Lima attempting an unsuccessful coup in 1960. Ydígoras was finally ousted by a military coup in 1963 with approval from Washington after Arévalo threatened to return to Guatemala to run in the next election, firmly putting the establishment in both Guatemala and Washington on edge.

During the subsequent military government of Alfredo Enrique Peralta Azurdia, Turcios Lima and Yon Sosa launched a guerrilla offensive from the eastern highlands, marking the beginning of a protracted armed conflict between leftist rebels and the Guatemalan government. Ironically, both had received U.S. military training while serving in the Guatemalan forces and now used their skills to attack local army garrisons. The battle was soon joined by another armed rebel group, the Fuerzas Armadas Rebeldes (FAR, Rebel Armed Forces). The PGT, meanwhile, formed an alliance with the rebels while advocating the return of Arévalo.

A self-proclaimed "third government of the revolution" came to power in 1966 under Julio Cesar Montenegro of the center-left Partido Revolucionario, who tried to continue in the vein of Arévalo and Árbenz. It was clear, however, that his hands were tied and power was in the hands of the military. Political violence escalated during his administration, with death squads killing hundreds of students, unionists, academics, and peasant leaders.

By the end of the decade the guerrilla movement had been virtually eliminated from the eastern highlands. FAR shifted its focus to Guatemala City, where it kidnapped and murdered the U.S. ambassador in 1968.

Electoral fraud and political violence, accompanied by economic decline, would mark much of Guatemala's history between 1970 and 1990. A reign of terror became firmly entrenched, with successive governments each going to greater lengths to contain the guerrilla threat and repress an increasingly unsatisfied populace from which the movement drew its support. At the heart of the matter was a system of government that ensured the continued prosperity of a wealthy minority to the detriment of a poor, landless, illiterate peasant class forced to work the elites' land. The demands of a growing urban middle class, meanwhile, were repressed with the help of the armed forces and right-wing death squads.

The United States, meanwhile, continued to pour money and logistical support into the increasingly bloody repression. Three years after the election of Carlos Arana Osorio in 1970, who was nicknamed "the butcher of Zacapa," 15,000 Guatemalans had been killed or disappeared. The United States did its share by training 32,000 Guatemalan police officers through the Agency for International Development (AID) via its public safety program. Guatemala's Policía Nacional was notoriously linked to the paramilitary death squads operating with impunity in the cities and countryside. Many off-duty police filled the ranks of these right-wing extremist groups working parallel to, but with unofficial sanction from, the more traditional forms of counterinsurgency.

In 1971, another guerrilla unit, the Organización Revolucionario del Pueblo en Armas (ORPA, Revolutionary Organization of the People in Arms), was formed. The unit was led by Rodrigo Asturias, the son of Nobel laureate novelist Miguel Ángel Asturias. It operated in the vicinity of Lake Atitlán, Quetzaltenango, San Marcos, and Suchitepéquez, setting up operations in a strategically important corridor between the highlands and the agriculturally rich coastal lowlands. ORPA spent eight years recruiting local combatants, then training and indoctrinating them into its ranks. Believed to be the most disciplined of the rebel organizations, it launched its first offensive in 1979 with the occupation of a coffee farm near Quetzaltenango.

Yet another guerrilla organization, the Ejército Guerrillero de los Pobres (EGP, Guerrilla Army of the Poor), exploded onto the scene in 1975 with the much-publicized execution of a notoriously ruthless Ixcán landlord. It had spent three years developing political consciousness among the peasantry in the remote Ixcán jungle where it operated prior to launching its first assault. The Guatemalan military began increasingly violent reprisals against the peasantry living in remote jungle outposts, some of whom kept the guerrillas fed and supplied. In Ixcán, as well as throughout Guatemala, peasants would become increasingly caught in the cross fire between the military and the rebel groups often serving as a scapegoat for the army's wrath.

On February 4, 1976, a massive earthquake struck the Guatemalan highlands, leaving 23,000 dead, 77,000 injured, and about a million homeless. The reconstruction efforts saw a renewed push to reform the inherent injustices of Guatemalan society with increased activity on behalf of the trade unions. In 1977, President Jimmy Carter, citing increasingly gross human rights violations, cut off military aid to Guatemala.

The 1978 elections were rigged to the benefit of Romeo Lucas García, who unleashed a fresh wave of repression against the usual victims, as well as academics, journalists, and trade unionists now. The guerrilla war grew increasingly strong in rural Guatemala at this time, with the number of total combatants estimated at 6,000 distributed among the four guerrilla groups, along with some 250,000 collaborators. The guerrillas actively recruited from a historically disenfranchised peasant base, particularly in the Ixil and Ixcán regions, which only strengthened the army's resolve to do away with the insurgency and intensified punitive measures against real and perceived collaborators. Peasants, priests, politicians, and anyone perceived to have ties to the guerrillas were massacred in the thousands. It is estimated that 25,000 Guatemalans were killed during the four-year Lucas regime.

Many atrocities were committed by the Lucas regime in a spiral of violence—making the Spanish conquest look increasingly benign by comparison—including an army massacre in the village of Panzós, Alta Verapaz, and the firebombing of the Spanish Embassy in Guatemala City during a peaceful occupation by peasant leaders. In Panzós, at least 35 peasants, including some children, lay murdered in the town square with dozens more injured or killed as they tried to make their escape. The occupation of Guatemala City's Spanish Embassy was carried out by the Guatemalan military on January 31, 1980. Without regard for embassy staff or the Spanish ambassador, Policía Nacional forces stormed the embassy and firebombed it. The sole survivor was the Spanish ambassador. The victims included the father of Nobel Peace Prize winner Rigoberta Menchú, who recounts this and other atrocities in her book, *I, Rigoberta Menchú*. Spain severed diplomatic relations with Guatemala

in the aftermath of the massacre, not restoring them until several years later.

In addition to the ambassador's survival, it should be noted that one of the peasant activists also survived the tragedy, only to be murdered a few days later by a paramilitary death squad while recovering in a local hospital.

In 1982, Guatemala's armed rebel groups—FAR, EGP, ORPA, and PGT-FA—consolidated to form the Unidad Revolucionaria Nacional Guatemalteca (URNG, Guatemalan National Revolutionary Unity), which would go on to fight for its ideals as a political force, while continuing armed resistance, and negotiate a peace treaty with the government in 1996.

Efraín Ríos Montt

The 1982 elections were again manipulated by the extreme right, this time to the benefit of Aníbal Guevara, but a coup on March 23 orchestrated by young military officers installed General Efraín Ríos Montt as the head of a three-member junta. The coup leaders cited the rigging of elections three times in eight years as justification for their actions, which were supported by most of the opposition parties. It was hoped Guatemala could be somehow steered once again on the path of peace, law, and order and that the terror would stop.

Ríos Montt was an evangelical Christian with ties to Iglesia El Verbo, one of several U.S.-based churches gaining ground in Guatemala after the 1976 earthquake. Among his many eccentricities was the delivery of weekly Sunday night sermons in which he expressed his desire to restore law and order, eliminate corruption, and defeat the guerrilla insurgency, allowing for the establishment of a true democracy.

On the surface things did seem to get better, particularly in the cities, thanks to an odd mix of heavy-handed discipline and strict moral guidelines governing all facets of government operations. Montt, for example, made a regular show of executions of alleged criminals before firing squads. He also offered amnesty to the guerrillas during the month of June 1982, but only a handful of these accepted. Some later

Forced Disappearance

Among the most horrific aspects of Guatemala's civil war were the kidnapping, torture, and murder of at least 50,000 citizens by an army bent on brutal counterinsurgency and the elimination of any and all political opposition, whether real or imagined. Parallel to the oppression at the hands of the military, death squads such as "White Hand" and "Eye for Eye" began operating independently of government forces but with their full knowledge and acquiescence. The kidnappings targeted people from all walks of life but especially journalists, union leaders, intellectuals, opposition party leaders, university students, laborers, teachers, and clergy.

In the 1970s the Inter-American Commission on Human Rights (IACHR), a branch of the Organization of American States, began issuing a series of annual human-rights reports on countries around the world. In 1985, it issued a scathing report on the human-rights situation in Guatemala, just before the country's return to democratic rule. As the stories of the tortured and disappeared are probably best told by the victims themselves, the 1985 report is significant in that it includes testimony from an actual kidnapping victim and torture survivor.

In addition to shedding light on the heinous crimes perpetrated against thousands of Guatemalans, the testimony is significant in that it demonstrates that the kidnappings and torture were carried out with surgical precision using methods undeniably linked to the training of counterinsurgency forces throughout Latin America by the United States's very own CIA. This and other documented cases of abuse by military and paramilitary forces, some involving U.S. citizens, offer irrefutable evidence of U.S. involvement in perpetuating widespread oppression and human-rights abuses via military aid and training to repressive regimes. This fact was acknowledged during President Clinton's visit to Guatemala in 1999, when he officially apologized for U.S. involvement in Guatemala's civil war.

Clinton's apology came shortly before the official release of a secret Guatemalan military document smuggled out by human-rights organizations that revealed the fate of more than 180 victims of forced disappearance between August 1983 and March 1985. The document's release provided the first news many of the victims' families had concerning the fate of their loved ones. After years of getting nowhere with Guatemalan authorities in the pursuit of justice against perpetrators of torture, murder, and forced disappearance, the relatives of 20 of the victims filed a suit against the Guatemalan government for denial of justice with the Inter-American Commission on Human Rights.

accounts of the Guatemalan civil war attribute this to communities' being either held hostage by guerrilla occupation and unable to make the trip down from the mountains or simply too frightened and distrustful of the military.

Whatever the reason, the cool response to Montt's amnesty offer unleashed a new wave of counterinsurgency terror against the guerrillas and the indigenous peoples believed to be aiding and abetting them. Under a scorched-earth campaign, entire villages were destroyed, with survivors being resettled into a series of so-called "model villages," allowing the army to keep a close watch on the peasantry while indoctrinating them with anticommunist rhetoric. The repression was made worse by a new system

of conscripted labor in the form of civil defense patrols (PACs) composed of rural peasants controlled by the army. PACs were forced to make routine night patrols and report any suspicious activities. Failure to do so would result in their own suspicion in the army's eyes, meaning further reprisals on their villages. In this way, two modern-day variants of important colonial structures survived well into Guatemala's recent history, the *congregación* and the *encomienda*.

An estimated 100,000 of Guatemala's indigenous Mayan descendants fled the violence, flooding refugee camps in neighboring Mexico or migrating farther north to the United States during the reign of Lucas García and Ríos Montt.

Cerezo and the Democratic Opening

Ríos Montt was eventually overthrown in August 1983 after just over a year in power by a military coup with U.S. backing. The underlying ideal was to get Guatemala firmly on the road back to democracy. Elections were called to take place in 1985 and General Mejía Víctores was installed as an interim chief-of-state. Repression in the countryside continued to escalate under the military's tireless scorched-earth campaign. The Ixil Triangle alone saw the displacement of 72 percent of its population and the destruction of 49 villages. Totals for Guatemala at this time included the destruction of 440 villages and more than 100,000 dead. In this context, the first free election in more than three decades took place. A new constitution was also drawn up.

Vinicio Cerezo Arévalo, a Christian Democrat, won the election with an overwhelming majority of the vote and widespread hope for change in Guatemala with the country firmly on the road to democracy. It was clear that the military still held the cards, however, and kept Cerezo under a tight leash via the Estado Mayor Presidencial, a notorious military security force officially charged with presidential protection but in reality designed to keep presidential power in check. Cerezo candidly admitted that the military still held 75 percent of the power.

Cerezo sought to give the democratic opening a chance, knowing that the military's power could not be broken in the five years his term in office would last, by taking a non-confrontational approach to the demands of Guatemala's various societal sectors. He kept a happy courtship with the powerful business interests, landowners, and generals. Among the latter was his defense minister, General Héctor Alejandro Gramajo, who curtailed much of the violence in the countryside and allowed Cerezo to survive numerous coup attempts.

In September of 1987 the Central American heads of state convened in the eastern highland town of Esquipulas, where they signed a treaty aimed at bringing the pacification and democratization of the region. Costa Rica's Oscar Arias Sánchez would later win the Nobel Peace Prize for his role in bringing the peace plan to fruition. Esquipulas II, as it was called, would open the doors for peace negotiations between the Guatemalan government and the URNG.

Although the levels of repression and violence dropped, they by no means disappeared. The armed struggle continued in remote corners of the highlands and Petén while death squads continued their reign of terror. Formal labor organization was once again given the official go-ahead, and widespread protests marked much of Cerezo's later years as the average Guatemalan saw little economic improvement.

Jorge Serrano Elías

Barred from running for a second term under the 1985 Constitution, Cerezo yielded power to his successor, Jorge Serrano Elías, in 1991. Also barred from running under the new constitution was Efraín Ríos Montt, though there was much speculation as to his role behind the scenes because Serrano had served in his government. The new constitution specifically prohibited anyone rising to power as the result of a military coup from running for president, a decision Montt has repeatedly tried unsuccessfully to have rescinded.

Indigenous-rights advocates, already enjoying greater freedom since the democratic opening, received a huge bolster from the awarding of the Nobel Peace Prize in 1992 to activist Rigoberta Menchú Tum for her efforts in bringing worldwide attention to the genocidal civil war still raging on in the countryside. The Guatemalan military issued an official protest to what it saw as disgraceful approval for an advocate of communist insurrection but removed its opposition on the wave of worldwide fanfare for the awarding of the prize to Menchú.

Guatemala's historical problems continued to plague the nation, and Serrano's incompetence at the helm soon became evident.

The peace process stalled with the Catholic Church's mediator accusing both sides of intransigence. Popular protests against Serrano's government, bolstered by corruption charges involving his suspected links with Colombian drug cartels, forced him to declare an autocoup in May 1993. He assumed dictatorial powers, citing the country's purported spiral into anarchy, and also dissolved congress, citing the gross corruption of the legislative body while calling for the election of a new one.

Widespread protests and the withdrawal of U.S. support for Serrano's government resulted in his removal from office just two days later. Congress met and voted on the appointment of Ramiro de León Carpio, the country's human-rights ombudsman, to succeed Serrano and finish out his term.

De León quickly set about rearranging the military high command in an attempt to purge some of the more radical elements and achieve a measure of political stability, though it was clear his powers over the military were limited. The URNG declared a cease-fire as a measure of goodwill toward the new administration. The guerrillas made some progress with the new administration, eventually signing an accord on indigenous rights and identity as well as a human rights accord establishing the creation of U.N.-mandated MINUGUA (United Nations Verification Mission in Guatemala) to oversee the implementation of the peace accords once the final agreement was reached. Although optimistic at first, Guatemalans soon lost hope in the De León administration when they saw he was incapable of addressing crime, constitutional reform, and land and tax issues.

Alvaro Arzú Irigoyen

Former Guatemala City mayor Alvaro Arzú Irigoyen won the 1996 presidential elections thanks to a strong showing in the capital despite widespread electoral abstention elsewhere. Arzú, a businessman, represented the Partido de Avanzada Nacional (PAN, National Advancement Party), with deep roots in the oligarchy and a commitment to economic growth fostered by the development of the private sector under a free market. He quickly appointed new defense, foreign, and economic ministers and set out to sign a final peace accord with the URNG.

The agreement for a "Firm and Lasting Peace" was signed on December 29, 1996, in the Palacio Nacional de la Cultura, which once served as the presidential palace. After years of bloodshed, the final death toll stood at 200,000 with about 50,000 being cases of forced disappearance. A subsequent U.N. report by the Historical Clarification Commission (CEH) squarely placed blame for most of the violence in the hands of the military and the civil-defense patrols, with 80 percent of the victims said to be of Mayan origin. "The majority of human rights violations occurred with the knowledge or by order of the highest authorities of the state," the report declared. It further stated: "State terror was applied to make it clear that those who attempted to assert their rights, and even their relatives, ran the risk of death by the most hideous means. The objective was to intimidate and silence society as a whole, in order to destroy the will for transformation, both in the short and long term."

The ambitious peace accords marked the culmination of years of negotiations between the government and guerrillas; if properly implemented, they would serve as the basis for the construction of a completely different Guatemala. Unfortunately, the provisions set forth in the accord have yet to be fully adopted. One example of this disappointing trend was the failure to amend the Constitution via a May 1999 referendum to officially redefine the country as "multiethnic, pluricultural, and multilingual," as stipulated in the accord on indigenous rights and identity. Voters stayed away from the polls in droves, and the few who did vote decided against the reforms.

The Catholic Church issued its own report on the violence during the country's civil war, which also placed the blame for the majority of the atrocities in the hands of the military. Two days after issuing his report, Bishop Juan Gerardi Conedera was murdered in his garage, much to the outrage of the general populace. By this time, most political killings had all but ceased, and the murder sent shock waves of indignation throughout Guatemalan society, which was clamoring for justice against Gerardi's killers. It soon became clear the act was a reprisal from military factions intent on demonstrating their continued hold on the country's power structure.

Subsequent investigations and attempts to bring the guilty parties to justice ended in frustration as key witnesses, prosecutors, and judges fled the country in the face of death threats. While political kidnappings and disappearances became mostly a thing of the past, the country's security situation drastically worsened in the aftermath of the civil war. Bank robberies, murders, extortionary kidnappings, and armed robbery were at an all-time high. Using many of the same methods as in the "disappearance" of thousands of Guatemalans, kidnappers unleashed a wave of terror in which 1,000 people were abducted in 1997 alone. The country, at the time, had the fourth-highest kidnapping rate in the world.

U.S. president Bill Clinton visited Guatemala in March 1999 for a summit meeting with the Central American presidents. In a surprising declaration, he expressed regret on behalf of the U.S. government for its role in the atrocities committed during the country's civil war, saying that U.S. support for military forces that "engaged in violent and widespread repression" in Guatemala "was wrong."

The crime spree was largely blamed on a power vacuum created during the departure of Guatemala's Policía Nacional and its subsequent replacement by the new Policía Nacional Civil, in accordance with the peace accords. The new police force was trained by experts from Spain, Chile, and the United States. It was hoped that a more professional police force would help bring greater security once fully established, but it quickly became evident that this was not the case. Meanwhile,

political murders such as the Gerardi murder remained unresolved, shedding light on the lackluster state of Guatemala's judicial system, a situation exacerbated by widespread lynching of supposed criminals in remote areas where the rule of law was merely a vague concept.

Security issues aside, Arzú was a gifted administrator, and government corruption remained at low levels, for Guatemala. Arzú's strengths as Guatemala City's mayor had always been infrastructure and public works. His time as president was no different in this regard, with various infrastructure projects being completed during his term in office. Guatemalans widely recognize his hard work backed by a concrete list of accomplishments, and he is still popular in opinion polls. He has served three consecutive terms in office as Guatemala City's mayor. Arzú also privatized many state entities, including the notoriously inefficient telephone company, as part of a neoliberal economic approach to state participation in the economy. Guatemala's telecommunications laws have subsequently been heralded for their contributions to vast improvements in service coverage, increased competition, and lowered prices. At the end of Arzú's presidency, however, many critics pointed to a perceived affinity for serving the interests of Guatemala's wealthy elite, a criticism his successor would play largely to his advantage at the polls in the 1999 election campaign.

THE 1996 PEACE ACCORDS

In addition to officially marking the end of hostilities between leftist insurgents and the Guatemalan government, the U.N.-brokered 1996 peace accords established a starting point from which to address historical grievances leading to the conflict and begin the construction of a more equitable society. From the start, the agreements established a fact-finding mission known as the Historical Clarification Commission (CEH) to investigate culpability for wartime atrocities committed largely against the country's Mayan population. The CEH and an independent wartime inquiries body created by Guatemala's Catholic Church, the Recuperation of the Historical Memory Project (REMHI), blamed the vast majority of atrocities on the army, with some violations also committed on the part of the guerrillas. Since the findings, many family members of victims of the civil war have sought to bring to justice those responsible for crimes against humanity, including genocide, torture, and illegal arrest. Because of the inadequacies of the Guatemalan judiciary, many have been forced to seek recourse in international courts, as in the case of the suit filed in a Spanish court under universal jurisdiction by the Rigoberta Menchú Foundation against eight government officials accused of crimes against humanity.

The accords also created an ambitious framework for reestablishing the rule of law as the country returned to peacetime while also seeking to address the war's underlying causes. In this regard, agreements were reached in the following areas: human rights, socioeconomic and agrarian issues, the strengthening of civil society and the role of the army in a democratic society, and rights and identity of indigenous peoples. Interestingly, these were negotiated by the establishment of a consensus among various sectors of society working with the Guatemalan government to have their interests and demands addressed at the negotiating table.

The far-reaching accords offer hope for the construction of a brand-new Guatemala among more equitable lines. The implementation of the reforms called for in the accords, however, has been a daunting task. It can be said that the peace accords have brought some degree of benefit to Guatemalan society. Some of the agreements have been fully complied with, state repression ended, and some opening for political participation has been created in recent years. There are still, however, many lingering issues, including lack of security, poverty, socioeconomic exclusion, and a high degree of confrontation between varying sectors of society. In essence, what we are seeing is a reflection of the peace accords' intimate connection to the process of Guatemala's continued democratization. It is this very process of democratization that will ensure that the spirit and the letter of the accords are eventually fulfilled.

POSTWAR GUATEMALA
Alfonso Portillo and the "Corporate Mafia State"

During the 1999 elections, Alfonso Portillo ran on a populist ticket, hoping to lure the lower classes away from his main opponent, who was fashioned after Arzú. He promised to cut poverty by ending corruption and tax evasion. His party, the Frente Republicano Guatemalteco (FRG, Guatemalan Republican Front), was actually the brainchild of Ríos Montt, the mastermind behind some of the worst atrocities against Guatemala's indigenous peoples during the army's scorched-earth campaign of the early 1980s. He was forbidden, once again, from running in the election. It never stopped him from trying.

Among the elements of Portillo's atrocious legacy was the solidifying of what analysts have called the "Corporate Mafia State," defined in a February 2002 Amnesty International report as, "The 'unholy alliance' between traditional sectors of the oligarchy, some 'new entrepreneurs,' elements of the police and military, and common criminals."

Highlighting the few achievements under the Portillo administration was the 2001 conviction of three persons involved in the Gerardi murder. Although two military officers and a priest were tried and convicted of the murder, the general consensus was that the intellectual authors of the crime were still at large. Progress was also made in the case of the long-running saga of the 1990 murder of anthropologist Myrna Mack, who was studying human rights violations of Guatemala's internally dispossessed during the civil war and was an outspoken critic of the government. The material author of the crime, Noel de Jesús Beteta, is currently serving a

25-year prison sentence. The intellectual author, Colonel Juan Valencia Osorio, was sentenced to 30 years in prison in 2002, but an appeals court granted his release the following year. Shortly after an order for his re-arrest and return to prison, Valencia escaped while in military custody and under dubious circumstances.

Meanwhile, Ríos Montt got himself elected president of congress. From his position, he and military interests were said to run the show via the creation of a parallel power structure while Portillo remained a convenient government front man. Corruption, always a problem plaguing Guatemala's governments, ballooned to unparalleled proportions. Scandals involved embezzlement by the interior minister as well as a highly publicized cover-up involving Ríos Montt himself.

In an event subsequently labeled "Guategate" by the local press, Ríos Montt and 19 other FRG members of congress were accused of secretly altering a liquor tax law, which had already been passed, at the behest of powerful liquor interests. The altered rate lowered the tariffs by as much as 50 percent. When opposition parties denounced the illegal changes to the law, congressional records from the meeting disappeared, while other documents were falsified. Although a popular outcry arose to have Ríos Montt and the other members of congress stripped of their diplomatic immunity to stand trial for their actions, the crime remained in impunity, as is so often the case in Guatemala.

In May 2003, the FRG nominated Ríos Montt as its presidential candidate in the elections to be held in November of that year. Once again, his candidacy was rejected by the electoral authorities and by two lower courts, in accordance with the constitutional ban on coup participants' running for presidential office. In July 2003 the Constitutional Court, with several judges appointed by the FRG, approved his candidacy for president, ignoring the constitutional ban that had prevented him from running in previous elections. Adding insult to injury, Ríos Montt had publicly (and correctly) predicted the margin by which he

would win the decision prior to its announcement. Days later, the Supreme Court suspended his campaign for the presidency and agreed to hear a complaint presented by two opposition parties.

Ríos Montt denounced the ruling as tampering with the judicial hierarchy and issued veiled threats concerning possible agitation by supporters of his candidacy. Days later, on July 24, a day known as Black Thursday, thousands of ski-masked and hooded FRG supporters invaded the Guatemala City streets armed with machetes, guns, and clubs. They had been bused in from the interior by the FRG and were led in organized fashion by well-known FRG militants, including several members of congress, who were photographed by the press while coordinating the actions.

The demonstrators quickly targeted the offices of outspoken media opposing Ríos Montt's candidacy, holding an entire building hostage for several hours after trying to occupy it. They also marched on the courts and opposition party headquarters, shooting out windows and burning tires in city streets. Journalists were attacked, including a TV camera operator who died of a heart attack while running away from an angry mob. The rioters finally disbanded after the second day of riots when Ríos Montt publicly called on them to return to their homes.

Following the unrest, the Constitutional Court, laden with allies of Ríos Montt and Portillo, overturned the Supreme Court decision and cleared the way for Ríos Montt to run for president. A majority of Guatemalans were disgusted with his actions and the corrupt legacy of his party. They expressed their discontent at the polls, where Ríos Montt finished a distant third in the presidential race.

Óscar Berger Perdomo

The winner after a second, runoff election between the top two candidates was Óscar Berger Perdomo of GANA (Gran Alianza Nacional or Grand National Alliance), a former Guatemala City mayor who represented the interests of the economic elite but surrounded himself with a diverse cabinet. Among them was Rigoberta Menchú, who was named the governmental goodwill ambassador for the peace accords, which the government promised to take up again.

The new government's first priority quickly became cleaning up the mess left behind by the FRG. The national treasury had been ransacked of more than $1 billion, with corruption on an unprecedented scale involving theft, money laundering, monetary transfers to the army, and creation of secret bank accounts in Panama, Mexico, and the United States by members of Portillo's staff. Berger promised to bring corrupt officials from the FRG government to justice. Remarkably, he was able to make good on his promises, and many corrupt officials are now behind bars awaiting trial, although some have managed to escape prosecution due to the inefficiency and corruption still rampant in the country's judicial system. Portillo was eventually extradited to the United States to face charges and even served time in a federal prison after accepting a plea bargain for a reduced sentence.

Crime and lack of security continued to be problems affecting a wide spectrum of the population. Gang violence plagued Guatemala City and numerous other cities and towns. The economic picture was severely disrupted when thousands of rural peasant farmers had their crops annihilated and their villages destroyed by Hurricane Stan in October 2005. Government reconstruction efforts in the storm's aftermath were slow in making it to affected communities.

Despite some public opposition, Berger was able to implement many of his neoliberal economic policies, including laws governing the concession of government services and construction projects to private entities, securing mining rights for multinational mining conglomerates, and the ratification of DR-CAFTA, the Central American Free Trade Agreement.

The judicial and legislative branches continued to come under fire for gross inefficiency and corruption charges. The existence of clandestine groups, a legacy of the corporate mafia state with links to state agents and organized crime, continued to plague the government. After numerous delays, a U.N.-sponsored commission, known as the International Commission Against Impunity in Guatemala (CICIG), was created. The responsibility for its creation was part of the 1996 peace accords, as it was clear to the international community that Guatemala would need some hand-holding in order to introduce the rule of law in the face of endemic impunity. The United States and other foreign governments offered financial support for the program, which was to be composed of expert international detectives providing material support to the Public Ministry in its investigations of parallel power structures. The creation of CICIG was approved by Guatemala's congress on August 1, 2007.

As Berger's presidency drew to a close, the general consensus was that his time as president was marked by mostly good intentions but also some modest gains, particularly in terms of a redress of Guatemala's historical ills. Among the glaring omissions was a long-term, inclusive strategy to develop rural areas, where the majority of Guatemala's indigenous peoples live. Delays in the reconstruction process after Hurricane Stan were continually cited as symptoms of weak leadership and an inability to coordinate efforts to reach a common goal.

The top two candidates in the 2007 presidential election were Álvaro Colom, a self-proclaimed social democrat of the UNE party (Unidad Nacional de la Esperanza, or National Unity for Hope), and Otto Pérez Molina of the Partido Patriota (Patriot Party), an ex-military hardliner whose main campaign promise was to combat Guatemala's rapidly deteriorating security situation with a "strong hand." Persistent rumors of ties to organized crime continued to haunt the UNE party during the campaign, but in the end Colom's appeals to Guatemala's mostly poor indigenous majority won him the victory in the countryside, though he was decidedly the loser among better-educated Guatemala City voters. As is usually the case for Guatemalan voters, their choice for president came down to what (or whom) they perceived to be the lesser of two evils.

Álvaro Colom

Shortly before taking office, Vice President Rafael Espada, a well-known former Houston heart surgeon, told MSNBC that, "Guatemala is sick, very sick, in intensive care." Colom chose Espada as a running mate in part because of his credibility with Guatemalan elites, though some had doubts regarding his limited political experience. The foreign press was generally kind in its assessment of Colom and was happy to back a social democrat with the U.S. government seal of approval. Colom told the Associated Press he was confident his government could make Guatemala more conciliatory and that he and Espada knew the country's problems inside and out.

As usual, however, campaign promises led to few tangible results during the early days of the administration, despite a much-touted "100 Day Plan" to combat nagging grievances such as spiraling crime rates and a generally somber economic outlook. These early days were marked by a palpable lack of direction on the part of the Colom government, as it reacted (or failed to react) to one issue after another.

At about the same time, the press began reporting on a surprising element of power behind the scenes: First Lady Sandra Torres de Colom. It became a matter of public scrutiny that she was also, in fact, presiding over cabinet meetings. Torres de Colom was placed at the helm of the newly created Council for Social Cohesion, which oversees the health and education ministries, among others. The legal framework creating this mechanism granted her tremendous powers and complete control over a $282 million budget free from any third-party oversight. Torres de Colom, according to several analysts, in fact became Guatemala's co-president, usurping powers that would normally fall under the jurisdiction of government ministers and the vice president. The Council for Social Cohesion

eventually implemented a program of *bolsas solidarias,* or rations of basic food items given to Guatemala's poor. Their continued distribution, however, was often conditioned by party support for UNE. The manipulated masses essentially became a platform for Torres de Colom's future presidential candidacy.

On May 10, 2009, prominent Guatemala City lawyer Rodrigo Rosenberg was assassinated while bicycling in Zona 14. The next day, a video surfaced in which he plainly accused the government of orchestrating his death. In the video, recorded just days before, Rosenberg states, "If you are hearing this message, it means that I, Rodrigo Rosenberg Marzano, was murdered by the president's private secretary, Gustavo Alejos, and his associate Gregorio Valdez, with the approval of Mr. Álvaro Colom and Sandra de Colom." The alleged reason for the murder given by Rosenberg claimed it was a government plot to silence opposition to government corruption in Guatemala's Banrural, including claims of money laundering and using it as a front to collect campaign funds for a future run for office by Sandra Torres de Colom. Khalil Musa had been appointed to Banrural's board of directors, but his appointment was withheld by the government over a period of three months prior to his murder in April 2009.

Rosenberg fought valiantly for the solving of the murders of Musa and his daughter Marjorie, and he had received death threats in the days leading up to his own murder. In light of these allegations, an outraged Guatemalan populace took to the streets demanding Colom's resignation. Colom, meanwhile, denied any wrongdoing and ordered a full investigation. He also orchestrated counter-demonstrations with the UNE party affiliates, busing in supporters to the capital from the provinces. The murders were investigated by CICIG, though many of the assertions made by Rosenberg in his video were corroborated through other sources, most importantly evidence of Musa's pending appointment to Banrural.

In January 2010, the results of CICIG's

investigation into the murder of Rosenberg were revealed. It was found that the lawyer orchestrated his own death with the unknowing help of friends and family members, who thought they were being recruited to arrange the execution of his would-be assassin. The truth in Guatemala is often harder to believe than lies.

In true Machiavellian fashion, Sandra Torres divorced Álvaro Colom in March 2011 with the intention of bypassing a Constitutional ban prohibiting family members of the sitting president from running for office. Her case would eventually make it to the highest court in the land after Guatemala's electoral authorities rejected her attempts to register her candidacy, citing the constitutional ban. In an Oscar-worthy performance Sandra Torres tearfully appealed to the magistrates of the *Corte de Constitucionalidad* for permission to run for office. The court unanimously rejected her candidacy in its final decision two days later.

The much-anticipated 2011 elections eventually came down to a runoff election between Manuel Baldizón, of the LIDER party, and Otto Perez Molina. Baldizón's platform was very similar to UNE's, and many believed he was a puppet of Sandra Torres. He made ridiculous campaign promises that could only appeal to the poor and uneducated masses, including bringing Guatemala's national soccer team to a World Cup showing and an extra yearly work bonus. A textbook narcissist, Baldizón had publicly (and unabashedly) stated he was a Clark Kent look-alike and seemed more concerned with his opponents' alleged copying of his fashion sense than in seriously debating any of the issues proposed during televised debates. Baldizón campaign posters in Guatemala City began morphing overnight with clown noses spray-painted on. Pérez Molina, and his vice-presidential candidate Roxana Baldetti, offered a more serious strategy to combat the country's drug cartels and other forms of organized crime while continuing social aid programs initiated by Colom. LIDER was quite evidently the loser

in Guatemala City, where Pérez Molina won overwhelmingly with over 70 percent majority. The national results revealed Pérez Molina was the victor by a 54 percent majority. In the days following the election, Pérez Molina and Baldetti quickly set to making strategic plans and new cabinet appointments (something never before seen in Guatemala) in preparation for their inauguration on January 14, 2012. The mood in Guatemala was particularly upbeat and hopeful going in to the new year.

Otto Pérez Molina

Hopes were dashed once it became clear the Pérez Molina government was not the answer to Guatemala's myriad problems. Crime and a number of other endemic problems continue to plague Guatemalans from all walks of life. An initial push by Pérez Molina to decriminalize drugs in Guatemala eventually fell silent in the face of opposition from Washington. In a candid interview with a South American news agency in November 2014, Pérez Molina hinted at an eventual decriminalization of certain substances before the end of his term in 2016. The reasons behind his push to decriminalize (and begin state regulation of) the drug trade, is the argument that Guatemala's violence is largely to blame on the drug cartels using the country as a transit point. He and others have argued that Guatemala is caught in a cross fire between powerful drug cartels who hash out the national territory in a turf war for control of trans-shipment points. Border areas, such as Huehuetenango and parts of Petén have been particularly susceptible. It should be noted that military patrols of rural areas have increased substantially under Pérez Molina, and this seems to have curbed the trend toward lawlessness and control by drug cartels previously in place, as evidenced by the massacre of 27 innocent peasants at the hands of Mexican Zetas on a rural Petén ranch in May 2011.

Guatemalan society seemed increasingly polarized in 2013, as Ríos Montt faced genocide charges before a Guatemalan court. On May 10, the court found him guilty of the massacre of 1,771 Ixil peasants during his 1980s scorched-earth campaign and sentenced him to 80 years in prison. Many in Guatemala thought the tide of impunity had finally turned, and it was possible to bring gross human rights violations and state terror to justice. Guatemala's Constitutional Court, citing a procedural error, eventually overturned the conviction 10 days later and ordered a new trial. The country's attorney general, Claudia Paz y Paz, had her term in office cut short soon after by the Constitutional Court and has since left the country. As José Luis Sanz, writing for Upside Down World, put it, "...the virtual dismissal of Attorney General Claudia Paz y Paz was the old order putting its collective foot down and demanding a return to power." Former governance minister Carlos Menocal told the same source, "The country's power elite thinks that if Ríos Montt were to stand trial, the general of all generals, the gendarme of the oligarchy, anyone could fall. It opened the door. It opened the dike, and the waters could drag you down. So the primary objective is to prevent the theme of genocide from advancing."

With so many problems, it's easy to see why many Guatemalans leave their country in search of something else. Illegal migration of Guatemalans to the United States continued its upward trend during the Pérez Molina administration. An increasing number of these migrants are children, as evidenced by an immigration crisis unleashed on the U.S. border in the summer of 2014. Gang violence in Guatemala's urban areas is increasingly to blame, as a desperate attempt at self-preservation. Some respite was offered by the Obama administration in November 2014 thanks to an executive order granting amnesty to some of the illegal immigrants in the United States. About 500,000 Guatemalans residing illegally in the U.S. stand to benefit from the new immigration policies.

The usual charges of corruption and cronyism plagued Pérez Molina and vice president Baldetti during much of their term in office. In April 2015, a CICIG investigation revealed the existence of a criminal organization known as La Línea, which operated clandestinely to permit tax evasion to the tune of millions of dollars. Several suspects implicated in the case were rounded up. Also directly implicated was Baldetti's personal secretary, Juan Carlos Monzón Rojas. The arrests happened as she and Monzón were traveling together in South Korea, where Baldetti was receiving an award from a university. Monzón fled justice while Baldetti returned to Guatemala several days later. Confronted by reporters, she was unable to answer questions about Monzón's whereabouts or the circumstances of her return to Guatemala. Her statement also contradicted what Pérez Molina had said about the day and time of her return. Wiretaps released by CICIG revealed the existence of a person high up in the La Línea criminal organization still at large and referred to as "La R" (The R), "La Dos" (Number Two), and "La Señora" (The Lady). Many believed this directly implicated Baldetti, protected while in office by immunity.

An outraged public took to Guatemala's central plaza to demand Baldetti's and Pérez Molina's resignations. A full-fledged citizen movement aimed at political and electoral reform began to take shape, strengthened by Baldetti's resignation on May 8. Elections were scheduled for the fall of 2015, as this book went to press. Manuel Baldizón, the would-be frontrunner in the elections, took the brunt of citizens' new level of disgust for partisan politics. His campaign events would be held privately after protesters stormed several events around the country. Among the many paradigms shattered during this time of awakening was that of the second-place finisher from the previous election having their turn "come up," an idea known as *te toca*. A popular hashtag online and in protests during May 2015 was #NoTeTocaBaldizon. Meanwhile, CICIG's mandate was renewed for another two years (despite Pérez Molina's quite obvious opposition) and it prepared to make new revelations based on investigations of campaign funding just in time for the elections.

Government

ORGANIZATION

Guatemala is a constitutional democracy. The president is the chief of state, assisted by a vice president, both of whom are elected to office for a single four-year term. The president is constitutionally barred from a second term, but the vice president may run for office after a four-year hiatus from office. The Congreso de la República is the national (unicameral) legislative body, consisting of 158 members. Congress members serve four-year terms running concurrently with the presidential term. Guatemala has 22 administrative subdivisions (departments) headed by governors appointed by the president. Popularly elected mayors or councils govern Guatemala City and 331 other municipalities.

JUDICIAL SYSTEM

The judicial branch is independent of the executive branch and the legislature and consists of a Constitutional Court and a Supreme Court of Justice. The Constitutional Court is the highest court in the land and consists of five judges elected for five-year terms, with each judge serving one year as president of the court. Congress, the Supreme Court of Justice, the Superior Council of the Universidad de San Carlos de Guatemala, and the bar association (Colegio de Abogados) each elect one judge and the president appoints the fifth. The Supreme Court of Justice consists of 13 magistrates who serve five-year terms and elect a president of the court each year from among their members. The judiciary suffers from a poor public image because of suspicions that it has become porous to influence from drug traffickers as well as being corrupt and inefficient, though it recently gained greater widespread respect with the rejection of Sandra Torres's presidential candidacy, in defense of the Constitution.

ELECTIONS

The current power balance is a product of the 1985 Constitution, formulated before the country's official return to democracy in 1986. A series of reforms in 1993 shortened terms of office for president, vice president, and members of congress from five years to four; for Supreme Court justices from six years to five; and increased terms for mayors and city councils from 2.5 years to four.

Between 1954 and 1986, Guatemala was ruled primarily by a military-oligarchy alliance that installed presidents periodically via widely fraudulent elections or military coups. In the few elections considered free and fair during this period, the military quickly stepped in to assert its dominant role while ensuring that the president remained a figurehead. All of the elections from 1985 onward have been considered free and fair, though the military still holds much power in Guatemala, probably more so than in any other Latin American country. Much of Guatemala's democratic process has consisted of a gradual strengthening of the state while trying to limit the power of the military. Other general characteristics of the democratic process have been the growth of citizen participation from all sectors of society in an atmosphere of greater freedom concurrent with the gradual strengthening of institutions having extremely limited experience with governance under a democratic system.

POLITICAL PARTIES

Guatemala's political parties constitute a veritable alphabet soup and change from year to year depending on the capricious nature of alliances between different factions. Parties are unstable, to say the least, and no party has won a presidential election on more than one occasion. As an election approaches, a fresh batch of newly formed parties begin to make the rounds. The ruling party following the 2011 elections was the Partido Patriota (PP). Other parties include the Unidad Nacional de la Esperanza (UNE), Libertad Democratica Renovada (LIDER), Frente Republicano Guatemalteco (FRG), Vision con Valores (VIVA), and Partido Unionista (PU). The Unidad Revolucionaria Nacional Guatemalteca (Guatemalan National Revolutionary Unity, also URNG-MAIZ) is the political party formed by the former guerrilla movement, which fought against the government during the country's 36-year civil war. It holds just a handful of congressional seats.

BUREAUCRACY

There is still a long way to go in the consolidation of a genuine functioning democracy in Guatemala. The judiciary and legislative branches are badly in need of reform and have lost virtually all credibility with their constituents. The current situation is still very much like that described in 2000 by the Guatemalan Institute of Political, Economic, and Social Studies, a nongovernmental organization:

In our society, agents or former agents of the state have woven a secret, behind-the-scenes network dedicated to obstructing justice. They have created a virtual alternative government that functions clandestinely with its own standardized and consistent modus operandi. In such a context, crimes are not clarified, and those responsible are not identified. Society finally forgets the cases and becomes resigned.

If the actual material authors left evidence at the scene of their crimes, they then decide who to implicate as scapegoats. If there are actually any inquiries and if these eventually lead to any arrests, these are always of low-ranking members of the army, or at best, an official not in active service.

When they can't pin the crime on some scapegoat, the scene of the crime is contaminated and legal proceedings are obstructed and proceed at a snail's pace. If, nonetheless, investigations still continue, these powerful forces hidden behind the scenes destroy the evidence. And of course it cannot be forgotten that pressure, threats, attacks, and corruption are all part of the efforts to undermine and demoralize the judiciary, who, knowing they are not able to count on a security apparatus that will guarantee that the law is enforced, feel obliged to cede in the face of this parallel power.

The powerlessness of the Guatemalan judiciary has forced some people to seek remedies for their grievances in international courts under universal jurisdiction established by the United Nations concerning crimes against humanity. One example is the suit filed before the Spanish National Court in 1999 by the Rigoberta Menchú Foundation against eight former Guatemalan officials, including General Efraín Ríos Montt, for murder, genocide, torture, terrorism, and illegal arrest. The case seeks to try those responsible for wartime abuses and centers around the 1980 attack on the Spanish Embassy in Guatemala City that claimed the lives of 37 peasant activists, among them Menchú's father, and embassy staff. The Spanish court has heard other cases involving genocide and established a precedent for universal jurisdiction in the 1998 arrest of Chile's General Augusto Pinochet in the United Kingdom. He remained in custody for 14 months until British authorities ruled Pinochet was unfit for trial and let him return to Chile.

In July 2006, a Spanish judge ordered the detention of all eight accused after an unfruitful visit to Guatemala with the intention of gathering testimonies from plaintiffs and questioning the accused. Ríos Montt and General Mejía Víctores effectively paralyzed the process with a series of appeals upheld by the Constitutional Court. Menchú admitted the difficulty of getting Guatemalan officials to execute the arrest orders, calling it "a test of the Guatemalan justice system."

As for the legislature, there is talk of reducing the number of members of congress, elected partly by proportional representation. The Guatemalan congress has suffered in recent years from a gradual erosion of confidence on the part of its constituents because of gross inefficiency, corruption, and growing suspicion of widespread links to drug trafficking. In essence, a majority of Guatemalans view their congressional body as practically useless and expensive to maintain.

Political parties, likewise, have suffered a gradual decline in credibility. The general pattern since 1986 has been one of great expectation for change prior to elections and the installation of a new government, followed by disappointment with the new government's failure to deliver on its promises, ending in frustration and renewed hope for change with the next round of elections. The government of Álvaro Colom appeared to be no exception to this pattern after its first year in power. Opinion polls point to a growing desire to see the emergence of better leadership and an authentic political class, something Guatemala still lacks.

Economy

According to the World Bank, Guatemala's gross domestic product in 2013 was $53.8 billion, an increase of 3.7 percent over the previous year, with a per capita GNI of about $3,340. Inflation was about 4 percent for the same year. Although it is the largest economy in Central America, large sectors of the population remain only marginally active in the economy. Guatemala is also the region's most populous country, with approximately 15.9 million inhabitants in 2014. The economy has been growing steadily since the 1996 peace accords and has demonstrated macroeconomic stability.

AGRICULTURE, TRADE, AND INDUSTRY

Agriculture accounts for 13 percent of GDP, with agricultural exports of coffee, sugar, bananas, cardamom, vegetables, flowers and plants, timber, rice, and rubber being the chief products. Guatemala exported $8 billion worth of goods in 2008, with 75 percent of these being agricultural products. Light industry contributes to 25 percent of the GDP, and manufactures include prepared food, clothing and textiles, construction materials, tires, and pharmaceuticals. The service sector accounts for 61 percent of Guatemala's GDP. The United States is Guatemala's biggest trading partner, accounting for more than half of the country's exports and 40 percent of its imports. Other important trading partners include the neighboring Central American countries, Mexico, South Korea, China, and Japan.

In terms of employment, agriculture is the largest employer, with half of the population employed by this sector. Services, bolstered by tourism, employ 35 percent of the population, and industry employs the remaining 15 percent. Unemployment in 2005 was 3 percent.

After the signing of the 1996 peace accords, Guatemala appeared poised for rapid economic growth, but a financial crisis in 1998 disrupted the expected pace. Despite gains in industry, the country's economy still showed much of its historical susceptibility to world commodity prices, specifically coffee. A collapse in coffee prices severely affected rural incomes and brought the industry into a serious recession, though exports of this commodity have bounced back since then.

Foreign investment has remained weak, with Guatemala unable to capitalize on foreign investment to the same degree as its neighbors. A notable exception is the privatization of utilities. Potential investors cite corruption, crime and security issues, and the lack of sufficient skilled labor as the principal barriers to new business.

Guatemala's economy is dominated by the private sector, which generates about 85 percent of the GDP. The government's involvement is small, with its business activities limited to public utilities, many of which have been privatized under a neoliberal economic model, and the operation of ports, airports, and several development-oriented financial institutions. The Berger administration passed legislation allowing for more private sector concessions of services in 2006.

The U.S.-Dominican Republic-Central America Free Trade Agreement (DR-CAFTA) was ratified by Guatemala on March 10, 2005. Priorities within DR-CAFTA include the elimination of customs tariffs on as many categories of goods as possible, opening services sectors, and creating clear and easily enforceable rules in areas such as investment, customs procedures, government procurement, electronic commerce, intellectual property protection, the use of sanitary measures for the protection of public health, and resolution of business disputes. Import tariffs were lowered as part of Guatemala's membership in the Central American Common Market, with most now below 15 percent. The implementation of DR-CAFTA has translated into a 95 percent increase in U.S. exports to Guatemala from pre-trade agreement levels, the region's second-highest growth levels. In 2013, the U.S. exported $5.5 billion worth of goods to Guatemala. U.S. imports from Guatemala were $4.2 billion in 2013, an increase of 33 percent from pre-CAFTA levels.

Another major contributor to Guatemala's economy is the money sent home by over 1.5 million expatriate Guatemalans living and working in the United States. In 2014, this amounted to $5.5 billion, which Guatemalans on the receiving end used to supplement their incomes, start businesses, and put into savings. This phenomenon has helped to widely

Guatemala's economy is still heavily based on agriculture.

ameliorate the country's endemic poverty and accounts for almost 12 percent of the GDP. Although income sent from abroad shows continued growth, Guatemalans fear that ever-present deportations of Guatemalan nationals from the United States will negatively impact the local economy.

DISTRIBUTION OF WEALTH

It remains to be seen whether DR-CAFTA will aggravate or alleviate Guatemala's skewed wealth- and land-distribution patterns, which are already some of the most unequal in the world. The wealthiest 10 percent of the population receives almost half of all income, and the top 20 percent receives two-thirds. More than half of the population lives in poverty, with about 15 percent living in extreme poverty and surviving on less than $2 a day. Underlying these patterns of wealth and income distribution are Guatemala's social-development indicators, such as infant mortality and illiteracy, which are among the worst in the hemisphere. Chronic malnutrition among the rural poor worsened with the onset of the late-1990s coffee crisis and devastation wrought by Hurricane Stan in 2005.

TOURISM

On a much more positive note, tourism has greatly impacted the economy in recent years, particularly since the end of the civil war in 1996. In 2004, Guatemala received one million visitors for the first time, and increased visitor numbers have continued in the years since. In 2014, Guatemala registered 2.14 million foreign arrivals with a tourism expenditure totaling $1.56 billion. Visitor arrivals were up 7.1 percent over the previous year. U.S. arrivals were only up 0.1 percent, attesting to a general absence of Guatemalan tourism marketing in U.S. media. In Central America, only Costa Rica receives more visitors.

About 30 percent of Guatemala's visitor arrivals come from North America, with another 34 percent coming from Central America, particularly El Salvador. U.S. visitors may be closing the gap, however, as statistics from the peak Easter travel season of 2006 show more Americans arriving in Guatemala than Salvadorans. Approximately 18 percent of Guatemala's tourists come from Europe, and another 18 percent come from various other countries.

Much of the money generated by tourism stays in local hands, as many communities have been able to capitalize on their proximity to area attractions by catering to the demands of an increasing number of visitors. Foreign tourism investment is limited mostly to main tourist areas, and local entrepreneurs have done an excellent job of filling in the void created by the lack of foreign investment.

The state tourism agency, INGUAT (Instituto Guatemalteco de Turismo) does a notoriously poor job of promoting the country's image abroad. Have you ever seen an ad for Guatemala in a U.S. magazine or television station? I didn't think so. The industry also largely failed to capitalize from the filming of the CBS television series *Survivor* in the rainforests of Petén, which aired in 2005.

The main obstacle to the continued growth of Guatemala's tourism industry is security, and the Guatemalan government is actively working to make travel safer for visitors to Guatemala.

Coffee is one of Guatemala's main exports.

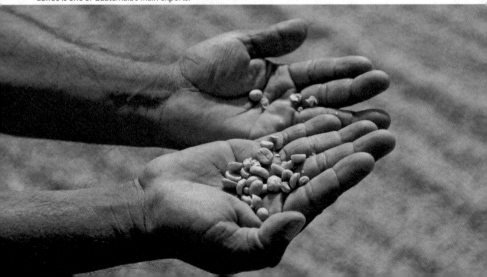

People and Culture

Guatemalans are a complex breed. First, there are the city-dwellers, who are as cosmopolitan as the residents of any North American city of comparable size. Social stratification, racism, and classicism also figure prominently into the makeup of many middle- and upper-class Guatemalans, in particular those living in urban areas. You may find some urban Guatemalans downright rude, though they are careful to put on their best appearances for foreigners.

Then there are Guatemala's rural poor and middle class. Most of them are warm and friendly; you may even be the object of their gracious hospitality. However, you may have to get past some cultural isolationism, as rural Guatemalans are naturally suspicious of outsiders once you are past the informal, superficial relationships of a passing traveler. This is not surprising given the country's penchant for violent social upheaval, class struggle, and an unfortunate more recent phenomenon, rising crime statistics.

Guatemala has its fair share of social problems. Perhaps the greatest challenges are the constant contradictions between wealth and poverty. It colors daily life in seemingly innocuous ways, such as traveling on a Guatemala City highway overlooking slums while driving to a fancy Zona 10 restaurant. It also colors day-to-day interactions with people, and you'll see it in the myriad ways Guatemalans treat each other.

It's no secret that the country has a legacy of violence from which it is still trying to recover. Its governments and leaders, with few exceptions, have mostly stayed in power long enough to rape the country of its resources and contribute to the wealth of fellow cronies while turning a blind eye to crime, social inequality, and widespread violence. The general populace seems resigned to live in a country where things simply happen, where governments make promises and then fail to deliver, where the rich continue to live privileged lives while the poor continue to somehow survive. Perhaps this is all the legacy of Spanish colonial government and the clashing of two very distinct cultures from opposite ends of the earth. Maybe it's the legacy of 36 years of civil war. What is certain is that Guatemala's cultural and sociopolitical makeup is a subject of much academic speculation, and you will certainly come to form your own opinions after some time traveling here.

I realize I haven't painted a very pretty picture of my fellow Guatemalans. It's sometimes difficult to spend time in such a beautiful country with so many sad contradictions. Part of traveling in Guatemala involves finding a way to live with these contradictions. It's all part of the experience.

ETHNICITY AND CLASS
Demographics

Guatemala's population is one of the fastest-growing in Latin America, with 2004 census figures placing the population at just over 14 million. The annual growth rate is 2.61 percent, and 43 percent of the population is under the age of 15. The country's population density is 116 people per square kilometer, with an urban-to-rural ratio of 38.7 percent to 61.3 percent. Population density is much lower in the northern Petén department, comprising a third of Guatemala's total land area but harboring only about 5 percent of the population. Urbanization is greatest in the Western Highlands region centered around Guatemala City and Quetzaltenango.

Ethnic Diversity

Guatemala has an incredible wealth of ethnic diversity, as attested to by the as-of-yet-unfulfilled push to amend the national constitution to officially describe the country as "pluricultural, multilingual, and multiethnic." The country is divided about evenly between descendants of indigenous Maya (comprising 21 different linguistic groups) and ladinos, who are of Mayan descent but have adopted European culture and dress in addition to the Spanish language. A sizable percentage of the population is a mixture of Mayan and European, also known as *mestizo*. A much smaller percentage of the population is of purely European descent, primarily from Spanish and German families, and they control a disproportionate fraction of the country's wealth. Many of these are direct descendants of the *criollo* (New World Spanish-born elite) families dominating the country's economy since colonial times. Indigenous Maya descendants are found in greatest numbers in the Western Highlands, with Guatemala City, the Pacific, Caribbean, and Petén lowlands being largely ladino.

Additionally, there are two non-Mayan ethnicities thrown into the mix, Xinca and Garífuna. Only about 100-250 Xinca-speakers remain, confined to a small area near the Salvadoran border. The Garinagu (plural of Garífuna), a mixture of Amerindian and African peoples, arrived from St. Vincent via Roatán, Honduras, in the early 1800s and settled in the Guatemalan Caribbean coastal town of Lívingston. Their culture is more similar to that of the Western Caribbean, with whom they identify more readily, than the rest of Guatemala.

Mayan Groups

Ethnicity and language are intertwined when it comes to Guatemala's principal Mayan groups, which include K'iche', Kaqchikel, Tz'utujil, Mam, Ixil, Q'eqchi', Poqomchi', Poqomam, and Q'anjob'al. By far the most numerous group is K'iche', with nearly one million speakers. A little more than 400,000 people speak Kaqchikel, and there are about 686,000 Mam speakers.

ECONOMIC CLASS STRUCTURES
The Oligarchy

The direct result of Guatemala's Spanish colonial legacy granting privileges to

More than half of Guatemalans are of Mayan descent.

Spanish-born elites is the modern-day oligarchy. In many cases, families can trace their roots to these colonial-era *criollo* families. As in neighboring El Salvador, where there is frequent reference to "The Fourteen Families," the Guatemalan oligarchy has a strong history of intermingling to the exclusion of outer echelons of society. For the purpose of this discussion, the oligarchy will also encompass the "new rich" and the subsequent generations of landowning business elites who remain firmly in control of Guatemala's politics and economy.

Much has been written about the Guatemalan elite's support for right-wing governments and military policies aimed at eliminating the threat of communist subversion during the country's civil war (1960-1996). Although the war had genocidal aspects, it was also very much related to the distribution of wealth and the 1950s-era reforms that threatened economic elites' hegemony. In essence, the oligarchy allied with the military in an attempt to maintain the status quo.

The oligarchy also found a willing ally in the Unites States, which was happy to support Guatemalan elites in their emulation of U.S. consumption patterns and the expansion of private enterprise. Stephen Connely Benz, in his book *Guatemalan Journey,* provides some interesting insights on Guatemala's oligarchy and the way in which U.S. government aid via the U.S. Agency for International Development (USAID) may have unknowingly exacerbated Guatemala's inequitable social structures. He argues that capitalism, prior to the arrival of USAID, already functioned in its most brutal form in Guatemala, and he points to the history of "the conservative oligarchy and the essentially feudalistic economic system that remained the principal obstacle to a more equitable distribution of wealth." He goes on to say that, "This oligarchy did not care for democracy, modernization, or even economic liberalism; what it cared for was the perpetuation of an extremely lucrative arrangement. . . . It was, in short, a

segment of society that had long gotten its way and was principally interested in maintaining its privileges—reform was the furthest thing from its interests, unless by economic reform one meant lower export taxes, privatization of services, and the liberalization of price controls." In essence, Benz argues, U.S. aid money given to support agro-industry and free enterprise went directly to the oligarchy and thus helped perpetuate the continuance of a "wildly unjust, cash-crop-driven economy that necessitated U.S. aid for the impoverished masses in the first place."

More recently, the Guatemalan elites' uncontested hold on the reins of power can be seen in the stalling of the 1996 peace accords. Although the accords contain many provisions that would contribute to make Guatemala a more just society, the vast majority of these reforms have fallen by the wayside. Ironically, the major economic reforms taking place since the signing of the peace accords largely involve the lower export taxes and privatization of services Benz speculated about.

On a practical level, you can see the Guatemalan elite at fancy restaurants, shopping malls, and hotel lobbies in Guatemala City. You'll recognize them by their entourage of bodyguards, nannies to mind the children, and chauffeur-driven late-model luxury cars. They'll greet each other in courteous fashion, and it will seem like everyone in the restaurant knows each other and is part of the same tight-knit clan. On a positive note, absent large quantities of U.S. foreign investment in Guatemalan real estate and tourism infrastructure, the oligarchy's presence has given Guatemala the condos, office buildings, and five-star hotels it would otherwise lack.

The Upper and Middle Classes

Guatemala's upper class has close ties to the oligarchy, and there is a bit of a gray area where the two intersect. Social class in Guatemala is very much about putting on appearances in an attempt to gain favor with

Endemic poverty is unfortunately still a reality for many Guatemalans.

Lower Classes

It's no surprise that, in a country where race and social standing go hand in hand, the vast majority of the country's poor are of Mayan descent. This applies to those living in poverty in highland villages and urban slums or trying to eke out a living in the Petén lowlands. About 80 percent of Guatemala's population lives in poverty, with about two-thirds of that number living in extreme poverty on less than $2 a day. Guatemala's social indicators, such as infant mortality and illiteracy, are among the worst in the hemisphere.

RELIGION

Religion in Guatemala is fairly complex, with traditional Mayan spirituality still very much a presence, particularly in the highlands, along with Catholicism and the more recent incursions of Evangelical Christianity. In much smaller numbers, Guatemala's Jewish population is centered in Guatemala City. There is also a small Muslim population with at least one mosque in Guatemala City.

Mayan Spirituality

Mayan spirituality has its origins in pre-Columbian religious practices and a cosmology that venerated natural phenomena, including rivers, mountains, and caves. The soaring temples built by the Mayan and other Mesoamerican civilizations were constructed to mimic mountains and were usually built in alignment with the cardinal directions. The solstices were very important in this regard, and many of their temple pyramids and observatories were built in precise fashion so as to mark these events. Caves were also sacred to the Maya and believed to be passages to the underworld, a belief that persists to this day. Archaeologists speculate that at least one powerful economic center, Cancuén, lacked buildings of strictly religious significance because of its proximity to the massive Candelaria cave network nearby.

The Mayan calendar is still in use in parts of Guatemala today, particularly in the Western Highlands, and is pegged closely

the upper echelons of society. Statistically, Guatemala has the third-highest per capita private aircraft ownership in the Americas, which gives you some idea of the purchasing power of wealthy Guatemalans. The country's wealth can also be seen in the fact that many homes that would be considered high-end in neighboring Central American countries such as Nicaragua and Honduras would be quite middle class in Guatemala. To give you an idea of how this is possible, keep in mind that the wealthiest 10 percent of the population receives almost half of all the income and the top 20 percent receives two-thirds.

Some might argue that Guatemala has no true middle class, but I would disagree. The middle class in Guatemala most certainly looks different than it does in the United States and even neighboring Central American countries. It's also proportionally smaller, but not altogether nonexistent. You'll find most of the country's middle class living in urban areas such as Guatemala City and Quetzaltenango.

to the agricultural cycle. Maize is a sacred crop and believed to have been the basis for the modern formation of man by the gods, as told in the K'iche' book of myths and legends, the *Popol Vuh,* discovered by a Spanish priest in Chichicastenango in the 18th century. Although the vast majority of sacred Mayan writings were burned by Bishop Diego de Landa in a 16th-century Yucatán bonfire, three Mayan texts, known as codices, survive in European museums. The *Chilam Balam* is another sacred book based on partially salvaged Yucatecan documents from the 17th and 18th centuries.

Modern-day Mayan religious practices, also known as *costumbre,* often take place in caves, archaeological sites, and volcanic summits. They often include offerings of candles, flowers, and liquor with the sacrifice of a chicken or other small animal thrown in for good measure.

Another curiosity of the Western Highlands is the veneration of a folk saint known alternatively as Maximón or San Simón, with a particularly persistent following in Santiago Atitlán and Zunil. The cigar-smoking, liquor-drinking idol is a thorn in the side of many Catholic and Evangelical groups, whose followers sometimes profess conversion to Christianity but often still hold allegiance to Maximón, who is thought to represent Judas or Pedro de Alvarado. Syncretism, combining Mayan religious beliefs and Catholicism, is a major player in highland Mayan spirituality.

The cult following of folk saints is also tied to the presence of *cofradías,* a form of Mayan community leadership with roots in Catholic lay brotherhoods wielding religious and political influences. The *cofradías* are responsible for organizing religious festivities in relation to particular folk saints and a different member of the *cofradía* harbors the Maximón idol in his home every year.

Many Mayan people practice syncretism, combining Catholicism and Maya rituals.

The Catholic Church

Catholicism has played an important role in Guatemala ever since colonial times, though the state increasingly took measures to limit its power starting in the late 19th century, when liberal reformers confiscated church property and secularized education. More recently, the church wrestled with its official mandate of saving souls and its moral obligation to alleviate the misery and injustice experienced by many of its subjects, particularly the Maya. Many parish priests, faced with the atrocities and injustices of the civil war, adopted the tenets of Liberation Theology, seeking a more just life in the here and now and officially opposing the military's scorched-earth campaign throughout the highlands. Many clergy paid for their beliefs with their lives or were forced into exile. Even after the civil war ended, Bishop Juan Gerardi was

Mayan Ethnolinguistic Groups

- **Achi':** Spoken in western Baja Verapaz, including Cubulco, Rabinal, San Miguel Chicaj, San Jerónimo, and Salamá.

- **Akateko:** Spoken in San Miguel Acatán and San Rafael La Independencia (Huehuetenango).

- **Awakateko:** Spoken in Aguacatán, Huehuetenango.

- **Ch'orti:** Spoken in La Unión (Zacapa) and Jocotán, Camotán, Olopa, and Quetzaltepeque (Chiquimula).

- **Chuj:** Spoken in San Mateo Ixtatán and parts of Nentón.

- **Itzá:** Spoken in Flores, San José, San Andrés, San Benito, La Libertad, and Sayaxché.

- **Ixil:** Spoken in Chajul, Cotzal, and Nebaj (El Quiché department).

- **Kaqchikel:** Spoken in 47 municipalities in seven departments, including Guatemala, Sacate-péquez, Chimaltenango, Escuintla, Sololá (Panajachel, Santa Catarina Palopó, San Antonio Palopó, Santa Cruz La Laguna, and San Marcos La Laguna), Suchitepéquez, and Baja Verapaz.

- **K'iche':** Guatemala's most widely spoken Mayan dialect, with speakers in 75 municipalities spanning six departments, including Sololá, Totonicapán, Quetzaltenango, El Quiché, Suchite-péquez, and Retalhuleu.

- **Mam:** Spoken in 55 municipalities in three departments, including Quetzaltenango, San Marcos, and Huehuetenango (Todos Santos and San Juan Atitán, among others).

- **Mopán:** Spoken in San Luis, Dolores, parts of Melchor de Mencos, and Poptún (Petén).

- **Popti (Jakalteko):** Spoken in parts of western Huehuetenango, including Jacaltenango, La Democracia, Concepción Huista, San Antonio Huista, Santa Ana Huista, and Nentón.

- **Poqomam:** Spoken in Mixco and Chinautla (Guatemala department), Palín (Escuintla), and Jalapa department.

- **Poqomchi':** Widely spoken in Alta and Baja Verapaz, including San Cristóbal Verapaz, Tactic, Tamahú, Tucurú, and Purulhá.

- **Q'anjob'al:** Spoken in Soloma, San Juan Ixcoy, Santa Eulalia, and Barillas (Huehuetenango).

- **Q'eqchi:** Most widely spoken in Alta Verapaz, including Cobán, Panzós, Senahú, San Pedro Carchá, San Juan Chamelco, Lanquín, Chisec, and Cahabón. Other locales include Uspantán (El Quiché department) and parts of Petén and Izabal.

- **Sakapulteko:** Spoken in parts of Sacapulas, El Quiché.

- **Sipakapense:** Spoken in Sipacapa, San Marcos.

- **Tektiteko:** Spoken in parts of Cuilco and Tectitán (Huehuetenango).

- **Tz'utujil:** Spoken in several of the Lake Atitlán villages, including San Lucas Tolimán, San Pablo La Laguna, San Juan La Laguna, San Pedro La Laguna, and Santiago Atitlán.

- **Uspanteko:** Spoken in Uspantán, El Quiché.

murdered in the days after his issuance of a scathing report on civil war atrocities perpetrated mostly by the military. The church remains a watchdog and defender of the poor, which is evident in the ongoing work of the Archbishop's Human Rights Office.

Although there are many churches throughout the country, the Catholic Church often has trouble finding priests to fill them, a factor that has contributed to the explosive growth of Evangelical Christianity. Pope John Paul II visited Guatemala three times during his term at the helm of the Vatican; the last visit was for the purpose of canonizing Antigua's beloved Hermano Pedro de San José Betancur.

Catholicism can still draw a big crowd, though, most noticeably during Holy Week, with its elaborate processions reenacting Christ's crucifixion, and the annual pilgrimage to Esquipulas on January 16 to pay homage to the Black Christ in the town's basilica.

Evangelical Christianity

According to some estimates, a third of Guatemala now claims adherence to Protestantism and, more specifically, Evangelical Christianity. The growth of this sect will become obvious as you travel around the country and hear the sounds of loud evening worship services, known as *cultos,* emanating from numerous churches, particularly in the highlands. The trend toward Evangelical Christianity dates to the aftermath of the 1975 earthquake, which destroyed several villages throughout the highlands. International aid agencies, several of them overtly Christian, rushed into Guatemala at a time of great need and gained many grateful converts in the process. During the worst of the civil war violence of the 1980s, many Guatemalans sought comfort in the belief of a better life despite the hardships of the present. Other factors making Evangelical Christianity attractive to Guatemalans include the tendency toward vibrant expressions of faith, spontaneity, and the lack of a hierarchy, which makes spiritual leaders more accessible to common people.

A notorious legacy of Guatemala's trend toward Protestantism was the dictatorship of Efraín Ríos Montt, a prominent member of Guatemala City's Iglesia El Verbo (Church of the Word), who sermonized Guatemalans on subjects including morality, Christian virtues, and the evils of communism via weekly TV broadcasts. Meanwhile, a scorched-earth campaign aimed at exterminating the guerrilla presence raged in the highlands, though violence in the cities was widely curtailed and order somewhat restored. He faced charges of genocide in a Guatemalan court and was even (briefly) found guilty, though it's doubtful he will ever be brought to justice. Also disturbing was the short presidency of Jorge Serrano Elías, another self-proclaimed Evangelical now exiled in Panama after he dissolved congress in a failed autocoup, which ended in his ouster a few days later. His government faced widespread corruption charges.

LANGUAGE

Guatemala's official language is Spanish, though as mentioned there are 23 other ethnolinguistic groups in this very diverse nation. Guatemalan Spanish is fairly clean and tends to avoid the dropping off of the last syllables in words, a common occurrence in Caribbean Spanish-speaking countries. This makes Guatemalan Spanish particularly easy to learn and understand for foreigners, a fact attested to by the overwhelming number of Spanish-language schools present in many parts of the country, but especially in Antigua and Quetzaltenango. Spanish schools are also present in Cobán, Huehuetenango, Todos Santos, San Andrés, San José (Petén), and Panajachel, to name a few. It's also possible to learn Mayan languages in many of these schools.

ARTS
Literature

Guatemala's first literary figure was Jesuit priest and poet Rafael Landívar (1731-1793). A native of Antigua, his most well-known work is *Rusticatio Mexicano,* a poem describing rural customs of the times. Landívar was forced to leave Guatemala in 1767 when his

A Few *Chapinismos*

The following is a listing of a few more commonly used Guatemalan expressions and slang terms. A full glossary can be found in the *Resources* chapter.

- *aguas!:* watch out!
- *a todo mecate:* full-speed ahead
- *babosadas:* lies or nonsense
- *cachito:* a little bit
- *canche:* blond or fair-skinned; also was a term used of guerrilla fighters during the civil war
- *capearse:* to play hooky
- *caquero:* arrogant or stuck-up, usually someone of wealth
- *casaca:* tall tales or embellishments
- *chapparro:* person of short stature
- *chupar:* to drink alcoholic beverages
- *clavos:* problems
- *(tener) conectes:* to have influence because of important or powerful friends
- *cuates:* buddies
- *goma (estar de):* to be hungover
- *güiro:* a child
- *jalón:* a lift or ride (in a vehicle)
- *mango:* a handsome man
- *mordida:* bribe
- *muco:* a person of low social class, usually used disdainfully by upper-class Guatemalans in reference to lower classes
- *pisto:* money
- *salsa:* to (mistakenly) think oneself cool and hip
- *sho (hacer):* to be quiet (shut up)
- *shuco:* dirty
- *shute:* nosy
- *vonós:* "let's go," a shortened version of *vámonos*

order was expelled from the Americas by the Spanish crown. The country's best-known writer is Miguel Ángel Asturias (1899-1974), winner of the 1967 Nobel Prize in literature. His most famous works include *El Señor Presidente* (1946), about the maniacal dictator Manuel Estrada Cabrera, and *Hombres de Maíz* (1949, translated as *Men of Maize*), about the Mayan peasantry. One of the characters in the latter is a guerrilla warrior by the name of Gaspar Ilom, a name that Asturias's son Rodrigo, influenced by his father's writings, would appropriate as a pseudonym while leading one of the guerrilla factions comprising the Guatemalan National Revolutionary Unity (URNG). His other well-known works include *El Papa Verde* (*The Green Pope,* 1954, about the United Fruit Company) and *Weekend en Guatemala* (1968, about the 1954 coup that ousted Jacobo Árbenz Guzmán).

Modern Guatemalan authors of note include Francisco Goldman, author of several novels, including *The Long Night of White Chickens,* which takes place mostly in Guatemala, *The Ordinary Seaman* (1997), and *The Divine Husband* (2004). Arturo Arias is another modern-day author known for having written the screenplay for the movie *El Norte* and the book *After the Bombs,* chronicling the Arbenz period and the aftermath of his overthrow. Víctor Perera has written several excellent books on Guatemalan culture and history, including *Unfinished Conquest* (1993) and *Rites: A Guatemalan Boyhood* (1986).

Visual Arts

Guatemala's rich history in the visual arts dates to pre-Columbian times, with the painting of exquisite murals and the carving of stelae by the Maya. The colonial period also left a substantial artistic legacy, mostly by anonymous artists. An exception is the work of Thomas de Merlo (1694-1739), whose paintings can still be seen in Antigua's Museo de Arte Colonial. Sculptor Quirio Cataño carved the Black Christ of Esquipulas in 1595, now an object of much veneration for pilgrims from all over Central America.

More recently, Kaqchikel painter Andrés Curruchich (1891-1969) pioneered the "primitivist" style of painting from his hometown in Comalapa, Chimaltenango. The currents of *indigenismo* ran strongly throughout the 20th century and were marked by an often-romanticized portrayal of indigenous culture, as evidenced by the murals found in Guatemala City's Palacio Nacional de la Cultura, which are the work of Alfredo Gálvez Suárez (1899-1946). Also in this vein was sculptor Ricardo Galeotti Torres (1912-1988), whose works include the giant marimba sculpture found in Quetzaltenango and the Tecún Umán statue in the plaza of Santa Cruz del Quiché.

Perhaps Guatemala's best-known visual artist, Carlos Mérida (1891-1984) was a contemporary of Pablo Picasso, whom he met while studying painting in Paris between 1908 and 1914. His *indigenista* art predates the work of Mexican muralists the likes of Diego Rivera by about seven years and sought to unify European modernism with themes more specific to the Americas. Mérida's work exhibits three major stylistic shifts throughout the years: a figurative period from 1907 to 1926, a surrealist phase from the late 1920s to the mid-1940s, and a geometric period from 1950 until his death in 1984. Many of his works can be seen in Guatemala City's Museum of Modern Art, which bears his name. Mérida's murals also grace the walls of several Guatemala City public buildings.

Another artist whose work adorns Guatemala City architecture is sculptor and engineer Efraín Recinos, designer of the city's Centro Cultural Miguel Ángel Asturias. A large Recinos mural composed of blue and green tiles was formerly housed inside La Aurora International Airport but was recently demolished as part of the airport renovation project. The large, white sculptures lining the airport's exterior facade were also created by Recinos and have been restored and incorporated into the terminal's new design.

In March 2007, Guatemala City hosted a sculpture festival with the participation of 12 internationally acclaimed artists working during a two-week period to create unique art pieces from blocks of marble. It was the first event of its kind held in Central America. The sculptures are now part of the city's artistic legacy and can be found along the boulevard connecting the international airport to Bulevar Liberación.

Architecture

In addition to the well-documented architectural legacy of the Maya, Guatemala is also known for its baroque architecture, found mostly in Antigua and Guatemala City cathedrals and government buildings. This style of architecture is a Spanish adaptation to local conditions, marked by the prevalence of earthquakes, with squat, thick-walled structures designed to weather numerous tremors throughout the years. Architecture in rural towns and villages tends to be rather functional, with a recent trend toward grotesque multistory concrete buildings replacing more traditional construction. Classic forms of rural architecture consist (or consisted) largely of whitewashed adobe houses with red-tile roofs.

Guatemala City has its fair share of assembly-line high-rise condominiums, though it also has some noteworthy modern architecture. If you have an interest in this topic, a recommended book is *Six Architects* (Ange Bourda, 2002), filled with wonderful color photographs chronicling the work of six Guatemala City architects who merged into a single firm and are responsible for several of the city's nicest buildings.

Music

Guatemala's national instrument is the marimba, a huge wooden xylophone with probable African origins. You'll often hear marimba in popular tourist regions such as Antigua, where its cheerful notes can be heard emanating from garden courtyards housed in the city's larger hotels. Pre-Columbian musical instruments consisted largely of drums, wooden flutes, whistles, and bone rasps. An excellent place to check out the history and

origins of Guatemala's highland Mayan musical traditions is Casa K'ojom, just outside Antigua in Jocotenango.

It's also not uncommon to hear music with Mexican influence in Guatemala, with the occasional mariachi band contracted to liven up a birthday party. Tejano and *ranchera* music can often be heard. You'll also hear North American rock bands here and there, sometimes on bus rides, though the sounds favored by bus drivers seem to have gotten stuck somewhere around 1984.

On the Caribbean Coast, the Garífuna population tends to favor the mesmerizing beats of *punta* and reggae, with variations including *punta rock* and *reggaeton,* English-Spanish rap laid over slowed-down Caribbean-style techno and reggae beats.

Grammy award-winning rock musician Ricardo Arjona is Guatemala's best-known international recording artist. He lives in Mexico City. Also enjoying recent success is Grammy-winning Gaby Moreno. Spanish-language pop and rock are, of course, also widely heard throughout Guatemala.

TV and Cinema

Guatemala has its very own cable TV channel, Guatevisión, which can be seen in the United States. It features a morning show based in Guatemala City as well as some fairly humorous entertainment programs that provide a glimpse of the nightlife and outdoor recreation scene throughout the country. Guatemala even had a celebrity newscaster of sorts, CNN's former Mexico City bureau chief Harris Whitbeck, who reported events around the world in English and Spanish. One of his more recent projects is a local TV show, *Entrémosle a Guate* (Let's Get in on Guate), with profiles of everyday Guatemalans who make the country a special place. He now lives in Antigua Guatemala, where he and his spouse own a restaurant. Also enjoying celebrity status is Guatemalan-born Oscar Isaac, starring in the latest installment of *Star Wars,* among numerous other films.

As for movies about Guatemala, *El Norte*

(1983, directed by Gregory Nava) is a classic tale of Guatemalan immigrants fleeing the civil war during the 1980s. More recently, in the summer of 2006, Antigua was the scene of on-location shooting for *Looking for Palladin,* a film about a young Hollywood go-getter who finds himself in Guatemala. Many folks in Antigua are hoping the film will open doors for more movies to be filmed in Guatemala.

CRAFTS

Guatemala is world famous for the artistic quality and variety of its crafts, with weaving at the top of the list. Each village has its unique style, and you can recognize villagers from a particular location based solely on their traditional attire. Among the most fascinating handwoven pieces are *huipiles,* embroidered blouses worn by highland Mayan women that feature colorful motifs that often include plants, animals, and lightning bolts in a dizzying array of colors. While you are

certainly welcome to buy village attire, it's never a good idea to wear it around while in Guatemala, as indigenous peoples will find this highly offensive (or downright hilarious, at best). Many people buy *huipiles* to frame and hang as home decor, laying the blouse flat with the large head opening at its center or hanging it from a wooden rod. You can see examples where this has been tastefully done in numerous Antigua boutique hotels.

Jade jewelry mined from local quarries is a popular item in upscale shops in Antigua. "Primitivist" paintings are popular in the villages of San Pedro and Santiago, on the shores of Lake Atitlán. For wool blankets, check out Momostenango, though you can also find them in markets throughout the country. The best wood carvings are found in the village of El Remate, in the northern Petén department, though traditional wooden ceremonial masks are still an item found exclusively in the Western Highlands.

a Guatemalan *huipil*

Essentials

Transportation

GETTING THERE
Air

Most international travelers to Guatemala arrive by plane. U.S. carriers have stepped up their presence in Guatemala in recent years and are expected to continue this trend, particularly in light of ever-increasing visitor arrivals and a growing population of Guatemalans living abroad.

As for airfares, the price of an average plane ticket from the United States to Guatemala varies widely depending on route and season, but ranges from about $350 to $850 roundtrip. Still, deals can be had if you know where to look and are willing to give up comforts like advance seat selection and ticket changeability. Internet sites offer discounted tickets and air ticket consolidators are worth checking out; a particularly useful tool for comparison shopping is www.kayak.com.

Guatemala has an open-skies agreement with the United States, meaning that any carrier from either country can fly to any point in the other. Guatemala once had an official flag-carrier, Aviateca, but Colombian-owned Avianca has since absorbed it. Avianca operates the majority of flights into and out of Guatemala, flying nonstop from a handful of gateway cities in the United States as well as via its hubs in San Salvador and Bogotá. The U.S. carriers also have a strong presence here. Several Latin American carriers, some of them noteworthy, operate here as well. The only European airline serving Guatemala at this time is Iberia, the Spanish flag-carrier.

AIRPORTS

Most international travelers flying to Guatemala arrive via Guatemala City's **La Aurora International Airport** (GUA). La Aurora could not be more conveniently located for Guatemala City residents, lying in the heart of the city just minutes from the business and hotel district. A recent renovation and expansion brought the once-obsolete La Aurora into the 21st century. The spacious glass-and-steel north and central terminals are vast improvements over La Aurora's former facilities and feature a number of good restaurants and duty-free shops. There's even a club lounge for United and Copa Airlines (Star Alliance) passengers. The flight departure check-in lobby, with a high, angular ceiling is actually part of the original construction dating back to the 1960s. It was given an updated look and restored to full functionality.

It can be a bit chaotic when exiting La Aurora, as families of arriving Guatemalans tend to load up cars (and sometimes entire buses) to welcome a returning loved one. The same is true for departing family members. Making your way out of the terminal (before merging with the crowds outside), you'll see an INGUAT tourist information kiosk. The English-speaking agents can provide maps and answer basic questions about ground transportation. Taxis and shuttle buses also operate out of kiosks found in the arrival area. A taxi to Zona 10 or Zona 14 costs about $9; trips to Carretera a El Salvador or elsewhere beyond the city limits cost more. Most of the Zona 10 hotels have courtesy shuttles to and from the airport. A shuttle bus to Antigua costs between $12 and $15. Likewise, car rentals can be booked from kiosks inside the airport terminal, located just after clearing customs.

Flores/Tikal, officially known as **Mundo Maya International Airport** (FRS), serves the northern department of Petén and the

---

ruins of Tikal. It now has air-conditioning and is a much-improved facility. Flights arrive several times daily from Guatemala City, Cancún, and Belize City. The flight to Flores from the Guatemalan capital takes about 50 minutes. Most travelers arriving here head straight for the ruins of Tikal, about an hour away via numerous minivans, or to the city of Flores, just five minutes away by taxi. A *colectivo* van to Tikal costs about $4. A taxi to Flores costs about $3. Arrival procedures are fairly straightforward thanks to the airport's smaller size.

FLIGHTS TO GUATEMALA CITY

The majority of nonstop flights come from a handful of North American hubs including Atlanta, Washington DC, Dallas/Ft. Worth, Fort Lauderdale, Houston, Los Angeles, Miami, New York (JFK), and New York/Newark. San Salvador and Panama City are becoming increasingly important as connecting points for flights from South America on Avianca and Copa Airlines, respectively. Madrid holds the distinction of being the sole European city with direct service to Guatemala City via a nonstop flight four times per week on Spanish flag-carrier Iberia.

Among U.S. carriers, **American Airlines** (tel. 800/433-7300 U.S., www.aa.com) flies nonstop three or four times daily to Guatemala City from Miami (depending on season) and daily nonstop from Dallas/Ft. Worth. It code shares with British Airways on flights from the U.K. and has excellent European connections of its own.

United Airlines (tel. 800/231-0856 U.S., www.united.com) has between two and four nonstops daily to Guatemala City from Houston Intercontinental (IAH), a nonstop flight from New York/Newark (EWR) operating anywhere from one to six times weekly, and twice-weekly nonstop service from Washington DC (IAD). First-class passengers and United Club members enjoy access to the Copa Club lounge, located next to gate 14.

Delta Air Lines (tel. 800/221-1212 U.S., www.delta.com) flies nonstop up to three times daily from Atlanta, twelve flights weekly from Los Angeles, and Saturday-only from New York's JFK to Guatemala City. Discount carrier **Spirit Airlines** (tel. 800/772-7117 U.S., www.spiritair.com) flies daily nonstop to Guatemala City from Fort Lauderdale.

As this book went to press, **Southwest Airlines** (www.southwest.com) was set to begin service to neighboring Belize and Costa Rica from Houston's Hobby Airport (HOU), aided by the construction of a new $156 million international terminal for flights to Mexico and Central America. Service to Guatemala seems likely as part of the airline's regional expansion and may be a reality by the time you read this.

Among foreign carriers, **Copa Airlines** (tel. 800/359-2672 U.S., www.copaair.com), the Panamanian flag-carrier, flies nonstop four times daily to Guatemala City from its hub in Panama City, with excellent connections to/from South America, the Caribbean, and Europe. The latter feed into KLM's daily Amsterdam-Panama City service and operate as a codeshare. There are additional flights between Guatemala and Panama stopping in Managua and San José. The airline operates a Copa Club lounge in conjunction with United at La Aurora airport and at Panama City's Tocumen airport.

The only nonstop service to Guatemala from Europe is on **Iberia** (www.iberia.com) four times per week (Mon., Tues., Thurs., Sat.) from its hub in Madrid with excellent connections to the rest of the continent. The return flight to Madrid stops in San Salvador, as nonstop flights to Europe from Guatemala City's short, high-altitude runway are a logistical impossibility.

Mexican flag carrier Mexicana went the way of the dodo bird in 2010, but competing carriers AeroMexico and Interjet have stepped in to fill the void in the Mexico City-Guatemala City market. **AeroMexico** (tel. 2278-9488, www.aeromexico.com) flies the route three times daily. **Interjet** (www.interjet.com) operates 11 weekly flights between Mexico City and Guatemala City.

Discount Mexican carrier **Volaris** (www. volaris.com) began twice-weekly service to Guatemala City from both Guadalajara and Cancún in June 2015. It has a decent route network for onward connections to the U.S. West Coast and Europe.

Avianca (tel. 800/400-8222 U.S., www. avianca.com) flies nonstop to Guatemala City from Miami and Los Angeles. Other nonstops include flights from Tegucigalpa and San Pedro Sula. There are numerous daily flights from Guatemala City to Avianca's hub in San Salvador as well as to San José, Costa Rica, with onward connections to/from South America. A new daily flight to Avianca's hub in Bogotá provides additional South American connecting flight opportunities.

In January 2014, Salvadoran discount carrier **VECA Airlines** (www.vecaairlines. com/en/sv) began offering flights between Guatemala City and San Salvador for about $100 each way. Plans call for service to Panama and Costa Rica via its hub in San Salvador (SAL).

FLIGHTS TO FLORES/TIKAL

Flights to Flores/Tikal arrive from Guatemala City and Belize City. **Avianca** (tel. 800/400-8222 U.S., www.avianca.com) operates two daily flights between Guatemala City and Flores using 68-passenger ATR-72 aircraft. **TAG** (800/528-8216 toll-free U.S. or 2332-1897 Guatemala) also has two daily flights to Flores from Guatemala City. The flights are operated with a 15-seat turboprop.

Tropic Air (tel. 800/422-3435, www.tropicair.com), a Belizean airline, flies to Flores/Tikal from Belize City daily.

Sea

Cruise ships dock at Puerto Quetzal, on the Pacific Coast, and Puerto Santo Tomás de Castilla, on the Caribbean side. Cruise lines offer a variety of activities for those wishing to disembark and explore Guatemalan shores, including visits to local resorts and beaches near Santo Tomás and inland trips to Antigua, Tikal, and Lake Atitlán or deep-sea fishing in the Pacific waters. For those wishing not to travel inland, there is not much to see and do in the immediate vicinity of either port of call, although the pier is usually packed with vendors selling everything from bags of Guatemalan coffee to colorful textiles and clothing. A land-based activity close to a port of call worth mentioning is hiking in the Cerro San Gil forest preserve near Santo Tomás de Castilla.

Ferry and water-taxi services connect the Guatemalan town of Lívingston with Punta Gorda, Belize (1.5 hours, $25), and Omoa, Honduras (1.25 hours, $16), both offered by Exotic Travel on Tuesdays and Fridays. A $10 departure tax applies when leaving Guatemala by sea.

If traveling to Guatemala on your own boat, you will most likely arrive on the Caribbean side and will need to check in with immigration officials in Lívingston before sailing up the Río Dulce, the most popular route with boaters.

River

The most popular route into Guatemala by river is via the Usumacinta River, which divides Mexico and Guatemala. Boats travel from the Mexican town of Frontera Corozal to La Técnica and Bethel, in Guatemala's northern Petén department. This is the route of choice for travelers wanting to combine visits to the Mexican sites of Palenque and Yaxchilán with trips to the various Petén ruins. Yaxchilán lies on the Mexican bank of the Usumacinta and is highly recommended. Buses from Palenque to the Mexican border are available via Transportes Montebello and Autotransportes Rio Chancala. Buses leave for the Petén departmental capital of Flores at 4am and 11am ($4, five hours). Buses leave Bethel for Flores at 5am, noon, 2pm, and 4pm, cost $4, and take four hours to make the trip. Package trips encompassing bus and boat transportation are available from various travel agencies in Palenque and Flores for travel in either direction for about $35.

Land

Many travelers enter Guatemala by bus, as part of larger explorations encompassing neighboring countries. If traveling by car or bus, try to make the border crossing as early in the day as possible, as there are few serviceable hotels and restaurants in border towns and they are notorious for their seedy atmosphere. Onward bus service tends to wind down further into the day, so try to get a move on while you can.

DRIVING FROM THE UNITED STATES

Many folks make the overland trip to Guatemala. The country's location in the northernmost reaches of Central America keeps border crossings to a minimum. The advent of the Internet has made it easy to find information for planning your road trip.

Most people cross into Mexico from the United States via Brownsville and then take the route through Mexico along the Pacific Coast. You can also travel via Mexico City or along the Atlantic side, but the Mexican capital's traffic and the inferior roads on the Atlantic side make the route less desirable. You'll need a tourist visa ($25) or a *transmigrante* visa to travel through Mexico, but many experienced road-trippers discourage getting the *transmigrante* visa, deeming it unnecessary and more difficult to process. For Mexican vehicle insurance, some travelers have recommended **Sanborn's Insurance** (www.sanbornsinsurance.com). More detailed information for planning the drive to Guatemala is available in the *Gringo's Guide to Driving Through Mexico and Central America* (www.drivemeloco.com).

FROM MEXICO

The main border crossings on the Pacific flatlands are Ciudad Hidalgo/Tecún Umán and Talismán/El Carmen, near Tapachula, Mexico. On the Pan-American Highway, the border crossing is at Ciudad Cuauhtémoc/La Mesilla between Comitán, Mexico, and Huehuetenango, Guatemala. Many travelers recommend this last route as the best entry point into Guatemala from Mexico when traveling in your own vehicle. All of these border towns have frequent bus service to nearby cities within both countries.

FROM BELIZE

The Belize border crossing into Guatemala is at Benque Viejo del Carmen/Melchor de Mencos. There is twice-daily bus service from Belize City to Flores via **Linea Dorada** (www.lineadorada.com.gt). The trip lasts 4-5 hours and costs $15. **San Juan Travel** (tel. 7926-0041 or 5461-6010) also has a daily bus covering the route.

FROM HONDURAS

The main border crossings are at El Florido (between Copán Ruinas, Honduras, and Chiquimula, Guatemala), Agua Caliente (between Nueva Ocotepeque, Honduras, and Esquipulas, Guatemala), and Corinto (between Omoa, Honduras, and Puerto Barrios, Guatemala). There are shuttle minibuses running between Copán, Guatemala City, and Antigua, as well as first-class bus service to Guatemala City from the main Honduran cities. **Hedman Alas** (www.hedmanalas.com) has daily service to Guatemala City via the El Florido border from Copán, San Pedro Sula, Tegucigalpa, and La Ceiba.

FROM EL SALVADOR

El Salvador's numerous borders with Guatemala are at Las Chinamas/Valle Nuevo (Highway CA-8), La Hachadura/Ciudad Pedro de Alvarado on Pacific Coast Highway (CA-2), San Cristóbal/San Cristóbal on the Pan-American Highway (CA-1), and Anguiatu/Anguiatu (Highway CA-10). Several bus lines operate service between Guatemala City and San Salvador, mostly via Las Chinamas, including **Pullmantur** (www.pullmantur.com).

TO AND FROM POINTS SOUTH

Tica Bus (www.ticabus.com) connects Guatemala City to San Salvador, Managua, San José, and Panama City, taking several days to make the trip and stopping in the listed capitals along the way. A one-way ticket from Guatemala City to San José, Costa Rica, costs about $50.

GETTING AROUND
Air

The only scheduled domestic service within Guatemala is between Guatemala City and Flores, although ongoing improvements to local infrastructure at many smaller airports may mean a small network of local flights may soon be up and running. Some of the flights to and from Flores operate using smaller aircraft, though the largest bird on this route nowadays is the 50-seat ATR-72. Airfares for this domestic service have are surprisingly expensive, particularly when taking into account the short distance involved in flying within Guatemala.

All of the domestic carriers flying out of Guatemala City operate from their private hangars, located on the east side of the runway, opposite the main terminal building. The only airline operating its domestic service from the main terminal at La Aurora airport is Avianca.

New domestic airports with passenger terminals are either complete or nearing completion in Quetzaltenango and Puerto San José. Plans call for terminals at the Pacific Coast leisure destination of Retalhuleu and the existing paved runway at Puerto Barrios. Cobán has a functional airstrip, though there is no scheduled service. Flights from Guatemala City to the above destinations may become a reality once the terminals are complete and investors make inroads into a market with certain potential. During the late 1990s, TACA (now Avianca) subsidiary Inter operated domestic air service between Guatemala City and Cobán, Quetzaltenango, Huehuetenango, and Puerto Barrios.

Land
BUSES AND SHUTTLE BUSES

Most travelers get around Guatemala by bus or shuttle bus. The majority of inter- and intracity buses are "chicken buses," as travelers have dubbed them, recycled U.S. school buses

Smaller planes cover the route between Flores and Guatemala City.

painted in lively colors. Cargo and carry-on baggage often consists of live animals, hence the name. Please be aware that robberies, including pickpocketing and armed hijacking, are increasingly common on these inexpensive public buses serving the interior. Chicken buses are also poorly maintained and frequently involved in traffic accidents in which the bus plunges into a ravine or makes a blind pass into a head-on collision. For the intrepid, the chicken bus is still an easy way to see Guatemala and get to virtually any part of the country cheaply.

Tourist shuttle buses plying the main tourist routes, though more expensive, have become increasingly popular for safety reasons and are highly recommended. Additionally, shuttle buses sometimes offer door-to-door service. Recommended shuttle buses are Atitrans, Turansa, and Grayline Tours.

Also reliable are first-class buses that run between Guatemala City and major cities such as Quetzaltenango, Huehuetenango, Puerto Barrios, Cobán, and Flores. Prices are comparable to shuttle buses, but service is aboard

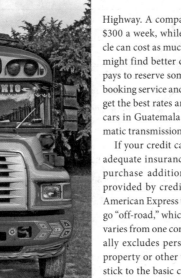

"Chicken buses" go all over Guatemala.

large luxury coaches, often with restrooms and onboard food service.

PICKUPS AND MINIVANS

Another common form of getting around, particularly in remote rural areas with infrequent bus service is via (roughly) scheduled service aboard pickup trucks. Minivans have also replaced cumbersome chicken buses in many rural areas with poor roads.

RENTAL CARS

Rental cars are plentiful in Guatemala and can be rented in Guatemala City, Panajachel, Antigua, Quetzaltenango, Cobán, and Flores. Some local agencies are also available. There's nothing like the freedom of having your own wheels when exploring new surroundings. Renting a car allows you to go wherever Guatemala's roads will take you. With that in mind, it's probably best to rent a four-wheel-drive vehicle. The only exception is if you plan to stick to urban areas such as Guatemala City and Antigua or along the Pan-American

Highway. A compact car will run you about $300 a week, while a four-wheel-drive vehicle can cost as much as $400-600 a week. You might find better deals online. It sometimes pays to reserve something through an online booking service and then call around locally to get the best rates and comparison shop. Most cars in Guatemala are stick shift, with automatic transmission often costing a bit more.

If your credit card company doesn't offer adequate insurance coverage, make sure to purchase additional insurance. Coverage provided by credit cards such as Visa and American Express usually doesn't apply if you go "off-road," which you likely will. Coverage varies from one company to the next, but usually excludes personal liability (damage to property or other vehicles) and theft. If you stick to the basic coverage offered by the car rental agency, your credit card will have to cover outrageous deductibles, often in the vicinity of $750-1,500. Purchasing full coverage from the rental agency can run $25 a day and really adds to the final bill, but some find it a small price to pay for peace of mind.

Before leaving the car rental lot, make sure to check the car over, paying attention to every minute detail. Rental agents will go over the car with you and document any scratches, dings, and dents. They'll inspect it again when you return the vehicle. Any new damage (or previously undocumented damage) might cost you dearly.

Never leave a vehicle parked on the street overnight and never leave personal belongings inside an unattended vehicle.

TAXIS

Taxicabs are available in almost any town or city. In smaller towns, the best way to find a taxi is in the central square, or *parque central*. In Guatemala City, taxis are available at the Zona 10 hotels, shopping malls, or (as a last resort) can be hailed from street corners. It's always best to call a cab, as certain city zones get more taxi traffic and not all companies are reliable. Highly recommended is **Taxis Amarillo Express** (tel. 1766); you must call

Rental Cars

The following U.S. car-rental agencies are represented in Guatemala and have kiosks at Guatemala City's La Aurora International Airport:

- **Alamo** (tel. 5219-7469 Guatemala City or 800/462-5266 toll-free U.S., www.alamo.com)

- **Avis** (tel. 2331-0017 Guatemala City or 800/331-1212 toll-free U.S., www.avis.com)

- **Budget** (tel. 2332-7744 Guatemala City or 800/472-3325 toll-free U.S., www.budget.com or www.budgetguatemala.com.gt)

- **Dollar** (tel. 2331-7185 Guatemala City or 800/800-4000 toll-free U.S., www.dollar.com)

- **Hertz** (tel. 2470-3800 Guatemala City or 800/654-3001 toll-free U.S., www.hertz.com)

- **Thrifty** (tel. 2379-8747 Guatemala City or 800/847-4389 toll-free U.S., www.thrifty.com)

for a cab and will need an exact address for pickup. They are one of the only companies to use taxi meters. As a final word of caution, the U.S. Embassy discourages travelers from hailing cabs off the street in Guatemala City.

In smaller towns and villages, you'll also find the Asian-style *tuk-tuks,* or motorized rickshaws powered by a motorcycle engine. These offer a lower-cost alternative to standard taxicabs and are great if you're traveling without luggage over short distances.

If you need to get around for days at a time, it might be worth renting a taxi by the day or week. This is particularly the case in Guatemala City, where there are many neighborhoods tucked into the varied terrain and certainly some places you'll wish to avoid. Many taxi drivers are willing to negotiate a daily or hourly rate, somewhere in the vicinity of $10 an hour or $75 a day. You can often get a really good deal if you negotiate for multiple days. Most Guatemalan taxi drivers are friendly and helpful, making great sources of conversation to gauge opinions on issues of daily life for the average Guatemalan. It seems almost everyone has a friend or a friend of a friend who is a taxi driver, and they may be able to recommend someone to you.

HITCHHIKING

Though hitchhiking in its traditional form is not widely practiced in Guatemala, a local adaptation exists in remote rural areas where there is limited or nonexistent bus service. People with pickup trucks will often give you a ride in the back of their trucks. The fee is usually nominal, if anything at all.

BOAT

In some areas, getting around by boat is the most practical option. This is particularly the case on the shores of Lake Atitlán, where regular ferry service and small motorboats make their way across the lake from Panajachel to the outlying villages. Boat service is also a major form of transportation in coastal areas, particularly in Izabal department along the Río Dulce, on Lake Izabal, and in coastal areas such as Lívingston and Puerto Barrios. On the Pacific side, motorboats traverse the Canal de Chiquimulilla, which separates the Pacific seaboard from the Guatemalan mainland along much of the coast.

Highway Overview

Roads in Guatemala are surprisingly good in some places, particularly on well-trodden paths like the Pan-American Highway. They are much better, overall, than the roads in neighboring Belize and Costa Rica. Roads in and around tourist areas are generally well marked, some courtesy of the Guatemala state tourism agency, INGUAT (Instituto Guatemalteco de Turismo). If while driving, you come across a large tree branch in the middle of the road, be prepared to stop. This is Guatemalans' way of officially signaling that danger lies ahead, usually in the form of a car stopped near the side of the road. Whether it be by bus or by car, do not travel on rural highways in Guatemala after dark.

Guatemala has several main highways. The **Pan-American Highway** (CA-1), also known as the Interamericana, runs from the Mexican border at La Mesilla through much of the Western Highlands, to Guatemala City and east to El Salvador at the San Cristóbal border. This is the road taken (at least for much of the journey) from Guatemala City to many of the main travel destinations, including La Antigua, Lake Atitlán, Quetzaltenango, and Huehuetenango. CA-1 has been expanded to four lanes from Guatemala City all the way to the Cuatro Caminos junction near Quetzaltenango.

The **Pacific Coast Highway** (CA-2) crosses the Pacific slope from the Mexican border at Tecún Umán all the way to Ciudad Pedro de Alvarado and El Salvador. A new, wider Pacific highway is in the planning stages. **Highway CA-9** runs from the Pacific Coast to Guatemala City, encompassing the country's only toll road: a good, fast *autopista*, or freeway. From Guatemala City, the highway heads east to Puerto Barrios and is being widened to four lanes from the capital to El Rancho Junction. CA-14 branches north from El Rancho into the departments of Baja and Alta Verapaz.

Continuing east along CA-9, the next junction is at Río Hondo, where CA-10 branches southeast to Zacapa and Chiquimula before linking up to eastbound CA-11 for Copán, Honduras. Back on the main branch of CA-9, CA-13 is the designation given to the road branching off at La Ruidosa Junction, just before Puerto Barrios, heading north to Río Dulce and continuing to Petén. It arrives in Flores and then branches eastward to the Belize border at Melchor de Mencos.

A road crossing the country from Izabal department west all the way to Huehuetenango, called the **Franja Transversal del Norte,** was under construction at the time of researching. Also in the works is an Anillo Departamental allowing traffic between CA-1 and eastbound Highway CA-9 to bypass traffic-congested Guatemala City altogether.

ESSENTIALS
TRANSPORTATION

Guatemala's roads can be extremely scenic.

Travel Companies

There is a relative absence of package tours from the United States to Guatemala, particularly as compared to Belize and Costa Rica. Still, there are a few good companies to recommend for travelers who want to visit Guatemala on a package tour or need the services of an established tour operator. This is certainly not an exhaustive list, but the following come highly recommended for the quality of service and established experience.

API-CULTURAL EMBRACE

Based in Austin, Texas, **API-Cultural Embrace** (tel. 512/469-9089, www.cultural-embracebyapi.com) offers volunteer and group travel opportunities to Guatemala with a focus on the Antigua area. Among the projects on offer are work with local orphanages, wildlife conservation, construction and renovation, environmental, wildlife conservation, medical and health, and community development. Included in service trips are 6-10 hours per week of language instruction and visits to area attractions such as Pacaya Volcano.

CAYAYA BIRDING

Bird-watchers will want to contact German-owned **Cayaya Birding** (tel. 5308-5160, www.cayaya-birding.com) for information on Guatemala's birding hot spots and to arrange trip details, including full itineraries. Knut Eisermann, an ornithologist living in Guatemala since 1997, runs the company.

CLARK TOURS

Highly recommended is **Clark Tours** (tel. 800/707-5275 U.S., www.saca.com/guat/intro.html), represented in the United States by Massachusetts-based SACA Tours. The company, established by an American living in Guatemala, has been around for 80 years. You will probably come across the company's large, luxurious tour buses more than once during your travels in Guatemala. Clark Tours has a variety of established itineraries and can also tailor custom itineraries to suit the needs of the most discriminating travelers. Clark Tours is also the local representative for American Express Travel Services and has offices in many Guatemala City luxury hotels, including the Barceló, Westin Camino Real, and Holiday Inn.

DO GUATEMALA

Based in Guatemala, **Do Guatemala** (14 Avenida A 3-06 Zona 1, 3rd floor, Quetzaltenango, tel. 4699-3614 or 7761-1369, www.do-guatemala.com) offers volunteer and language study programs in Antigua and Quetzaltenango. Programs focus on education, children, the elderly, medical projects, environment, and construction. There are set group travel dates (usually during the busy summer high season) with an extensive 13-day itinerary that covers most of Guatemala's highlights.

GEORGE'S TRAVEL CLUB OF GUATEMALA

George's Travel Club of Guatemala (tel. 202/436-9983 U.S., 502/5175-9974 Guatemala, www.georges-travelclub.com) is an Antigua-based travel company owned by a U.S. expat. Well-thought-out travel itineraries include luxurious accommodations, four-wheel-drive road trips, sea fishing, kayaking, volcano climbs, and exploring Mayan ruins.

MAYA EXPEDITIONS

Rated one of the top eco-outfitters in the world by *Condé Nast Traveler*, **Maya Expeditions** (13 Avenida 14-70, Zona 10, tel. 2366-9950, www.mayaexpeditions.com) is a Guatemala-based adventure-travel outfitter that comes highly recommended for its adventurous itineraries, particularly white-water rafting. Company founder Tammy Ridenour, a Colorado native, started the company in 1987 and is credited with pioneering ecotourism in Guatemala. Among the company's various offerings, which also include archaeological and cultural tourism, is a trip retracing the steps of the wildly popular *Survivor Guatemala* television series.

NO LIMIT EXPEDITIONS

Based in La Antigua Guatemala, **No Limit Expeditions** (tel. 720/295-4880, www.nolimitx.com) runs recommended adventure four-wheel-drive expeditions to far-flung locales deep in the rainforests of northern Guatemala and Belize aboard Land Rovers. Accommodations include comfortable jungle camps and luxury ecolodges. The "Ruins and Rainforests" expedition includes some of the greatest Mayan cities (Tikal, Uaxactún, Caracol, Yaxhá) and seldom-visited locales such as the murals at San Bartolo. They also run expeditions to El Mirador and the Mayan Highlands.

Visas and Officialdom

TOURIST REQUIREMENTS

Citizens of the United States traveling to Guatemala will need a U.S. passport valid for at least six months beyond their intended length of stay and ticket documents for onward or return travel. Stays of up to 90 days are permitted without a visa. The United States now requires passports as the sole travel document for all travelers returning to the United States by air.

Requirements for other countries, including Australia, Canada, the European Union, Israel, Japan, New Zealand, and Switzerland, include a passport valid for at least three months beyond the intended length of stay and ticket documents for onward or return travel. Entry is limited to 30 days. Extensions are allowed by going through the local Migración (Immigration) office.

Foreigners are required to carry their passport (or a clear photocopy) with them at all times. If you are driving a rental car and happen to be stopped, the police officer will ask for your passport in addition to your driver's license.

In June 2006, Guatemala entered into an agreement with El Salvador, Honduras, and Nicaragua known as the **CA-4 Border Control Agreement.** Under its terms, citizens of these four countries may travel freely across each other's land borders without completing entry and exit formalities at Immigration checkpoints. United States citizens and other eligible foreign nationals who legally enter any of the four member countries may also travel within the CA-4 without obtaining additional visas or tourist entry permits for the other three countries. Immigration officials at the first port of entry determine the length of stay, up to a maximum of 90 days. Foreign tourists who wish to remain in the four-country region beyond the length of stay initially granted for their visit will need to request a one-time extension from local Immigration authorities or travel to a country outside the CA-4 region and then reenter.

For visa extensions, head to the **Departamento de Extranjería** (7a Avenida 1-17 Zona 4, INGUAT Building, Guatemala City, tel. 2361-8476, 8am-2pm Mon.-Fri.). You'll need to show evidence of financial solvency as well as an onward ticket.

CUSTOMS

Foreign travelers to Guatemala may import the following items duty-free: personal effects, including clothing, jewelry, medicine, photography and video equipment, sports equipment, a personal computer, a wheelchair if the traveler has disabilities, 500 grams of tobacco, and three liters of alcoholic beverages. INGUAT can provide assistance to professional photographers and videographers needing to bring in large amounts of equipment.

Recreation

PARKS AND PROTECTED AREAS

Guatemala has more than 90 protected areas encompassing about 28 percent of the country's total land area. Among the different types of protected areas are biosphere reserves, national parks, biotopes, natural monuments, wildlife refuges, and private nature reserves. Several of these are encompassed within larger areas, as is the case with the national parks and biotopes making up the larger Maya Biosphere Reserve. Most of Guatemala's protected areas, including the biosphere reserves, have been created since 1990. All of Guatemala's volcanoes are protected areas. There are also laws in effect to protect endangered wildlife species; among these are Guatemala's big cats and parrots.

The National Protected Areas Council (CONAP) is the entity charged with administering Guatemala's protected areas. It was created in 1990, along with the National Environmental Commission (CONAMA), which oversees broader environmental matters and was replaced in 2000 by the Ministry of the Environment and Natural Resources (MARN). CONAP has been historically underfunded and understaffed, leaving few resources with which to protect vast areas of land from invasion. Private conservation groups have stepped in to assist CONAP in its mandate, and there are now several parks coadministered or primarily administered by private organizations. A specially trained police force began operating in Guatemala's protected areas in 2005, particularly in the Maya Biosphere Reserve, aided by M-16s and AK-47s to combat well-armed timber and wildlife poachers. All the parks have at least rudimentary ranger stations. In an ongoing effort to attract more park visitation, many have excellent facilities for guest accommodations and well-marked trails.

Biosphere Reserves

Privately managed by conservation group Defensores de la Naturaleza, **Sierra de las Minas Biosphere Reserve** is a vast, 236,000-hectare mountain park encompassing a diverse variety of ecosystems, including cloud forests harboring several species of endemic conifers, as well as tropical moist and rainforests. The peaks of Sierra de las Minas surpass 3,000 meters (9,800 feet) in elevation and are home to healthy populations of quetzals and jaguars, among other exotic animals. Sixty-two permanent streams have their source in the upper slopes of the biosphere reserve, making it an important watershed supplying the Motagua and Polochic Rivers. Together with the adjacent Bocas del Polochic Wildlife Refuge, the parks account for 80 percent of Guatemala's biodiversity.

The 1.6-million-hectare **Maya Biosphere Reserve** is composed of Tikal National Park, Laguna del Tigre National Park, Mirador-Dos Lagunas-Rio Azul National Park, Sierra del Lacandón National Park, Biotopo El Zotz-San Miguel La Palotada, Yaxhá-Nakum-Naranjo Natural Monument, and multiple-use and buffer zones. This large swath of land encompasses roughly a third of the Petén department and is Guatemala's last hope for preserving a sizable part of the Petén forests. Contiguous with large parks in neighboring Mexico and Belize, it is part of the largest protected tropical forest in Mesoamerica. The various parks are protected, on paper at least, from all human activity, though a sizable multiple-use zone exists in large areas of the park, permitting sustainable extraction of forest products such as *xate* palm and chicle, oil drilling (present before the park's creation), and community forestry concessions. Standing between the core zones and the deforestation characterizing much of the rest of Petén is an ever-shrinking buffer zone increasingly porous to the advance of the

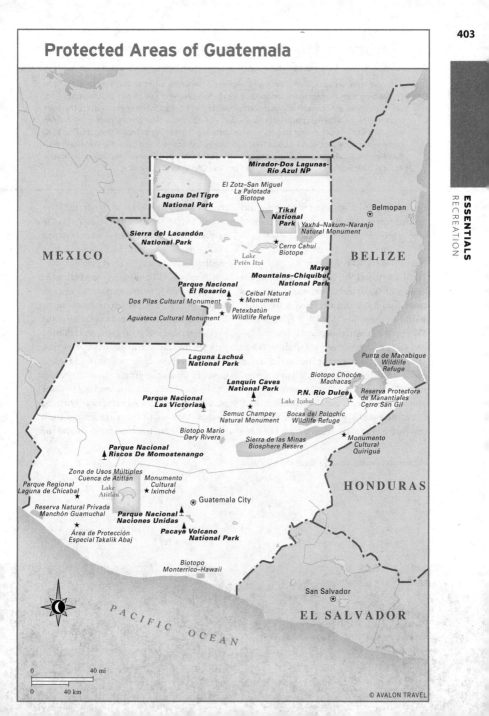

Protected Areas of Guatemala

Mirador-Dos Lagunas-Río Azul NP

Laguna Del Tigre National Park

El Zotz–San Miguel La Palotada Biotope

Tikal National Park

Belmopan

Yaxhá–Nakum–Naranjo Natural Monument

Sierra del Lacandón National Park

MEXICO

Cerro Cahuí Biotope

Lake Petén Itzá

BELIZE

Maya Mountains–Chiquibul National Park

Parque Nacional El Rosario

Ceibal Natural Monument

Dos Pilas Cultural Monument

Aguateca Cultural Monument

Petexbatún Wildlife Refuge

Laguna Lachuá National Park

Punta de Manabique Wildlife Refuge

Biotopo Chocón Machacas

Lanquín Caves National Park

P.N. Río Dulce

Reserva Protectora de Manantiales Cerro San Gil

Parque Nacional Las Victorias

Lake Izabal

Semuc Champey Natural Monument

Bocas del Polochíc Wildlife Refuge

Biotopo Mario Dary Rivera

Sierra de las Minas Biosphere Resere

Monumento Cultural Quiriguá

Parque Nacional Riscos De Momostenango

Zona de Usos Múltiples Cuenca de Atitlán

Monumento Cultural Iximché

HONDURAS

Parque Regional Laguna de Chicabal

Lake Atitlán

Guatemala City

Reserva Natural Privada Manchón Guamuchal

Parque Nacional Naciones Unidas

Área de Protección Especial Takalik Abaj

Pacaya Volcano National Park

Biotopo Monterrico–Hawaii

San Salvador

PACIFIC OCEAN

EL SALVADOR

0   40 mi
0   40 km

© AVALON TRAVEL

Safety in the Maya Biosphere Reserve

Potential travelers to Guatemala's Maya Biosphere Reserve are urged to contact one of the conservation groups managing the individual parks before planning a visit, so as to ascertain current safety conditions. As conservationists and archaeologists working in the field can attest, there are too many illegal activities perpetrated by heavily armed men, and far too many stories of run-ins with them, to be out running around in these parts oblivious to the potential dangers. That said, some well-established parks such as Tikal and Yaxhá can be considered generally safe, along with some well-established ecotourism circuits in the Maya Biosphere Reserve, including the Scarlet Macaw Trail, trips to El Zotz-San Miguel La Palotada, and treks to El Mirador.

agricultural frontier. The individual parks making up the biosphere reserve are covered here in their respective sections.

National Parks

Tikal National Park, the oldest and best known of Guatemala's national parks, was created in 1956 and declared a UNESCO World Heritage Site in 1979. It encompasses 357 square kilometers of primary tropical forest and protects a vast array of wildlife, as well as harboring the remains of one of the Mayan civilization's greatest cities. Tikal is understandably high on the list of priorities for any visitor to Guatemala and shouldn't be missed.

Laguna del Tigre National Park is a vast park on the northwestern corner of Petén encompassing important wetlands, the largest in Central America. It also contains the only remaining populations of scarlet macaws in Guatemala, which are being protected via ongoing conservation efforts at a biological research station. Oil drilling, present before the park's creation, continues inside the reserve, despite protests from environmental groups and its having been declared a violation of the park's intended use. Also going on inside the park are the clandestine activities of loggers, wildlife poachers, drug traffickers, and smugglers of illegal immigrants across the border to Mexico. Archaeologists working in these parts enter under the escort of heavily armed guards. Visitors to this park should limit their activities to those centered around the

Guatemala's impressive Maya Biosphere Reserve

Scarlet Macaw Biological Research Station, as the current lawless conditions prevent my recommending more in-depth explorations of this wild frontier.

Sierra del Lacandón National Park is a densely forested, rugged mountain park said to harbor one of the largest populations of jaguars in all of Central America as well as an incredible degree of biodiversity. Hidden in the forests are the remains of several Mayan sites, the most important of which is Piedras Negras, deep inside the park along the Usumacinta River, which marks the western border with Mexico. The park is privately administered by Fundación Defensores de la Naturaleza. In June 2006, together with The Nature Conservancy, it completed the purchase of 31,000 hectares (77,000 acres) of privately owned land in the core zone of Sierra del Lacandón. There are a number of ranger stations inside the park, the most prominent of which is at Piedras Negras.

A large park in the northern section of the Maya Biosphere Reserve near the Mexican border, **Mirador-Dos Lagunas-Río Azul National Park** protects vast expanses of tropical forests and the remains of several Mayan cities. Among the most impressive ruins are those at El Mirador, including El Tigre temple, which is 18 stories high with a base the size of three football fields. Other sites inside the park include Río Azul and Nakbé, visible from the top of El Mirador's massive temples. Access to the park is by foot, a full day's walk from the village of Carmelita, or helicopter.

Laguna Lachuá National Park consists of a circular lagoon in the Ixcán jungle west of Cobán surrounded by 14,500 hectares of tropical forest and several miles of hiking trails. The karst limestone nature of this placid pool makes it a very attractive turquoise. A high concentration of mahogany trees in the surrounding forests has made it vulnerable to clandestine logging.

One of Guatemala's oldest protected areas encompassing the watershed of its namesake river connecting Lake Izabal with the Caribbean Sea, **Río Dulce National Park** covers 7,200 hectares along its 30-kilometer-long course. In many places, the banks of the river are shrouded in dense tropical forest punctuated at one point by a large canyon with high rock faces.

Natural Monuments

Television reality-show aficionados might recall **Yaxhá-Nakum-Naranjo Natural Monument** as the setting for *Survivor Guatemala,* filmed here during the summer of 2005. The park encompasses the ruins of three Mayan cities set amid dense tropical forest adjacent to Tikal National Park. Also in the park is Yaxhá Lagoon, with its healthy numbers of crocodiles.

The site of **Semuc Champey Natural Monument** is high in the Alta Verapaz mountains, where the Río Cahabón flows into a giant cave before reemerging a few hundred feet downstream. Atop the churning turmoil is a natural bridge holding a splendid series of turquoise limestone pools surrounded by tropical forest. It is probably Guatemala's finest swimming hole.

Biotopes

Guatemala's biotopes are administered by **CECON** (Avenida La Reforma 0-63 Zona 10, Guatemala City, tel. 2361-5450 or 2331-0904), the Center for Conservation Studies of Guatemala's San Carlos University (USAC). The biotopes are the brainchild of former USAC Dean Mario Dary Rivera, who was murdered when the establishment of the Quetzal Biotope in Alta Verapaz conflicted with local lumber interests. The biotopes were created with the protection and study of a particular animal species in mind. Biotopes protect sea turtles on the Pacific Coast, manatees in the Izabal region, and bats in the Petén forests, among others.

Biotopo Mario Dary Rivera, also known as the Biotopo del Quetzal (Quetzal Biotope), is a cloud forest preserve conveniently situated along the road to Cobán near the village of Purulhá, in Baja Verapaz department. It covers 1,022 hectares with ranges in elevation up to 2,300 meters (7,500 feet). In the early morning, it is easily one of the best places to see Guatemala's national bird, the resplendent quetzal. The cloud forest vegetation consists largely of conifers, broadleaf trees, orchids, mosses, ferns, and bromeliads. There is an excellent network of nature trails, some of which lead to waterfalls and excellent views of the surrounding areas. Other amenities include information and visitor centers, a store, a cafeteria, showers, and cooking facilities. A variety of accommodations are found nearby.

On Guatemala's Pacific Coast, **Biotopo Monterrico-Hawaii** was designated for the protection of Guatemala's endangered sea turtles, which come to lay their eggs on its black-sand beaches. Between May and September, local residents are actively involved in collecting eggs for hatching at a local nursery in exchange for being allowed to keep part of the booty. After incubation, the hatchlings are released with the help of tourists, who jump at the opportunity to hold one of the tiny hatchlings in hand before sending them on their journey across the sand and into the sea. Monterrico is a popular beach with Guatemalans and foreigners alike. Nearby Hawaii is substantially quieter. The park also protects important mangrove forests and marshes in addition to several species of plants and animals. There is also an iguana-breeding program at the site.

Biotopo Chocón Machacas, within Río Dulce National Park, encompasses 7,600 hectares and was created with the protection of the manatee in mind, though studies suggest very few of these creatures remain anywhere in Guatemala. The park is in an area known as El Golfete and features old-growth forests, flooded forests, mangrove swamps, canals, and lagoons. In addition to manatees, the park also harbors important populations of crocodiles, otters, and jungle cats.

Also in Petén, on the shores of Lake Petén Itzá, **Biotopo Cerro Cahuí** covers 650 hectares and consists of a small hill varying in altitude 200-300 meters (650-985 feet). The preserve was created to protect the Petén

ocellated turkey and consists mostly of secondary-growth forest. There are several lookouts with excellent views of the lake along the park's well-marked trails. It is a popular spot for bird-watching, with a good range of nearby accommodations.

HIKING

Guatemala's terrain, featuring mountains, volcanoes, and vast forested flatlands, is a hiker's dream. Adding to the allure of hiking in Guatemala is the opportunity to interact with locals along the way. Many hiking circuits in Guatemala, particularly in the Verapaz cloud forests and the plateaus of the Western Highlands region, are operated via local community tourism initiatives. In addition to providing the opportunity to see the environment and culture through the eyes of local inhabitants, hiring the services of community guides also provides locals with a much-needed source of income and instills a sense of pride in their home. It also speaks loudly to the value (both economic and moral) of conserving precious ecosystems when tourists come from faraway lands to enjoy them.

Among the most popular hikes are the summits of several of Guatemala's 33 volcanoes (some active), including Agua, Acatenango, Pacaya, San Pedro, Santa María, and Tajumulco.

Many tourism circuits operated by local community tourism initiatives include adequate visitors centers, and there are often campsites. The same is true for the government-run system of parks and protected areas.

BIKING

Road biking is a fairly popular sport in Guatemala, particularly in the highlands, where mountain roads offer unique challenges to strength and endurance. The country even has its own version of the Tour de France, known as La Vuelta Ciclística a Guatemala (The Biking Circuit of Guatemala). The event takes place yearly sometime in August.

More popular with visitors, **mountain biking** is increasingly popular in the hills around Antigua and Lake Atitlán thanks in part to a number of excellent local outfitters.

ROCK CLIMBING

Rock climbing is a relatively new phenomenon in Guatemala, though there are now at least two outfitters specializing in this activity. The rock faces fronting Lake Amatitlán, near Guatemala City, and an area known as "La Muela" (The Molar, also known as "Cerro Quemado"), near Quetzaltenango, are the prime climbing spots. Difficulty ratings of the various routes range from 5.8 to 5.13. It's also possible to rappel inside a waterfall, also known as canyoning, in Jalapa and other areas.

BEACHES

While Guatemala is not as well known for its beaches as some of its Central American neighbors, it nonetheless boasts some nice stretches on both the Pacific and Caribbean Coasts. On the Pacific, the wild black-sand beaches found along the coast near the **Manchón Guamuchal** wetlands are one of the region's best-kept secrets. The closest beach to Guatemala City is **Puerto San José,** reached in about 90 minutes by a four-lane highway, though it's certainly not the most

pleasant of the country's beaches. Just west of San José is **Chulamar,** with at least one recommended resort hotel.

Farther east, there are also some lovely stretches between **Iztapa** and **Monterrico.** The 25-kilometer road connecting both towns is experiencing a modest construction boom of stylish resort hotels, with land speculators quickly snapping up the remaining parcels of oceanfront property. East of Monterrico, **Hawaii** also has pretty stretches of nearly deserted beaches, though there are increasing numbers of Guatemala's elite building vacation homes here.

On the Caribbean Coast, Guatemala has some fairly decent white-sand beaches on the **Punta de Manabique** promontory. Along the coastline between Lívingston and the Belize border, the nicest beaches are at palm-fringed **Playa Blanca.** For talcum-powder white-sand beaches lapped by turquoise waters, head off the coast to the Belize Barrier Reef, where you'll find the **Zapotillo cayes.**

FISHING
Sailfishing

The Pacific Ocean waters off the port of Iztapa are hailed as the "Sailfish Capital of the World," with world records for single-day

hiking on Acatenango Volcano

catch-and-release firmly supporting these claims. Apparently, a unique pattern of swirling ocean currents between Mexico and El Salvador creates an eddy unusually rich in pelagic fish, such as herring and mackerel, right on Guatemala's doorstep. Sailfish and marlin gather to feed on this bait, along with large concentrations of dorado, yellowfin tuna, and wahoo. The result is some of the world's best sailfishing.

Numerous outfitters have set up shop in Iztapa offering sailfishing year-round, though the most active season is between November and May because of the colder weather prevalent in the North American region from which most anglers hail.

Lake Fishing

Thanks to grand plans for recreational options to be offered on behalf of now-departed Pan American Airways, Lake Atitlán saw the introduction of largemouth bass in the late 1950s. The lake's extreme depths make catching the larger fish said to inhabit the deeper waters quite a challenge, which only adds to the allure of fishing these waters. Your best bet for catching "the big one" is during the annual spring spawning season, between March and May.

WATER SPORTS
White-Water Rafting and Kayaking

Guatemala has a number of white-water rivers with rapids ranging from Class II-VI (Class VI being unpassable waterfalls). The most popular river for rafting and kayaking is the **Río Cahabón,** found in the region of Las Verapaces. It features some of Central America's finest stretches of white water complemented by jungles, caves, hot springs, and waterfalls.

For more sedate kayaking on ocean kayaks, Lakes Petén Itzá and Atitlán are good bets.

Scuba Diving and Snorkeling

It's possible to scuba dive off the Caribbean Coast near **Punta de Manabique,** though you're probably better off heading just a bit farther north to the exquisite **Zapotillo cayes,** part of the Belize Barrier Reef. Several outfitters arrange trips from Lívingston. Scuba diving is also a popular activity in **Lake Atitlán,** where you might even be able to feel the heat emanating from underwater lava flows in this still-active volcanic region. Another peculiarity of diving here is that the lake is at a rather high altitude just over 1,500 meters (5,000 feet), adding another variable to the mix.

Surfing

An emerging surfing scene is centered around the Pacific Coast village of **Sipacate,** which enjoys excellent breaks. **Iztapa** also reportedly has good breaks, as does **Monterrico.** A useful website for checking out Guatemala's surf scene is www.surfinguatemala.com.

Boating

Boaters will find marinas on both Guatemalan coasts. On the Pacific, a new marina was built with partial backing from Dutch interests near the aging port facilities of **Champerico.** Farther east, the **Marina Pez Vela** caters to sportfishing boats and is adjacent to the **Puerto Quetzal Cruise Ship Terminal.** It has restaurants and good tourism infrastructure. On the Caribbean Coast, you'll find many boats traveling up the **Río Dulce** from the Caribbean Coast and docking at any of a number of marinas in the river's namesake town.

GOLF

Guatemala has some excellent golf courses, mostly around Guatemala City, housed in private clubs open to foreign visitors. Some afford excellent views of the city, and all enjoy spectacular locations in the mountains flanking the urban area. Antigua Guatemala also has a phenomenal golf course with volcano views.

SPECTATOR SPORTS
Fútbol

Guatemalans love their soccer, known as *fútbol*. It is by far the most widely played sport in the country, with every town or village having at least something that resembles a soccer field. Almost everywhere you go, you'll find games being played on Sunday afternoons. As for professional soccer playing, the two most popular teams in the country's four-team national soccer league, denoted by the colors of their jerseys, are the Rojos (Municipales) and Cremas (Comunicaciones). The two usually end up going head to head at the end of the season for the championship title.

Games can be seen at Guatemala City's Estadio Mateo Flores, but be advised that the crowds can get quite rowdy. In 1996, things got so out of hand that a stampede ensued when stands collapsed, killing 100 people. The soccer stadium has been remodeled in the aftermath. If you've always wanted to see a Latin American soccer match, you might want to check it out. Guatemala also has a few star players in U.S. Major League Soccer and on some European teams.

International games played by the national squad are a big event, as Guatemala has never been to a World Cup. Guatemala is part of CONCACAF, the Caribbean, North, and Central American Confederation. CONCACAF gets four slots for the World Cup, three of which usually end up going to the United States, Mexico, and Costa Rica. In 2004-2005, the national squad (also known as *la bicolor*) got closer than it's ever been, advancing into the Final Round of the World Cup qualifiers tied in points with Costa Rica after beating Honduras 1-0. Postgame celebrations spilled into the streets and lasted into the wee hours of the morning. Unfortunately, the high hopes ended in bitter disappointment. Things got off to a great start with a 5-1 routing of Trinidad and Tobago, but Guatemala then lost 2-0 to the United States and never fully recovered.

Baseball

Known locally as *béisbol,* games can be seen at Parque Minerva's ballpark. The game has become increasingly popular in recent years, and you'll often see league games going on at area ballparks, usually on Saturday mornings.

Accommodations

Options for accommodations in Guatemala vary from the backpacker's basic $3-a-night room in cheap, blue-light hotels or hostels to ultraswanky boutique hotels and five-star international chain hotels and resorts. It's possible to tour the country entirely on either end of the budget spectrum. There are certainly plenty of options in between, as well as the more recent development of attractive ecolodges in areas adjacent to pristine natural areas. Camping is also another fairly common alternative, particularly at the national parks, though RV hookups are still virtually nonexistent. The government levies a 12 percent sales tax in addition to a 10 percent tax that goes to INGUAT (Guatemala Tourist Commission), bringing the total to a whopping 22 percent. Most of the budget and many of the midrange hotels include these taxes in the prices they'll quote you, but this is not the case in higher-end accommodations.

In popular tourist areas, you'll often be approached by *comisionistas* offering to find you a place to stay. These people work with local hotels and are paid commissions for each person they bring to a particular property. Usually, the places they work with aren't the best deals in town since they have to pay these people, an expense that simply gets added to the room rates. Also, more reputable hotels with good clientele and favorable word of mouth are rarely the kinds of places that would need the services of these freelancers.

HOSPEDAJES, HOSTELS, AND CHEAP HOTELS

Guatemala is a major stop along the Central American backpacking circuit, so it's no surprise that there are a plethora of low-budget hotels to choose from. Many of these are *hospedajes* or *pensiones* with very basic rooms run by local families. The rooms at the most basic places may all be on a shared-bath (*baño compartido*) basis. This is particularly the case in some of the very remote mountain villages in the Western Highlands region. The next-highest level in comfort consists of rooms with private bath (*baño privado*). A recent trend in areas with heavy tourist presence is the establishment of excellent *hostales* (hostels), where several travelers share dormitory-type bedrooms and bathrooms. Antigua, Copán, Guatemala City, Flores, and Cobán, to name a few, have some excellent hostels.

The key thing to look for when scoping out hotels with bargain-basement prices is cleanliness. All of the hotels recommended in this guidebook pass the cleanliness standard, as there are some budget hotels that are truly filthy. I'm all about making my dollar go as far as possible, but I draw the line here. If you do end up staying in a hotel room of questionable cleanliness, break out the sleeping bag. It's always a good idea to pack one along if you're traveling on a budget. Rooms in the highlands tend to suffer from mold problems, so keep this in mind if you're allergic. For rooms in tropical areas, make sure there is a fan, preferably a ceiling fan, as this will make for a much more restful night's sleep.

Another consideration in budget hotels is the quality of the mattresses. Definitely check this out, as the quality of beds varies widely. In some tropical areas, beds might consist of a thin mattress atop a concrete block. This peculiar arrangement has been called to attention in hotel descriptions where applicable.

The cheapest of the cheap hotels may not offer hot water or may not have it on during the whole day. Always inquire about this. In many budget hotels, the hot water comes from an electric hot-water heater attached to the showerhead. These can often look scary, with wires jutting out all over the place. It's a good idea to check out your water-heater situation before taking a room. Be very careful not to touch the showerhead while in the shower, unless, of course, you enjoy being mildly electrocuted. As a final note, bring flip-flops or some other type of shower shoe to avoid catching a nasty fungus in shared bathrooms.

MIDRANGE HOTELS

There are a number of good-value, moderately priced hotels throughout Guatemala charging somewhere in the vicinity of $25-50 per night. Spending $50-100 a night in Guatemala gets you a very nice spread indeed. Despite its newfound popularity, you can still get some very good travel deals in Guatemala. You'll certainly get more bang for your buck than in Belize or Costa Rica, but it's anyone's guess as to how much longer this will last. In the $25-50 range, you'll be surprised at what you'll find. Many rooms in this category come with a private bathroom and almost all moderately priced rooms have cable TV (with channels in English), so you can catch up on the news back home or keep up with your favorite sports team while on the road. Decent mattresses and air-conditioning are also available in some of the better-value accommodations in this category.

Spending $50-100 on a hotel room in Guatemala City will land you in the chic Zona Viva district very close to the airport and near the best restaurants and nightlife venues. In Antigua, you can book a decent boutique property or even stay in a resort. Ditto for the coasts, Petén, and Lake Atitlán.

HIGH-END HOTELS AND RESORTS
Luxury Hotels

Guatemala City boasts the presence of many luxury chains, including Crowne Plaza, Westin, and InterContinental, among others.

You'll also find luxury hotels in Antigua, Lake Atitlán, and the vicinity of Tikal and Flores, in Petén. Antigua has some of the nicest boutique hotels anywhere in the world, and plenty of them. Rates at Guatemala's nicer hotels can range $100-900 a night. Many Guatemala City luxury hotels cater to business travelers and deals might be available for weekend stays. These are usually advertised on their websites. Near Retalhuleu, the Hostales del IRTRA seem like a bit of a misnomer, as the complex is less like a hostel and more like a large resort complex with some truly luxurious suites with all the look and feel of a Four Seasons. There are plans in the works for a convention center and golf resort.

Beach Resorts

This category has gained relevance only in recent years as the Pacific Coast's long-neglected beaches have become the target of tourism development. Most of the Pacific Coast's resorts are along the Iztapa-Monterrico corridor or in either of these towns, including brand-new Cayman Suites and Dos Mundos Pacific Resort. West of Puerto San José, Chulamar features the sprawling Soleil Pacífico, a sizable all-inclusive resort fronting black-sand beaches. It's popular on weekends, but you may have the place all to yourself during the week if a cruise ship isn't docked at nearby Puerto Quetzal.

On the Caribbean Coast near Puerto Barrios, Amatique Bay Resort is a sizable complex fronting an artificial white-sand beach with its own marina and three restaurants. Across the bay near Puerto Santo Tomás de Castilla and its new cruise-ship terminal, Green Bay Hotel also fronts an artificial beach along a lagoon and provides easy access to nearby nature preserves.

Ecolodges

Another recent trend is the development of ecolodges springing up seemingly everywhere. These vary from somewhat simple community-run ecolodges to downright stylish, with Francis Ford Coppola's La Lancha (on Lake Petén Itzá) at the forefront of the latter category. Most ecolodges are found in Petén department and in the regions of Izabal and Las Verapaces.

Food

WHAT TO EAT

Guatemalan food may at first seem a bit odd to gringo palates, though the freshness and pungency of local ingredients, including a bounty of tropical fruits and vegetables, soon have many people enticed by the local flavors. Guatemalan dishes are based largely on corn, a staple crop with Guatemala's indigenous population. Corn is ground and made into a dough, which in turn is used to make tortillas, cooked over an open fire on a *comal*. Tortillas are a staple with Indians and ladinos alike, and the average Guatemalan family consumes several dozen tortillas per week. In the countryside, tortillas with a dash of lemon and salt, along with beans, form the basis of meals in many low-income households. Even in the cities, tortillas are bought from the local *tortillería* or, in many cases, delivered fresh daily. Unlike revenge, tortillas are not a dish best served cold. Guatemalans like them piping hot, and they usually arrive in a basket wrapped in traditional cloth to keep them warm. Many restaurants will have a *tortillería* at the front of the restaurant, where you can watch the tortillas being made, attesting to their freshness.

Other Guatemalan dishes include *tamales*, made from corn meal, pork or turkey, tomato sauce, and olives wrapped in a banana leaf and boiled. Traditionally, Guatemalans will eat a *tamal* at midnight on Christmas Eve. *Chuchitos* are a delicious combination of cornmeal with turkey and tomato sauce wrapped in a cornhusk. *Paches* are similar to *tamales*, but they are made from potato-based dough instead of corn. Guatemalans are no strangers to tacos, though the local version is a corn tortilla filled with pork or chicken, rolled up, fried, and covered with tomato sauce and traditional cheese bits. Tostadas are flat, fried corn tortillas topped with tomato sauce or bean paste, shredded parsley, and cheese bits.

Among Guatemala's dishes are also a variety of spicy stews found regionally. Found in the northern region of Las Verapaces, *kakik* is a turkey stew requiring 24 ingredients. Served along the Caribbean Coast of Izabal, *tapado* is a seafood stew made with plantains and coconut milk. Spicy meat dishes include *pollo en jocón* (chicken in a tomatillo-cilantro sauce) and *pollo en pepián* (chicken in a tomato-pumpkin seed sauce).

In addition to three meals a day, Guatemalans are also big fans of the *refacción,* a midafternoon snack consisting of a light sandwich or pastry and coffee. The prominence of bakeries and cake shops throughout the country attests to the popularity of this extra half-meal. Not all Guatemalans can afford to eat three square meals a day—a large part of the population subsists on less than $2 daily. In many places, meat is a luxury few can afford. Dinner is usually late for North American tastes and is usually eaten sometime around 8pm.

Besides traditional food, heavy European influences on Guatemalan culture throughout the years have resulted in a wide array of culinary tastes. You'll see plenty of evidence of this in Guatemala City and Antigua, where there are numerous options for dining in addition to some very interesting fusions of Guatemalan and international flavors. In food and culture, Guatemalans love to emulate the consumption patterns of their North American neighbors. You'll see plenty of fast-food franchises, mostly in Guatemala City, but also with surprising frequency in other urban areas. Guatemala City also has its fair share of U.S. casual dining franchises the likes of T.G.I. Friday's, Chili's, and Applebee's. But, since you didn't come all this way to eat the same food you'd have back home, you'll need a few tips on where to eat locally.

WHERE TO EAT

You can expect to find table service and menus in *restaurantes. Comedores* are much simpler eateries, sometimes with a menu but other times with a set dish for the day. The best *comedores* are easy to spot: They'll have the greatest number of locals eating there. You'll find Guatemalans often eat at streetside stalls serving greasy tacos, fried chicken, and the like. These places are often referred to in jest as *shucos* (dirties) and are best avoided by international travelers unless you have a very strong stomach or have developed resistance to intestinal critters through continued exposure to food of questionable cleanliness south of the border.

ORDERING AND PAYING

The menu is known as *la carta* or *el menú.* To request the check, order *la cuenta* or ask, *"¿cuánto le debo?"* ("How much do I owe you?"). Tips are not required at simple eateries and may already be included on your bill in many midrange restaurants. Check to see. If not, a standard tip in Guatemala is 10 percent.

BUYING GROCERIES

Corner stores known as *tiendas* carrying basic food items are common in cities and towns throughout the country. Larger grocery stores are found in Guatemala City and some of the larger cities. Major grocery chains include Paiz (recently acquired by WalMart) and La Torre. Every town and village has a *mercado* (market), where folks go to buy fruits and vegetables as well as meats. Try to avoid the butcher section if you don't take well to displays of raw flesh covered with flies. Inquire about the price per pound of any required items instead of just picking up an odd-numbered assortment and then asking how much it is, because that's the best way to get ripped off.

BEVERAGES
Non-Alcoholic Drinks

Although Guatemala produces some of the world's finest coffee, most of it is set aside for export. Still, you can find an excellent cup of java in Antigua, Guatemala City, Cobán, and other tourist places, though the coffee served at many less expensive restaurants is not usually the greatest. There's almost always at least one decent place in town for coffee.

With the wide variety of fruits available in Guatemala's myriad vegetation zones, fruit smoothies (often made with milk and called *licuados*) are common beverages. At simpler smoothie stands, you should always be careful to make sure the water used in making your drink is purified. Also, try to get fruit smoothies made from produce that requires peeling, rather than from fruits that are found on or close to the ground. Good, safe bets are pineapple or cantaloupe (or, even better, these mixed together). Strawberries sold locally are notorious for carrying amoebas and other parasites, so unless you plan on disinfecting them yourself or are in a place where you have assurance that this has been done, stick to fruits with peels. Orange juice served in Guatemala is often freshly squeezed and delicious, a delightful surprise for North American palates that have become all too accustomed to the taste of juice made from concentrate.

Sodas and carbonated beverages are widely available, as you'll guess from the ubiquitous advertising on town walls. Although plastic soda bottles and cans have become more widely available in recent years, you'll still see plenty of glass bottles in use. If you plan on buying a soda and taking the glass bottle with you, you'll have to fork over a few extra bills for the glass deposit. Otherwise, you can have it put in a sandwich bag with a straw, which is a bit unnerving for first-time visitors but perfectly normal and hygienic.

Alcoholic Beverages

Guatemala's eastern region produces Zacapa Centenario, a highly acclaimed rum that has won numerous international awards. It makes a great gift for folks back home. If you're not heading to the eastern lowlands of Zacapa or don't want to lug your purchase around the country during the rest of your travels, keep in mind the Guatemala City airport has a Zacapa Centenario Duty Free shop where you can buy a bottle or two on your way out of the country. In the Mayan highland towns and villages, the liquor of choice is *aguardiente,* locally made moonshine also known as *guaro.* Popular brands include *Quezalteca Especial* and *Venado. Rompopo* and *caldo de frutas* are two types of alcoholic beverages made in the town of Salcajá, near Quetzaltenango. The first is essentially a spiked eggnog and the latter is made from fermented fruits.

Cervecería Centroamericana produces most of Guatemala's beers from its brewery in Guatemala City, including Gallo, a lager that is Guatemala's national brew. You can find it in the United States under the name Famosa, as Ernest and Julio Gallo Wines holds the rights to the use of the Gallo name in North America. *Gallo* means rooster in Spanish, and the beer is easily identifiable by the stylized rooster on its label. Other beers brewed by Cervecería Centroamericana include Dorada Draft, smooth export pilsner Monte Carlo, and dark beer Moza. Brewed by Cervecería Nacional and available only in and around Quetzaltenango, Cabro is another good beer. Cervecería Centroamericana once enjoyed uncontested dominion of the Guatemalan beer market but has seen competition in recent years with the arrival of competing brands, most notably Brazilian Brahva.

Conduct and Customs

You'll find most Guatemalans are warm and friendly. In many instances, they will be very curious about you as a foreigner, particularly in areas that are still getting accustomed to a growing presence of gringo travelers. Urban and rural settings have varying degrees of formality, though politeness and good manners are appreciated by Guatemalans from all walks of life and will get you far.

DRESS AND APPEARANCE

Guatemala is in many ways a rather formal and conservative country, probably owing to its legacy of colonialism and its status as the main base of regional power for the Spanish colonial aristocracy. It's a very class-conscious society, with good grooming, neat dress, and cleanliness expected. In many instances, the way you look is the way you'll be treated. You'll notice this the first time you go to a Guatemala City shopping mall (especially on weekends) and see well-dressed urbanites going for a cup of coffee or heading out to see a movie. Sneakers and shorts are considered much too casual for many events foreigners would find perfectly acceptable. This is starting to change, however, and you'll also see younger Guatemalans wearing shorts, T-shirts, and flip-flops typical of the Abercrombie & Fitch look that is also wildly popular with Guatemalan youth from wealthy families. If you plan on going out to dance clubs, be sure to bring a good pair of shoes, as you won't make it past the front door wearing sneakers. Dress is much more relaxed at the beach or in the countryside.

For business travelers, suits are still very much the norm for men. Professional women tend to wear conservative dresses or two-piece suits. The less affluent will pay careful attention to dress as neatly as possible, especially for trips to the capital or other urban centers.

Backpackers, known as *mochileros,* often get a bum rap as an unkempt group who contribute very little to the economy and only cause trouble for hotel owners and tourist service operators. This is generally manifested as a form of marked distrust, though this is usually not the case in places that cater to these types of travelers as their main clientele, such as budget hostels.

ETIQUETTE

The formality of Guatemalan culture also extends to etiquette. Guatemalans take titles seriously (including *doctor* or *doctora* for doctors and *licenciado(a)* for an attorney or holder of a bachelor's degree). Whenever possible, they should be used when addressing the individual in person or via correspondence. Women usually greet men and each other with air kisses. Men will greet friends with a handshake different from the standard business handshake. Grips tend to be firm. When meeting someone for the first time, it's customary to say, *"mucho gusto"* (a shortened version of "nice to meet you"). Simply saying *"hola"* is considered too casual. Other greetings include *"buenos días"* (good morning), *"buenas tardes"* (good afternoon), and *"buenas noches"* (good evening). Particularly in rural areas, people will greet each other with one of these as they pass each other along the trail, road, or street. In urban settings, you'll often hear one of these greetings when someone walks into a place of business, such as a doctor's office, for example. Another formality is the use of *"buen provecho"* when walking into a restaurant where people are eating and *"muchas gracias"* upon getting up from the table after a meal.

PHOTOGRAPHIC ETIQUETTE

It's never a good idea to photograph Mayan people without their permission, as they consider it highly offensive and it intrudes upon their spiritual beliefs. The old photographers' rule contending that it's easier to apologize (for taking a candid photo) than to ask permission doesn't really apply in Guatemala. This is especially true concerning photographs of children, and you should be careful not to show them undue interest and attention, as persistent rumors of foreigners involved in child-snatching of Guatemalan children for organ transplant abroad have led to mob incidents on at least two occasions, with two people killed and one seriously injured. (The last incident was in 2000 in the village of Todos Santos.) In both cases, the foreigners were trying to photograph a child. This scenario is most plausible in the highlands, though not exclusively so.

It can be understandably difficult at times to refrain from taking photographs because Mayan children (and Mayan people in general) are especially photogenic and can provide some wonderful opportunities for portraiture or candid shots. On the up side, the situation forces you to interact with the locals and get to know them. You'll soon find that many are willing to let you photograph them (often for the promise of sending them a photo) and your photographs will be better because of the rapport you've established with the subject.

SMOKING

As of February 2009, it is no longer possible to smoke in public places in Guatemala, including bars, restaurants, office buildings, and airports. Some foreigners (especially European travelers) may not yet know about this law; you may have to kindly but firmly point this out, or ask the property manager do so on your behalf.

GUATEMALAN BEHAVIOR
Confianza and Saving Face
One of the main traits of Guatemalan behavior is what is known as being en confianza. Attaining this level in your interpersonal relationships means having a high level of openness, trust, and comfort with those you are en confianza (in confidence) with. Once you have reached this level in your relationship with someone, you will most likely be visiting their home and sharing a few meals. Confianza is just as important for making friends as it is for doing business and overall success in Guatemalan society. You can erode your confianza by displaying character flaws such as losing your temper in public or dressing inappropriately, but Guatemalans will never confront you directly. Instead they will do what is known as "saving face." There may be a perceptible chill in their demeanor toward you.

Another player in the Guatemalan social lingo is the concept of pena, directly linked to the concept of saving face. To have pena is to feel badly, as in the case of imposing on your host or needing to say something unpleasant or accusatory. North Americans are very direct and to the point, which is not at all how Guatemalans are. They will go to great lengths to avoid the pena of having to tell you something or ask something of you they are not comfortable with.

North Americans (or those who have spent extended periods of time there) often find this idiosyncrasy quite frustrating. Former Vice President Rafael Espada, who spent several years as a prominent surgeon in Houston prior to being elected to office, highlighted this characteristic during an interview with Prensa Libre following his first year back in Guatemala. He said this face-saving mechanism, whereby people will tell you what they think you want to hear, was one of his biggest frustrations. Espada said it was hard to get things done when people have given you assurances that the wheels are set in motion, when often they haven't even started what you asked them to do in the first place.

Conversation
Guatemalans tend to use the vos form of tu (you), a derivative of the archaic vosotros now used only in Spain. This is particularly the case with two men of the same age or similar

social standing. It shouldn't be used to address a person of perceived lesser social stature, as it's somewhat demeaning when used in this way, though upper-class Guatemalans tend to do it anyway. Stick to the formal *usted* unless the person switches to the informal *tu* or *vos*.

Personal Space and Privacy

Guatemalans might be a bit "touchy feely" by North American standards. It's not uncommon to see two heterosexual male friends walking with their arms around each other. This is more common with school-age children, however. Guatemalans generally greet each other with hugs and kisses (or air kisses if it's a stranger of the opposite gender). They may also grab your arm when trying to emphasize a point.

North Americans' love of privacy might at times seem strange to Guatemalans. This is something to keep in mind if you are staying with a host family. What might seem like a normal degree of privacy to you may seem like seclusion and isolation, on your part, to them. Most host families who have had a number of North American visitors have grown accustomed to this.

Travel Tips

OPPORTUNITIES FOR STUDY AND VOLUNTEER WORK
Language Study

Guatemala is a popular place for Spanish-language study, particularly Antigua and Quetzaltenango. Here are a few basic things to look out for when deciding where to study Spanish in Guatemala. First of all, you'll want to decide what sort of environment you're looking for to choose a location. Antigua and Quetzaltenango offer some fine institutions in addition to the chance to combine your language instruction with time spent in interesting urban locales. Both towns have a lively nightlife scene and a fairly substantial presence of foreign travelers. This might be a pro or a con, depending on how you look at it. If you're looking to make new friends and traveling companions after your courses are finished, then this will certainly suit you. But if you're looking for a total language-immersion experience, you might find yourself speaking English outside of classroom time more often than not.

There are a few highland towns and villages with language schools that offer good instruction with (for now) a relatively small foreign presence. These include the language schools in Nebaj, Cobán, and remote areas of Huehuetenango. For the altruistic, Quetzaltenango offers the chance for language instruction in an environment oozing with fellow travelers, volunteers, and NGO workers plugged into a variety of projects hoping to make life better for people in Guatemala's impoverished Western Highlands.

Virtually all of Guatemala's language schools offer one-on-one instruction, and your choice of an instructor is particularly important to your progress. You should never feel locked into a deal with a particular instructor. If you find that you and the instructor just aren't jiving, don't hesitate to ask for a new one. All of the recommended schools get their strength from the quality of their individual instructors, so finding one that's right for you shouldn't be too difficult if you know where to look.

In terms of cost, you'll find it fairly accessible. The bulk of Guatemala's schools charge somewhere between $150 and $250 per week, including at least 20 hours of instruction per week and room and board with a local host family. Some schools, particularly in Antigua and Quetzaltenango, provide the option of staying in on- or off-campus housing or apartments.

As a final note, Guatemalan Spanish is relatively clear of the accents found in Caribbean, Mexican, and even Costa Rican Spanish. Guatemalans also tend to speak more slowly than Caribbean Spanish speakers. It's actually a very melodic Spanish, and you'll soon recognize its singsong sound. In terms of value for the money you spend and variety of locales in which to learn, you really can't beat Spanish-language instruction in Guatemala.

Volunteer Opportunities

The country is also the focus of many relief and development projects on the part of NGOs, some of which are almost always looking for volunteers. Many of these are linked to local language schools. Areas with a particularly heavy concentration of NGOs include Quetzaltenango, the Ixil Triangle, and Petén.

Foreign Study Programs

For college students seeking a study-abroad opportunity, **The University of Arizona** (www.studyabroad.arizona.edu), in partnership with the Center for Mesoamerican Research (CIRMA), offers semester- and year-long programs in Antigua focusing on intensive Spanish-language instruction in addition to Central American history, politics, and culture. Likewise, the **University of Texas at Austin** (www.utexas.edu) offers a semester abroad at its Casa Herrera facility in the heart of Antigua Guatemala. Topics include pre-Columbian art, archaeology, history, and culture.

TRAVELING WITH CHILDREN

Guatemalans love children, and traveling with them will often be all that you need to break the ice with locals. Guatemala's cultural and natural wealth can also form the basis for a very educational trip allowing children to see and experience what they might only read about in textbooks and classrooms.

Guatemala has also been a popular place for U.S. citizens to adopt Guatemalan children. The U.S. government discouraged adoptions from Guatemala because of deficient legal parameters ensuring the protection of adopting parents and adopted children in line with international standards. Adoptions in Guatemala are suspended at this time. However, legislation has been passed to be in compliance with the tenets of the Hague convention governing international adoption.

Guatemala makes a great place for Spanish-language study.

Kid-Friendly Guatemala

Latin Americans are very family oriented, and Guatemalans are no exception. There is plenty to see and do in Guatemala for families traveling with children of all ages. The following is a list of kid- and family-friendly attractions throughout the country.

GUATEMALA CITY

Among the city's museums, none is more kid friendly than the **Museo de los Niños** (Children's Museum), in Zona 13 near the airport. There are a number of interactive displays as well as opportunities for play. Just across the street, you'll find the city's excellent **La Aurora Zoo,** harboring a good collection of animals from Guatemala and around the world. Cages are being gradually phased out.

LAKE ATITLÁN

On the lake's beautiful shores, there are plenty of places to stay for families traveling with children. Among the best are the family-sized villas at **San Buenaventura de Atitlán,** equipped with a kitchen and several rooms. Nearby, kids (and outdoor-loving parents) will enjoy the **Reserva Natural Atitlán,** where they can see monkeys and coatimundis along the nature trails leading to waterfalls. There are also a butterfly farm and private lake beach in addition to an excellent visitors center.

Kids enjoy Hostal Palajunoj, one of the Hostales del IRTRA.

PACIFIC COAST

The Pacific Coast is extremely family friendly, primarily thanks to the presence of the twin theme parks of **Xocomil** and **Xetulul,** near Retalhuleu. Xocomil is a water park on par with the finest in the United States, and Xetulul includes re-creations of famous Spanish, French, Italian, and Guatemalan landmarks along with an exhilarating roller coaster and assorted other rides. After the parks close, the fun continues across the street at the excellent accommodations of **Hostales del IRTRA,** with numerous swimming pools, restaurants, and activities. Also in this area is the new **Dino Park**, with animatronic dinosaurs straight out of Jurassic Park. For some seaside fun, head to **Monterrico,** where (in season) you can participate in a race involving newly hatched sea turtles making their maiden voyage across the sandy beach to their ocean home. Kids will also get a kick out of the **Auto-Safari Chapín,** in Taxisco about 90 minutes from Guatemala City. It's a drive-through safari experience, in which you can see several of kids' favorite animals, including lions, zebras, and parrots.

PETÉN

Children will certainly be impressed by the Mayan ruins at **Tikal,** along with the abundant wildlife found along the various nature trails crisscrossing the park or swinging from the trees. At the entrance to Tikal, older kids and adults will enjoy the **Tikal Canopy Tour,** allowing them to zip across the forest canopy along metallic cables while strapped to a harness. If you want to see more of the forest canopy on slightly less adrenaline-inducing conditions, head to **Parque Natural Ixpanpajul,** where there are plenty of outdoor activities, including walks along hanging bridges connecting forested jungle canyons.

ACCESS FOR TRAVELERS WITH DISABILITIES

Guatemala is a somewhat challenging country for people with disabilities, as there is little in the way of public infrastructure specifically catering to the needs of travelers with disabilities. Antigua might be a bit cumbersome for travelers in wheelchairs because of its cobblestone streets but nonetheless it has ramps for wheelchair access on every street corner. There are a few exceptions to the general lack of access for those with disabilities. Guatemala City's new public transportation system, the Transmetro, was said to offer wheelchair access as part of its innovative infrastructure. The international airport now also features several elevators as part of its recent renovation. Modern Guatemala City hotels housed in high-rise buildings also have these amenities. For intercity travel, the best option for travelers with disabilities is to take shuttle buses.

WOMEN TRAVELING ALONE

As elsewhere in Latin America, men in Guatemala tend to be chauvinistic, particularly the country's ladinos. Women traveling alone might find themselves the object of unwanted attention. Guatemalan women are accustomed to fairly constant harassment by men on the street, including catcalls, whistling, and horn honking, which they tend to ignore. This is usually the best tactic, though it's somewhat difficult to put into practice. Take a deep breath and count to 10. Your best bet as a preventive measure in this regard is to dress demurely, particularly in urban areas. After dark, take a cab, but try to find someone to share it with.

GAY AND LESBIAN TRAVELERS

The prevalence of *machismo* (male-dominated culture) can make things difficult, if not downright dangerous, for gay and lesbian couples choosing to express mutual affection publicly. Gay travelers and residents will want to keep a low profile while in public areas in Guatemala so as not to attract unwanted attention. Homosexuality is still not widely accepted in Guatemala, and many commonly used slurs and epithets apply directly to gays. Still, things may be starting to change, as Guatemalans are quick to emulate the cultural standards they see on international TV, specifically the greater acceptance of gay men and lesbians portrayed in the U.S. media. Acceptance of homosexuality, in this way, appears directly linked to socioeconomic status—or at least access to cable television. Some openly gay Guatemalans live with their partners and are open about their relationships with friends and family, though financial and social independence figure prominently into this decision.

Religious beliefs and prejudices vary and affect how gay men and lesbian women are treated in any society. It all depends on the individual. I've witnessed innkeepers issue disparaging remarks about gay guests behind their backs, but I've also run into uncommon acceptance of homosexuality from cabdrivers gushing about their gay clients.

As in many international cities, there's a growing gay-rights movement in Guatemala City, and there are a number of gay bars and nightclubs, mostly in Zona 1. As with most venues, things are constantly changing, so log on to www.gayguatemala.com for the latest.

Health and Safety

Guatemala's status as a poor, developing nation translates into a variety of health and safety risks for the foreign traveler. Many of these are directly related to poor hygiene. When it comes to safety and law enforcement, the **Policía Nacional Civil** (created by the 1996 peace accords) has not lived up to its expectations as an efficient, incorruptible, and professional police force. On a positive note, the **Tourism Police** have demonstrated proficiency in helping travelers as well as making areas somewhat safer with patrols and group escorts. Private initiatives, as they almost always do in Guatemala, have stepped in to fill the gaps, also providing some measure of protection for foreign visitors.

Travelers might want to consider buying traveler's insurance before heading to Guatemala. Several different types of insurance with varying degrees of coverage are available in the United States, Canada, and Europe. The Guatemala Tourist Commission (INGUAT) also provides assistance to travelers in need via its **Programa de Asistencia al Turista**. They can be reached by dialing 1500.

BEFORE YOU GO

Officially, no vaccinations are required for entry into Guatemala, though it's a good idea to be up to date on rabies, typhoid, measles-mumps-rubella (MMR), yellow fever, and tetanus shots. A hepatitis vaccine is now widely available and probably also a good idea. If you plan on taking preventive medications against malaria, you'll need to start them a few weeks before potential exposure to the disease. The Centers for Disease Control and Prevention (CDC) maintains an international travelers' hotline, which can be reached at 888/232-3228, and a travel health home page found at www.cdc.gov/travel.

PREVENTATIVE MAINTENANCE

As the saying goes, "An ounce of prevention is worth a pound of cure." This is certainly the case for travel in Guatemala, as there are certain measures you can take to avoid succumbing to many of the most common ailments. Washing hands frequently and drinking only bottled water will help keep you free of stomach ailments as will consuming only cooked foods or peeled fruits such as bananas and oranges. Lettuce and strawberries are two common culprits, often leading to severe gastrointestinal distress. Likewise, stay away from ice cubes unless you have complete assurance that they come from purified water. By law, all ice cubes served in Guatemalan restaurants must come from purified water, a good idea in theory but certainly not always the case. I've often had my doubts even about supposedly purified ice cubes in restaurants after falling ill. When in doubt, leave the ice out. Be careful not only with what you eat, but where you eat. Stay away from street stalls selling cheap food, referred to jokingly by locals as *shucos* (literally, "dirties"). While Guatemalan stomachs have developed immunity through the years to nasty food-borne bugs, the average gringo traveler's has not.

FOOD- OR WATER-BORNE DISEASES

Despite these precautions, many travelers to Guatemala might find themselves experiencing a classic case of "the runs" as their digestive tracts adjust to new flora. This usually lasts only a day or two. If the problem persists, it may be a sign of more serious issues. In some cases, it may be food poisoning, which can occur just as easily back home. If this is the case, drink plenty of water and get some rest. You'll probably end up just having to ride it out for a few days and may want to take an anti-diarrhea medicine such as Pepto Bismol or Lomotil.

Travelers' Diarrhea

In addition to diarrhea, symptoms of this often-acquired malady include nausea, vomiting, bloating, and weakness. The usual culprit is *E. coli* bacteria from contaminated food or water. It's important to stay hydrated. Drink plenty of water and clear fluids and keep your strength up by eating bland foods such as crackers or steamed rice. As with food poisoning, you may want to take some over-the-counter anti-diarrhea medication.

Dysentery

Characterized by many of the same symptoms as described above, along with the possibility of bloody stools and generally prolonged malaise, dysentery comes in two flavors: bacillic (bacterial) and amoebic (parasitic). The onset of bacillic dysentery is usually sudden, characterized by vomiting, diarrhea, and fever. Treatment is via antibiotics, to which it responds well. Amoebic dysentery, on the other hand, has an incubation period and symptoms may not show up for several days. It's also harder to get rid of. It is usually treated with a weeklong course of Flagyl (Metronidazole), an extremely potent drug that will wipe out all intestinal flora—good and bad. It also has some marked side effects, such as a bitter taste in the mouth, irritability, and dizziness. You should avoid alcohol while taking this drug, as the combination can make you violently ill.

As with all gastrointestinal issues, it's very important to stay hydrated. Also, see a doctor to get an exact diagnosis. Because of the prevalence of gastrointestinal diseases among Guatemalans, most cities have at least one clinic that can take a stool sample and diagnose the exact nature of the problem.

Cholera

Not entirely unheard of in Guatemala, cholera can be an issue in poorer neighborhoods lacking adequate sanitation, which are usually not visited by foreign travelers. Today's cholera strains are not nearly as deadly as those of the past, though there have been outbreaks in Guatemala in years past. It's best to avoid raw fish and ceviche, a marinated raw-seafood salad popular throughout Latin America.

INSECT-BORNE DISEASES

Mosquitoes are the main carriers of insect-borne illnesses common throughout tropical areas around the world. The best approach to avoiding malaria and other mosquito-borne illnesses is to avoid being bitten by mosquitoes in the first place. Mosquitoes are most abundant during the rainy season, so take special care to protect against mosquito bites during this time of year. Some travelers favor liberal application of bug spray with DEET as the active ingredient, which seems to be the most effective at keeping the critters at bay. Plant-based bug sprays seem to be less effective. It's also possible to buy clothing treated with permethrin, a bug-repellent chemical. It's also possible to buy it separately and treat your clothing with it. Treated garments are scentless in addition to being highly insect repellent. You can find these products in camping and outdoor stores.

Malaria

Malaria is transmitted by the female *Anopheles* mosquito and is prevalent in the Caribbean lowlands and Petén jungles, though not in the highlands. Anopheles mosquitoes tend to bite at night. Flulike symptoms of malaria include high fever, chills, headaches, muscle pain, and fatigue. It can be fatal if left untreated.

Some travelers also opt to take antimalarial drugs, available locally without a prescription (and quite cheaply). The most widely used is chloroquine, known by its brand name Aralen. Although chloroquine-resistant strains of malaria are found in other parts of the world, including South America, this is not the case in Guatemala. You'll need to start taking the drug (500 mg) a week before arriving in malarial zones, weekly while there, and continue to take it once a week for at least four weeks after you've left the malarial zone. Other travelers opt to take two 500 mg doses with them to use if and only if the disease strikes.

Some people experience marked side effects while taking chloroquine, including nausea, headaches, fever, rashes, and nightmares. A newer antimalarial drug, malarone, was approved by the FDA in 2000, supposedly with fewer side effects than traditional drugs and which does not need to be taken for as long. It is not yet widely available in Guatemala.

Dengue

Dengue is also transmitted by mosquitoes and prevalent in lowland areas, though it is far less common than malaria and only rarely fatal. Although there is no treatment, most people recover from its debilitating symptoms, which include a fever that can last 5-7 days, headache, severe joint pain, and skin rashes. The disease may last up to another week after the fever has lifted. Tylenol can help reduce the fever and counteract the headaches. Dengue is transmitted by a mosquito that bites during the daytime, the *Aëdes aegypti*. A far less common, though potentially fatal, form of dengue is hemorrhagic dengue. It needs to be treated within a few days of the appearance of symptoms, which are a carbon copy of regular dengue symptoms until severe hemorrhaging sets in, making medical treatment well advised at the first sign of dengue.

Chikungunya

Chikungunya is another mosquito-borne illness that has more recently come over to the Americas from Africa. The culprit is also the *Aëdes aegypti* mosquito. Symptoms are similar to those of dengue and include fever lasting up to a week, body aches, and/or severe joint pain and stiffness that can last weeks, months, or even years. A rash, headache, fatigue, nausea, and vomiting are also possible symptoms. There is currently no treatment for the disease other than bed rest and painkillers to numb the discomfort. Travelers to Guatemala's Pacific Coast, in particular, should be wary of mosquitoes due to chikungunya's prevalence in this region. An ounce of prevention is worth a pound of cure.

BITES AND STINGS
Sand Fleas and Sand Flies

Among the more annoying *bichos* (bugs) are sand fleas, which are virtually imperceptible but can leave a trail of welts on feet and ankles. The best way to avoid bites is by washing off after walking on sandy areas. Annoying and also extremely painful are the bites of sand flies known as *tábanos* inhabiting coastal areas, mostly on the Caribbean Coast. They look like a cross between a bee and housefly. You may not feel them on you until it's too late, as they have a knack for landing gently on their victims. Tábano infestations are worst during the dry months, when breezes off the ocean are greatly reduced. If traveling to remote beaches, go prepared with pants, long sleeves, bandana, hat, and bug spray. It may seem silly going to the beach with pants and long sleeves, but it sure beats the very unpleasant experience of being bitten and pursued by these persistent critters (I speak from experience).

Snakes

Lowland Guatemala is home to some of the world's deadliest snakes, including the aggressive fer-de-lance, a pit viper also known as *barba amarilla* for the yellow coloring under its mouth. It's easily distinguishable by its diamond-shaped head and intricate diamond patterns on its skin. It is fairly common in Petén, Izabal, and the Verapaces. Bites are usually fatal unless the victim receives medical attention within a few hours. Other poisonous snakes include rattlesnakes, the red, black, and yellow-banded coral snake, and the eyelash viper, which you should be particularly wary of, as it tends to blend in to vegetation, especially palm trees.

Wear high boots and long pants for hiking in the jungle. Always watch where you step and be particularly careful of woodpiles and rocks. Snakes tend to hang out near jungle watering holes and gaps created by fallen trees. For extended trips into the jungle, it's a good idea to go with a guide. Let guides lead the way, as their eyes are keenly attuned to the presence of snakes and they are usually armed with a machete.

HIV/AIDS

AIDS is a growing concern in Guatemala, particularly because of the widespread use of prostitutes in a society ruled by *machismo*. Certainly not making things any better is the economic need of infected prostitutes who continue working after being infected. If you plan on sleeping with a stranger or friend met in your travels, be sure to use a condom, available almost anywhere and known as *preservativos* or *condones*.

MEDICAL ATTENTION
Doctors and Hospitals

Medical services in Guatemala City are generally top-notch, particularly in many private hospitals. Outside the capital, there are several private hospitals providing quality medical care in urban areas. Public facilities such as the Instituto Guatemalteco de Seguridad Social (IGSS) should be avoided, as they are set up to cater to low-income people with no other alternative and are notoriously understaffed and underfunded. Rural areas are extremely lacking in health care, which has resulted in the presence of Cuban doctors in parts of the highlands who have arrived to help bridge the health-care gap.

Pharmacies

In many cases pharmacists sometimes serve as de facto doctors, as prescriptions are not necessary for medications in Guatemala. Patients will often describe symptoms and take something on the pharmacist's recommendation. Still, it's always best to see a doctor. Many drugs can be found more cheaply in Guatemala, as they are produced locally by a handful of pharmaceutical companies.

In almost every town, at least one pharmacy will be open all night thanks to a system known as *farmacia de turno* (on-call pharmacy), in which the local pharmacies stay open on a rotating basis. Local newspapers publish a listing of these pharmacies and sometimes the outlets themselves have a neon sign stating as such.

SAFETY
Crime

Crime has been a problem throughout Guatemala in the aftermath of the civil war, though statistics show most foreign travelers enjoy their visit to the country without any problems. As many veteran travelers to Guatemala like to point out, you're still safer here than in many large U.S. cities.

Among Guatemala's urban areas, Guatemala City has by far the greatest prevalence of crime. Much of this consisted of groups perpetrating robberies against arriving passengers heading into the city from La Aurora International Airport. Private vehicles, taxis, and shuttle buses have been targeted indiscriminately. Authorities were investigating suspected groups while simultaneously opening security checkpoints and police kiosks to provide greater police presence along this route. It remains to be seen whether large-scale infrastructural improvements involving roads adjacent to the airport (as part of the airport renovation project) will make things safer for arriving passengers.

A related issue is that of highway holdups on rural roads, a very unpleasant topic that I must nonetheless cover here. Sometimes, groups will use bends in the road and speed bumps to their advantage, stopping vehicles as they slow down and robbing passengers of valuables. In the most spectacular cases of highway banditry, pickup trucks carrying armed men will pursue a vehicle and then pass it. Another car might come alongside the victim's vehicle while the car in front shoots at it in an attempt to make the driver stop the car. In addition to taking the passengers' possessions, perpetrators occasionally drag the car's occupants out of the vehicle, tie them up, and steal the car.

Guatemalans who sniff out an impending carjacking have been known to speed up as would-be perpetrators signal them to slow down, not without significant risk of being harmed by the bullets that are often landed on the car by frustrated assailants. If you are stopped and robbed, it's best to remain calm and give them what they want. Opposing a robbery will only make things worse, as the thieves will see this as an invitation to use greater force (I speak from a personal experience in Mexico). It's hard to predict where robberies may occur, though certain areas do seem more prone to this type of crime than others. Among these areas are RN-11, along the southeastern side of Lake Atitlán, the road to El Salvador outside the Guatemala City area (Salvadorans are a favorite target), and some rural Petén roads.

For more on this topic, read the U.S. government's Consular Information Sheet, found online at www.travel.state.gov. Another useful site is that concerning recent incidents of crime against foreigners in Guatemala, available at http://guatemala.usembassy.gov/recent_incidents.html. It will give you an idea of what can happen, but try not to let it alarm you.

Gang violence is also a growing concern. The groups, known as *maras,* operate in parts of Guatemala City not usually frequented by international travelers as well as in some urban areas throughout the country.

Kidnappings reached an all-time high after the civil war, usually involving prominent citizens held for ransom and sometimes returned to their families, depending on whether or not the ransom money was collected. They seem to have subsided in more recent years and rarely, if ever, involve foreigners.

During your trip to Guatemala, there are a number of commonsense measures you can take to avoid becoming the victim of street crime. Don't walk around wearing flashy jewelry and carry only the amount of cash you need for the day in a concealed place. Use safety-deposit boxes for important documents such as passports. In crowded cities, carry your backpack in front of you and be aware of your surroundings at all times. Always keep an eye on your luggage at the airport, bus terminals, and hotels. At night, take a cab and don't go walking out and about after dark. At the beach, be sure not to bring too many things that might tempt thieves while you're in the water. Also, be careful not to walk along isolated stretches of beach, particularly around the Caribbean city of Lívingston. It's never a good idea to climb volcanic summits without a guide, particularly those around Antigua and Lake Atitlán, as these are especially prone to robberies.

That being said, there are still many areas of the country that are beautiful for backcountry hiking and remain crime-free, particularly the Western Highlands region of the Ixil Triangle, where you can explore freely. Before embarking on a backcountry hike or volcano climb, always inform someone who is not going with you of your plans and when you plan to return.

Police

The Policía Nacional Civil (PNC) was created after the civil war with help from Chilean and Spanish security forces but has not been the efficient security force it was hoped it would be. In addition to widespread allegations of corruption, it is perceived as being grossly inefficient. Corrupt agents are suspected of involvement with drug trafficking and the highway holdups, as many robberies occur shortly after travelers are stopped at police checkpoints and perpetrators are often described as wearing police uniforms. Despite these conditions, if you are stopped by police it is best not to offer a bribe, as straight cops will not hesitate to throw you in jail. It's best to go through the usual mechanisms and pay the fine (if applicable). After being stopped,

Guatemala's well-armed police at Tikal National Park

Drugs

Guatemala is a major transshipment point for cocaine coming into the United States from South America, as evidenced by the many clandestine landing strips found in isolated areas of Petén department. Marijuana is grown in remote lowland areas of Guatemala and poppy (the basis for heroin) is grown in the Western Highlands, particularly in the department of San Marcos.

High-ranking military officials have been implicated in drug smuggling, working with local cartels linked to Colombia's powerful Cali cartel. United States drug officials have begun referring to Guatemala as *la bodega* (the warehouse), as it houses a large share of the cocaine continuing north to Mexico, from where it makes its final entry into the United States. Among the local cartels, the most prominent are based in the eastern lowlands near Zacapa (not an area frequented by foreign tourists), Izabal department, and the southern part of Petén department near Sayaxché. Some travelers have reported run-ins with local drug traffickers on private lands, but you're unlikely to be harmed as long as you adopt a live-and-let-live attitude.

Cocaine consumption is an increasing problem among affluent Guatemalans, particularly in Guatemala City night clubs. Drug use is strictly forbidden by law, and you will be thrown in jail without hesitation for violations. If you are arriving in Guatemala by air from elsewhere in Latin America, drug-sniffing dogs will probably be on hand to greet your flight, and you may be questioned by authorities after clearing immigration procedures.

be particularly mindful of your surroundings and especially on the lookout for vehicles that might be following you a little too closely.

The Guatemalan military sometimes jointly patrols areas with police forces because of the latter's demonstrated inability to provide a security presence that dissuades criminal activity. In contrast, Tourism Police (Politur) are generally helpful and have been dispatched to patrol tourist areas. They have been particularly effective at curbing robberies in areas where criminal activity was once getting out of hand, including Tikal National Park and areas in the vicinity of Antigua.

Information and Services

MONEY

Prices throughout this guide are quoted in U.S. dollars unless otherwise noted. Guatemala's currency is the quetzal, which is pegged to the U.S. dollar and denoted by Q. The exchange rate was about Q7.68 to US$1, and it has remained at about the same rate for several years now. Bills come in denominations of 5, 10, 20, 50, and 100 quetzales, though the new polymer Q1, Q5, and Q200 bills are now in circulation. The Q500 bills might surface soon. Coins come in denominations of 1, 5, 10, 25, 50 *centavos* (Q0.01, Q0.05, Q0.10, Q0.25, Q.50) and Q1, though other than the one-quetzal coin they are more of a nuisance than anything else. Often, if your change is a few centavos, the merchant will keep it.

In smaller towns and villages, you might have trouble breaking Q100 (or larger) notes, so bring smaller bills with you if possible.

Exchange

Travelers have the option of getting around with cash U.S. dollars (which you will need to at least partially exchange for local currency), travelers checks (American Express being the most widely recognized and accepted), wire transfers (most expensive option), Visa or MasterCard cash advances (watch those interest rates), or through ATMs linked to international networks (recommended).

Banks

Banks in Guatemala tend to keep long hours, typically 9am-6pm Monday-Friday and 9am-1pm on Saturday. Changing money and travelers checks at banks is relatively painless and routine, though you'll probably be asked to show your passport or at least a photocopy of it for identification. You'll also notice that banks, like convenience stores and other businesses, are heavily guarded by armed security.

In border areas, you'll typically be approached by money changers offering slightly better rates than local banks. It's perfectly safe to change your money with them, though it's probably a good idea to exchange only what you might need for the first day or two in the new country. Try not to pull out a wad of bills for all to see.

Travelers Checks

This is still the safest way to carry money during your travels, though you'll be able to exchange them only in urban areas and tourist destinations with full-service banks. There's also a bit more bureaucracy involved in exchanging travelers checks, and you might be asked to show your original purchase receipt. American Express is by far the most widely accepted type of travelers check. The local American Express representative is **Clark Tours** (7a Avenida 14-76, Plaza Clark, Zona 9, Guatemala City, tel. 2412-4700, www.clark-tours.com).

Wire Transfers

Because of the widespread phenomenon of remittances sent home by Guatemalan nationals living abroad, several companies have set up shop all over Guatemala. This may be your best bet if you happen to run short of cash during your travels. Many local banks and businesses are Western Union affiliates. For a list of these affiliates in Guatemala, visit the website at www.westernunion.com. You can also send money via American Express MoneyGram. Keep in mind these companies make their money off exorbitant fees charged for their services in addition to a poor exchange rate for the money, which you'll end up getting in local currency.

Credit Cards and ATMs

Credit cards have become more and more commonplace in Guatemala, though they are still accepted mainly in urban centers, major tourist attractions, and luxury hotels or expensive restaurants and shops. Some smaller merchants may charge a fee, usually 7 to 10 percent of the transaction amount, the justification being that they are charged this amount by the credit card companies and can't afford to absorb the cost because of their smaller sales volume. Visa and MasterCard are the most widely accepted.

ATMs in Guatemala are hooked up to international networks and most travelers have no problems accessing their bank accounts in this way. It's always a good idea to keep an eye on transactions online while you're on the road if you're able to and report any inconsistencies immediately. You will never be required to enter your pin number on a pad to enter an ATM kiosk, a common scam to steal card and PIN numbers that has fooled some travelers. Always be aware of your surroundings and try not to visit the ATM at night or unaccompanied.

You can search for Visa ATM locations in Guatemala online at http://visa.via.infonow.net/ and MasterCard ATMs at www.mastercard.com/atm. A useful listing of Banco Industrial Visa ATMs throughout Guatemala can be found at www.bi.com.gt. This will give you an idea of the availability of ATMs along your planned travel route.

COMMUNICATIONS AND MEDIA
Postal Services

Guatemala's postal service, known as El Correo, was privatized a few years back and placed in the very capable hands of a Canadian company, making it much more reliable than it once was. It's also fairly inexpensive, though a letter to the United States might take three weeks to arrive at its destination. International couriers such as FedEx, UPS, and DHL also have a sizable presence here, along with several local companies used largely by Guatemalan expats living in the United States. The latter are substantially more affordable.

Telephone Service

Guatemala's country code is 502. There are no separate area or city codes. All phone numbers, save a few emergency numbers, are eight digits long. There are also a few toll-free numbers belonging to airlines and services that begin with 1-801. The national telephone service was privatized in 1999 and is now known as Telgua. A number of other phone companies, including Spanish Telefónica also operate here, providing some welcome competition. Each of the local phone companies has its own dialing codes for calling the United States from a land line, which will save you money. Most travelers, however, end up using any of the numerous phone centers in major tourist cities, from where you can call fairly cheaply to anywhere in the world. (These are covered in the appropriate geographical sections and are almost always housed in the same places offering Internet services.) Telgua also has call centers in major cities.

The most convenient and cheapest way to call home (and be able to call hotels and make reservations while on the road) is to have a cell phone. The most popular phone network is **Tigo** (www.tigo.com.gt), which likewise has the widest coverage and charges by the second, saving you money in the long run. Rates for domestic calls are about $0.16 a minute and you can call the United States for about $0.12 a minute. You can buy a phone locally, with the cheapest somewhere around $45, or bring one with you and use it in Guatemala if it's an unlocked phone. If you're an iPhone enthusiast, or if your cell phone uses the latest 4G technology, you'll be happy to know that both **Movistar** (www.movistar.com.gt) and **Claro** (www.claro.com.gt) sell iPhones locally. All three carriers have 4G networks with various plans to suit your needs, and with prices comparable to those in the United States. These companies also offer videophone service for phones equipped with this feature.

Internet

Internet access is widely available in most cities and tourist destinations throughout

Guatemala City Embassies and Consulates

Most embassies and consulates tend to be open only during weekday mornings.

- **Austria:** 6a Avenida 20-25, Edificio Plaza, Zona 10, tel. 2364-3460
- **Belize:** Avenida La Reforma 8-50, Edificio El Reformador, Suite 803, Zona 9, tel. 2334-5531
- **Canada:** 13 Calle 8-44, 6th Floor, Edificio Edyma Plaza, Zona 10, tel. 2333-6102
- **Colombia:** 5a Avenida 5-55, Edificio Europlaza, Torre I, Zona 14, tel. 2385-3432
- **Costa Rica:** 1a Avenida 15-52 Zona 10, tel. 2363-1345
- **Cuba:** 13 Calle 5-72 Zona 10, tel. 2333-7627
- **El Salvador:** 5a Avenida 8-15 Zona 9, tel. 2360-7660
- **France:** Edificio Marbella, 11th Floor, 16 Calle 4-53 Zona 10, tel. 2337-3639
- **Germany:** Edificio Plaza Marítima, 20 Calle 6-20 Zona 10, tel. 2364-6700
- **Honduras:** 19 Avenida "A" 20-19 Zona 10, tel. 2366-5640
- **Israel:** 13 Avenida 14-07 Zona 10, Colonia Oakland, tel. 2363-5665
- **Italy:** 5a Avenida 8-59 Zona 14, tel. 2337-4851
- **Mexico:** 15 Calle 3-20 Zona 10, tel. 2333-7254
- **Netherlands:** 16 Calle 0-55, 13th Floor, Torre Internacional, Zona 10, tel. 2367-4761
- **Nicaragua:** 10a Avenida 14-72 Zona 10, tel. 2368-0785
- **Panama:** 10a Avenida 18-53 Zona 14, tel. 2368-2805
- **Spain:** 6a Calle 6-48 Zona 9, tel. 2379-3530
- **Sweden:** 8a Avenida 15-07 Zona 10, tel. 2333-6536
- **Switzerland:** Torre Internacional, 16 Calle 0-65 Zona 10, tel. 2367-5520
- **United Kingdom:** Torre Internacional, 16 Calle 0-65, 11th Floor, Zona 10, tel. 2367-5520
- **United States:** Avenida La Reforma 7-01 Zona 10, tel. 2331-1541

the country. You'll have no trouble finding places to check your email or surf the web. Hourly rates are usually in the $1-2 range. Many hotels and restaurants offer free wireless Internet.

Newspapers and Magazines

Prensa Libre is Guatemala's most widely circulated newspaper and is highly respected. You can find the online version at www.prensalibre.com.gt. Other excellent newspapers include *Siglo XXI* (www.sigloxxi.com) and *elPeriódico* (www.elperiodico.com.gt). All of these are tabloid, rather than broadsheet, in format. A tabloid in the sense of being filled with plenty of yellow journalism, scandal, and not much else of use is *Nuestro Diario*, which nonetheless seems to be somewhat popular in the country's interior. Guatemala's respectable newspapers are an excellent source of information and make a great way to practice reading Spanish. They have a long tradition of investigative reporting and have done a wonderful job of uncovering numerous scandals

Guatemala's corrupt politicians would probably get away with (at least without public knowledge) were it not for the work of these intrepid journalists. Journalism can still be a dangerous occupation in Guatemala, though press freedom has come a long way since the dark times of the civil war.

Published in Antigua, the monthly *Revue magazine* has tons of helpful tips and contact information for hotels, restaurants, and businesses in Guatemala as well as parts of Honduras and El Salvador. There are also well-written stories on topics of interest to locals and visitors alike. It's available in tourist shops, hotels, and restaurants free of charge.

Television

Guatemala has a handful of local channels, though cable TV with channels beamed in from the United States is also widely available. The country also has its own cable network, Guatevisión, with a morning show and some entertaining programs covering recreational options throughout the country.

MAPS AND TOURIST INFORMATION

Maps

Recently introduced, **Mapas de Guatemala** (www.mapasdeguatemala.com) makes an excellent series of beautifully illustrated full-color maps of Guatemala's main tourist regions, which also include helpful information on local businesses. The free maps are available at INGUAT as well as tourist gift shops and restaurants throughout the country. If you need a good map before leaving for Guatemala, **ITMB Publishing** (530 W. Broadway, Vancouver, BC, Canada, 604/879-3621, www.itmb.com) publishes an excellent *International Travel Map of Guatemala* ($10.95), which is weatherproof and can be found at well-known bookstores in the United States.

Tourist Information

The Guatemala Tourist Commission (INGUAT) provides tourist information from its offices in major tourist areas and the country's two international airports. It is also in charge of promoting Guatemala internationally, and you may see ads for Guatemala in travel magazines from time to time. Unfortunately, it's not the catchiest advertising, and chances are you missed it.

INGUAT does a fairly good job with its mandate and has been instrumental in the organization of community-based tourism providers. It also participates in international tourism fairs promoting Guatemala, provides logistical support for travel journalists covering the country for international publications, keeps tabs on hotel pricing standards, and is credited with wooing airlines to begin service to Guatemala.

INGUAT's central office is in Guatemala City's Zona 4 at 7a Avenida 1-17 and its website is www.visitguatemala.com.

WEIGHTS AND MEASURES

Time

Guatemala is six hours behind GMT and in the same time zone as U.S. Central Standard Time. Hours of daylight do not vary greatly between seasons, but daylight savings time is sometimes observed, depending on the whims of individual governments. It was observed in the summer of 2006 and has not been observed since.

Electricity

Nearly all outlets are 110 volts, 60 cycles with outlets for plugs consisting of parallel flat blades just like the ones found in the United States, Canada, and Mexico. Power outages and electrical surges are common in rural areas, especially during unusually arid dry seasons or very wet rainy seasons in thunderstorms. Be extra careful with sensitive equipment such as laptop computers.

Measurements

Like the American and European influences

on its culture, Guatemala uses a sometimes confusing mixture of weights and measures from both the metric and old English systems. Fruits and vegetables are weighed by the pound, but folks weigh themselves in kilos; gas is dispensed in gallons but distances are computed in kilometers, and so on and so forth.

Another commonly used distance measurement is the *vara*, equivalent to 0.84 meters or a little less than a yard. For measuring land areas, the *manzana* equals about 0.7 hectare or 1.7 acres and the *caballería* covers a little more than 45 hectares or 111.5 acres. The *quintal* is widely used for weighing coffee and is the equivalent of 46 kilos.

Resources

Glossary

aduana: customs

agua: literally "water" but also used in reference to soda pop

agua pura: bottled water

aguardiente: cane alcohol or moonshine

aguas termales: hot springs

alcalde: mayor

alfombra: a colorful carpet made of sawdust and flowers central to Holy Week celebrations in Antigua and elsewhere in Guatemala

altense: a resident of Quetzaltenango

al tiempo: referring to drinks at room temperature

altiplano: the highlands

artesanías: handicrafts

avenida: avenue

ayudante: in cheap public buses, the man who helps the driver in collecting fares and helping passengers with baggage

bajo: lowland swampy areas of the Petén lowlands

balneario: a bathing or swimming hole

baño compartido/general: shared bath (in reference to accommodations)

baño privado: private bathroom

barranco: a ravine

baule: a leatherback turtle

billares: pool or billiards

billete: a banknote or bill

bistec: beef steak

bolo: drunk; also *borracho*

brujo: a male witch or sorcerer

cajero automático: automated teller machine (ATM)

calle: street

camioneta: a second-class bus

campesino: peasant farmer

canícula: a brief one- or two-week dry spell during the rainy summer months of July and August

cantina: a seedy bar

caoba: mahogany

casa de huéspedes: a guesthouse

cayuco: canoe

cerveza: beer

champa: thatched-roof, wall-less structure

chapín/chapina: what Guatemalans call themselves

chichicaste: a stinging plant somewhat like poison ivy

chiclero: a tapper of chewing-gum resin of the jungle Petén region

coche: a pig, not a car, as in other parts of Latin America

cofradía: traditional political-religious organization present in some highland Mayan communities

comedor: a simple eatery

corte: traditional wraparound skirt worn by Mayan women

costumbre: traditional Mayan religious practices that include offerings of flowers, candles, and sometimes animal sacrifices

coyote: a smuggler of undocumented immigrants across Mexico and into the United States

criollo: Guatemalan of Spanish heritage

cucurucho: costumed carriers of procession parade floats during Semana Santa celebrations *curandero:* traditional healer or shaman

edificio: a building; used in street addresses in urban areas

encomienda: a colonial system enabling landholders to exact tribute and labor from the local indigenous population

farmacia de turno: a pharmacy that remains open all night on a rotating basis

finca: a farm of any type but usually referring to a coffee farm

hospedaje: inexpensive family-run accommodations

huipil: traditional embroidered dress

ingenio: a sugar mill

invierno: literally "winter" but used to describe the May-October rainy season

IVA: short for *impuesto al valor agregado* (value added tax) VAT; in Guatemala it's 12 percent

ladino: a person of indigenous descent who has adopted European ways

lancha: small motorboat

latifundia: large landholding in the form of a plantation or hacienda

lavandería: laundry

machista: a male chauvinist

maquiladora: an industrial plant where clothes are assembled for reexport by cheap local labor; more commonly known in the United States as a "sweatshop"

mara: a gang, but also used to describe a "gang" in the manner referring to an agglomeration of people or a crowd

mestizo: person of mixed Spanish and Indian descent

milpa: a maize or corn plant; also sometimes used in reference to a cornfield

minifundia: small landholdings, usually in the hands of Mayan peasantry

morería: small crafts shop producing costumes and masks for traditional dancing

palapa: a high-ceilinged thatched-roof structure commonly used in restaurant or hotel architecture

parlama: green sea turtle

parque nacional: national park

pensión: inexpensive accommodations

petate: a reed mat

picop: pickup truck

Pullman: a first-class bus, though to varying degrees of newness and quality

rancho: a simple thatched structure; also sometimes referred to in its diminutive *ranchito*

recargo: a surcharge; usually associated with credit card transactions

refacción: snack time between lunch and dinner; also on menus as *refacciones* consisting of pastries and sandwiches

repatriado: returned civil war refugee, usually from Mexico

reserva natural privada: a privately owned nature preserve

reserva protectora de manantiales: a watershed protection preserve

retablo: an altarpiece in a colonial church

revueltos: scrambled (eggs)

ron: rum

sacbe: once-paved Mayan causeways present in the modern-day lowlands of Petén and still used as footpaths

stela (stelae): pre-Columbian stone monuments, usually carved

timbre: a type of stamp sold in banks used in paying fees such as visa renewals

traje: traditional Mayan costume worn by inhabitants of individual highland villages

túmulo: a speed bump

verano: literally "summer," but usually in reference to the height of the dry season between March and the beginning of the rainy season in May

zafra: sugarcane harvest in the Pacific lowlands

zancudo: mosquito

zona: a city zone into which Guatemala's principal urban areas are divided

Spanish Phrasebook

Spanish commonly uses 30 letters—the familiar English 26, plus four straightforward additions: ch, ll, ñ, and rr, which are consonants.

PRONUNCIATION

Spanish pronunciation rules are straightforward and easy to learn, because—in contrast to English—they don't change. Spanish vowels generally sound softer than in English. (Note: The capitalized syllables below receive stronger accents.)

Vowels

a like ah, as in "hah": *agua* AH-gooah (water), *pan* PAHN (bread), and *casa* CAH-sah (house)

e like ay, as in "may:" *mesa* MAY-sah (table), *tela* TAY-lah (cloth), and *de* DAY (of, from)

i like ee, as in "need": *diez* dee-AYZ (10), *comida* ko-MEE-dah (meal), and *fin* FEEN (end)

o like oh, as in "go": *peso* PAY-soh (weight), *ocho* OH-choh (eight), and *poco* POH-koh (a bit)

u like oo, as in "cool": *uno* OO-noh (one), *cuarto* KOOAHR-toh (room), and *usted* oos-TAYD (you); when it follows a "q" the u is silent; when it follows an "h" or has an umlaut, it's pronounced like "w"

Consonants

b, ch, d, f, k, l, m, n, p, q, s, t, v, w, x, y, z pronounced almost as in English; h occurs, but is silent (not pronounced at all)

c like k as in "keep": *cuarto* KOOAR-toh (room), *corazón* kor-a-SOHN (heart); when it precedes "e" or "i," pronounce c like s, as in "sit": *cerveza* sayr-VAY-sah (beer), *encima* ayn-SEE-mah (atop).

g like g as in "gift" when it precedes "a," "o," "u," or a consonant: *gato* GAH-toh (cat), *hago* AH-goh (I do, make); otherwise, pronounce g like h as in "hat": *giro* HEE-roh (money order), *gente* HAYN-tay (people)

j like h, as in "has": *jueves* HOOAY-vays (Thursday), *mejor* may-HOR (better)

ll like y, as in "yes": *toalla* toh-AH-yah (towel), *ellos* AY-yohs (they, them)

ñ like ny, as in "canyon": *año* AH-nyo (year), *señor* SAY-nyor (Mr., sir)

r is lightly trilled, with tongue at the roof of your mouth like a very light English r, as in "ready": *pero* PAY-roh (but), *tres* TRAYS (three), *cuatro* KOOAH-troh (four).

rr like a Spanish r, but with much more emphasis and trill. Let your tongue flap. Practice with *burro* (donkey), *carretera* (highway), and *Carrillo* (proper name), then really let go with *ferrocarril* (railroad).

Note: The single small but common exception to all of the above is the pronunciation of Spanish y when it's being used as the Spanish word for "and," as in *Ron y Kathy*. In such case, pronounce it like the English ee, as in "keep": Ron "ee" Kathy (Ron and Kathy).

Accent

Native English speakers often make errors of pronunciation by ignoring accented, or stressed, syllables. All Spanish vowels—a, e, i, o, and u—may carry accents determining which syllable of a word is emphasized.

The rule for accent, the relative stress given to syllables within a given word, is straightforward. If a word ends in a vowel, an n, or an s, accent the next-to-last syllable; if not, accent the last syllable.

Pronounce *gracias* GRAH-seeahs (thank you), *orden* OHR-dayn (order), and *carretera* kah-ray-TAY-rah (highway) with stress on the next-to-last syllable.

Otherwise, accent the last syllable: *venir* vay-NEER (to come), *ferrocarril* fay-roh-cah-REEL (railroad), and *edad* ay-DAHD (age).

Exceptions to the accent rule are always marked with an accent sign: (á, é, í, ó, or ú), such as *teléfono* tay-LAY-foh-noh (telephone), *jabón* hah-BON (soap), and *rápido* RAH-pee-doh (rapid).

BASIC AND COURTEOUS EXPRESSIONS

Most Spanish-speaking people consider formalities important. Whenever approaching anyone for information or some other reason, do not forget the appropriate salutation—good morning, good evening, and so forth. Standing alone, the greeting *hola* (hello) can sound brusque.

Hello. *Hola.*
Good morning. *Buenos días.*
Good afternoon. *Buenas tardes.*
Good evening. *Buenas noches.*
How are you? *¿Cómo está usted?*
Very well, thank you. *Muy bien, gracias.*
Okay; good. *Bien.*
Not okay; bad. *Mal, feo.*
So-so. *Más o menos.*
And you? *¿Y usted?*
Thank you. *Gracias.*
Thank you very much. *Muchas gracias.*
You're very kind. *Muy amable.*
You're welcome. *De nada.*
Good-bye. *Adios.*
See you later. *Hasta luego.*
please *por favor*
yes *sí*
no *no*
I don't know. *No sé.*
Just a moment, please. *Momentito, por favor.*
Excuse me, please (when you're trying to get attention). *Disculpe* or *Con permiso.*
Excuse me (when you've made a mistake). *Lo siento.*
Pleased to meet you. *Mucho gusto.*
What is your name? *¿Cómo se llama usted?*
Do you speak English? *¿Habla usted inglés?*
Is English spoken here? (Does anyone here speak English?) *¿Se habla inglés?*
I don't speak Spanish well. *No hablo bien el español.*
I don't understand. *No entiendo.*

How do you say... in Spanish? *¿Cómo se dice...en español?*
My name is... *Me llamo...*
Would you like... *¿Quisiera usted...*
Let's go to... *Vamos a...*

TERMS OF ADDRESS

When in doubt, use the formal *usted* (you) as a form of address.

I *yo*
you (formal) *usted*
you (familiar) *tu*
he/him *él*
she/her *ella*
we/us *nosotros*
you (plural) *ustedes*
they/them *ellos* (all males or mixed gender); *ellas* (all females)
Mr., sir *señor*
Mrs., madam *señora*
miss, young lady *señorita*
wife *esposa*
husband *esposo*
friend *amigo* (male); *amiga* (female)
sweetheart *novio* (male); *novia* (female)
son; daughter *hijo; hija*
brother; sister *hermano; hermana*
father; mother *padre; madre*
grandfather; grandmother *abuelo; abuela*

TRANSPORTATION

Where is...? *¿Dónde está...?*
How far is it to...? *¿A cuánto está...?*
from...to... *de...a...*
How many blocks? *¿Cuántas cuadras?*
Where (Which) is the way to...? *¿Dónde está el camino a...?*
the bus station *la terminal de autobuses*
the bus stop *la parada de autobuses*
Where is this bus going? *¿Adónde va este autobús?*
the taxi stand *la parada de taxis*
the train station *la estación de ferrocarril*
the boat *el barco*
the airport *el aeropuerto*
I'd like a ticket to... *Quisiera un boleto a...*
first (second) class *primera (segunda) clase*

round-trip *ida y vuelta*
reservation *reservación*
baggage *equipaje*
Stop here, please. *Pare aquí, por favor.*
the entrance *la entrada*
the exit *la salida*
the ticket office *la oficina de boletos*
(very) near; far *(muy) cerca; lejos*
to; toward *a*
by; through *por*
from *de*
the right *la derecha*
the left *la izquierda*
straight ahead *recto*
in front *en frente*
beside *al lado*
behind *atrás*
the corner *la esquina*
the stoplight *el semáforo*
a turn *una vuelta*
right here *aquí*
somewhere around here *por acá*
right there *allí*
somewhere around there *por allá*
street; boulevard *calle; bulevar*
highway *carretera*
bridge; toll *puente; peaje*
address *dirección*
north; south *norte; sur*
east; west *oriente (este); poniente (oeste)*

ACCOMMODATIONS

hotel *hotel*
Is there a room? *¿Hay cuarto?*
May I (may we) see it? *¿Puedo (podemos) verlo?*
What is the rate? *¿Cuál es el precio?*
Is that your best rate? *¿Es su mejor precio?*
Is there something cheaper? *¿Hay algo más económico?*
a single room *un cuarto sencillo*
a double room *un cuarto doble*
double bed *cama matrimonial*
twin beds *camas gemelas*
with private bath *con baño*
hot water *agua caliente*
shower *ducha*
towels *toallas*

soap *jabón*
toilet paper *papel higiénico*
blanket *frazada; chamarra*
sheets *sábanas*
air-conditioned *aire acondicionado*
fan *ventilador*
key *llave*
manager *gerente*

FOOD

I'm hungry. *Tengo hambre.*
I'm thirsty. *Tengo sed.*
menu *lista; menú*
order *orden*
glass *vaso*
fork *tenedor*
knife *cuchillo*
spoon *cuchara*
napkin *servilleta*
soft drink *refresco*
coffee *café*
tea *té*
drinking water *agua pura; agua potable*
bottled carbonated water *agua mineral*
bottled uncarbonated water *agua sin gas*
beer *cerveza*
wine *vino*
milk *leche*
juice *jugo*
cream *crema*
sugar *azúcar*
cheese *queso*
snack *refacción*
breakfast *desayuno*
lunch *almuerzo*
daily lunch special *el menú del día*
dinner *cena*
the check *la cuenta*
eggs *huevos*
bread *pan*
salad *ensalada*
fruit *fruta*
mango *mango*
watermelon *sandía*
papaya *papaya*
banana *banano*
apple *manzana*

orange *naranja*
plantain *plátano*
lime *limón*
fish *pescado*
shellfish *mariscos*
shrimp *camarones*
meat (without) *(sin) carne*
chicken *pollo*
pork *puerco*
beef; steak *res; bistec*
bacon; ham *tocino; jamón*
fried *frito*
roasted *asada*
barbecue; barbecued *barbacoa; al carbón*

SHOPPING

money *dinero*
money-exchange bureau *casa de cambio*
I would like to exchange travelers checks. *Quisiera cambiar cheques de viajero.*
What is the exchange rate? *¿Cuál es el tipo de cambio?*
How much is the commission? *¿Cuánto cuesta la comisión?*
Do you accept credit cards? *¿Aceptan tarjetas de crédito?*
money order *giro*
How much does it cost? *¿Cuánto cuesta?*
What is your final price? *¿Cuál es su último precio?*
expensive *caro*
cheap *barato; económico*
more *más*
less *menos*
a little *un poco*
too much *demasiado*

HEALTH

Help me please. *Ayúdeme por favor.*
I am ill. *Estoy enfermo.*
Call a doctor. *Llame un doctor.*
Take me to... *Lléveme a...*
hospital *hospital; sanatorio*
drugstore *farmacia*
pain *dolor*
fever *fiebre*
headache *dolor de cabeza*

stomach ache *dolor de estómago*
burn *quemadura*
cramp *calambre*
nausea *náusea*
vomiting *vomitar*
medicine *medicina*
antibiotic *antibiótico*
pill; tablet *pastilla*
aspirin *aspirina*
ointment; cream *pomada; crema*
bandage *venda*
cotton *algodón*
sanitary napkins use brand name, e.g., Kotex
birth control pills *pastillas anticonceptivas*
contraceptive foam *espuma anticonceptiva*
condoms *preservativos; condones*
toothbrush *cepillo dental*
dental floss *hilo dental*
toothpaste *crema dental*
dentist *dentista*
toothache *dolor de muelas*

POST OFFICE AND COMMUNICATIONS

long-distance telephone *teléfono de larga distancia*
I would like to call... *Quisiera llamar a...*
collect *a cobrar*
station to station *a quien contesta*
person to person *persona a persona*
credit card *tarjeta de crédito*
post office *correo*
general delivery *lista de correo*
letter *carta*
stamp *estampilla, timbre*
postcard *postal*
air mail *correo aéreo*
registered *registrado*
money order *giro*
package; box *paquete; caja*
string; tape *cuerda; cinta*

AT THE BORDER

border *frontera*
customs *aduana*
immigration *migración*

tourist card *tarjeta de turista*
inspection *inspección; revisión*
passport *pasaporte*
profession *profesión*
marital status *estado civil*
single *soltero*
married; divorced *casado; divorciado*
widowed *enviudado*
insurance *seguros*
title *título*
driver's license *licencia de conducir*
gas station *gasolinera*
car *carro*
gasoline *gasolina*
unleaded *sin plomo*
full, please *lleno, por favor*
tire *llanta*
tire repair shop *vulcanizadora* or *pinchazo*
air *aire*
water *agua*
oil (change) *(cambio de) aceite*
grease *grasa*
My...doesn't work. *Mi...no sirve.*
battery *batería*
radiator *radiador*
alternator *alternador*
generator *generador*
tow truck *grúa*
repair shop *taller mecánico*
tune-up *afinación* or *tune-up*

VERBS

Verbs are the key to getting along in Spanish. They employ mostly predictable forms and come in three classes, which end in *ar, er,* and *ir,* respectively:

to buy *comprar*
I buy, you (he, she, it) buys *compro, compra*
we buy, you (they) buy *compramos, compran*

to eat *comer*
I eat, you (he, she, it) eats *como, come*
we eat, you (they) eat *comemos, comen*

to climb *subir*

I climb, you (he, she, it) climbs *subo, sube*
we climb, you (they) climb *subimos, suben*

Here are more (with irregularities indicated):

to do or make *hacer* (regular except for *hago,* I do or make)
to go *ir* (very irregular: *voy, va, vamos, van*)
to go (walk) *andar*
to love *amar*
to work *trabajar*
to want *desear, querer*
to need *necesitar*
to read *leer*
to write *escribir*
to repair *reparar*
to stop *parar*
to get off (the bus) *bajar*
to arrive *llegar*
to stay (remain) *quedar*
to stay (lodge) *hospedar*
to leave *salir* (regular except for *salgo,* I leave)
to look at *mirar*
to look for *buscar*
to give *dar* (regular except for *doy,* I give)
to carry *llevar*
to have *tener* (irregular but important: *tengo, tiene, tenemos, tienen*)
to come *venir* (similarly irregular: *vengo, viene, venimos, vienen*)

Spanish has two forms of "to be":

to be *estar* (regular except for *estoy,* I am)
to be *ser* (very irregular: *soy, es, somos, son*)

Use *estar* when speaking of location or a temporary state of being: "I am at home." *"Estoy en casa."* "I'm sick." *"Estoy enfermo."* Use *ser* for a permanent state of being: "I am a doctor." *"Soy doctora."*

NUMBERS
zero *cero*
one *uno*

two *dos*
three *tres*
four *cuatro*
five *cinco*
six *seis*
seven *siete*
eight *ocho*
nine *nueve*
10 *diez*
11 *once*
12 *doce*
13 *trece*
14 *catorce*
15 *quince*
16 *dieciseis*
17 *diecisiete*
18 *dieciocho*
19 *diecinueve*
20 *veinte*
21 *veinte y uno* or *veintiuno*
30 *treinta*
40 *cuarenta*
50 *cincuenta*
60 *sesenta*
70 *setenta*
80 *ochenta*
90 *noventa*
100 *cien*
101 *ciento y uno*
200 *doscientos*
500 *quinientos*
1,000 *mil*
10,000 *diez mil*
100,000 *cien mil*
1,000,000 *millón*
one-half *medio*
one-third *un tercio*
one-fourth *un cuarto*

TIME

What time is it? *¿Qué hora es?*
It's one o'clock. *Es la una.*

It's three in the afternoon. *Son las tres de la tarde.*
It's 4am. *Son las cuatro de la mañana.*
six-thirty *seis y media*
a quarter till eleven *un cuarto para las once*
a quarter past five *las cinco y cuarto*
an hour *una hora*
today *hoy*
tomorrow *mañana*
yesterday *ayer*
a week *una semana*
a month *un mes*
a year *un año*
after *después*
before *antes*
last night *anoche*
the next day *el día siguiente*

DAYS OF THE WEEK

Monday *Lunes*
Tuesday *Martes*
Wednesday *Miércoles*
Thursday *Jueves*
Friday *Viernes*
Saturday *Sábado*
Sunday *Domingo*

MONTHS

January *Enero*
February *Febrero*
March *Marzo*
April *Abril*
May *Mayo*
June *Junio*
July *Julio*
August *Agosto*
September *Septiembre*
October *Octubre*
November *Noviembre*
December *Diciembre*

Suggested Reading

HISTORY
Pre-Columbian History

Coe, Michael D. *Breaking the Maya Code.* New York: Thames and Hudson, 1999. Chronicles the work of several scholars involved in the eventual decipherment of the meaning behind the Mayan glyphs.

Coe, Michael D. *The Maya,* 7th edition. New York: Thames and Hudson, 2005. A classic reference manual on the Maya and essential guide for the traveler that includes useful color plates.

Demarest, Arthur. *Ancient Maya: The Rise and Fall of a Rainforest Civilization.* Cambridge: Cambridge University Press, 2005. Written by a prominent archaeologist who has worked on numerous projects in Guatemala, this book explores the ecological aspects of the rise of Mayan civilization and the role of internecine warfare in its demise.

Harrison, Peter. *The Lords of Tikal: Rulers of an Ancient Maya City.* New York: Thames and Hudson, 2000. Traces the history of Tikal from its humble beginning to its apogee in the late 9th century AD.

Montgomery, John. *Tikal: An Illustrated History of the Ancient Maya Capital.* New York: Hippocrene Books, 2000. Wonderfully illustrated with photos, maps, and drawings, this is a good introduction to Tikal for the visitor and casual Mayanist.

Colonial Era

Lovell, W. George. *Conquest and Survival in Colonial Guatemala: A Historical Geography of the Cuchumatán Highlands,* 3rd edition. Kingston, Ontario: McGill-Queen's University Press, 2004. Quickly becoming a classic, this landmark work covers the Spanish conquest and the survival of the local indigenous culture despite the ravages of colonial legacies while linking the roots of the past to more recent sociopolitical conditions.

Civil War

Arnson, Cynthia J., editor. *Comparative Peace Processes in Latin America.* Washington, DC: Woodrow Wilson Center Press, 1999. Provides a good analysis of the peace process that led to a negotiated settlement of the civil war in Guatemala and other countries as well as issues concerning the roles of truth-telling reports, the search for justice, and reconciliation.

Burgos-Debray, Elizabeth, editor. *I, Rigoberta Menchú: An Indian Woman in Guatemala.* London: Verso, 1984. The classic autobiography of Nobel Peace Prize winner Rigoberta Menchú.

Goldman, Francisco. *The Art of Political Murder: Who killed the Bishop?* New York: Grove/Atlantic, 2008. A fascinating look into the inner workings of Guatemala's political and justice systems vis-à-vis the murder of Bishop Juan Gerardi and its subsequent investigation. This well-researched book details the machinations involved in hiding the culprits in one of Guatemala's most notorious high-profile murders and the admirable work of a handful of investigators who sought the truth against all odds.

Grandin, Greg. *The Last Colonial Massacre: Latin America in the Cold War.* Chicago: The University of Chicago Press, 2004. This thought-provoking book argues that the Latin American Cold War was actually a struggle between two differing notions of democracy, with its main achievement being the elimination of grassroots attempts at building social democracy. It uses Guatemala as a case study and concludes, somewhat convincingly, that the version of democracy now being extolled as the best option in the war against terror is itself a product of the same.

Handy, Jim. *Revolution in the Countryside: Rural Conflict and Agrarian Reform in Guatemala, 1944–1954.* Chapel Hill: University of North Carolina Press, 1994. A good in-depth look at the Agrarian Reform Law and the Guatemalan political scene during the Arévalo and Arbenz years.

Manz, Beatriz. *Paradise in Ashes: A Guatemalan Journey of Courage, Terror, and Hope.* Berkeley: University of California Press, 2004. Written by an anthropologist, this book centers around the Ixcán village of Santa María Tzejá, whose inhabitants were caught in the violence between the guerrillas and military during the civil war.

Perera, Víctor. *Unfinished Conquest: The Guatemalan Tragedy.* Berkeley: University of California Press, 1993. A must-read for travelers to Guatemala, covering sociopolitical aspects of the Guatemalan civil war as well as environmental issues in a well-written travel narrative style.

Sanford, Victoria. *Buried Secrets: Truth and Human Rights in Guatemala.* New York: Palgrave Macmillan, 2004. A highly recommended read with well-researched information from a number of different sources, including eyewitness testimonies from massacre survivors, interviews with members of forensic teams, human rights workers, high-ranking military officers, guerrillas, and government officials. It is an instrumental book for understanding the full scale of the genocidal civil war and the attempt to rebuild society in its aftermath.

Schlesinger, Stephen C., and Stephen Kinzer. *Bitter Fruit: The Story of the American Coup in Guatemala.* Cambridge: Harvard University Press, 2005. This is a classic book on Guatemala and its historical relationship with the United States. First published in 1982, it covers in much detail the 1954 CIA-orchestrated coup ousting Jacobo Árbenz.

Stoll, David. *Between Two Armies in the Ixil Towns of Guatemala.* New York: Columbia University Press, 1993. A controversial book postulating the theory that the Ixil Maya of Nebaj, Chajul, and Cotzal were not so much enamored with revolutionary possibilities for social change as much as simply caught between the opposing fires of the military and guerrilla forces with widely differing sociopolitical agendas.

Stoll, David. *Rigoberta Menchú and the Story of All Poor Guatemalans.* Boulder, Colorado: Westview Press, 1999. Also quite controversial, this work directly challenges much of the testimony presented by Rigoberta Menchú in her autobiography as embellishments or fabrications while granting that the atrocities described therein were accurate depictions of events during the civil war.

Wilkinson, Daniel. *Silence on the Mountain: Stories of Terror, Betrayal, and Forgetting in Guatemala.* New York: Houghton Mifflin, 2002. Part travelogue and part history book, this is a fascinating, well-written account of the American author's experience in Guatemala; it manages to uncover many of the issues relating to the origins and unfolding of Guatemala's civil war as told by those who survived the violence.

Central America

LaFeber, Walter. *Inevitable Revolutions: The United States in Central America.* New York: W. W. Norton, 1993. Traces the historical roots of Central America's armed conflicts along with the role of U.S. hegemony in perpetuating them.

POLITICS

Grandin, Greg. *The Guatemala Reader: History, Culture, Politics (The Latin America Readers)*. Duke University Press Books, 2011. An excellent resource for those wanting to explore the history and culture of Guatemala in a wide array of facets not limited solely to its dark history. It provides a well-rounded look at Guatemala in a contemporary context.

O'Neill, Kevin Lewis. *Securing the City: Neoliberalism, Space, and Insecurity in Postwar Guatemala*. Duke University Press Books, 2011. A collection of essays forming an excellent comparative study of the effects of neoliberalist approaches to postwar security in Guatemala's violent capital. Among the issues it explores are the further entrenchment of deep chasms between city and country, and the exacerbation of Guatemala's deeply rooted structures of inequality and ethnic discrimination.

TRAVELOGUES

Benz, Stephen Connely. *Guatemalan Journey*. Austin: University of Texas Press, 1996. A humorous, insightful, and well-written account of an American traveler's experiences living in Guatemala during the late 1980s.

Huxley, Aldous. *Beyond the Mexique Bay*. New York: Harper and Brothers Publishers, 1934. A classic take on early-20th-century travel in Guatemala by a well-known author.

Shaw, Christopher. *Sacred Monkey River: A Canoe Trip with the Gods*. New York: W. W. Norton, 2000. A superbly written adventure-travel narrative packed with historical and natural history anecdotes about the mighty Usumacinta River, which flows along the Mexico-Guatemala border.

Sherer, Michael. *Our Man in Antigua*. A well-written, well-researched, and frequently updated guide to Antigua's ever-changing dining, nightlife, and accommodations scenes. The author lives in Antigua, has traveled Guatemala extensively, and is skilled at picking out worthwhile entertainment options.

Stephens, John Lloyd. *Incidents of Travel in Central America, Chiapas and Yucatán*. New York: Dover Publications, 1969. A classic book and a must-read for the traveler to Guatemala, also featuring the fantastic illustrations of Stephens's friend and traveling companion Frederick Catherwood. It created quite an interest in the region, particularly its Mayan sites, when it was first published in 1841.

Wright, Ronald. *Time Among the Maya: Travels in Belize, Guatemala and Mexico*. New York: Grove/Atlantic, 2000. Another good read with insights on culture, history, adventure, and anthropology by a writer with an evident love for the modern-day Mayan people.

FICTION

Goldman, Francisco. *The Long Night of White Chickens*. New York: Grove/Atlantic, 1998. This well-written novel is a tale of intrigue set in 1980s Guatemala governed by military dictatorships. It's an entertaining read and does a nice job of bridging the gap between the seemingly parallel worlds of the United States and Guatemala.

ART

Gieseman, Peter, and Ange Bourda. *Six Architects*. Bogotá: Villegas Editores, 2003. An art-photography book documenting the architecture of the Guatemala City *Seis Arquitectos* firm.

Moller, Jonathan. *Our Culture Is Our Resistance: Repression, Refuge and Healing in Guatemala*. New York: PowerHouse Books,

2004. A beautiful photographic collection of highland Mayan culture in the aftermath of the civil war with wonderful guest commentaries from Rigoberta Menchú, Francisco Goldman, and various other authors of books on Guatemala.

NATURAL HISTORY

Beletsky, Les. *Traveller's Wildlife Guides: Belize and Northern Guatemala*. Northampton: Interlink Books, 2005.

Lee, Julian C. *Field Guide to the Amphibians and Reptiles of the Maya World: The Lowlands of Mexico, Northern Guatemala and Belize*. Ithaca: Cornell University Press, 2000.

Peterson, Roger Tory, and Edward L. Chalif. *A Field Guide to Mexican Birds: Mexico, Guatemala, Belize, El Salvador*. New York: Houghton Mifflin, 1999. Describes and illustrates 1,038 species.

Primack, Richard B., et al., eds. *Timber, Tourists, and Temples: Conservation and Development in the Maya Forest of Belize, Guatemala, and Mexico*. Washington, DC: Island Press, 1998. Covers the delicate political and social issues implicated in conserving the region's remaining rainforests as told from the perspective of social scientists, conservationists, and biologists working in the field.

ADOPTION

Michelini, Gil. *Daddy, Come & Get Me: A Dad's Adventure Through a Guatemalan Adoption*. CreateSpace, 2012. A fascinating read chronicling a father's mission to adopt a child from Guatemala and the sacrifices endured by the child's birth mother in handing her over for adoption. The title comes from the author's dream in which he heard a child calling out these words from a mountaintop.

O'Dwyer, Jessica. *Mamalita: An Adoption Memoir*. Berkeley, Calif.: Seal Press, 2010. An at times harrowing account of the difficulties in adopting a Guatemalan child vis-à-vis shady adoption agencies and bureaucratic red tape, and one woman's persistence in the face of such trials.

Internet Resources

GENERAL INFORMATION

www.prensalibre.com.gt
www.sigloxxi.com
www.elperiodico.com.gt
If you can read Spanish (or want to practice reading Spanish), Guatemala's main newspapers all have decent websites.

http://guatemalapost.com
An English-language wrap-up of news on Guatemala from various sources.

http://lanic.utexas.edu/la/ca/guatemala
The University of Texas has compounded a comprehensive list of links on everything pertaining to Guatemala.

www.revuemag.com
The highly recommended *Revue* magazine (in English) can be downloaded online in PDF format.

TRAVEL AND ENVIRONMENT

www.planeta.com
An excellent website with plenty of information on ecotravel in Guatemala and elsewhere in Latin America.

www.visitguatemala.com
The Guatemala Tourist Commission (INGUAT) website with a variety of information on Guatemala.

http://senderonatural.com
A Guatemalan-run website dedicated to sustainable tourism in Guatemala with a variety of good recreational options and recommended accommodations.

SPANISH LANGUAGE
www.123teachme.com
www.guatemala365.com
Both sites have reviews and rankings made by former students in the recommended language schools.

VOLUNTEERING
www.idealist.org
International volunteer website listing several opportunities in Guatemala.

www.volunteeradventures.com
Features a few Guatemala projects looking for international volunteers, mainly in the areas of wildlife conservation and opportunities to teach English.

www.entremundos.org
Quetzaltenango-based organization with tons of information on volunteer opportunities in the Western Highlands.

DESTINATION-SPECIFIC SITES
Chisec
www.puertamundomaya.com

Cobán
www.cobanav.net

Guatemala City
www.muniguate.com

Lívingston
www.livingston.com.gt

Nebaj
www.nebaj.com

Pachalum
www.pachalum.com

Quetzaltenango
www.xelawho.com
www.xelapages.com
www.xelapages.net

Semuc Champey
www.semucchampey.com

Uspantán
www.uspantan.com

Index

List of Maps

Acknowledgments

This guidebook would not have been possible without the help and inspiration of several folks to whom I owe my gratitude. First, I'd like to thank G-d for life and omnipresent love and inspiration. I'd also like to thank my parents for their support, for planting in me a love for both Guatemala and the United States, and allowing me to experience the best of both worlds. They have made Antigua Guatemala their home since the last edition in 2012. I had the wonderful opportunity to stay with them and even travel to several locations together, where they discovered new parts of their home country.

In Antigua, thanks go to Victor Ferrell at O.X. Outdoor Excursions for facilitating a trip to one of Guatemala's most amazing attractions, Acatenango Volcano. Antigua has a wonderful expat community and I'm glad to be in touch with many of its wonderful folks such as Elizabeth Bell, John Heaton, Harris Whitbeck, Shaun Paul Griffiths, and Stephanie Jolluck, who contributed to the production of this guidebook in ways they might not even be aware of.

In Guatemala City, a big shout out to Marcos Romero-Close for taking time out from his busy schedule to show me around the capital by bike. His enthusiasm for Guatemala and that of his brother Manuel Romero-Close are worthy of emulation. It's contagious, in fact. If you haven't checked out the "Perhaps you need a little Guatemala" Facebook page, you should do so immediately.

There were many innkeepers who helped me out with a place to stay during my travels and to them I also owe my gratitude for the gracious hospitality.

I almost missed out on visiting El Mirador due to government red tape, but Sandra Esteban of Expedición Extrema came to my rescue. The epic chopper trip to the Maya site in March 2015 will be forever engrained in my memory. We had a blast and the poignant conversation with my fellow Guatemalans about the state of Guatemalan affairs seems almost prophetic in retrospect given the tumultuous nature of things in 2015. Let's hope for the best...

I'd like to thank all the Moon Guatemala Facebook fans and all those who have written in with their comments and suggestions for future editions. Thanks, dear reader, for making this possible with your purchase and support!

Finally, I'd like to thank the staff at Avalon Travel, especially my editor, Kathryn Ettinger, and production coordinator, Elizabeth Jang, for all their hard work and help in making this book read and look its best. I'm stoked to finally have a full-color edition on this magical country in print!

Also Available

MAP SYMBOLS

▭▭▭ Expressway	○	City/Town	✈	Airport	⚲	Golf Course
▭▭▭ Primary Road	◉	State Capital	✈	Airfield	Ⓟ	Parking Area
▭▭▭ Secondary Road	⊛	National Capital	▲	Mountain	⛢	Archaeological Site
┈┈┈ Unpaved Road	★	Point of Interest	✛	Unique Natural Feature	⚲	Church
▬▬▬ Feature Trail	•	Accommodation				Gas Station
- - - Other Trail	▼	Restaurant/Bar	⚑	Waterfall	⬮	Glacier
⋯⋯ Ferry	▪	Other Location	♠	Park	▨	Mangrove
▭▭▭ Pedestrian Walkway	▲	Campground	⬛	Trailhead	▨	Reef
⬚⬚⬚ Stairs			⛷	Skiing Area	▨	Swamp

CONVERSION TABLES

°C = (°F - 32) / 1.8
°F = (°C x 1.8) + 32
1 inch = 2.54 centimeters (cm)
1 foot = 0.304 meters (m)
1 yard = 0.914 meters
1 mile = 1.6093 kilometers (km)
1 km = 0.6214 miles
1 fathom = 1.8288 m
1 chain = 20.1168 m
1 furlong = 201.168 m
1 acre = 0.4047 hectares
1 sq km = 100 hectares
1 sq mile = 2.59 square km
1 ounce = 28.35 grams
1 pound = 0.4536 kilograms
1 short ton = 0.90718 metric ton
1 short ton = 2,000 pounds
1 long ton = 1.016 metric tons
1 long ton = 2,240 pounds
1 metric ton = 1,000 kilograms
1 quart = 0.94635 liters
1 US gallon = 3.7854 liters
1 Imperial gallon = 4.5459 liters
1 nautical mile = 1.852 km

MOON GUATEMALA
Avalon Travel
a member of the Perseus Books Group
1700 Fourth Street
Berkeley, CA 94710, USA
www.moon.com

Editor and Series Manager: Kathryn Ettinger
Copy Editor: Ashley Benning
Graphics Coordinator: Elizabeth Jang
Production Coordinator: Elizabeth Jang
Cover Design: Faceout Studios, Charles Brock
Moon Logo: Tim McGrath
Map Editor: Mike Morgenfeld
Cartographers: Sierra Willems, Brian Shotwell
Indexer: Greg Jewett

ISBN-13: 978-1-63121-131-7
ISSN: 1533-4201

Printing History
1st Edition — 2001
5th Edition — October 2015
5 4 3 2 1

Front cover photo: Finca El Zapote botanical gardens © Al Argueta

Title page: Acatenango trail © Al Argueta

Interior photos: all photos © Al Argueta, except page 21 © Marie Ann Daloia/123rf.com; page 66 © Marcos Romero Close; page 187 (top) and page 204 © Scott Ruprecht; page 235 © Stefan Ember/123rf.com

Back cover photo: embroidery detail of a Guatemalan *huipil* © Al Argueta

Printed in Canada by Friesens

KEEPING CURRENT

If you have a favorite gem you'd like to see included in the next edition, or see anything that needs updating, clarification, or correction, please drop us a line. Send your comments via email to feedback@moon.com, or use the address above.

31901056852512